**IF FOUND, please notify and arrange return to owner.** This written test book is important for the owner's/pilot's preparation for the Federal Aviation Administration Written Test for the Instrument Rating*. Thank you.

Pilot's Name _____

Address _____

_____
City                                           State     Zip Code

Telephone    (      ) _____

*Also used for the instrument ground instructor (IGI) and flight instructor -- instrument (CFII).

Additional copies of *Instrument Pilot FAA Written Exam* are available from

Gleim Publications, Inc.
P.O. Box 12848
University Station
Gainesville, Florida 32604
(904) 375-0772
(800) 87-GLEIM

The price is $16.95 (subject to change without notice). Orders must be prepaid. Use the order form on page 478. Shipping and handling charges will be added to telephone orders. Add applicable sales tax to shipments within Florida.

Gleim Publications, Inc. guarantees the immediate refund of all resalable materials returned in 30 days. Shipping and handling charges are nonrefundable.

---

**ALSO AVAILABLE FROM GLEIM PUBLICATIONS, INC.**

*ORDER FORM ON PAGE 478.*

    *PRIVATE PILOT AND RECREATIONAL PILOT FAA WRITTEN EXAM*
    *PRIVATE PILOT FAA PRACTICAL TEST PREP*
    *PRIVATE PILOT HANDBOOK*
    *RECREATIONAL PILOT FLIGHT MANEUVERS*
    *AVIATION WEATHER AND WEATHER SERVICES*

**Advanced Pilot Training Books**

    *INSTRUMENT PILOT FAA PRACTICAL TEST PREP*
    *COMMERCIAL PILOT FAA WRITTEN EXAM*
    *COMMERCIAL PILOT FAA PRACTICAL TEST PREP*
    *FLIGHT/GROUND INSTRUCTOR FAA WRITTEN EXAM*
    *FUNDAMENTALS OF INSTRUCTING FAA WRITTEN EXAM*
    *FLIGHT INSTRUCTOR FAA PRACTICAL TEST PREP*
    *AIRLINE TRANSPORT PILOT FAA WRITTEN EXAM*

# REVIEWERS AND CONTRIBUTORS

Maria M. Bolanos, B.A., University of Florida, has 10 years of production experience in scientific and technical publications. Ms. Bolanos coordinated the production of the text and reviewed the final manuscript.

Gillian Hillis, B.A., University of Florida, is our editor. Ms. Hillis reviewed the entire manuscript and revised it for readability.

Barry A. Jones, CFII, B.S. in Air Commerce/Flight Technology, Florida Institute of Technology, is a charter pilot and flight instructor with Gulf Atlantic Airways in Gainesville, FL. Mr. Jones drafted answer explanations, incorporated numerous revisions, assisted in assembling the text, and provided technical assistance throughout the project.

Heiko E. Kallenbach, ATP, CFII, MEI, MFA, Carnegie Mellon University, is a pilot for a commuter airline. Mr. Kallenbach drafted answer explanations, reviewed the manuscript, and provided technical assistance during production of the 4th edition.

Kristopher B. Murphy, CFII, is a flight instructor in single engine airplanes with Gator Aire in Gainesville, FL. Mr. Murphy reviewed selected chapters and assisted in editing the text.

John F. Rebstock, B.S., School of Accounting, University of Florida, reviewed the entire edition and composed the page layout.

Robert H. Thompson, CFII, B.S., Florida State University, is first officer on a CE-500 Citation. Mr. Thompson reviewed selected chapters and assisted in editing the text.

The CFIs who have worked with me throughout the years to develop and improve my pilot training materials.

The many FAA employees who helped, in person or by telephone, primarily in Gainesville, Orlando, Oklahoma City, and Washington, DC.

The many pilots and student pilots who have provided comments and suggestions about *Instrument Pilot FAA Practical Test Prep* and *Instrument Pilot FAA Written Exam* during the past 7 years.

# A PERSONAL THANKS

This manual would not have been possible without the extraordinary efforts and dedication of Jim Collis and Connie Steen, who typed the entire manuscript and all revisions, as well as prepared the camera-ready pages.

The author also appreciates the proofreading and production assistance of Laura David, Michelle Grubert, Kim Houellemont, and Terri Talley, and the production assistance of Robert Barrett.

Finally, I appreciate the encouragement, support, and tolerance of my family throughout this project.

CAUTION: The FAA issues new written test books in the Spring, and they usually expire September 1, two years later. Thus for about 6 months after a new written test book is issued, FAA written test examiners can test you with either the old FAA edition or the new FAA edition. Talk to your written test examiner to determine which edition (s)he will use. The dates of our editions are on the cover. Call with any questions.

# FIFTH (1993-1995) EDITION

# INSTRUMENT PILOT

# FAA WRITTEN EXAM

by Irvin N. Gleim, Ph.D., CFII

## ABOUT THE AUTHOR

Irvin N. Gleim earned his private pilot certificate in 1965 from the Institute of Aviation at the University of Illinois, where he subsequently received his Ph.D. He is a commercial pilot and flight instructor (instrument) with multiengine and seaplane ratings, and is a member of the Aircraft Owners and Pilots Association, American Bonanza Society, Civil Air Patrol, Experimental Aircraft Association, and Seaplane Pilots Association. He is also author of Practical Test Prep books for the private, instrument, commercial, and flight instructor certificates/ratings, and study guides for the private/ recreational, instrument, commercial, flight/ground instructor, fundamentals of instructing, and airline transport pilot FAA written tests. Two additional pilot training books are *Private Pilot Handbook* and *Aviation Weather and Weather Services*.

Dr. Gleim has also written articles for professional accounting and business law journals, and is the author of the most widely used review manuals for the CIA exam (Certified Internal Auditor), the CMA exam (Certified Management Accountant), and the CPA exam (Certified Public Accountant). He is Professor Emeritus, Fisher School of Accounting, University of Florida, and is a CIA, CMA, and CPA.

P.O. Box 12848
University Station
Gainesville, Florida 32604
(904) 375-0772
(800) 87-GLEIM

Library of Congress Catalog Card No. 93-79833
ISBN 0-917539-44-3
Third Printing: May 1994

Copyright © 1993 by Gleim Publications, Inc.

ALL RIGHTS RESERVED. No part of this material may be reproduced in any form whatsoever
without express written permission from Gleim Publications, Inc.

---

## SOURCES USED IN INSTRUMENT PILOT FAA WRITTEN EXAM

The first lines of the answer explanations contain citations to authoritative sources of the answers. These publications can be obtained from the FAA, the Government Printing Office, and aviation bookstores. These citations are abbreviated as provided below:

| | | | |
|---|---|---|---|
| AC | Advisory Circular | | |
| ACL | Aeronautical Chart Legend | Fl Comp | Flight Computer |
| A/FD | Airport/Facility Directory | FTH | Flight Training Handbook |
| AFNA | Aerodynamics for Naval | IFH | Instrument Flight Handbook |
| | Aviators | MHP | Medical Handbook for Pilots |
| AIM | Airman's Information Manual | NTSB | National Transportation Safety |
| AvW | Aviation Weather | | Board Regulations |
| AWS | Aviation Weather Services | P/C Glossary | Pilot/Controller Glossary (AIM) |
| FAA-P-8740-50 | On Landings, Part III | PHAK | Pilot's Handbook of Aeronautical |
| FAR | Federal Aviation Regulations | | Knowledge |

---

## HELP !!

This is the Fifth Edition designed specifically for private pilots who aspire to the Instrument Rating. It will continue to be revised biennially. Please send any corrections and suggestions for subsequent editions to the author, c/o Gleim Publications, Inc. The last page in this book has been reserved for you to make comments and suggestions. It can be torn out and mailed to us.

A companion volume, *Instrument Pilot FAA Practical Test Prep*, is also available. Additionally, you may want to obtain *Aviation Weather and Weather Services*, which combines all of the information from the FAA's *Aviation Weather* (AC 00-6A), *Aviation Weather Services* (AC 00-45D), and numerous FAA publications into one easy-to-understand book. Save time, money, and frustration -- order these books today! See the order form on page 478. Please bring these books to the attention of flight instructors, fixed base operators, and others with a potential interest in instrument flying. Wide distribution of these books and increased interest in flying depend on your assistance, good word, etc. Thank you.

**NOTE: ANSWER DISCREPANCIES and ERRATA SHEETS**

Our answers have been carefully researched and reviewed. Inevitably there will be differences with competitors' books and even the FAA. If necessary we will develop an ERRATA SHEET for *Instrument Pilot FAA Written Exam*. Please write us about any discrepancies. We will respond to all inquiries.

# TABLE OF CONTENTS

> **Instrument Ground Instructor** -- The FAA's written test for IGI is also taken from this book and consists of 50 questions. It is comparable to the Instrument Rating Airplane written test; i.e., just follow the instructions in Chapter 1 to pursue the IGI written test. Note that the IGI test will have a few helicopter and/or glider questions that are not in this book. Take a guess without any advance preparation. You only need 35 right out of 50 to pass the test.
>
> **Certificated Flight Instructor/Instrument (airplane)** -- The CFII written test, which consists of 50 questions, is also taken from the questions in this book.

# PREFACE

The primary purpose of this book is to provide you with the easiest, fastest, and least expensive means of passing the instrument rating (airplane) written test.  We have

1.  Reproduced 898 actual FAA airplane test questions which can possibly appear on your FAA written test (airplane).

2.  Reordered the questions into 86 logical topics.

3.  Organized the 86 topics into 10 chapters.

4.  Explained the answer immediately to the right of each question.

5.  Provided an easy-to-study outline of exactly what you need to know (and no more) at the beginning of each chapter.

Accordingly, you can thoroughly prepare for the FAA written test by

1.  Studying the brief outlines at the beginning of each chapter.

2.  Answering the question on the left side of each page while covering up the answer explanations on the right side of each page.

3.  Reading the answer explanation for each question that you answer incorrectly or have difficulty with.

4.  Our *FAA Test Prep* software facilitates this process.

The secondary purpose of this study aid is to introduce *Instrument Pilot FAA Practical Test Prep*, which is a similar book for the FAA's practical test.  Just as this book thoroughly prepares you for the FAA written test, *Instrument Pilot FAA Practical Test Prep* prepares you for success on your practical test.  It will also save you many hours of flight training and study.

Most books create additional work for the user.  In contrast, my books facilitate your effort.  They are easy to use.  The outline format, type styles, and spacing are designed to improve readability.  Concepts are often presented as phrases rather than as complete sentences.

Read Chapter 1, The FAA Written Test, carefully.  Also, recognize that this study manual is concerned with **airplane** flight training, not helicopter training.  I am confident this manual will facilitate speedy completion of your written test.  I also wish you the very best as you complete your instrument rating, in subsequent flying, and in obtaining additional ratings and certificates.

Enjoy Flying -- Safely!

*Irvin N. Gleim*

September 1993

# CHAPTER ONE
# THE FAA WRITTEN TEST

The beginning of this chapter provides an overview of the process to obtain an instrument rating. The remainder of the chapter explains the content and procedure of the Federal Aviation Administration (FAA) written test and how the test can be taken at a computer testing center. Learning to fly using IFR (Instrument Flight Rules) and getting an instrument rating are fun. Begin today!

*Instrument Pilot FAA Written Exam* is one of three related books for obtaining an instrument rating. The other two are Gleim's *Instrument Pilot FAA Practical Test Prep* and *Aviation Weather and Weather Services*, both in outline/illustration format.

*Instrument Pilot FAA Practical Test Prep* is a comprehensive, carefully organized presentation of everything you will need to know for your practical (flight) test. It integrates material from over 100 FAA publications and other sources. This book will transfer knowledge to you and give you the confidence to do well on your FAA practical test.

*Aviation Weather and Weather Services* combines all of the information from the FAA's *Aviation Weather* (AC 00-6A), *Aviation Weather Services* (AC 00-45D), and numerous FAA publications into one easy-to-understand book. It will help you study all aspects of aviation weather and provide you a single reference book.

Note this 1993 revision of *Instrument Pilot FAA Written Exam* was prompted by a revised FAA written test book to accommodate changed airspace classification terminology. Nonetheless, most of the charts herein contain old airspace terminology. Memory aid: list A down to G (no F) and match old airspace classifications based on height from highest to lowest: A = PCA, B = TCA, C = ARSA, D = ATA, E = general controlled, and G = uncontrolled.

## 1.1 WHAT IS AN INSTRUMENT RATING?

An instrument rating is added to your private or commercial pilot certificate. A new certificate will be issued to you by the FAA upon satisfactory completion of your training program, a written test, and a practical test. A sample private pilot certificate with an instrument rating is reproduced on page 2.

## 1.2 REQUIREMENTS TO OBTAIN AN INSTRUMENT RATING

1.  Hold at least a private pilot certificate.

2.  Be able to read, speak, and understand the English language.

3.  Hold a current FAA medical certificate.

    a.  You must undergo a routine medical examination which may only be administered by FAA-designated doctors called aviation medical examiners (AME).

    b.  Even if you have a physical handicap, medical certificates can be issued in many cases.  Operating limitations may be imposed depending upon the nature of the disability.

    c.  Your certificated flight instructor-instrument (CFII) or fixed base operator (FBO) will be able to recommend an AME.

        1)  CFII is a flight instructor who has an instrument rating on his/her flight instructor certificate and is authorized to provide instruction for the instrument rating.

        2)  An FBO is an airport business that gives flight lessons, sells aviation fuel, repairs airplanes, etc.

        3)  Also, the FAA publishes a directory that lists all authorized AMEs by name and address.  Copies of this directory are kept at all FAA offices, ATC facilities, and Flight Service Stations (FSS).

4.  Receive appropriate ground instruction (such as studying this book, *Instrument Pilot FAA Practical Test Prep*, and *Aviation Weather and Weather Services*) to learn

    a.  Federal Aviation Regulations (FAR) applicable to instrument pilots
    b.  IFR navigation
    c.  Aviation weather
    d.  Safe and efficient operation of an airplane under instrument weather conditions.

5.  Pass a written test with a score of 70% or better.  Most FAA written tests are administered by FAA designated examiners.  This test is administered at some FAA Flight Standards District Offices (FSDO) and at some airport FBOs.  The instrument rating written test consists of 60 multiple-choice questions selected from the 898 airplane-related questions

among the 943 questions in the FAA's Instrument Rating Written Test Book (FAA-T-8080-20A); the balance of 45 questions are for helicopters. Each of the FAA's 898 airplane questions is reproduced in this book with complete explanations to the right of each question.

6.  Flight experience (FAR 61.65)

   a.  125 hr. pilot flight time.

   b.  50 hr. pilot in command on cross-country flight more than 50 NM from departure point (after becoming a private pilot, i.e., solo cross-country as a student pilot does NOT count).

      1)  Each cross-country flight must have a landing at least 50 NM from the departure point.

   c.  40 hr. of simulated or actual instrument time (of which up to 20 hr. may be in an FAA-approved ground simulator).

   d.  15 hr. of instrument flight instruction (at least 5 must be in an airplane).

7.  Flight instruction and skill (FAR 61.65). A logbook sign-off by your CFII on the following pilot operations:

   a.  *Control and accurate maneuvering of an airplane solely by reference to instruments.*

   b.  *IFR navigation by the use of the VOR and ADF systems, including compliance with air traffic control instructions and procedures.*

   c.  *Instrument approaches to published minimums using the VOR, ADF, and ILS systems (instruction in the use of the ADF and ILS may be received in an instrument ground trainer).*

   d.  *Cross-country flying in simulated or actual IFR conditions, on Federal airways, or as routed by ATC, including one such trip of at least 250 NM, including VOR, ADF, and ILS approaches at different airports.*

   e.  *Simulated emergencies, including the recovery from unusual attitudes, equipment or instrument malfunctions, loss of communications, engine-out emergencies if a multiengine airplane is used, and missed approach procedure.*

8.  An alternative is to enroll in an FAA-certificated pilot school that has an approved instrument rating course (airplane).

   a.  These schools are known as Part 141 schools because they are authorized by Part 141 of the FARs.

      1)  All other regulations concerning the certification of pilots are found in Part 61 of the FARs.

   b.  The Part 141 course must consist of at least 30 hr. of ground instruction and 35 hr. of flight instruction.

9.  Successfully complete a practical test which will be given as a final exam by an FAA inspector or designated pilot examiner. The practical test will be conducted as specified in the FAA's Instrument Rating Practical Test Standards (FAA-S-8081-4A, dated March 1989).

   a.  FAA inspectors are FAA employees and do not charge for their services.

   b.  FAA-designated pilot examiners are proficient, experienced flight instructors and pilots who are authorized by the FAA to conduct flight tests. They do charge a fee.

   c.  The FAA's Instrument Rating Practical Test Standards are outlined and reprinted in Gleim's *Instrument Pilot FAA Practical Test Prep.*

## 1.3 FAA WRITTEN TEST

This written test book is designed to help you prepare for and successfully take the FAA written test for the instrument rating (airplane), instrument flight instructor (airplane), and the instrument ground instructor.

1.  The remainder of this chapter explains the FAA written test procedures.

2.  All of the 898 questions in the FAA's Instrument Rating Written Test Book (FAA-T-8080-20A) that are applicable to airplanes have been grouped into the following 10 categories, which are the titles of Chapters 2 through 11:

    Chapter  2 -- Airplane Instruments
    Chapter  3 -- Airports and Air Traffic Control
    Chapter  4 -- Aviation Weather
    Chapter  5 -- Federal Aviation Regulations
    Chapter  6 -- Navigation
    Chapter  7 -- Flight Physiology
    Chapter  8 -- Flight Operations
    Chapter  9 -- Instrument Approaches
    Chapter 10 -- IFR En Route
    Chapter 11 -- Comprehensive IFR Trip Review

    Note that in the official FAA Instrument Rating Written Test Book (FAA-T-8080-20A) containing all of the questions, the FAA's questions are **not** grouped together by topic. We have unscrambled them for you in this book.

3.  Within each of the chapters listed, questions relating to the same subtopic (e.g., missed approaches, holding patterns, turn rates, etc.) are grouped together to facilitate your study program. Each subtopic is called a module.

4.  To the right of each question are

    a.  The correct answer,
    b.  The FAA question number, and
    c.  A reference for the answer explanation.

        1)  See page iv for a listing of abbreviations used for authoritative sources.
        2)  EXAMPLE: *IFH Chap V* means *Instrument Flying Handbook*, Chapter V.

5.  Each chapter begins with an outline of the material tested on the FAA written test. The outlines in this part of the book are very brief and have only one purpose: to help you pass the FAA written test for the instrument rating.

    a.  **CAUTION:** The **sole purpose** of this book is to expedite your passing the FAA written test for the instrument rating. Accordingly, all extraneous material (i.e., not directly tested on the FAA written test) is omitted even though much more information and knowledge are necessary to fly safely. This additional material is presented in two related books: Gleim's *Instrument Pilot FAA Practical Test Prep* and *Aviation Weather and Weather Services*.

Follow the suggestions given throughout this chapter and you will have no trouble passing the written test the first time you take it.

## 1.4 HOW TO PREPARE FOR THE FAA WRITTEN TEST

1.  Begin by carefully reading the rest of this chapter. You need to have a complete understanding of the examination process prior to beginning to study for it. This knowledge will make your studying more efficient.

2.  After you have spent an hour studying this chapter, set up a study schedule, including a target date for taking your written test.

    a.  Do not let the study process drag on because it will be discouraging, i.e., the quicker the better.

    b.  Consider enrolling in an organized ground school course at your local FBO, community college, etc.

    c.  Determine where and when you are going to take your written test.

3.  Work through each of Chapters 2 through 11.

    a.  Each chapter begins with a list of its module titles. The number in parentheses after each title is the number of FAA questions that cover the information in that module. The two numbers following the parentheses are the page numbers on which the outline and the questions for that particular module begin, respectively.

    b.  Begin by studying the outlines slowly and carefully.

    c.  Cover the answer explanations on the right side of each page with your hand or a piece of paper while you answer the multiple-choice questions.

        1)  Remember, it is very important to the learning (and understanding) process that you honestly commit yourself to an answer. If you are wrong, your memory will be reinforced by having discovered your error. Therefore, it is crucial to cover up the answer and make an honest attempt to answer the question before reading the answer.

        2)  Study the answer explanation for each question that you answer incorrectly, do not understand, or have difficulty with.

4.  Note that this written test book (in contrast to most other question and answer books) contains the FAA questions grouped by topic. Thus, some questions may appear repetitive, while others may be duplicates or near-duplicates. Accordingly, do not work question after question (i.e., waste time and effort) if you are already conversant with a topic and the type of questions asked.

5.  As you move from module to module and chapter to chapter you may need further explanation or clarification of certain topics. You may wish to obtain and use the following Gleim books:

    a.  *Instrument Pilot FAA Practical Test Prep*, which covers in detail all the information in the FAA Instrument Rating Practical Test Standards, and other information relevant to instrument pilots from various FAA publications.

    b.  *Aviation Weather and Weather Services* combines all the information in the FAA's *Aviation Weather*, *Aviation Weather Services*, and various other FAA publications into one easy-to-read book in an outline/illustration format.

6.  Keep track of your work!!! As you complete a module in Chapters 2 through 11, grade yourself with an A, B, C, or ? (use a ? if you need help on the subject) next to the module title at the front of the respective chapter.

    a.  The A, B, C, or ? is your self-evaluation of your comprehension of the material in that module and your ability to answer the questions.

        A     means a good understanding
        B     means a fair understanding
        C     means a shaky understanding
        ?     means to ask your CFII or others about the material and/or questions and
              read the pertinent sections in *Instrument Pilot FAA Practical Test Prep* and/or
              *Aviation Weather and Weather Services*.

b.   This procedure will provide you with the ability to quickly see (by looking at the first page of Chapters 2 through 11) how much studying you have done (and how much remains) and how well you have done.

c.   This procedure will also facilitate review.  You can spend more time on the modules you had difficulty with.

## 1.5  WHEN TO TAKE THE WRITTEN TEST

1.   You must be at least 15 years of age to take the instrument rating written test.

2.   You must prepare for the test by successfully completing a ground instruction course under the supervision of your CFII, i.e., studying this book.

a.   See Module 1.10, Authorization to Take the Written Test, on page 8.

3.   Take the written test within the next 30 days.  Get the test behind you.

a.   Your flight test must follow within 24 months or you will have to retake your written test.

## 1.6  WHERE TO TAKE THE WRITTEN TEST

1.   Most FAA written tests are administered by FAA designated examiners.  Written tests are also administered by some FSDOs and other FAA facilities.

a.   There are also testing centers where you may take FAA written tests on a computer.  See Module 1.7, Computer Testing Centers, below.

2.   Ask your CFII or call a nearby FBO to inquire about the nearest FAA facility administering written tests.

a.   There is no charge to take the written test at an FAA facility.

b.   Call the FAA facility to make sure that the facility you are considering administers written tests (some do not).

3.   Also, many FBOs in conjunction with an FAA designated examiner administer written tests for a nominal fee, e.g., $25.  Check with your flight or ground instructor.

## 1.7  COMPUTER TESTING CENTERS

The FAA has contracted with several computer testing services to administer FAA written tests. The advantage is that you get an immediate Airman Computer Test Report upon completion of the test.  Thus, you do not have to wait to have your written test sent to the FAA in Oklahoma City for grading and then have the results mailed to you.

Each of these computer testing services has testing centers throughout the country.  You register by calling an 800 number.  Call the following testing services for information regarding the location of their testing center most convenient to you and the time allowed and cost to take their instrument rating (airplane) written test.

CATS        (800) 947-4228
DRAKE       (800) 359-3278
SYLVAN      (800) 967-1100

Also, about twenty Part 141 schools use the AVTEST computer testing system, which is very similar to the computer testing services described above.

Note that the FAA corrects (rewrites) defective questions on the computer tests, which it cannot do in the written test books. Thus, it is important to carefully study questions that are noted to have no correct answer or a "best" answer in this book. On the written test, you will get credit for these defective questions, but on computer tests, the questions will probably have been rephrased.

## 1.8 GLEIM'S *FAA TEST PREP* SOFTWARE

Computer testing is consistent with modern aviation's use of computers (e.g., DUAT, flight simulators, computerized cockpits, etc.). In the future, all FAA tests will be taken on computers. Computer testing is already the choice of most pilots because of the immediate test results and the ease of using a computer.

Computer testing is natural after computer study. Computer assisted instruction is a very efficient and effective method of study. Gleim's *FAA Test Prep* software is designed to prepare you for computer testing. *FAA Test Prep* contains all of the questions in this book (but not the outlines and figures). You choose either STUDY MODE or TEST MODE.

In STUDY MODE, the software provides you with an explanation of each answer you choose (correct or incorrect). You design each study session:

> Topic(s) you wish to cover
> Number of questions
> Order of questions -- FAA, Gleim, or random
> Order of answers to each question -- FAA or random
> Questions missed from last session -- test, study, or both
> Questions missed from all sessions -- test, study, or both
> Questions never answered correctly

In TEST MODE, you decide the format -- CATS, DRAKE, SYLVAN, AVTEST, or Gleim. When you finish your test, you can study the questions missed and access answer explanations. The software imitates the operation of the FAA-approved computer testing companies listed above. Thus, you have a complete understanding of exactly how to take an FAA computer test before you go to a computer testing center.

To use *FAA Test Prep* you need an IBM-compatible computer with a hard disk and 1.5 MB (2.0 MB for *Airline Transport Pilot*) of disk space. Just call (800) 87-GLEIM and we will send a diskette for you to try at NO obligation on your part. If you like the software and desire unlimited use, you may license it for $25 by telephone, FAX, or mail.

Unlicensed software permits you to use the STUDY MODE with a sample set of questions. Once you license the software, you will have access to all questions and be able to use the TEST MODE.

## 1.9 PART 141 SCHOOLS WITH WRITTEN TEST EXAMINING AUTHORITY

The FAA permits some FAR Part 141 schools to develop, administer, and grade their own written tests as long as they use the FAA written test books, i.e., those with the same questions as in this book. The FAA does not provide the correct answers to the Part 141 schools and the FAA only reviews the Part 141 school test question selection sheets. Thus, some of the answers used by Part 141 test examiners may not agree with the FAA or those in this book. The latter is not a problem, but may explain why you may miss a question on a Part 141 written test using an answer presented in this book.

## 1.10 AUTHORIZATION TO TAKE THE WRITTEN TEST

Before taking the written test, FAR 61.65 requires applicants for the instrument rating to have received ground instruction, or have logged home study in at least the following areas of aeronautical knowledge:

1. The regulations ... that apply to flight under IFR conditions, the Airman's Information Manual, and the IFR air traffic system and procedures;

2. Dead Reckoning appropriate to IFR navigation, IFR navigation by radio aids using the VOR, ADF, and ILS systems, and the use of IFR charts and instrument approach plates;

3. The procurement and use of aviation weather reports and forecasts, and the elements of forecasting weather trends on the basis of that information and personal observation of weather conditions; and

4. The safe and efficient operation of airplanes or helicopters, as appropriate, under instrument weather conditions.

For your convenience, a standard authorization form for the instrument rating written test is reproduced on page 479 which can be easily completed, signed by a flight or ground instructor, torn out, and taken to the written test site.

## 1.11 FORMAT OF THE WRITTEN TEST

The FAA's instrument rating written test for airplanes consists of 60 multiple-choice questions selected from the 898 questions that appear in the next 10 chapters.

Note that the FAA test will be taken from exactly the same questions that are reproduced in this book. If you study the next 10 chapters (including all the questions and answers) and do well on our practice test (see Module 1.20 on page 16), **you should be assured of passing your FAA written test.**

## 1.12 WHAT TO TAKE TO THE FAA WRITTEN TEST

1. The same flight computer that you have used to solve the test questions in this book, i.e., one you are familiar with and have used before.

2. Navigational plotter.

3. A pocket calculator you are familiar with and have used before (no instructional material for the calculator is allowed).

4. Authorization to take the examination (see page 479).

5. Picture identification of yourself.

6. Note: Paper and pencils are supplied at the examination site.

## 1.13 COMPUTER TEST PROCEDURES

To register for the written test by computer, you should call one of the computer testing services listed in Module 1.7, Computer Testing Centers, on page 6, or you may call one of their testing centers. These testing centers and telephone numbers are listed in Gleim's *FAA Test Prep* software under Vendors in the main menu. When you register, you will pay the fee with a credit card.

When you arrive at the computer testing center, you will be required to provide positive proof of identification and documentary evidence of your age. The identification presented must include your

photograph, signature, and actual residential address, if different from the mailing address. This information may be presented in more than one form of identification. Next, you sign in on the testing center's daily log. On the logsheet there must be a statement that your signature certifies that, if this is a retest, you meet the applicable requirements (see Module, 1.18, Failure on the Written Test, on page 15) and that you have not taken and passed this written test in the past 2 years. Finally, you will present your logbook endorsement or authorization form from your instructor, which authorizes you to take the test. A standard authorization form is provided on page 479 for your use.

Next, you will be taken into the testing room and seated at a computer terminal. A person from the testing center will assist you in logging on the system and you will be asked to confirm your personal data (e.g., name, Social Security number, etc.). Then you will be prompted and given an on-line introduction to the computer testing system and you will take a sample test. If you have used our *FAA Test Prep* software, you will be conversant with the computer testing methodology and environment and you will probably want to skip the sample test and begin the actual test immediately. You will be allowed approximately 2.5 hr. to complete the actual test. When you have completed your test, an Airman Computer Test Report will be printed out, validated (usually with an embossed seal), and given to you by a person from the testing center. Before you leave, you will be required to sign out on the testing center's daily log.

Each testing center has certain idiosyncrasies in its paperwork, scheduling, telephone procedures, as well as in its software. It is for this reason that our *FAA Test Prep* software emulates each of these FAA-approved computer testing companies.

## 1.14 WRITTEN TEST PROCEDURES

When you arrive at the written test site, you will register for the test by completing the information section of the answer sheet. If you are taking your test by computer, refer to the previous section and ignore the following discussion of how to take the written test. The answer sheet is labeled Airman Written Test Application. A sample answer sheet is presented on page 10. It is important that you complete all items.

The Test No. at the upper right comes from the Question Selection Sheet. A question selection sheet similar to the one you will be given is presented on page 11. The question selection sheet tells you which 60 of the 898 airplane-related questions you are to answer.

1. The 898 questions are in the FAA's Instrument Rating Written Test Book (FAA-T-8080-20A). The number on the front of the FAA book should be the same as the number on top of the question selection sheet. For example, the number on the sample question selection sheet on page 11 is FAA-T-8080-20A. Bring any discrepancy to the attention of the person in charge of the test.

After you complete the information section (top) of the Airman Written Test Application (hereafter referred to as the answer sheet), you will be given

1. The answer sheet (returned to you by the person in charge of the test after (s)he has checked to see that you have completed the application portion properly).
2. The question selection sheet.
3. Instrument Rating Written Test Book (FAA-T-8080-20A).
4. Pencils and scratch paper (otherwise use the back of the question selection sheet as scratch paper).
5. Plastic overlays.

4186895

DEPARTMENT OF TRANSPORTATION — FEDERAL AVIATION ADMINISTRATION

# AIRMAN WRITTEN TEST APPLICATION

| DATE OF TEST | | | TITLE OF TEST | TEST NO. |
|---|---|---|---|---|
| MONTH | DAY | YEAR | INSTRUMENT RATING - AIRPLANE | 775062 |

PLEASE PRINT ONE LETTER IN EACH SPACE—LEAVE A BLANK SPACE AFTER EACH NAME

NAME (LAST, FIRST, MIDDLE)

| DATE OF BIRTH | | |
|---|---|---|
| MONTH | DAY | YEAR |

MAILING ADDRESS    NO. AND STREET, APT. #, P.O. BOX, OR RURAL ROUTE

DESCRIPTION

| HEIGHT | WEIGHT | HAIR | EYES |
|---|---|---|---|

CITY, TOWN OR POST OFFICE. AND STATE        ZIP CODE

BIRTHPLACE (City and State, or foreign country)    CITIZENSHIP    SOCIAL SECURITY NO.    IF A SOCIAL SECURITY NUMBER HAS NEVER BEEN ISSUED CHECK THIS BLOCK ➞ ☐

Is this a retest? ☐No ☐Yes, date of last test    Have you taken or are you taking an FAA approved course for this test? ☐No ☐Yes *(If "yes" give details below)*

Graduation date:    NAME OF SCHOOL    CITY AND STATE

CERTIFICATION: I CERTIFY that all of the statements made in this application are true, complete, and correct to the best of my knowledge and belief and are made in good faith. Signature _ _ _ _ _ _ _ _ _

— — DO NOT WRITE IN THIS BLOCK — — FOR USE OF FAA OFFICE ONLY — —

Applicant's identity established by:

| CARD A | | | | | | CARD B | | |
|---|---|---|---|---|---|---|---|---|
| CATEGORY | TEST NUMBER | TAKE NO. | SECTIONS 1 2 3 4 5 6 7 | EXPIRATION MONTH DAY YEAR | | CERTIFICATED SCHOOL NUMBER | MECH EXP DATE BY SECTION 1 2 3 | ID |

FIELD OFFICE DESIGNATION

SIGNATURE of FAA Representative

INSTRUCTIONS FOR MARKING THE ANSWER SHEET. Completely darken only one circle for each question. DO NOT USE (X) OR (✓). Use black lead pencil furnished by examiner. To make corrections, open answer sheet so erasure marks will not show on page 2. Then erase incorrect response on page 4. On page 2 (copy) mark the incorrect response with a slash (/). Questions are arranged in VERTICAL sequence as indicated by the arrows.

```
 1 ①②③④   23 ①②③④   45 ①②③④   67 ①②③④   89 ①②③④   111 ①②③④   133 ①②③④
 2 ①②③④   24 ①②③④   46 ①②③④   68 ①②③④   90 ①②③④   112 ①②③④   134 ①②③④
 3 ①②③④   25 ①②③④   47 ①②③④   69 ①②③④   91 ①②③④   113 ①②③④   135 ①②③④
 4 ①②③④   26 ①②③④   48 ①②③④   70 ①②③④   92 ①②③④   114 ①②③④   136 ①②③④
 5 ①②③④   27 ①②③④   49 ①②③④   71 ①②③④   93 ①②③④   115 ①②③④   137 ①②③④
 6 ①②③④   28 ①②③④   50 ①②③④   72 ①②③④   94 ①②③④   116 ①②③④   138 ①②③④
 7 ①②③④   29 ①②③④   51 ①②③④   73 ①②③④   95 ①②③④   117 ①②③④   139 ①②③④
 8 ①②③④   30 ①②③④   52 ①②③④   74 ①②③④   96 ①②③④   118 ①②③④   140 ①②③④
 9 ①②③④   31 ①②③④   53 ①②③④   75 ①②③④   97 ①②③④   119 ①②③④   141 ①②③④
10 ①②③④   32 ①②③④   54 ①②③④   76 ①②③④   98 ①②③④   120 ①②③④   142 ①②③④
11 ①②③④   33 ①②③④   55 ①②③④   77 ①②③④   99 ①②③④   121 ①②③④   143 ①②③④
12 ①②③④   34 ①②③④   56 ①②③④   78 ①②③④  100 ①②③④   122 ①②③④   144 ①②③④
13 ①②③④   35 ①②③④   57 ①②③④   79 ①②③④  101 ①②③④   123 ①②③④   145 ①②③④
14 ①②③④   36 ①②③④   58 ①②③④   80 ①②③④  102 ①②③④   124 ①②③④   146 ①②③④
15 ①②③④   37 ①②③④   59 ①②③④   81 ①②③④  103 ①②③④   125 ①②③④   147 ①②③④
16 ①②③④   38 ①②③④   60 ①②③④   82 ①②③④  104 ①②③④   126 ①②③④   148 ①②③④
17 ①②③④   39 ①②③④   61 ①②③④   83 ①②③④  105 ①②③④   127 ①②③④   149 ①②③④
18 ①②③④   40 ①②③④   62 ①②③④   84 ①②③④  106 ①②③④   128 ①②③④   150 ①②③④
19 ①②③④   41 ①②③④   63 ①②③④   85 ①②③④  107 ①②③④   129 ①②③④
20 ①②③④   42 ①②③④   64 ①②③④   86 ①②③④  108 ①②③④   130 ①②③④
21 ①②③④   43 ①②③④   65 ①②③④   87 ①②③④  109 ①②③④   131 ①②③④
22 ①②③④   44 ①②③④   66 ①②③④   88 ①②③④  110 ①②③④   132 ①②③④
```

Chapter 1: The FAA Written Test
11

DEPARTMENT OF TRANSPORTATION    FEDERAL AVIATION ADMINISTRATION

# QUESTION SELECTION SHEET

Use only with
Question Book
FAA-T-8080-20A

| TITLE | TEST NO. |
|---|---|
| **INSTRUMENT RATING -- AIRPLANE** | **775062** |

NAME _____

**NOTE: IT IS PERMISSIBLE TO MARK ON THIS SHEET.**

| On Answer Sheet for Item No. | Answer Question Number | On Answer Sheet for Item No. | Answer Question Number | On Answer Sheet for Item No. | Answer Question Number |
|---|---|---|---|---|---|
| 1 | 4035 | 21 | 4314 | 41 | 4612 |
| 2 | 4063 | 22 | 4315 | 42 | 4637 |
| 3 | 4066 | 23 | 4316 | 43 | 4655 |
| 4 | 4076 | 24 | 4318 | 44 | 4659 |
| 5 | 4078 | 25 | 4320 | 45 | 4680 |
| 6 | 4081 | 26 | 4321 | 46 | 4707 |
| 7 | 4088 | 27 | 4339 | 47 | 4737 |
| 8 | 4090 | 28 | 4410 | 48 | 4748 |
| 9 | 4108 | 29 | 4419 | 49 | 4771 |
| 10 | 4118 | 30 | 4437 | 50 | 4789 |
| 11 | 4130 | 31 | 4452 | 51 | 4797 |
| 12 | 4161 | 32 | 4463 | 52 | 4817 |
| 13 | 4167 | 33 | 4494 | 53 | 4824 |
| 14 | 4193 | 34 | 4505 | 54 | 4836 |
| 15 | 4217 | 35 | 4515 | 55 | 4874 |
| 16 | 4234 | 36 | 4530 | 56 | 4891 |
| 17 | 4241 | 37 | 4558 | 57 | 4899 |
| 18 | 4249 | 38 | 4566 | 58 | 4900 |
| 19 | 4312 | 39 | 4593 | 59 | 4910 |
| 20 | 4313 | 40 | 4603 | 60 | 4932 |

*For Official Use Only*

The plastic overlays are to put over pages on which you must mark, e.g., routes between airports on en route chart excerpts. The actual book of test questions is reused continually, and the FAA asks that you make no marks directly on it. Thus, plastic overlays permit you to write on the plastic (which is erasable), rather than on the pages in the exam question book itself.

1.  Answer the questions in order. **Carefully** refer to the question selection sheet for the FAA question number you are to answer.

2.  Watch your time. You will have 4 hr. to complete the 60 questions on your test. This is 4 min. per question (60 questions in 240 min.). Most candidates finish in about 1 to 2 hr.

3.  As you read each question, ignore (or cover up) the answer selections. Most people taking tests skim a question to get on to the answers.

    a.  When reading the question, pay particular attention to the requirement; i.e., **Exactly what is required**?

        1)  If you do not completely understand the requirements, you will probably answer the question incorrectly.

    b.  Then go back and use the data in the question and any related charts, diagrams, etc., to solve the question.

    c.  Select the best answer.

    d.  Mark the answer on the answer sheet.

        1)  Another approach is to set your answer sheet aside at the beginning of the test, write each answer on your question selection sheet next to the question, and transfer your answers to the answer sheet when you have completed the test. This reduces the risk of recording your answers improperly on your answer sheet.

    e.  If you are relatively sure of your answer, line out the question number on the question selection sheet.

        1)  The FAA permits you to mark on the question selection sheet.

        2)  As you line out these numbers on the question selection sheet, look back to the answer sheet to make sure it was the last question answered and also that you have put the answer where it should be on the answer sheet.

        3)  Be careful. Do not skip or omit a line on the answer sheet. The computer that grades the answer sheet has no way to determine whether you completed the answer sheet incorrectly or did not know the answer.

    f.  If you are unsure about a question, put a question mark on the question selection sheet rather than lining out the number on the question sheet.

    g.  If you temporarily skip a question, put an "X" on the question selection sheet rather than lining out the question number.

        1)  This will facilitate your returning to the question later.

    h.  After working through all 60 questions, go back and answer all the questions that you marked with a "?" or an "X."

        1)  If you do not know an answer, guess. There is no deduction or penalty for wrong answers.

        2)  If you guess, try to eliminate one answer and select the remaining answer that appears best.

    i.  Before turning in your answer sheet, check to see that the first 60 answers are marked and that only one answer is marked for each question.

        1)  If you change an answer, make sure the erasures are complete.

    j.    Note that the FAA answer sheet is numbered to 150 instead of 60.  This is because the answer sheet is designed to accommodate all FAA exams.  You are only to mark answers 1 through 60 (the number of questions on the FAA Instrument Rating Written Test).

    4.    There may be a few bad questions, i.e., no correct answers.  In these cases, any answer selection will be graded as correct.  Choose the best answer.

        a.    See Module 1.15, FAA Questions with Typographical Errors, below.

    5.    Finally, remember that you only need 70% to pass.  70% of 60 questions is 42 questions.  Thus, you can miss 18 and still pass.

        a.    While you should seriously attempt every question, do not become obsessed with making a perfect score.  If you do, you may become rattled if you have trouble with a question.  Also, you will begin to spend too much time on each question and become fatigued before you complete the test.

## 1.15  FAA QUESTIONS WITH TYPOGRAPHICAL ERRORS

Occasionally, FAA test questions contain typographical errors such that there is no correct answer.  The FAA test development process involves many steps and people, and as you would expect, glitches occur in the system that are beyond the control of any one person.  We have indicated an X as the answer to such questions on the cross reference list on pages 467 through 475.  We also indicate "best" rather than "correct" answers for some questions.  Use these "best" answers and any answer (except X) for questions with no correct answer if they appear on your written test.

Note that the FAA corrects (rewrites) defective questions on the computer tests, which it cannot do in the written test books.  Thus, it is important to carefully study questions that are noted to have no correct answer or a "best" answer in this book.  On the written test, you will get credit for these defective questions, but on computer tests, the questions will probably have been rephrased.

## 1.16  FAA WRITTEN TEST INSTRUCTIONS

The page of general instructions that appears in the test book is reproduced on page 14.  Study them now and reread them when you take the written test.

## 1.17  HOW THE FAA NOTIFIES YOU OF YOUR WRITTEN TEST SCORE

    1.    The results of your written test will be sent to you from the FAA Aeronautical Center in Oklahoma City where it is graded.

    2.    You will receive your Airman Written Test Report (AC Form 8080-2) approximately 2 to 3 weeks after you take the examination.  An example AC Form 8080-2 is reproduced on page 15.

        a.    Note that you will receive only one grade as illustrated.

        b.    The expiration date is the date by which you must take your FAA practical test.

        c.    The report lists the FAA subject matter knowledge codes of the questions you missed, so you can review the topics you missed prior to your flight test.

    3.    Use the FAA Listing of Subject Matter Knowledge Codes on pages 455 to 466 to determine which topics you had difficulty with.

        a.    Look them over and review them with your CFII so (s)he can certify that (s)he reviewed the deficient areas and found you competent in them when you take your practical test.

# GENERAL INSTRUCTIONS

## MAXIMUM TIME ALLOWED FOR TEST: 4 HOURS

Maximum time allowed for each test is based upon previous experience and educational statistics. This time is considered more than adequate for applicants with proper preparation and instruction.

### MATERIALS

Materials to be used with this written test book when used for airman certification testing:

1. AC Form 8080-3, Airman Written Test Application, which includes the answer sheet.

2. Question selection sheet which identifies the questions to be answered.

3. Plastic overlay sheet which can be placed over performance charts for plotting purposes.

### TEST INSTRUCTIONS

1. Read the instructions on page 1 of AC Form 8080-3, and complete page 4 of the form. Incomplete or erroneous personal information entered on this form delays the scoring process.

2. The questions in this written test book are numbered consecutively beginning with 4001. Refer to the question selection sheet to determine which questions to answer.

3. For each question number on the answer sheet, find the appropriate question in the written test book.

4. Mark your answer in the space provided for each question number on the answer sheet. Spaces 1, 2, or 3 left unmarked will be counted by the computer scanner as a miss.

5. The test questions are of the multiple-choice type. Until revised, answer sheets contain selections listed as 1, 2, 3, and 4 and should be interpreted as A, B, and C respectively. Selection 4 should never be used.

6. The supplementary material required to answer the questions will be found in apendixes 2 and 3.

7. Read each question carefully and avoid hasty assumptions. Do not answer until you understand the question. Do not spend too much time on any one question. Answer all of the questions that you readily know and then reconsider those you find difficult. Be careful to make necessary conversions when working with temperatures, speeds, and distances.

8. If a regulation or operations procedure is changed after this written test book is printed, you will receive credit for the affected question.

## DO NOT USE THIS BOOK UNLESS IT CORRESPONDS WITH THE BOOK NUMBER ON THE TEST.

### THE MINIMUM PASSING GRADE IS 70.

**Note:** The computer testing services allow 2.5 hr. for the instrument rating test. Ask about the time permitted when you call their 800 number.

4. Keep your Airman Written (or Computer) Test Report in a safe place because you must submit it to the FAA examiner when you take your final practical test.

| DO NOT DESTROY THIS TEST REPORT<br>This Test Report must be presented<br>for retesting or certification. | | DEPARTMENT OF TRANSPORTATION · FEDERAL AVIATION ADMINISTRATION<br>**AIRMAN WRITTEN TEST REPORT (RIS: AC 8080-2)** | | | | | | | | | 1466    41<br>SSN 434-80-6677 | |
|---|---|---|---|---|---|---|---|---|---|---|---|---|
| **TEST** | | **GRADES BY SECTION** | | | | | | | **FAA OFFICE NO.** | **TEST DATE** | **EXPIRATION DATE** | |
| **TAKE NO.** | **TITLE** * | 1 | 2 | 3 | 4 | 5 | 6 | 7 | | | | |
| 01 | IRA | 77 | | | | | | | SO 07 | **09-16-93** | **09-30-95** | |

| EXPIRATION DATE<br>*(Last day of month)* | | | | | | | |
|---|---|---|---|---|---|---|---|

◄—— **MECHANICS ONLY · EXPIRATION DATE CODES**
The first character designates the month; the second and third characters, the year. January through September as shown by numbers 1 through 9; October as "O"; November as "N"; December as "D".

*\*See codes on reverse side:*

LAST NAME, FIRST MIDDLE
FLANAGAN WILLIAM PATRICK JR
4720 NW 39TH ST
GAINESVILLE FL      32601

**EXAMPLES:**
Month (June) _____ 6   75
Year (1975) _____
Month (December) _____ D   75
Year (1975) _____

1    A20 B10 I05 I31 I52 J14 J33 J40

When applicable, an authorized instructor may complete and sign this statement:

I HAVE GIVEN THIS APPLICANT ADDITIONAL INSTRUCTION IN EACH OF THE SUBJECT AREAS FAILED AND CONSIDER THE APPLICANT COMPETENT TO PASS THE TEST.

LAST_____INITIAL_____CERTIFICATE NO._____TYPE_____*INSTRUCTOR'S SIGNATURE*_____
   *INSTRUCTOR'S NAME (Print)*
**FRAUDULENT ALTERATION OF THIS FORM BY ANY PERSON IS A BASIS FOR SUSPENSION OR REVOCATION OF ANY CERTIFICATES OR RATINGS HELD BY THAT PERSON.**
AC Form 8080-2 (10-83)      ISSUED BY:    ADMINISTRATOR<br>                                         FEDERAL AVIATION ADMINISTRATION

## 1.18 FAILURE ON THE WRITTEN TEST

1. If you fail (less than 70%) the written test (almost impossible if you follow the above instructions), you may retake it after 30 days.

   a. You can retake the test sooner than 30 days after a first failure only if your flight or ground instructor endorses the bottom of your Airman Written (or Computer) Test Report certifying that you have received the necessary ground instruction to retake the test.

2. Upon retaking the test, everything is the same except you must also submit your Airman Written (or Computer) Test Report indicating the previous failure to the examiner.

3. Note that the pass rate on the instrument rating written test is about 70%, i.e., 3 out of 10 fail the test initially. Reasons for failure include

   a. Failure to study the material tested (contained in the outlines at the beginning of Chapters 2 through 11 of this book);

   b. Failure to practice working the FAA exam questions under test conditions (all of the FAA questions on airplanes appear in Chapters 2 through 11 of this book); and

   c. Poor examination technique, such as

      1) Not reading questions and understanding the requirements, and

      2) Failure to complete the answer sheet correctly, e.g., getting answers out of sequence.

## 1.19 REORGANIZATION OF FAA QUESTIONS

1.  The questions in the FAA Instrument Rating Written Test Book (FAA-T-8080-20A) are numbered 4001 to 4943. The FAA questions appear to be presented randomly.

    a.  We have reorganized the FAA questions into chapters and modules.

    b.  The FAA question number is presented in the middle of the first line of the explanation of each answer.

2.  Pages 467 through 475 contain a list of the FAA questions numbers 4001 to 4943 with cross-references to the chapters and question numbers in this book.

    a.  For example, we have coded question 4002 as 5-18, which means it is found in Chapter 5 as question 18.

    b.  Note that, although 4001 to 4943 implies 943 questions, only 898 apply to airplanes.

        1)  The remaining 45 questions relate to gliders, balloons, etc., and have been omitted from this book.

            a)  These questions are indicated as NA in our cross-reference table beginning on page 467.

        2)  In summary, 898 in this book + 45 nonairplane = 943 questions.

With this overview of exam requirements, you are ready to begin the easy-to-study outlines and rearranged questions with answers to build your knowledge and confidence and PASS THE FAA's INSTRUMENT RATING WRITTEN TEST. The feedback we receive from users of our books and software indicates that they reduce anxiety, improve FAA test scores, and build knowledge. Studying for each test becomes a useful step toward advanced certificates and ratings.

## 1.20 SIMULATED FAA PRACTICE TEST

Appendix A, Instrument Rating Practice Test, beginning on page 447, allows you to practice taking the FAA written test without the answers next to the questions. This test has 60 questions that have been randomly selected from the 898 airplane-related questions in the FAA's Instrument Rating Written Test Book (FAA-T-8080-20A). Topical coverage in this practice test is similar to that of the FAA Instrument Rating--Airplane test.

It is very important that you answer all 60 questions at one sitting. You should not consult the answers, especially when being referred to figures (charts, tables, etc.) throughout this book where the questions are answered and explained. Analyze your performance based on the answer key which follows the practice test in Appendix A.

---

If this Gleim written test book saves you time and frustration in preparing for the FAA instrument rating written test, you should use Gleim's *Instrument Pilot FAA Practical Test Prep* to prepare for the FAA practical test. *Instrument Pilot FAA Practical Test Prep* will assist you in developing the competence and confidence to pass your FAA practical test, just as this book organizes and explains the knowledge needed to pass your FAA written test.

Also, flight maneuvers are quickly perfected when you understand exactly what to expect before you get into an airplane to practice the flight maneuvers. You must be ahead of (not behind) your CFII and your airplane. Gleim's practical test prep books explain and illustrate all flight maneuvers so the maneuvers and their execution are intuitively appealing to you.

Call **(800) 87-GLEIM** and order these books today!

---

# END OF CHAPTER

# CHAPTER TWO
# AIRPLANE INSTRUMENTS

This chapter contains outlines of major concepts tested, all FAA test questions and answers regarding the major instrument systems in an airplane, and an explanation of each answer. The subtopics or modules within this chapter are listed above, followed in parentheses by the number of questions from the FAA written test pertaining to that particular module. The two numbers following the parentheses are the page numbers on which the outline and questions begin for that module.

**CAUTION:** Recall that the **sole purpose** of this book is to expedite your passing the FAA written test for the instrument rating. Accordingly, all extraneous material (i.e., topics or regulations not directly tested on the FAA written test) is omitted, even though much more information and knowledge are necessary to fly safely. This additional material is presented in *Instrument Pilot FAA Practical Test Prep* and *Aviation Weather and Weather Services*, available from Gleim Publications, Inc. See the order form on page 478.

## 2.1 COMPASS ERRORS (Questions 1-11)

1. During taxi, you should check your compass to see that it is swinging freely and indicating known headings.

2. The difference between direction indicated by a magnetic compass not installed in an airplane and one installed in an airplane is called compass deviation.

    a. Magnetic fields produced by metals and electrical accessories in an airplane disturb the compass needle.

3. Magnetic compasses can only be considered accurate during straight-and-level flight at constant airspeed.

    a. When turning and accelerating/decelerating, the fluid level and compass card do not remain level and magnetic force pulls "down" as well as toward the pole.

    b. These are known as the magnetic dip characteristics.

4. In the Northern Hemisphere, acceleration/deceleration error occurs when on an easterly or westerly heading.

    a. A magnetic compass will indicate a turn toward the north during acceleration on an easterly or westerly heading.

    b. A magnetic compass will indicate a turn toward the south during deceleration on an easterly or westerly heading.

    c. Acceleration/deceleration error does not occur on a northerly or southerly heading.

5.  In the Northern Hemisphere, compass turning error occurs when turning from a northerly or southerly heading.

    a.  A magnetic compass will lag (and at the start of a turn indicate a turn in the opposite direction) when turning from a northerly heading.

        1)  If turning to the east (right), the compass will initially indicate a turn to the west and then lag behind the actual heading until your airplane is headed east (at which point there is no error).

        2)  If turning to the west (left), the compass will initially indicate a turn to the east and then lag behind the actual heading until your airplane is headed west (at which point there is no error).

    b.  A magnetic compass will lead or precede the turn when turning from a southerly heading.

    c.  Turning errors do not occur when turning from or through an easterly or westerly heading; i.e., turning errors are minimized at 90° and 270° headings.

6.  These magnetic dip errors diminish as acceleration/deceleration or turns are completed.

## 2.2 PITOT-STATIC SYSTEM (Questions 12-21)

1.  When both the airspeed indicator pitot tube and the drain hole are blocked, the airspeed indicator acts as an altimeter.

    a.  At a given altitude, airspeed changes would not change the indicated airspeed.

    b.  During climbs, the indicated airspeed will increase.

    c.  During descents, the indicated airspeed will decrease.

    d.  These changes occur as a result of the differential between the pressure of the air locked in the pitot tube and the static air vent pressure.

2.  If an alternate static source is vented inside an unpressurized airplane, the static pressure is usually lower than outside pressure due to the Venturi Effect of the outside air flowing over the cockpit.

    a.  The airspeed indicator will indicate a faster-than-actual airspeed.
    b.  The vertical speed indicator (VSI) will momentarily show a climb.
    c.  The altimeter will read higher than actual.

3.  If the pitot tube becomes clogged with ice during flight, only the airspeed indicator will be affected.

    a.  The altimeter and vertical speed indicator depend upon the static air vents.

    b.  If the static ports are iced over, the vertical speed indicator will not reflect climbs and descents because the change in air pressure cannot be detected by the VSI.

4.  If the vertical speed indicator is not calibrated correctly (e.g., continually indicates a descent or climb), it can still be used for IFR flight by adjusting for the error when interpreting the indications.

    a.  The VSI is not a required instrument for IFR flight. (Nonetheless, the FAA requires you to report the inability to climb/descend at least 500 fpm and the Instrument PTS requires constant rate climbs/descents.)

5.  The Mach meter or Mach indicator shows the ratio of aircraft true airspeed to the speed of sound at flight altitude by means of the pressure differential between static and impact sources, with correction for temperature and altitude.

6.  If the outside air temperature increases during a flight at constant power and a constant indicated altitude, true airspeed (TAS) and true altitude will increase.

**2.3 ALTIMETER** (Questions 22-46)

1. The altimeter indicates the true altitude at the field elevation if the local altimeter setting is used in an accurate altimeter.

    a. Thus the altimeter indicates altitude in relation to the pressure level set in the barometric window.

2. Altimeters have three "hands" (like a clock's hour, minute, and second hands).

3. The three hands on the altimeter are generally arranged as follows:

    a. 10,000-ft. interval (thin needle with a flared triangular tip)
    b. 1,000-ft. interval (short, fat needle)
    c. 100-ft. interval (long, medium-thickness needle)

4. Altimeters are numbered 0 through 9.

5. To read an altimeter,

    a. First, determine whether the thin needle with the flared triangular tip rests between 0 and 1 (for 1-10,000 ft.), 1 and 2 (10,000-20,000 ft.), or 2 and 3 (20,000-30,000 ft.).

    b. Second, determine whether the shortest needle is between 0 and 1 (0-1,000 ft.), 1 and 2 (1,000-2,000), etc.

    c. Third, determine at which number the medium needle is pointing, e.g., 1 for 100 ft., 2 for 200 ft., etc.

6. The altimeter setting dial allows adjustment for nonstandard pressure.

    a. A window in the face of the altimeter shows a barometric scale that can be rotated.

    b. Rotating the setting dial simultaneously changes the scale and the altimeter hands in the same direction.

7. Atmospheric pressure decreases about 1 in. Hg for every 1,000 ft. of altitude gained.

    a. Changing the altimeter setting changes the indicated altitude in the same direction and by 1,000 ft. for every in. change.

    b. For example, changing from 29.92 in. to 30.92 in. increases indicated altitude by 1,000 ft., or from 30.15 in. to 30.25 in. increases indicated altitude by 100 ft.

8. Prior to takeoff, the altimeter should be set to the current local altimeter setting.

    a. With the current altimeter setting, the indicated altitude of the airplane on the ground should be within 75 ft. of the actual elevation of the airport for acceptable accuracy.

    b. If the current local altimeter setting is not available, use the departure airport elevation.

    c. The local altimeter setting should be used by all pilots in a particular area, primarily to provide for better vertical separation of aircraft.

    d. During an IFR flight in Class E airspace below 18,000 ft. MSL, ATC will periodically provide the current altimeter setting.

9. The standard temperature and pressure at sea level are 15°C and 29.92 in. Hg (59°F and 1013.2 millibars of mercury).

    a. Pressure altitude is the indicated altitude when the altimeter setting is adjusted to 29.92 in. Hg.

    b. Pressure altitude is used in computations of density altitude, true altitude, and true airspeed.

    c. Pressure altitude will equal true altitude when standard atmospheric conditions exist.

    d. Pressure altitude and density altitude are the same at standard temperature.

10.   The altimeter must be set to pressure altitude when flying at or above 18,000 ft. MSL.

a.    This guarantees vertical separation of airplanes above 18,000 ft. MSL.

11.   Since altimeter readings are adjusted for changes in barometric pressure but not for temperature changes, an airplane will be at lower-than-indicated altitude when flying in colder-than-standard air.

a.    On warm days, you will be at a higher altitude (i.e., true altitude) than your altimeter indicates.

12.   When pressure lowers en route, your altimeter will register higher-than-actual altitude until you adjust the altimeter for the new altimeter setting.

## 2.4 GYROSCOPES  (Questions 47-48)

1.    Listen to your electric gyroscopes for funny noises after the battery is turned on but before the engine is started.

2.    One of the characteristics of a gyro is that it is resistant to deflection of the spinning wheel, which is based on two of Newton's laws of motion.

a.    A body at rest will continue at rest and a body in motion will continue in motion in a straight line until acted upon by an outside force.

b.    Deflection of a moving body is proportional to the deflective force applied and inversely proportional to the body's weight and speed.

## 2.5 HEADING INDICATOR  (Questions 49-52)

1.    The heading indicator (HI) should be set to the correct magnetic heading 5 min. after the engine is started.

a.    Prior to takeoff, check the heading indicator to determine that it continues to maintain the correct heading after taxi turns.

2.    The remote indicating compass (RIC) combines the functions of the magnetic compass and heading indicator.  One component of the RIC is the slaving control and compensator unit, as shown in Fig. 143 on page 34.

a.    This unit contains a slaving meter needle which indicates the difference between the displayed heading and the actual magnetic heading.

1)    A right deflection (+) indicates a clockwise (right) error in the heading indicator compass card (i.e., the correct magnetic heading is to the right of the indicated heading).

a)    Depressing the right (counterclockwise) heading drive button will move the heading indicator compass card to the left, thus increasing (+) the indicated heading toward the correct value (i.e., from 180° to 190°).

2)    A left deflection (−) indicates a counterclockwise (left) error in the heading indicator compass card (i.e., the correct magnetic heading is to the left of the indicated heading).

a)    Depressing the left (clockwise) heading drive button will move the heading indicator compass card to the right, thus decreasing (−) the indicated heading toward the correct value (i.e., from 190° to 180°).

b.    To make corrections to the RIC, the system must be placed in the free gyro mode.

1)    After corrections are made the system is returned to the slaved mode, which is the normal mode of operation.

## 2.6 ATTITUDE INDICATOR  (Questions 53-61)

1.  Prior to IFR flight, the pilot should check the horizon bar, which should be erect and stable within 5 min. of engine warm-up.

    a.  The horizon bar should not tilt more than 5° when making taxi turns.

    b.  Remember, you can adjust the position of the miniature airplane but it is the horizon bar that moves to indicate attitude in flight.

        1)  The horizon bar remains parallel to the horizon as the airplane's attitude changes.

2.  Precession errors (both pitch and bank) on attitude indicators are greatest when rolling out of a 180° steep turn in either direction.

    a.  As the airplane returns to straight-and-level coordinated flight, the miniature aircraft will show a slight climb and a turn in the direction opposite to the turn just made.

        1)  If you indicate straight-and-level, you will be descending and turning in the direction of the turn just made.

    b.  These precession errors during turns (including coordinated turns) are caused by centrifugal force acting on the pendulous vanes (erection mechanism in the attitude indicator).  It results in the precession of the gyro toward the inside of the turn.

3.  Attitude indicators also reflect an error during skidding turns which precesses the gyro toward the inside of the turn.

    a.  As the airplane returns to straight-and-level coordinated flight, the miniature aircraft shows a turn in the direction opposite to the skid.  Pitch indication is not affected.

4.  Deceleration precession makes some attitude indicators incorrectly indicate a descent.

    a.  Conversely, acceleration, through precession, may result in attitude indicators incorrectly indicating a climb.

## 2.7 TURN-AND-SLIP INDICATOR  (Questions 62-63)

1.  Prior to engine start, the turn-and-slip indicator should indicate the needle centered, the tube full of fluid, and the ball approximately centered.

2.  During taxi turns, the needle should deflect in the direction of the turn and the ball should move freely opposite the turn due to centrifugal force.

## 2.8 TURN COORDINATOR  (Questions 64-68)

1.  The turn coordinator indicates rate of roll and rate of turn.

    a.  When the bank is changing, the rate of roll is indicated.
    b.  When the bank is constant, the rate of turn is indicated.
    c.  Thus, the angle of bank is only indirectly indicated.

2.  On taxi turns, the miniature aircraft indicates a turn in the direction of the taxiing turn and the ball moves to the outside of the turn due to centrifugal force.

---

**QUESTIONS AND ANSWER EXPLANATIONS**

All the FAA questions from the written test for the instrument rating relating to the major instrument systems in an airplane and the material outlined previously are reproduced on the following pages in the same modules as the outlines. To the immediate right of each question are the correct answer and answer explanation. You should cover these answers and answer explanations with your hand or a piece of paper while responding to the questions. Refer to the general discussion in Chapter 1 on how to take the examination.

Remember that the questions from the FAA Instrument Rating Question Book have been reordered by topic, and the topics have been organized into a meaningful sequence. Accordingly, the first line of the answer explanation gives the FAA question number and the citation of the authoritative source for the answer.

---

## 2.1 Compass Errors

**1.**
**4834.** On the taxi check, the magnetic compass should

A— swing opposite to the direction of turn when turning from north.
B— exhibit the same number of degrees of dip as the latitude.
C— swing freely and indicate known headings.

**Answer (C) is correct (4834).** *(IFH Chap IV)*
When taxiing, the magnetic compass should be checked to make sure that the compass card is swinging freely and indicating known headings.
Answer (A) is incorrect because the compass exhibits turning errors only when the airplane is airborne and in a bank. Answer (B) is incorrect because compass turning errors occur in flight as a result of magnetic dip.

**2.**
**4877.** What should be the indication on the magnetic compass as you roll into a standard rate turn to the left from an east heading in the Northern Hemisphere?

A— The compass will initially indicate a turn to the right.
B— The compass will remain on east for a short time, then gradually catch up to the magnetic heading of the aircraft.
C— The compass will indicate the approximate correct magnetic heading if the roll into the turn is smooth.

**Answer (C) is correct (4877).** *(IFH Chap IV)*
If you roll into a smooth, coordinated, standard-rate turn to the left or right from an east or west heading, the compass will indicate the approximate correct magnetic heading. There are no turning errors on turns from east or west headings.
Answer (A) is incorrect because the compass will initially indicate a turn in the opposite direction of a bank only when turning from a north heading. Answer (B) is incorrect because when turning from an east heading, the compass will immediately indicate a turn, if the roll into the turn is smooth.

**3.**
**4886.** What should be the indication on the magnetic compass as you roll into a standard rate turn to the right from an easterly heading in the Northern Hemisphere?

A— The compass will initially indicate a turn to the left.
B— The compass will remain on east for a short time, then gradually catch up to the magnetic heading of the aircraft.
C— The compass will indicate the approximate correct magnetic heading if the roll into the turn is smooth.

**Answer (C) is correct (4886).** *(IFH Chap IV)*
If you roll into a smooth, coordinated, standard-rate turn to the left or right from an east or west heading, the compass will normally indicate the approximate correct magnetic heading. Acceleration, not turning errors, are found in east or west headings in the Northern Hemisphere.
Answer (A) is incorrect because the compass will initially indicate a turn in the opposite direction of a bank only when turning from a north heading. Answer (B) is incorrect because when turning from an east heading, the compass will immediately indicate a turn, if the roll into the turn is smooth.

**4.**
**4887.** What should be the indication on the magnetic compass as you roll into a standard rate turn to the right from a south heading in the Northern Hemisphere?

A— The compass will indicate a turn to the right, but at a faster rate than is actually occurring.
B— The compass will initially indicate a turn to the left.
C— The compass will remain on south for a short time, then gradually catch up to the magnetic heading of the aircraft.

**5.**
**4888.** On what headings will the magnetic compass read most accurately during a level 360° turn, with a bank of approximately 15°?

A— 135° through 225°.
B— 90° and 270°.
C— 180° and 0°.

**6.**
**4889.** What causes the northerly turning error in a magnetic compass?

A— Coriolis force at the mid-latitudes.
B— Centrifugal force acting on the compass card.
C— The magnetic dip characteristic.

**7.**
**4890.** What should be the indication on the magnetic compass when you roll into a standard rate turn to the left from a south heading in the Northern Hemisphere?

A— The compass will indicate a turn to the left, but at a faster rate than is actually occurring.
B— The compass will initially indicate a turn to the right.
C— The compass will remain on south for a short time, then gradually catch up to the magnetic heading of the aircraft.

**8.**
**4891.** What should be the indication on the magnetic compass as you roll into a standard rate turn to the right from a westerly heading in the Northern Hemisphere?

A— The compass will initially show a turn in the opposite direction, then turn to a northerly indication but lagging behind the actual heading of the aircraft.
B— The compass will remain on a westerly heading for a short time, then gradually catch up to the actual heading of the aircraft.
C— The compass will indicate the approximate correct magnetic heading if the roll into the turn is smooth.

**Answer (A) is correct (4887).** *(IFH Chap IV)*
In turns from a southerly heading in the Northern Hemisphere, the compass leads the turn. That is, it indicates a turn in the proper direction, but at a faster rate than is actually occurring.
Answer (B) is incorrect because the compass will initially indicate a turn in the opposite direction if the turn is made from a north (not south) heading. Answer (C) is incorrect because it describes a shallower than standard turn from a north (not south) heading.

**Answer (B) is correct (4888).** *(IFH Chap IV)*
When making a turn through north or south, the compass indication will usually be incorrect. But when turning through east or west, the compass indication is usually accurate. Therefore, the compass should be indicating properly when passing through 90° and 270°. This only holds true for medium to shallow bank turns, e.g., 15-30°.
Answer (A) is incorrect because the compass leads the heading when turning through south. Answer (C) is incorrect because compass turning errors are greatest at north and south headings.

**Answer (C) is correct (4889).** *(IFH Chap IV)*
Magnetic dip causes a compass needle to point both down toward the earth as well as to the magnetic pole. This causes turning errors.
Answer (A) is incorrect because the Coriolis force of the spinning Earth affects winds rather than compass indications. Answer (B) is incorrect because centrifugal force is not related to compass turning errors.

**Answer (A) is correct (4890).** *(IFH Chap IV)*
In turns from a southerly heading in the Northern Hemisphere, the compass leads the turn. That is, it indicates a turn in the proper direction, but at a faster rate than is actually occurring.
Answer (B) is incorrect because the compass will initially indicate a turn in the opposite direction if the turn is made from a north (not south) heading. Answer (C) is incorrect because it describes a shallower than standard turn from a north (not south) heading.

**Answer (C) is correct (4891).** *(IFH Chap IV)*
If you roll into a smooth, coordinated, standard-rate turn to the left or right from an east or west heading, the compass will indicate the approximate correct magnetic heading. There are no turning errors on turns from east or west headings.
Answer (A) is incorrect because the compass will initially indicate a turn in the opposite direction of a bank only when turning from a north heading. Answer (B) is incorrect because when turning from an east heading, the compass will immediately indicate a turn, if the roll into the turn is smooth.

**9.**
**4892.** What should be the indication on the magnetic compass as you roll into a standard rate turn to the right from a northerly heading in the Northern Hemisphere?

A— The compass will indicate a turn to the right, but at a faster rate than is actually occurring.
B— The compass will initially indicate a turn to the left.
C— The compass will remain on north for a short time, then gradually catch up to the magnetic heading of the aircraft.

**Answer (B) is correct (4892).** *(IFH Chap IV)*
In turns from a northerly heading in the Northern Hemisphere, the compass will initially indicate a turn to the opposite direction. Then the compass heading will lag behind the actual heading until the airplane approaches an east or west heading.
Answer (A) is incorrect because it describes a turn to the right from a southerly heading. Answer (C) is incorrect because it describes a shallower than standard turn from north.

**10.**
**4893.** What should be the indication on the magnetic compass as you roll into a standard rate turn to the left from a west heading in the Northern Hemisphere?

A— The compass will initially indicate a turn to the right.
B— The compass will remain on west for a short time, then gradually catch up to the magnetic heading of the aircraft.
C— The compass will indicate the approximate correct magnetic heading if the roll into the turn is smooth.

**Answer (C) is correct (4893).** *(IFH Chap IV)*
If you roll into a smooth, coordinated, standard-rate turn to the left or right from an east or west heading, the compass will indicate the approximate correct magnetic heading. Turning errors appear on turns from north or south headings, not east or west.
Answer (A) is incorrect because the compass will initially indicate a turn in the opposite direction of a bank only when turning from a north heading. Answer (B) is incorrect because when turning from an east heading, the compass will immediately indicate a turn, if the roll into the turn is smooth.

**11.**
**4894.** What should be the indication on the magnetic compass as you roll into a standard rate turn to the left from a north heading in the Northern Hemisphere?

A— The compass will indicate a turn to the left, but at a faster rate than is actually occurring.
B— The compass will initially indicate a turn to the right.
C— The compass will remain on north for a short time, then gradually catch up to the magnetic heading of the aircraft.

**Answer (B) is correct (4894).** *(IFH Chap IV)*
In turns from a northerly heading in the Northern Hemisphere, the compass will initially indicate a turn to the opposite direction and the compass heading will lag behind actual until the airplane approaches an east or west heading.
Answer (A) is incorrect because it describes a turn to the left from a southerly heading. Answer (C) is incorrect because it describes a shallower than standard turn from north.

## 2.2 Pitot-Static System

**12.**
**4909.** During flight, if the pitot tube becomes clogged with ice, which of the following instruments would be affected?

A— The airspeed indicator only.
B— The airspeed indicator and the altimeter.
C— The airspeed indicator, altimeter, and Vertical Speed Indicator.

**Answer (A) is correct (4909).** *(IFH Chap IV)*
The pitot-static system is a source of pressure for the altimeter, vertical speed indicator, and airspeed indicator. The pitot tube is connected directly to the airspeed indicator, and the static vents are connected directly to all three. The pressure of air coming into the pitot tube (impact air pressure) is compared with the air pressure at the static system vents to determine airspeed.
Answer (B) is incorrect because the pitot tube is connected only to the airspeed indicator (not the altimeter). Answer (C) is incorrect because the pitot tube is connected only to the airspeed indicator (not the altimeter or vertical speed indicator).

**13.**
**4830.** If both the ram air input and the drain hole of the pitot system are blocked, what reaction should you observe on the airspeed indicator when power is applied and a climb is initiated out of severe icing conditions?

A— The indicated airspeed would show a continuous deceleration while climbing.
B— The airspeed would drop to, and remain at, zero.
C— No change until an actual climb rate is established, then indicated airspeed will increase.

Answer (C) is correct (4830). *(IFH Chap IV)*
When the airspeed indicator pitot tube and drain hole are blocked, the airspeed indicator will react as an altimeter. There will be a constant pressure within the pitot tube, and as the pressure from the static source decreases during a climb, the indicated airspeed on the altimeter will increase.
Answer (A) is incorrect because, as there is an increase in altitude, the airspeed indicator will show an increase in airspeed as the air pressure within the pitot tube is relatively greater than that of the static air. Answer (B) is incorrect because this reaction would occur if the ram air input, but not the drain hole, were blocked.

**14.**
**4854.** What indication should a pilot observe if an airspeed indicator ram air input and drain hole are blocked?

A— The airspeed indicator will react as an altimeter.
B— The airspeed indicator will show a decrease with an increase in altitude.
C— No airspeed indicator change will occur during climbs or descents.

Answer (A) is correct (4854). *(IFH Chap IV)*
When the airspeed indicator pitot tube and drain hole are blocked, the airspeed indicator will react as an altimeter. There will be a constant pressure within the pitot tube, and as the pressure from the static source decreases during a climb, the indicated airspeed on the altimeter will increase.
Answer (B) is incorrect because indicated airspeed will increase (not decrease) with increases in altitude. Answer (C) is incorrect because differential pressure between the pitot tube and static air source changes, and so does indicated airspeed.

**15.**
**4821.** If both the ram air input and drain hole of the pitot system are blocked, what airspeed indication can be expected?

A— No variation of indicated airspeed in level flight even if large power changes are made.
B— Decrease of indicated airspeed during a climb.
C— Constant indicated airspeed during a descent.

Answer (A) is correct (4821). *(IFH Chap IV)*
If both the pitot tube input and the drain hole on the pitot system are blocked, the airspeed indication will be constant at any given altitude.
Answer (B) is incorrect because, during a climb, it will indicate an increase (not decrease) due to the stronger differential pressure in the blocked pitot tube relative to the static vents. Answer (C) is incorrect because indicated airspeed would change with changes in altitude.

**16.**
**4913.** If the outside air temperature increases during a flight at constant power and at a constant indicated altitude, the true airspeed will

A— decrease and true altitude will increase.
B— increase and true altitude will decrease.
C— increase and true altitude will increase.

Answer (C) is correct (4913). *(IFH Chap III)*
As temperature increases, pressure levels increase and true altitude increases given a constant indicated altitude. As altitude increases with constant power, true airspeed increases.
Answer (A) is incorrect because TAS increases (not decreases). Answer (B) is incorrect because true altitude will increase (not decrease).

**17.**
**4908.** If, while in level flight, it becomes necessary to use an alternate source of static pressure vented inside the airplane, which of the following should the pilot expect?

A— The altimeter to read lower than normal.
B— The vertical speed to momentarily show a descent.
C— The vertical speed to momentarily show a climb.

Answer (C) is correct (4908). *(IFH Chap IV)*
Most aircraft equipped with a pitot-static system are provided with an alternate source of static pressure for emergency use. This source is usually vented inside the cabin. The pressure within an unpressurized cockpit is slightly lower than the pressure outside the airplane because of the Venturi effect of the air moving past the outside of the cockpit. When the alternate static source is used, the altimeter will read higher than actual and the vertical speed indicator will momentarily show a climb.
Answer (A) is incorrect because the altimeter will indicate higher (not lower) than actual because of the lower relative air pressure from the alternate static air vent. Answer (B) is incorrect because the VSI indication will be a momentary climb, not a descent.

**18.**
**4930.**  If while in level flight, it becomes necessary to use an alternate source of static pressure vented inside the airplane, which of the following variations in instrument indications should the pilot expect?

A— The altimeter will read lower than normal, airspeed lower than normal, and the VSI will momentarily show a descent.

B— The altimeter will read higher than normal, airspeed greater than normal, and the VSI will momentarily show a climb.

C— The altimeter will read lower than normal, airspeed greater than normal, and the VSI will momentarily show a climb and then a descent.

**19.**
**4879.**  What would be the indication on the VSI during entry into a 500 FPM actual descent from level flight if the static ports were iced over?

A— The indication would be in reverse of the actual rate of descent (500 FPM climb).

B— The initial indication would be a climb, then descent at a rate in excess of 500 FPM.

C— The VSI pointer would remain at zero regardless of the actual rate of descent.

**20.**
**4056.**  You check the flight instruments while taxiing and find the vertical speed indicator (VSI) indicates a descent of 100 feet per minute.  In this case, you

A— must return to the parking area and have the instrument corrected by an authorized instrument repairman.

B— may take off and use 100 feet descent as the zero indication.

C— may not take off until the instrument is corrected by either the pilot or a mechanic.

**21.**
**4864.**  What information does a Mach meter present?

A— The ratio of aircraft true airspeed to the speed of sound.

B— The ratio of aircraft indicated airspeed to the speed of sound.

C— The ratio of aircraft equivalent airspeed, corrected for installation error, to the speed of sound.

Answer (B) is correct (4930).  *(IFH Chap IV)*
Most aircraft equipped with a pitot-static system are provided with an alternate source of static pressure for emergency use.  This source is usually vented inside the cabin.  The pressure within an unpressurized cockpit is slightly lower than the pressure outside the airplane because of the Venturi effect of the air moving past the outside of the cockpit.  When the alternate static source is used, the altimeter will read higher than actual and the vertical speed indicator will momentarily show a climb.
Answer (A) is incorrect because the altimeter and airspeed indicators will read higher (not lower) than normal, and the vertical speed indicator will momentarily show a climb (not a descent).  Answer (C) is incorrect because the altimeter will read higher (not lower) than normal, and the vertical speed indicator will show level flight (not a descent) after the momentary climb.

Answer (C) is correct (4879).  *(IFH Chap IV)*
The vertical speed indicator operates from the static pressure source and indicates change in pressure.  Thus, if the static pressure ports became iced over, there would be no change in the static pressure and there would be no indication of descent or climb.
Answer (A) is incorrect because, with no change in pressure, the indication would be level (not a climb).  Answer (B) is incorrect because, with no change in pressure, the indication would be level (not a climb or descent).

Answer (B) is correct (4056).  *(IFH Chap IV)*
The needle of the vertical speed indicator should indicate zero when the aircraft is on the ground or maintaining a constant pressure level in flight.  If it does not indicate zero, you must allow for the error when interpreting the indications in flight.  Since the VSI is not a required instrument, you may fly when it is out of adjustment.
Answer (A) is incorrect because the VSI can be used by making allowances in flight.  Answer (C) is incorrect because the VSI can be used by making allowances in flight.

Answer (A) is correct (4864).  *(IFH Chap IV)*
The Mach meter indicates the ratio of aircraft true airspeed to the speed of sound at flight altitude.  It uses the pressure differential between the impact and static air sources and corrects automatically for temperature and altitude.
Answer (B) is incorrect because the Mach meter uses true (not indicated) airspeed.  Answer (C) is incorrect because equivalent airspeed is the calibrated airspeed of an aircraft corrected for compressibility flow at a particular altitude.  The Mach meter uses true airspeed.

## 2.3  Altimeter

**22.**
**4402.** How should you preflight check the altimeter prior to an IFR flight?

A— Set the altimeter to 29.92" Hg. With current temperature and the altimeter indication, determine the true altitude to compare with the field elevation.
B— Set the altimeter first with 29.92" Hg and then the current altimeter setting. The change in altitude should correspond to the change in setting.
C— Set the altimeter to the current altimeter setting. The indication should be within 75 feet of the actual elevation for acceptable accuracy.

Answer (C) is correct (4402). *(IFH Chap IV)*
Set the altimeter to the local altimeter setting before taking off and verify that the indication is within 75 ft. of the actual elevation. If greater than 75 ft., you should consult an instrument repair shop.
Answer (A) is incorrect because setting the altimeter to 29.92 and adjusting for temperature gives density (not true) altitude. Answer (B) is incorrect because only indicated altitude (not change in altitude) is checked.

**23.**
**4880.** How should you preflight check the altimeter prior to an IFR flight?

A— Set the altimeter to the current temperature. With current temperature and the altimeter indication, determine the calibrated altitude to compare with the field elevation.
B— Set the altimeter first with 29.92" Hg and then the current altimeter setting. The change in altitude should correspond to the change in setting.
C— Set the altimeter to the current altimeter setting. The indication should be within 75 feet of the actual elevation for acceptable accuracy.

Answer (C) is correct (4880). *(IFH Chap IV)*
Set the altimeter to the local altimeter setting before taking off and verify that the indication is within 75 ft. of the actual elevation. If greater than 75 ft., you should consult an instrument repair shop.
Answer (A) is incorrect because an altimeter can be adjusted for nonstandard pressure, not temperature. Answer (B) is incorrect because only indicated altitude (not change in altitude) is checked.

**24.**
**4923.** The altimeter indicates the aircraft altitude in relation to

A— sea level.
B— the standard datum plane.
C— the pressure level set in the barometric window.

Answer (C) is correct (4923). *(PHAK Chap III)*
The altimeter indicates the airplane altitude in relationship to the pressure level set in the barometric window. These altimeter settings are intended to reflect height above sea level in the vicinity of the reporting station. Therefore, you must adjust your altimeter setting as the flight progresses from one station to the next.
Answer (A) is incorrect because the height above sea level (true altitude) is only indicated when the altimeter is set to the correct altimeter setting. Answer (B) is incorrect because the height above the standard datum plane (pressure altitude) is only indicated when the altimeter is set to 29.92.

**25.**
**4910.** The local altimeter setting should be used by all pilots in a particular area, primarily to provide for

A— the cancellation of altimeter error due to nonstandard temperatures aloft.
B— better vertical separation of aircraft.
C— more accurate terrain clearance in mountainous areas.

Answer (B) is correct (4910). *(IFH Chap IV)*
Because the altimeter in each airplane is equally affected by temperature and pressure variation errors, use of the local altimeter setting in a given area provides for better vertical separation of aircraft.
Answer (A) is incorrect because the altimeter setting does not compensate for nonstandard temperatures aloft. Rather, all altimeters in the area will reflect the same uncompensated amount. Answer (C) is incorrect because temperatures aloft must also be considered to assure terrain clearance.

**26.**
**4484.** (Refer to figure 84 below.) Which altimeter depicts 8,000 feet?

A— 1.
B— 2.
C— 3.

Answer (B) is correct (4484). *(IFH Chap IV)*
8,000 ft. is indicated on the altimeter in the accompanying figure by the short hand (1,000-ft. intervals) on 8, the long hand (100-ft. intervals) on zero, and the thin hand with flared tip (10,000-ft. intervals) just below 1.
Answer (A) is incorrect because both the thin hand and the short hand are on 8, which would indicate something in the vicinity of 88,000 ft. Answer (C) is incorrect because the thin hand is on zero, which is indicating 800 ft.

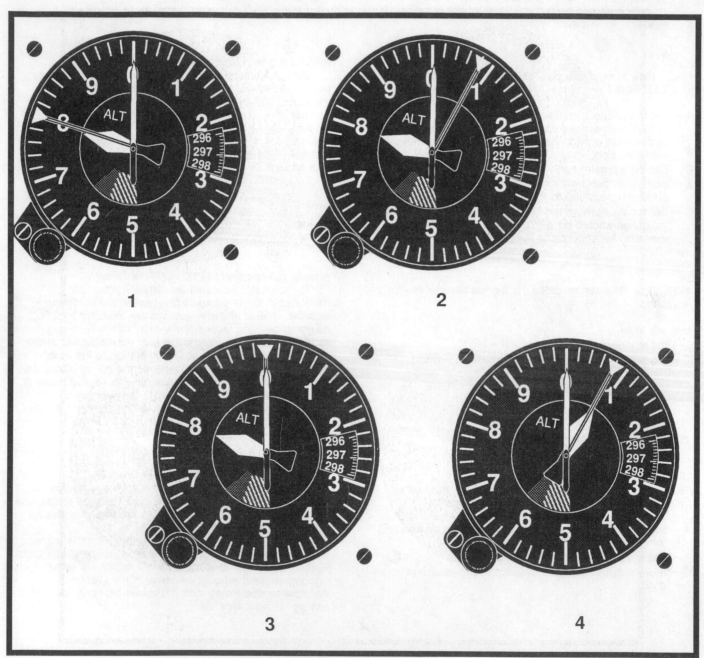

FIGURE 84.—Altimeter/8,000 Feet.

**27.**
**4483.** (Refer to figure 83 below.) Which altimeter depicts 12,000 feet?

A— 2.
B— 3.
C— 4.

Answer (C) is correct (4483). *(IFH Chap IV)*
    When indicating 12,000 ft., an altimeter has the long hand (100-ft intervals) on 0, the short hand (1,000-ft intervals) on 2, and the thin hand with flared tip (10,000-ft. intervals) just over 1.
    Answer (A) is incorrect because the thin hand is above 2 and the short hand is on 1, indicating 21,000 ft. Answer (B) is incorrect because the short hand is on 1, the long hand is on 2, and the thin hand is above 1, indicating about 11,200 ft.

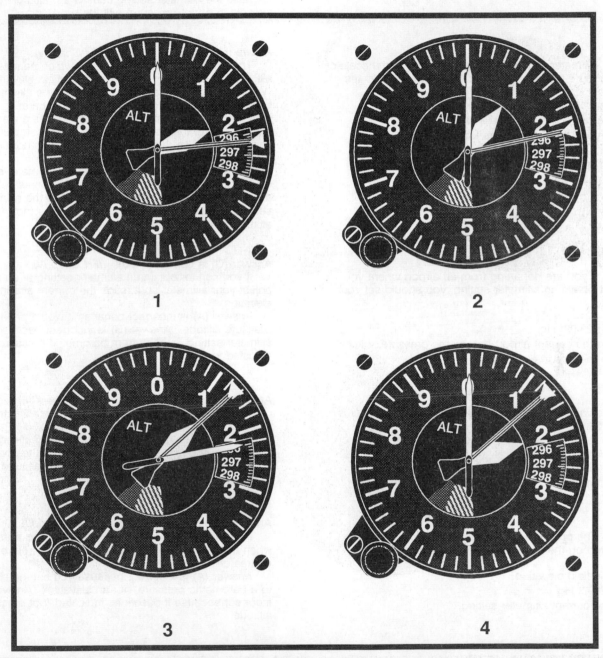

FIGURE 83.—Altimeter/12,000 Feet.

**28.**
**4922.** Altimeter setting is the value to which the scale of the pressure altimeter is set so the altimeter indicates

A— pressure altitude at sea level.
B— true altitude at field elevation.
C— pressure altitude at field elevation.

Answer (B) is correct (4922). *(PHAK Chap III)*
    The altimeter setting is the value which permits the altimeter to indicate the true altitude at field elevation. Within the vicinity of a particular airport, the altimeter setting provides an accurate means of separating traffic vertically and also provides obstruction clearance. Note that the use of the word "true" here is not completely accurate because the altimeter setting does not correct for nonstandard temperature.
    Answer (A) is incorrect because the altimeter setting causes the altimeter to indicate true (not pressure) altitude at field (not sea) level. Answer (C) is incorrect because the altimeter setting causes the altimeter to indicate true (not pressure) altitude.

**29.**
**4111.** Altimeter setting is the value to which the scale of the pressure altimeter is set so the altimeter indicates

A— true altitude at field elevation.
B— pressure altitude at field elevation.
C— pressure altitude at sea level.

Answer (A) is correct (4111). *(IFH Chap IV)*
    The altimeter setting is the value which permits the altimeter to indicate the true altitude at field elevation. Within the vicinity of a particular airport, the altimeter setting provides an accurate means of separating traffic vertically and also provides obstruction clearance. Note that the use of the word "true" here is not completely accurate because the altimeter setting does not correct for nonstandard temperature.
    Answer (B) is incorrect because the altimeter setting causes the altimeter to indicate true (not pressure) altitude. Answer (C) is incorrect because the altimeter setting causes the altimeter to indicate true (not pressure) altitude at field (not sea) level.

**30.**
**4480.** If you are departing from an airport where you cannot obtain an altimeter setting, you should set your altimeter

A— on 29.92" Hg.
B— on the current airport barometric pressure, if known.
C— to the airport elevation.

Answer (C) is correct (4480). *(IFH Chap IV)*
    If you cannot obtain an altimeter setting at an airport, adjust your altimeter so it reads the current airport elevation.
    Answer (A) is incorrect because it would provide only pressure altitude. Answer (B) is incorrect because the altimeter setting is the current barometric pressure adjusted to sea level.

**31.**
**4479.** Which altitude is indicated when the altimeter is set to 29.92" Hg?

A— Density.
B— Pressure.
C— Standard.

Answer (B) is correct (4479). *(PHAK Chap III)*
    Pressure altitude is indicated when the altimeter is set to 29.92.
    Answer (A) is incorrect because density altitude is pressure altitude corrected for nonstandard temperature. Answer (C) is incorrect because standard altitude is a nonsense concept in this context.

**32.**
**4912.** The pressure altitude at a given location is indicated on the altimeter after the altimeter is set to

A— the field elevation.
B— 29.92" Hg.
C— the current altimeter setting.

Answer (B) is correct (4912). *(PHAK Chap III)*
    Pressure altitude by definition is indicated altitude when the altimeter setting is 29.92. This is true regardless of area or true altitude.
    Answer (A) is incorrect because you set the altimeter to a barometric pressure, not an elevation. Answer (C) is incorrect because it describes indicated (not pressure) altitude.

**33.**
**4478.** How can you determine the pressure altitude at an airport without a tower or FSS?

A— Set the altimeter to 29.92" Hg and read the altitude indicated.

B— Set the altimeter to the current altimeter setting of a station within 100 miles and correct this indicated altitude with local temperature.

C— Use your computer and correct the field elevation for temperature.

**34.**
**4477.** How can you obtain the pressure altitude on flights below 18,000 feet?

A— Set your altimeter to 29.92" Hg.

B— Use your computer to change the indicated altitude to pressure altitude.

C— Contact an FSS and ask for the pressure altitude.

**35.**
**4911.** At an altitude of 6,500 feet MSL, the current altimeter setting is 30.42" Hg. The pressure altitude would be approximately

A— 7,500 feet.

B— 6,000 feet.

C— 6,500 feet.

**36.**
**4482.** How does a pilot normally obtain the current altimeter setting during an IFR flight in Class E airspace below 18,000 feet?

A— The pilot should contact ARTCC at least every 100 NM and request the altimeter setting.

B— FSS's along the route broadcast the weather information at 15 minutes past the hour.

C— ATC periodically advises the pilot of the proper altimeter setting.

**37.**
**4110.** Which of the following defines the type of altitude used when maintaining FL 210?

A— Indicated.

B— Pressure.

C— Calibrated.

Answer (A) is correct (4478). *(PHAK Chap III)*
The pressure altitude is determined by setting your altimeter to 29.92 and reading the altitude indicated. No matter what altitude or location, the altimeter reads pressure altitude when the barometric window is set to 29.92" Hg.
Answer (B) is incorrect because it describes true altitude. Answer (C) is incorrect because correcting field elevation for temperature is a nonsense concept.

Answer (A) is correct (4477). *(PHAK Chap III)*
Pressure altitude can be determined anywhere by setting the altimeter to 29.92.
Answer (B) is incorrect because it is much, much easier just to change the altimeter to 29.92. Answer (C) is incorrect because the FSS does not maintain pressure altitude data.

Answer (B) is correct (4911). *(IFH Chap IV)*
Rotating the altimeter's setting knob to a higher (or lower) barometric setting moves the hands to higher (or lower) indicated altitude at the rate of 1" Hg to 1,000 ft. of altitude. Given the current altimeter setting of 30.42 and the indicated altitude of 6,500 ft., resetting the window to 29.92 would lower indicated altitude by 500 ft. (30.42 – 29.92 = 0.5" Hg = 500 ft.). The new indicated altitude would be 6,000 ft. MSL, which would be pressure altitude.
Answer (A) is incorrect because a pressure change of 0.5" Hg results in an altitude change of 500 ft. (not 1,000 ft.). Answer (C) is incorrect because pressure altitude is equal to actual altitude only when the current altimeter setting is 29.92.

Answer (C) is correct (4482). *(IFH Chap IV)*
During IFR flight in Class E airspace below 18,000 ft. MSL, ATC periodically provides altimeter settings. Thus, you will continually hear the altimeter settings given to other pilots as you monitor ATC.
Answer (A) is incorrect because ATC provides the altimeter setting without being asked. Answer (B) is incorrect because FSSs do not broadcast the altimeter setting regularly.

Answer (B) is correct (4110). *(IFH Chap IV)*
Above 18,000 MSL (FL 180), pressure altitude is used to separate traffic. Pressure altitude is the altitude indicated on an altimeter when it is set to 29.92" Hg.
Answer (A) is incorrect because "indicated" is whatever altitude appears on the face of the altimeter. Answer (C) is incorrect because all altimeters are calibrated.

**38.**
**4444.** What is the procedure for setting the altimeter when assigned an IFR altitude of 18,000 feet or higher on a direct flight off airways?

A— Set the altimeter to 29.92" Hg before takeoff.
B— Set the altimeter to the current altimeter setting until reaching the assigned altitude, then set to 29.92" Hg.
C— Set the altimeter to the current reported setting for climbout and 29.92" Hg upon reaching 18,000 feet.

Answer (C) is correct (4444). *(FAR 91.121)*
When at an altitude of 18,000 ft. MSL (FL 180) or higher, the altimeter should be set to 29.92, which is pressure altitude. It does not matter whether you are on an airway.
Answer (A) is incorrect because indicated altitude (using local altimeter settings) should be used up to FL 180. Answer (B) is incorrect because you should set the altimeter to 29.92 upon reaching FL 180 (not your assigned altitude).

**39.**
**4446.** While you are flying at FL 250, you hear ATC give an altimeter setting of 28.92" Hg in your area. At what pressure altitude are you flying?

A— 24,000 feet.
B— 25,000 feet.
C— 26,000 feet.

Answer (B) is correct (4446). *(IFH Chap IV)*
The pressure altitude is 25,000 ft. in your area because at FL 250 your altimeter should be set at 29.92. A flight level (FL) by definition means a pressure altitude.
Answer (A) is incorrect because FL 250 by definition means a pressure altitude of 25,000 ft. Answer (C) is incorrect because FL 250 by definition means a pressure altitude of 25,000 ft.

**40.**
**4445.** En route at FL 290, the altimeter is set correctly, but not reset to the local altimeter setting of 30.57" Hg during descent. If the field elevation is 650 feet and the altimeter is functioning properly, what is the approximate indication upon landing?

A— 715 feet.
B— 1,300 feet.
C— Sea level.

Answer (C) is correct (4445). *(IFH Chap IV)*
One in. of pressure equals approximately 1,000 ft. of altitude. If an altimeter should be set to 30.57 but is set to 29.92, it is set .65" Hg too low, and thus will indicate 650 ft. (1,000 ft. x .65) less than actual altitude. Thus, if the airplane lands at an airport with a field elevation of 650 ft., the altimeter will indicate sea level, i.e., 650 ft. elevation minus the 650 ft. altimeter setting error.
Answer (A) is incorrect because 715 ft. is obtained by adding 65 ft. rather than subtracting 650 ft. Answer (B) is incorrect because 1,300 ft. is obtained by adding 650 ft. rather than subtracting 650 ft.

**41.**
**4481.** En route at FL 290, your altimeter is set correctly, but you fail to reset it to the local altimeter setting of 30.26" Hg during descent. If the field elevation is 134 feet and your altimeter is functioning properly, what will it indicate after landing?

A— 100 feet MSL.
B— 474 feet MSL.
C— 206 feet below MSL.

Answer (C) is correct (4481). *(IFH Chap IV)*
One in. of pressure equals approximately 1,000 ft. of altitude. If an altimeter should be set to 30.26 but is set to 29.92, it is set .34" Hg too low and thus will indicate 340 ft. (1,000 ft. x .34) less than actual altitude. Thus, if the airplane lands at an airport with a field elevation of 134 ft., the altimeter will indicate 206 ft. below sea level (134 ft. airport elevation – 340 altimeter setting error).
Answer (A) is incorrect because 100 ft. is obtained by subtracting 34 ft. rather than subtracting 340 ft.
Answer (B) is incorrect because 474 ft. is obtained by adding 340 ft. rather than subtracting 340 ft.

**42.**
**4090.** Under which condition will pressure altitude be equal to true altitude?

A— When the atmospheric pressure is 29.92" Hg.
B— When standard atmospheric conditions exist.
C— When indicated altitude is equal to the pressure altitude.

Answer (B) is correct (4090). *(IFH Chap IV)*
Pressure altitude will equal true altitude when standard atmospheric conditions exist at the current altitude, i.e, 29.92" Hg and 15°C at sea level.
Answer (A) is incorrect because, to get true altitude from an altimeter, both temperature and pressure must be standard. Answer (C) is incorrect because nonstandard temperatures will make indicated altitude deviate from true altitude.

**43.**

**4089.** Under what condition is pressure altitude and density altitude the same value?

A— At standard temperature.
B— When the altimeter setting is 29.92" Hg.
C— When indicated, and pressure altitudes are the same value on the altimeter.

Answer (A) is correct (4089). *(IFH Chap IV)*
Density altitude, by definition, is pressure altitude adjusted for nonstandard temperature. Accordingly, pressure altitude will equal density altitude at standard temperature.
Answer (B) is incorrect because pressure altitude has not been adjusted for nonstandard temperature. Answer (C) is incorrect because neither indicated nor pressure altitude is adjusted for nonstandard temperature.

**44.**

**4109.** Under what condition will true altitude be lower than indicated altitude with an altimeter setting of 29.92" Hg?

A— In warmer than standard air temperature.
B— In colder than standard air temperature.
C— When density altitude is higher than indicated altitude.

Answer (B) is correct (4109). *(IFH Chap IV)*
When temperature lowers en route, you are lower than your altimeter indicates. Similarly, when you are in colder than standard air temperatures, true altitude is lower than pressure altitude.
Answer (A) is incorrect because, when you are in warmer than standard air, the true altitude is above pressure altitude. Answer (C) is incorrect because, assuming an altimeter setting of 29.92, if density altitude is higher than indicated altitude, the air is thinner and, thus, warmer. When you are in warmer than standard air, the true altitude is above indicated altitude.

**45.**

**4093.** When an altimeter is changed from 30.11" Hg to 29.96" Hg, in which direction will the indicated altitude change and by what value?

A— Altimeter will indicate 15 feet lower.
B— Altimeter will indicate 150 feet lower.
C— Altimeter will indicate 150 feet higher.

Answer (B) is correct (4093). *(IFH Chap IV)*
Altimeter settings vary approximately 1" Hg for each 1,000 ft. of altitude. When the altimeter setting is changed from 30.11 to 29.96, it is lower by .15" Hg. Thus, the altimeter will indicate 150 ft. lower (1,000 ft. x .15). Remember the indicated altitude and altimeter setting vary directly, i.e., when the altimeter setting is adjusted up, indicated altitude increases and vice versa.
Answer (A) is incorrect because .15" Hg is equal to 150 ft. (not 15 ft.). Answer (C) is incorrect because, when the altimeter setting is lowered, indicated altitude decreases (not increases).

**46.**

**4091.** Which condition would cause the altimeter to indicate a lower altitude than actually flown (true altitude)?

A— Air temperature lower than standard.
B— Atmospheric pressure lower than standard.
C— Air temperature warmer than standard.

Answer (C) is correct (4091). *(IFH Chap IV)*
When temperatures are warmer than standard, the pressure levels are raised. That is, the altimeter will indicate an altitude lower than that at which the aircraft is actually flying.
Answer (A) is incorrect because in colder than standard air, pressure levels drop. Thus, the altimeter reads higher (not lower) than true altitude. Answer (B) is incorrect because using the correct altimeter setting adjusts for nonstandard pressure.

## 2.4 Gyroscopes

**47.**

**4881.** Which practical test should be made on the electric gyro instruments prior to starting an engine?

A— Check that the electrical connections are secure on the back of the instruments.
B— Check that the attitude of the miniature aircraft is wings level before turning on electrical power.
C— Turn on the electrical power and listen for any unusual or irregular mechanical noise.

Answer (C) is correct (4881). *(IFH Chap V)*
Electric gyro instruments can be checked for irregular noises by listening to them when the battery is turned on but prior to starting the engine. You should notice any bearing clatters, clicks, or other unusual noises. Additionally, you can look at the instruments to see if they are in their expected positions. There are additional tests to pursue after the engine is started.
Answer (A) is incorrect because pilots should not be handling or touching electrical connections behind the instrument panel. Answer (B) is incorrect because the attitude of the miniature aircraft will probably not be wings level before the gyro starts spinning.

**48.**
**4902.** One characteristic that a properly functioning gyro depends upon for operation is the

A— ability to resist precession 90° to any applied force.
B— resistance to deflection of the spinning wheel or disc.
C— deflecting force developed from the angular velocity of the spinning wheel.

Answer (B) is correct (4902). *(IFH Chap IV)*
Newton's second law of motion states that the deflection of a moving body is proportional to the deflective force applied and is inversely proportional to its weight and speed. For a gyro, the resistance to deflection is proportional to the deflective force. This property is used by the attitude indicator.
Answer (A) is incorrect because precession is the name for the reaction to deflection. The gyro uses precession, not resists it. Answer (C) is incorrect because the deflective force is applied to (not developed by) the gyro.

## 2.5 Heading Indicator

**49.**
**4885.** What pre-takeoff check should be made of a vacuum-driven heading indicator in preparation for an IFR flight?

A— After 5 minutes, set the indicator to the magnetic heading of the aircraft and check for proper alignment after taxi turns.
B— After 5 minutes, check that the heading indicator card aligns itself with the magnetic heading of the aircraft.
C— Determine that the heading indicator does not precess more than 2° in 5 minutes of ground operation.

Answer (A) is correct (4885). *(IFH Chap V)*
Vacuum-driven gyros take several minutes to get up to speed. After about 5 min., set the heading indicator to the correct magnetic heading. After taxiing to the runup area, verify that the heading indicator still indicates the correct magnetic heading.
Answer (B) is incorrect because non-slaved heading indicators must be manually set to the correct magnetic heading. Answer (C) is incorrect because a precession error of no more than 3° in 15 min. (not 2° in 5 min.) is acceptable for normal operations.

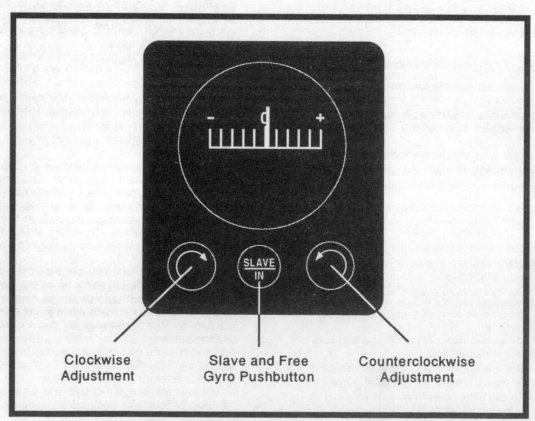

Clockwise Adjustment     Slave and Free Gyro Pushbutton     Counterclockwise Adjustment

FIGURE 143.—Slaved Gyro Illustration.

**50.**
**4827.** (Refer to figure 143 on page 34.) The heading on a remote indicating compass is 120° and the magnetic compass indicates 110°. What action is required to correctly align the heading indicator with the magnetic compass?

A— Select the free gyro mode and depress the counter-clockwise heading drive button.
B— Select the slaved gyro mode and depress the clockwise heading drive button.
C— Select the free gyro mode and depress the clockwise heading drive button.

**51.**
**4828.** (Refer to figure 143 on page 34.) When the system is in the free gyro mode, depressing the clockwise manual heading drive button will rotate the remote indicating compass card to the

A— right to eliminate left compass card error.
B— right to eliminate right compass card error.
C— left to eliminate left compass card error.

**52.**
**4829.** (Refer to figure 143 on page 34.) The heading on a remote indicating compass is 5° to the left of that desired. What action is required to move the desired heading under the heading reference?

A— Select the free gyro mode and depress the clockwise heading drive button.
B— Select the slaved gyro mode and depress the clockwise heading drive button.
C— Select the free gyro mode and depress the counter-clockwise heading drive button.

## 2.6 Attitude Indicator

**53.**
**4842.** What pre-takeoff check should be made of the attitude indicator in preparation for an IFR flight?

A— The horizon bar does not vibrate during warmup.
B— The miniature airplane should erect and become stable within 5 minutes.
C— The horizon bar should erect and become stable within 5 minutes.

Answer (C) is correct (4827). (IFH Chap IV)
Some remote indicating compasses (RIC) have a separate slaving control and compensator unit with a deviation meter. The instrument shows any difference between the displayed heading and the magnetic heading. It also provides the controls shown in Fig. 143 to correct any errors. To correct from 120° indicated on the RIC to the magnetic heading of 110°, select the free gyro mode and depress the clockwise heading drive button until 110° heading on RIC is indicated **and** the deviation meter is centered.
Answer (A) is incorrect because using the counterclockwise drive button would increase the indicated headings, e.g., from 120° to 130° indicated. Answer (B) is incorrect because the RIC must be in the free gyro mode to use the heading drive button.

Answer (A) is correct (4828). (IFH Chap IV)
A left compass card error means that the card has rotated too far to the left, i.e., it reads too high a heading. The clockwise adjustment rotates the indicating compass card to the right to eliminate left compass card error. For example, this would change a 120° heading to 110°.
Answer (B) is incorrect because you adjust to the right for left (not right) error. Answer (C) is incorrect because the clockwise manual heading drive button rotates the compass card to the right, not left.

Answer (C) is correct (4829). (IFH Chap IV)
If the heading on the compass is left of that desired, then the compass has rotated too far to the right, which is a right compass error. Thus, the slaving control must be placed in the free mode, and the counter-clockwise drive button depressed.
Answer (A) is incorrect because the clockwise heading drive button would correct a left (not a right) card error. Answer (B) is incorrect because the RIC must be in the free gyro mode to use the heading drive button and the counterclockwise heading drive button should be depressed.

Answer (C) is correct (4842). (IFH Chap V)
The pretakeoff check for attitude indicators is that within the 5-min. warm-up, the horizon bar should erect to the horizontal position and remain at the correct position. It should remain stable during straight taxiing and taxi turns.
Answer (A) is incorrect because the horizon bar usually vibrates during warm-up as the gyro gets up to speed. Answer (B) is incorrect because the miniature airplane can be adjusted manually but otherwise remains stationary. It is the horizon bar that moves within the instrument face.

**54.**
**4835.** Which condition during taxi is an indication that an attitude indicator is unreliable?

A— The horizon bar tilts more than 5° while making taxi turns.
B— The horizon bar vibrates during warmup.
C— The horizon bar does not align itself with the miniature airplane after warmup.

**55.**
**4861.** During coordinated turns, which force moves the pendulous vanes of a vacuum-driven attitude indicator resulting in precession of the gyro toward the inside of the turn?

A— Acceleration.
B— Deceleration.
C— Centrifugal.

**56.**
**4901.** If a 180° steep turn is made to the right and the aircraft is rolled out to straight-and-level flight by visual reference, the miniature aircraft will

A— show a slight climb and turn to the left.
B— show a slight climb and turn to the right.
C— show a slight skid and climb to the right.

**57.**
**4860.** During normal coordinated turns, what error due to precession should you observe when rolling out to straight-and-level flight from a 180° steep turn to the right?

A— A straight-and-level coordinated flight indication.
B— The miniature aircraft would show a slight turn indication to the left.
C— The miniature aircraft would show a slight descent and wings-level attitude.

**58.**
**4857.** During normal operation of a vacuum-driven attitude indicator, what attitude indication should you see when rolling out from a 180° skidding turn to straight-and-level coordinated flight?

A— A straight-and-level coordinated flight indication.
B— A nose-high indication relative to level flight.
C— The miniature aircraft shows a turn in the direction opposite the skid.

Answer (A) is correct (4835).   *(IFH Chap V)*
The horizon bar in an attitude indicator should not tilt more than 5° while making taxi turns.  If it does, it is unreliable and should not be used for IFR flight.
Answer (B) is incorrect because the horizon bar will vibrate as the gyros get up to speed during warm-up.  Answer (C) is incorrect because the horizon bar aligns itself with the center of the dial, indicating level flight.  Then the miniature airplane must be adjusted to align with the horizon bar from the pilot's perspective.

Answer (C) is correct (4861).   *(IFH Chap IV)*
The altitude indicator normally erects itself by discharging air equally through four exhaust ports, each of which is partially covered by a pendulous vane.  During coordinated (and skidding) turns, centrifugal force moves the vanes from their vertical position, precessing the gyro toward the inside of the turn.
Answer (A) is incorrect because acceleration is a force that induces climb/descent errors in the attitude indicator.  Answer (B) is incorrect because deceleration is a force that induces climb/descent errors in the attitude indicator.

Answer (A) is correct (4901).   *(IFH Chap IV)*
In 180° coordinated steep turns, when the airplane is rolled out to straight-and-level flight, the attitude indicator will indicate a turn to the opposite direction along with a slight climb.  Thus, the indicated turn would be to the left if the steep turn were made to the right.
Answer (B) is incorrect because the turning error is to the left (not to the right) in response to rolling out of a right turn.  Answer (C) is incorrect because evidence of a skid error cannot be read from the miniature airplane of the attitude indicator, and because the turn error would be to the left, not to the right.

Answer (B) is correct (4860).   *(IFH Chap IV)*
In 180° coordinated steep turns, when the airplane is rolled out to straight-and-level flight, the attitude indicator will indicate a turn to the opposite direction along with a slight climb.  Thus, the indicated turn would be to the left if the steep turn were made to the right.
Answer (A) is incorrect because the attitude indicator will show a slight climb to the left (not straight-and-level), and it does not indicate coordinated flight.  Answer (C) is incorrect because it will indicate a slight climb (not descent) and a turning error.

Answer (C) is correct (4857).   *(IFH Chap IV)*
Similarly to coordinated turns, the attitude indicator will show a bank in the opposite direction when the aircraft is rolled out of a skidding turn.  However, there will be no nose-up indication.
Answer (A) is incorrect because the attitude indicator will show a slight turn in the opposite direction (not straight-and-level), and it does not indicate coordinated flight.  Answer (B) is incorrect because a nose-high indication would only result when rolling out of a coordinated turn.

**59.**
**4900.** Errors in both pitch and bank indication on an attitude indicator are usually at a maximum as the aircraft rolls out of a

A— 180° turn.
B— 270° turn.
C— 360° turn.

Answer (A) is correct (4900). *(IFH Chap IV)*
Errors for both pitch and bank indication on an attitude indicator are greatest when rolling out of a 180° turn. This precession error, normally between 3° and 5°, is self-correcting by the part of the heading indicator called the erecting mechanism.
Answer (B) is incorrect because pitch and bank errors are usually the greatest after 180° (not 270°) of turn. Answer (C) is incorrect because pitch and bank errors are usually the greatest after 180° (not 360°) of turn.

**60.**
**4919.** When an airplane is decelerated, some attitude indicators will precess and incorrectly indicate a

A— left turn.
B— climb.
C— descent.

Answer (C) is correct (4919). *(IFH Chap IV)*
Deceleration affects some attitude indicators through precession to incorrectly indicate a descent.
Answer (A) is incorrect because acceleration and deceleration result in erroneous pitch readings, not turning errors. Answer (B) is incorrect because acceleration (not deceleration) may result in precession-related errors indicating a climb.

**61.**
**4918.** When an airplane is accelerated, some attitude indicators will precess and incorrectly indicate a

A— climb.
B— descent.
C— right turn.

Answer (A) is correct (4918). *(IFH Chap IV)*
Acceleration affects some attitude indicators through precession to incorrectly indicate a climb.
Answer (B) is incorrect because deceleration (not acceleration) may result in precession-related errors indicating a descent. Answer (C) is incorrect because acceleration and deceleration result in erroneous pitch readings, not turning errors.

## 2.7 Turn-and-Slip Indicator

**62.**
**4882.** Prior to starting an engine, you should check the turn-and-slip indicator to determine if the

A— needle indication properly corresponds to the angle of the wings or rotors with the horizon.
B— needle is approximately centered and the tube is full of fluid.
C— ball will move freely from one end of the tube to the other when the aircraft is rocked.

Answer (B) is correct (4882). *(IFH Chap V)*
Prior to starting an engine, the turn-and-slip indicator should indicate the needle approximately centered and the tube should be full of fluid with the ball also approximately centered if the airplane is on a level surface.
Answer (A) is incorrect because the needle corresponds to rate and direction of turn (not wing or rotor angle). Answer (C) is incorrect because rocking the aircraft is not necessary. Freedom of movement of the ball is checked during taxi.

**63.**
**4883.** What indications should you observe on the turn-and-slip indicator during taxi?

A— The ball moves freely opposite the turn, and the needle deflects in the direction of the turn.
B— The needle deflects in the direction of the turn, but the ball remains centered.
C— The ball deflects opposite the turn, but the needle remains centered.

Answer (A) is correct (4883). *(IFH Chap V)*
While taxiing, the turn-and-slip indicator ball should move freely opposite the direction of any turn since centrifugal force forces the ball to the outside. Also, the rate of turn indicator should indicate a turn in the proper direction.
Answer (B) is incorrect because the ball will deflect opposite to the direction of the turn. Answer (C) is incorrect because the needle deflects in the direction of the turn.

## 2.8 Turn Coordinator

**64.**
**4847.** What indications are displayed by the miniature aircraft of a turn coordinator?

A— Rate of roll and rate of turn.
B— Direct indication of bank angle and pitch attitude.
C— Indirect indication of bank angle and pitch attitude.

Answer (A) is correct (4847). *(IFH Chap IV)*
The turn coordinator indicates rate of roll and rate of turn. When the bank is constant, the rate of turn is indicated. When the bank is changing, the rate of roll is also indicated.
Answer (B) is incorrect because the turn coordinator only indirectly indicates bank angle and has no relationship to pitch attitude. Answer (C) is incorrect because the turn coordinator has no relationship to pitch attitude.

**65.**
**4839.** What does the miniature aircraft of the turn coordinator directly display?

A— Rate of roll and rate of turn.
B— Angle of bank and rate of turn.
C— Angle of bank.

Answer (A) is correct (4839). *(IFH Chap IV)*
The turn coordinator indicates rate of roll and rate of turn. When the bank is constant, the rate of turn is indicated. When the bank is changing, the rate of roll is also indicated.
Answer (B) is incorrect because the angle of bank is not directly indicated by the turn coordinator. Answer (C) is incorrect because the angle of bank is not directly indicated by the turn coordinator.

**66.**
**4856.** What indication is presented by the miniature aircraft of the turn coordinator?

A— Indirect indication of the bank attitude.
B— Direct indication of the bank attitude and the quality of the turn.
C— Quality of the turn.

Answer (A) is correct (4856). *(IFH Chap IV)*
The miniature aircraft of the turn coordinator indicates the rate of roll when bank is changing. When the rotation around the longitudinal axis is zero, the instrument indicates the rate of turn. Thus, it provides only an indirect indication of the angle of bank.
Answer (B) is incorrect because the turn coordinator does NOT provide a direct indication of bank. Answer (C) is incorrect because the ball in the turn coordinator (not the miniature aircraft) provides information on the quality of the turn.

**67.**
**4921.** The displacement of a turn coordinator during a coordinated turn will

A— indicate the angle of bank.
B— remain constant for a given bank regardless of airspeed.
C— increase as angle of bank increases.

Answer (C) is correct (4921). *(IFH Chap IV)*
The displacement of a turn coordinator increases as angle of bank (in coordinated flight) increases because the turn coordinator shows rate of turn which increases as angle of bank increases.
Answer (A) is incorrect because the angle of bank is only indirectly indicated. Answer (B) is incorrect because, when the rate of roll is zero, the turn coordinator provides information concerning the rate of turn, which in turn changes as airspeed changes given a constant bank.

**68.**
**4831.** What indication should be observed on a turn coordinator during a left turn while taxiing?

A— The miniature aircraft will show a turn to the left and the ball remains centered.
B— The miniature aircraft will show a turn to the left and the ball moves to the right.
C— Both the miniature aircraft and the ball will remain centered.

Answer (B) is correct (4831). *(IFH Chap V)*
On a taxiing turn to the left, the turn coordinator shows a turn to the left and the ball moves to the right. The centrifugal force of the turn, which is not offset by bank when taxiing, forces the ball opposite to the turn.
Answer (A) is incorrect because the ball moves to the outside of the turn due to centrifugal force. Answer (C) is incorrect because the miniature aircraft reacts to yaw and shows a turn to the left, and the ball reacts to centrifugal force by moving right.

# END OF CHAPTER

# CHAPTER THREE
# AIRPORTS AND AIR TRAFFIC CONTROL

This chapter contains outlines of major concepts tested, all FAA Instrument Rating test questions and answers regarding airports and Air Traffic Control, and an explanation of each answer. The subtopics or modules within this chapter are listed above, followed in parentheses by the number of questions from the FAA written test pertaining to that particular module. The two numbers following the parentheses are the page numbers on which the outline and questions begin for that module.

On September 16, 1993 the U.S. airspace was reclassified to conform with the International Civil Aviation Organization (ICAO) standards.

1.   Class A -- formerly known as the PCA
2.   Class B -- formerly known as a TCA
3.   Class C -- formerly known as an ARSA
4.   Class D -- formerly known as an Airport Traffic Area and Control Zone
5.   Class E -- formerly known as general controlled airspace and the Continental Control Area
6.   Class G -- formerly known as uncontrolled airspace

**CAUTION:** Recall that the **sole purpose** of this book is to expedite your passing the FAA written test for the instrument rating. Accordingly, all extraneous material (i.e., topics or regulations not directly tested on the FAA written test) is omitted, even though much more information and knowledge are necessary to fly safely. This additional material is presented in *Instrument Pilot FAA Practical Test Prep* and *Aviation Weather and Weather Services*, available from Gleim Publications, Inc. See the order form on page 478.

## 3.1 PRECISION INSTRUMENT RUNWAY MARKINGS  (Questions 1-8)

1.    The figure below depicts a precision instrument runway.

   a.    The distance from the runway threshold to the fixed distance marker is 1,000 ft. (distance A).

   b.    The distance from the runway threshold to the touchdown zone marker is 500 ft. (distance B).

   c.    The distance from the beginning of the touchdown zone marker to the beginning of the fixed distance marker is 500 ft. (distance C).

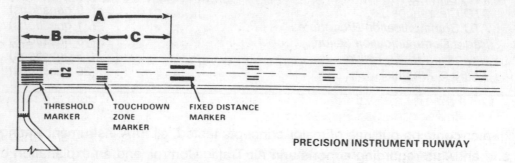

PRECISION INSTRUMENT RUNWAY

2.    A displaced threshold is a threshold that is not at the beginning of a runway.  It is indicated by arrows in the middle of the runway pointing to a broad, solid line across the runway.  The remainder of the runway, following the displaced threshold, is the landing portion of the runway.

   a.    The paved area before the displaced threshold is available for taxiing, the landing rollout, and the takeoff of aircraft but not landing.

   b.    In Fig. 138 on page 49, the approach end of the runway is on the right.  Thus, taxiing and takeoff are permitted toward the green threshold lights (marked by the arrow).

3.    Runway end identifier lights (REIL) consist of a pair of synchronized flashing lights, one on each side of the runway threshold facing the approach area.

   a.    REIL permit the rapid and positive identification of a runway surrounded by other lighting, lacking contrast with surrounding terrain, and/or during reduced visibility.

4.    Hydroplaning occurs when an aircraft's tires are separated from the runway by water.

   a.    It usually occurs at high speeds when water is standing on a smooth runway.

## 3.2 VISUAL APPROACH SLOPE INDICATOR (VASI)  (Questions 9-20)

1.    Visual approach slope indicators (VASI) are a system of lights that provide visual descent information during the approach to a runway.

2.    The standard VASI consists of a two-barred tier of lights.  You are

   a.    Below the glide path if both light bars appear red (remember this with "red means dead").

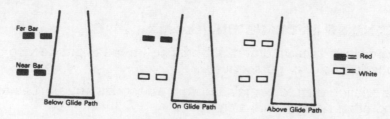

   b.   On the glide path if the far lights (on top visually) appear red and the near lights (on bottom visually) appear white.

        1)   This glide path is normally set at 3°.

   c.   Above the glide path if both light bars appear white.

3.  Actually, each light bar marks a separate glide path. The far light bar marks a higher glide path than the glide path extended from the nearer light bar. You are between them when you are lower than the higher glide path and above the lower glide path.

   a.   Remember, red over white (i.e., R before W alphabetically) is the desired sequence.

        1)   White over red is impossible.

4.  VASIs also may have three light bars which provide a lower glide path and a higher glide path. The higher glide path marked by the middle and far light bars is intended for use by high cockpit aircraft.

   a.   If the nearest light bar is white and the two farther light bars are red you are on the lower glide path, usually 3°.

   b.   If the farthest light bar is red and the two nearest light bars are white, you are on the upper glide path, usually 3.25°.

   c.   Above both glide paths, all light will be white. Below both glide paths, all lights will be red.

5.  If all VASI lights appear red as you reach the MDA, you should level off momentarily to intercept the proper glide path.

6.  A tricolor VASI is a single light unit projecting three colors visible for ½ to 1 mi. in daylight and about 5 mi. at night.

   a.   The below glide path indicator is red.
   b.   The above glide path indicator is amber.
   c.   The on glide path indicator is green.

7.  VASI only provides glide path guidance and provides safe obstruction clearance within ±10° of the extended runway centerline from as far as 4 NM from the runway threshold.

   a.   It provides no information on alignment with the runway.

## 3.3 PRECISION APPROACH PATH INDICATOR (PAPI)  (Questions 21-25)

1.  PAPI lights are similar to VASIs but they are installed in a single row of either two or four lights.

2.  If two of the lights are red and two are white, you are on the glide path (3°).

3.  When three of the four lights indicate red, you are slightly below the glide path (2.8°).

4.  When all four lights are red, you are low (on a glide path of less than 2.5°).

5.  If three lights are white, you are slightly above the glide path (3.2°).

6.  If all four lights are white, you are high (on a glide path of more than 3.5°).

## 3.4 IFR FLIGHT PLANNING INFORMATION  (Questions 26-32)

1.  Every pilot should receive a preflight briefing from a Flight Service Station (FSS), whether by telephone, radio, or personal visit.

   a.   The briefing should contain weather advisories and notices about en route airports and other navigational aids.

2.  The Notice to Airmen (NOTAM) system disseminates time-critical aeronautical information that is temporary in nature or not known in time to publish on charts or in procedural publications.

    a.  NOTAMs include airport or primary runway closures, changes in the status of navigational aids, instrument landing systems, radar service availability, and other information that could affect a pilot's decision to make a flight.

3.  There are three categories of NOTAMs:

    a.  NOTAM (D) -- distant NOTAMs contain information for all participating navigational facilities.

    b.  NOTAM (L) -- local NOTAMs contain information about facilities in the FSS area only.

    c.  FDC NOTAMs are temporary or permanent regulatory changes published as needed by the National Flight Data Center (FDC).

        1)  FDC NOTAMs advise of changes in flight data which affect instrument approach procedures, and amend aeronautical charts and flight restrictions prior to normal publication.

4.  NOTAMs are disseminated in two classes:

    a.  Class I NOTAMs -- the most current data, disseminated via telecommunications. They are included as part of a routine pilot weather briefing given by an FSS specialist.

    b.  Class II NOTAMS -- The Notice to Airmen (Class II) publication is printed and mailed biweekly.

        1)  Once published, Class II NOTAMs are not provided during pilot weather briefing unless specifically requested.

5.  The best source of airport conditions would be to combine data available from

    a.  The Airport/Facility Directory
    b.  NOTAMs (L)
    c.  NOTAMs (D).

6.  Automatic Terminal Information Service (ATIS) broadcasts are updated whenever any official weather data are received, regardless of content change or reported values, or when there is a change in other pertinent data such as active runway, instrument approach in use, etc.

    a.  Absence of the sky condition and visibility from the ATIS broadcast specifically implies that the ceiling is more than 5,000 ft. and visibility is more than 5 SM.

7.  In Class B, C, or D airspace, operation of an airport beacon during daylight hours usually indicates IFR conditions (ground visibility less than 3 SM and/or ceiling less than 1,000 ft.).

## 3.5 IFR FLIGHT PLAN (Questions 33-43)

1.  To operate under Instrument Flight Rules in controlled airspace, you are required to file an IFR Flight Plan.

    a.  The FAA's standard flight plan form appears in Fig. 1 on page 56.

2.  When you file a composite (part VFR, part IFR) flight plan, you should check both VFR and IFR in Block 1.

3. In Block 3, you are to indicate the aircraft type and special equipment.

   a. After the aircraft type, a slash is followed by a letter indicating the combination of

      1) Usable transponder
      2) DME
      3) Area navigation (RNAV) equipment.

   b. Not reported are ADF or airborne radar capability.

4. When an IFR flight plan has different altitudes for different legs, you should only enter the altitude for the first leg in Block 7.

5. Time en route (Block 10) should be based on arrival at the point of first intended landing.

6. The fuel on board time (Block 12) should be based upon the total usable fuel on board.

7. On composite flight plans for which the first portion of the flight is IFR, the flight plan should be a standard IFR flight plan, including

   a. Points of transition from one airway to another,

   b. Fixes defining direct route segments, and

   c. The clearance limit fix, i.e., the point at which you will begin the VFR portion of the flight.

8. When transitioning from VFR to IFR on a composite flight plan, you should contact the nearest FSS to close the VFR portion and request an ATC IFR clearance.

   a. You must obtain an IFR clearance before entering IFR conditions.

9. IFR flight plans can only be canceled if you are flying in VFR conditions outside Class A airspace.

10. When landing at an airport without a control tower, the pilot must initiate IFR flight plan cancellation. The pilot may cancel

    a. By radio while airborne if conditions are VFR.
    b. By radio or telephone as soon as (s)he is on the ground.

11. A waypoint on an IFR flight is a predetermined geographical position used for an RNAV route or RNAV instrument approach identification or progress reporting. It is defined relative to a VORTAC position **or** by longitude and latitude, i.e., it does not have to be relative to a VORTAC.

## 3.6 ATC CLEARANCES (Questions 44-52)

1. Pilots of airborne aircraft should read back ATC clearances concerning altitude assignments and/or vectors and any part requiring verification.

2. An abbreviated IFR clearance includes

   a. Destination airport

   b. Initial altitude

   c. SID (Standard Instrument Departure) name and number with transition, if appropriate.

3. When a departure clearance from a noncontrolled airport contains a void time, the pilot must advise ATC as soon as possible (but no later than 30 min. after the void time) if a decision is made NOT to take off.

4. A cruise clearance assigns a pilot a block of airspace from the minimum IFR altitude up to and including the altitude specified in the cruise clearance.

   a. Climb and descent within the block is at the discretion of the pilot.

## 3.7 ATC COMMUNICATION PROCEDURES  (Questions 53-73)

1. When flying IFR, the pilot must maintain continuous contact with assigned ATC frequencies.

   a. All radio frequency changes are made at the direction of ATC.

2. When climbing or descending per ATC clearance, the pilot should use the optimum rate consistent with the aircraft to 1,000 ft. above or below the assigned altitude and then climb or descend at the rate of between 500 and 1,500 fpm until attaining the assigned altitude.

   a. It is sufficient to use a cruise climb rather than a maximum angle of climb.
   b. If you cannot climb or descend at least 500 fpm, you should notify ATC.
   c. You should lead your turns so that you remain in the center of the airway.

3. The reports that a pilot must make to ATC without a specific ATC request include

   a. At all times:

      1) When unable to climb or descend at a rate of at least 500 fpm.

      2) Change in the average true airspeed at cruising altitude when it varies by more than 5% or 10 kt. from that filed in your flight plan.

      3) Before changing assigned altitude.

      4) When you have missed an approach.

      5) When leaving at any assigned holding fix or point.

      6) The time and altitude when reaching holding fix or clearance limit.

      7) Loss of communication or navigation capability or anything else affecting the safety of flight.

   b. When not in radar contact:

      1) When leaving final approach fix inbound on final approach.
      2) To correct an estimate which appears to be more than 3 min. in error.
      3) When passing certain reporting points:

         a) Compulsory reporting points as marked by solid black triangles on En Route Charts.

         b) Over each fix used in the flight plan to define the route of flight on a direct flight not flown on radials or courses of established airways or routes.

4. Your Mode C transponder should always be set to Mode C and turned ON unless otherwise requested by ATC.

5. When receiving traffic advisories from ATC, remember that the controller only sees the airplane's direction of travel, not the airplane heading.

   a. You must adjust traffic reports for any wind correction you are holding.

6. "Radar contact" means your airplane has been identified on the radar screen and radar flight following will be provided until radar identification is terminated by the controller.

7. "Resume own navigation" means that you continue to be under ATC radar surveillance but you are responsible for your own navigation. No more vectors will be given.

   a. You are still in radar contact with ATC. Thus, you do not need to make position reports.

8. "Radar service terminated" means that you are no longer under ATC radar surveillance and you must resume position reports at compulsory reporting points.

9. IFR flights receive separation from all IFR aircraft and participating VFR aircraft operating in Class C airspace.

10. When flying VFR on practice instrument approaches, you must avoid IFR conditions. You do not have an IFR clearance.

11. While you should comply with all headings and altitudes assigned by ATC, you should feel free to question any assigned altitude or heading believed to be incorrect. The pilot has ultimate responsibility for safe flight.

12. When ATC requests a specified airspeed, you are expected to maintain the speed plus or minus 10 kt. based upon indicated airspeed.

13. If on descent and approach you cancel IFR, you must contact the control tower at your landing destination at least 4.3 NM (5 SM) from the center of the airport, i.e., before you enter Class D airspace.

14. At controlled airports having Flight Service Stations, the FSS will provide Local Airport Advisory (LAA) service when the control tower is not in operation.

    a. The FSS provides advisory data on runways, weather, traffic patterns, etc. It does NOT constitute ATC clearance or other authoritative ATC actions.

    b. Remember, if ATC is not operating, you must cancel your own flight plan by notifying the FSS.

15. "Minimum fuel" is just an advisory to ATC that indicates an emergency situation is possible should any undue delay occur.

## 3.8 RADIO COMMUNICATION FAILURE (Questions 74-78)

1. In the event of two-way communications failure, ATC will assume the pilot is operating in accordance with FAR 91.185.

    a. As always, pilot judgment is the final determinant of safest flying.

2. According to FAR 91.185, if you lose two-way communications

    a. When holding, and you have received an expected further clearance (EFC) time, you should leave the holding pattern at the EFC time.

    b. When you are on an IFR flight in VFR conditions, you should continue your flight under VFR and land as soon as practicable.

    c. When you are in IFR conditions, you should continue on the route specified in your clearance (for each leg of your flight) at the highest of

        1) The last assigned altitude,
        2) Expected altitude per ATC, or
        3) MEA (minimum en route altitude).

3. When losing radio communications, you should alert ATC by setting your transponder code to 7600.

    a. If you are in an emergency situation, you should set and leave the transponder at 7700.

## 3.9 NAVIGATION RADIO FAILURE (Questions 79-81)

1. If your DME fails above FL 240, you should notify ATC of the failure and continue to the next airport of intended landing at which repairs or replacement of the equipment can be made.

2. When operating IFR, you must immediately report to ATC the loss of VOR, TACAN, ADF, or LF navigation receiver capability, complete or partial loss of ILS receiver, and/or any impairment of radio communications capability.

## 3.10 TYPES OF AIRSPACE  (Questions 82-101)

1.  En Route Low Altitude Charts show Class B, Class C, Class D, Class E, and special use airspace.

    a.  But not Class A airspace.

2.  Class G (uncontrolled) airspace is airspace where ATC does not control air traffic.

3.  Transition areas are Class E airspace and are designated to contain IFR operations while moving between the terminal area and en route flight.

    a.  When designated in conjunction with an airport which has a prescribed instrument approach, Class E airspace extends upward from 700 ft. AGL.

    b.  When designated in conjunction with airway route structures, etc., Class E airspace extends upward from 1,200 ft.

    c.  Both types of transition areas terminate at the base of overlying controlled airspace, i.e., Class A airspace.

4.  Class A airspace is from 18,000 ft. MSL to FL 600.

5.  Military Operations Areas (MOA) consist of airspace established for the purpose of separating certain military training activities from IFR traffic.

    a.  Both IFR and VFR traffic are permitted but they should exercise extreme caution.

6.  Class C airspace consists of controlled airspace within which all aircraft are subject to the operating rules and pilot and equipment requirements specified in FAR Part 91.

    a.  No specific pilot certification is required to operate in Class C airspace.

    b.  Aircraft must be equipped with two-way radio communications and a Mode C transponder.

7.  Class C airspace consists of an inner circle and outer circle and an outer area.

    a.  The inner circle is a 5-NM radius from the primary Class C airport.

        1)  Extending from the surface to 4,000 ft. above the primary airport.

    b.  The outer circle is a 10-NM radius from the primary Class C airport.

        1)  Extending from 1,200 ft. AGL to 4,000 ft. above the primary airport (i.e., the same height as the inner circle).

    c.  The outer area extends outward from the primary Class C airport with about a 20-NM radius, with some site-specific variation.

        1)  Extends from the lower limits of the radar coverage up to the ceiling of approach control's delegated airspace.

8.  The maximum altitude at which Class G airspace will exist is 14,500 ft. MSL (excluding the airspace less than 1,500 ft. AGL).

9.  The maximum altitude for Class B airspace may vary with airport.

10. The normal lateral limits for Class D airspace are approximately 4 NM.

---

## QUESTIONS AND ANSWER EXPLANATIONS

All the FAA questions from the written test for the instrument rating relating to airports and Air Traffic Control and the material outlined previously are reproduced on the following pages in the same modules as the outlines. To the immediate right of each question are the correct answer and answer explanation. You should cover these answers and answer explanations with your hand or a piece of paper while responding to the questions. Refer to the general discussion in Chapter 1 on how to take the FAA written test.

Remember that the questions from the FAA Instrument Rating Question Book have been reordered by topic, and the topics have been organized into a meaningful sequence. Accordingly, the first line of the answer explanation gives the FAA question number and the citation of the authoritative source for the answer.

---

### 3.1 Precision Instrument Runway Markings

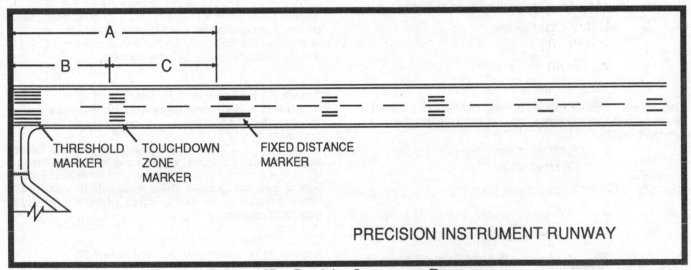

FIGURE 137.—Precision Instrument Runway.

**1.**
**4791.** (Refer to figure 137 above.) What is the distance (A) from the beginning of the runway to the fixed distance marker?

A— 500 feet.
B— 1,000 feet.
C— 1,500 feet.

Answer (B) is correct (4791). *(AIM Para 2-22)*
The fixed distance marker on precision instrument runways consists of two heavy lines parallel to the direction of the runway, 1,000 ft. from the runway threshold.
Answer (A) is incorrect because the six parallel lines (somewhat lighter and narrower than the fixed distance marker) 500 ft. from the threshold of the runway are the touchdown zone marker. Answer (C) is incorrect because the marker at roughly 1,500 ft. from the threshold is the next marker beyond the fixed distance marker, not the fixed distance marker.

**2.**
**4792.** (Refer to figure 137 above.) What is the distance (B) from the beginning of the runway to the touchdown zone marker?

A— 250 feet.
B— 500 feet.
C— 750 feet.

Answer (B) is correct (4792). *(AIM Para 2-22)*
The distance from the runway threshold to the touchdown zone marker is 500 ft. The touchdown zone marker consists of six lines parallel to the runway.
Answer (A) is incorrect because there is no standardized marking 250 ft. from the beginning of the runway. Answer (C) is incorrect because there is no standardized marking 750 ft. from the beginning of the runway.

**3.**
**4793.** (Refer to figure 137 on page 47.) What is the distance (C) from the beginning of the touchdown zone marker to the beginning of the fixed distance marker?

A— 1,000 feet.
B— 500 feet.
C— 250 feet.

**Answer (B) is correct (4793).** *(AIM Para 2-22)*
Since the touchdown zone marker is 500 ft. from the runway threshold and the fixed distance marker is 1,000 ft. from the runway threshold, the distance from the beginning of the touchdown zone marker to the beginning of the fixed distance marker is 500 ft. (1,000 – 500).
Answer (A) is incorrect because 1,000 ft. is the distance from the beginning of the runway to the fixed distance marker. Answer (C) is incorrect because 250 ft. is not a standard distance between runway markings.

**4.**
**4796.** The primary purpose of runway end identifier lights, installed at many airfields, is to provide

A— rapid identification of the approach end of the runway during reduced visibility.
B— a warning of the final 3,000 feet of runway remaining as viewed from the takeoff or approach position.
C— rapid identification of the primary runway during reduced visibility.

**Answer (A) is correct (4796).** *(AIM Para 2-3)*
Runway end identifier lights (REIL) are effective for rapid and positive identification of the approach end of a runway which is surrounded by a preponderance of other lighting, which lacks contrast with surrounding terrain, and/or during reduced visibility. They are white strobe lights one on each side of the runway threshold.
Answer (B) is incorrect because it describes runway remaining lights in the center of the runway, not REIL. Answer (C) is incorrect because REIL of other than the primary runway may be used to help identify the airport. In other words, REIL may be flashing at the end of a runway which is not the primary runway.

**5.**
**4795.** Which type of runway lighting consists of a pair of synchronized flashing lights, one on each side of the runway threshold?

A— RAIL.
B— HIRL.
C— REIL.

**Answer (C) is correct (4795).** *(AIM Para 2-3)*
Runway end identifier lights (REIL) consist of a pair of synchronized flashing lights, one on each side of the runway threshold.
Answer (A) is incorrect because RAIL refers to runway alignment indicator lights, which are sequenced flashing lights that are used in combination with other approach lighting systems. Answer (B) is incorrect because HIRL refers to high-intensity runway lights, which is a runway edge light system.

**6.**
**4794.** Which runway marking indicates a displaced threshold on an instrument runway?

A— Arrows leading to the threshold mark.
B— Centerline dashes starting at the threshold.
C— Red chevron marks in the nonlanding portion of the runway.

**Answer (A) is correct (4794).** *(AIM Para 2-22)*
On any runway, a displaced threshold is marked with a series of arrows in the middle of the runway pointing to the threshold mark, which is a solid line across the runway. A displaced threshold is available for taxiing, landing rollout, and takeoff, but not landing.
Answer (B) is incorrect because it describes the centerline marking of a runway. Answer (C) is incorrect because chevron marks are usually yellow. They indicate a nonusable portion of the runway that is only available for emergency use (overrun and stopway areas).

**7.**

**4797.** (Refer to figure 138 below.) What night operations, if any, are authorized between the approach end of the runway and the threshold lights?

A— No aircraft operations are permitted short of the threshold lights.

B— Only taxi operations are permitted in the area short of the threshold lights.

C— Taxi and takeoff operations are permitted, providing the takeoff operations are toward the visible green threshold lights.

Answer (C) is correct (4797). *(AIM Para 2-4)*

On displaced thresholds, runway edge lights appear red when taxiing toward the green threshold lights and white when taxiing away from the threshold to the departure end of the runway. The area behind the displaced runway threshold is available for taxiing, landing rollout, and takeoff of aircraft.

Answer (A) is incorrect because overrun areas are where only emergency operations are permitted. Overrun areas do not have any runway edge lights. Answer (B) is incorrect because landing rollout and takeoff operations are also permitted behind displaced thresholds.

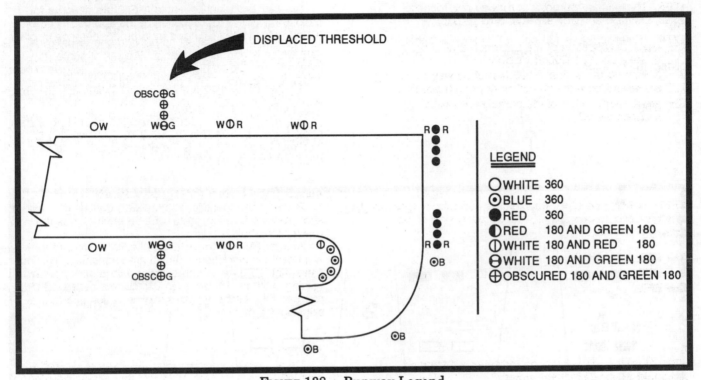

FIGURE 138.—Runway Legend.

**8.**

**4738.** Under which conditions is hydroplaning most likely to occur?

A— When rudder is used for directional control instead of allowing the nosewheel to contact the surface early in the landing roll on a wet runway.

B— During conditions of standing water, slush, high speed, and smooth runway texture.

C— During a landing on any wet runway when brake application is delayed until a wedge of water begins to build ahead of the tires.

Answer (B) is correct (4738). *(FAA-P-8740-50)*

In hydroplaning, the aircraft tire is separated from the runway by water. It is more apt to happen at higher speeds, when there is standing water or slush on the runway, and when the runway has a smooth texture.

Answer (A) is incorrect because the nosewheel cannot hydroplane if it is not put down to the runway surface. Answer (C) is incorrect because hydroplaning occurs regardless of brake timing.

## 3.2 Visual Approach Slope Indicator (VASI)

**9.**
**4781.** Which approach and landing objective is assured when the pilot remains on the proper glidepath of the VASI?

A— Continuation of course guidance after transition to VFR.
B— Safe obstruction clearance in the approach area.
C— Course guidance from the visual descent point to touchdown.

Answer (B) is correct (4781). *(AIM Para 2-2)*
The VASI system provides visual descent guidance and provides safe obstruction clearance within plus or minus 10° of the extended runway centerline from as far as 4 NM from the runway threshold.
Answer (A) is incorrect because VASI does not provide course guidance. Answer (C) is incorrect because VASI does not provide course guidance.

**10.**
**4774.** (Refer to figure 134 below.) Unless a higher angle is necessary for obstacle clearance, what is the normal glidepath angle for a 2-bar VASI?

A— 2.75°.
B— 3.00°.
C— 3.25°.

Answer (B) is correct (4774). *(AIM Para 2-2)*
Two-bar VASI installations provide one visual glide path which is normally set at 3°. Angles at some locations may be as high as 4.5°, however, to give proper obstacle clearance. This greater angle may necessitate increased runway allowed for landing and rollout of some high-performance airplanes.
Answer (A) is incorrect because the normal glide path angle for a 2-bar VASI is 3°, not 2.75°. Answer (C) is incorrect because 3.25° is the normal upper glide path provided by a 3-bar VASI.

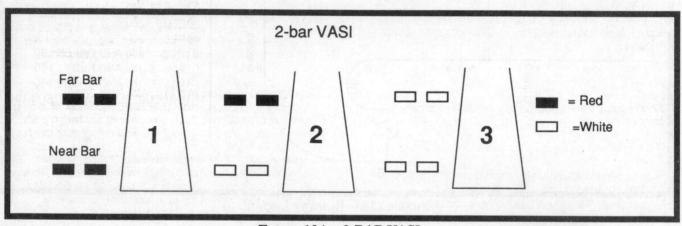

FIGURE 134.—2-BAR VASI.

**11.**
**4775.** Which of the following indications would a pilot see while approaching to land on a runway served by a 2-bar VASI?

A— If on the glidepath, the near bars will appear red, and the far bars will appear white.
B— If departing to the high side of the glidepath, the far bars will change from red to white.
C— If on the glidepath, both near bars and far bars will appear white.

Answer (B) is correct (4775). *(AIM Para 2-2)*
As you move to the high side of a VASI glide slope, the far bar will change from red to white. When you are on the glide slope, the far bar is red. When you are above the glide slope, the far bar is white.
Answer (A) is incorrect because, if you are on the glide slope, the near bars are white (not red) and the far bars are red (not white) (the opposite is impossible). Answer (C) is incorrect because, if both near and far bars are white, you are above (not on) the glide slope.

**12.**
**4778.** When on the proper glidepath of a 2-bar VASI, the pilot will see the near bar as

A— white and the far bar as red.
B— red and the far bar as white.
C— white and the far bar as white.

Answer (A) is correct (4778). *(AIM Para 2-2)*
When on the proper glide path of a 2-bar VASI, the near lights will be white and the far lights red.
Answer (B) is incorrect because white over red is impossible. Answer (C) is incorrect because white over white means you are above (not on) the glide path.

**13.**
**4779.** If an approach is being made to a runway that has an operating 3-bar VASI and all the VASI lights appear red as the airplane reaches the MDA, the pilot should

A— start a climb to reach the proper glidepath.
B— continue at the same rate of descent if the runway is in sight.
C— level off momentarily to intercept the proper approach path.

Answer (C) is correct (4779). *(AIM Para 2-2)*
If all three VASI bars are red, you are beneath both glide paths and should level off momentarily to intercept the proper approach path.
Answer (A) is incorrect because a climb is not necessary. If you level off you will soon be back on the glide path. Answer (B) is incorrect because you should briefly stop (not continue) your rate of descent to get back on the desired glide path.

**14.**
**4776.** The middle and far bars of a 3-bar VASI will

A— both appear white to the pilot when on the upper glidepath.
B— constitute a 2-bar VASI for using the lower glidepath.
C— constitute a 2-bar VASI for using the upper glidepath.

Answer (C) is correct (4776). *(AIM Para 2-2)*
On 3-bar VASIs, the lower glide path is provided by the near and middle bars at a 3° glide slope. The middle and far bars normally have a 1/4° greater glide slope and are used for the upper glide path.
Answer (A) is incorrect because, when both the middle and far bars are white, the airplane is above both glide paths. Answer (B) is incorrect because the near and middle bars are used for the lower glide path.

**15.**
**4777.** Tricolor Visual Approach Indicators normally consist of

A— a single unit, projecting a three-color visual approach path.
B— three separate light units, each projecting a different color approach path.
C— three separate light projecting units of very high candle power with a daytime range of approximately 5 miles.

Answer (A) is correct (4777). *(AIM Para 2-2)*
Tricolor Visual Approach Indicators consist of a single light unit projecting a three-color visual approach path. It has a useful range of ½ to 1 mi. in daylight and as much as 5 mi. at night.
Answer (B) is incorrect because Tricolor Visual Approach Indicators have only one light unit and have only one glide path. Answer (C) is incorrect because Tricolor VASIs have only one projecting unit with a daytime range of about 1, not 5, mi.

**16.**
**4780.** Which is a feature of the tricolor VASI?

A— One light projector with three colors: red, green, and amber.
B— Two visual glidepaths for the runway.
C— Three glidepaths, with the center path indicated by a white light.

Answer (A) is correct (4780). *(AIM Para 2-2)*
Tricolor VASIs normally consist of a single light unit projecting a three-color visual approach path. The colors are amber (above the glide path), green (on the path), and red (below the path).
Answer (B) is incorrect because two visual glide paths for the runway is a feature of a 3-bar (not tricolor) VASI. Answer (C) is incorrect because it is a nonsense concept, i.e., there is not a three glide path VASI.

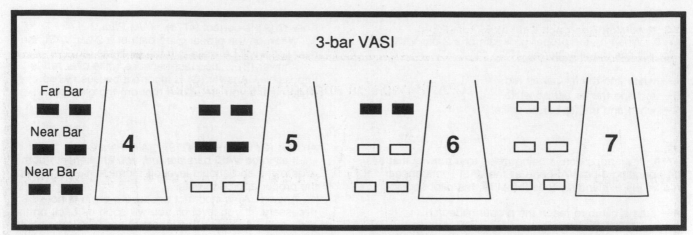

FIGURE 135.—3-BAR VASI.

**17.**
**4782.** (Refer to figure 135 above.) Unless a higher angle is required for obstacle clearance, what is the normal glidepath for a 3-bar VASI?

A— 2.3°.
B— 2.75°.
C— 3.0°.

Answer (C) is correct (4782). *(AIM Para 2-2)*
The normal glide path for a 3-bar VASI (the lower glide path) is 3°. The upper glide path is usually a 3.25° slope. Higher-angle glide slopes, up to 4.5°, are used in some places for adequate obstruction clearance.
Answer (A) is incorrect because 2.3° is not a VASI glide path angle. Answer (B) is incorrect because 2.75° is not a VASI glide path angle.

**18.**
**4783.** (Refer to figure 135 above.) Which illustration would a pilot observe when on the lower glidepath?

A— 4.
B— 5.
C— 6.

Answer (B) is correct (4783). *(AIM Para 2-2)*
On the lower glide path of a 3-bar VASI, the near lights should be white and the middle and far bars will be red, which is illustration 5.
Answer (A) is incorrect because illustration 4 indicates you are below both glide paths. Answer (C) is incorrect because illustration 6 indicates you are on the upper glide path.

**19.**
**4784.** (Refer to figure 135 above.) Which illustration would a pilot observe if the aircraft is above both glidepaths?

A— 5.
B— 6.
C— 7.

Answer (C) is correct (4784). *(AIM Para 2-2)*
When above both glide paths on a 3-bar VASI, all three rows of lights appear white, which is illustration 7.
Answer (A) is incorrect because illustration 5 indicates you are on the lower glide path. Answer (B) is incorrect because illustration 6 indicates you are on the upper glide path.

**20.**
**4785.** (Refer to figure 135 above.) Which illustration would a pilot observe if the aircraft is below both glidepaths?

A— 4.
B— 5.
C— 6.

Answer (A) is correct (4785). *(AIM Para 2-2)*
When below both glide paths on a 3-bar VASI, all three rows of lights would appear red, which is illustration 4.
Answer (B) is incorrect because illustration 5 indicates you are on the lower glide path. Answer (C) is incorrect because illustration 6 indicates you are on the upper glide path.

## 3.3 Precision Approach Path Indicator (PAPI)

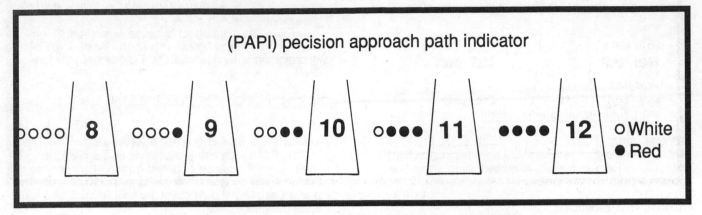

FIGURE 136.—Precision Approach Path Indicator (PAPI).

**21.**
**4786.** (Refer to figure 136 above.) Which illustration depicts an "on glidepath" indication?

A— 8.
B— 10.
C— 11.

Answer (B) is correct (4786). *(AIM Para 2-2)*
The Precision Approach Path Indicator (PAPI) uses light units similar to the VASI but they are installed in a single row of either two or four units, rather than bars. If all the light units indicate white, you are above the glide slope. If all indicate red, you are below the glide slope. If two lights indicate red and two lights indicate white, you are on the glide slope such as illustration 10.
Answer (A) is incorrect because illustration 8 indicates you are above the glide slope. Answer (C) is incorrect because illustration 11 indicates you are slightly below (2.8°) the glide slope.

**22.**
**4787.** (Refer to figure 136 above.) Which illustration depicts a "slightly low" (2.8°) indication?

A— 9.
B— 10.
C— 11.

Answer (C) is correct (4787). *(AIM Para 2-2)*
On PAPI, you are slightly below (2.8°) the glide path when three of the four lights indicate red as in illustration 11.
Answer (A) is incorrect because illustration 9 indicates you are slightly above (3.2°) the glide path. Answer (B) is incorrect because illustration 10 indicates you are on (3.0°) the glide path.

**23.**
**4788.** (Refer to figure 136 above.) Which illustration would a pilot observe if the aircraft is on a glidepath higher than 3.5°?

A— 8.
B— 9.
C— 11.

Answer (A) is correct (4788). *(AIM Para 2-2)*
Higher than the glide path on PAPIs means 3.5° or more. It is indicated by all white lights as in illustration 8.
Answer (B) is incorrect because illustration 9 indicates you are slightly high (3.2°). Answer (C) is incorrect because illustration 11 indicates you are slightly low (2.8°).

**24.**
**4789.** (Refer to figure 136 above.) Which illustration would a pilot observe if the aircraft is "slightly high" (3.2°) on the glidepath?

A— 8.
B— 9.
C— 11.

Answer (B) is correct (4789). *(AIM Para 2-2)*
Slightly high on a PAPI is about 3.2°. It would appear as three of the four lights indicating white. The remaining light indicates red such as illustration 9.
Answer (A) is incorrect because illustration 8 indicates high or more than 3.5° glide slope. Answer (C) is incorrect because illustration 11 indicates slightly low or about a 2.8° glide slope.

**25.**
**4790.** (Refer to figure 136 on page 53.) Which illustration would a pilot observe if the aircraft is less than 2.5°?

A— 10.
B— 11.
C— 12.

Answer (C) is correct (4790). *(AIM Para 2-2)*
On PAPI systems, low is indicated by all red such as illustration 12. It means the aircraft is on a less than 2.5° glide slope.
Answer (A) is incorrect because illustration 10 indicates you are on the glide path (3.0°). Answer (B) is incorrect because illustration 11 indicates slightly low (2.8°).

### 3.4 IFR Flight Planning Information

**26.**
**4405.** The most current en route and destination flight information for planning an instrument flight should be obtained from

A— the ATIS broadcast.
B— the FSS.
C— Notices to Airmen (Class II).

Answer (B) is correct (4405). *(AIM Para 5-1)*
The FAA urges every pilot to receive a preflight briefing, which may be obtained from a Flight Service Station (FSS) by telephone, radio, or personal visit. The preflight briefing should cover weather, airport, and en route navigation data.
Answer (A) is incorrect because the ATIS (Automatic Terminal Information Service) broadcasts only information pertaining to landing and departing operations at one airport. ATIS does not provide any en route information. Answer (C) is incorrect because Notices to Airmen (Class II) is a biweekly publication containing current NOTAMs. It is only one aspect of a complete flight briefing.

**27.**
**4080.** What is the purpose of FDC NOTAMs?

A— To provide the latest information on the status of navigation facilities to all FSS facilities for scheduled broadcasts.
B— To issue notices for all airports and navigation facilities in the shortest possible time.
C— To advise of changes in flight data which affect instrument approach procedures (IAP), aeronautical charts, and flight restrictions prior to normal publication.

Answer (C) is correct (4080). *(AIM Para 5-3)*
FDC (Flight Data Center) NOTAMs are regulatory in nature and issued to establish restrictions to flight or amend charts or published instrument approach procedures. FDC NOTAMs are published as needed, and indexed in the biweekly Class II NOTAMs publication.
Answer (A) is incorrect because NOTAM (D), not FDC NOTAMs, provide information for status of navigational facilities. These NOTAMs are appended to the hourly weather reports. Answer (B) is incorrect because the purpose of NOTAM (D) or (L) is to issue notices for all public use airports and navigation facilities in the shortest possible time.

**28.**
**4406.** From what source can you obtain the latest FDC NOTAM's?

A— In Notices to Airmen (Class II NOTAM's).
B— At an FAA FSS.
C— In the Airport/Facility Directory.

Answer (B) is correct (4406). *(AIM Para 5-3)*
The National Flight Data Center occasionally publishes regulatory changes (either permanent or temporary) in FDC (Flight Data Center) NOTAMs. They are also used to advertise temporary flight restrictions caused by such things as natural disasters, large public events, and other events that may generate congested air traffic. FSSs are required to keep a file of current FDC NOTAMs.
Answer (A) is incorrect because Class II NOTAMs are only published biweekly. The FSSs may have more current data. Answer (C) is incorrect because the Airport/Facility Directory is only published every 56 days. The A/FD only includes permanent changes that were known at the time of publication.

**29.**
**4079.** Which sources of aeronautical information, when used collectively, provide the latest status of airport conditions (e.g., runway closures, runway lighting, snow conditions)?

A— Airman's Information Manual, aeronautical charts, and Distant (D) Notice to Airmans (NOTAM's).
B— Airport Facility Directory, FDC NOTAM's, and Local (L) NOTAM's.
C— Airport Facility Directory, Distant (D) NOTAM's, and Local (L) NOTAM's.

Answer (C) is correct (4079). *(AIM Para 5-3)*
The latest status of airport conditions can be determined by using the Airport/Facility Directory for items that have been known for some time, and Distant (D) NOTAMs and Local (L) NOTAMs, which contain the most up-to-date data.
Answer (A) is incorrect because the Airman's Information Manual (AIM) is a source of basic flight information and ATC procedures (not specific airport information), and Aeronautical Charts do not indicate the latest status of runway conditions. Answer (B) is incorrect because FDC NOTAMs deal with regulatory changes or unusual air traffic congestion, not local airport conditions.

**30.**
**4403.** When are ATIS broadcasts updated?

A— Every 30 minutes if weather conditions are below basic VFR; otherwise, hourly.
B— Upon receipt of any official weather, regardless of content change or reported values.
C— Only when the ceiling and/or visibility changes by a reportable value.

Answer (B) is correct (4403). *(AIM Para 4-12)*
ATIS broadcasts are updated upon the receipt of any official weather regardless of content change or reported values. A new recording will also be made when there is a change in other pertinent data such as runway change, instrument approach in use, etc.
Answer (A) is incorrect because the frequency of ATIS updates does not differ under VFR or IFR conditions. Answer (C) is incorrect because the recording will be updated whenever official weather is received, even if there is no change.

**31.**
**4404.** Absence of the sky condition and visibility on an ATIS broadcast specifically implies that

A— the ceiling is more than 5,000 feet and visibility is 5 miles or more.
B— the sky condition is clear and visibility is unrestricted.
C— the ceiling is at least 3,000 feet and visibility is 5 miles or more.

Answer (A) is correct (4404). *(AIM Para 4-12)*
The ATIS broadcast generally includes the latest weather sequence, sky conditions, temperature, dew point, wind direction and velocity, altimeter, runways in use, etc. Absence of the sky condition and visibility on an ATIS broadcast specifically implies that the ceiling is more than 5,000 ft. and visibility is more than 5 SM.
Answer (B) is incorrect because the absence of the sky condition and visibility on an ATIS broadcast implies that ceilings are more than 5,000 ft. (not clear) and visibility 5 SM or more, not unrestricted. Answer (C) is incorrect because the absence of the sky condition on an ATIS broadcast implies a ceiling of more than 5,000 ft., not at least 3,000 ft.

**32.**
**4408.** The operation of an airport rotating beacon during daylight hours may indicate that

A— the in-flight visibility is less than 3 miles and the ceiling is less than 1,500 feet within Class E airspace.
B— the ground visibility is less than 3 miles and/or the ceiling is less than 1,000 feet in Class B, C, or D airspace.
C— an IFR clearance is required to operate within the airport traffic area.

Answer (B) is correct (4408). *(AIM Para 2-8)*
Operation of an airport beacon during daylight hours often indicates that the ground visibility is less than 3 SM and/or the ceiling is less than 1,000 ft. in Class B, C, or D airspace. Pilots should not rely solely on the beacon to indicate weather conditions because there is no regulatory requirement for daylight operation of the airport's rotating beacon.
Answer (A) is incorrect because the operation of an airport rotating beacon during daylight hours at an airport located in Class E airspace may indicate that in-flight visibility (if ground is not reported) is less than 3 SM and/or the ceiling is less than 1,000 ft., not 1,500 ft. Answer (C) is incorrect because an IFR clearance is required only in controlled airspace when IMC exists, not because an airport's rotating beacon is on during the day.

## 3.5 IFR Flight Plan

**33.**
**4072.** (Refer to figure 1 below.) Which item(s) should be checked in block 1 for a composite flight plan?

A— VFR with an explanation in block 11.
B— IFR with an explanation in block 11.
C— VFR and IFR.

Answer (C) is correct (4072). *(AIM Para 5-7)*
If a composite VFR/IFR flight plan is being filed, you should check both VFR and IFR in Block 1 of the flight plan. A DVFR flight plan is required for flights through air defense identification zones (ADIZ) for national security reasons.
Answer (A) is incorrect because both VFR and IFR should be checked. Answer (B) is incorrect because both VFR and IFR should be checked.

**34.**
**4075.** (Refer to figure 1 below.) Which equipment determines the code to be entered in block 3 as a suffix to aircraft type on the flight plan form?

A— DME, ADF, and airborne radar.
B— DME, transponder, and ADF.
C— DME, transponder, and RNAV.

Answer (C) is correct (4075). *(AIM Para 5-7)*
Block 3 asks for the aircraft type and special equipment. After the aircraft type, a slash is followed by a letter indicating the combination of transponder, DME, and area navigation (RNAV) equipment that you have in the airplane.
Answer (A) is incorrect because you need not report ADF (automatic direction finder) or airborne radar. Answer (B) is incorrect because an ADF is not considered a special type of navigation equipment.

**35.**
**4074.** (Refer to figure 1 below.) What information should be entered in block 7 of an IFR flight plan if the flight has three legs, each at a different altitude?

A— Altitude for first leg.
B— Altitude for first leg and highest altitude.
C— Highest altitude.

Answer (A) is correct (4074). *(AIM Para 5-7)*
Block 7 of IFR flight plans is for altitude. You should only enter the initial request for altitude. When more than one altitude or flight level is desired along the route of flight, it is best to make subsequent requests direct to the controller.
Answer (B) is incorrect because initial (not highest) altitude is to be submitted on your flight plan. Answer (C) is incorrect because initial (not highest) altitude is to be entered on your flight plan.

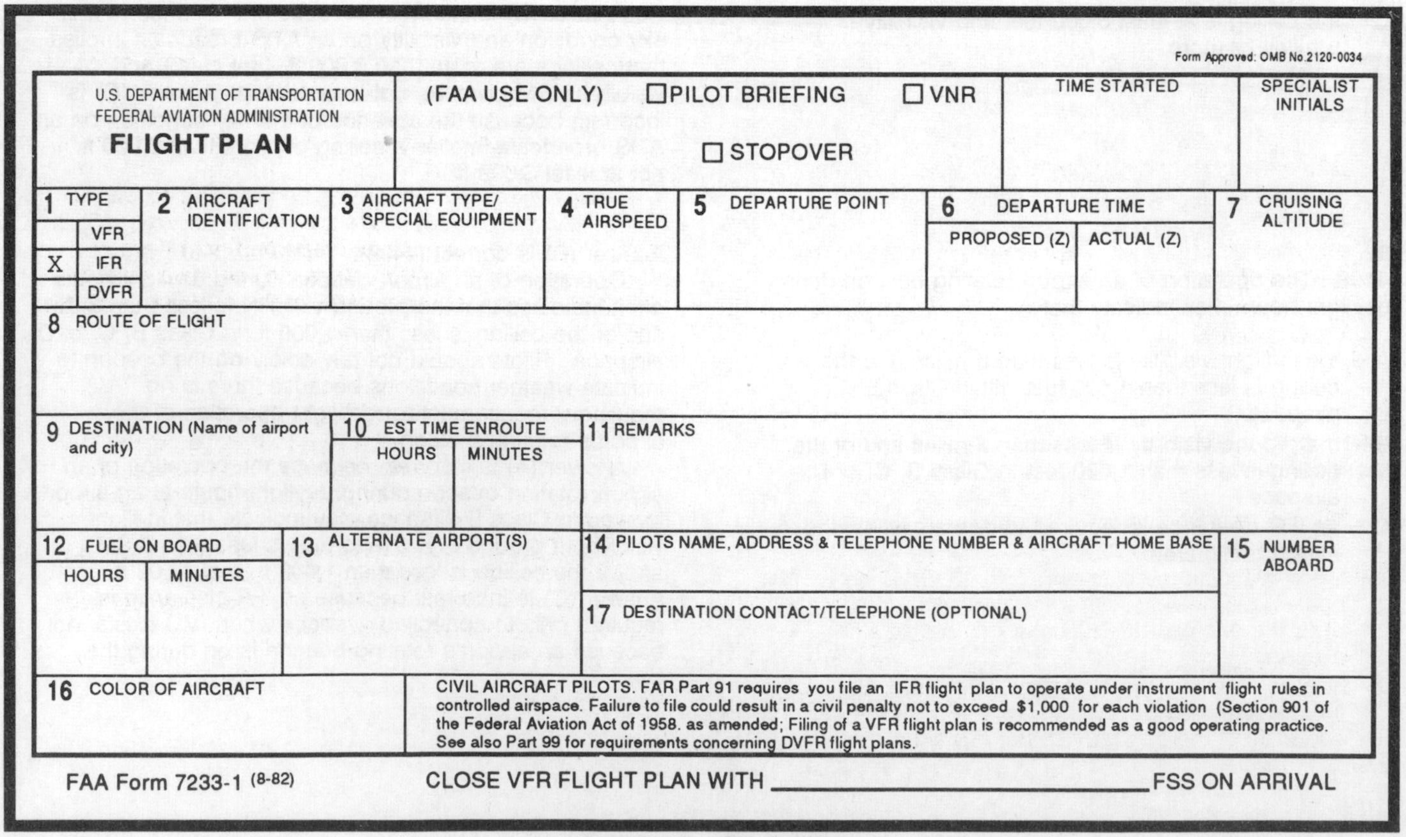
Form Approved: OMB No.2120-0034

U.S. DEPARTMENT OF TRANSPORTATION
FEDERAL AVIATION ADMINISTRATION
**FLIGHT PLAN**

(FAA USE ONLY) ☐ PILOT BRIEFING ☐ VNR ☐ STOPOVER | TIME STARTED | SPECIALIST INITIALS

1 TYPE: VFR; X IFR; DVFR
2 AIRCRAFT IDENTIFICATION
3 AIRCRAFT TYPE/ SPECIAL EQUIPMENT
4 TRUE AIRSPEED
5 DEPARTURE POINT
6 DEPARTURE TIME — PROPOSED (Z) — ACTUAL (Z)
7 CRUISING ALTITUDE
8 ROUTE OF FLIGHT
9 DESTINATION (Name of airport and city)
10 EST TIME ENROUTE — HOURS — MINUTES
11 REMARKS
12 FUEL ON BOARD — HOURS — MINUTES
13 ALTERNATE AIRPORT(S)
14 PILOTS NAME, ADDRESS & TELEPHONE NUMBER & AIRCRAFT HOME BASE
15 NUMBER ABOARD
17 DESTINATION CONTACT/TELEPHONE (OPTIONAL)
16 COLOR OF AIRCRAFT

CIVIL AIRCRAFT PILOTS. FAR Part 91 requires you file an IFR flight plan to operate under instrument flight rules in controlled airspace. Failure to file could result in a civil penalty not to exceed $1,000 for each violation (Section 901 of the Federal Aviation Act of 1958. as amended; Filing of a VFR flight plan is recommended as a good operating practice. See also Part 99 for requirements concerning DVFR flight plans.

FAA Form 7233-1 (8-82) CLOSE VFR FLIGHT PLAN WITH ______________ FSS ON ARRIVAL

FIGURE 1.—Flight Plan.

**36.**
**4073.** (Refer to figure 1 on page 56.) The time entered in block 12 for an IFR flight should be based on which fuel quantity?

A— Total fuel required for the flight.
B— Total useable fuel on board.
C— The amount of fuel required to fly to the destination airport, then to the alternate, plus a 45-minute reserve.

**37.**
**4761.** What point at the destination should be used to compute estimated time en route on an IFR flight plan?

A— The final approach fix on the expected instrument approach.
B— The initial approach fix on the expected instrument approach.
C— The point of first intended landing.

**38.**
**4059.** When may a pilot file a composite flight plan?

A— When requested or advised by ATC.
B— Any time a portion of the flight will be VFR.
C— Any time a landing is planned at an intermediate airport.

**39.**
**4060.** When filing a composite flight plan where the first portion of the flight is IFR, which fix(es) should be indicated on the flight plan form?

A— All points of transition from one airway to another, fixes defining direct route segments, and the clearance limit fix.
B— Only the fix where you plan to terminate the IFR portion of the flight.
C— Only those compulsory reporting points on the IFR route segment.

**40.**
**4061.** What is the recommended procedure for transitioning from VFR to IFR on a composite flight plan?

A— Prior to transitioning to IFR, contact the nearest FSS, close the VFR portion, and request ATC clearance.
B— Upon reaching the proposed point for change to IFR, contact the nearest FSS and cancel your VFR flight plan, then contact ARTCC and request an IFR clearance.
C— Prior to reaching the proposed point for change to IFR, contact ARTCC, request your IFR clearance, and instruct them to cancel the VFR flight plan.

Answer (B) is correct (4073). *(AIM Para 5-7)*
Block 12 should be filled in with the time at normal cruising speed using total usable fuel on board. It should be computed from the departure point.
Answer (A) is incorrect because total fuel required for the flight is determined in your flight planning, but is not an item that is listed on an IFR flight plan. Answer (C) is incorrect because it describes the IFR fuel requirement.

Answer (C) is correct (4761). *(FAR 91.169)*
Estimated time en route on an IFR flight plan should be the time from takeoff at the departure airport to touchdown at the point of first intended landing.
Answer (A) is incorrect because, due to varying weather conditions, runways in use, traffic, etc., there is no way of accurately telling which approach will be used. Answer (B) is incorrect because, due to varying weather conditions, runways in use, traffic, etc., there is no way of accurately telling which approach will be used.

Answer (B) is correct (4059). *(AIM Para 5-6)*
A composite flight plan should be filed whenever VFR operation is specified for one portion of the flight and IFR for another portion.
Answer (A) is incorrect because ATC does not request or advise on the type of flight plan to file other than IFR flight plans required in certain weather conditions and in the positive control area. Answer (C) is incorrect because you are not required to convert a flight plan from or to IFR or VFR when landing is planned at an intermediate airport.

Answer (A) is correct (4060). *(AIM Para 5-6)*
On composite flight plans for which the first portion of the flight is IFR, the flight plan should be a standard IFR flight plan, which includes points of transition from one airway to another, fixes defining direct route segments, and the clearance limit fix.
Answer (B) is incorrect because you have to define the route to get to your clearance limit fix. Answer (C) is incorrect because compulsory reporting points are not listed on an IFR flight plan unless they define a point of transition, direct route segments, or the clearance limit fix.

Answer (A) is correct (4061). *(AIM Para 5-6)*
Prior to transitioning from VFR to IFR, you close the VFR portion with FSS and request ATC clearance. You must remain in VFR weather conditions until operating in accordance with the IFR clearance.
Answer (B) is incorrect because you must obtain an IFR clearance before beginning IFR operations. Answer (C) is incorrect because you should cancel your VFR flight plan with FSS, not ATC.

**41.**
**4076.** When may a pilot cancel the IFR flight plan prior to completing the flight?

A— Any time.
B— Only if an emergency occurs.
C— Only in VFR conditions outside positive controlled airspace.

Answer (C) is correct (4076).  *(AIM Para 5-13)*
An IFR flight plan may be canceled at any time you are operating in VFR conditions outside positive control airspace by stating, "Cancel my IFR flight plan" to ATC. Once accepted by ATC, you should change to the appropriate communications frequency, transponder code, and altitude.
Answer (A) is incorrect because you cannot proceed VFR under IFR conditions or when flying above FL 180 (i.e., in the positive control area).  Answer (B) is incorrect because ATC will provide needed assistance in emergencies while operating under an IFR flight plan.

**42.**
**4058.** How is your flight plan closed when your destination airport has IFR conditions and there is no control tower or flight service station (FSS) on the field?

A— The ARTCC controller will close your flight plan when you report the runway in sight.
B— You may close your flight plan any time after starting the approach by contacting any FSS or ATC facility.
C— Upon landing, you must close your flight plan by radio or by telephone to any FSS or ATC facility.

Answer (C) is correct (4058).  *(AIM Para 5-13)*
IFR flight plans are automatically closed by ATC if you land at an airport with an operating control tower. However, if operating on an IFR flight plan to an airport with no functioning control tower, the pilot must cancel the IFR flight plan.  You may cancel your IFR flight plan while airborne only if weather permits.  If your destination airport has IFR conditions and there is no tower or FSS on the field, you should close your IFR flight plan upon landing by radio or telephone to any FSS or ATC facility.
Answer (A) is incorrect because you (not ATC) must close your IFR flight plan at uncontrolled airports. Answer (B) is incorrect because, when an airport has IFR conditions, you require IFR clearances until you have safely landed.

**43.**
**4069.** What is a waypoint when used for an IFR flight?

A— A predetermined geographical position used for an RNAV route or an RNAV instrument approach.
B— A reporting point defined by the intersection of two VOR radials.
C— A location on a victor airway which can only be identified by VOR and DME signals.

Answer (A) is correct (4069).  *(IFH Chap VII)*
A waypoint on an IFR flight is a predetermined geographical position used for an RNAV route or an RNAV instrument approach definition or progress reporting purposes.  It is defined relative to a VORTAC position or in terms of latitude/longitude coordinates.
Answer (B) is incorrect because a point defined by the intersection of two VOR radials is called an intersection, not a waypoint.  Answer (C) is incorrect because a location on a victor airway which can only be identified by VOR and DME signals is called a DME fix, not a waypoint.

## 3.6 ATC Clearances

**44.**
**4395.** What response is expected when ATC issues an IFR clearance to pilots of airborne aircraft?

A— Read back the entire clearance as required by regulation.
B— Read back those parts containing altitude assignments or vectors and any part requiring verification.
C— Read-back should be unsolicited and spontaneous to confirm that the pilot understands all instructions.

Answer (B) is correct (4395).  *(AIM Para 4-86)*
Pilots of airborne aircraft should read back those parts of ATC clearances and instructions containing altitude assignments or vectors and any part requiring verification.  The read-back serves as a double-check between pilots and ATC and reduces the kinds of communications errors that occur when a number is either misheard or is incorrect.
Answer (A) is incorrect because the read-back is an expected procedure, but there is no regulatory requirement to read back an ATC clearance.  Only those parts containing altitude assignments or vectors and any part requiring verification (not the entire clearance) should be read back.  Answer (C) is incorrect because only those parts containing altitude assignments or vectors and any part requiring verification (not all instructions) should be read back.

**45.**
**4396.** Which clearance items are always given in an abbreviated IFR departure clearance? (Assume radar environment.)

A— Altitude, destination airport, and one or more fixes which identify the initial route of flight.
B— Destination airport, altitude, and SID Name-Number-Transition, if appropriate.
C— Clearance limit, and SID Name, Number, and/or Transition, if appropriate.

Answer (B) is correct (4396). *(AIM Para 5-23)*
An abbreviated IFR departure clearance will include the destination airport. En route altitude will be stated in the clearance and the pilot will be advised to expect an assigned or filed altitude within a given time or at a certain point after departure. Any SID (Standard Instrument Departure) will also be specified by ATC stating the SID name, the current number, and the SID transition name.
Answer (A) is incorrect because the fixes are already included in the flight plan and do not need to be repeated in an abbreviated IFR departure clearance. Answer (C) is incorrect because an en route altitude is always given in an abbreviated IFR departure clearance.

**46.**
**4414.** Which information is always given in an abbreviated clearance?

A— SID or transition name and altitude to maintain.
B— Name of destination airport or specific fix and altitude.
C— Altitude to maintain and code to squawk.

Answer (B) is correct (4414). *(AIM Para 5-23)*
An abbreviated IFR departure clearance always contains the name of your destination airport or clearance limit, altitude, and, if a SID is to be flown, the SID name, the current number, and the SID transition name.
Answer (A) is incorrect because the destination airport or clearance limit is always given in an abbreviated clearance. Answer (C) is incorrect because the destination airport or clearance limit is always given in an abbreviated clearance.

**47.**
**4486.** An abbreviated departure clearance "...CLEARED AS FILED..." will always contain the name

A— and number of the STAR to be flown when filed in the flight plan.
B— of the destination airport filed in the flight plan.
C— of the first compulsory reporting point if not in a radar environment.

Answer (B) is correct (4486). *(AIM Para 5-23)*
An abbreviated IFR departure clearance will include the destination airport. En route altitude will be stated, and the pilot will be advised to expect an assigned or filed altitude by a certain time or at a certain point after departure either separately or as part of a SID. The abbreviated clearance also includes the SID Name-Number-Transition, if appropriate.
Answer (A) is incorrect because, if a SID is given in an abbreviated clearance, the controller is required to state the SID name, the current number, and the SID transition name. Answer (C) is incorrect because compulsory reporting points are not given in an abbreviated clearance.

**48.**
**4398.** On the runup pad, you receive the following clearance from ground control:

CLEARED TO DALLAS-LOVE AIRPORT AS FILED — MAINTAIN SIX THOUSAND — SQUAWK ZERO SEVEN ZERO FOUR JUST BEFORE DEPARTURE — DEPARTURE CONTROL WILL BE ONE TWO FOUR POINT NINER.

An abbreviated clearance, such as this, will always contain the

A— departure control frequency.
B— transponder code.
C— assigned altitude.

Answer (C) is correct (4398). *(AIM Para 5-23)*
An en route altitude will be stated, or the pilot will be advised to expect an assigned or filed altitude within a given time or at a certain point after departure. This may be done separately or as part of a SID.
Answer (A) is incorrect because an abbreviated clearance is based on the flight-planned route of the flight. The departure control frequency is given after the abbreviated (route) clearance. Answer (B) is incorrect because an abbreviated clearance is based on the route of flight. The transponder code is given after the abbreviated (route) clearance.

**49.**
**4394.** When departing from an airport not served by a control tower, the issuance of a clearance containing a void time indicates that

A— ATC will assume the pilot has not departed if no transmission is received before the void time.
B— the pilot must advise ATC as soon as possible, but no later than 30 minutes, of their intentions if not off by the void time.
C— ATC will protect the airspace only to the void time.

Answer (B) is correct (4394). *(AIM Para 5-24)*
If operating from an airport not served by a control tower, the pilot may receive a clearance containing a provision that if the flight has not departed by a specific time (void time), the clearance is void. In this situation, the pilot who does not depart prior to the void time must advise ATC of his/her intentions as soon as possible, but no later than 30 min. after the void time.
Answer (A) is incorrect because ATC will assume a departure unless they hear from the pilot. Answer (C) is incorrect because the airspace is protected until ATC hears from the pilot.

**50.**
**4443.** What is the significance of an ATC clearance which reads "...CRUISE SIX THOUSAND..."?

A— The pilot must maintain 6,000 until reaching the IAF serving the destination airport, then execute the published approach procedure.
B— It authorizes a pilot to conduct flight at any altitude from minimum IFR altitude up to and including 6,000.
C— The pilot is authorized to conduct flight at any altitude from minimum IFR altitude up to and including 6,000, but each change in altitude must be reported to ATC.

Answer (B) is correct (4443). *(AIM Para 4-83)*
The term "cruise" in a clearance assigns a pilot a block of airspace from the minimum IFR altitude up to and including the specified altitude (e.g., 6,000 ft. MSL). The pilot may level off at any intermediate altitude within this block of airspace. Climb and descent within the block is to be made at the discretion of the pilot. However, once the pilot starts descent and verbally reports leaving an altitude in the block, (s)he may not return to that altitude without additional ATC clearance.
Answer (A) is incorrect because the pilot need not maintain 6,000 ft. Answer (C) is incorrect because the pilot may change altitude without reporting to ATC.

**51.**
**4392.** What is the significance of an ATC clearance which reads "...CRUISE SIX THOUSAND..."?

A— The pilot must maintain 6,000 feet until reaching the IAF serving the destination airport, then execute the published approach procedure.
B— Climbs may be made to, or descents made from, 6,000 feet at the pilot's discretion.
C— The pilot may utilize any altitude from the MEA/MOCA to 6,000 feet, but each change in altitude must be reported to ATC.

Answer (B) is correct (4392). *(AIM Para 4-83)*
The term "cruise" in a clearance assigns a pilot a block of airspace from the minimum IFR altitude up to and including the specified altitude (e.g., 6,000 ft. MSL). The pilot may climb to, level off at, or descend from any intermediate altitude within this block of airspace. Once the pilot starts descent and verbally reports leaving an altitude in the block, however, (s)he may not return to that altitude without additional ATC clearance.
Answer (A) is incorrect because the pilot need not maintain 6,000 ft. Answer (C) is incorrect because the pilot is assigned all the airspace from the minimum IFR altitude to 6,000 ft. MSL and may change altitudes without reporting to ATC.

**52.**
**4458.** A "CRUISE FOUR THOUSAND FEET" clearance would mean that the pilot is authorized to

A— vacate 4,000 feet without notifying ATC.
B— climb to, but not descend from 4,000 feet, without further ATC clearance.
C— use any altitude from minimum IFR to 4,000 feet, but must report leaving each altitude.

Answer (A) is correct (4458). *(AIM Para 4-83)*
The term "cruise" in a clearance assigns a pilot a block of airspace from the minimum IFR altitude up to and including the specified altitude (e.g., 4,000 ft. MSL). The pilot may level off at any intermediate altitude within this block of airspace. Climb and descent within the block is to be made at the discretion of the pilot. However, once the pilot starts descent and verbally reports leaving an altitude, (s)he may not return to that altitude without additional ATC clearance.
Answer (B) is incorrect because any airspace between the minimum IFR altitude and 4,000 ft. MSL may be used without further ATC clearance. Answer (C) is incorrect because cruise clearances do not require reporting a change in altitude to ATC.

## 3.7 ATC Communication Procedures

**53.**
**4420.** During a takeoff into IFR conditions with low ceilings, when should the pilot contact departure control?

A— Before penetrating the clouds.
B— When advised by the tower.
C— Upon completing the first turn after takeoff or upon establishing cruise climb on a straight-out departure.

**Answer (B) is correct (4420).** *(AIM Para 5-25)*
Pilots should not change to the departure control frequency until advised by ATC. Because the pilot maintains continuous contact with assigned ATC frequencies, all frequency changes are at the direction of ATC.
Answer (A) is incorrect because the tower will advise the pilot when to contact departure control, and it is not based on whether the aircraft has penetrated the clouds. Answer (C) is incorrect because the tower will advise the pilot when to contact departure control, which may or may not be upon completion of the first turn after takeoff or establishment of a cruise climb on departure.

**54.**
**4393.** What is the recommended climb procedure when a nonradar departure control instructs a pilot to climb to the assigned altitude?

A— Maintain a continuous optimum climb until reaching assigned altitude and report passing each 1,000-foot level.
B— Climb at a maximum angle of climb to within 1,000 feet of the assigned altitude, then 500 feet per minute the last 1,000 feet.
C— Maintain an optimum climb on the centerline of the airway without intermediate level-offs until 1,000 feet below assigned altitude, then 500 feet per minute.

**Answer (C) is correct (4393).** *(AIM Para 4-89)*
When ATC clearances are given to descend or climb to a certain altitude, the pilot should use the optimum rate consistent with the operating characteristics of the aircraft to 1,000 ft. above or below the assigned altitude and then attempt to descend or climb at a rate of between 500 and 1,500 fpm until reaching the assigned altitude. Also, on airways, one should climb and descend on the centerline of the airway with no intermediate level-offs.
Answer (A) is incorrect because the pilot is not required to report passing each 1,000 ft. of altitude. Answer (B) is incorrect because one should normally use a cruise climb rather than a maximum angle of climb.

**55.**
**4555.** To comply with ATC instructions for altitude changes of more than 1,000 feet, what rate of climb or descent should be used?

A— As rapidly as practicable to 500 feet above/below the assigned altitude, and then at 500 feet per minute until the assigned altitude is reached.
B— 1,000 feet per minute during climb and 500 feet per minute during descents until reaching the assigned altitude.
C— As rapidly as practicable to 1,000 feet above/below the assigned altitude, and then between 500 and 1,500 feet per minute until reaching the assigned altitude.

**Answer (C) is correct (4555).** *(AIM Para 4-89)*
When ATC clearances are given to descend or climb to a certain altitude, the pilot should use the optimum rate consistent with the operating characteristics of the aircraft to 1,000 ft. above or below the assigned altitude and then attempt to descend or climb at a rate of between 500 and 1,500 fpm until reaching the assigned altitude. Also, one should climb and descend on the centerline of the airway with no intermediate level-offs.
Answer (A) is incorrect because the rate should be between 500 and 1,500 fpm after you are within 1,000 (not 500) ft. of the target altitude. Answer (B) is incorrect because the rate of climb and descent should be based upon aircraft capability and when 1,000 ft. above or below the assigned altitude, then attempt to descend or climb at a rate of between 500 and 1,500 fpm until the assigned altitude is reached.

**56.**
**4380.** When ATC has not imposed any climb or descent restrictions and aircraft are within 1,000 feet of assigned altitude, pilots should attempt to both climb and descend at a rate of between

A— 500 feet per minute and 1,000 feet per minute.
B— 500 feet per minute and 1,500 feet per minute.
C— 1,000 feet per minute and 2,000 feet per minute.

**Answer (B) is correct (4380).** *(AIM Para 4-89)*
When ATC clearances are given to descend or climb to a certain altitude, the pilot should use the optimum rate consistent with the operating characteristics of the aircraft to 1,000 ft. above or below the assigned altitude and then attempt to descend or climb at a rate of between 500 and 1,500 fpm until reaching the assigned altitude. Also, on airways, one should climb and descend on the centerline of the airway with no intermediate level-offs.
Answer (A) is incorrect because within 1,000 ft. of the assigned altitude pilots should attempt to climb/descend at a rate of between 500 and 1,500 (not 1,000) fpm. Answer (C) is incorrect because within 1,000 ft. of the assigned altitude pilots should attempt to climb/descend at a rate of between 500 (not 1,000) and 1,500 (not 2,000) fpm.

**57.**
**4456.** Which report should be made to ATC without a specific request when not in radar contact?

A— Entering instrument meteorological conditions.
B— When leaving final approach fix inbound on final approach.
C— Correcting an E.T.A. any time a previous E.T.A. is in error in excess of 2 minutes.

Answer (B) is correct (4456). *(AIM Para 5-33)*
The following reports (in addition to those that are made at all times) should be made to ATC without a specific request when not in radar contact:

1. When leaving final approach fix inbound on final approach (non-precision approach) or when leaving the outer marker or fix used in lieu of the outer marker inbound on final approach (precision approach).
2. Position reports over compulsory reporting points.
3. A corrected ETA to a reporting point at any time it becomes apparent that an estimate as previously submitted is in error in excess of 3 min.

Answer (A) is incorrect because a report should be made to ATC whether or not in radar contact any time you encounter any type of weather conditions that have not been forecast. If IMC were forecast, no report is necessary. Answer (C) is incorrect because a report should be made to ATC when correcting an ETA any time a previous ETA is in error in excess of 3 min., not 2 min.

**58.**
**4078.** Where are the compulsory reporting points, if any, on a direct flight not flown on radials or courses of established airways or routes?

A— Fixes selected to define the route.
B— There are no compulsory reporting points unless advised by ATC.
C— At the changeover points.

Answer (A) is correct (4078). *(AIM Para 5-32)*
The compulsory reporting points (when not in radar contact) on a direct flight not flown on radials or courses of established airways or routes are those fixes selected to define the route on the flight plan.
Answer (B) is incorrect because on a direct flight the compulsory reporting points are those fixes used to define the route. Answer (C) is incorrect because some navigation systems used on direct flights do not require COPs to prevent the loss of navigation guidance, e.g., LORAN.

**59.**
**4390.** When should your transponder be on Mode C while on an IFR flight?

A— Only when ATC requests Mode C.
B— At all times if the equipment has been calibrated, unless requested otherwise by ATC.
C— When passing 12,500 feet MSL.

Answer (B) is correct (4390). *(AIM Para 4-18)*
If your airplane's transponder is equipped to reply on Mode C, it should be on at all times unless deactivation is directed by ATC.
Answer (A) is incorrect because Mode C should only be turned off (not on) when directed by ATC. Answer (C) is incorrect because Mode C is a requirement any time you are flying above 10,000 ft. MSL, not 12,500 ft. MSL.

**60.**
**4421.** During a flight, the controller advises "traffic 2 o'clock 5 miles southbound." The pilot is holding 20° correction for a crosswind from the right. Where should the pilot look for the traffic?

A— 40° to the right of the airplane's nose.
B— 20° to the right of the airplane's nose.
C— Straight ahead.

Answer (A) is correct (4421). *(AIM Para 4-13)*
ATC issues traffic advisories in terms of the airplane's course (i.e., ground track), not its heading. Allowance must be made for drift correction or course change made simultaneously with the radar traffic information. 2 o'clock is approximately 60° to the right of the airplane's course. Since the pilot is already holding a 20° right wind correction, the pilot need to look only 40° to the right of the airplane's nose for the traffic.
Answer (B) is incorrect because 20° to the right of the airplane's nose is 40° to the right of the airplane's track, which is between 1 and 2 o'clock. Answer (C) is incorrect because straight ahead is 20° (wind correction) to the right of the airplane's track, which is between 12 and 1 o'clock.

**61.**
**4605.** During the en route phase of an IFR flight, the pilot is advised "Radar service terminated." What action is appropriate?

A— Set transponder to code 1200.
B— Resume normal position reporting.
C— Activate the IDENT feature of the transponder to re-establish radar contact.

Answer (B) is correct (4605). *(AIM Para 5-32)*
During the en route phase of an IFR flight, you are advised that "radar service terminated" or "radar contact lost," you should resume normal position reporting as required when not in radar contact.
Answer (A) is incorrect because you should set the transponder to code 1200 (VFR) only when you cancel your IFR flight plan with ATC and you are instructed to squawk VFR. Answer (C) is incorrect because you should activate the IDENT feature of the transponder only upon the request of ATC.

**62.**
**4423.** What does the ATC term "Radar Contact" signify?

A— Your aircraft has been identified and you will receive separation from all aircraft while in contact with this radar facility.
B— Your aircraft has been identified on the radar display and radar flight-following will be provided until radar identification is terminated.
C— You will be given traffic advisories until advised the service has been terminated or that radar contact has been lost.

Answer (B) is correct (4423). *(P/C Glossary)*
The term "Radar Contact" is used by ATC to inform an aircraft that it is identified on the radar display and radar flight following will be provided until radar service is terminated. Reporting over compulsory reporting points is not required when an aircraft is in radar contact.
Answer (A) is incorrect because separation from all aircraft only occurs in Class A, B, and C airspace. Answer (C) is incorrect because traffic advisory service is only provided to the extent possible. Higher priority duties take precedence, such as controlling or other limitations, volume of traffic, frequency congestion, or controller workload.

**63.**
**4422.** What is meant when departure control instructs you to "resume own navigation" after you have been vectored to a Victor airway?

A— You should maintain the airway by use of your navigation equipment.
B— Radar service is terminated.
C— You are still in radar contact, but must make position reports.

Answer (A) is correct (4422). *(P/C Glossary)*
Assuming you have been vectored to an airway on your intended route of flight, you should maintain your course along the airway by use of your navigation equipment when ATC advises you to resume your own navigation.
Answer (B) is incorrect because "resume navigation" means that the radar controller will stop vectoring you, not stop observing you. Answer (C) is incorrect because position reporting is not required when you are in radar contact with ATC.

**64.**
**4424.** Upon intercepting the assigned radial, the controller advises you that you are on the airway and to "RESUME OWN NAVIGATION." This phrase means that

A— you are still in radar contact, but must make position reports.
B— radar services are terminated and you will be responsible for position reports.
C— you are to assume responsibility for your own navigation.

Answer (C) is correct (4424). *(P/C Glossary)*
Assuming you have been vectored to an airway on your intended route of flight, you should maintain your course along the airway by use of your navigation equipment when ATC advises you to resume your own navigation.
Answer (A) is incorrect because position reporting is not required when in radar contact. Answer (B) is incorrect because "resume navigation" only means that the radar controller is going to stop vectoring you, not stop observing you.

**65.**
**4409.** What service is provided by departure control to an IFR flight when operating from an airport within Class C airspace?

A— Separation from all aircraft operating in Class C airspace.
B— Position and altitude of all traffic within 2 miles of the IFR pilot's line of flight and altitude.
C— Separation from all IFR aircraft and participating VFR aircraft.

Answer (C) is the best answer (4409). *(FAR 91.130)*
In Class C airspace, ATC provides an IFR flight with separation from all IFR aircraft and participating VFR aircraft. VFR aircraft are only required to establish and maintain two-way radio communication with ATC and to be equipped with a Mode C transponder.
Answer (A) is incorrect because an IFR flight is only provided traffic advisories and conflict resolution with VFR aircraft. Answer (B) is incorrect because ATC provides position and altitude of aircraft that may conflict, not position and altitude of all traffic within 2 NM of your line of flight.

**66.**
**4758.** If during a VFR practice instrument approach, Radar Approach Control assigns an altitude or heading that will cause you to enter the clouds, what action should be taken?

A— Enter the clouds, since ATC authorization for practice approaches is considered an IFR clearance.
B— Avoid the clouds and inform ATC that altitude/ heading will not permit VFR.
C— Abandon the approach.

**Answer (B) is correct (4758).** *(AIM Para 4-71)*
During a VFR practice instrument approach, you are responsible to comply with basic visual flight rules. Thus, if radar approach assigns an altitude or heading that will cause you to enter the clouds, you must avoid the clouds and inform ATC that that altitude/heading will not permit VFR.
Answer (A) is incorrect because pilots may not enter clouds without an IFR clearance. Answer (C) is incorrect because the pilot need only modify, not abandon the approach, to maintain VFR.

**67.**
**4726.** You are being vectored to the ILS approach course, but have not been cleared for the approach. It becomes evident that you will pass through the localizer course. What action should be taken?

A— Turn outbound and make a procedure turn.
B— Continue on the assigned heading and query ATC.
C— Start a turn to the inbound heading and inquire if you are cleared for the approach.

**Answer (B) is correct (4726).** *(AIM Para 5-43)*
Normally, you will be informed by ATC when it is necessary to vector across the final approach course for spacing or other reasons. If you have not been cleared for the approach and it becomes evident that you will cross the approach course, you must continue on your assigned heading and question ATC.
Answer (A) is incorrect because while being radar vectored, a procedure turn is not authorized unless cleared by ATC. Answer (C) is incorrect because you must maintain your assigned heading, not turn inbound on the final approach course.

**68.**
**4725.** What is the pilot in command's responsibility when flying a propeller aircraft within 20 miles of the airport of intended landing and ATC requests the pilot to reduce speed to 160? (Pilot complies with speed adjustment.)

A— Reduce TAS to 160 knots and maintain until advised by ATC.
B— Reduce IAS to 160 MPH and maintain until advised by ATC.
C— Reduce IAS to 160 knots and maintain that speed within 10 knots.

**Answer (C) is correct (4725).** *(AIM Para 4-91)*
ATC will express all speed adjustments in terms of kt. based on indicated airspeed (IAS) in 10-kt. increments below FL 240. When complying with an ATC speed adjustment to reduce to 160, you should reduce IAS to 160 kt. and maintain that speed within 10 kt.
Answer (A) is incorrect because ATC speed restrictions are based on indicated airspeed (IAS), not true airspeed (TAS). Answer (B) is incorrect because airspeeds are given in kt., not MPH.

**69.**
**4071.** For which speed variation should you notify ATC?

A— When the groundspeed changes more than 5 knots.
B— When the average true airspeed changes 5 percent or 10 knots, whichever is greater.
C— Any time the groundspeed changes 10 MPH.

**Answer (B) is correct (4071).** *(AIM Para 5-33)*
There are a number of things a pilot needs to report to ATC without being requested. One is a change in the average TAS at cruising altitude when it varies by 5% or 10 kt. (whichever is greater) from that filed in the flight plan.
Answer (A) is incorrect because ATC should be notified if TAS (not groundspeed) varies more than 10 (not 5) kt. or 5%, whichever is greater. Answer (C) is incorrect because ATC should be notified if TAS (not groundspeed) varies more than 10 kt. (not MPH) or 5%, whichever is greater.

**70.**
**4469.** When are you required to establish communications with the tower, if you cancel your IFR flight plan 10 miles from the destination?

A— Immediately after canceling the flight plan.
B— When advised by ARTCC.
C— At least 5 miles from the center of the airport.

Answer (C) is correct (4469). *(FAR 91.129)*
When flying within Class D airspace, you must be in communication with the tower. Class D airspace normally has a 4.3-NM (5-SM) radius from the center of the airport with an operating tower. Accordingly, you must notify the tower of your position and intentions prior to entering Class D airspace.
Answer (A) is incorrect because, while it is a good operating practice to make an initial call to the tower up to 15 SM, it is only required before entering Class D airspace (i.e., 4.3 NM out). Answer (B) is incorrect because, while ARTCC may advise you to contact the tower when the controller accepts your IFR flight plan cancellation, you are only required to contact the tower prior to entering Class D airspace.

**71.**
**4415.** If a control tower and an FSS are located on the same airport, which tower function is assumed by the FSS during those periods when the tower is closed?

A— Automatic closing of the IFR flight plan.
B— Approach control clearance.
C— Airport Advisory Service.

Answer (C) is correct (4415). *(AIM Para 4-8)*
An FSS located on an airport will provide Local Airport Advisory (LAA) service at that airport when there is no operating control tower. This service provides arriving and departing aircraft with wind direction and speed, favored runway, altimeter setting, pertinent known traffic, pertinent known field condition, and airport taxi routes and traffic patterns. The information is advisory in nature.
Answer (A) is incorrect because the pilot must initiate cancellation of the IFR plan if operating IFR to an airport with no functioning control tower. Answer (B) is incorrect because FSS personnel can only issue advisories (not ATC clearances) to pilots.

**72.**
**4416.** Which service is provided for IFR arrivals by a FSS located on an airport without a control tower?

A— Automatic closing of the IFR flight plan.
B— Airport advisories.
C— All functions of approach control.

Answer (B) is correct (4416). *(AIM Para 4-8)*
An FSS located on an airport will provide Local Airport Advisory (LAA) service at that airport if there is no operating control tower. This service provides arriving and departing aircraft with wind direction and speed, favored runway, altimeter setting, pertinent known traffic, pertinent known field condition, and airport taxi routes and traffic patterns. The information is advisory in nature.
Answer (A) is incorrect because the pilot must initiate cancellation of the IFR plan if operating IFR to an airport with no operating control tower. Answer (C) is incorrect because FSS personnel can only issue advisories (not ATC clearances and instructions) to pilots.

**73.**
**4379.** What does declaring "minimum fuel" to ATC imply?

A— Traffic priority is needed to the destination airport.
B— Emergency handling is required to the nearest useable airport.
C— Merely an advisory that indicates an emergency situation is possible should any undue delay occur.

Answer (C) is correct (4379). *(AIM Para 5-85)*
You should advise ATC of your minimum fuel status when your fuel supply has reached a state where, upon reaching your destination, you cannot accept any undue delay. Be aware this is not an emergency situation, but merely an advisory that indicates an emergency situation is possible should any undue delay occur.
Answer (A) is incorrect because priority may be issued when declaring an emergency, not when declaring minimum fuel. Answer (B) is incorrect because minimum fuel advisory is not an emergency situation.

## 3.8 Radio Communication Failure

**74.**
**4462.** You enter a holding pattern at a fix, not the same as the approach fix, and receive an EFC time of 1530. At 1520 you experience complete two-way communications failure. Which procedure should you follow to execute the approach to a landing?

A— Depart the holding fix to arrive at the approach fix as close as possible to the EFC time and complete the approach.

B— Depart the holding fix at the EFC time, and complete the approach.

C— Depart the holding fix at the EFC time or earlier if your flight planned ETA is before the EFC.

Answer (B) is correct (4462). *(FAR 91.185)*
If you experience two-way radio communication failure at a holding fix that is not the same as the approach fix, leave the holding fix at the EFC time, and complete the approach.
Answer (A) is incorrect because you leave for, not arrive at, the approach fix at the EFC time. Answer (C) is incorrect because the EFC time takes precedence over the flight plan ETA.

**75.**
**4463.** Which procedure should you follow if you experience two-way communications failure while holding at a holding fix with an EFC time? (The holding fix is not the same as the approach fix.)

A— Depart the holding fix to arrive at the approach fix as close as possible to the EFC time.

B— Depart the holding fix at the EFC time.

C— Proceed immediately to the approach fix and hold until EFC.

Answer (B) is correct (4463). *(FAR 91.185)*
If you experience two-way radio communication failure at a holding fix that is not the same as the approach fix, leave the holding fix at the EFC time, and complete the approach.
Answer (A) is incorrect because you would leave for, not arrive at, the approach fix at the EFC time.
Answer (C) is incorrect because you should not leave the holding fix to go to the approach fix until the EFC time.

**76.**
**4464.** You are in IMC and have two-way radio communications failure. If you do not exercise emergency authority, what procedure are you expected to follow?

A— Set transponder to code 7600, continue flight on assigned route and fly at the last assigned altitude or the MEA, whichever is higher.

B— Set transponder to code 7700 for 1 minute, then to 7600, and fly to an area with VFR weather conditions.

C— Set transponder to 7700 and fly to an area where you can let down in VFR conditions.

Answer (A) is correct (4464). *(FAR 91.185, AIM Para 6-32)*
When you lose two-way radio capability, you should alert ATC by changing your transponder to code 7600. If you experience two-way radio communication failure while in IMC, continue your flight on the assigned route and maintain the last assigned altitude or the MEA, whichever is higher.
Answer (B) is incorrect because the transponder should be set on 7600 at all times, not 7700 for 1 min., and you must maintain your assigned route and altitude (or MEA). If VMC are encountered, then continue the flight under VFR and land as soon as practicable. Answer (C) is incorrect because you should set the transponder to 7600. While in IMC, you must maintain your assigned route and altitude (or MEA).

**77.**
**4466.** What altitude and route should be used if you are flying in IMC and have two-way radio communications failure?

A— Continue on the route specified in your clearance, fly at an altitude that is the highest of last assigned altitude, altitude ATC has informed you to expect, or the MEA.

B— Fly direct to an area that has been forecast to have VFR conditions, fly at an altitude that is at least 1,000 feet above the highest obstacles along the route.

C— Descend to MEA and, if clear of clouds, proceed to the nearest appropriate airport. If not clear of clouds, maintain the highest of the MEA's along the clearance route.

Answer (A) is correct (4466). *(FAR 91.185)*
When you lose two-way radio communication in IMC, continue the flight by the route assigned by the last ATC clearance or by the route that ATC has advised may be expected to be assigned, or by the flight plan. Use the highest of: the altitude assigned in the last ATC clearance, the MEA, or the flight level ATC may be expected to assign.
Answer (B) is incorrect because you should continue the assigned route. Answer (C) is incorrect because you should use the highest altitude: assigned, expected to be assigned, or MEA.

**78.**
**4465.** Which procedure should you follow if, during an IFR flight in VFR conditions, you have two-way radio communications failure?

A— Continue the flight under VFR and land as soon as practicable.
B— Continue the flight at assigned altitude and route, start approach at your ETA, or, if late, start approach upon arrival.
C— Land at the nearest airport that has VFR conditions.

**Answer (A) is correct (4465).** *(FAR 91.185)*
If a radio failure occurs during an IFR flight in VFR conditions or if VFR conditions are encountered after the failure, the pilot should continue the flight under VFR and land as soon as practicable.
Answer (B) is incorrect because it only applies if you are in instrument meteorological conditions, not VFR. Answer (C) is incorrect because the pilot retains the prerogative of exercising good judgment and is not required to land at an unauthorized airport, at an airport unsuitable for the type of aircraft flown, or to land only minutes short of the destination.

## 3.9 Navigation Radio Failure

**79.**
**4448.** What action should you take if your DME fails at FL 240?

A— Advise ATC of the failure and land at the nearest available airport where repairs can be made.
B— Notify ATC that it will be necessary for you to go to a lower altitude, since your DME has failed.
C— Notify ATC of the failure and continue to the next airport of intended landing where repairs can be made.

**Answer (C) is correct (4448).** *(FAR 91.205)*
When required DME fails at or above FL 240, the pilot should notify ATC immediately and may continue operations at and above FL 240 to the next airport of intended landing at which repairs or replacement of the equipment can be made.
Answer (A) is incorrect because you can continue to your destination (not the nearest airport) and have repairs made there. Answer (B) is incorrect because you need not descend to a lower altitude after you notify ATC. You can continue to operate at or above FL 240.

**80.**
**4459.** What is the procedure when the DME malfunctions at or above 24,000 feet MSL?

A— Notify ATC immediately and request an altitude below 24,000 feet.
B— Continue to your destination in VFR conditions and report the malfunction.
C— After immediately notifying ATC, you may continue to the next airport of intended landing where repairs can be made.

**Answer (C) is correct (4459).** *(FAR 91.205)*
When required DME fails at or above FL 240, the pilot should notify ATC immediately and may continue operations at and above FL 240 to the next airport of intended landing at which repairs or replacement of the equipment can be made.
Answer (A) is incorrect because there is no need to descend to a lower altitude. You can continue to your destination and have repairs made there. Answer (B) is incorrect because you can continue your flight as normal, even if IFR, and make repairs at your destination.

**81.**
**4460.** What action should you take if your No. 1 VOR receiver malfunctions while operating in controlled airspace under IFR? Your aircraft is equipped with two VOR receivers. The No. 1 receiver has Omni/Localizer/Glide Slope capability, and the No. 2 has only Omni.

A— Report the malfunction immediately to ATC.
B— Continue the flight as cleared; no report is required.
C— Continue the approach and request a VOR or NDB approach.

**Answer (A) is correct (4460).** *(FAR 91.187)*
When operating under IFR in controlled airspace, you must immediately report to ATC as soon as practical any malfunctions of navigational, approach, or communication equipment occurring in flight. Each report should include:

1. Aircraft identification,
2. Equipment affected,
3. Degree to which the capability of the pilot to operate under IFR in the ATC system is impaired, and
4. Nature and extent of assistance desired from ATC.

Answer (B) is incorrect because a report to ATC is required. Answer (C) is incorrect because ATC will know that you need a VOR or NDB approach if you report the ILS receiver inoperative.

## 3.10 Types of Airspace

**82.**
**4077.** Which airspaces are depicted on the En Route Low Altitude Chart?

A— Class D, Class C, Class B, Class E, and special use airspace.
B— Class A, special use airspace, Class D, and Class E.
C— Special use airspace, Class E, Class D, Class A, Class B, and Class C.

Answer (A) is correct (4077). *(ACL)*
En Route Low Altitude Charts depict Class B, Class C, Class D, Class E, and special use airspace up to but not including 18,000 ft. MSL. The legend for a Low Altitude En Route Chart in Chapter 10 of this book will also appear in your FAA Instrument Rating Question Book.
Answer (B) is incorrect because Class A airspace is airspace above FL 180. It is not depicted on En Route Low Altitude Charts. Answer (C) is incorrect because Class A airspace is not depicted on En Route Low Altitude Charts.

**83.**
**4475.** Class G airspace is that airspace where

A— ATC does not control air traffic.
B— ATC controls only IFR flights.
C— the minimum visibility for VFR flight is 3 miles.

Answer (A) is correct (4475). *(AIM Para 3-11)*
Class G airspace is that portion of the airspace that has not been designated as Class A, Class B, Class C, Class D, or Class E. In Class G airspace, ATC has neither the authority nor the responsibility for exercising control over air traffic in any weather condition.
Answer (B) is incorrect because ATC does not control IFR flight in Class G airspace. Answer (C) is incorrect because the minimum visibility for VFR flight is 1 SM, not 3 SM, in Class G airspace during the day when below 10,000 ft. MSL.

**84.**
**4473.** Which airspace is defined as a transition area when designated in conjunction with an airport which has a prescribed IAP?

A— The Class E airspace extending upward from 700 feet or more above the surface and terminating at the base of the overlying controlled airspace.
B— That Class D airspace extending from the surface and terminating at the base of the continental control area.
C— The Class C airspace extending from the surface to 700 or 1,200 feet AGL, where designated.

Answer (A) is correct (4473). *(FAR 71.71)*
Transition areas are Class E airspace that extends upward from 700 ft. or more above the surface when designated in conjunction with an airport for which an instrument approach procedure (IAP) has been prescribed. Class E airspace extends up to but not including 18,000 ft. MSL, i.e., the base of Class A airspace.
Answer (B) is incorrect because a transition area is classified as Class E, not Class D airspace. Answer (C) is incorrect because transition areas are Class E, not Class C, airspace and extend upward from, not to, 700 ft.

**85.**
**4476.** What are the vertical limits of a transition area that is designated in conjunction with an airport having a prescribed IAP?

A— Surface to 700 feet AGL.
B— 1,200 feet AGL to the base of the overlying controlled airspace.
C— 700 feet AGL or more to the base of the overlying controlled airspace.

Answer (C) is correct (4476). *(FAR 71.71)*
Transition Areas are controlled airspace extending upward from 700 ft. or more above the surface when designated in conjunction with an airport for which an instrument approach procedure has been prescribed. Transition Areas terminate at the base of overlying controlled airspace (i.e., Class A airspace).
Answer (A) is incorrect because a Transition Area begins at 700 ft. AGL, not the surface, when it is designated in conjunction with an IAP. Answer (B) is incorrect because Transition Areas begin at 1,200 ft. AGL when designated in conjunction with an airway route structure or segment, not with an airport with an instrument approach.

**86.**
**4474.** The vertical extent of the Class A airspace throughout the conterminous U.S. extends from

A— 18,000 feet to and including FL 450.
B— 18,000 feet to and including FL 600.
C— 12,500 feet to and including FL 600.

Answer (B) is correct (4474). *(AIM Para 3-12)*
Class A airspace extends from 18,000 ft. MSL to and including FL 600.
Answer (A) is incorrect because FL 450 is the top of the jet routes. Answer (C) is incorrect because the base of Class A airspace is 18,000 ft. MSL, not 12,500 ft. MSL.

**87.**
**4434.** MOAs are established to

A— prohibit all civil aircraft because of hazardous or secret activities.
B— separate certain military activities from IFR traffic.
C— restrict civil aircraft during periods of high-density training activities.

Answer (B) is correct (4434). *(AIM Para 3-45)*
MOAs consist of airspace of defined vertical and lateral limits established for the purpose of separating certain military training activities from IFR traffic. When an MOA is in use, nonparticipating IFR traffic may be cleared to fly through if ATC can provide IFR separation. Otherwise, ATC will reroute or restrict nonparticipating IFR traffic.
Answer (A) is incorrect because a prohibited area (not MOA) would prohibit all aircraft because of reasons of national security. Answer (C) is incorrect because a restricted area (not an MOA) would be used to restrict aircraft during certain periods.

**88.**
**4526.** (Refer to figure 93 below.) What is the floor of Class E airspace when designated in conjunction with an airway?

A— 700 feet AGL.
B— 1,200 feet AGL.
C— 1,500 feet AGL.

Answer (B) is correct (4526). *(FAR 71.71)*
The floor of Class E airspace when designated in conjunction with an airway is 1,200 ft. AGL.
Answer (A) is incorrect because 700 ft. AGL is the floor of Class E airspace when designated in conjunction with an airport which has an approved IAP, not with an airway. Answer (C) is incorrect because the floor of Class E airspace when designated in conjunction with an airway is 1,200 ft. AGL, not 1,500 ft. AGL.

**89.**
**4527.** (Refer to figure 93 below.) Which altitude is the normal vertical limit for Class D airspace?

A— 1,000 feet AGL.
B— 2,500 feet AGL.
C— 4,000 feet AGL.

Answer (B) is correct (4527). *(AIM Chap 3)*
Class D airspace extends from the surface up to and including 2,500 ft. AGL.
Answer (A) is incorrect because 1,000 ft. AGL is the normal traffic pattern altitude for piston aircraft, not the ceiling of Class D airspace. Answer (C) is incorrect because 4,000 ft. AGL is the vertical limit for Class C, not Class D, airspace.

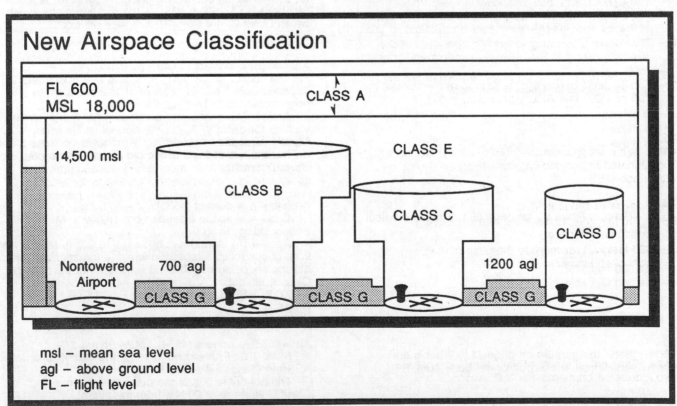

FIGURE 93.—New Airspace Classification.

**90.**
**4528.** (Refer to figure 93 on page 69.) What is the floor of Class E airspace when designated in conjunction with an airport which has an approved IAP?

A— 500 feet AGL.
B— 700 feet AGL.
C— 1,200 feet AGL.

Answer (B) is correct (4528). *(FAR 71.71)*
The floor of Class E airspace when designated in conjunction with an airport which has an approved IAP is 700 ft. AGL.
Answer (A) is incorrect because 500 ft. AGL is not an altitude which defines airspace. Answer (C) is incorrect because 1,200 ft. AGL is the floor of Class E airspace when designated in conjunction with an airway, not an approved IAP.

**91.**
**4529.** (Refer to figure 93 on page 69.) Which altitude is the vertical limit for Class A airspace?

A— 14,500 feet MSL.
B— 18,000 feet MSL.
C— 60,000 feet MSL.

Answer (C) is correct (4529). *(FAR 71.33)*
Class A airspace extends from 18,000 ft. MSL to and including 60,000 ft. MSL (i.e., FL 600).
Answer (A) is incorrect because 14,500 ft. MSL is the vertical limit for Class G, not Class A, airspace. Answer (B) is incorrect because 18,000 ft. MSL is the floor, not the vertical limit, of Class A airspace.

**92.**
**4530.** (Refer to figure 93 on page 69.) What is the maximum altitude that Class G airspace will exist? (Does not include airspace less than 1,500 feet AGL.)

A— 18,000 feet MSL.
B— 14,500 feet MSL.
C— 14,000 feet MSL.

Answer (B) is correct (4530). *(AIM Chap 3)*
The maximum altitude at which Class G airspace will exist (not including airspace less than 1,500 ft. AGL) is 14,500 ft. MSL.
Answer (A) is incorrect because 18,000 ft. MSL is the floor of Class A airspace, not the maximum altitude at which Class G airspace will exist. Answer (C) is incorrect because 14,000 ft. MSL is not an altitude which defines airspace.

**93.**
**4531.** (Refer to figure 93 on page 69.) What is the maximum altitude that Class B airspace will exist?

A— 4,000 feet MSL.
B— 14,500 feet MSL.
C— May vary with airport.

Answer (C) is correct (4531). *(AIM Chap 3)*
The maximum altitude at which Class B airspace will exist may vary with airport.
Answer (A) is incorrect because 4,000 ft. MSL is not an altitude which defines airspace. Answer (B) is incorrect because 14,500 ft. MSL is the maximum altitude at which Class G, not Class B, airspace will exist.

**94.**
**4532.** (Refer to figure 93 on page 69.) What are the normal lateral limits for Class D airspace?

A— 3 miles.
B— 4 miles.
C— 5 miles.

Answer (B) is correct (4532). *(AIM Chap 3)*
The normal lateral limits for Class D airspace are approximately 4 NM. Note that all lateral distances are now referenced to NM, not SM.
Answer (A) is incorrect because 3 SM is the minimum visibility for basic VFR, not the normal lateral limits, in Class D airspace. Answer (C) is incorrect because 5 SM defines the lateral limits of the old Airport Traffic Area, not Class D airspace.

**95.**
**4533.** (Refer to figure 93 on page 69.) What is the floor of Class A airspace?

A— 10,000 feet MSL.
B— 14,500 feet MSL.
C— 18,000 feet MSL.

Answer (C) is correct (4533). *(FAR 71.33)*
Class A airspace extends from 18,000 ft. MSL up to, and including, FL 600.
Answer (A) is incorrect because 10,000 ft. MSL is the floor of controlled airspace in which a transponder with altitude encoding capability is required, not the floor of Class A airspace. Answer (B) is incorrect because 14,500 ft. MSL is a floor of Class E, not Class A, airspace.

**96.**
**4534.** (Refer to figure 94 on page 71.) What is the normal radius from the airport of the outer area, B?

A— 10 miles.
B— 20 miles.
C— 25 miles.

Answer (B) is correct (4534). *(AIM Para 3-31)*
Note: The FAA did not change the classification of an ARSA to Class C airspace in Fig. 94.
The normal radius of the outer area surrounding Class C airspace is 20 NM from the airport.
Answer (A) is incorrect because 10 NM is the radius of the outer circle, not area, of Class C airspace. Answer (C) is incorrect because 25 NM does not pertain to any set radius of Class C airspace.

# Airport Radar Service Area (ARSA)

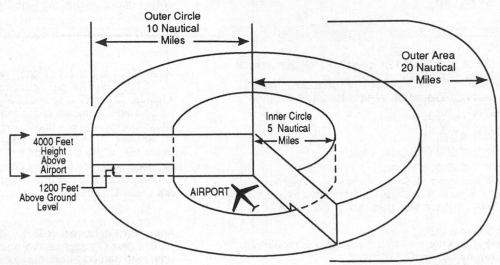

Services upon establishing two-way radio communication
and radar contact:

Sequencing Arrivals
IFR/VFR Standard Separation
IFR/VFR Traffic Advisories and Conflict Resolution
VFR/VFR Traffic Advisories

Note: The normal radius of the Outer Area, will be
20nm, with some site specific variations.

IFR:　Instrument Flight Rules
VFR:　Visual Flight Rules

FIGURE 94.—Airport Radar Service Area (ARSA).

**97.**
**4535.** (Refer to figure 94 above.) What is the radius
from the airport of the inner circle, C?

A— 5 miles.
B— 7 miles.
C— 10 miles.

Answer (A) is correct (4535). *(AIM Para 3-31)*
　Note:　The FAA did not change the classification of an
ARSA to Class C airspace in Fig. 94.
　The radius of the inner circle of Class C airspace is
5 NM from the airport.
　Answer (B) is incorrect because 7 NM is not
established as the radius for any portion of Class C
airspace. Answer (C) is incorrect because 10 NM is the
radius of the outer, not inner, circle of Class C airspace.

**98.**
**4536.** (Refer to figure 94 above.) What is the radius
from the airport of the outer circle, A?

A— 5 miles.
B— 10 miles.
C— 15 miles.

Answer (B) is correct (4536). *(AIM Para 3-31)*
　Note:　The FAA did not change the classification of an
ARSA to Class C airspace in Fig. 94.
　The radius of the outer circle of Class C airspace is
10 NM from the airport.
　Answer (A) is incorrect because 5 NM is the radius of
the inner, not outer, circle of Class C airspace.
Answer (C) is incorrect because 15 NM is not established
as the radius for any area of Class C airspace.

**99.**
**4537.** (Refer to figure 94 on page 71.) Which altitude is applicable to the base of the outer circle?

A— 700 feet AGL.
B— 1,000 feet AGL.
C— 1,200 feet AGL.

Answer (C) is correct (4537). *(AIM Para 3-31)*
Note: The FAA did not change the classification of an ARSA to Class C airspace in Fig. 94.
The base of the outer circle of Class C airspace is 1,200 ft. AGL.
Answer (A) is incorrect because 700 ft. AGL is not applicable to Class C airspace; it is the base of transition areas. Answer (B) is incorrect because 1,000 ft. AGL is not applicable to Class C airspace; it is the normal traffic pattern altitude for propeller airplanes.

**100.**
**4538.** (Refer to figure 94, box 1 on page 71.) Which altitude is applicable to the vertical extent of the inner and outer circles?

A— 3,000 feet AGL.
B— 3,000 feet above airport.
C— 4,000 feet above airport.

Answer (C) is correct (4538). *(AIM Para 3-31)*
Note: The FAA did not change the classification of an ARSA to Class C airspace in Fig. 94.
The vertical extent of the inner and outer circles of Class C airspace is 4,000 ft. above the airport.
Answer (A) is incorrect because 3,000 ft. AGL pertains to the top of the old airport traffic area, not Class C airspace. Answer (B) is incorrect because 3,000 ft. above airport pertains to the top of the old airport traffic area, not Class C airspace.

**101.**
**4539.** What minimum aircraft equipment is required for operation within Class C airspace?

A— Two-way communications and Mode C transponder.
B— Two-way communications.
C— Transponder and DME.

Answer (A) is correct (4539). *(AIM Para 3-32)*
In Class C airspace, the equipment requirement is an operating two-way communications radio and a Mode C transponder.
Answer (B) is incorrect because a Mode C transponder is also required. Answer (C) is incorrect because two-way communications and Mode C capability are also required and DME is not required.

# END OF CHAPTER

# CHAPTER FOUR
# AVIATION WEATHER

This chapter contains outlines of major concepts tested, all FAA Instrument Rating test questions and answers regarding weather, and an explanation of each answer. The subtopics or modules within this chapter are listed above, followed in parentheses by the number of questions from the FAA written test pertaining to that particular module. The two numbers following the parentheses are the page numbers on which the outline and questions begin for that module.

**CAUTION:** Recall that the **sole purpose** of this book is to expedite your passing the FAA written test for the instrument rating. Accordingly, all extraneous material (i.e., topics or regulations not directly tested on the FAA written test) is omitted, even though much more information and knowledge are necessary to fly safely. This additional material is presented in *Instrument Pilot FAA Practical Test Prep*, and *Aviation Weather and Weather Services*, available from Gleim Publications, Inc. See the order form on page 478.

## 4.1 CAUSES OF WEATHER (Questions 1-15)

1. Every physical process of weather is accompanied by or is the result of heat exchanges.

2. Unequal heating of the Earth's surface causes differences in pressure and thus, altimeter settings.

    a. On weather maps, the lines drawn to connect points of equal pressure show pressure contours. They are called isobars.

3. Three of the forces at work on winds are

    a. The pressure gradient force, which causes wind to flow from an area of high pressure to one of low pressure.

        1) This flow is thus perpendicular to the isobars.

    b. Coriolis force, which deflects winds to the right in the Northern Hemisphere. It is caused by the Earth's rotation.

        1) The Coriolis force is at a right angle to wind direction and directly proportional to wind speed. Its effect is more forceful at greater altitudes (above approximately 2,000 ft. AGL) because surface winds are slowed by friction.

        2) It deflects winds so strongly that they flow parallel to isobars.

    c. Friction with the Earth's surface weakens the wind.

        1) Since these winds are slower, they are less affected by Coriolis force. The pressure gradient becomes stronger than Coriolis force and the wind flows across, rather than parallel to, the isobars.

4. An air mass is an extensive body of air having uniform moisture and temperature properties.

5. The average height of the layer of the Earth's atmosphere called the troposphere is about 37,000 ft. in mid-latitudes. It varies between approximately 25,000 ft. at the poles to 65,000 ft. at the equator.

6. The boundary between the troposphere and the stratosphere is the thin layer called the tropopause.

    a. Temperature and wind vary greatly in the vicinity of the tropopause.
    b. It is associated with an abrupt change in the temperature lapse rate.

7. The stratosphere is the layer of atmosphere above the tropopause.

    a. It is characterized by low moisture content and absence of clouds.
    b. It has relatively small changes in temperature with an increase in altitude.

8. The jet stream is a narrow, disjointed, wandering "river" of maximum winds.

    a. It moves with pressure ridges and troughs in the upper atmosphere near the tropopause.

    b. It blows from a generally westerly direction, and by definition has a speed of 50 kt. or more.

    c. The jet stream is normally weaker and farther north in the summer.

    d. The jet stream is normally stronger and farther south in the winter.

9. A front is the zone of transition between two air masses of different temperature, humidity, and wind.

    a. There is always a change in wind when you fly across a front.

    b. The threat of low-level wind shear occurs just before the warm front passes the airport.

   c.   With a cold front, the most critical period for wind shear occurs just as or just after the cold front passes the airport.

10.   Frontal waves and cyclones (and areas of low pressure) usually form in slow-moving cold fronts or in stationary fronts.

11.   Squall lines usually develop ahead of a cold front.

## 4.2 STABILITY OF AIR MASSES (Questions 16-28)

1.   The lapse rate is a measure of how much temperature decreases (or possibly increases) with an increase in altitude. This is the actual temperature change associated with increases in altitude and sometimes is referred to as the ambient lapse rate.

   a.   In contrast to the ambient or actual lapse rate is the adiabatic lapse rate. The adiabatic or "expansional cooling" lapse rate is the temperature decrease is due only to expansion of air as it rises. The adiabatic lapse rate means no heat gain or loss -- just a decrease in temperature because of expansion.

      1)   The dry adiabatic lapse rate is 3°C per 1,000 ft.

      2)   The adiabatic rate varies from about 1.1°C to 2.8°C based on moisture content of the air.

      3)   The average adiabatic rate is 2°C per 1,000 ft.

2.   The ambient lapse rate can thus be used by pilots to determine the stability of air masses.

   a.   The greater the ambient lapse rate (more than 2°C per 1,000 ft.) and the higher the humidity, the more unstable the air -- and more thunderstorms are expected.

   b.   Moist air is less stable than dry air because it cools adiabatically at a slower rate, which means that moist air must rise higher before its temperature cools to that of the air around it (i.e., cumulus build-up).

3.   Cloud formation after lifting is determined by the stability of the air before lifting.

   a.   Turbulence and clouds with vertical development (cumuliform) result when unstable air rises (due to convective currents).

   b.   Moist, stable air moving up a mountain slope produces stratiform clouds as it cools.

      1)   Unstable air moving up a mountain slope produces clouds with extensive vertical development.

4.   When a cold air mass moves over a warm surface, heating from below provides unstable lifting action, giving rise to cumuliform clouds, turbulence, and good visibility.

5.   The growth rate of precipitation is enhanced by upward air currents carrying water droplets upward where condensation increases droplet size.

6.   Stable air characteristics:
   a.   Stratiform clouds and fog
   b.   Smooth air
   c.   Continuous (steady) precipitation
   d.   Fair to poor visibility in haze and smoke

7.   Unstable air characteristics:
   a.   Cumuliform clouds
   b.   Turbulent air
   c.   Good visibility
   d.   Showery precipitation

## 4.3 TEMPERATURE INVERSIONS  (Questions 29-32)

1.  Normally, temperature decreases as altitude increases.  A temperature inversion occurs when temperature increases as altitude increases.

2.  Temperature inversions usually result in a stable layer of warm air below the inversion.

3.  A temperature inversion often develops near the ground on clear, cool nights when the wind is light.

    a.  It is caused by terrestrial radiation.

4.  Smooth air with restricted visibility (due to fog, haze, or low clouds) is usually found beneath a low-level temperature inversion.

## 4.4 TEMPERATURE/DEW POINT AND FOG  (Questions 33-45)

1.  When the air temperature is within 5°F of the dew point and the temperature/dew point spread is decreasing, you should expect fog and/or low clouds.

    a.  Air temperature largely determines how much water vapor can be held by the air.

    b.  Dew point is the temperature at which the air will be saturated with moisture, i.e., 100% humidity.

    c.  Frost forms on collecting surfaces when their temperature is below the dew point of the surrounding air and the dew point is below freezing.

2.  Water vapor becomes visible as it condenses into clouds, fog, or dew.

    a.  Evaporation is the conversion of liquid water to water vapor.
    b.  Sublimation is the conversion of ice to water vapor, or water vapor to ice.

3.  Radiation fog is most likely to occur when there is a clear sky, little or no wind, and a small temperature/dew point spread over a land surface (especially low, flatland areas).

    a.  As the ground cools rapidly due to radiation, the air close to the surface cools more quickly than slightly higher air.

        1)  This is the most frequent type of surface-based temperature inversion.

    b.  As the air reaches its dew point, radiation fog forms.

4.  Advection fog forms as a result of moist air condensing as it moves over a colder surface (i.e., water or ground).

    a.  It requires wind to force the movement.

    b.  Advection fog is most likely to occur in coastal areas, when air moves inland from the coast in winter.

5.  Upslope fog results from warm, moist air being cooled as it is forced up sloping terrain.

6.  Precipitation-induced fog results from warm fronts (warmer air over cooler air), i.e., when warm rain or drizzle falls through the cooler air.

    a.  Evaporation from the precipitation saturates the cooler air, causing fog.

7.  Fog can also form easily in industrial areas where combustion pollution provides a high concentration of condensation nuclei (tiny particles on which moisture can condense as the air cools).

## 4.5 CLOUDS (Questions 46-53)

1. Clouds are divided into four families based on their height:

    a. High clouds (consist of ice crystals and do not pose an icing threat)
    b. Middle clouds
    c. Low clouds
    d. Clouds with extensive vertical development

2. Lifting action, unstable air, and moisture are the ingredients for the formation of cumulonimbus clouds.

    a. Fair weather cumulus clouds form in convective currents and often indicate turbulence at and below the cloud level.

    b. Nimbus means rain cloud.

    c. Towering cumulus are early stages of cumulonimbus.

    d. The greatest turbulence is in cumulonimbus clouds (thunderstorms).

3. Standing lenticular altocumulus clouds (ACSL) are almond or lens-shaped, and form on the crests of waves created by barriers in the wind flow (e.g., on the leeward side of a mountain).

    a. The presence of these clouds indicate very strong turbulence.

## 4.6 THUNDERSTORMS (Questions 54-63)

1. Thunderstorms have three phases in their life cycle:

    a. Cumulus: The building stage of a thunderstorm when there are continuous updrafts.

    b. Mature: The time of greatest intensity when there are both updrafts and downdrafts (causing severe wind shear and turbulence).

        1) The commencing of rain on the Earth's surface indicates the beginning of the mature stage of a thunderstorm.

    c. Dissipating: Characterized predominantly by downdrafts; i.e., the storm is raining itself out.

2. A thunderstorm, by definition, always has lightning because that is what causes thunder.

3. Thunderstorms are produced by cumulonimbus clouds. They form when there is

    a. Sufficient water vapor,
    b. An unstable lapse rate, and
    c. An initial upward boost (i.e., a lifting action) to start the process.

4. Thunderstorms produce wind shear turbulence, a hazardous and invisible phenomenon, particularly for airplanes landing and taking off.

    a. If a thunderstorm is penetrated, a pilot should fly straight ahead, set power for recommended turbulence penetration airspeed, and attempt to maintain a level attitude.

5. The most severe thunderstorm conditions (heavy hail, destructive winds, tornadoes, etc.) are generally associated with squall line thunderstorms.

    a. A squall line is a nonfrontal, narrow band of thunderstorms usually ahead of a cold front.

6. A squall (not squall line) is defined as sudden increases in wind speed of at least 15 kt. to a peak of 20 kt. or more and lasting 1 min. or longer.

    a. A gust is defined as a brief increase in wind speed of at least 10 kt.

7. Embedded thunderstorms are obscured because they occur in very cloudy conditions or thick haze layers.

8. Airborne weather-avoidance radar detects only precipitation drops. It does not detect minute cloud droplets (i.e., clouds and fog).

   a. Thus, airborne weather-avoidance radar provides no assurance of avoiding instrument weather conditions.

## 4.7 ICING (Questions 64-71)

1. Structural icing requires two conditions:

   a. Flight through visible moisture, and
   b. The temperature at freezing or below.

2. Freezing rain usually causes the greatest accumulation of structural ice.

   a. Freezing rain indicates that temperatures are above freezing at some higher altitude.

3. Ice pellets are caused when rain droplets freeze at a higher altitude, i.e., freezing rain exists above.

4. Heavy, wet snow indicates the temperature is above freezing at your altitude.

   a. The snow formed above you but is on the verge of melting when it appears heavy and wet.

5. Frost on wings disrupts the airflow over the wings causing early airflow separation resulting in a loss of lift. It should be removed before flight is attempted.

6. Test data indicate that ice, snow, or frost having a thickness and roughness similar to medium or coarse sandpaper on the leading edge and upper surface of a wing can reduce wing lift by as much as 30% and increase drag by 40%.

7. With a standard (average) temperature lapse rate of 2°C per 1,000 ft., the freezing level can be determined by knowing the current temperature and elevation.

   a. EXAMPLE: At a field elevation of 1,350 ft. MSL, the temperature is +8°C. To reach the freezing level the temperature must drop 8°C. Thus the freezing level is 4,000 ft. (8°C ÷ 2°C/1,000 ft.) up, or at 5,350 ft. MSL.

## 4.8 WIND SHEAR (Questions 72-77)

1. Wind shear is any change in wind velocity (speed and/or direction).

2. If the change is abrupt and of more than slight magnitude, it can be an extreme hazard to flight.

3. Wind shear can occur at any level in the atmosphere and be horizontal and/or vertical, i.e., whenever adjacent air flows in different directions and/or speeds.

4. It is an atmospheric condition that may be associated with a low-level temperature inversion, a jet stream, or a frontal zone.

5. Light turbulence momentarily causes slight, erratic changes in altitude and/or attitude.

6. Severe turbulence and wind shear may be found on all sides of a thunderstorm, including directly beneath it and as much as 20 mi. laterally.

7. Hazardous wind shear is commonly encountered near the ground during periods of strong temperature inversion and near thunderstorms.

   a. Expect wind shear in a temperature inversion whenever wind speed at 2,000 to 4,000 ft. AGL is 25 kt. or more.

## 4.9 AIRMETS AND SIGMETS (Questions 78-83)

1. SIGMETs and AIRMETs are issued to notify en route pilots of the possibility of encountering hazardous flying conditions.

2. SIGMET advisories include weather phenomena which are potentially hazardous to all aircraft.

    a. Convective SIGMETs

        1) Tornadoes

        2) Lines of thunderstorms

        3) Embedded thunderstorms

        4) Thunderstorm areas greater than or equal to thunderstorm intensity level 4 with an area coverage of 40% or more

        5) Hail greater than or equal to ¾ in. diameter

    b. Other SIGMETs

        1) Severe and extreme turbulence

        2) Severe icing

        3) Widespread duststorms, sandstorms, or volcanic ash lowering visibilities to less than 3 SM.

3. AIRMETs apply to light aircraft to notify of

    a. Moderate icing
    b. Moderate turbulence
    c. Visibility less than 3 SM or ceilings less than 1,000 ft.
    d. Sustained winds of 30 kt. or more at the surface
    e. Extensive mountain obscurement

4. More information regarding any AIRMET or SIGMET can be obtained from an FSS.

    a. AIRMETs are broadcast on receipt and H+15 and H+45 during the first hour after issuance.

        1) SIGMETs are broadcast on the same schedule as AIRMETs.
        2) Convective SIGMETs are broadcast on receipt and at 15-min. intervals.

    b. The maximum forecast period for an AIRMET is 6 hr.

5. Pilots should realize that the primary function of ATC is to separate aircraft. Other services such as weather avoidance can be provided when it does not interfere with traffic separation.

## 4.10 SURFACE AVIATION WEATHER REPORTS (Questions 84-91)

1. Surface aviation weather reports are actual weather observations made once an hour at each reporting station.

    a. They are available by computer in all Flight Service Stations. They are coded by the letters "SA."

    b. They are also referred to as sequence reports.

2. Three-letter station identifiers are listed on the left side of the report and are followed by

    a. The designation or type of report, i.e., SA.

    b. The time the weather observations were made using Coordinated Universal Time (i.e, Z).

    c. The weather observation at that station.

3.   The weather is presented as

    a.   The basic sky conditions and ceilings

        1)   X means sky is obscured
        2)   W means indefinite ceiling

    b.   Visibility (SM)
    c.   Weather and obstructions to vision
    d.   Sea level pressure (millibars)
    e.   Temperature (°F) and dew point (°F)
    f.   Wind direction (reference to true north), speed (kt.), and character
    g.   Altimeter setting (inches of Hg)
    h.   Remarks

4.   EXAMPLE:  SLC SA 1251 E11Ø OVC 3Ø Ø79/53/28/1916G24/981/RF2 RB12

    a.   SLC is Salt Lake City.

    b.   SA means a record observation (i.e., an hourly weather observation).

    c.   1251 is the time (Z) of the weather observations.

    d.   E11Ø OVC is an estimated ceiling at 11,000 ft. AGL which is overcast.

    e.   Visibility is 30 SM.

    f.   Pressure is 1007.9 millibars.

    g.   Temperature is 53°F.

    h.   Dew point is 28°F.

    i.   Wind is from 190° at 16 kt., gusting to 24 kt.

    j.   Altimeter setting is 29.81 in. of Hg.

    k.   Remarks:  Rain and fog obscuring two-tenths of the sky.  Rain began 12 min. past the hour.

5.   Ceiling is the height above the Earth's surface of the lowest layer of clouds that is reported as broken, overcast, or obscured (but not those classified as thin, partial, or scattered).

6.   Pilot weather reports (PIREPs) are frequently attached to surface aviation weather reports.

    a.   EXAMPLE:    UA/OV MRB-PIT/TM 1600/FL 100/TP BE55 /SK 024 BKN 032/042 BKN-OVC/TA -12/IC LGT-MDT RIME 055-080/RM WND COMP HEAD 020 MH310 TAS 180.

        DECODED:    Pilot report, Martinsburg to Pittsburgh at 1600Z at 10,000 ft.  Type of aircraft is a Beechcraft Baron.  First cloud layer has base at 2,400 ft. broken top 3,200 ft.  Second cloud layer base is 4,200 ft. broken occasionally overcast with no tops reported.  Outside air temperature is −12°C.  Light to moderate rime icing reported between 5,500-8,000 ft.  Headwind component is 20 kt.  Magnetic heading is 310° and true air speed is 180 kt.

b.   PIREPs are transmitted in the format illustrated below.

### Encoding Pilot Weather Reports (PIREP)

1. **UA** -   Routine PIREP, **UUA** - Urgent PIREP

2. **/OV** -   Location: Use 3-letter NAVAID idents only.
   a. Fix: /OV ABC, /OV ABC 090025.
   b. Fix to fix: /OV ABC-DEF, /OV ABC-DEF 120020,
   /OV ABC  045020-DEF  120005, /OV ABC-DEF-GHI.

3. **/TM** -   Time: 4 digits in GMT: /TM 0915.

4. **/FL** -   Altitude/Flight Level: 3 digits for hundreds of
   feet. If not known, use UNKN: /FL095,
   /FL310, /FLUNKN.

5. **/TP** -   Type aircraft: 4 digits maximum, If not known use UNKN:
   /TP L329,/TP B727, /TP UNKN.

6. **/SK** -   Cloud layers: Describe as follows:
   a. Height of cloud base in hundreds of feet. If
   unknown, use UNKN.
   b. Cloud cover symbol.
   c. Height of cloud tops in hundreds of feet.
   d. Use solidus (/) to separate layers.
   e. Use a space to separate each sub element.
   f. Examples: /SK 038 BKN, /SK 038 OVC 045,
   /SK 055 SCT 073/085 BKN 105, /SK UNKN OVC

7. **/WX** -   Weather: Flight visibility reported first.
   Use standard weather symbols, Intensity is not
   reported: /WX FV02 R H, /WX FV01 TRW.

8. **/TA** -   Air temperature in Celsius: If below zero, prefix with
   a hyphen: /TA 15, /TA -06.

9. **/WV** -   Wind: Direction and speed in six digits.
   /WV 270045, /WV 280110.

10. **/TB** -   Turbulence: Use standard contractions for intensity and
   type (use CAT or CHOP when appropriate). Include altitude only
   if different from /FL.
   /TB EXTRM, /TB LGT-MDT BLO-090.

11. **/IC** -   Icing: Describe using standard intensity and type contractions.
   Include altitude only if different than /FL: /IC LGT-MDT RIME, /IC SVR CLR
   026-045.

12. **/RM** -   Remarks: Use free form to clarify the report. Most hazardous element first:
   /RM LLWS -15KT SFC-003 DURGC RNWY 22 JFK.
   Refer to FAAH 7110.10 for expanded explanation of TEI coding.

#### Examples of Completed PIREPS

UA /OV RFD 170030/TM 1315/FL160/TP PA60 /SK 025 OVC 095/180 OVC
/TA -21/WV 270048

UA /OV DHT 360015-AMA-CDS/TM 2116/FL050/TP PA32 /SK UNKN OVC/WX FV03 R
/TB LGT/TA 04/RM HVY RAIN

✦ U.S. GPO: 1985—461-823/21543

# PIREP FORM

**Pilot Weather Report**                                    ➡ ≡ *Space Symbol*
3-Letter SA Identifier

1. **UA**➡____  **UUA**➡____
➡ — —                    *Routine*          *Urgent*
                         *Report*           *Report*

2. **/OV**➡   Location:

3. **/TM**➡   Time:

4. **/FL**   Altitude/Flight Level:

5. **/TP**   Aircraft Type:

*Items 1 through 5 are mandatory for all PIREPs*

6. **/SK**➡   Sky Cover:

7. **/WX**➡   Flight Visibility and Weather:

8. **/TA**   Temperature (Celsius):

9. **/WV**   Wind:

10. **/TB**➡   Turbulence:

11. **/IC**➡   Icing:

12. **/RM**➡   Remarks:

FAA FORM 7110-2 (1-89) Supersedes Previous Edition

## 4.11  WEATHER DEPICTION CHARTS  (Questions 92-94)

1.   A weather depiction chart is a map of the United States depicting sky conditions at the time stated on the chart based on surface aviation (SA) reports.

   a.   Reporting stations are marked with a little circle (sky symbol).

      1)   If the sky is clear, the circle is open; if overcast, the circle is solid; if scattered, the circle is 1/4 solid; if broken, the circle is 3/4 solid.  If the sky is obscured, there is an "X" in the circle.

      2)   The height of clouds is expressed in hundreds of feet above ground level and is located beneath the sky symbol; e.g., 120 means 12,000 ft.

2.   Areas with ceilings below 1,000 ft. and/or visibility less than 3 mi. (i.e., below VFR) are bracketed with solid black contour lines and are shaded.

   a.   Visibility is indicated to the left of the sky symbol, e.g., 2 stands for 2 SM visibility.

   b.   Areas of marginal VFR with ceilings of 1,000 to 3,000 ft. and/or visibility at 3 to 5 SM are bracketed by solid black contour lines and are unshaded.

   c.   Ceilings greater than 3,000 ft. and visibility greater than 5 SM are not indicated by contour lines on weather depiction charts.

3.    Significant weather is indicated by the following symbols:

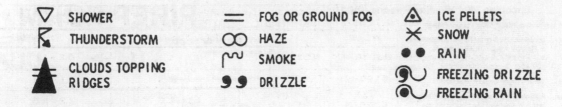

4.    The weather depiction chart quickly shows pilots where weather conditions reported are above or below VFR minimums.

5.    Example sky symbols and related weather data:

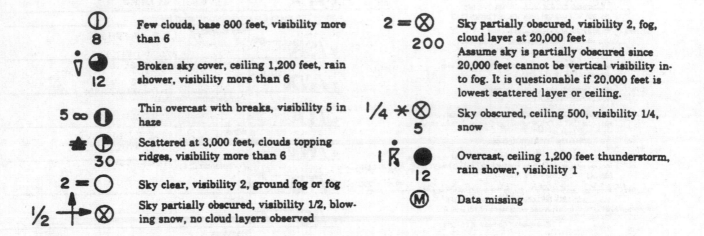

## 4.12 RADAR SUMMARY CHARTS (Questions 95-103)

1.    Radar summary charts graphically display a collection of radar reports concerning the intensity and movement of precipitation, e.g., squall lines, specific thunderstorm cells, and other areas of hazardous precipitation.

2.    During preflight planning, the pilot should combine the radar summary chart information with indications of other charts, reports, and forecasts to gain a three-dimensional understanding of the weather.

3.    Information presented on the radar summary chart includes

    a.    Echo pattern and coverage

    b.    Weather associated with echoes (using the same weather symbols as SAs)

        1)    EXAMPLE: TRW+ means increasing thunderstorms and rainshowers.

    c.    Intensity (contours)

    d.    Trend (+ or −) of precipitation

    e.    Height of echo bases and tops

    f.    Movement of echoes

4. The following symbols are used on radar summary charts.

| VIP LEVEL | ECHO INTENSITY | PRECIPITATION INTENSITY | RAINFALL RATE in/hr STRATIFORM | RAINFALL RATE in/hr CONVECTIVE |
|---|---|---|---|---|
| 1 | WEAK | LIGHT | LESS THAN 0.1 | LESS THAN 0.2 |
| 2 | MODERATE | MODERATE | 0.1 - 0.5 | 0.2 - 1.1 |
| 3 | STRONG | HEAVY | 0.5 - 1.0 | 1.1 - 2.2 |
| 4 | VERY STRONG | VERY HEAVY | 1.0 - 2.0 | 2.2 - 4.5 |
| 5 | INTENSE | INTENSE | 2.0 - 5.0 | 4.5 - 7.1 |
| 6 | EXTREME | EXTREME | MORE THAN 5.0 | MORE THAN 7.1 |

Highest precipitation top in area in hundreds of feet MSL. (45,000 FEET MSL)

\* The numbers representing the intensity level do not appear on the chart. Beginning from the first contour line, bordering the area, the intensity level is 1-2; second contour is 3-4; and third contour is 5-6.

——— SYMBOLS USED ON CHART ———

**SYMBOL   MEANING**

| | |
|---|---|
| R | RAIN |
| RW | RAIN SHOWER |
| HAIL | HAIL |
| S | SNOW |
| IP | ICE PELLETS |
| SW | SNOW SHOWER |
| L | DRIZZLE |
| T | THUNDERSTORM |
| ZR,ZL | FREEZING PRECIPITATION |
| NE | NO ECHOES OBSERVED |
| NA | OBSERVATIONS UNAVAILABLE |
| OM | OUT FOR MAINTENANCE |
| STC | STC ON - all precipitation may not be seen |
| ROBEPS | RADAR OPERATING BELOW PERFORMANCE STANDARDS |
| RHINO | RANGE HEIGHT INDICATOR NOT OPERATING |

**SYMBOL   MEANING**

| | |
|---|---|
| + | INTENSITY INCREASING OR NEW ECHO |
| − | INTENSITY DECREASING |
| NO SYMBOL | NO CHANGE IN INTENSITY |
| 35 | CELL MOVEMENT TO NE AT 35 KNOTS |
| | LINE OR AREA MOVEMENT TO EAST AT 20 KNOTS |
| LM | LITTLE MOVEMENT |
| MA | ECHOES MOSTLY ALOFT |
| PA | ECHOES PARTLY ALOFT |

**SYMBOL   MEANING**

| | |
|---|---|
| | LINE OF ECHOES |
| SLD | 8/10 OR GREATER COVERAGE IN A LINE |
| WS999 | SEVERE THUNDERSTORM WATCH |
| WT999 | TORNADO WATCH |
| LEWP | LINE ECHO WAVE PATTERN |
| HOOK | HOOK ECHO |

RAINFALL RATES SHOULD BE USED WITH CAUTION

5. The height of the precipitation tops and bases of echoes are shown on the chart in hundreds of feet above mean sea level.

   a. Tops are entered above a short line while any available bases are entered below.

      1) Top heights displayed are the highest in the indicated area.

   b. EXAMPLES:

      450   Maximum top 45,000 ft.

      220
      ———
      080   Bases 8,000 ft.; maximum top 22,000 ft.

## 4.13 TERMINAL FORECASTS (Questions 104-110)

1. Terminal forecasts (FT) are weather forecasts for large airports throughout the country. They are a source of weather to expect at your ETA.

   a. The FT is a forecast for the area within a 5-NM radius of the center of the runway complex.

2. Forecasts are issued three times a day for the next 24-hr. period.

   a. The last 6 hr. are an "outlook" rather than a forecast.

3.  The components of the forecast for each station are

    a.  Station identifier.

    b.  Date-time group: first 2 digits indicate the date; second 2 digits indicate the time in Zulu when the forecast begins today; third 2 digits indicate the time in Zulu when the forecast ends tomorrow.

        1)  Zulu is Coordinated Universal Time (also abbreviated UTC).

    c.  The first 6-hr. forecast begins with cloud and wind forecasts.

    d.  Each subsequent 6-hr. forecast is preceded by the time Zulu it begins.

4.  EXAMPLE: GNV 181010 100 SCT 250 −BKN 1615. 18Z C80 BKN 1815. 00Z C50 BKN 3215. 04Z MVFR CIG.

    a.  GNV is Gainesville.

    b.  181010. The forecast is valid beginning on the 18th day of the month from 1000Z to 1000Z on the 19th.

    c.  100 SCT 250 −BKN 1615. This means clouds at 10,000 ft. scattered, 25,000 ft. thin broken, with surface wind from 160° at 15 kt.

    d.  18Z C80 BKN 1815. This means by 1800Z, the ceiling is forecast to be 8,000 ft. broken with surface wind from 180° at 15 kt.

    e.  00Z C50 BKN 3215. This means by 0000Z, the ceiling is forecast to be 5,000 ft. broken with surface wind from 320° at 15 kt.

    f.  04Z MVFR CIG. This means from 0400Z until 1000Z (the end of the forecast period), marginal VFR is forecast due to ceilings.

5.  When there is no wind entry, it is expected to be less than 6 kt.

    a.  The word WND in the categorical outlook means the wind is expected to be 25 kt. or stronger.

6.  When there is no visibility entry, it is expected to be more than 6 SM.

## 4.14 AREA FORECASTS (Questions 111-114)

1.  Area forecasts (FA) are for several states and/or portions of states. They include information about frontal movement, turbulence, and icing conditions for a specific area. FAs are issued three times a day and consist of a

    a.  12-hr. forecast, and
    b.  An additional 6-hr. categorical outlook.

2.  The area forecast is in a three-section format.

    a.  The first is "Hazards/Flight Precautions" and is identified by the letter "H."

        1)  Area identifier followed by "H."
        2)  Heading (FA) with effective date/time group.
        3)  Hazards explained with valid time.

    b.  The second section, "Synopsis, VFR Clouds/Weather, " is identified by the letter "C."

        1)  Area identifier followed by "C."
        2)  Heading (FA) with effective date/time group.
        3)  Synopsis.
        4)  Clouds and weather.

    c.  The third section is a state by state summary of the forecast.

3.  SIG CLDS AND WX ("significant clouds and weather") provides a summary of cloudiness and weather significant to flight operations, broken down by state or other geographical areas.

4.  FLT PRCTN ("flight precautions") summarizes expected hazardous weather.

5.  The TWEB route forecast provides information similar to an FA, but in a route format.

    a.  This includes expected sky cover, cloud tops, visibility, weather, and obstructions to vision.

## 4.15 WINDS AND TEMPERATURES ALOFT FORECASTS (Questions 115-124)

1.  Forecast winds and temperatures are provided at specified altitudes for specific locations in the United States are presented in table form.

2.  A four-digit group (used when temperatures are not forecast) shows wind direction with reference to **true** north and the wind speed in **knots**.

    a.  The first two digits indicate wind direction after you add a zero.
    b.  The next two digits indicate the wind speed.

3.  A six-digit group includes the forecast temperature aloft.

    a.  The last two digits indicate the temperature in degrees Celsius.

    b.  Plus or minus is indicated before the temperature, except at higher altitudes (above 24,000 ft. MSL) where it is always below freezing.

    c.  The ISA (International Standard Atmosphere) temperature is 15°C at the surface with a standard lapse rate of 2°C per 1,000 ft.

4.  When the wind speed is less than 5 kt., the forecast is coded 9900, which means that the wind is light and variable.

5.  Note that at some of the lower levels the wind and temperature information is omitted.

    a.  Winds aloft are not forecast for levels within 1,500 ft. of the station elevation.

    b.  No temperatures are forecast for the 3,000-ft. level or for a level within 2,500 ft. of the station elevation.

6.  If the wind speed is forecast to be 100 to 199 kt., the forecaster adds 50 to the direction and subtracts 100 from the speed. To decode, you must do the reverse: subtract 50 from the direction and add 100 to the speed.

    a.  EXAMPLE: If the forecast for the 39,000-ft. level appears as "731960," subtract 50 from 73 and add 100 to 19. The wind would be 230° at 119 kt. with a temperature of −60°C (above 24,000 ft.).

    b.  It is easy to know when the coded direction has been increased by 50. Coded direction (in tens of degrees) normally ranges from 01 (010°) to 36 (360°). Any coded direction with a numerical value greater than 36 indicates a wind of 100 kt. or greater. The coded direction for winds of 100 to 199 kt. thus ranges from 51 through 86.

7.  If the wind speed is forecast to be 199 kt. or more, the wind group is coded as 199 kt.; e.g., "7799" is decoded 270° at 199 kt. or more.

8.  EXAMPLES: Decode these FD winds and temperatures:

| Coded | Decoded |
| --- | --- |
| 9900 + 00 | Winds light and variable, temperature 0°C |
| 2707 | 270° at 7 kt. |
| 850552 | 85 − 50 = 35; 05 + 100 = 105 |
|  | 350° at 105 kt., temperature −52°C |

## 4.16 LOW-LEVEL PROGNOSTIC CHARTS (Questions 125-132)

1. Low-level prognostic charts contain four charts (panels).

    a. The two upper panels forecast significant weather from the surface up to 24,000 ft.: one for 12 hr. and the other for 24 hr. from the time of issuance.

    b. The two lower panels forecast surface conditions: one for 12 hr. and the other for 24 hr. from time of issuance.

    c. See Fig. 6 on page 121.

2. The top panels show

    a. Ceilings less than 1,000 ft. and/or visibility less than 3 SM (IFR) by a solid line around the area;

    b. Ceilings 1,000 to 3,000 ft. and/or visibility 3 to 5 SM (MVFR) by a scalloped line around the area;

    c. Moderate or greater turbulence by a broken line around the area; and

        1) Altitudes "up to" are above a line; e.g., 120 is up to 12,000 ft.

        2) Altitudes "down to" are below a line; e.g., 90 is down to 9,000 ft.

    d. Freezing levels given by a dashed line corresponding to the height of the freezing level.

3. The bottom panels show location of

    a. Highs, lows, fronts, and
    b. Other areas of significant weather.

4. The following symbols are used on "prog" charts:

    a. Standard weather symbols.

| Symbol | Meaning | Symbol | Meaning |
|---|---|---|---|
| | Moderate turbulence | | Rain shower |
| | Severe turbulence | | Snow shower |
| | Moderate icing | | Thunderstorms |
| | Severe icing | | Freezing rain |
| | Rain | | Tropical storm |
| | Snow | | Hurricane (typhoon) |
| | Drizzle | | |

NOTE: Character of stable precipitation is the manner in which it occurs. It may be intermittent or continuous. A single symbol denotes intermittent and a pair of symbols denotes continuous.

Examples,

| | Intermittent | Continuous | |
|---|---|---|---|
| | ● | ● ● | Rain |
| | ໑ | ໑໑ | Drizzle |
| | ✳ | ✳✳ | Snow |

b.   Significant weather symbols.

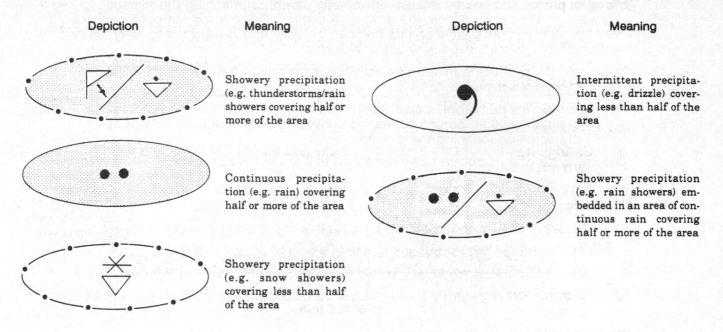

| Depiction | Meaning | Depiction | Meaning |
|---|---|---|---|
| | Showery precipitation (e.g. thunderstorms/rain showers covering half or more of the area | | Intermittent precipitation (e.g. drizzle) covering less than half of the area |
| | Continuous precipitation (e.g. rain) covering half or more of the area | | Showery precipitation (e.g. rain showers) embedded in an area of continuous rain covering half or more of the area |
| | Showery precipitation (e.g. snow showers) covering less than half of the area | | |

## 4.17 SEVERE WEATHER OUTLOOK CHARTS  (Questions 133-136)

1.   The Severe Weather Outlook Chart (AC) is a preliminary 24-hr. outlook for thunderstorm activity presented in two panels.

   a.   The top panel covers the 12-hr. period 1200Z - 0000Z.
   b.   The bottom panel covers the remaining 12 hr., 0000Z - 1200Z.
   c.   This manually prepared chart is issued once daily in the morning.

2.   General thunderstorms.  A line with an arrowhead delineates an area of probable general thunderstorm activity.

   a.   As you face the direction of the arrow, activity is expected to the right of the line.

   b.   An area labeled APCHG indicates probable general thunderstorm activity may approach severe intensity.

      1)   "Approaching" means winds greater than or equal to 35 kt. but less than 50 kt. and/or hail greater than or equal to ½ in. in diameter but less than ¾ in. (surface conditions).

3.   Severe thunderstorms.  The single-hatched area indicates possible severe thunderstorms.

   a.   Slight risk (SLGT) -- 2 to 5% coverage or 4 to 10 radar grid boxes containing severe thunderstorms per 100,000 square mi.

   b.   Moderate risk (MDT) -- 6 to 10% coverage or 11 to 21 radar grid boxes containing severe thunderstorms per 100,000 square mi.

   c.   High risk -- more than 10% coverage or more than 21 radar grid boxes containing severe thunderstorms per 100,000 square mi.

4.   Tornadoes.  Tornado watches are plotted only if a tornado watch is in effect at chart time. The watch area is cross-hatched.

5.   The Severe Weather Outlook Chart is strictly for advanced planning.  It alerts all interests to the possibility of future storm development.

### 4.18 MICROBURSTS  (Questions 137-144)

1.  Microbursts are small-scale intense downdrafts which, on reaching the surface, spread outward in all directions from the downdraft center.  This causes the presence of both vertical and horizontal wind shears that can be extremely hazardous to all types and categories of aircraft, especially at low altitudes.

2.  Parent clouds producing microburst activity can be any of the low or middle layer convective cloud types.

    a.  Microbursts commonly occur within the heavy rain portion of thunderstorms, but also in much weaker, benign-appearing convective cells that have little or no precipitation reaching the ground.

3.  The life cycle of a microburst as it descends in a convective rain shaft is illustrated below.

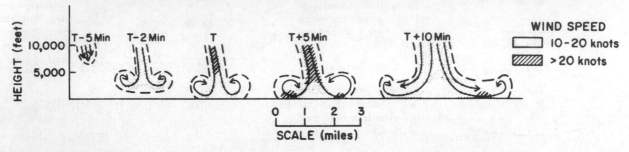

4.  Characteristics of microbursts include:

    a.  Size -- The microburst downdraft is typically less than 1 mi. in diameter as it descends from the cloud base to about 1,000-3,000 ft. above the ground.

        1)  In the transition zone near the ground, the downdraft changes to a horizontal outflow that can extend to approximately 2½ mi. in diameter.

    b.  Intensity -- The downdrafts can be as strong as 6,000 fpm.

        1)  Horizontal winds near the surface can be as strong as 45 kt. resulting in a 90-kt. shear (headwind to tailwind change for a traversing aircraft) across the microburst.

        2)  These strong horizontal winds occur within a few hundred feet of the ground.

    c.  Visual signs -- Microbursts can be found almost anywhere there is convective activity.

        1)  They may be embedded in heavy rain associated with a thunderstorm or in light rain in benign-appearing virga.

        2)  When there is little or no precipitation at the surface accompanying the microburst, a ring of blowing dust may be the only visual clue of its existence.

    d.  Duration -- An individual microburst will seldom last longer than 15 min. from the time it strikes the ground until dissipation.

        1)  The horizontal winds continue to increase during the first 5 min. with the maximum intensity winds lasting approximately 2-4 min.

        2)  An important consideration for pilots is that the microburst intensifies for about 5 min. after it strikes the ground.

5.  Microburst wind shear may create a severe hazard for aircraft within 1,000 ft. of the ground, particularly during the approach to landing and landing and takeoff phases.

    a.  The aircraft may encounter a headwind (performance increasing) followed by a downdraft and tailwind (both performance decreasing), possibly resulting in terrain impact.

    b.  See Fig. 13 on page 124.

## 4.19 OTHER WEATHER CHARTS (Questions 145-150)

1. Constant Pressure Charts provide information about the observed temperature, wind, and temperature/dew point spread along your proposed route.

2. The Surface Analysis Chart provides locations of pressure systems, wind, dew points, and obstructions to vision at the valid time of the chart.

3. The Convective Outlook Report describes the prospects for general thunderstorm activity during the following 24 hr.

    a. Areas with a high, moderate, or slight risk of severe thunderstorms are included, as well as areas where thunderstorms may approach severe limits.

4. The most accurate information on icing conditions would be in PIREPs, AIRMETs, and SIGMETs.

## 4.20 TROPOPAUSE DATA CHARTS (Questions 151-164)

1. The tropopause chart is tested on the instrument written test. It consists of four panels:

    a. High level significant prog chart (Figure 7, page 129).
    b. Tropopause height/Vertical wind shear prog chart (Figure 10, page 130).
    c. Observed winds aloft for 34,000 ft. (Figure 12, page 132).
    d. Tropopause pressure temperature and winds chart (Figure 11, page 134).

2. The high level significant weather prognosis chart covers 24,000 ft. MSL to 63,000 ft. MSL.

    a. Large dashed lines enclose areas of probable moderate or greater turbulence not caused by convective activity. Symbols denote intensity, base, and top.

    b. Small scalloped lines enclose areas of expected cumulonimbus development. "CB" denotes cumulonimbus.

        1) CB refers to the occurrence or expected occurrence of an area of widespread cumulonimbus clouds or cumulonimbus clouds along a line with little space between the individual clouds.

        2) It also depicts cumulonimbus clouds embedded in cloud layers or concealed by haze or dust.

        3) It does not refer to isolated or scattered cumulonimbus clouds not embedded in cloud layers or concealed by haze.

        4) Cumulonimbus clouds imply moderate or greater turbulence or icing.

    c. EXAMPLES:

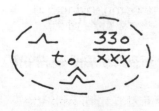

Moderate to severe turbulence from below lower limit of the prog (24,000 feet) to 33,000 feet. (Consult low-level prog for turbulence forecasts below 24,000 feet.)

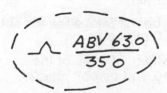

Moderate turbulence from 35,000 feet to above upper limit of the prog.

ISOL embedded (less than one-eight) cumulonimbus, tops 42,000 feet. Bases are below 24,000 ft.—the lower limit of the prog.

1/8 to 4/8 coverage, embedded cumulonimbus, tops 52,000 feet, bases below 24,000 feet.

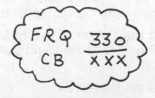

5/8 to 8/8 coverage cumulonimbus, bases below 24,000 feet and tops 33,000 feet.

    d.   Tropopause height is depicted in rectangular boxes in hundreds of feet MSL.

3.   The tropopause height/vertical wind shear prognosis chart depicts height of the tropopause in terms of pressure altitude.

    a.   Solid lines trace the intersection of the tropopause with standard constant pressure surfaces, e.g., FL 180, 210, 240, 270, 300, 340, 390, etc.

       1)   Heights are in hundreds of feet and are preceded by the letter F.

    b.   Vertical wind shear is in kt. per 1,000 ft. depicted by dashed lines at 2-kt. intervals.

       1)   Wind shear is averaged through a layer from about 8,000 ft. below to 4,000 ft. above the tropopause.

4.   Observed winds aloft charts for selected levels are sent out twice daily. For each upper air observing station, the pressure, temperature, and wind are reported at the tropopause.

    a.   The wind direction and speed at each station is shown by arrows the same as forecast charts.

       1)   The tens digit of the wind direction is presented at one end of the arrow, e.g., 2 for 320, 7 for 070, 6 for 160, etc.

       2)   The temperature in Celsius is presented at the other end of the wind arrow (end away from the wind velocity symbols).

       3)   Wind velocity is indicated by the sum of 3 types of indicators:

                         ▲ = 50 kts.          / = 10 kts.          / = 5 kts.

       4)   EXAMPLES:

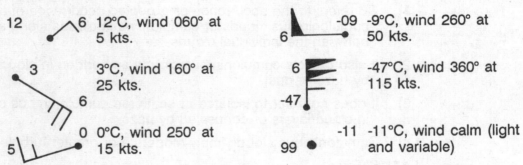

    b.   Note that observed winds aloft at various fixed altitudes, e.g., 34,000 ft., are very similar to the tropopause observed winds and temperatures.

5.   The tropopause pressure temperature and winds chart shows for each upper air observing station at the tropopause the pressure, temperature, and wind.

EXAMPLE:

200
ABQ
4

ABQ reports at the tropopause wind 240° at 115 kt., pressure 200 millibars.

---

**QUESTIONS AND ANSWER EXPLANATIONS**

All the FAA questions from the written test for the instrument rating relating to weather and the material outlined previously are reproduced on the following pages in the same modules as the outlines. To the immediate right of each question are the correct answer and answer explanation. You should cover these answers and answer explanations with your hand or a piece of paper while responding to the questions. Refer to the general discussion in Chapter 1 on how to take the examination.

Remember that the questions from the FAA Instrument Rating Question Book have been reordered by topic, and the topics have been organized into a meaningful sequence. Accordingly, the first line of the answer explanation gives the FAA question number and the citation of the authoritative source for the answer.

---

## 4.1 Causes of Weather

**1.**
**4096.** The primary cause of all changes in the Earth's weather is

A— variation of solar energy received by the Earth's regions.
B— changes in air pressure over the Earth's surface.
C— movement of the air masses.

Answer (A) is correct (4096). *(AvW Chap 2)*
Every physical process of weather is accompanied by or is the result of a heat exchange. Unequal solar heating of the Earth's surface causes differences in air pressure, which result in all changes in the Earth's weather.
Answer (B) is incorrect because changes in air pressure are a result of varying temperatures. Answer (C) is incorrect because movement of air masses (wind) is a result of varying temperatures and pressures.

**2.**
**4108.** Which force, in the Northern Hemisphere, acts at a right angle to the wind and deflects it to the right until parallel to the isobars?

A— Centrifugal.
B— Pressure gradient.
C— Coriolis.

Answer (C) is correct (4108). *(AvW Chap 4)*
Coriolis force is a result of the Earth's rotation. As the wind moves perpendicular to the isobars (from high to low pressure), it is apparently deflected to the right in the Northern Hemisphere, until it is moving parallel to the isobars. This effect is most pronounced above 2,000 ft. AGL.
Answer (A) is incorrect because centrifugal force is a force that acts outwardly on any object moving in a curved path. Answer (B) is incorrect because pressure gradient causes the wind to move perpendicular to the isobars. It is then deflected by Coriolis force.

**3.**
**4107.** What relationship exists between the winds at 2,000 feet above the surface and the surface winds?

A— The winds at 2,000 feet and the surface winds flow in the same direction, but the surface winds are weaker due to friction.
B— The winds at 2,000 feet tend to parallel the isobars while the surface winds cross the isobars at an angle toward lower pressure and are weaker.
C— The surface winds tend to veer to the right of the winds at 2,000 feet and are usually weaker.

Answer (B) is correct (4107). *(AvW Chap 4)*
Generally, winds near the surface are weaker than those aloft due to the friction between the Earth's surface and the wind. Also, because they are slower, winds near the surface are less affected by the Coriolis force. The pressure gradient forces are thus stronger near the surface and the winds cross the isobars at an angle instead of flowing parallel to them.
Answer (A) is incorrect because the Coriolis force is less at the surface, so surface winds flow in a direction different from those aloft. Answer (C) is incorrect because the winds aloft veer to the right of surface winds, not the opposite.

**4.**
**4106.** Winds at 5,000 feet AGL on a particular flight are southwesterly while most of the surface winds are southerly. This difference in direction is primarily due to

A— a stronger pressure gradient at higher altitudes.
B— friction between the wind and the surface.
C— stronger Coriolis force at the surface.

**5.**
**4105.** What causes surface winds to flow across the isobars at an angle rather than parallel to the isobars?

A— Coriolis force.
B— Surface friction.
C— The greater density of the air at the surface.

**6.**
**4158.** An air mass is a body of air that

A— has similar cloud formations associated with it.
B— creates a wind shift as it moves across the Earth's surface.
C— covers an extensive area and has fairly uniform properties of temperature and moisture.

**7.**
**4097.** A characteristic of the stratosphere is

A— an overall decrease of temperature with an increase in altitude.
B— a relatively even base altitude of approximately 35,000 feet.
C— relatively small changes in temperature with an increase in altitude.

**8.**
**4155.** A jetstream is defined as wind of

A— 30 knots or greater.
B— 40 knots or greater.
C— 50 knots or greater.

Answer (B) is correct (4106). *(AvW Chap 4)*
Southerly winds at the surface will become southwesterly winds at 5,000 ft. because the Coriolis force deflects winds aloft to the right. This force has less effect on surface winds which have been slowed by friction with the Earth's surface.
Answer (A) is incorrect because the pressure differentials are approximately uniform through the altitudes. Answer (C) is incorrect because the Coriolis force at the surface is weaker with slower wind speed.

Answer (B) is correct (4105). *(AvW Chap 4)*
Generally, winds near the surface are weaker than those aloft due to the friction between the Earth's surface and the wind. Also, because they are slower, winds near the surface are less affected by the Coriolis force. The pressure gradient forces are thus stronger near the surface and the winds cross the isobars at an angle instead of flowing parallel to them.
Answer (A) is incorrect because the Coriolis force is directly proportional to wind speed. At higher altitudes (above 2,000 to 3,000 ft. AGL), winds not slowed by surface friction are so deflected by the Coriolis force that they flow parallel to the isobars, not across them. Answer (C) is incorrect because the greater air density at the surface has little effect on the relationship of winds to the isobars.

Answer (C) is correct (4158). *(AvW Chap 8)*
An air mass is an extensive body of air within which the conditions of temperature and moisture in a horizontal plane are essentially uniformly distributed. Generally, an air mass takes on the properties of the large area it overlies.
Answer (A) is incorrect because an air mass may have cloud formations or it may be clear and dry. Answer (B) is incorrect because changes in wind, temperature, etc., indicate a frontal zone between two air masses.

Answer (C) is correct (4097). *(AvW Chap 1)*
The stratosphere is the atmospheric layer above the tropopause. It is the band of altitude from about 7 to 22 mi. It is characterized by a slight average increase in temperature from base to top and thus is very stable. It also has a low moisture content and an absence of clouds.
Answer (A) is incorrect because there is a slight increase, not decrease, in temperature with increase in altitude. Answer (B) is incorrect because the base of the stratosphere is considerably higher at the equator than at the poles.

Answer (C) is correct (4155). *(AvW Chap 13)*
The jet stream is a roughly horizontal stream of wind of 50 kt. or more (by definition) concentrated within a narrow band imbedded in the westerly winds in the high troposphere. It occurs in an area of intensified pressure gradients. A second or even third jet stream may form at one time, and these may not be continuous.
Answer (A) is incorrect because a jet stream, by definition, is a wind of 50 kt. (not 30 kt.) or greater. Answer (B) is incorrect because a jet stream, by definition, is a wind of 50 kt. (not 40 kt.) or greater.

**9.**
**4154.** The average height of the troposphere in the middle latitudes is

A— 20,000 feet.
B— 25,000 feet.
C— 37,000 feet.

Answer (C) is correct (4154). *(AvW Chap 1)*
In the mid-latitudes, the average height of the troposphere is about 37,000 ft. It is 25,000-30,000 ft. at the poles and 55,000-65,000 ft. at the equator. It is generally higher in summer than in winter.
Answer (A) is incorrect because the average height of the troposphere is 25,000-30,000 ft. at the poles (not the mid-latitudes). Answer (B) is incorrect because the average height of the troposphere is 25,000-30,000 ft. at the poles (not the mid-latitudes).

**10.**
**4168.** The strength and location of the jetstream is normally

A— stronger and farther north in the winter.
B— weaker and farther north in the summer.
C— stronger and farther north in the summer.

Answer (B) is correct (4168). *(AvW Chap 13)*
In the mid-latitudes, the wind speed in the jet stream averages considerably less in the summer than in the winter. Also, the jet stream shifts further north in summer than in winter.
Answer (A) is incorrect because the jet stream is usually farther south (not north) in winter. Answer (C) is incorrect because the jet stream is usually weaker (not stronger) in summer.

**11.**
**4227.** Which feature is associated with the tropopause?

A— Absence of wind and turbulent conditions.
B— Absolute upper limit of cloud formation.
C— Abrupt change in temperature lapse rate.

Answer (C) is correct (4227). *(AvW Chap 13)*
The tropopause is the transition layer of atmosphere between the troposphere (surface to about 7 to 22 mi.) and the stratosphere. A characteristic of the tropopause is that there is an abrupt change in the temperature lapse rate, i.e., the rate at which temperature decreases with height.
Answer (A) is incorrect because there are usually very strong winds in the tropopause. These create narrow zones of wind shear, which may generate hazardous turbulence. Answer (B) is incorrect because clouds may form above the tropopause even though there is little moisture in the stratosphere.

**12.**
**4136.** Which weather phenomenon is always associated with the passage of a frontal system?

A— A wind change.
B— An abrupt decrease in pressure.
C— Clouds, either ahead or behind the front.

Answer (A) is correct (4136). *(AvW Chap 8)*
Whenever a front passes, a wind shift will always occur. This discontinuity may be in direction, speed, or both.
Answer (B) is incorrect because the pressure and/or temperature may not change significantly as a weak front passes. Answer (C) is incorrect because some fronts do not contain enough moisture to produce clouds. Therefore, clouds are not always associated with a frontal system.

**13.**
**4140.** Which is a characteristic of low-level wind shear as it relates to frontal activity?

A— With a warm front, the most critical period is before the front passes the airport.
B— With a cold front, the most critical period is just before the front passes the airport.
C— Turbulence will always exist in wind-shear conditions.

Answer (A) is correct (4140). *(AvW Chap 8)*
Wind shear associated with a warm front occurs above an airport before the front passes the airport. A warm front is warmer air overtaking colder air.
Answer (B) is incorrect because cold front wind shear occurs just as or just after the front passes rather than before it passes. Answer (C) is incorrect because wind shear can sometimes occur with no forewarning from turbulence.

**14.**
**4127.** Frontal waves normally form on

A— slow moving cold fronts or stationary fronts.
B— slow moving warm fronts and strong occluded fronts.
C— rapidly moving cold fronts or warm fronts.

Answer (A) is correct (4127). *(AvW Chap 8)*
Frontal waves and cyclones (areas of low pressure) usually form in slow-moving cold fronts or in stationary fronts.
Answer (B) is incorrect because frontal waves are usually not associated with warm fronts or occluded fronts. Answer (C) is incorrect because frontal waves usually form on slow (not rapidly) moving cold fronts and not on warm fronts.

**15.**
**4137.** Where do squall lines most often develop?

A— In an occluded front.
B— In a cold air mass.
C— Ahead of a cold front.

Answer (C) is correct (4137). *(AvW Chap 8)*
A squall line is a nonfrontal band of active thunderstorms that sometimes develops ahead of a cold front.
Answer (A) is incorrect because squall lines are usually associated with a fast-moving cold front. Answer (B) is incorrect because they occur ahead of the cold front, not behind the front in the cold air.

## 4.2 Stability of Air Masses

**16.**
**4128.** Which are characteristics of an unstable cold air mass moving over a warm surface?

A— Cumuliform clouds, turbulence, and poor visibility.
B— Cumuliform clouds, turbulence, and good visibility.
C— Stratiform clouds, smooth air, and poor visibility.

Answer (B) is correct (4128). *(AvW Chap 9)*
When a cold air mass moves over a warm surface, the warm air near the surface rises and creates an unstable situation. These convective currents give rise to cumuliform clouds, turbulence, and good visibility.
Answer (A) is incorrect because unstable air lifts and blows haze away, resulting in good (not poor) visibility. Answer (C) is incorrect because unstable conditions produce cumuliform rather than stratiform clouds. Also, the air is turbulent and there is good visibility.

**17.**
**4119.** What are the characteristics of stable air?

A— Good visibility, steady precipitation, and stratus-type clouds.
B— Poor visibility, intermittent precipitation, and cumulus-type clouds.
C— Poor visibility, steady precipitation, and stratus-type clouds.

Answer (C) is correct (4119). *(AvW Chap 8)*
Stable air is air which is still or moving horizontally but without vertical movement. As a result, the pollutants hang in the air and visibility is poor. Also, stable air forms stratus-type clouds since the air is moving in layers. Reladely, precipitation spreads out over a wide area and is relatively steady.
Answer (A) is incorrect because the visibility is poor rather than good in stable air. Answer (B) is incorrect because the precipitation is steady and the clouds are stratiform.

**18.**
**4118.** What type clouds can be expected when an unstable air mass is forced to ascend a mountain slope?

A— Layered clouds with little vertical development.
B— Stratified clouds with considerable associated turbulence.
C— Clouds with extensive vertical development.

Answer (C) is correct (4118). *(AvW Chap 6)*
Air which is unstable has a greater lapse rate. Because the air above is much colder than the air below, the lower (warmer) air tends to rise very easily. When an unstable air mass is forced to ascend up a mountain slope it will probably continue to ascend beyond the mountain slope. Once the air expands and cools to the dew point, cumulus clouds will form with considerable vertical development. Any unstable air mass movement will usually result in turbulence as well.
Answer (A) is incorrect because layered clouds are associated with stable air. Answer (B) is incorrect because stratified clouds are associated with stable air and no turbulence.

**19.**
**4117.** Which is a characteristic of stable air?

A— Fair weather cumulus clouds.
B— Stratiform clouds.
C— Unlimited visibility.

Answer (B) is correct (4117). *(AvW Chaps 6, 7)*
Stratiform clouds, i.e., layer-type clouds, characteristically form in stable air. A stable atmosphere resists any upward or downward displacement, so clouds tend to lie horizontally instead of developing vertically.
Answer (A) is incorrect because cumulus clouds indicate unstable conditions. Answer (C) is incorrect because restricted, not unlimited, visibility near the ground is an indication of stable air.

**20.**
**4116.** The general characteristics of unstable air are

A— good visibility, showery precipitation, and cumuliform-type clouds.
B— good visibility, steady precipitation, and stratiform-type clouds.
C— poor visibility, intermittent precipitation, and cumuliform-type clouds.

Answer (A) is correct (4116). *(AvW Chaps 6, 7)*
Unstable air is moving vertically and usually produces cumulus clouds. The precipitation from cumulus clouds is showery. The lifting associated with unstable air generally clears smoke and other pollution away and visibility is relatively good.
Answer (B) is incorrect because unstable air generally has showery (not steady) precipitation and cumulus (not stratiform) clouds. Answer (C) is incorrect because unstable air generally has good (not poor) visibility.

**21.**
**4115.** What type of clouds will be formed if very stable moist air is forced upslope?

A— First stratified clouds and then vertical clouds.
B— Vertical clouds with increasing height.
C— Stratified clouds with little vertical development.

Answer (C) is correct (4115). *(AvW Chap 6)*
Even when being forced upslope, stable air forms stratus-type clouds. This is because the air resists any further upward movement.
Answer (A) is incorrect because there would be vertical clouds if the air were unstable rather than stable. Answer (B) is incorrect because there would be vertical clouds if the air were unstable rather than stable.

**22.**
**4098.** Steady precipitation, in contrast to showers, preceding a front is an indication of

A— stratiform clouds with moderate turbulence.
B— cumuliform clouds with little or no turbulence.
C— stratiform clouds with little or no turbulence.

Answer (C) is correct (4098). *(AvW Chap 6)*
Steady precipitation is a characteristic of stable air because of its lack of lifting action. Also characteristic are stratiform clouds with relatively little turbulence.
Answer (A) is incorrect because stable air has little or no turbulence. Answer (B) is incorrect because stratiform rather than cumuliform clouds form in stable air.

**23.**
**4159.** What enhances the growth rate of precipitation?

A— Advective action.
B— Upward currents.
C— Cyclonic movement.

Answer (B) is correct (4159). *(AvW Chap 5)*
The growth rate of precipitation is enhanced by upward currents which carry moisture particles to cooler levels. The particles grow in size and weight (due to condensation) until the atmosphere can no longer hold them (saturation point) and they fall as precipitation.
Answer (A) is incorrect because advective action usually refers to the horizontal transport of atmospheric properties by wind, such as warm advection (warm land air moving out over colder water). Answer (C) is incorrect because cyclonic movement refers to the counterclockwise movement around a low pressure area.

**24.**

**4123.** Which of the following combinations of weather producing variables would likely result in cumuliform-type clouds, good visibility, rain showers, and possible clear-type icing in clouds?

A— Unstable, moist air, and no lifting mechanism.
B— Stable, dry air, and orographic lifting.
C— Unstable, moist air, and orographic lifting.

**25.**

**4122.** What determines the structure or type of clouds which form as a result of air being forced to ascend?

A— The method by which the air is lifted.
B— The stability of the air before lifting occurs.
C— The amount of condensation nuclei present after lifting occurs.

**26.**

**4121.** Stability can be determined from which measurement of the atmosphere?

A— Low-level winds.
B— Ambient lapse rate.
C— Atmospheric pressure.

**27.**

**4120.** What are some characteristics of unstable air?

A— Nimbostratus clouds and good surface visibility.
B— Turbulence and poor surface visibility.
C— Turbulence and good surface visibility.

**28.**

**4124.** Unsaturated air flowing upslope will cool at the rate of approximately (dry adiabatic lapse rate)

A— 3 °C per 1,000 feet.
B— 2 °C per 1,000 feet.
C— 2.5 °C per 1,000 feet.

Answer (C) is correct (4123). *(AvW Chap 6)*
Cumuliform clouds, good visibility, and showery rain are produced as unstable, moist air is lifted into higher, cooler regions. When the lifting is the result of movement over terrain (e.g., up a mountain slope), it is called orographic lifting. Clear icing is formed from large drops such as those found in cumuliform clouds.
Answer (A) is incorrect because, without a lifting mechanism, there would be no vertical development of clouds to result in showery rain and icing in clouds. Answer (B) is incorrect because stable conditions result in stratiform rather than cumuliform clouds, and dry air does not result in showery rain or icing even when lifted.

Answer (B) is correct (4122). *(AvW Chap 6)*
The structure of clouds is determined by the stability of the air before it is lifted. If unstable, the clouds will have vertical development. If stable, the clouds will be horizontal, i.e., stratiform.
Answer (A) is incorrect because the stability of the air (not the lifting mechanism) determines the type of cloud formations. Answer (C) is incorrect because condensation nuclei encourage the formation of rain droplets or ice, but have no effect on the type of cloud formations.

Answer (B) is correct (4121). *(AvW Chap 2)*
The ambient lapse rate is the actual rate of decrease in temperature with height. A great decrease in temperature as altitude increases encourages warm air from below to rise and creates an unstable air mass. Lifting is inhibited by lesser or very small temperature decreases with altitude (i.e., a low lapse rate).
Answer (A) is incorrect because stability refers to vertical air movement, not horizontal air movement. Answer (C) is incorrect because atmospheric pressure is a measure of the weight or downward force of air, and does not affect air stability.

Answer (C) is correct (4120). *(AvW Chaps 6, 7)*
The lifting tendency of unstable air creates turbulence and clears the surface air of clouds, dust, and other pollution.
Answer (A) is incorrect because stratus clouds are characteristic of stable (not unstable) air. Answer (B) is incorrect because poor surface visibility is a characteristic of stable (not unstable) air.

Answer (A) is correct (4124). *(AvW Chap 6)*
The dry adiabatic lapse rate signifies a prescribed rate of expansional cooling or compressional heating. The dry adiabatic rate is 3°C for each 1,000 ft. Note this differs from the average normal lapse rate of 2°C for each 1,000 ft. of altitude. The latter is NOT dry air, but rather air with "average" humidity.
Answer (B) is incorrect because 2°C per 1,000 ft. is the standard lapse rate in stable air. Answer (C) is incorrect because 2.5°C per 1,000 ft. is the rate at which the temperature and dew point converge in a convective current of unsaturated air.

## 4.3 Temperature Inversions

**29.**

**4114.** What feature is associated with a temperature inversion?

A— A stable layer of air.
B— An unstable layer of air.
C— Air mass thunderstorms.

**Answer (A) is correct (4114).** *(AvW Chaps 2, 6)*
A temperature inversion is defined as an increase in temperature with height; i.e., the lapse rate is less than standard. The cooler air stays near the surface and there is little or no vertical movement.
Answer (B) is incorrect because instability occurs when the temperature decreases (not increases as in a temperature inversion) with an increase in height, and the warmer air continues to rise. Answer (C) is incorrect because air mass thunderstorms result from instability. They do not occur when there is a temperature inversion.

**30.**

**4200.** Which weather conditions should be expected beneath a low-level temperature inversion layer when the relative humidity is high?

A— Smooth air and poor visibility due to fog, haze, or low clouds.
B— Light wind shear and poor visibility due to haze and light rain.
C— Turbulent air and poor visibility due to fog, low stratus-type clouds, and showery precipitation.

**Answer (A) is correct (4200).** *(AvW Chap 2)*
A temperature inversion is an increase in temperature as altitude increases, i.e., normally temperature decreases with increases in altitude. In an inversion, warm air rises to its own temperature and forms a stable layer of air. A low level inversion results in poor visibility by trapping fog, smoke, dust, etc., into low levels of the atmosphere.
Answer (B) is incorrect because wind shear may be expected within (not beneath) a low-level temperature inversion. Answer (C) is incorrect because an inversion forms a stable layer of air thus making it smooth (not turbulent), and causing steady (not showery) precipitation.

**31.**

**4125.** A temperature inversion will normally form only

A— in stable air.
B— in unstable air.
C— when a stratiform layer merges with a cumuliform mass.

**Answer (A) is correct (4125).** *(AvW Chap 2)*
In a temperature inversion, warm air overlies colder air; i.e., the lapse rate is inverted. By definition, this is a stable condition, since there is no lifting action.
Answer (B) is incorrect because unstable air has colder air above warm air. Answer (C) is incorrect because a merger of stratus and cumulus clouds is associated with an occluded front, not necessarily a temperature inversion.

**32.**

**4094.** A common type of ground or surface based temperature inversion is that which is produced by

A— warm air being lifted rapidly aloft in the vicinity of mountainous terrain.
B— the movement of colder air over warm air, or the movement of warm air under cold air.
C— ground radiation on clear, cool nights when the wind is light.

**Answer (C) is correct (4094).** *(AvW Chap 2)*
A temperature inversion means the temperature becomes warmer rather than cooler with increases in altitude. A ground- or surface-based temperature inversion is produced when the air near the surface is cooled faster than the overlying air as a result of radiation of heat on a clear, still night. The air very close to the surface is thus cooler than the air a few hundred feet above.
Answer (A) is incorrect because when warm air is lifted, unstable (not stable) air is the result. Answer (B) is incorrect because a temperature inversion consists of warm air over colder air (not colder over warm).

## 4.4 Temperature/Dew Point and Fog

**33.**

**4169.** Which conditions are favorable for the formation of radiation fog?

A— Moist air moving over colder ground or water.
B— Cloudy sky and a light wind moving saturated warm air over a cool surface.
C— Clear sky, little or no wind, small temperature/dewpoint spread, and over a land surface.

**Answer (C) is correct (4169).** *(AvW Chap 12)*
Conditions favorable for radiation fog are a clear sky, little or no wind, and a small temperature/dew point spread. The fog forms as terrestrial radiation cools the ground. The air near the ground is cooled to dew point and fog forms.
Answer (A) is incorrect because it describes advection fog. Answer (B) is incorrect because it describes advection fog.

**34.**
**4167.** What situation is most conducive to the formation of radiation fog?

A— Warm, moist air over low, flatland areas on clear, calm nights.
B— Moist, tropical air moving over cold, offshore water.
C— The movement of cold air over much warmer water.

Answer (A) is correct (4167). *(AvW Chap 12)*
Conditions favorable for radiation fog are a clear sky, little or no wind, and a small temperature/dew point spread. The fog forms as terrestrial radiation cools the ground. The air close to the surface cools more quickly than the slightly higher air. The air near the ground is cooled to dew point and fog forms.
Answer (B) is incorrect because advection fog forms as a result of warm air moving over a colder surface. Answer (C) is incorrect because steam fog forms when cold air moves over a warmer surface.

**35.**
**4112.** The most frequent type of ground- or surface-based temperature inversion is that produced by

A— radiation on a clear, relatively still night.
B— warm air being lifted rapidly aloft in the vicinity of mountainous terrain.
C— the movement of colder air under warm air, or the movement of warm air over cold air.

Answer (A) is correct (4112). *(AvW Chap 2)*
An inversion often develops near the ground on clear, cool nights when the wind is light. The ground radiates heat and cools much faster than the overlying air. Air in contact with the ground becomes cold while the temperature a few hundred feet above changes very little. Thus temperature increases with height.
Answer (B) is incorrect because it describes orographic lifting. Answer (C) is incorrect because it describes a cold front and a warm front, respectively.

**36.**
**4166.** What types of fog depend upon a wind in order to exist?

A— Steam fog and downslope fog.
B— Precipitation-induced fog and ground fog.
C— Advection fog and upslope fog.

Answer (C) is correct (4166). *(AvW Chap 12)*
Upslope fog forms as a result of moist, stable air being cooled as it moves up a sloping terrain. Advection fog forms when moist air is blown over a cold surface, decreasing the moist air's temperature to its dew point. Thus, both upslope fog and advection fog depend on air moving from one area to another, i.e., depend on wind.
Answer (A) is incorrect because downslope fog is a nonsense term. Answer (B) is incorrect because precipitation fog forms when warm rain or drizzle falls through cool air, and ground fog requires little or no wind.

**37.**
**4165.** In what localities is advection fog most likely to occur?

A— Coastal areas.
B— Mountain slopes.
C— Level inland areas.

Answer (A) is correct (4165). *(AvW Chap 12)*
Advection fog forms when moist air moves over colder ground or water. This type of fog is thus most common along coastal areas. During the winter, advection fog over the central and eastern United States results when moist air from the Gulf of Mexico spreads northward over cold ground.
Answer (B) is incorrect because mountain slopes are required for upslope (not advection) fog. Answer (C) is incorrect because level inland areas will most likely produce radiation (not advection) fog.

**38.**
**4164.** In which situation is advection fog most likely to form?

A— An air mass moving inland from the coast in winter.
B— A light breeze blowing colder air out to sea.
C— Warm, moist air settling over a warmer surface under no-wind conditions.

Answer (A) is correct (4164). *(AvW Chap 12)*
Advection fog forms when moist air moves over colder ground or water. This type of fog is most likely to form when an air mass moves from the warmer water inland from the coast in winter. As the air moves over the cooler land, it cools to the dew point and forms advection fog.
Answer (B) is incorrect because colder air blowing out to sea results in steam (not advection) fog. Answer (C) is incorrect because warm, moist air settling over a warmer surface would not cool, so fog would not form.

**39.**

**4163.** Fog is usually prevalent in industrial areas because of

A— atmospheric stabilization around cities.
B— an abundance of condensation nuclei from combustion products.
C— increased temperatures due to industrial heating.

Answer (B) is correct (4163). (AvW Chap 12)
Fog often forms in industrial areas because the combustion products leave dust in the air on which water can condense. These particles are called condensation nuclei.
Answer (A) is incorrect because cities, per se, have no effect on air stability. Answer (C) is incorrect because the amount of heat that factories release into the air is not significant in the formation of fog.

**40.**

**4162.** Which weather condition can be expected when moist air flows from a relatively warm surface to a colder surface?

A— Increased visibility.
B— Convective turbulence due to surface heating.
C— Fog.

Answer (C) is correct (4162). (AvW Chap 12)
When moist air flows from a relatively warm surface to a colder surface, the warm, moist air is cooled to its dew point and advection fog is produced.
Answer (A) is incorrect because fog forms, which decreases (not increases) visibility. Answer (B) is incorrect because the surface cools the air, resulting in stable air with little or no convective turbulence.

**41.**

**4156.** Under which condition does advection fog usually form?

A— Moist air moving over colder ground or water.
B— Warm, moist air settling over a cool surface under no-wind conditions.
C— A land breeze blowing a cold air mass over a warm water current.

Answer (A) is correct (4156). (AvW Chap 12)
Advection fog forms when moist air moves over colder ground or water. The moist air is cooled to the dew point and fog forms.
Answer (B) is incorrect because it describes radiation fog. Answer (C) is incorrect because it describes steam fog.

**42.**

**4103.** The amount of water vapor which air can hold largely depends on

A— relative humidity.
B— air temperature.
C— stability of air.

Answer (B) is correct (4103). (AvW Chap 5)
Air temperature largely determines how much water vapor can be held by the air. Warm air, which is less dense, can hold more water vapor than cold air.
Answer (A) is incorrect because relative humidity is the ratio of the existing amount of water vapor in the air at a given temperature to the maximum amount that could be held at that temperature. Answer (C) is incorrect because air stability is related to the temperature lapse rate (not moisture).

**43.**

**4104.** Clouds, fog, or dew will always form when

A— water vapor condenses.
B— water vapor is present.
C— the temperature and dewpoint are equal.

Answer (A) is correct (4104). (AvW Chap 5)
As water vapor condenses, it becomes visible as clouds, fog, or dew.
Answer (B) is incorrect because some water vapor is usually present, but it does not necessarily form clouds, fog, or dew. Answer (C) is incorrect because, even at 100% humidity (when the dew point equals actual temperature), water vapor may not condense if sufficient condensation nuclei are not present.

**44.**

**4101.** To which meteorological condition does the term "dewpoint" refer?

A— The temperature to which air must be cooled to become saturated.
B— The temperature at which condensation and evaporation are equal.
C— The temperature at which dew will always form.

Answer (A) is correct (4101). (AvW Chap 5)
Dew point refers to the temperature to which air must be cooled to become saturated by the water vapor in the air. Dew point when related to air temperature in aviation weather reports reveals how close the air is to saturation and possible cloud, fog, or precipitation formation.
Answer (B) is incorrect because condensation (vapor to water) occurs at low temperatures and evaporation (water to vapor) occurs at high temperatures. Answer (C) is incorrect because the formation of dew depends on relative humidity and the temperature of the collecting surface.

**45.**
**4100.** Which conditions result in the formation of frost?

A— The temperature of the collecting surface is at or below freezing and small droplets of moisture are falling.
B— When dew forms and the temperature is below freezing.
C— Temperature of the collecting surface is below the dewpoint of surrounding air and the dewpoint is colder than freezing.

**Answer (C) is correct (4100).** *(AvW Chap 5)*
If the air temperature drops below the dew point, the air becomes more dense and can no longer hold the water vapor.  The water vapor will condense to form visible moisture.  Frost will form only if the temperature of the collecting surfaces is below the dew point of the surrounding air AND the dew point is below freezing.
Answer (A) is incorrect because the dew point must also be below freezing and droplets of moisture are not necessary.  Answer (B) is incorrect because the formation of dew is not required, and the dew point of surrounding air must be below freezing and the temperature of the collecting surface must be less than the dew point.

## 4.5  Clouds

**46.**
**4134.** What are the four families of clouds?

A— Stratus, cumulus, nimbus, and cirrus.
B— Clouds formed by updrafts, fronts, cooling layers of air, and precipitation into warm air.
C— High, middle, low, and those with extensive vertical development.

**Answer (C) is correct (4134).** *(AvW Chap 7)*
For identification purposes, clouds are divided into four "families" based on their height range.  The families are:  high clouds, middle clouds, low clouds, and clouds with extensive vertical development.
Answer (A) is incorrect because it describes cloud formation and characteristic.  Answer (B) is incorrect because it describes the way various clouds are formed.

**47.**
**4133.** Which family of clouds is least likely to contribute to structural icing on an aircraft?

A— Low clouds.
B— High clouds.
C— Clouds with extensive vertical development.

**Answer (B) is correct (4133).** *(AvW Chaps 7, 10)*
High clouds are least likely to contribute to structural icing since they usually consist entirely of ice crystals.  Since ice is already frozen, it will not freeze onto the structural surface of the airplane.
Answer (A) is incorrect because low clouds can contain supercooled water, which freezes on contact with the airplane.  Answer (C) is incorrect because clouds with extensive vertical development can contain supercooled water, which freezes on contact with the airplane.

**48.**
**4132.** The presence of standing lenticular altocumulus clouds is a good indication of

A— a jetstream.
B— very strong turbulence.
C— heavy icing conditions.

**Answer (B) is correct (4132).** *(AvW Chaps 7, 9)*
When stable air crosses a mountain barrier, it tends to flow in layers.  The barrier may set up waves in these layers, which remain stationary while the wind blows rapidly through them.  Wave crests extend well above the highest mountain tops.  Under each wave crest is a rotary circulation, which can create very violent turbulence.  Crests of the standing waves may be marked by stationary lens-shaped clouds known as standing lenticular clouds.
Answer (A) is incorrect because the jet stream flows around the world at high altitudes and at varying latitudes.  Answer (C) is incorrect because standing lenticular clouds occur at varying temperatures, not only below freezing.

**49.**
**4131.** The suffix "nimbus", used in naming clouds, means a

A— cloud with extensive vertical development.
B— raincloud.
C— dark massive, towering cloud.

**Answer (B) is correct (4131).** *(AvW Chap 7)*
The prefix "nimbo" or the suffix "nimbus" means rain-cloud.  For example, stratified clouds from which rain is falling are called nimbostratus clouds.  A heavy, swelling, cumulus-type cloud which produces precipitation is called a cumulonimbus cloud.
Answer (A) is incorrect because "cumulo" (not "nimbus") denotes a cloud with extensive vertical development.  Answer (C) is incorrect because it specifies a cumulonimbus cloud, not any nimbus cloud.

**50.**
**4130.**  Standing lenticular clouds, in mountainous areas, indicate

A— an inversion.
B— unstable air.
C— turbulence.

Answer (C) is correct (4130).  *(AvW Chaps 7, 9)*
The "waves" generated as wind flows across a mountain barrier may form standing lenticular clouds at the crest of each wave.  Their presence indicates very strong turbulence, and they should be avoided.
Answer (A) is incorrect because stratus (not standing lenticular) clouds indicate stable air which may be the result of a temperature inversion.  Answer (B) is incorrect because cumulus (not standing lenticular) clouds indicate unstable air.

**51.**
**4129.**  Which clouds have the greatest turbulence?

A— Towering cumulus.
B— Cumulonimbus.
C— Altocumulus castellanus.

Answer (B) is correct (4129).  *(AvW Chap 11)*
Cumulonimbus clouds are thunderstorms and the ultimate manifestation of instability.  They are huge vertically developed clouds with dense, billowy tops often crowned with thick veils of dense cirrus, called the "anvil." Nearly the entire spectrum of flying hazards is contained in these clouds, including violent turbulence.
Answer (A) is incorrect because towering cumulus clouds are only a preliminary stage of the cumulonimbus cloud.  Answer (C) is incorrect because altocumulus castellanus is a middle-level convective cloud which indicates rough turbulence with some icing, but thunderstorms are far more turbulent.

**52.**
**4157.**  A high cloud is composed mostly of

A— ozone.
B— condensation nuclei.
C— ice crystals.

Answer (C) is correct (4157).  *(AvW Chap 7)*
The high cloud family is cirriform.  It includes cirrus, cirrocumulus, and cirrostratus clouds.  They are composed almost entirely of ice crystals.  Their bases range from 16,500 ft. to 45,000 ft.
Answer (A) is incorrect because ozone is an unstable form of oxygen.  The heaviest concentrations are in the stratosphere, not in clouds.  Answer (B) is incorrect because condensation nuclei are the small particles in the air onto which water vapor condenses or sublimates.

**53.**
**4149.**  Fair weather cumulus clouds often indicate

A— turbulence at and below the cloud level.
B— poor visibility.
C— smooth flying conditions.

Answer (A) is correct (4149).  *(AvW Chap 7)*
Fair weather cumulus clouds form in convective currents and are characterized by relatively flat bases and dome-shaped tops.  They indicate a shallow layer of instability, some turbulence, and no significant icing.
Answer (B) is incorrect because the instability producing the cumulus clouds provides good (not poor) visibility.  Answer (C) is incorrect because the instability producing the cumulus clouds creates some turbulence, not smooth conditions.

## 4.6  Thunderstorms

**54.**
**4148.**  What are the requirements for the formation of a thunderstorm?

A— A cumulus cloud with sufficient moisture.
B— A cumulus cloud with sufficient moisture and an inverted lapse rate.
C— Sufficient moisture, an unstable lapse rate, and a lifting action.

Answer (C) is correct (4148).  *(AvW Chap 11)*
For a thunderstorm to form, the air must have sufficient water vapor, an unstable lapse rate, and an initial upward lifting to start the storm process in motion.  Surface heating, converging winds, sloping terrain, a frontal surface, or any combination of these can provide the lift.
Answer (A) is incorrect because a lifting action is needed.  Answer (B) is incorrect because lifting action and an unstable (not inverted) lapse rate are needed.

**55.**
**4147.** What is an indication that downdrafts have developed and the thunderstorm cell has entered the mature stage?

A— The anvil top has completed its development.
B— Precipitation begins to fall from the cloud base.
C— A gust front forms.

**Answer (B) is correct (4147).** *(AvW Chap 11)*
    The mature stage of a thunderstorm is signaled when rain begins falling at the surface. This means that the downdrafts have developed sufficiently to carry water all the way through the thunderstorm.
    Answer (A) is incorrect because an anvil top does not necessarily develop over every thunderstorm. Answer (C) is incorrect because gust front is a nonsense term.

**56.**
**4146.** Which procedure is recommended if a pilot should unintentionally penetrate embedded thunderstorm activity?

A— Reverse aircraft heading or proceed toward an area of known VFR conditions.
B— Reduce airspeed to maneuvering speed and maintain a constant altitude.
C— Set power for recommended turbulence penetration airspeed and attempt to maintain a level flight attitude.

**Answer (C) is correct (4146).** *(AvW Chap 11)*
    If a thunderstorm is penetrated, the pilot should always attempt to maintain a constant attitude at or below the maneuvering or turbulence penetration speed recommended for the airplane. Note that the airspeed cannot always be kept constant, but the power can be set so that one will be operating generally at or below the maneuvering speed.
    Answer (A) is incorrect because a straight course will probably take you out of the storm most quickly. Also, turning maneuvers increase stresses on the aircraft. Answer (B) is incorrect because it may be impossible to maintain a constant airspeed ($V_A$) in updrafts and downdrafts. It is best to set power so you will operate at or below $V_A$. Also, attempting to maintain constant altitude, not attitude, increases the stress on the airplane.

**57.**
**4145.** Which thunderstorms generally produce the most severe conditions, such as heavy hail and destructive winds?

A— Warm front.
B— Squall line.
C— Air mass.

**Answer (B) is correct (4145).** *(AvW Chap 11)*
    A squall line is a nonfrontal narrow band of active thunderstorms. It often contains severe, steady-state thunderstorms and presents the single most intense weather hazard to airplanes.
    Answer (A) is incorrect because warm fronts indicate stable air, which does not usually produce thunderstorms. Answer (C) is incorrect because an air mass thunderstorm is the least severe type of thunderstorm.

**58.**
**4144.** Which weather phenomenon is always associated with a thunderstorm?

A— Lightning.
B— Heavy rain showers.
C— Supercooled raindrops.

**Answer (A) is correct (4144).** *(AvW Chap 11)*
    A thunderstorm, by definition, has lightning, because lightning causes the thunder. Lightning is the discharge of electricity generated by thunderstorms.
    Answer (B) is incorrect because hail may occur instead of heavy rain showers. Answer (C) is incorrect because supercooled raindrops may not occur if the lifting process does not extend above the freezing level.

**59.**
**4143.** During the life cycle of a thunderstorm, which stage is characterized predominately by downdrafts?

A— Cumulus.
B— Dissipating.
C— Mature.

**Answer (B) is correct (4143).** *(AvW Chap 11)*
    Thunderstorms have 3 life cycles: cumulus, mature, and dissipating. In the dissipating stage, the storm is characterized by downdrafts as the storm rains itself out.
    Answer (A) is incorrect because the cumulus stage is the building stage characterized by updrafts. Answer (C) is incorrect because the mature stage has both updrafts and downdrafts, which create strong wind shears.

**60.**

**4142.** If squalls are reported at your destination, what wind conditions should you anticipate?

A— Sudden increases in windspeed of at least 15 knots to a peak of 20 knots or more, lasting for at least 1 minute.

B— Peak gusts of at least 35 knots for a sustained period of 1 minute or longer.

C— Rapid variation in wind direction of at least 20° and changes in speed of at least 10 knots between peaks and lulls.

**Answer (A) is correct (4142).** *(AvW Chap 11)*
A squall is a sudden increase in wind speed by at least 15 kt. to a peak of 20 kt. or more and lasting for at least 1 min. In contrast, a wind gust is a brief increase in wind with a variation between peaks and lulls of at least 10 kt. Note that these definitions involve variations in wind speed, not wind direction.
Answer (B) is incorrect because the phrase, "at least 35 kt.," refers to a "peak wind" which is reported in a surface aviation weather report. Answer (C) is incorrect because squalls refer to changes in wind speed (not direction).

**61.**

**4141.** What is indicated by the term "embedded thunderstorms"?

A— Severe thunderstorms are embedded within a squall line.

B— Thunderstorms are predicted to develop in a stable air mass.

C— Thunderstorms are obscured by massive cloud layers and cannot be seen.

**Answer (C) is correct (4141).** *(AvW Chap 11)*
The term "embedded thunderstorms" means that the storms are embedded in clouds or thick haze layers and cannot be seen.
Answer (A) is incorrect because a squall line consists of severe thunderstorms which can usually be seen. Answer (B) is incorrect because thunderstorms do not usually occur in stable air masses.

**62.**

**4126.** Which weather phenomenon signals the beginning of the mature stage of a thunderstorm?

A— The start of rain at the surface.

B— Growth rate of cloud is maximum.

C— Strong turbulence in the cloud.

**Answer (A) is correct (4126).** *(AvW Chap 11)*
The mature stage of a thunderstorm is indicated when rain begins falling at the surface. This means that downdrafts have developed sufficiently to carry water all the way through the thunderstorm.
Answer (B) is incorrect because maximum growth rate occurs in the first or cumulus stage. Answer (C) is incorrect because strong turbulence can occur in all stages.

**63.**

**4092.** Which is true regarding the use of airborne weather-avoidance radar for the recognition of certain weather conditions?

A— The radarscope provides no assurance of avoiding instrument weather conditions.

B— The avoidance of hail is assured when flying between and just clear of the most intense echoes.

C— The clear area between intense echoes indicates that visual sighting of storms can be maintained when flying between the echoes.

**Answer (A) is correct (4092).** *(AvW Chap 11)*
Weather-avoidance radar provides information on precipitation based on echo returns. Avoiding the heaviest areas of precipitation will often (not always) keep you out of the greatest turbulence. Radar does not show water vapor. Thus, clouds and fog, i.e., instrument weather conditions, are not indicated.
Answer (B) is incorrect because intense thunderstorms can often hurl hail for miles. Answer (C) is incorrect because visual sighting of storms is not assured, because clouds and fog are not shown by radar.

## 4.7 Icing

**64.**

**4152.** In which meteorological environment is aircraft structural icing most likely to have the highest rate of accumulation?

A— Cumulonimbus clouds.

B— High humidity and freezing temperature.

C— Freezing rain.

**Answer (C) is correct (4152).** *(AvW Chap 10)*
The condition most favorable for very hazardous icing is the presence of many large, supercooled water drops (i.e., freezing rain). The heaviest icing will usually be found at altitudes at or slightly above the freezing level where the temperature is never more than a few degrees below freezing.
Answer (A) is incorrect because icing does not necessarily occur in thunderstorms due to large variation in temperature in thunderstorms. Answer (B) is incorrect because visible moisture, not just high humidity, must be present for icing.

**65.**
**4171.** Test data indicate that ice, snow, or frost having a thickness and roughness similar to medium or coarse sandpaper on the leading edge and upper surface of a wing can

A— reduce lift by as much as 50 percent and increase drag by as much as 50 percent.
B— increase drag and reduce lift by as much as 25 percent.
C— reduce lift by as much as 30 percent and increase drag by 40 percent.

Answer (C) is correct (4171). *(AC 120-58)*
Test data indicate that ice, snow, or frost formations having a thickness and surface roughness similar to medium or coarse sandpaper on the leading edge and upper surface of a wing can reduce wing lift by as much as 30% and increase drag by 40%. These changes in lift and drag significantly increase stall speed, reduce controllability, and alter aircraft flight characteristics.
Answer (A) is incorrect because ice, snow, or frost having a thickness or roughness similar to medium or coarse sandpaper on the leading edge and upper surface of a wing can reduce lift by as much as 30%, not 50%, and increase drag by 40%, not 50%. Answer (B) is incorrect because ice, snow, or frost having a thickness or roughness similar to medium or coarse sandpaper on the leading edge and upper surface of a wing can reduce lift by as much as 30%, not 25%, and increase drag by 40%, not 25%.

**66.**
**4161.** Which precipitation type normally indicates freezing rain at higher altitudes?

A— Snow.
B— Hail.
C— Ice pellets.

Answer (C) is correct (4161). *(AvW Chap 8)*
Ice pellets normally indicate that rain droplets are freezing at a higher altitude. Warmer air above exists from which rain is falling and freezing on the way down, as it enters cooler air (i.e., freezing rain exists above).
Answer (A) is incorrect because snow indicates that the temperature of the air above you is well below freezing. Answer (B) is incorrect because hail indicates instability of the air aloft where supercooled droplets above the freezing level begin to freeze. Once a drop has frozen, other drops latch on to it, and the hailstone grows.

**67.**
**4153.** What is an operational consideration if you fly into rain which freezes on impact?

A— You have flown into an area of thunderstorms.
B— Temperatures are above freezing at some higher altitude.
C— You have flown through a cold front.

Answer (B) is correct (4153). *(AvW Chap 10)*
Rain which freezes on impact is called freezing rain. If rain falls through freezing air, it will usually form supercooled water droplets, i.e., freezing rain. It indicates that temperatures somewhere above the airplane are above freezing.
Answer (A) is incorrect because freezing rain does not necessarily indicate the presence of thunderstorms. Answer (C) is incorrect because freezing rain does not necessarily indicate the presence of cold fronts.

**68.**
**4102.** What temperature condition is indicated if wet snow is encountered at your flight altitude?

A— The temperature is above freezing at your altitude.
B— The temperature is below freezing at your altitude.
C— You are flying from a warm air mass into a cold air mass.

Answer (A) is correct (4102). *(AvW Chap 5)*
If snow is wet at your altitude, you are in above-freezing temperatures because the snow has started to melt.
Answer (B) is incorrect because the wet snow indicates above freezing (not below freezing) at your altitude. Answer (C) is incorrect because the temperature is lower above you, but not necessarily in front of you.

**69.**
**4099.** The presence of ice pellets at the surface is evidence that

A— there are thunderstorms in the area.
B— a cold front has passed.
C— there is freezing rain at a higher altitude.

Answer (C) is correct (4099). *(AvW Chap 5)*
Ice pellets form as a result of rain freezing at a higher altitude. Rain droplets cool as they fall from a warmer layer through air with a temperature below freezing.
Answer (A) is incorrect because thunderstorms do not necessarily cause ice pellets. Answer (B) is incorrect because cold fronts do not necessarily cause ice pellets.

**70.**
**4151.** Why is frost considered hazardous to flight operation?

A— Frost changes the basic aerodynamic shape of the airfoil.
B— Frost decreases control effectiveness.
C— Frost causes early airflow separation resulting in a loss of lift.

Answer (C) is correct (4151). *(AvW Chap 10)*
Frost spoils the smooth flow of air, thus causing a slowing of the airflow. This causes early airflow separation over the affected airfoil, resulting in a loss of lift. A heavy coat of hard frost will cause a 5 to 10% increase in stall speed. Even a small amount of frost on airfoils may prevent an aircraft from becoming airborne at normal takeoff speed.
Answer (A) is incorrect because frost is very thin. It does not change the airfoil shape as structural icing does. Answer (B) is incorrect because frost has no bearing on control effectiveness, only airfoil lift.

**71.**
**4113.** If the air temperature is +8 °C at an elevation of 1,350 feet and a standard (average) temperature lapse rate exists, what will be the approximate freezing level?

A— 3,350 feet MSL.
B— 5,350 feet MSL.
C— 9,350 feet MSL.

Answer (B) is correct (4113). *(AvW Chap 2)*
The decrease of temperature with altitude is defined as the lapse rate. The standard lapse rate is 2°C per 1,000 ft. To reach the freezing level you must have a drop of 8°C. Thus the freezing level is 4,000 ft. (8/2 x 1,000 ft.) up, or at 5,350 ft. MSL (1,350 + 4,000).
Answer (A) is incorrect because it represents a standard lapse rate of 4° per 1,000 ft. Answer (C) is incorrect because it represents a standard lapse rate of 1° per 1,000 ft.

## 4.8 Wind Shear

**72.**
**4150.** What is an important characteristic of wind shear?

A— It is an atmospheric condition that is associated exclusively with zones of convergence.
B— The Coriolis phenomenon in both high- and low-level air masses is the principal generating force.
C— It is an atmospheric condition that may be associated with a low-level temperature inversion, a jet stream, or a frontal zone.

Answer (C) is correct (4150). *(AvW Chap 9)*
Wind shear can occur at any level where winds are blowing in different directions or at different speeds. It is an atmospheric condition associated with low-level temperature inversions, the jet stream, or a frontal zone.
Answer (A) is incorrect because zones of convergence are low pressure areas. Wind shear can occur in highs as well as lows. Answer (B) is incorrect because the Coriolis force is the deflective force of the Earth's rotation which affects all wind flows, not just wind shear.

**73.**
**4210.** A pilot reporting turbulence that momentarily causes slight, erratic changes in altitude and/or attitude should report it as

A— light turbulence.
B— moderate turbulence.
C— light chop.

Answer (A) is correct (4210). *(AWS Sect 14)*
Light turbulence is defined as a disturbed air flow that momentarily causes slight erratic changes in altitude and/or attitude.
Answer (B) is incorrect because moderate turbulence is more intense. It is sufficient to cause changes in altitude, but the pilot maintains control throughout. Answer (C) is incorrect because light chop means slight or moderate, rapid, and somewhat rhythmic bumpiness without appreciable changes in altitude or attitude.

**74.**
**4139.** What is an important characteristic of wind shear?

A— It is primarily associated with the lateral vortices generated by thunderstorms.
B— It usually exists only in the vicinity of thunderstorms, but may be found near a strong temperature inversion.
C— It may be associated with either a wind shift or a windspeed gradient at any level in the atmosphere.

Answer (C) is correct (4139). *(AvW Chap 9)*
Wind shear can occur at any level where winds are blowing in different directions or at different speeds.
Answer (A) is incorrect because wind shear is found in conditions other than thunderstorm turbulence, e.g., mountain waves, fronts, etc. Answer (B) is incorrect because wind shear is found in conditions other than thunderstorm turbulence, e.g., mountain waves, fronts, etc.

**75.**
**4135.** Where can wind shear associated with a thunderstorm be found? Choose the most complete answer.

A— In front of the thunderstorm cell (anvil side) and on the right side of the cell.
B— In front of the thunderstorm cell and directly under the cell.
C— On all sides of the thunderstorm cell and directly under the cell.

Answer (C) is correct (4135). *(AvW Chap 11)*
     Wind shear associated with thunderstorms may be found on all sides of the thunderstorm cell, including directly beneath it and as much as 20 mi. laterally.
     Answer (A) is incorrect because wind shear may be found on all sides and beneath the thunderstorm cell. Answer (B) is incorrect because wind shear may be found on all sides and beneath the thunderstorm cell.

**76.**
**4138.** Where does wind shear occur?

A— Exclusively in thunderstorms.
B— Wherever there is an abrupt decrease in pressure and/or temperature.
C— With either a wind shift or a windspeed gradient at any level in the atmosphere.

Answer (C) is correct (4138). *(AvW Chap 9)*
     Wind shear can occur at any level where winds are blowing in different directions (wind shift) or at different speeds (a wind speed gradient).
     Answer (A) is incorrect because wind shear is also caused by barriers to wind flow, behind and below airplanes generating lift, etc. Answer (B) is incorrect because wind shear is the result of wind change, not temperature or pressure, per se.

**77.**
**4238.** Hazardous wind shear is commonly encountered near the ground

A— during periods when the wind velocity is stronger than 35 knots.
B— during periods when the wind velocity is stronger than 35 knots and near mountain valleys.
C— during periods of strong temperature inversion and near thunderstorms.

Answer (C) is correct (4238). *(AvW Chap 9)*
     Thunderstorms produce hazardous wind shear near the ground. Wind shear during temperature inversions is also hazardous when at low levels as it affects aircraft approaching and departing airports.
     Answer (A) is incorrect because any wind (not wind shear) is hazardous when in excess of 35 kt.
Answer (B) is incorrect because wind shear usually occurs on the leeward side of mountains, not in valleys.

## 4.9  AIRMETs and SIGMETs

**78.**
**4467.** At what time are current AIRMET's broadcast by the FSS?

A— 15 minutes after the hour only.
B— Every 15 minutes until the AIRMET is canceled.
C— 15 and 45 minutes after the hour during the first hour after issuance.

Answer (C) is correct (4467). *(AIM Para 7-5)*
     AIRMETs are broadcast when received by an FSS, at 15 min. past the hour, and at 45 min. past the hour during the first hour after issuance.
     Answer (A) is incorrect because an AIRMET is also transmitted at 45 min. past the hour during the first hour of issuance. Answer (B) is incorrect because AIRMETs are only broadcast for the first hour.

**79.**
**4187.** What is the maximum forecast period for AIRMET's?

A— Two hours.
B— Four hours.
C— Six hours.

Answer (C) is correct (4187). *(AWS Sect 4)*
     The maximum forecast period for AIRMETs is 6 hr. If conditions persist beyond 6 hr., the AIRMET must be updated and reissued.
     Answer (A) is incorrect because convective SIGMETs (not AIRMETs) are valid for up to 2 hr. Answer (B) is incorrect because SIGMETs (not AIRMETs) are valid for up to 4 hr.

**80.**
**4181.** SIGMET's are issued as a warning of weather conditions potentially hazardous

A— particularly to light aircraft.
B— to all aircraft.
C— only to light aircraft operations.

Answer (B) is correct (4181). *(AIM Para 7-5)*
     SIGMETs warn of weather considered potentially hazardous to all categories of aircraft. SIGMETs are forecasts of tornadoes, lines of thunderstorms, embedded thunderstorms, large hail, severe and extreme turbulence, severe icing, and widespread sandstorms and snowstorms.
     Answer (A) is incorrect because SIGMETs apply to all aircraft. Answer (C) is incorrect because AIRMETs, not SIGMETs, apply to light aircraft.

**81.**

**4183.** Which meteorological condition is issued in the form of a SIGMET (WS)?

A— Widespread sand or duststorms lowering visibility to less than 3 miles.
B— Moderate icing.
C— Sustained winds of 30 knots or greater at the surface.

Answer (A) is correct (4183). *(AIM Para 7-5)*
   SIGMETs are issued for severe and extreme turbulence, severe icing, and widespread duststorms, sandstorms, or volcanic ash lowering visibility below 3 mi.
   Answer (B) is incorrect because moderate icing is issued in the form of an AIRMET (not a SIGMET). Answer (C) is incorrect because sustained winds of 30 kt. or greater at the surface are issued in the form of an AIRMET (not a SIGMET).

**82.**

**4468.** Pilots of IFR flights seeking ATC in-flight weather avoidance assistance should keep in mind that

A— ATC radar limitations and, frequency congestion may limit the controllers capability to provide this service.
B— circumnavigating severe weather can only be accommodated in the en route areas away from terminals because of congestion.
C— ATC Narrow Band Radar does not provide the controller with weather intensity capability.

Answer (A) is correct (4468). *(AIM Para 7-12)*
   The controllers' primary function is to provide safe separation between aircraft. Any additional service, such as weather avoidance, can only be provided to the extent it does not interfere with the primary function. Unfortunately, the separation workload is usually greater when weather disrupts the normal flow of traffic.
   Answer (B) is incorrect because controllers can provide weather circumnavigation in terminal areas when workload permits. Answer (C) is incorrect because the new "Narrowband Radar" is replacing digitized radar weather displays in ARTCC facilities to provide even better measurement of precipitation density.

**83.**

**4241.** If you hear a SIGMET alert, how can you obtain the information in the SIGMET?

A— ATC will announce the hazard and advise you when to listen to an FSS broadcast.
B— Contact a weather watch station.
C— Contact the nearest FSS and ascertain whether the advisory is pertinent to your flight.

Answer (C) is correct (4241). *(AIM Para 7-9)*
   Pilots, upon hearing the alert notice, if they have not received the advisory or are in doubt, should contact the nearest FSS and ascertain whether the advisory is pertinent to their flights.
   Answer (A) is incorrect because the pilot should contact FSS directly, not wait for a broadcast. Answer (B) is incorrect because FSSs (not weather watch stations) disseminate weather information to pilots.

## 4.10  Surface Aviation Weather Reports

**84.**

**4205.** What is meant by the entry in the remarks section of this Surface Aviation Weather Report for BOI?

   BOI SA 1854 -X M7 OVC1 1/2R+F
   990/63/61/3205/980/RF2 RB12

A— Runway fog, visibility 2 miles; base of the rainclouds 1200 feet.
B— Rain and fog obscuring 2/10 of the sky; rain began 12 minutes before the hour.
C— Rain and fog obscuring 2/10 of the sky; rain began at 1812.

Answer (C) is correct (4205). *(AWS Sect 2)*
   When there is a partial obscuration of the sky, the remarks section reports the portion that is obscured in 10ths. Here, the remarks section reads "RF2 RB12." This means that rain and fog obscure 2/10ths of the sky. "RB12" means rain began 12 min. after the hour or 1812 since this was issued at 1854.
   Answer (A) is incorrect because RF stands for rain and fog, not runway fog, and RB stands for rain began, not base of rain clouds. Answer (B) is incorrect because the two digits following "RB" indicate min. after (not before) the hour.

**85.**

**4204.** What is the significance of the "F2" in the remarks portion of this Surface Aviation Weather Report for CLE?

CLE SP 1350-X E80 BKN 150 OVC 1GF
169/67/67/2105/003/R23LVV11/2 F2

A— The restriction to visibility is caused by fog and the prevailing visibility is 2 SM.
B— The partial obscuration is caused by fog and the visibility value is variable, 1 and ½ to 2 SM.
C— Fog is obscuring 2/10 of the sky.

Answer (C) is correct (4204). *(AWS Sect 2)*
   The remarks section reads "R23LVV11/2 F2." This means "runway 23 left, visibility value 1-1/2 SM, fog obscuring 2/10 of the sky."
   Answer (A) is incorrect because the prevailing visibility is 1½ SM, not 2 SM. Answer (B) is incorrect because the visibility value is 1½ SM and not variable. If it were variable, it would state 11/2 V2, not 11/2 F2.

**86.**
**4202.** A ceiling is defined as the height of the

A— highest layer of clouds or obscuring phenomena aloft that covers over 6/10 of the sky.
B— lowest layer of clouds that contributed to the overall overcast.
C— lowest layer of clouds or obscuring phenomena aloft that is reported as broken or overcast.

Answer (C) is correct (4202). *(AWS Sect 2)*
A ceiling is defined as the height of the lowest layer of clouds or obscuring phenomenon aloft that is reported as broken or overcast and not classified as thin.
Answer (A) is incorrect because the ceiling is the base of the lowest (not highest) layer of clouds. Answer (B) is incorrect because the lowest layer of clouds must be broken or overcast, not simply a contributor to the overall overcast.

**87.**
**4203.** The reporting station originating this Surface Aviation Weather Report has a field elevation of 1,000 feet. If the reported sky cover is one continuous layer, what is its thickness?

MDW RS 1856 M7 OVC11/2R+F 990/63/61/3205/980/...
UA.../SK OVC 65

A— 4,800 feet.
B— 5,000 feet.
C— 5,800 feet.

Answer (A) is correct (4203). *(AWS Sect 2)*
"UA.../SK OVC 65" in the remarks section indicates a pilot report stating the top of the overcast layer is 6,500 ft. MSL. Note that the base is a measured 700 ft. AGL and the surface is given as 1,000 ft. MSL. Accordingly, the sky cover base is 1,700 ft. MSL. Given the tops at 6,500 ft. MSL, the thickness is 4,800 ft. (6,500 − 1,700).
Answer (B) is incorrect because the airport elevation would have to be 800 ft. (not 1,000 ft.) for the sky cover to be 1,000 ft. thick. Answer (C) is incorrect because the height of the ceiling is 700 ft. AGL (not MSL).

**88.**
**4196.** The station originating the following weather report has a field elevation of 1,800 feet MSL. If the sky cover is one continuous layer, what is its thickness?

W8X1FK 174/74/73/0000/004/OVC/35

A— 900 feet.
B— 1,700 feet.
C— 2,700 feet.

Answer (A) is correct (4196). *(AWS Sect 2)*
"OVC/35" in the remarks section of the SA means the top of the overcast is 3,500 ft. MSL. "W8" indicates an indefinite ceiling of 800 ft. This means that the ceiling was determined by measuring vertical visibility into an obscured sky. Thus, the sky cover extends from 2,600 ft. MSL (1,800 ft. field elevation + 800 ft. ceiling) to 3,500 ft. MSL and is 900 ft. thick.
Answer (B) is incorrect because the ceiling is 800 ft. AGL (not at the surface). Answer (C) is incorrect because the ceiling is at 800 ft. AGL (not MSL).

**89.**
**4182.** What significant cloud coverage is reported by a pilot in this SA?

MOB...M9...OVC 2LF 131/44/43/3212/991/UA/OV
15NW MOB 1355/SK OVC 025/045 OVC 090

A— Three separate overcast layers exist with bases at 2,500, 7,500, and 13,500 feet.
B— The top of lower overcast is 2,500 feet; base and top of second overcast layer is 4,500 and 9,000 feet, respectively.
C— The base of second overcast layer is 2,500 feet; top of second overcast layer is 7,500 feet; base of third layer is 13,500 feet.

Answer (B) is correct (4182). *(AWS Sect 3)*
The pilot reports that the top of the first layer of overcast is 2,500 ft MSL. The base is a measured 900 ft. AGL. The base of the second layer is 4,500 with the top 9,000. Note that in a pilot report (UA), the base of the cloud coverage precedes the sky cover symbol, and the top of the coverage follows the sky coverage symbol.
Answer (A) is incorrect because the report does not mention 7,500 ft. or 13,500 ft. Answer (C) is incorrect because the report does not mention 7,500 ft. or 13,500 ft.

**90.**
**4220.** Interpret this PIREP.

UA/OVR MRB FL060/SK INTMTLY BL/TB MDT/RM R
TURBC INCRS WWD.

A— Ceiling 6,000 feet intermittently below moderate thundershowers; turbulence increasing westward.
B— FL 60,000, intermittently below clouds; moderate rain, turbulence increasing with the wind.
C— At 6,000 feet; intermittently between layers; moderate turbulence; moderate rain; turbulence increasing westward.

Answer (C) is the best answer (4220). *(AWS Sect 3)*
The PIREP reads over MRB at 6,000 ft. MSL; intermittently between layers; turbulence moderate; remarks: rain and turbulence increasing westward. (Note that rain is not actually described as moderate. Rather, it along with turbulence is increasing westward.)
Answer (A) is incorrect because the flight level (not the ceiling) is 6,000 ft., and TB MDT means moderate turbulence (not thundershowers). Answer (B) is incorrect because the flight level is 6,000 ft. (not 60,000 ft.), and BL means between layers (not below clouds).

**91.**
**4198.** Interpret the PIREP.

UA/OV 20S ATL 1620 FL050/TP BE 18/IC
MDT RIME ICE

A— 20 NM south of Atlanta at 1620Z, a pilot flying at 5,000 feet in a Beech 18 reported moderate rime ice.
B— 20 minutes after the hour snow began at Atlanta, wind 160° at 20 knots; a Beech 18 reported moderate rime ice at 5,000 feet.
C— Snow encountered at 2,000 feet over Atlanta at 1620Z; a Beech 18 encountered rime ice at 5,000 feet.

**Answer (A) is correct (4198).** *(AWS Sect 3)*
This PIREP reads "over 20 NM south of Atlanta at 1620Z at 5,000 ft. MSL a Beechcraft 18 reports moderate rime ice."
Answer (B) is incorrect because 20S ATL means 20 NM south of ATL (not 20 min. past the hour and snow) and 1620 means 1620Z (not wind direction and speed). Answer (C) is incorrect because 20S ATL means 20 NM south of ATL (not snow at 2,000 ft.)

## 4.11 Weather Depiction Charts

**92.**
**4208.** (Refer to figure 4 on page 110.) The Weather Depiction Chart indicates that the coastal sections of Texas and Louisiana are reporting

A— all ceilings at or above 20,000 feet with visibilities of 20 miles or more.
B— marginal VFR conditions due to broken ceilings of 2,000 feet.
C— VFR conditions with scattered clouds at 2,000 feet and higher cirroform.

**Answer (C) is correct (4208).** *(AWS Sect 6)*
On the coastal sections of Texas and Louisiana in Fig. 4, the small circles with one-quarter coverage mean scattered clouds. Some indicate 20, which means 2,000 ft., and others indicate 200 and 250, which means high cirrus (20,000 ft. and 25,000 ft.).
Answer (A) is incorrect because visibilities are shown not by numbers but by shaded areas, i.e., IFR, marginal VFR, and VFR. Answer (B) is incorrect because marginal VFR is a nonshaded outlined area. It does not appear in any of the mentioned coastal areas.

**93.**
**4207.** (Refer to figure 4 on page 110.) The Weather Depiction Chart indicates the heaviest precipitation along the front is occurring in

A— Missouri.
B— Illinois.
C— Kansas.

**Answer (B) is correct (4207).** *(AWS Sect 6)*
Along the front in Illinois in Fig. 4, there are a number of what appear to be Rs with an arrow on the leg, which indicate thunderstorms. Additionally, a single small dot means intermittent rain. Continuous rain is indicated by two dots located horizontally. The three dots in a triangular form that appear in central Illinois indicate continuous moderate rain.
Answer (A) is incorrect because Missouri has only one thunderstorm symbol and a couple of rain dots. Answer (C) is incorrect because Kansas contains no rain dots.

**94.**
**4206.** (Refer to figure 4 on page 110.) The Weather Depiction Chart indicates that northern Illinois and southern Wisconsin are reporting

A— marginal VFR conditions due to reduced visibility in drizzle and fog.
B— low IFR conditions due to ceilings below 500 feet with drizzle.
C— IFR conditions due to overcast ceilings less than 1,000 feet with reduced visibility in rain and rain showers.

**Answer (C) is correct (4206).** *(AWS Sect 6)*
In Fig. 4, northern Illinois and southern Wisconsin are in a shaded area, which means IFR. IFR, in contrast to MVFR or VFR, means ceilings less than 1,000 ft. and/or visibility less than 3 mi.
Answer (A) is incorrect because it is IFR, not marginal VFR. Also, drizzle is shown by apostrophes, and fog is shown by three horizontal lines, such as in southeast Iowa. Answer (B) is incorrect because, in southern Wisconsin, some of the ceilings are 700 ft. (not below 500 ft.).

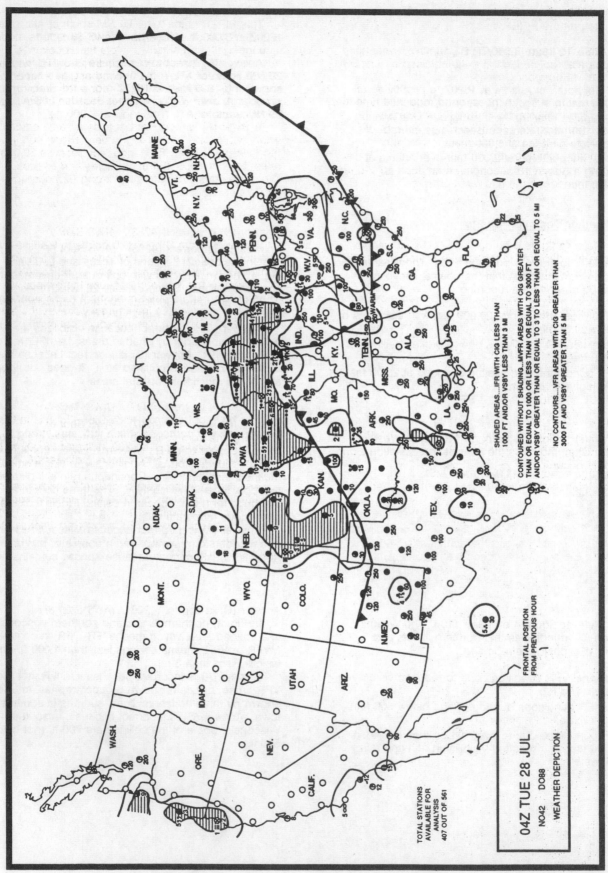

FIGURE 4.—Weather Depiction Chart.

## 4.12 Radar Summary Charts

**95.**
**4230.** (Refer to figure 8 on page 112.) What weather conditions are depicted in the area indicated by arrow A on the Radar Summary Chart?

A— Moderate to strong echoes; echo tops 30,000 feet MSL; line movement toward the northwest.
B— Weak to moderate echoes; average echo bases 30,000 feet MSL; cell movement toward the southeast; rain showers with thunder.
C— Strong to very strong echoes; echo tops 30,000 feet MSL; thunderstorms and rain showers.

**Answer (C) is correct (4230).** *(AWS Sect 7)*
On Fig. 8, find arrow A. Note that it points to a dot indicating the highest top in hundreds of feet, which is 30,000 ft. It lies within the second ring in a circuit, which makes it level 3 to 4, which is strong to very strong. The entire area is TRW-RW, which is thundershowers and rainshowers.
Answer (A) is incorrect because an area contained within two circles has strong to very strong echoes (not moderate). Answer (B) is incorrect because 30,000 ft. refers to echo tops, not echo bases and an area within two circles has strong to very strong (not near to moderate) echoes.

**96.**
**4233.** (Refer to figure 8 on page 112.) What weather conditions are depicted in the area indicated by arrow B on the Radar Summary Chart?

A— Weak echoes, heavy rain showers, area movement toward the southeast.
B— Weak to moderate echoes, rain showers increasing in intensity.
C— Strong echoes, moderate rain showers, no cell movement.

**Answer (B) is correct (4233).** *(AWS Sect 7)*
The arrow from B on Fig. 8 points to the first level of contours, which are weak to moderate echoes with rainshowers increasing in intensity as indicated by RW+.
Answer (A) is incorrect because the echoes are weak to moderate with the area movement to the northeast, not southeast. Answer (C) is incorrect because the echoes are weak to moderate (first contour), not strong.

**97.**
**4232.** (Refer to figure 8 on page 112.) What weather conditions are depicted in the area indicated by arrow C on the Radar Summary Chart?

A— Average echo bases 2,800 feet MSL, thundershowers, and intense to extreme echo intensity.
B— Cell movement toward the northwest at 20 knots, intense echoes, and echo bases 28,000 feet MSL.
C— Area movement toward the northeast at 20 knots, strong to very strong echoes, and echo tops 28,000 feet MSL.

**Answer (C) is correct (4232).** *(AWS Sect 7)*
The point of the arrow from C on Fig. 8 is in the second level of contours, which indicates strong to very strong echo intensity. The 280 indicates 28,000 ft. MSL tops. The arrow with two feathers indicates 20 kt. northeast movement.
Answer (A) is incorrect because 280 indicates tops of 28,000 MSL, not bases of 2,800 MSL and the second level of contours indicates strong to very strong (not intense) echoes. Answer (B) is incorrect because the second level of contours indicates strong to very strong (not intense) echoes.

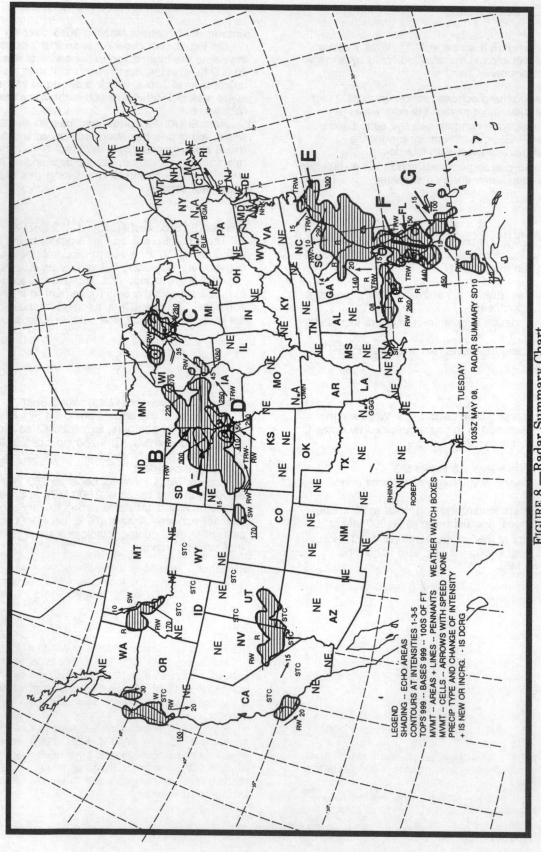

FIGURE 8.—Radar Summary Chart.

**98.**
**4231.** (Refer to figure 8 on page 112.) What weather conditions are depicted in the area indicated by arrow D on the Radar Summary Chart?

A— Echo tops 4,100 feet MSL, strong to very strong echoes within the smallest contour, and area movement toward the northeast at 50 knots.

B— Intense to extreme echoes within the smallest contour, echo tops 29,000 feet MSL, and cell movement toward the northeast at 50 knots.

C— Strong to very strong echoes within the smallest contour, echo bases 29,000 feet MSL, and cell in northeast Nebraska moving northeast at 50 knots.

**Answer (B) is correct (4231).** *(AWS Sect 7)*
The arrow extending from D in Fig. 8 is in the third contour, which means that the echo intensity is intense to extreme. The 290 indicates tops of 29,000 ft. MSL. The arrow with the 50 on top of it indicates movement to the northeast at 50 kt.
Answer (A) is incorrect because the 410 is for another area of echoes to the northeast of the D arrow, with tops of 41,000 ft. MSL (not 4,100 ft.). Answer (C) is incorrect because the tops, not bases, are 29,000 ft. MSL and the echoes are intense to extreme (not strong to very strong).

**99.**
**4234.** (Refer to figure 8 on page 112.) What weather conditions are depicted in the area indicated by arrow E on the Radar Summary Chart?

A— Highest echo tops 30,000 feet MSL, weak to moderate echoes, thunderstorms and rain showers, and cell movement toward northwest at 15 knots.

B— Echo bases 29,000 to 30,000 feet MSL, strong echoes, rain showers increasing in intensity, and area movement toward northwest at 15 knots.

C— Thundershowers decreasing in intensity; area movement toward northwest at 15 knots; echo bases 30,000 feet MSL.

**Answer (A) is correct (4234).** *(AWS Sect 7)*
The end of the arrow extending from E in Fig. 8 is in the first contour. Accordingly, the echoes are weak to moderate. The 300 indicates tops of 30,000 ft. MSL. The TRW indicates thunderstorms and rain showers. The arrow to the northwest with a 15 at the end indicates movement to the northwest at 15 kt.
Answer (B) is incorrect because the tops (not the bases) are 29,000 ft. MSL and the echoes are weak to moderate (not strong). Answer (C) is incorrect because the tops (not the bases) are 30,000 ft. MSL. Also, if thundershowers were decreasing in intensity, the TRW would have a minus (–) after it.

**100.**
**4237.** (Refer to figure 8 on page 112.) What weather conditions are depicted in the area indicated by arrow F on the Radar Summary Chart?

A— Line of echoes; thunderstorms; highest echo tops 46,000 feet MSL; no line movement indicated.

B— Echo bases vary from 15,000 feet to 46,000 feet MSL; thunderstorms increasing in intensity; line of echoes moving rapidly toward the north.

C— Line of severe thunderstorms moving from south to north; echo bases vary from 4,400 feet to 4,600 feet MSL; extreme echoes.

**Answer (A) is the best answer (4237).** *(AWS Sect 7)*
The solid line to which the arrow from F in Fig. 8 is pointing is a line of echoes. They are thunderstorms as indicated by TRW. The highest echo tops are 45,000 ft. MSL, which appears as 450. No movement of the line itself is indicated. Note: It appears that the FAA has not updated the highest echo top from the previous edition of the test.
Answer (B) is incorrect because the tops, not the bases, are approximately 46,000 ft. MSL. No movement or change in intensity is indicated. Answer (C) is incorrect because the tops are 44,000 to approximately 46,000 ft. MSL, not 4,400 to 4,600. No movement of the line is indicated.

**101.**
**4236.** (Refer to figure 8 on page 112.) What weather conditions are depicted in the area indicated by arrow G on the Radar Summary Chart?

A— Echo bases 10,000 feet MSL; cell movement toward northeast at 15 knots; weak to moderate echoes; rain.

B— Area movement toward northeast at 15 knots; rain decreasing in intensity; echo bases 1,000 feet MSL; strong echoes.

C— Strong to very strong echoes; area movement toward northeast at 15 knots; echo tops 10,000 feet MSL; light rain.

**Answer (A) is correct (4236).** *(AWS Sect 7)*
The arrow from G in Fig. 8 points to an area of echoes with bases of 10,000 ft. MSL moving to the northeast at 15 kt. Since the echoes are in the first level of contours, they are weak to moderate. The R indicates rain.
Answer (B) is incorrect because the bases are 10,000 ft. MSL, not 1,000 ft. MSL. Also, decreasing intensity would be indicated by a minus sign after the R. Answer (C) is incorrect because there is only one contour level, signifying weak to moderate intensity, not strong to very strong.

**102.**
**4174.** What important information is provided by the Radar Summary Chart that is not shown on other weather charts?

A— Lines and cells of hazardous thunderstorms.
B— Types of precipitation between reporting stations.
C— Areas of cloud cover and icing levels within the clouds.

Answer (A) is correct (4174). *(AWS Sect 7)*
The Radar Summary Chart shows lines of thunderstorms and hazardous cells that are not shown on other weather charts.
Answer (B) is incorrect because other weather charts show areas of precipitation. Answer (C) is incorrect because icing conditions cannot be detected by radar.

**103.**
**4235.** For the most effective use of the Radar Summary Chart during preflight planning, a pilot should

A— consult the chart to determine more accurate measurements of freezing levels, cloud cover, and wind conditions between reporting stations.
B— compare it with the charts, reports, and forecasts of a three-dimensional picture of clouds and precipitation.
C— utilize the chart as the only source of information regarding storms and hazardous conditions existing between reporting stations.

Answer (B) is correct (4235). *(AWS Sect 7)*
The Radar Summary Chart graphically indicates a collection of radar reports, i.e., reports of echoes from thunderstorms and heavy precipitation. In conjunction with the Weather Depiction Chart, which is a composite of Surface Aviation Weather Reports, the Radar Summary Chart provides a more three-dimensional picture of clouds and precipitation.
Answer (A) is incorrect because the Radar Summary Chart does not show freezing levels, cloud cover, or wind conditions. Answer (C) is incorrect because the Radar Summary Chart must be used in conjunction with other reports and forecasts for an accurate picture of weather conditions.

## 4.13 Terminal Forecasts

**104.**
**4228.** From which primary source should you obtain information regarding the weather expected to exist at your destination at your estimated time of arrival?

A— Weather Depiction Chart.
B— Radar Summary and Weather Depiction Chart.
C— Terminal Forecast.

Answer (C) is correct (4228). *(AWS Sect 4)*
A Terminal Forecast (FT) is a description of the surface weather expected to occur at an airport. It includes cloud heights and amounts, visibility, weather, and relative flight operations within 5 mi. of the center of the airport. Thus, an FT would provide expected weather for your arrival at another airport.
Answer (A) is incorrect because a Weather Depiction Chart provides a national (not local) report of current (not forecast) conditions. Answer (B) is incorrect because a Radar Summary Chart and a Weather Depiction Chart provide a national (not local) report of current (not forecast) conditions.

**105.**
**4179.** The word "wind" in the categorical outlook in the Terminal Forecast means that the wind during that period is forecast to be

A— 10 knots or stronger.
B— less than 25 knots.
C— 25 knots or stronger.

Answer (C) is correct (4179). *(AWS Sect 4)*
When WIND or WND appears in categorical outlooks of a Terminal Forecast, the wind is forecast to be 25 kt. or stronger.
Answer (A) is incorrect because "wind" means 25 kt. (not 10 kt.) or stronger. Answer (B) is incorrect because "wind" means 25 kt. or stronger (not less).

**106.**
**4180.** What expected windspeed is specifically implied at 2200Z by this Terminal Forecast for Memphis?

MEM 251010 C5 X 1/2F 1710 OCNL C0 X 1/2F.
16Z C25 BKN 11/2F 1720. 22Z 20 SCT. 00Z CLR.

A— Less than 6 knots.
B— Less than 10 knots.
C— Calm and variable.

Answer (A) is correct (4180). *(AWS Sect 4)*
By 2200Z, the forecast (22Z 2Ø SCT) is for 2,000 ft. scattered. There is no wind entry. When there is no wind entry, the wind is forecast to be less than 6 kt.
Answer (B) is incorrect because the absence of a wind entry in the FT means that the wind is forecast to be less than 6 kt. (not 10 kt.). Answer (C) is incorrect because the absence of a wind entry in the FT means that the wind is forecast to be less than 6 kt. (not calm and variable).

**107.**
**4178.** The absence of a visibility entry in a Terminal Forecast specifically implies that the surface visibility

A— exceeds 10 miles.
B— exceeds 6 miles.
C— is at least 15 miles in all directions from the center of the runway complex.

**Answer (B) is correct (4178).** *(AWS Sect 4)*
When a visibility entry in a Terminal Forecast is omitted, it means that visibility will be more than 6 SM.
Answer (A) is incorrect because the absence of a visibility entry in the FT means that the visibility is forecast to exceed 6 SM (not 10 SM). Answer (C) is incorrect because the absence of a visibility entry in the FT means that the visibility is forecast to exceed 6 SM (not 15 SM).

**108.**
**4177.** Omission of a wind entry in a Terminal Forecast specifically implies that the wind is expected to be less than

A— 5 knots.
B— 6 knots.
C— 8 knots.

**Answer (B) is correct (4177).** *(AWS Sect 4)*
Omission of a wind entry in a Terminal Forecast implies that the wind is expected to be less than 6 kt.
Answer (A) is incorrect because the absence of a wind entry in the FT means that the wind is forecast to be less than 6 kt. (not 5 kt.). Answer (C) is incorrect because the absence of a wind entry in the FT means that the wind is forecast to be less than 6 kt. (not 8 kt.).

**109.**
**4176.** Which primary source should be used to obtain forecast weather information at your destination for the planned ETA?

A— Area Forecast.
B— Radar Summary and Weather Depiction Charts.
C— Terminal Forecast.

**Answer (C) is correct (4176).** *(AWS Sect 4)*
A Terminal Forecast (FT) is a description of the surface weather expected to occur at an airport. The forecast includes cloud heights and amounts, visibility, weather, and relative flight operations within 5 mi. of the center of the airport. Thus, an FT would provide expected weather for your arrival at another airport.
Answer (A) is incorrect because an Area Forecast is for a multi-state section of the United States. It is not a forecast for a specific destination. Answer (B) is incorrect because Weather Depiction Charts and Radar Summary Charts are national weather maps. They provide current (not forecast) conditions.

**110.**
**4170.** The body of a Terminal Forecast covers a geographical area within

A— a 5-mile radius of the center of a runway complex.
B— 25 miles of the center of an airport.
C— 10 miles of the station originating the FT.

**Answer (A) is correct (4170).** *(AWS Sect 4)*
A Terminal Forecast (FT) is a description of the surface weather expected to occur at an airport. It includes cloud heights and amounts, visibility, weather, and wind relative to flight operations within 5 NM of the center of the runway complex. If the FT includes the word "vicinity" (VCNTY), it refers to a band from 5 NM to 25 NM surrounding the runway complex.
Answer (B) is incorrect because FTs are for an area with a 5-NM (not 25-NM) radius of a specific airport. Answer (C) is incorrect because FTs are for an area with a 5-NM (not 10-NM) radius of a specific airport.

## 4.14 Area Forecasts

**111.**
**4201.** What is the single source reference that contains information regarding frontal movement, turbulence, and icing conditions for a specific area?

A— Terminal Forecast.
B— Weather Depiction Chart.
C— Area Forecast.

**Answer (C) is correct (4201).** *(AWS Sect 4)*
An Area Forecast (FA) is a forecast of general weather conditions over an area the size of several states. It is used to determine en route weather. It includes information about frontal movement, turbulence, and icing conditions for a specific area.
Answer (A) is incorrect because a Terminal Forecast (FT) is the surface weather expected to occur at an airport and does not include information on frontal movement, turbulence, and icing conditions. Answer (B) is incorrect because a Weather Depiction Chart is a computer analysis of surface aviation reports that gives a broad overview of observed weather at the time of the chart and does not include information on turbulence or icing.

**112.**
**4175.** The section of the Area Forecast entitled "significant clouds and weather" contains a

A— summary of cloudiness and weather significant to flight operations broken down by states or other geographical areas.
B— summary of forecast sky cover, cloud tops, visibility, and obstructions to vision along specific routes.
C— statement of Airmen's Meteorological Information (AIRMET's) and Significant Meteorological Information (SIGMET) still in effect at the time of issue.

Answer (A) is correct (4175). *(AWS Sect 4)*
   The "significant clouds and weather" section of an Area Forecast (FA) contains a 12-hr. forecast of clouds and significant flight operations plus a 6-hr. categorical outlook. Surface visibility and obstructions to vision are included when the forecast visibility is 5 SM or less. Precipitation, thunderstorms, and sustained winds of 30 kt. or greater are always included. The breakdown may be by state or other geographical areas or in reference to location or movement of a pressure system or front.
   Answer (B) is incorrect because it describes TWEBs. Answer (C) is incorrect because AIRMETs and SIGMETs, i.e., adverse weather warnings, are found in the hazards/flight precautions section of an FA.

**113.**
**4186.** The section of the Area Forecast entitled "Hazards/Flight Precautions" contains

A— a 12-hour forecast that identifies and locates aviation weather hazards.
B— a statement listing those AIRMET's still in effect.
C— a summary of general weather conditions over several states.

Answer (A) is correct (4186). *(AWS Sect 4)*
   The hazards/flight precautions section of an Area Forecast identifies and locates aviation weather hazards which meet in-flight advisory criteria and thunderstorms that are forecast to be at least scattered in area coverage.
   Answer (B) is incorrect because AIRMETs are explained, not just listed by title. Answer (C) is incorrect because a summary of general weather conditions is in the significant clouds and weather section.

**114.**
**4185.** Which forecast provides specific information concerning expected sky cover, cloud tops, visibility, weather, and obstructions to vision in a route format?

A— DFW FA 131240.
B— MEM FT 132222.
C— 249 TWEB 252317.

Answer (C) is correct (4185). *(AWS Sect 4)*
   The TWEB Route Forecast provides information similar to that provided by an Area Forecast but in a route format.
   Answer (A) is incorrect because it is an Area Forecast, indicated by FA. Answer (B) is incorrect because it is a Terminal Forecast, as indicated by FT.

## 4.15  Winds and Temperatures Aloft Forecasts

**115.**
**4193.** (Refer to figure 2 on page 117.) What approximate wind direction, speed, and temperature (relative to ISA) should a pilot expect when planning for a flight over ALB at FL 270?

A— 270° magnetic at 97 knots; ISA –4 °C.
B— 260° true at 110 knots; ISA +5 °C.
C— 275° true at 97 knots; ISA +4 °C.

Answer (C) is correct (4193). *(AWS Sect 4)*
   For conditions at FL 270 over ALB in Fig. 2, you must interpolate between values at FL 240 and FL 300. First, decode the two given flight levels:

| | | | |
|---|---|---|---|
| FL 240 | = | 270° at | 77 kt. and –28°C |
| FL 300 | = | 280° at | 118 kt. and –42°C |
| Difference | = | 10° | 41 kt.    –14°C |

Interpolation for each value gives:

   FL 270  =  275° at   97 kt. and –35°C

Finally, note that the answer asks for ISA (standard temperature). At 2° per 1,000 ft., ISA would be 54°C (27 x 2) less than surface standard of 15°C. Thus, at FL 270, the standard temperature is 15° – 54° = –39°C. Thus the –35°C forecast temperature is ISA + 4°C.
   Answer (A) is incorrect because winds aloft are always given in true (not magnetic) direction. Answer (B) is incorrect because interpolating between 270° and 280° results in 275° (not 260°).

| VALID 141200Z FOR USE 0900-1500Z.  TEMPS NEG ABV 24000 | | | | | | | | |
| FT | 3000 | 6000 | 9000 | 12000 | 18000 | 24000 | 30000 | 34000 | 39000 |
| --- | --- | --- | --- | --- | --- | --- | --- | --- | --- |
| EMI | 2807 | 2715-07 | 2728-10 | 2842-13 | 2867-21 | 2891-30 | 751041 | 771150 | 780855 |
| ALB | 0210 | 9900-07 | 2714-09 | 2728-12 | 2656-19 | 2777-28 | 781842 | 760150 | 269658 |
| PSB | | 1509+04 | 2119+01 | 2233-04 | 2262-14 | 2368-26 | 781939 | 760850 | 780456 |
| STL | 2308 | 2613+02 | 2422-03 | 2431-08 | 2446-19 | 2461-30 | 760142 | 782650 | 760559 |

FIGURE 2.—Winds and Temperatures Aloft Forecast.

**116.**
**4192.** (Refer to figure 2 above.)  What approximate wind direction, speed, and temperature (relative to ISA) should a pilot expect when planning for a flight over PSB at FL 270?

A— 260° magnetic at 93 knots; ISA +7 °C.
B— 280° true at 113 knots; ISA +3 °C.
C— 255° true at 93 knots; ISA +6 °C.

Answer (C) is correct (4192).  *(AWS Sect 4)*
For conditions at FL 270 over PSB in Fig. 2, you must interpolate between values at FL 240 and FL 300.  First, decode the two given flight levels:

| FL 240 | = | 230° at | 68 kt. and | –26.0°C |
| FL 300 | = | 280° at | 119 kt. and | –39.0°C |
| Difference | = | 50° | 51 kt. | –13.0°C |

Interpolation for each value gives:

FL 270 = 255° at 93 kt. and –33°C

Finally, note that to compare the temperature to standard, subtract the lapse rate at FL 270 [(27,000/1,000) x 2° = 54°] from surface standard of 15°C to get FL 270 standard of –39°C.  The forecast temperature of about –33°C at FL 270 is thus 6°C warmer than standard.
Answer (A) is incorrect because winds aloft are always given in true (not magnetic) direction.  Answer (B) is incorrect because interpolating between 230° and 280° results in 255° (not 280°).

**117.**
**4194.** (Refer to figure 2 above.)  What approximate wind direction, speed, and temperature (relative to ISA) should a pilot expect when planning for a flight over EMI at FL 270?

A— 265° true; 100 knots; ISA +3 °C.
B— 270° true; 110 knots; ISA +5 °C.
C— 260° magnetic; 100 knots; ISA –5 °C.

Answer (A) is correct (4194).  *(AWS Sect 4)*
For conditions at FL 270 over EMI in Fig. 2, you must interpolate between values at FL 240 and FL 300.  First, decode the two given flight levels:

| FL 240 | = | 280° at | 91 kt. and | –30°C |
| FL 300 | = | 250° at | 110 kt. and | –41°C |
| Difference | = | 30° | 19 kt. | –11°C |

Interpolation for each value gives approximately

FL 270 = 265° at 100 kt. and –36°C

Finally, note that to compare the temperature to standard, subtract the lapse rate at FL 270 [(27,000/1,000) x 2° = 54°] from surface standard of 15°C to get FL 270 standard of –39°C.  The forecast temperature of about –36°C at FL 270 is thus 3°C warmer than standard.
Answer (B) is incorrect because interpolating between 250° and 280° results in 265° (not 270°).  Answer (C) is incorrect because winds aloft are given in true (not magnetic) direction.

**118.**
**4199.** A station is forecasting wind and temperature aloft at FL 390 to be 300° at 200 knots; temperature −54 °C. How would this data be encoded in the FD?

A— 300054.
B— 809954.
C— 309954.

Answer (B) is correct (4199). *(AWS Sect 4)*
At FL 390, a 300° wind at 200 kt. is encoded as 809954. Note that the first two digits are the direction. The second two digits are velocity. 200 kt. or greater wind speeds are coded as 99 for the speed and a 5 is added to the first digit of the direction. Here, the direction is 80 for 300°. The temperature is the last two digits, and minus signs are omitted above 24,000 ft. MSL.
Answer (A) is incorrect because it indicates winds from 300° at 0 kt. However, when forecast speed is less than 5 kt., the code is 9900 for wind direction and speed. Answer (C) is incorrect because it indicates a 99 kt. wind speed from 300°.

**119.**
**4095.** How much colder than standard temperature is the actual temperature at 9,000 feet, as indicated in the following excerpt from the Winds and Temperature Aloft Forecast?

| FT | 6000 | 9000 |
|----|------|------|
|    | 0737-04 | 1043-10 |

A— 3 °C.
B— 10 °C.
C— 7 °C.

Answer (C) is correct (4095). *(AWS Sect 4)*
At 9,000 ft., the forecast temperature is −10°C. Standard temperature is 15°C at sea level with a lapse rate of 2°C per 1,000 ft., which would bring the standard temperature to −3°C at 9,000 ft. (15° − 18°). Therefore, the forecast temperature of −10°C is 7° colder than the standard temperature of −3°C.
Answer (A) is incorrect because standard temperature at 9,000 ft. is −3°C (not −7°C). Answer (B) is incorrect because standard temperature at 9,000 ft. is −3°C (not 0°C).

**120.**
**4172.** What wind direction and speed is represented by the entry 9900+00 for 9,000 feet, on an Winds and Temperatures Aloft Forecast (FD)?

A— Light and variable; less than 5 knots.
B— Vortex winds exceeding 200 knots.
C— Light and variable; less than 10 knots.

Answer (A) is correct (4172). *(AWS Sect 4)*
The entry 9900 on a Winds and Temperatures Aloft Forecast indicates light and variable winds. +00 is the air temperature on the Celsius scale.
Answer (B) is incorrect because an example of the code for winds over 200 kt. would be 7099, for 200° at 199+ kt. Answer (C) is incorrect because light and variable means less than 5 kt. (not 10 kt.).

**121.**
**4189.** When is the wind-group at one of the forecast altitudes omitted at a specific location or station in the Winds and Temperatures Aloft Forecast (FD)? When the wind

A— is less than 5 knots.
B— is less than 10 knots.
C— at the altitude is within 1,500 feet of the station elevation.

Answer (C) is correct (4189). *(AWS Sect 4)*
No winds are forecast within 1,500 ft. of the station elevation. No temperatures are forecast for the 3,000-ft. MSL or for a level within 2,500 ft. of station elevation.
Answer (A) is incorrect because, when forecast wind speed is less than 5 kt., the code 9900 is used for direction and velocity. Answer (B) is incorrect because, when forecast wind speed is less than 5 kt. (not 10 kt.), the code 9900 is used for direction and velocity.

**122.**
**4188.** When is the temperature at one of the forecast altitudes omitted at a specific location or station in the Winds and Temperatures Aloft Forecast (FD)?

A— When the temperature is standard for that altitude.
B— For the 3,000-foot altitude (level) or when the level is within 2,500 feet of station elevation.
C— Only when the winds are omitted for that altitude (level).

Answer (B) is correct (4188). *(AWS Sect 4)*
No temperatures are forecast for the 3,000-ft. level or for a level within 2,500 ft. of station elevation. No winds are forecast within 1,500 ft. of the station elevation.
Answer (A) is incorrect because temperatures are reported whether standard or not. Answer (C) is incorrect because the winds are omitted within 1,500 ft. of the ground and temperatures are omitted within 2,500 ft. of the ground.

**123.**
**4190.** Decode the excerpt from the Winds and Temperature Aloft Forecast (FD) for OKC at 39,000 feet.

| FT | 3000 | 6000 | 39000 |
|---|---|---|---|
| OKC | | | 830558 |

A— Wind 130° at 50 knots, temperature –58 °C.
B— Wind 330° at 105 knots, temperature –58 °C.
C— Wind 330° at 205 knots, temperature –58 °C.

Answer (B) is correct (4190). *(AWS Sect 4)*
At OKC at 39,000 ft., the 83 for wind direction means that 100 kt. have been deducted from the wind speed and 50 added to the wind direction. Thus, the wind speed is 105 kt. Also, subtract 50 from the first two-digit code for direction to get 330°. Above 24,000 ft., the temperatures are always negative.
Answer (A) is incorrect because 130° at 50 kt. and –58°C would be 135058. Answer (C) is incorrect because 330° at 205 kt. and –58°C would be 839958.

**124.**
**4191.** Which values are used for winds aloft forecasts?

A— Magnetic direction and knots.
B— Magnetic direction and MPH.
C— True direction and knots.

Answer (C) is correct (4191). *(AWS Sect 4)*
Winds aloft are forecast in true direction and kt.
Answer (A) is incorrect because true (not magnetic) direction is used. Answer (B) is incorrect because true (not magnetic) direction and kt. (not MPH) are used.

## 4.16 Low-Level Prognostic Charts

**125.**
**4214.** A prognostic chart depicts the conditions

A— existing at the surface during the past 6 hours.
B— which presently exist from the 1,000-millibar through the 700-millibar level.
C— forecast to exist at a specific time in the future.

Answer (C) is correct (4214). *(AWS Sect 8)*
Prognostic charts show conditions as they are forecast to be at the valid time (UTC or Zulu) for the chart. The charts are issued four times daily.
Answer (A) is incorrect because prognostic charts relate to the future, not the past. Answer (B) is incorrect because prognostic charts relate to the future, not the present.

**126.**
**4213.** (Refer to figure 5 below.) What is the meaning of the symbol depicted as used on the U.S. Low-Level Significant Weather Prognostic Chart?

A— Showery precipitation (e.g. rain showers) embedded in an area of continuous rain covering half or more of the area.
B— Continuous precipitation (e.g. rain) covering half or more of the area.
C— Showery precipitation (e.g. thunderstorms/rain showers) covering half or more of the area.

Answer (A) is correct (4213). *(AWS Sect 8)*
The dot over the triangle in Fig. 5 indicates showery precipitation. The two heavy, solid dots indicate continuous rain. The shaded area indicates that more than one-half of the area is obscured.
Answer (B) is incorrect because the dot over the triangle indicates showery precipitation within the area of continuous precipitation. Answer (C) is incorrect because thunderstorms are indicated by an R with an arrow on the leg.

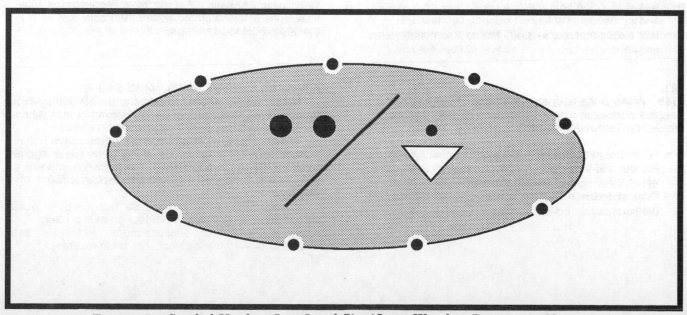

FIGURE 5.—Symbol Used on Low-Level Significant Weather Prognostic Chart.

**127.**
**4212.** Which meteorological conditions are depicted by a prognostic chart?

A— Conditions existing at the time of the observation.
B— Interpretation of weather conditions for geographical areas between reporting stations.
C— Conditions forecast to exist at a specific time shown on the chart.

Answer (C) is correct (4212). *(AWS Sect 8)*
    Prognostic charts show conditions as they are forecast to be at the valid time for the chart. The charts are issued four times daily.
    Answer (A) is incorrect because prognostic charts relate to the future, not the present. Answer (B) is incorrect because prognostic charts relate to the future, not the present.

**128.**
**4211.** The Low-Level Significant Weather Prognostic Chart depicts weather conditions

A— that are forecast to exist at a valid time shown on the chart.
B— as they existed at the time the chart was prepared.
C— that existed at the time shown on the chart which is about 3 hours before the chart is received.

Answer (A) is correct (4211). *(AWS Sect 8)*
    Prognostic charts show conditions as they are forecast to be at the valid time for the chart. The charts are issued four times daily.
    Answer (B) is incorrect because the Low-Level Prog Chart consists of 12- and 24-hr. forecasts. Answer (C) is incorrect because prognostic charts look to the future, they do not report the past.

**129.**
**4219.** (Refer to figure 6 on page 121.) The chart symbols over southern California on the 12-Hour Significant Weather Prognosis Chart indicate

A— expected top of moderate turbulent layer to be 12,000 feet MSL.
B— expected base of moderate turbulent layer to be 12,000 feet MSL.
C— light turbulence expected above 12,000 feet MSL.

Answer (A) is correct (4219). *(AWS Sect 8)*
    On the 12-Hour Significant Weather Prog (upper left of Fig. 6), the symbol ⌃ indicates moderate turbulence. The expected top and base of the turbulent layer appear above and below a short line in hundreds of feet MSL. Absence of a figure below the line (as here) indicates turbulence from the surface up. No figure above the line indicates turbulence extending above the upper limit of the chart. Thus, in southern California, moderate turbulence is expected from the surface up to 12,000 ft.
    Answer (B) is incorrect because 12,000 ft. is the top of the turbulence, not the base. Answer (C) is incorrect because the symbol shows moderate (not light) turbulence and it is below (not above) 12,000 ft. MSL.

**130.**
**4218.** (Refer to figure 6 on page 121.) The 12-Hour Significant Weather Prognosis Chart indicates that eastern Kentucky and eastern Tennessee can expect probable ceilings

A— less than 1,000 feet and/or visibility less than 3 miles.
B— less than 1,000 feet and/or visibility less than 3 miles, and moderate turbulence below 10,000 feet MSL.
C— less than 1,000 feet and/or visibility less than 3 miles, and moderate turbulence above 10,000 feet MSL.

Answer (A) is correct (4218). *(AWS Sect 8)*
    The 12-Hour Significant Weather Prog is on the upper left of Fig. 6. Eastern Kentucky and eastern Tennessee are enclosed in a solid line, which indicates IFR, i.e., ceiling less than 1,000 ft. and/or visibility less than 3 SM.
    Answer (B) is incorrect because no turbulence is indicated for eastern Kentucky and Tennessee on the 12-hr. prog. Answer (C) is incorrect because no turbulence is indicated for eastern Kentucky and Tennessee on the 12-hr. prog.

**131.**
**4217.** (Refer to figure 6 on page 121.) The 12-Hour Significant Weather Prognosis Chart indicates that West Virginia will likely experience

A— continuous or showery precipitation covering half or more of the area.
B— thunderstorms and rain showers covering half or more of the area.
C— continuous rain covering less than half of the area.

Answer (A) is correct (4217). *(AWS Sect 8)*
    Note the FAA incorrectly refers to the 12-hr. Significant Weather Prog Chart (upper panel) instead of the 12-hr. Surface Prog Chart (lower panel).
    The shaded area covering West Virginia on the 12-hr. Surface Prog Chart (lower left of Fig. 6) indicates 50% or more coverage. The two solid dots indicate continuous rain. The small dot over the triangle indicates rain showers.
    Answer (B) is incorrect because thunderstorms would be indicated by an R with an arrow on its front leg. Answer (C) is incorrect because more than half (not less than half) of the area is forecast to be in rain/rain showers.

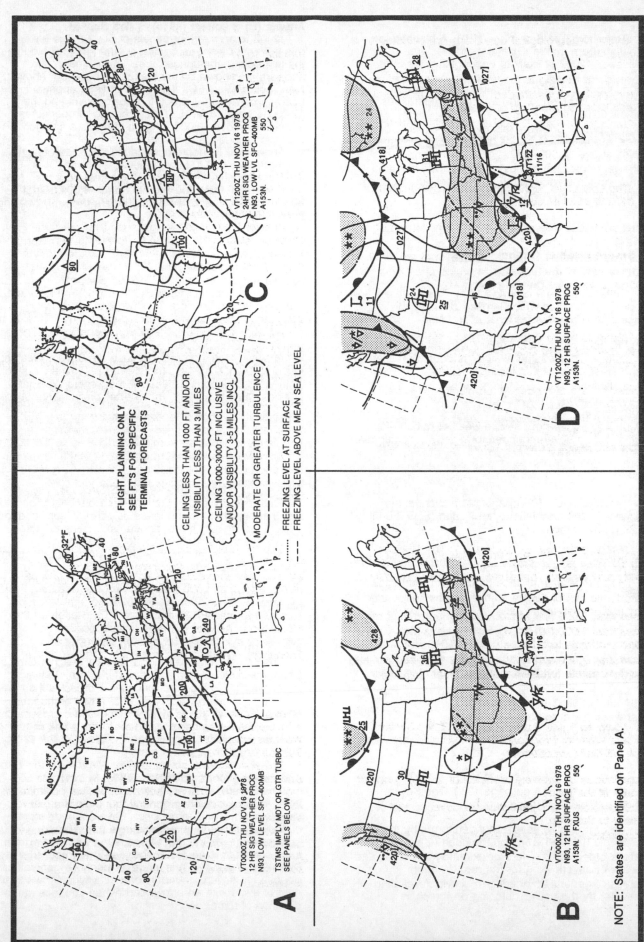

FLIGHT PLANNING ONLY
SEE FTS FOR SPECIFIC
TERMINAL FORECASTS

CEILING LESS THAN 1000 FT AND/OR
VISIBILITY LESS THAN 3 MILES

CEILING 1000-3000 FT INCLUSIVE
AND/OR VISIBILITY 3-5 MILES INCL

MODERATE OR GREATER TURBULENCE

FREEZING LEVEL AT SURFACE
FREEZING LEVEL ABOVE MEAN SEA LEVEL

FIGURE 6.—Low-Level Significant Prognostic Chart.

NOTE: States are identified on Panel A.

**132.**
**4216.** (Refer to figure 6 on page 121.) A planned low altitude flight from central Oklahoma to western Tennessee at 1200Z is likely to encounter

A— continuous or intermittent rain or rain showers, moderate turbulence, and freezing temperatures below 8,000 feet.

B— continuous or showery rain over half or more of the area, moderate turbulence, and freezing temperatures above 10,000 feet.

C— showery precipitation covering less than half the area, no turbulence below 18,000 feet, and freezing temperatures above 12,000 feet.

Answer (B) is correct (4216). *(AWS Sect 8)*
1200Z is on the right panels of Fig. 6. The lower panel (Panel D) shows continuous rain as indicated by the two dots in the shaded area. Additionally, rain showers are shown by the triangle with the dot above it. Now look on Panel C. The route of flight appears to be half-way between the 8,000-ft. freezing level and the 12,000-ft. freezing level. Thus, freezing temperatures should be above 10,000 ft. Also, there is a symbol indicating moderate turbulence.
Answer (A) is incorrect because the route of flight is south of the 8,000-ft. freezing level. Answer (C) is incorrect because the shading indicates more than 50% rain coverage, the turbulence is up to 18,000 ft., not above 18,000 ft., and temperatures are probably freezing above 10,000 ft.

## 4.17 Severe Weather Outlook Charts

**133.**
**4239.** (Refer to figure 9 on page 123.) The Severe Weather Outlook Chart which is used primarily for advance planning, provides what information?

A— An 18-hour categorical outlook with a 48-hour valid time for severe weather watch, thunderstorm lines, and areas of expected tornado activity.

B— A preliminary 12-hour outlook for severe thunderstorm activity and probable convective turbulence.

C— A preliminary 24-hour severe weather outlook for general and severe thunderstorm activity, tornadoes, and watch areas.

Answer (C) is correct (4239). *(AWS Sect 11)*
A Severe Weather Outlook Chart (AC) in Fig. 9 is a preliminary 24-hr. outlook for thunderstorm activity presented in two panels. The top panel covers the 12-hr. period from 12Z to 00Z; the bottom panel covers the remaining 12-hr. period.
Answer (A) is incorrect because the Severe Weather Outlook Chart is a 24-hr. (not 18-hr.) preliminary outlook. Answer (B) is incorrect because the Severe Weather Outlook Chart is a 24-hr. (not 12-hr.) preliminary outlook.

**134.**
**4240.** (Refer to figure 9 on page 123.) What is the significance of the annotations "MDT" and "SLGT" on the 00Z-12Z panel of the AC?

A— Moderate risk area, surrounded by a slight risk area, of possible severe turbulence.

B— Slight to moderate chance of low-level wind shear.

C— Moderate risk of severe thunderstorms surrounded by a slight risk area.

Answer (C) is correct (4240). *(AWS Sect 11)*
The Severe Weather Outlook area on the top panel in Fig. 9 shows that the moderate risk area is surrounded by a slight risk area. The moderate risk means 6-10% coverage and the slight risk is 2-5% coverage.
Answer (A) is incorrect because the chart depicts the risk of severe thunderstorms, not severe turbulence, per se. Answer (B) is incorrect because the chart depicts the risk of severe thunderstorms, not low-level wind shear, per se.

**135.**
**4248.** (Refer to figure 9 on page 123.) The crosshatched area on the Severe Weather Outlook Chart indicates

A— moderate risk of thunderstorms.

B— forecast risk of tornados.

C— forecast risk of heavy thunderstorms.

Answer (B) is correct (4248). *(AWS Sect 11)*
The crosshatched area on a Severe Weather Outlook Chart indicates an area that is under a tornado watch.
Answer (A) is incorrect because a crosshatched area indicates a tornado watch area (not a risk of thunderstorms). Answer (C) is incorrect because a crosshatched area indicates a tornado watch area (not a risk of thunderstorms).

**136.**
**4197.** (Refer to figure 9 on page 123.) The Severe Weather Outlook Chart depicts

A— areas of probable severe thunderstorms by the use of single hatched areas on the chart.

B— areas of forecast, severe or extreme turbulence, and areas of severe icing for the next 24 hours.

C— areas of general thunderstorm activity (excluding severe) by the use of hatching on the chart.

Answer (A) is correct (4197). *(AWS Sect 11)*
The Severe Weather Outlook Chart is a preliminary 24-hr. outlook depicting general thunderstorms, severe thunderstorms, and tornadoes. Severe thunderstorm outlook areas are marked by single hatching.
Answer (B) is incorrect because severe and extreme turbulence and icing are announced (not forecast) in SIGMETs. Answer (C) is incorrect because general, as opposed to severe, thunderstorm activity is shown to the right of a line with an arrowhead (when you face in the direction of the arrow).

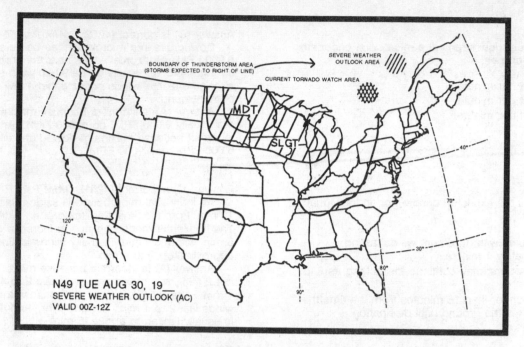

N49 TUE AUG 30, 19__
SEVERE WEATHER OUTLOOK (AC)
VALID 00Z-12Z

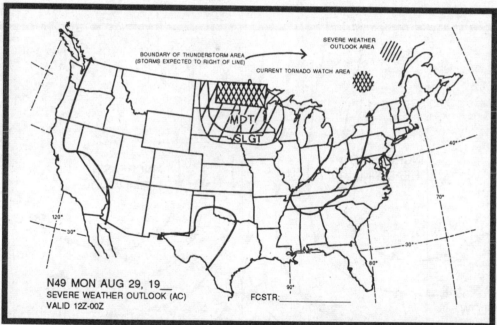

N49 MON AUG 29, 19__
SEVERE WEATHER OUTLOOK (AC)
VALID 12Z-00Z

FCSTR:_____

FIGURE 9.—Severe Weather Outlook Charts.

### 4.18 Microbursts

**137.**
**4253.** An aircraft that encounters a headwind of 45 knots, within a microburst, may expect a total shear across the microburst of

A— 40 knots.
B— 80 knots.
C— 90 knots.

Answer (C) is correct (4253). *(AIM Para 7-24)*

If a headwind in a microburst is 45 kt., the wind will be going in the opposite direction on the other side of the microburst at presumably the same 45 kt., resulting in a wind shear between the headwind and tailwind of 90 kt.

Answer (A) is incorrect because the total wind shear expected across a microburst is twice the initial headwind, e.g., 45 kt. x 2 = 90 kt. (not 40 kt.). Answer (B) is incorrect because the total wind shear expected across a microburst is twice the initial headwind, e.g., 45 kt. x 2 = 90 kt. (not 80 kt.).

**138.**
**4252.** Maximum downdrafts in a microburst encounter may be as strong as

A— 8,000 feet per minute.
B— 7,000 feet per minute.
C— 6,000 feet per minute.

Answer (C) is correct (4252).  *(AIM Para 7-24)*
    Downdrafts in a microburst can be as strong as 6,000 FPM.  Horizontal winds near the surface can be as strong as 45 kt., resulting in a 90-kt. wind shear.  The strong horizontal winds occur within a few hundred feet of the ground.
    Answer (A) is incorrect because maximum downdrafts are usually 6,000 FPM, not 8,000 FPM.  Answer (B) is incorrect because maximum downdrafts are usually 6,000 FPM, not 7,000 FPM.

**139.**
**4251.** What is the expected duration of an individual microburst?

A— Two minutes with maximum winds lasting approximately 1 minute.
B— One microburst may continue for as long as 2 to 4 hours.
C— Seldom longer than 15 minutes from the time the burst strikes the ground until dissipation.

Answer (C) is correct (4251).  *(AIM Para 7-24)*
    An individual microburst will seldom last longer than 15 min. from the time it strikes ground until dissipation.  The horizontal winds continue to increase during the first 5 min. with maximum intensity winds lasting approximately 2 to 4 min.
    Answer (A) is incorrect because microbursts last 15, not 2 min., and maximum winds last 2 to 4 min., not 1 min.  Answer (B) is incorrect because the maximum winds last 2 to 4 min., not 2 to 4 hr., and the microburst is usually limited to about 15 min.

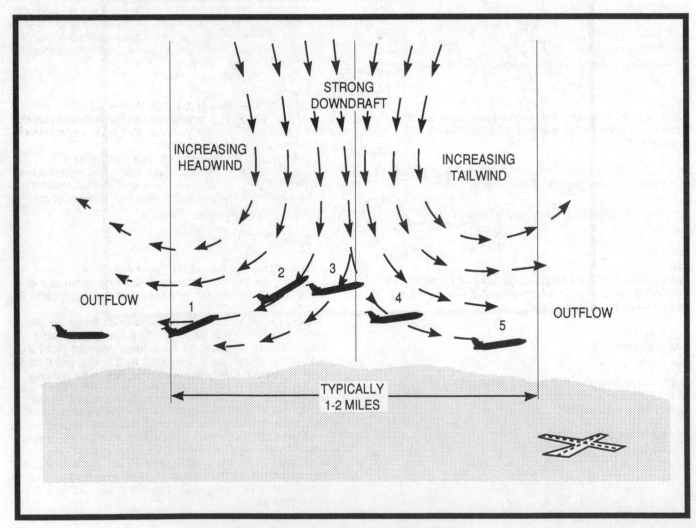

FIGURE 13.—Microburst Section Chart.

**140.**
**4255.** (Refer to figure 13 on page 124.) When penetrating a microburst, which aircraft will experience an increase in performance without a change in pitch or power?

A— 3.
B— 2.
C— 1.

Answer (C) is correct (4255). *(AIM Para 7-24)*
Refer to Fig. 13 and note that as airplane at point 1 approaches the microburst it will experience an increasing headwind and increasing performance.
Answer (A) is incorrect because at point 3 the airplane is experiencing a strong downdraft. Answer (B) is incorrect because at point 2 the airplane is experiencing a decreasing headwind component.

**141.**
**4256.** (Refer to figure 13 on page 124.) The aircraft in position 3 will experience which effect in a microburst encounter?

A— Decreasing headwind.
B— Increasing tailwind.
C— Strong downdraft.

Answer (C) is correct (4256). *(AIM Para 7-24)*
At point 3 in Fig. 13 the airplane is experiencing a strong downdraft as it is approaching the center of the microburst.
Answer (A) is incorrect because at point 2, not 3, the airplane encounters decreasing headwind. Answer (B) is incorrect because at point 5 the airplane encounters an increasing tailwind and it may result in an extreme situation as pictured, i.e., just before impact.

**142.**
**4257.** (Refer to figure 13 on page 124.) What effect will a microburst encounter have upon the aircraft in position 4?

A— Strong tailwind.
B— Strong updraft.
C— Significant performance increase.

Answer (A) is correct (4257). *(AIM Para 7-24)*
At point 4 in Fig. 13 the airplane is encountering a strong tailwind in addition to a strong downdraft.
Answer (B) is incorrect because there are no updrafts in microbursts, only downdrafts. Answer (C) is incorrect because the significance in performance increase occurs at point 1 (not 4) where there is an increase in headwind.

**143.**
**4258.** (Refer to figure 13 on page 124.) How will the aircraft in position 4 be affected by a microburst encounter?

A— Performance increasing with a tailwind and updraft.
B— Performance decreasing with a tailwind and downdraft.
C— Performance decreasing with a headwind and downdraft.

Answer (B) is correct (4258). *(AIM Para 7-24)*
In Fig. 13, point 4 represents decreased performance as a result of both the windshear shift from a headwind to a tailwind and a strong downdraft.
Answer (A) is incorrect because performance decreases at point 4 due to the tailwind and also there is a downdraft, not an updraft. Answer (C) is incorrect because the performance decreases as a result of the tailwind, not headwind.

**144.**
**4254.** (Refer to figure 13 on page 124.) If involved in a microburst encounter, in which aircraft positions will the most severe downdraft occur?

A— 4 and 5.
B— 2 and 3.
C— 3 and 4.

Answer (C) is correct (4254). *(AIM Para 7-24)*
In Fig. 13, the most severe downdrafts occur at the center of the microburst, which are indicated by points 3 and 4.
Answer (A) is incorrect because point 5 has significantly less downdraft even though it has considerably more tailwind. Answer (B) is incorrect because point 2 has not so significant a downdraft as 3 and 4, but it contains significant headwind even though it is decreasing.

## 4.19 Other Weather Charts

**145.**
**4184.** A pilot planning to depart at 1100Z on an IFR flight is particularly concerned about the hazard of icing. What sources reflect the most accurate information on icing conditions (current and forecast) at the time of departure?

A— Low-Level Significant Weather Prognostic Chart, and the Area Forecast.
B— The Area Forecast, and the Freezing Level Chart.
C— Pilot weather reports (PIREP's), AIRMET's, and SIGMET's.

Answer (C) is correct (4184). *(AWS Sect 4)*
The most accurate information on icing would be in PIREPs, AIRMETs, and SIGMETs. AIRMETs are issued for moderate icing and SIGMETs for severe icing. PIREPS in the vicinity of a planned route are also useful to determine icing hazards.
Answer (A) is incorrect because Low Level Prog Charts are not issued for icing hazards. Answer (B) is incorrect because, while FAs and Freezing Level Charts provide information about general icing forecasts, AIRMETs and SIGMETs are more specific and PIREPs are the most accurate of all.

**146.**
**4195.** What flight planning information can a pilot derive from constant pressure charts?

A— Clear air turbulence and icing conditions.
B— Levels of widespread cloud coverage.
C— Winds and temperatures aloft.

Answer (C) is correct (4195). *(AWS Sect 12)*
Constant Pressure Charts provide information about the observed temperature, wind, and temperature/dew point spread along your proposed route.
Answer (A) is incorrect because clear air turbulence is shown on the Low-Level Prog Chart. Answer (B) is incorrect because areas and levels of widespread cloud coverage are shown on the Weather Depiction and Surface Analysis charts.

**147.**
**4173.** What conclusion(s) can be drawn from a 500-millibar Constant Pressure Chart for a planned flight at FL 180?

A— Winds aloft at FL 180 generally flow across the height contours.
B— Observed temperature, wind, and temperature/dewpoint spread along the proposed route can be approximated.
C— Upper highs, lows, troughs, and ridges will be depicted by the use of lines of equal pressure.

Answer (B) is correct (4173). *(AWS Sect 12)*
A Constant Pressure Chart is an upper-air weather map which includes information on wind direction, height of constant pressure, temperature, and temperature/dew point spread.
Answer (A) is incorrect because the winds usually flow parallel to the height contours. Answer (C) is incorrect because heights of the specified pressure for each station are depicted via solid lines called contours to give a height pattern. The contours depict high height centers and low height centers, not highs and lows.

**148.**
**4226.** Which weather forecast describes prospects for an area coverage of both severe and general thunderstorms during the following 24 hours?

A— Terminal Forecast.
B— Convective outlook.
C— Severe Weather Watch Bulletin.

Answer (B) is correct (4226). *(AWS Sect 4)*
The Convective Outlook (AC) describes the prospects for general thunderstorm activity during the following 24 hr. Areas with a high, moderate, or a slight risk of severe thunderstorms are included, as well as areas where thunderstorms may approach severe limits.
Answer (A) is incorrect because a Terminal Forecast is for a 5-NM radius area around a specific airport. Answer (C) is incorrect because a Severe Weather Watch Bulletin defines areas of possible severe thunderstorms and tornado activity in one region.

**149.**
**4209.** The Surface Analysis Chart depicts

A— actual pressure systems, frontal locations, cloud tops, and precipitation at the time shown on the chart.
B— frontal locations and expected movement, pressure centers, cloud coverage, and obstructions to vision at the time of chart transmission.
C— actual frontal positions, pressure patterns, temperature, dewpoint, wind, weather, and obstructions to vision at the valid time of the chart.

**150.**
**4215.** What information is provided by a Convective Outlook (AC)?

A— It describes areas of probable severe icing and severe or extreme turbulence during the next 24 hours.
B— It provides prospects of both general and severe thunderstorm activity during the following 24 hours.
C— It indicates areas of probable convective turbulence and the extent of instability in the upper atmosphere (above 500 MB).

## 4.20 Tropopause Data Charts

**151.**
**4225.** (Refer to figure 7 on page 129.) What information is indicated by arrow A?

A— The height of the tropopause in meters above sea level.
B— The height of the existing layer of CAT.
C— The height of the tropopause in hundreds of feet above MSL.

**152.**
**4223.** (Refer to figure 7 on page 129.) What weather conditions are depicted within the area indicated by arrow C?

A— Severe CAT forecast within the area outlined by dashes from 32,000 feet MSL to below the lower limit of the chart.
B— Moderate turbulence at FL 320 within the area outlined by dashes.
C— Moderate to severe CAT has been reported at FL 320.

Answer (C) is correct (4209). *(AWS Sect 5)*
The Surface Analysis Chart provides the locations of pressure systems, dew points, wind, and obstructions to vision at the valid time of the chart.
Answer (A) is incorrect because the Surface Analysis Chart does not depict cloud tops. Answer (B) is incorrect because expected movement of weather systems is not depicted. This chart depicts current conditions at the time of issuance.

Answer (B) is correct (4215). *(AWS Sect 4)*
The Convective Outlook describes the prospects for general thunderstorm activity during the following 24 hr. Areas with a high, moderate, or a slight risk of severe thunderstorms are included, as well as areas where thunderstorms may approach severe limits.
Answer (A) is incorrect because severe icing and severe or extreme turbulence are the subjects of SIGMETs. Answer (C) is incorrect because it describes a 500 mb Constant Pressure Analysis Chart.

Answer (C) is correct (4225). *(AWS Sect 8)*
On the High Level Significant Prog Chart, Fig. 7, tropopause heights are depicted in rectangular boxes in hundreds of feet MSL, i.e., 240, 300, 340, 390, 450, and 530. As you look at the map you can see how the tropopause height varies around the center.
Answer (A) is incorrect because the height is in hundreds of feet, not meters. Answer (B) is incorrect because areas of clear air turbulence (CAT) are bounded by heavy dashed lines.

Answer (A) is correct (4223). *(AWS Sect 8)*
On the High Level Significant Prog Chart, the arrow from C on Fig. 7 points to information that belongs in the dashed area consisting primarily of Arizona and New Mexico. It indicates that severe turbulence is forecast from below FL 240 to FL 320.
Answer (B) is incorrect because the symbol indicates turbulence. The extra "hat" indicates that the turbulence is severe. Answer (C) is incorrect because only the symbol for severe turbulence (not CAT) is used for the vertical area from below FL 240 to FL 320.

**153.**
**4224.** (Refer to figure 7 on page 129.) What weather conditions are depicted within the area indicated by arrow B?

A— Light to moderate turbulence at and above 33,000 feet MSL.
B— Moderate to severe turbulence from below 24,000 feet MSL to 33,000 feet MSL.
C— Moderate to severe CAT is forecast to exist at FL 330.

Answer (B) is correct (4224). *(AWS Sect 8)*
On the High Level Significant Prog Chart, the arrow from B on Fig. 7 refers to an area bounded by heavy dashed lines, which means clear air turbulence (CAT). The designation ⋀ to ⋀ means moderate to severe. The XXX beneath the line means the base is below FL 240 (the lower limit of all High-Level Progs), and the 330 means the top of the forecast CAT, FL 300.
Answer (A) is incorrect because the turbulence is moderate to severe, not light to moderate. Answer (C) is incorrect because CAT is forecast from below FL 240 to FL 330. The high level significant weather prog is for 24,000 ft. MSL to 63,000 ft. MSL.

**154.**
**4222.** (Refer to figure 7 on page 129.) What weather conditions are depicted within the area indicated by arrow D?

A— Existing isolated cumulonimbus, tops above 41,000 feet and less than one-fifth coverage.
B— Forecast isolated embedded cumulonimbus, bases below 24,000 feet MSL, tops at 41,000 feet MSL and less than one-eighth coverage.
C— Forecast isolated thunderstorms, tops at FL 410, less than two-fifths coverage.

Answer (B) is correct (4222). *(AWS Sect 8)*
The arrow from D on Fig. 7 points to an area depicting thunderstorms and cumulonimbus clouds (CB). They are isolated (which means less than one-eighth coverage), but they are embedded from below FL 240 to FL 410.
Answer (A) is incorrect because this chart gives forecast (not existing) weather, the cumulonimbus clouds are embedded, and there is less than one-eighth coverage. Answer (C) is incorrect because the cumulonimbus clouds are embedded and there is less than one-eighth coverage.

**155.**
**4221.** (Refer to figure 7 on page 129.) What weather conditions are depicted within the area indicated by arrow E?

A— Frequent embedded thunderstorms, less than one-eighth coverage, tops at FL 370.
B— Frequent lightning in thunderstorms at FL 370.
C— Frequent cumulonimbus, five-eighths to eight-eighths coverage, bases below 24,000 feet MSL and tops at 37,000 feet MSL.

Answer (C) is correct (4221). *(AWS Sect 8)*
The arrow from E on Fig. 7 points to an area indicating frequent (FRQ), i.e., 5/8 to 8/8 coverage of cumulonimbus and thunderstorms. They are from below FL 240 to FL 370.
Answer (A) is incorrect because the thunderstorms are not embedded. Also, there is 5/8 to 8/8 area coverage (FRQ). Answer (B) is incorrect because the High-Level Prog does not indicate lightning.

**156.**
**4229.** (Refer to figure 7 on page 129.) What weather conditions are depicted within the area indicated by arrow F?

A— Two-eighths to six-eighths coverage, occasional embedded thunderstorms, tops at FL 510.
B— One-eighth to four-eighths coverage, occasional embedded thunderstorms, maximum tops at 51,000 feet MSL.
C— Occasionally embedded cumulonimbus, bases from 18,000 feet to 51,000 feet.

Answer (B) is correct (4229). *(AWS Sect 8)*
The scalloped area (on Fig. 7) to which the arrow from F points shows occasional (1/8 to 4/8) embedded cumulonimbus from below 24,000 ft. MSL to 51,000 ft. MSL.
Answer (A) is incorrect because the coverage codes range includes ISOL (to 1/8), OCNL (1/8 to 4/8), and FRQ (5/8 to 8/8), not 2/8 to 6/8. Answer (C) is incorrect because the High Level Significant Weather Prog is limited to 24,000 ft. MSL and up, and the cumulonimbus bases are frequent, not occasional.

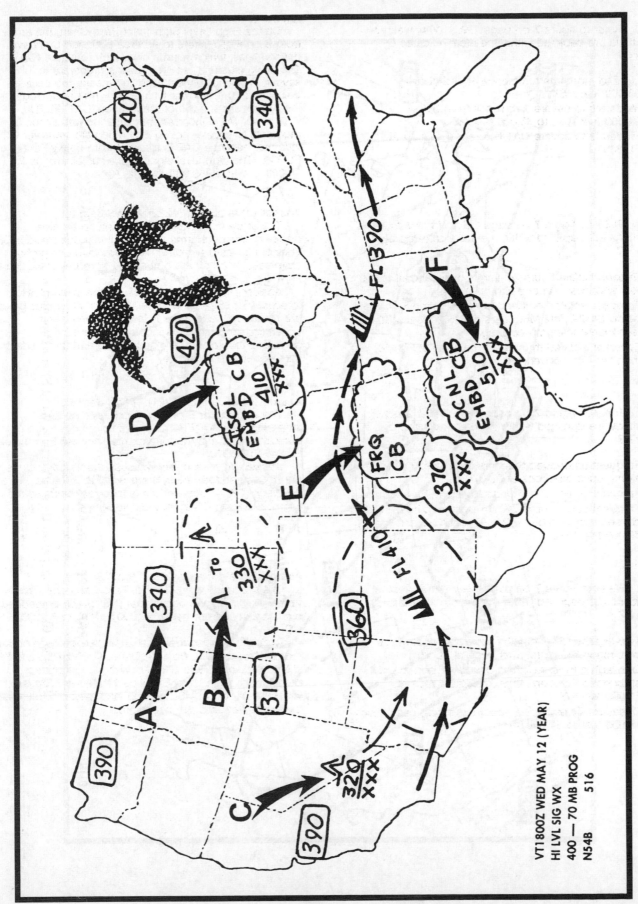

FIGURE 7.—High-Level Significant Weather Prognostic Chart.

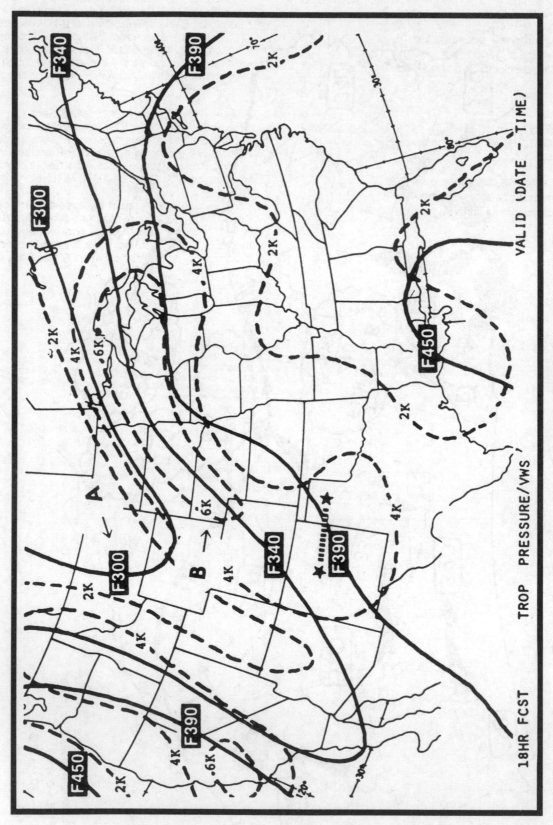

FIGURE 10. —Tropopause Height/Vertical Wind Shear Prognostic Chart.

**157.**
**4245.** (Refer to figure 10 on page 130.) The reference to 6K (see arrow B) indicates

A— vertical wind shear per 1,000 feet.
B— wind velocity at 34,000 feet.
C— vertical wind velocity at 34,000 feet.

**158.**
**4242.** (Refer to figure 10 on page 130.) The symbol on the TROP.WIND SHEAR PROG indicated by arrow A represents the

A— wind direction at the tropopause (300°).
B— FL of the tropopause.
C— height of maximum wind shear (30,000 feet).

Answer (A) is correct (4245). *(AWS Sect 13)*
See Fig. 10. The Tropopause Height/Vertical Wind Shear Prog Chart depicts vertical wind shear in kt. per 1,000 ft. by using dashed lines at 2-kt. intervals.
Answer (B) is incorrect because the Tropopause Height/Vertical Wind Shear Prog Chart depicts vertical wind not horizontal wind. Answer (C) is incorrect because wind shear, not wind velocity, is reported.

Answer (B) is correct (4242). *(AWS Sect 13)*
See Fig. 10. Solid lines trace intersections of the tropopause with standard constant pressure surfaces. Heights are preceded by the letter F and are in hundreds of feet. Thus, "F300" indicates the height of the tropopause is FL 300 (30,000 ft. MSL) along that solid line.
Answer (A) is incorrect because the Tropopause Wind Prog Chart (this is the Trop Wind Shear Prog) depicts wind direction. Answer (C) is incorrect because the height of maximum wind shear is not identified on the Tropopause Height/Vertical Wind Shear Prog Chart.

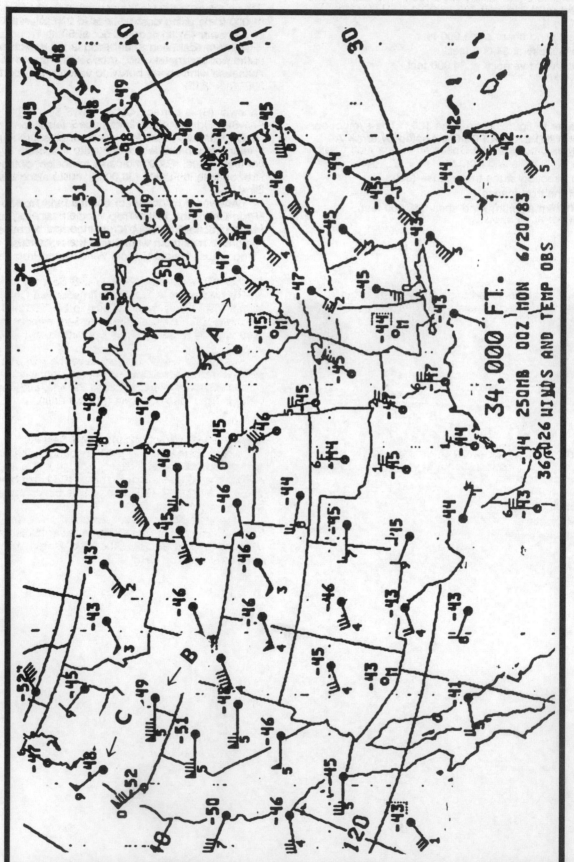

FIGURE 12.—Observed Winds Aloft for 34,000 Feet.

**159.**
**4246.** (Refer to figure 12 on page 132.) What is the approximate wind direction and velocity at 34,000 feet (see arrow C)?

A— 290°/50 knots.
B— 330°/50 knots.
C— 090°/48 knots.

Answer (A) is correct (4246). *(AWS Sect 13)*
Refer to arrow C in Fig. 12 (in Oregon) for Portland. The line is from the Northwest with a 9 next to it which means 290°. On the line is a solid triangle which means 50 kt. So the wind is from 290° at 50 kt.
Answer (B) is incorrect because the 9 next to a northwest line means 290° (not 330°). Answer (C) is incorrect because the 9 next to a northwest line means 290° (not 090°).

**160.**
**4247.** (Refer to figure 12 on page 132.) The wind direction and velocity on the Observed Winds Aloft Chart (see arrow A) is indicated from the

A— northeast at 35 knots.
B— northwest at 47 knots.
C— southwest at 35 knots.

Answer (C) is correct (4247). *(AWS Sect 13)*
Refer to arrow A in Fig. 12 (in southern Ohio). A line from the southwest with a 3 next to it = 230°. On the line are three 10-kt. symbols and one 5-kt. symbol indicating wind velocity of 35 kt. Thus the wind is from 230° at 35 kt.
Answer (A) is incorrect because the line, and thus the wind, is from the southwest (not the northeast). Answer (B) is incorrect because the line, and thus the wind, is from the southwest (not the northwest).

**161.**
**4249.** (Refer to figure 12 on page 132.) What is the approximate wind direction and velocity at CVG at 34,000 feet (see arrow A)?

A— 040°/35 knots.
B— 097°/40 knots.
C— 230°/35 knots.

Answer (C) is correct (4249). *(AWS Sect 13)*
Refer to arrow A in Fig. 12 (in southern Ohio). A line from the southwest with a 3 next to it = 230°. On the line are three 10-kt. symbols and one 5-kt. symbol indicating wind velocity of 35 kt. Thus the wind is from 230° at 35 kt.
Answer (A) is incorrect because the line, and thus the wind, is from the southwest (not the northeast). Answer (B) is incorrect because the line, and thus the wind, is from the southwest (not the east).

**162.**
**4250.** (Refer to figure 12, arrow B, on page 132.) What is the approximate wind direction and velocity at BOI (see arrow B)?

A— 270°/55 knots.
B— 250°/95 knots.
C— 080°/95 knots.

Answer (B) is correct (4250). *(AWS Sect 13)*
Refer to arrow B in Fig. 12 (in Idaho). The line plotted is from the southwest with a 5 by it, thus it is 250°. Adding the 50-kt. symbol with four 10-kt. symbols and one 5-kt. symbol the wind velocity is 95 kt. Thus the wind is from 250° at 95 kt.
Answer (A) is incorrect because the line has a 5 next to it, indicating 250° (not 270°). Answer (C) is incorrect because the line, and thus the wind, is from the southwest (not the east).

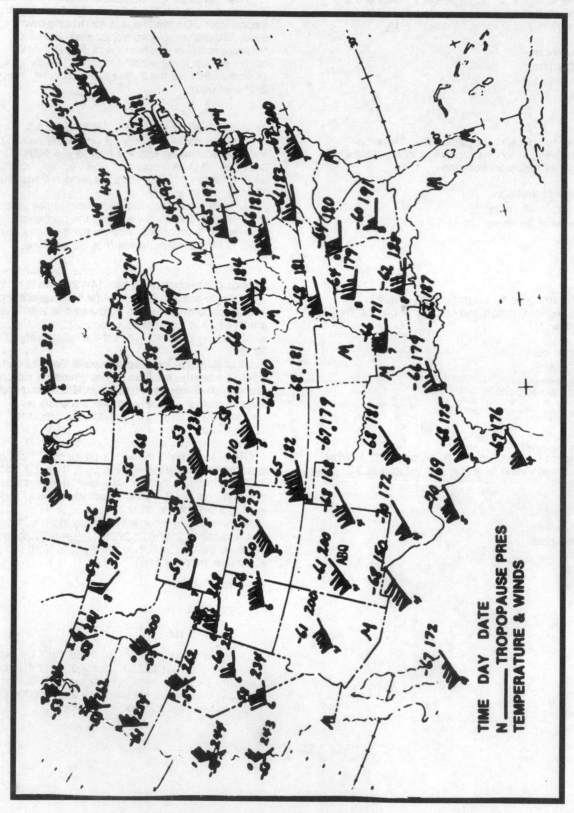

FIGURE 11.—Tropopause Pressure Temperature and Winds.

**163.**
**4243.** (Refer to figure 11 on page 134.) What is the pressure in millibars on the tropopause pressure, temperature, and winds chart for ABQ?

A— 150.
B— 172.
C— 200.

Answer (C) is correct (4243). *(AWS Sect 13)*
Refer to Fig. 11, Tropopause Pressure, Temperature, and Winds. The plotted data for ABQ (Albuquerque) is tropopause wind, 240° at 115 kt.; tropopause temperature, –61°C; and tropopause pressure 200 millibars.

Temp. in Celsius          Pressure in Millibars
     -61                            200
                                        ABQ

4  Wind Direction (out of the range
    180° to 270° the 4 means 240°)

= 50 kts

= 10 kts

= 5 kts

Answer (A) is incorrect because the pressure, indicated on the non-feathered end of the line, is 200 (not 150). Answer (B) is incorrect because the pressure, indicated on the non-feathered end of the line, is 200 (not 172).

**164.**
**4244.** (Refer to figure 11 on page 134.) What is the approximate wind direction and velocity at ABQ?

A— 220°/200 knots.
B— 060°/61 knots.
C— 240°/115 knots.

Answer (C) is correct (4244). *(AWS Sect 13)*
Refer to Fig. 11, Tropopause Pressure, Temperature, and Winds. The plotted data for ABQ (Albuquerque) is tropopause wind, 240° at 115 kt.; tropopause temperature, –61°C; and tropopause pressure 200 millibars.

Temp. in Celsius          Pressure in Millibars
     -61                            200
                                        ABQ

4  Wind Direction (out of the range
    180° to 270° the 4 means 240°)

= 50 kts

= 10 kts

= 5 kts

Answer (A) is incorrect because the 4 by the feathered end means 240° (not 220°) and the 200 means pressure (not wind velocity). Answer (B) is incorrect because the wind is shown to be 240° (not 060°) and –61 refers to temperature (not wind velocity).

# END OF CHAPTER

# CHAPTER FIVE
# FEDERAL AVIATION REGULATIONS

This chapter contains outlines of major concepts tested, all FAA test questions and answers regarding Federal Aviation Regulations (FARs), and an explanation of each answer. The subtopics or modules within this chapter are listed above, followed in parentheses by the number of questions from the FAA written test pertaining to that particular module. The two numbers following the parentheses are the page numbers on which the outline and questions begin for that module.

On September 16, 1993, the U.S. airspace was reclassified to conform with the International Civil Aviation Organization (ICAO) standards.

1. Class A -- formerly known as the PCA
2. Class B -- formerly known as a TCA
3. Class C -- formerly known as an ARSA
4. Class D -- formerly known as an Airport Traffic Area and Control Zone
5. Class E -- formerly known as general controlled airspace and the Continental Control Area
6. Class G -- formerly known as uncontrolled airspace

**CAUTION:** Recall that the **sole purpose** of this book is to expedite your passing the FAA written test for the instrument rating. Accordingly, all extraneous material (i.e., topics or regulations not directly tested on the FAA written test) is omitted, even though much more information and knowledge are necessary to fly safely. This additional material is presented in *Instrument Pilot FAA Practical Test Prep* and *Aviation Weather and Weather Services*, available from Gleim Publications, Inc. See the order form on page 478.

## 5.1 FAR PART 61
### 61.3 Requirements for Certificates, Ratings, and Authorizations (Questions 1-2)

1.  The pilot in command must hold an instrument rating when operating under IFR or in weather conditions less than the minimums prescribed for VFR flight.

2.  An IFR clearance is required when operating in Class A airspace (formerly the Positive Control Area or route segment).

### 61.51 Pilot Logbooks (Questions 3-5)

1.  Instrument flight time may be logged when flight is solely by reference to instruments under actual or simulated flight conditions.

    a.  The place and type of each instrument approach completed, and the name of the safety pilot, must be included in the logbook for each simulated instrument flight.

2.  An instrument flight instructor may log instrument time when acting as an instrument flight instructor in actual instrument weather conditions.

### 61.57 Recent Flight Experience: Pilot in Command (Questions 6-15)

1.  In order to act as pilot in command under IFR, one must have logged 6 hr. of instrument time (actual or simulated) within the previous 6 months.

    a.  At least 3 hr. must be in the category of aircraft involved.

    b.  At least 6 instrument approaches must be performed in any aircraft or any approved instrument ground trainer, or any combination of these.

    c.  Alternatively, the pilot must have passed an instrument competency check in the aircraft category involved.

2.  An instrument pilot who does not meet the experience requirements during the prescribed time or 6 months thereafter must then pass an instrument competency check,

    a.  This may be conducted by an FAA inspector, an FAA-designated examiner, or a certificated instrument flight instructor.

### 61.129 Airplane Rating: Aeronautical Experience (Questions 16-20)

1.  Commercial pilots without an instrument rating cannot carry passengers for hire on cross-country flights during the day beyond a radius of 50 NM.

    a.  Carrying passengers at night is also prohibited without an instrument rating.

## 5.2 FAR PART 91

### 91.3 Responsibility and Authority of the Pilot in Command (Question 21)

1. The pilot in command is directly responsible for, and the final authority as to, determining the airworthiness and operation of that aircraft prior to each flight.

### 91.103 Preflight Action (Questions 22-23)

1. Before beginning any IFR flight, the pilot must obtain and become familiar with information about weather reports and forecasts, fuel requirements, alternatives available if the planned flight cannot be completed, any known traffic delays, runway lengths at airports of intended use, and takeoff and landing distance information.

### 91.109 Flight Instruction; Simulated Instrument Flight and Certain Flight Tests (Question 24)

1. To operate an airplane in simulated instrument flight, you must have at least a private pilot who is appropriately rated in your aircraft occupying the other control seat as a safety pilot.

### 91.123 Compliance with ATC Clearances and Instructions (Questions 25-27)

1. If you deviate from an ATC clearance in an emergency, you must notify ATC as soon as possible.

2. If you are given priority by ATC in an emergency, ATC may request that you submit a detailed report within 48 hr. to the manager of that ATC facility.

    a. This may be required even though no rule has been violated.

3. During an IFR flight in IMC, if a distress condition is encountered, the pilot should immediately declare an emergency and obtain an amended clearance.

    a. Distress is a condition of being threatened by serious and/or imminent danger and of requiring immediate assistance.

### 91.129 Operations in Class D Airspace (Question 28)

1. If an aircraft's transponder fails during flight within Class D airspace, no deviation is required because a transponder is not required in Class D airspace.

    a. Class D airspace was formerly known as an Airport Traffic Area and a Control Zone.

### 91.131 Operations in Class B Airspace (Questions 29-30)

1. Operations in Class B airspace (formerly TCA) require two-way radio communications with ATC and a Mode C transponder.

    a. If operating IFR, you must have a VOR receiver.

2. If it is necessary to conduct training operations within Class B airspace, procedures established by ATC for these flights within the Class B airspace will be followed.

### 91.135 Operations in Class A Airspace (Questions 31-34)

1. An IFR flight plan is required when flying in IFR conditions in controlled airspace, and at all times in Class A airspace.

    a. Class A airspace includes the airspace from 18,000 ft. MSL up to and including FL 600.

## 91.155  Basic VFR Weather Minimums  (Questions 35-41)

### Cloud Clearance and Visibility Required for VFR

| Airspace | Flight Visibility | Distance from Clouds | | Airspace | Flight Visibility | Distance from Clouds |
|---|---|---|---|---|---|---|
| Class A | Not applicable | Not applicable | | Class G: | | |
| | | | | 1,200 ft. or less above the surface (regardless of MSL altitude). | | |
| Class B | 3 SM | Clear of clouds | | Day, except as provided in 1. below | 1 SM | Clear of clouds |
| | | | | Night, except as provided in 1. below | 3 SM | 500 ft. below 1,000 ft. above 2,000 ft. horiz. |
| Class C | 3 SM | 500 ft. below 1,000 ft. above 2,000 ft. horiz. | | | | |
| | | | | More than 1,200 ft. above the surface but less than 10,000 ft. MSL | | |
| Class D | 3 SM | 500 ft. below 1,000 ft. above 2,000 ft. horiz. | | Day | 1 SM | 500 ft. below 1,000 ft. above 2,000 ft. horiz. |
| Class E: | | | | Night | 3 SM | 500 ft. below 1,000 ft. above 2,000 ft. horiz. |
| Less than 10,000 ft. MSL | 3 SM | 500 ft. below 1,000 ft. above 2,000 ft. horiz. | | More than 1,200 ft. above the surface and at or above 10,000 ft. MSL | 5 SM | 1,000 ft. below 1,000 ft. above 1 SM horiz. |
| At or above 10,000 ft. MSL | 5 SM | 1,000 ft. below 1,000 ft. above 1 SM horiz. | | | | |

1.  An airplane may be operated clear of clouds in Class G airspace at night below 1,200 ft. AGL when the visibility is less than 3 SM but more than 1 SM in an airport traffic pattern and within ½ NM of the runway.

2.  When flying under a "VFR-on-Top" clearance on IFR flights, you must fly at VFR altitudes and comply with VFR visibility and distance from clouds criteria.

## 91.157  Special VFR Weather Minimums  (Question 42)

1.  With some exceptions, special VFR clearances can be requested in Class B, Class C, Class D, or Class E airspace areas.

    a.  The flight requirements are to remain clear of clouds and have visibility of at least 1 SM.

2.  Flight under special VFR clearance at night is only permitted if the pilot is instrument rated and the airplane is IFR equipped.

## 91.167 Fuel Requirements for Flight in IFR Conditions (Questions 43-44)

1.  When flying IFR, you must carry sufficient fuel to fly to the first airport of intended landing, fly to the alternate airport (if required), and then fly for 45 min. at normal cruising speed.

2.  An alternate airport is not required if the destination airport has

    a.  At least one approved instrument approach procedure (IAP), and
    b.  From 1 hr. before to 1 hr. after the ETA, a forecast of at least

        1)  2,000 ft. ceiling and
        2)  3 SM visibility.

## 91.169 IFR Flight Plan: Information Required (Questions 45-54)

1.  Intended airports of landing on an IFR flight must have a forecast ceiling of at least 2,000 ft. and visibility of at least 3 SM for 1 hr. before and 1 hr. after the ETA. Otherwise, an alternate must be listed on your IFR flight plan.

2.  When a pilot elects to proceed to the selected alternate airport, the landing minimums used should be the minimums specified for the approach procedure selected.

3.  To list an airport with a nonprecision approach as an alternate, the forecast weather must be for at least an 800-ft. ceiling and 2 SM visibility at your ETA.

4.  To list an airport with a precision approach as an alternate, the forecast weather must indicate at least a 600-ft. ceiling and 2 SM visibility at your ETA.

5.  If no instrument approaches are prescribed, the minimums for listing an airport as an alternate on an IFR flight are forecast weather allowing descent from the MEA, approach, and landing under basic VFR.

## 91.171 VOR Equipment Check for IFR Operations (Questions 55-60)

1.  When making VOR operation checks, the date, place, bearing error, and pilot signature should be placed in the aircraft log or other record.

2.  Operational checks of VORs must be made every 30 days.

3.  The maximum allowable tolerance when performing an operational check of a dual VOR system is 4° variation between the two indicated bearings.

    a.  When performing an operational check using a VOT, the maximum tolerance is ±4°.

4.  In addition to the VOR check that must be made at least every 30 days, the altimeter system and the transponder must have been inspected within 24 calendar months.

## 91.173 ATC Clearance and Flight Plan Required (Questions 61-65)

1.  No person may operate an aircraft in controlled airspace under IFR unless that person has

    a.  Filed an IFR flight plan, and
    b.  Received an appropriate ATC clearance.

## 91.177 Minimum Altitudes for IFR Operations (Question 66)

1.  Except when necessary for takeoff or landing, the minimum altitude for IFR flight (if none are prescribed in FAR Parts 95 or 97) is

    a.  2,000 ft. above the highest obstacle within a horizontal distance of 4 NM over designated mountainous terrain, or

    b.  1,000 ft. above the highest obstacle within a horizontal distance of 4 NM over nonmountainous terrain.

## 91.205 Powered Civil Aircraft with Standard Category U.S. Airworthiness Certificates: Instrument and Equipment Requirements (Questions 67-69)

1.  For IFR flight, navigation equipment must be appropriate to the ground facilities to be used.

2.  Above 24,000 ft. MSL, DME is required if VOR navigational equipment is required.

3.  Gyroscopic directional indicator, gyroscopic attitude indicator, and a gyroscopic rate-of-turn indicator are required for IFR flight.

## 91.211 Supplemental Oxygen (Questions 70-73)

1.  At cabin pressure altitudes above 15,000 ft. MSL, each passenger of the aircraft must be provided with supplemental oxygen.

2.  At cabin pressure altitudes above 14,000 ft. MSL, the required minimum flight crew must be provided and use supplemental oxygen during the entire flight time at those altitudes.

3.  Pilots can fly at cabin pressure altitudes above 12,500 ft. MSL up to and including 14,000 ft. MSL for up to 30 min. without supplemental oxygen.

    a.  If a flight is conducted at these altitudes for more than 30 min., oxygen must be provided to and used by the required minimum flight crew for the time in excess of 30 min.

## 91.215 ATC Transponder and Altitude Reporting Equipment and Use (Questions 74-77)

1.  All aircraft must have and use an altitude encoding transponder (Mode C) when operating:

    a.  Within Class B airspace,
    b.  Within 30 NM of the primary Class B airport,
    c.  Within and above Class C airspace,
    d.  Above 10,000 ft. MSL except at and below 2,500 ft. AGL, and
    e.  In Class A airspace.

2.  Request for deviations must be made to the controlling ATC facility.

    a.  If the transponder fails during flight, ATC may authorize the aircraft to continue to the airport of ultimate destination.

    b.  For operation of an aircraft that is not equipped with a transponder, the request for a deviation must be made at least 1 hr. before the proposed operation.

        1)  An aircraft with an operating transponder but without Mode C can request a deviation at any time.

## 91.411 Altimeter System and Altitude Reporting Equipment Tests and Inspections (Questions 78-79)

1.  Each static pressure system and altimeter instrument must be tested and inspected by the end of the 24th calendar month following the current inspection.

## 5.3 NTSB PART 830 NOTIFICATION AND REPORTING OF AIRCRAFT ACCIDENTS OR INCIDENTS AND OVERDUE AIRCRAFT, AND PRESERVATION OF AIRCRAFT WRECKAGE, MAIL, CARGO, AND RECORDS (Question 80)

1.  NTSB Part 830 covers the procedures required for aircraft accident and incident reporting responsibilities for pilots.

## 5.1 FAR PART 61
### 61.3 Requirements for Certificates, Ratings, and Authorizations

**1.**
**4031.** Under which condition must the pilot in command of a civil aircraft have at least an instrument rating?

A— When operating in the Continental Control Area.
B— For a flight in VFR conditions while on an IFR flight plan.
C— For any flight above an altitude of 1,200 feet AGL, when the visibility is less than 3 miles.

Answer (B) is correct (4031). *(FAR 61.3)*
No person may act as pilot in command of a civil aircraft under IFR or in weather conditions less than the minimums prescribed for VFR flight unless (s)he holds an instrument rating.
Answer (A) is incorrect because an instrument rating is required at all times when operating in Class A, not Class E, airspace. Answer (C) is incorrect because VFR is permitted in uncontrolled airspace during the day with visibilities of as little as 1 SM when more than 1,200 ft. AGL but below 10,000 ft. MSL.

**2.**
**4025.** The pilot in command of a civil aircraft must have an instrument rating only when operating

A— under IFR in controlled airspace and in a positive control area or positive control route segment.
B— under IFR, in weather conditions less than the minimum for VFR flight, and in a positive control area or route segment.
C— in weather conditions less than the minimum prescribed for VFR flight.

Answer (B) is correct (4025). *(FAR 61.3 and 91.135)*
No person may act as pilot in command of a civil aircraft under IFR, in weather conditions less than the minimums prescribed for VFR flight, or in Class A airspace unless (s)he holds an instrument rating.
Answer (A) is incorrect because it omits the requirement to be instrument rated if flying in IFR conditions in uncontrolled airspace. Answer (C) is incorrect because it omits flying in VFR conditions with an IFR clearance.

### 61.51 Pilot Logbooks

**3.**
**4010.** Which flight time may be logged as instrument time when on an instrument flight plan?

A— All of the time the aircraft was not controlled by ground references.
B— Only the time you controlled the aircraft solely by reference to flight instruments.
C— Only the time you were flying in IFR weather conditions.

Answer (B) is correct (4010). *(FAR 61.51)*
A pilot may log as instrument flight time only that time during which (s)he operates the aircraft solely by reference to instruments, under actual or simulated instrument flight conditions.
Answer (A) is incorrect because VFR flight can be conducted above a cloud layer without visual ground references, i.e., VFR-on-top. Answer (C) is incorrect because time under the hood (i.e., simulated IFR) as well as actual IFR conditions counts as instrument time.

**4.**

**4009.** What portion of dual instruction time may a certificated instrument flight instructor log as instrument flight time?

A— All time during which the instructor acts as instrument instructor, regardless of weather conditions.

B— All time during which the instructor acts as instrument instructor in actual instrument weather conditions.

C— Only the time during which the instructor flies the aircraft by reference to instruments.

**Answer (B) is correct (4009).** *(FAR 61.51)*

An instrument flight instructor may log as instrument time that time during which (s)he acts as instrument flight instructor in actual instrument weather conditions.

Answer (A) is incorrect because the flight conditions must be IMC for the instructor to log flight instruction as instrument time. Answer (C) is incorrect because instructing in (as well as flying in) actual IFR weather conditions can be logged as instrument time by the instructor.

**5.**

**4008.** If a pilot enters the condition of flight in the pilot logbook as simulated instrument conditions, what qualifying information must also be entered?

A— Place and type of each instrument approach completed and name of safety pilot.

B— Number and type of instrument approaches completed and route of flight.

C— Name and pilot certificate number of safety pilot and type of approaches completed.

**Answer (A) is correct (4008).** *(FAR 61.51)*

A pilot may log as instrument flight time only that time during which (s)he operates the aircraft solely by reference to instruments, under actual or simulated instrument flight conditions. Each entry must include the place and type of each instrument approach completed and the name of the safety pilot for each simulated instrument flight.

Answer (B) is incorrect because the place (not number) and type of instrument approaches must be entered along with the safety pilot's name, not the route of flight. Answer (C) is incorrect because the place is required and the safety pilot's certificate number is not.

## 61.57 Recent Flight Experience: Pilot in Command

**6.**

**4021.** How long does a pilot remain current for IFR flight after successfully completing an instrument competency check if no further IFR flights are made?

A— 90 days.
B— 6 months.
C— 12 months.

**Answer (B) is correct (4021).** *(FAR 61.57)*

No pilot may act as pilot in command when operating under IFR or in weather conditions less than the minimums prescribed for VFR unless (s)he has, within the past 6 months, logged at least 6 hr. of instrument time under actual or simulated IFR conditions, at least three of which were in the category of aircraft involved, including at least six instrument approaches. An alternative way to remain current is to pass an instrument competency check in the category of aircraft involved.

Answer (A) is incorrect because 90 days refers to takeoff and landing currency to carry passengers. Answer (C) is incorrect because 12 months is the time whereafter another instrument competency check is required.

**7.**

**4027.** To meet the minimum required instrument experience to remain current for IFR operations, you must accomplish during the past 6 months at least six instrument approaches

A— and 6 hours of instrument time; 3 of the 6 hours in flight in the category of aircraft to be flown.

B— and 6 hours of instrument time in any aircraft.

C— three of which must be in the same category and class of aircraft to be flown, and 6 hours of instrument time in any aircraft.

**Answer (A) is correct (4027).** *(FAR 61.57)*

No pilot may act as pilot in command when operating under IFR or in weather conditions less than the minimums prescribed for VFR unless (s)he has, within the past 6 months, logged at least 6 hr. of instrument time under actual or simulated IFR conditions, at least three of which were in the category of aircraft involved, including at least six instrument approaches.

Answer (B) is incorrect because 3 of the 6 hr. of instrument time must be in the category of aircraft to be flown. Answer (C) is incorrect because there is no requirement that the approaches must be in an aircraft, and only 3 of the 6 hr. of instrument time must be in the same category of aircraft, not any aircraft.

**8.**

**4012.** The minimum instrument time required, within the last 6 months, to be current for IFR is

A— 6 hours; at least 3 of the 6 hours in the category of aircraft to be flown.

B— 6 hours in the same category aircraft.

C— 6 hours in the same category aircraft, and at least 3 of the 6 hours in actual conditions.

**Answer (A) is correct (4012).** *(FAR 61.57)*
No pilot may act as pilot in command when operating under IFR or in weather conditions less than the minimums prescribed for VFR unless (s)he has, within the past 6 months, logged at least 6 hr. of instrument time under actual or simulated IFR conditions, at least three of which were in the category of aircraft involved, including at least six instrument approaches.
Answer (B) is incorrect because only 3 of the 6 hr. need be in the same category of aircraft. Answer (C) is incorrect because currency requirements may be met in simulated IFR flight.

**9.**

**4023.** What minimum conditions are necessary for the instrument approaches required for IFR currency in an airplane?

A— A minimum of six in any approved instrument ground trainer or aircraft within the past 6 months.

B— A minimum of six, at least three of which must be in an aircraft within the past 6 months.

C— A minimum of six in an aircraft, at least three of which must be in the same category within the past 6 months.

**Answer (A) is correct (4023).** *(FAR 61.57)*
The only requirement is to have logged six instrument approaches. These approaches may be in any approved instrument ground trainer or aircraft (or any combination of these) within the past 6 months.
Answer (B) is incorrect because all six approaches may be done in an approved instrument ground trainer, not necessarily in an aircraft. Answer (C) is incorrect because all six approaches may be done in an approved instrument ground trainer, not necessarily in an aircraft.

**10.**

**4014.** An instrument rated pilot, who has not logged any instrument time in 1 year or more, cannot serve as pilot in command under IFR, unless the pilot

A— completes the required 6 hours and six approaches, followed by an instrument competency check given by an FAA-designated examiner.

B— passes an instrument competency check in the category of aircraft involved, given by an approved FAA examiner, instrument instructor, or FAA inspector.

C— passes an instrument competency check in the category of aircraft involved, followed by 6 hours and six instrument approaches, 3 of those hours in the category of aircraft involved.

**Answer (B) is correct (4014).** *(FAR 61.57)*
A pilot who does not meet the recent instrument experience requirements during the prescribed time or 6 months thereafter may not serve as pilot in command under IFR or in weather conditions less than the minimums prescribed for VFR until (s)he passes an instrument competency check in the category of aircraft involved, given by an FAA inspector, a member of an armed force of the U.S. authorized to conduct flight tests, an FAA-approved check pilot, or a certificated instrument flight instructor. The FAA may authorize part or all of this check in a pilot ground trainer equipped for instruments or an aircraft simulator.
Answer (A) is incorrect because an instrument competency check by itself provides currency. Additional hours and approaches are not required. Answer (C) is incorrect because an instrument competency check by itself provides currency. Additional hours and approaches are not required.

**11.**

**4013.** After your recent IFR experience lapses, how much time do you have before you must pass an instrument competency check to act as pilot in command under IFR?

A— 6 months.

B— 90 days.

C— 12 months.

**Answer (A) is correct (4013).** *(FAR 61.57)*
A pilot who does not meet the recent instrument experience requirements during the prescribed time or 6 months thereafter may not serve as pilot in command under IFR or in weather conditions less than the minimums prescribed for VFR until (s)he passes an instrument competency check.
Answer (B) is incorrect because 90 days refers to the takeoff and landing currency requirements to carry passengers. Answer (C) is incorrect because 12 months is the time from when you gain IFR currency to when you require another instrument competency check (assuming you have not maintained currency since you gained competency).

**12.**
**4017.** What minimum conditions are necessary for the instrument approaches required for IFR currency?

A— The approaches may be made in an aircraft, approved instrument ground trainer, or any combination of these.

B— At least three approaches must be made in the same category of aircraft to be flown.

C— At least three approaches must be made in the same category and class of aircraft to be flown.

Answer (A) is correct (4017). *(FAR 61.57)*
The only requirement is to have logged six instrument approaches. These approaches may be in any approved instrument ground trainer or aircraft (or any combination of these) within the past 6 months.
Answer (B) is incorrect because all six approaches may be done in an approved instrument ground trainer, not necessarily in an aircraft. Answer (C) is incorrect because all six approaches may be done in an approved instrument ground trainer, not necessarily in an aircraft.

**13.**
**4015.** A pilot's recent IFR experience expires on July 1 of this year. What is the latest date the pilot can meet the IFR experience requirement without having to take an instrument competency check?

A— December 31, this year.

B— June 30, next year.

C— July 31, this year.

Answer (A) is correct (4015). *(FAR 61.57)*
A pilot who does not meet the recent instrument experience requirements during the prescribed time or 6 months thereafter may not serve as pilot in command under IFR or in weather conditions less than the minimums prescribed for VFR until (s)he passes an instrument competency check. If the 6 months' recency experience period expires on July 1, the 6 months thereafter would expire on December 31 this year.
Answer (B) is incorrect because this is 12 months instead of 6 months. Answer (C) is incorrect because this is 1 month instead of 6 months.

**14.**
**4020.** How may a pilot satisfy the recent instrument experience requirement necessary to act as pilot in command in IMC?

A— Log 6 hours of instrument time under actual or simulated IFR conditions within the last 6 months, including six instrument approaches of any kind. Three of the 6 hours must be in flight in the category of aircraft involved.

B— Log 6 hours of instrument time under actual or simulated IFR conditions within the last 6 months, including at least three instrument approaches of any kind. Three of the 6 hours must be in flight in the category of aircraft involved.

C— Log 6 hours of instrument time under actual or simulated IFR conditions within the last 3 months, including at least six instrument approaches of any kind. Three of the 6 hours must be in flight in any category aircraft.

Answer (A) is correct (4020). *(FAR 61.57)*
No pilot may act as pilot in command under IFR or in weather conditions less than the minimums prescribed for VFR unless (s)he has, within the past 6 months, logged at least 6 hr. of instrument time under actual or simulated IFR conditions, at least three of which were in the category of aircraft involved, including at least six instrument approaches.
Answer (B) is incorrect because six, not three, instrument approaches are required. Answer (C) is incorrect because the experience is required within the last 6, not 3, months. Also only 3 of the 6 hr. must be in the category of aircraft you are current in (not any category of aircraft).

**15.**
**4026.** Which additional IFR experience allows you to meet the recent IFR experience requirements to act as pilot in command of an airplane under IFR?

Your present instrument experience within the past 6 months is:

3 hours and one instrument approach in a simulator

3 hours and one instrument approach in an airplane

A— Four instrument approaches in an approved simulator.

B— Three hours of simulated or actual instrument flight time in a helicopter and two instrument approaches in an airplane or helicopter.

C— Three instrument approaches in a helicopter.

Answer (A) is correct (4026). *(FAR 61.57)*
No pilot may act as pilot in command under IFR or in weather conditions less than the minimums prescribed for VFR unless (s)he has, within the past 6 months, logged at least 6 hr. of instrument time under actual or simulated IFR conditions, at least three of which were in the category of aircraft involved, including at least six instrument approaches. Since you have 6 hr. of IFR experience, with 3 hr. in an airplane, and two approaches, you need four additional approaches in any aircraft or approved simulator.
Answer (B) is incorrect because 4 (not 2) additional approaches are required and no helicopter time is required. Answer (C) is incorrect because 4 (not 3) additional approaches are required.

## 61.129  Airplane Rating:  Aeronautical Experience

**16.**

**4035.** To carry passengers for hire in an airplane on cross-country flights of more than 50 NM from the departure airport, the pilot in command is required to hold at least

A— a Category II pilot authorization.
B— a First-Class Medical certificate.
C— a Commercial Pilot Certificate with an instrument rating.

Answer (C) is correct (4035). *(FAR 61.129)*
    To carry passengers for hire, the pilot in command is required to hold at least a Commercial Pilot Certificate. Additionally, to carry those passengers for hire in an airplane on cross-country flights of more than 50 NM (or at night), (s)he must also hold an instrument rating on the commercial certificate.
    Answer (A) is incorrect because Category II refers to an authorization for reduced ILS approach minimums. Answer (B) is incorrect because a First-Class Medical Certificate is required for operations requiring an airline transport pilot certificate.

**17.**

**4034.** Which limitation is imposed on the holder of a Commercial Pilot Certificate if that person does not hold an instrument rating?

A— That person is limited to private pilot privileges at night.
B— The carrying of passengers or property for hire on cross-country flights at night is limited to a radius of 50 NM.
C— The carrying of passengers for hire on cross-country flights is limited to 50 NM and the carrying of passengers for hire at night is prohibited.

Answer (C) is correct (4034). *(FAR 61.129)*
    The applicant for a commercial pilot certificate must hold an instrument rating (airplane), or the commercial pilot certificate is endorsed with a limitation prohibiting the carriage of passengers for hire in airplanes on cross-country flights of more than 50 NM, or at night.
    Answer (A) is incorrect because that person may exercise commercial pilot privileges at night, but with limitations.  Answer (B) is incorrect because no passengers may be carried at night without an instrument rating.

**18.**

**4002.** What limitation is imposed on a newly certificated commercial airplane pilot if that person does not hold an instrument pilot rating?

A— The carrying of passengers or property for hire on cross-country flights at night is limited to a radius of 50 nautical miles (NM).
B— The carrying of passengers for hire on cross-country flights is limited to 50 NM for night flights, but not limited for day flights.
C— The carrying of passengers for hire on cross-country flights is limited to 50 NM and the carrying of passengers for hire at night is prohibited.

Answer (C) is correct (4002). *(FAR 61.129)*
    The applicant for a commercial pilot certificate must hold an instrument rating (airplane), or the commercial pilot certificate is endorsed with a limitation prohibiting the carriage of passengers for hire in airplanes on cross-country flights of more than 50 NM, or at night.
    Answer (A) is incorrect because the carriage of property (freight) is not limited at night.  Answer (B) is incorrect because no passengers may be carried at night and the flight is limited to 50 NM (not unlimited) for day flights without an instrument rating.

**19.**

**4028.** A certificated commercial pilot who carries passengers for hire in an airplane at night is required to have at least

A— an associated type rating if the airplane is of the multiengine class.
B— a First-Class Medical Certificate.
C— an airplane instrument pilot rating.

Answer (C) is correct (4028). *(FAR 61.129)*
    A certificated commercial pilot who carries passengers for hire in an airplane at night is required to have an instrument rating (airplane).
    Answer (A) is incorrect because, even if the airplane requires a type rating, the commercial pilot must have at least an instrument rating to carry passengers for hire at night.  Answer (B) is incorrect because only a Second-Class Medical Certificate is required of commercial pilots.  First-Class Medical Certificates are required of airline transport pilots.

**20.**
**4029.** You intend to carry passengers for hire on a night VFR flight in a single-engine airplane within a 25-mile radius of the departure airport. You are required to possess at least which rating(s)?

A— A Commercial Pilot Certificate with a single-engine land rating.
B— A Commercial Pilot Certificate with a single-engine and instrument (airplane) rating.
C— A Private Pilot Certificate with a single-engine land and instrument airplane rating.

Answer (B) is correct (4029). *(FAR 61.129)*
A commercial pilot certificate with a single-engine airplane rating is required to carry passengers for hire and to operate that class of aircraft. Also, an applicant for a commercial pilot certificate must hold an instrument rating (airplane), or the commercial pilot certificate will be endorsed with a limitation prohibiting carrying passengers for hire on cross-country flights of more than 50 NM or at night.
Answer (A) is incorrect because to carry passengers for hire at night one must have an instrument rating as well as a commercial pilot certificate. Answer (C) is incorrect because a commercial (not private) pilot certificate is required to carry passengers for hire.

## 5.2 FAR PART 91
### 91.3 Responsibility and Authority of the Pilot in Command

**21.**
**4039.** Who is responsible for determining that the altimeter system has been checked and found to meet FAR requirements for a particular instrument flight?

A— Owner.
B— Operator.
C— Pilot in command.

Answer (C) is correct (4039). *(FAR 91.3)*
The pilot in command of an aircraft is directly responsible for, and is the final authority as to, the airworthiness and operation of that aircraft.
Answer (A) is incorrect because the owner is primarily responsible for maintaining the aircraft, but the pilot in command is responsible for determining that the aircraft is airworthy, i.e., the aircraft is in compliance with the FARs. Answer (B) is incorrect because the operator is primarily responsible for maintaining the aircraft, but the pilot in command is responsible for determining that the aircraft is airworthy, i.e., the aircraft is in compliance with the FARs.

### 91.103 Preflight Action

**22.**
**4033.** Before beginning any flight under IFR, the pilot in command must become familiar with all available information concerning that flight. In addition, the pilot must

A— list an alternate airport on the flight plan and become familiar with the instrument approaches to that airport.
B— list an alternate airport on the flight plan and confirm adequate takeoff and landing performance at the destination airport.
C— be familiar with the runway lengths at airports of intended use, and the alternatives available if the flight cannot be completed.

Answer (C) is correct (4033). *(FAR 91.103)*
Each pilot in command shall, before beginning a flight, familiarize him/herself with all available information concerning that flight. For a flight under IFR or a flight not in the vicinity of an airport, this information should include weather reports and forecasts, fuel requirements, alternatives available if the planned flight cannot be completed, and any known traffic delays of which (s)he has been advised by ATC. For any flight, the preflight information should include runway lengths at airports of intended use and takeoff and landing distance information.
Answer (A) is incorrect because listing an alternate airport is not required for all IFR flights, i.e., when the destination is forecast to have ceilings above 2,000 ft. and visibility at least 3 SM. Answer (B) is incorrect because listing an alternate airport is not required for all IFR flights, i.e., when the destination is forecast to have ceilings above 2,000 ft. and visibility at least 3 SM.

**23.**
**4003.** Before beginning any flight under IFR, the pilot in command must become familiar with all available information concerning that flight. In addition, the pilot must

A— be familiar with all instrument approaches at the destination airport.
B— list an alternate airport on the flight plan and confirm adequate takeoff and landing performance at the destination airport.
C— be familiar with the runway lengths at airports of intended use, and the alternatives available if the flight cannot be completed.

Answer (C) is correct (4003). *(FAR 91.103)*
Each pilot in command shall, before beginning a flight, familiarize him/herself with all available information concerning that flight. For a flight under IFR or a flight not in the vicinity of an airport, this information should include weather reports and forecasts, fuel requirements, alternatives available if the planned flight cannot be completed, and any known traffic delays of which (s)he has been advised by ATC. For any flight, the preflight information should include runway lengths at airports of intended use and takeoff and landing distance information.
Answer (A) is incorrect because, while it is a good operating procedure to know what approaches are available, it is not a required preflight action. Answer (B) is incorrect because listing an alternate airport is not required for all IFR flights, i.e., when the destination is forecast to have ceilings above 2,000 ft. and visibility at least 3 SM.

## 91.109 Flight Instruction; Simulated Instrument Flight and Certain Flight Tests

**24.**
**4011.** What are the minimum qualifications for a person who occupies the other control seat as safety pilot during simulated instrument flight?

A— Appropriately rated in the aircraft.
B— Private pilot.
C— Private pilot with instrument rating.

Answer (A) is correct (4011). *(FAR 91.109)*
No person may operate a civil aircraft in simulated instrument flight unless the other control seat is occupied by a safety pilot who possesses at least a private pilot certificate with category and class ratings appropriate to the aircraft being flown. Appropriately rated in the aircraft implies at least a private pilot certificate.
Answer (B) is incorrect because the safety pilot's certificate must carry an appropriate category and class rating, e.g., a private pilot (helicopter) may not act as safety pilot in an airplane. Answer (C) is incorrect because the safety pilot does not need to be instrument rated.

## 91.123 Compliance with ATC Clearances and Instructions

**25.**
**4407.** When may ATC request a detailed report of an emergency even though a rule has not been violated?

A— When priority has been given.
B— Any time an emergency occurs.
C— When the emergency occurs in controlled airspace.

Answer (A) is correct (4407). *(FAR 91.123)*
Each pilot in command who is given priority by ATC in an emergency (even though no FAR has been violated) shall, if requested by ATC, submit a detailed report of that emergency within 48 hr. to the manager of that ATC facility.
Answer (B) is incorrect because a written report may be requested when priority is given in an emergency, not any time an emergency occurs. Answer (C) is incorrect because a written report may be requested when priority is given in an emergency, regardless of where the emergency occurs.

**26.**
**4461.** While on an IFR flight, a pilot has an emergency which causes a deviation from an ATC clearance. What action must be taken?

A— Notify ATC of the deviation as soon as possible.
B— Squawk 7700 for the duration of the emergency.
C— Submit a detailed report to the chief of the ATC facility within 48 hours.

Answer (A) is correct (4461). *(FAR 91.123)*
Each pilot in command who, in an emergency, deviates from an ATC clearance or instruction shall notify ATC of that deviation as soon as possible.
Answer (B) is incorrect because, in an emergency, you must report a deviation from an ATC clearance as soon as possible, not just squawk 7700 during the emergency. Answer (C) is incorrect because a report in 48 hr. is only required if you are given priority during the emergency and ATC requests such a report.

**27.**
**4381.** During an IFR flight in IMC, a distress condition is encountered, (fire, mechanical, or structural failure). The pilot should

A— not hesitate to declare an emergency and obtain an amended clearance.
B— wait until the situation is immediately perilous before declaring an emergency.
C— contact ATC and advise that an urgency condition exists and request priority consideration.

Answer (A) is correct (4381). *(FAR 91.123 and P/C Glossary)*
Distress is a condition of being threatened by serious and/or imminent danger and of requiring immediate assistance. Thus, during an IFR flight in IMC, if a distress condition is encountered, you should immediately declare an emergency and obtain an amended clearance.
Answer (B) is incorrect because a distress condition is perilous and you should not hesitate to declare an emergency. Answer (C) is incorrect because you should contact ATC and declare an emergency (not urgency) condition exists and obtain an amended clearance, not a request for consideration.

## 91.129 Operations in Class D Airspace

**28.**
**4375.** The aircraft's transponder fails during flight within Class D airspace.

A— The pilot should immediately request clearance to depart the Class D airspace.
B— No deviation is required because a transponder is not required in Class D airspace.
C— Pilot must immediately request priority handling to proceed to destination.

Answer (B) is correct (4375). *(FAR 91.129)*
If an aircraft's transponder fails during flight within Class D airspace, no deviation is required because a transponder is not required in Class D airspace.
Answer (A) is incorrect because, since a transponder is not required in Class D airspace, the pilot does not need to depart the Class D airspace. Answer (C) is incorrect because, since a transponder is not required in Class D airspace, a pilot does not need priority handling to proceed to his/her destination.

## 91.131 Operations in Class B Airspace

**29.**
**4426.** In addition to a VOR receiver and two-way communications capability, which additional equipment is required for IFR operation in Class B airspace?

A— Another VOR and communications receiver and a coded transponder.
B— Standby communications receiver, DME, and coded transponder.
C— An operable coded transponder having Mode C capability.

Answer (C) is correct (4426). *(FAR 91.131)*
Unless otherwise authorized by ATC, no person may operate an aircraft within Class B airspace unless that aircraft is equipped with

1. An operable two-way radio,
2. An operable 4096-code transponder having Mode C capability, and
3. For IFR operations, an operable VOR or TACAN receiver.

Answer (A) is incorrect because dual communication and navigation equipment is not required, and the transponder must have Mode C capability. Answer (B) is incorrect because a standby radio receiver and DME are not required, and the transponder must have Mode C capability.

**30.**
**4440.** Which of the following is required equipment for operating an airplane within Class B airspace?

A— A 4096 code transponder with automatic pressure altitude reporting equipment.
B— A VOR receiver with DME.
C— A 4096 code transponder.

Answer (A) is correct (4440). *(FAR 91.131)*
Unless otherwise authorized by ATC, no person may operate an aircraft within Class B airspace unless that aircraft is equipped with

1. An operable two-way radio,
2. An operable 4096-code transponder having Mode C capability, and
3. For IFR operations, an operable VOR or TACAN receiver.

Answer (B) is incorrect because DME is not required and a VOR receiver is only required when operating IFR. Answer (C) is incorrect because the 4096 code transponder must also have Mode C capability.

## 91.135 Operations in Class A Airspace

**31.**
**4024.** Under which condition are you required to have an instrument rating for flight in VMC?

A— Flight through an MOA.
B— Flight into an ADIZ.
C— Flight in a positive control area.

Answer (C) is correct (4024). *(FAR 91.135)*
   No person may operate an aircraft within Class A airspace at any time unless (s)he is rated for instrument flight, and is on an instrument flight plan.
   Answer (A) is incorrect because an instrument rating is not required for flight through an MOA in VMC. Answer (B) is incorrect because an instrument rating is not required for flight into an ADIZ (Air Defense Identification Zone) in VMC.

**32.**
**4066.** When is an IFR clearance required during VFR weather conditions?

A— When operating in the Class E airspace.
B— When operating in a Class A airspace.
C— When operating in airspace above 14,500 feet.

Answer (B) is correct (4066). *(FAR 91.135, 91.173)*
   No person may operate an aircraft within Class A airspace unless the aircraft is operated under an IFR clearance, regardless of the weather conditions. Class A airspace includes the airspace from 18,000 ft. MSL up to and including FL 600.
   Answer (A) is incorrect because an IFR clearance is not required in VMC in Class E airspace. Answer (C) is incorrect because an IFR clearance is not required in VMC in Class E airspace from 14,500 ft. MSL up to but not including 18,000 ft. MSL.

**33.**
**4062.** When is an IFR flight plan required?

A— When less than VFR conditions exist in either Class E or Class G airspace and in Class A airspace.
B— In all Class E airspace when conditions are below VFR, in Class A airspace, and in defense zone airspace.
C— In Class E airspace when IMC exists or in Class A airspace.

Answer (C) is correct (4062). *(FAR 91.135, 91.173)*
   No person may operate an aircraft in Class E airspace in IMC unless (s)he has filed an IFR flight plan and received an appropriate ATC clearance. Furthermore, under FAR 91.135, no one may operate in Class A airspace unless the aircraft is operated under IFR at a specific flight level assigned by ATC. This implies having filed an IFR flight plan for these airspaces also.
   Answer (A) is incorrect because, while an instrument rating is required, an IFR flight plan is not required in Class G airspace. Answer (B) is incorrect because VFR flights are permitted when VFR weather conditions exist in air defense identification zones (ADIZ).

**34.**
**4067.** Operation in which airspace requires filing an IFR flight plan?

A— Any airspace when the visibility is less than 1 mile.
B— Class E airspace with IMC and positive control area.
C— Positive control area, Continental Control Area, and all other airspace, if the visibility is less than 1 mile.

Answer (B) is correct (4067). *(FAR 91.135, 91.173)*
   No person may operate an aircraft in Class E airspace in IMC unless (s)he has filed an IFR flight plan and received an appropriate ATC clearance. Furthermore, under FAR 91.135, no one may operate in Class A airspace unless the aircraft is operated under IFR at a specific flight level assigned by ATC. This implies having filed an IFR flight plan for these airspaces also.
   Answer (A) is incorrect because an IFR flight plan is not required in Class G airspace. Answer (C) is incorrect because an IFR flight plan is not required in uncontrolled Class G airspace.

## 91.155   Basic VFR Weather Minimums

**35.**
**4519.**  What is the required flight visibility and distance from clouds if you are operating in Class E airspace at 9,500 feet MSL with a VFR-on-Top clearance during daylight hours?

A— 3 SM, 1,000 feet above, 500 feet below, and 2,000 feet horizontal.
B— 5 SM, 500 feet above, 1,000 feet below, and 2,000 feet horizontal.
C— 3 SM, 500 feet above, 1,000 feet below, and 2,000 feet horizontal.

**Answer (A) is correct (4519).  *(FAR 91.155)***
In Class E airspace below 10,000 ft. MSL, the basic VFR weather minimums are flight visibility of 3 SM and a distance from clouds of 500 ft. below, 1,000 ft. above, and 2,000 ft. horizontal.
Answer (B) is incorrect because the visibility requirement is 3, not 5, SM and the distances from clouds above and below are reversed.  It should be 1,000 ft. above and 500 ft. below.  Answer (C) is incorrect because the distances from clouds above and below are reversed.  It should be 1,000 ft. above and 500 ft. below.

**36.**
**4518.**  What is the minimum flight visibility and distance from clouds for flight at 10,500 feet with a VFR-on-Top clearance during daylight hours?  (Class E airspace.)

A— 3 SM, 1,000 feet above, 500 feet below, and 2,000 feet horizontal.
B— 5 SM, 1,000 feet above, 1,000 feet below, and 1 mile horizontal.
C— 5 SM, 1,000 feet above, 500 feet below, and 1 mile horizontal.

**Answer (B) is correct (4518).  *(FAR 91.155)***
In Class E airspace at or above 10,000 ft. MSL, the basic VFR weather minimums are flight visibility of 5 SM and a distance from clouds of 1,000 ft. above or below and 1 SM horizontal.
Answer (A) is incorrect because 3 SM, 1,000 ft. above, 500 ft. below, and 2,000 ft. horizontal are the minimum flight visibility and distance from clouds in Class E airspace below, not at or above, 10,000 ft. MSL.  Answer (C) is incorrect because the vertical separation from clouds is 1,000 ft. both above and below.

**37.**
**4524.**  (Refer to figure 92* on page 153.)  What is the minimum in-flight visibility and distance from clouds required for an airplane operating less than 1,200 feet AGL during daylight hours in area 6?

A— 3 miles; (I) 1,000 feet; (K) 2,000 feet; (L) 500 feet.
B— 1 mile; (I) clear of clouds; (K) clear of clouds; (L) clear of clouds.
C— 1 mile; (I) 500 feet; (K) 1,000 feet; (L) 500 feet.

**Answer (B) is correct (4524).  *(FAR 91.155)***
In Class G airspace at or below 1,200 ft. AGL (Area 6 in Fig. 92), the basic VFR weather minimums during daylight hours are in-flight visibility of 1 SM and clear of clouds.
Answer (A) is incorrect because 3 SM visibility, 1,000 ft. above, 500 ft. below, and 2,000 ft. horizontal are the minimum visibility and distance from clouds in VFR flight in Area 6 at night, not in daylight.  Answer (C) is incorrect because no such combination of requirements exists in any airspace.

**38.**
**4522.**  (Refer to figure 92* on page 153.)  What is the minimum in-flight visibility and distance from clouds required in VFR conditions above clouds at 13,500 feet MSL (above 1,200 feet AGL) in Class G airspace during daylight hours for area 2?

A— 5 miles; (A) 1,000 feet; (C) 2,000 feet; (D) 500 feet.
B— 3 miles; (A) 1,000 feet; (C) 1 mile; (D) 1,000 feet.
C— 5 miles; (A) 1,000 feet; (C) 1 mile; (D) 1,000 feet.

**Answer (C) is correct (4522).  *(FAR 91.155)***
In Class G airspace at more than 1,200 ft. AGL and at or above 10,000 ft. MSL (Area 2 in Fig. 92), the basic VFR weather minimums are in-flight visibility of 5 SM and a distance from clouds of 1,000 ft. above or below and 1 SM horizontal.
Answer (A) is incorrect because 1,000 ft. above, 2,000 ft. horizontal, and 500 ft. below are the minimum cloud distances for VFR in Class G airspace above 1,200 ft. AGL and below, not at or above, 10,000 ft. MSL.  Answer (B) is incorrect because visibility minimum is 5 SM, not 3 SM.

**39.**
**4523.**  (Refer to figure 92* on page 153.)  What in-flight visibility and distance from clouds is required for a flight at 8,500 feet MSL (above 1,200 feet AGL) in Class G airspace in VFR conditions during daylight hours in area 4?

A— 1 mile; (E) 1,000 feet; (G) 2,000 feet; (H) 500 feet.
B— 3 miles; (E) 1,000 feet; (G) 2,000 feet; (H) 500 feet.
C— 5 miles; (E) 1,000 feet; (G) 1 mile; (H) 1,000 feet.

**Answer (A) is correct (4523).  *(FAR 91.155)***
In Class G airspace at more than 1,200 ft. AGL but less than 10,000 ft. MSL (Area 4 in Fig. 92), the basic VFR weather minimums during daylight hours are in-flight visibility of 1 SM and a distance from clouds of 500 ft. below, 1,000 ft. above, and 2,000 ft. horizontal.
Answer (B) is incorrect because the in-flight visibility of 3 SM is required for a night, not day, flight.  Answer (C) is incorrect because in-flight visibility of 5 SM and a distance from clouds of 1,000 ft. above or below and 1 SM horizontal are the VFR weather minimums in Class G airspace above 1,200 ft. AGL and at or above, not below, 10,000 ft. MSL.

*Note that Fig. 92 incorrectly shows 1,200 ft. MSL instead of 1,200 ft. AGL.

**40.**
**4520.** (Refer to figure 92* below.) What is the minimum in-flight visibility and distance from clouds required for a VFR-on-Top flight at 9,500 feet MSL (above 1,200 feet AGL) during daylight hours for area 3?

A— 2,000 feet; (E) 1,000 feet; (F) 2,000 feet; (H) 500 feet.
B— 5 miles; (E) 1,000 feet; (F) 2,000 feet; (H) 500 feet.
C— 3 miles; (E) 1,000 feet; (F) 2,000 feet; (H) 500 feet.

**41.**
**4521.** (Refer to figure 92* below.) A flight is to be conducted in VFR-on-Top conditions at 12,500 feet MSL (above 1,200 feet AGL). What is the in-flight visibility and distance from clouds required for operation in Class E airspace during daylight hours for area 1?

A— 5 miles; (A) 1,000 feet; (B) 2,000 feet; (D) 500 feet.
B— 5 miles; (A) 1,000 feet; (B) 1 mile; (D) 1,000 feet.
C— 3 miles; (A) 1,000 feet; (B) 2,000 feet; (D) 1,000 feet.

Answer (C) is correct (4520). *(FAR 91.155)*
In Class E airspace at less than 10,000 ft. MSL (Area 3 in Fig. 92), the basic VFR weather minimums are in-flight visibility of 3 SM and a distance from clouds of 500 ft. below, 1,000 ft. above, and 2,000 ft. horizontal.
Answer (A) is incorrect because the visibility required is 3 SM, not 2,000 ft. Answer (B) is incorrect because the visibility required is 3 SM, not 5 SM.

Answer (B) is correct (4521). *(FAR 91.155)*
In Class E airspace at or above 10,000 ft. MSL (Area 1 in Fig. 92), the basic VFR weather minimums are in-flight visibility of 5 SM and a distance from clouds of 1,000 ft. above or below and 1 SM horizontal.
Answer (A) is incorrect because the distance from cloud requirements listed are for below, not at or above, 10,000 ft. MSL. Answer (C) is incorrect because the visibility requirement is 5 SM, not 3 SM, and the horizontal separation requirement from clouds is 1 SM, not 2,000 ft.

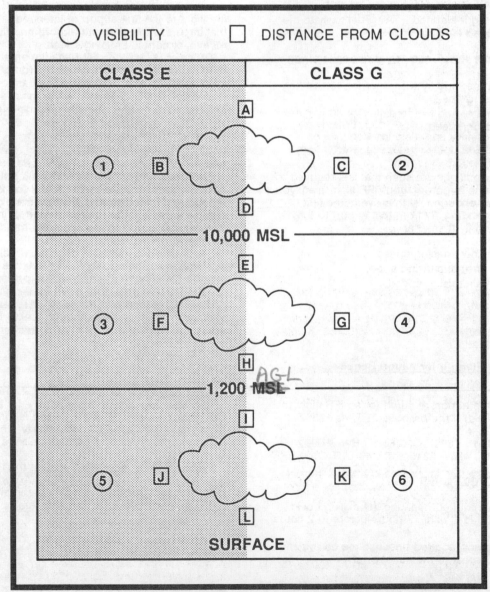

FIGURE 92.—Minimum In-Flight Visibility and Distance from Clouds.

*Note that Fig. 92 incorrectly shows 1,200 ft. MSL instead of 1,200 ft. AGL.

## 91.157 Special VFR Weather Minimums

**42.**
**4525.** (Refer to figure 92 on page 153.) What is the minimum in-flight visibility and distance from clouds required for an airplane operating less than 1,200 feet AGL under special VFR during daylight hours in area 5?

A— 1 mile; (I) 2,000 feet; (J) 2,000 feet; (L) 500 feet.
B— 3 miles; (I) clear of clouds; (J) clear of clouds; (L) 500 feet.
C— 1 mile; (I) clear of clouds; (J) clear of clouds; (L) clear of clouds.

**Answer (C) is correct (4525).** *(FAR 91.157)*
Note that Fig. 92 incorrectly shows 1,200 ft. MSL instead of 1,200 ft. AGL.
In Class E airspace when operating an airplane under special VFR, the distance from clouds requirement is clear of clouds. No one may take off or land an airplane under special VFR unless ground visibility is at least 1 SM. If ground visibility is not reported, the in-flight visibility during takeoff or landing must be at least 1 SM.
Answer (A) is incorrect because special VFR permits operation just clear of clouds. Answer (B) is incorrect because special VFR permits just clear of clouds and with a minimum visibility of 1 SM, not 3 SM.

## 91.167 Fuel Requirements for Flight in IFR Conditions

**43.**
**4032.** What are the minimum fuel requirements for airplanes in IFR conditions, if the first airport of intended landing is forecast to have a 1,500-foot ceiling and 3 miles visibility at flight-planned ETA? Fuel to fly to the first airport of intended landing,

A— and fly thereafter for 45 minutes at normal cruising speed.
B— fly to the alternate, and fly thereafter for 45 minutes at normal cruising speed.
C— fly to the alternate, and fly thereafter for 30 minutes at normal cruising speed.

**Answer (B) is correct (4032).** *(FAR 91.167)*
In general, no person may operate a civil aircraft in IFR conditions unless it carries enough fuel (considering weather reports, forecasts, and conditions) to complete the flight to the first airport of intended landing; fly from that airport to the alternate airport; and fly after that for 45 min. at normal cruising speed.
Answer (A) is incorrect because an alternate airport is required because the destination airport, from 1 hr. before to 1 hr. after ETA has a forecast ceiling of less than 2,000 ft. AGL. Answer (C) is incorrect because the fuel requirement after the alternate is 45 min., not 30 min.

**44.**
**4005.** If weather conditions are such that it is required to designate an alternate airport on your IFR flight plan, you should plan to carry enough fuel to arrive at the first airport of intended landing, fly from that airport to the alternate airport, and fly thereafter for

A— 30 minutes at slow cruising speed.
B— 45 minutes at normal cruising speed.
C— 1 hour at normal cruising speed.

**Answer (B) is correct (4005).** *(FAR 91.167)*
No person may operate a civil aircraft in IFR conditions unless it carries enough fuel (considering weather reports and forecasts and weather conditions) to complete the flight to the first airport of intended landing, fly from that airport to the alternate, and fly after that for 45 min. at normal cruising speed.
Answer (A) is incorrect because a helicopter (not an airplane) is required to fly from the first airport of intended landing to the alternate airport, and fly thereafter for 30 min. at normal (not slow) cruising speed. Answer (C) is incorrect because, after reaching the alternate, you must have enough fuel to fly for an additional 45 min. (not 1 hr.) at normal cruising speed.

## 91.169 IFR Flight Plan: Information Required

**45.**
**4082.** Is an alternate airport required for an IFR flight to ATL (Atlanta Hartsfield) if the proposed ETA is 1930Z?

ATL FT AMD 1 161615 1630Z C20 BKN 6RW-VRBL 20 SCT C40 BKN OCNL 4RW- 3315. 18Z 40 SCT C100 BKN 3110 OCNL C20 BKN 6RW-CHC C10 OVC 3TRW 3310G20 AFT 21Z. 09Z MVFR CIG R.

A— An alternate is required because the ceiling could fall below 2,000 feet within 2 hours before to 2 hours after the ETA.
B— An alternate is not required because the ceiling and visibility are forecast to remain at or above 1,000 feet and 3 miles, respectively.
C— An alternate is not required because the ceiling and visibility are forecast to be at or above 2,000 feet and 3 miles within 1 hour before to 1 hour after the ETA.

**Answer (C) is correct (4082).** *(FAR 91.169)*
An alternate airport is not required if for at least 1 hr. before to 1 hr. after ETA the ceiling is forecast to be at least 2,000 ft. AGL and 3 SM visibility. In the Terminal Forecast, the chance of 1,000-ft. ceilings due to overcast is after 2100Z.
Answer (A) is incorrect because the time frame is 1 (not 2) hr. before and after ETA. Answer (B) is incorrect because the ceiling must remain at least 2,000 ft., not 1,000 ft., for an alternate not to be required.

**46.**
**4719.** When a pilot elects to proceed to the selected alternate airport, which minimums apply for landing at the alternate?

A— 600-1 if the airport has an ILS.
B— Ceiling 200 feet above the published minimum; visibility 2 miles.
C— The landing minimums for the approach to be used.

**47.**
**4630.** If a pilot elects to proceed to the selected alternate, the landing minimums used at that airport should be the

A— minimums specified for the approach procedure selected.
B— alternate minimums shown on the approach chart.
C— minimums shown for that airport in a separate listing of "IFR Alternate Minimums."

**48.**
**4081.** What minimum weather conditions must be forecast for your ETA at an airport that has only a VOR approach with standard alternate minimums, for the airport to be listed as an alternate on the IFR flight plan?

A— 800-foot ceiling and 1 statute mile (SM) visibility.
B— 800-foot ceiling and 2 SM visibility.
C— 1,000-foot ceiling and visibility to allow descent from minimum en route altitude (MEA), approach, and landing under basic VFR.

**49.**
**4083.** What minimum conditions must exist at the destination airport to avoid listing an alternate airport on an IFR flight plan when a standard IAP is available?

A— From 2 hours before to 2 hours after ETA, forecast ceiling 2,000, and visibility 2 and ½ miles.
B— From 2 hours before to 2 hours after ETA, forecast ceiling 3,000, and visibility 3 miles.
C— From 1 hour before to 1 hour after ETA, forecast ceiling 2,000, and visibility 3 miles.

Answer (C) is correct (4719). *(FAR 91.169)*
When one goes to an alternate airport to land, the landing minimums for the particular approach, not the minimums for listing the airport as an alternate, are the minimums to be used for the approach.
Answer (A) is incorrect because, to be listed on the flight plan as an alternate airport, the weather conditions at the estimated time of arrival at the alternate must be a 600-ft. ceiling and 2 (not 1) SM visibility. Answer (B) is incorrect because the published approach minimums, not some adjustment thereof, should be used.

Answer (A) is correct (4630). *(FAR 91.169)*
When one goes to an alternate airport to land, the landing minimums for the particular approach, not the minimums for listing the airport as an alternate, are the approach minimums to be used for the approach.
Answer (B) is incorrect because alternate minimums shown on the approach chart refer to the weather conditions required to list that airport as an alternate on your IFR flight plan (not to land there). Answer (C) is incorrect because alternate minimums shown on the approach chart refer to the weather conditions required to list that airport as an alternate on your IFR flight plan (not to land there).

Answer (B) is correct (4081). *(FAR 91.169)*
Unless otherwise authorized, no one may include an alternate airport with only a nonprecision approach in an IFR flight plan unless current weather forecasts indicate that, at the ETA at the alternate airport, the ceiling will be at least 800 ft. and 2 SM visibility.
Answer (A) is incorrect because the visibility requirement is 2 (not 1) SM. Answer (C) is incorrect because, if no instrument approach procedure is available at an airport, the ceiling and visibility minimums are those allowing descent from the MEA, approach, and landing under basic VFR.

Answer (C) is correct (4083). *(FAR 91.169)*
An alternate airport is not required to be listed on an IFR flight plan if the destination airport has a standard instrument approach procedure available and, for at least 1 hr. before and 1 hr. after the estimated time of arrival, the weather reports or forecasts, or any combination of them, indicate:

1. The ceiling will be at least 2,000 ft. above the airport elevation; and
2. The visibility will be at least 3 SM.

Answer (A) is incorrect because the destination weather condition forecast is from 1 (not 2) hr. before and after ETA, and the visibility must be at least 3 (not 2½) SM. Answer (B) is incorrect because the destination weather condition forecast is from 1 (not 2) hr. before and after ETA, and the ceiling must be at least 2,000 (not 3,000) ft. AGL.

**50.**
**4086.** What are the minimum weather conditions that must be forecast to list an airport as an alternate when the airport has no approved IAP?

A— The ceiling and visibility at ETA, 2,000 feet and 3 miles, respectively.
B— The ceiling and visibility from 2 hours before until 2 hours after ETA, 2,000 feet and 3 miles, respectively.
C— The ceiling and visibility at ETA must allow descent from MEA, approach, and landing, under basic VFR.

**51.**
**4085.** What standard minimums are required to list an airport as an alternate on an IFR flight plan if the airport has VOR approach only?

A— Ceiling and visibility at ETA, 800 feet and 2 miles, respectively.
B— Ceiling and visibility from 2 hours before until 2 hours after ETA, 800 feet and 2 miles, respectively.
C— Ceiling and visibility at ETA, 600 feet and 2 miles, respectively.

**52.**
**4087.** What minimum weather conditions must be forecast for your ETA at an airport that has a precision approach procedure, with standard alternate minimums, in order to list it as an alternate for the IFR flight?

A— 600-foot ceiling and 2 SM visibility at your ETA.
B— 600-foot ceiling and 2 SM visibility from 2 hours before to 2 hours after your ETA.
C— 800-foot ceiling and 2 SM visibility at your ETA.

**53.**
**4760.** What are the alternate minimums that must be forecast at the ETA for an airport that has a precision approach procedure?

A— 400-foot ceiling and 2 miles visibility.
B— 600-foot ceiling and 2 miles visibility.
C— 800-foot ceiling and 2 miles visibility.

Answer (C) is correct (4086). *(FAR 91.169)*
Unless otherwise authorized, no one may include an alternate airport that has no instrument approach in an IFR flight plan unless current weather forecasts indicate that, at the ETA at the alternate airport, the ceiling and visibility will allow descent from the MEA, approach, and landing under basic VFR.
Answer (A) is incorrect because an alternate must be listed on your IFR flight plan unless the weather at your destination is forecast, from 1 hr. before to 1 hr. after ETA, to have a ceiling of 2,000 ft. and visibility of 3 SM. Answer (B) is incorrect because an alternate must be listed on your IFR flight plan, unless the weather at your destination is forecast, from 1 (not 2) hr. before to 1 hr. after ETA, to have at least 2,000 ft. ceiling and 3 SM.

Answer (A) is correct (4085). *(FAR 91.169)*
Unless otherwise authorized, no person may include an alternate airport that has only a VOR (i.e., nonprecision) approach in an IFR flight plan unless current weather forecasts indicate that at the ETA at the alternate airport the ceiling is at least 800 ft. and visibility is 2 SM.
Answer (B) is incorrect because the alternate airport weather minimums apply to the ETA, not 2 hr. plus or minus. Answer (C) is incorrect because 600 ft. and 2 SM are the alternate airport weather minimums for a precision approach, i.e., ILS.

Answer (A) is correct (4087). *(FAR 91.169)*
Unless otherwise authorized, no person may include an alternate airport that has a precision (ILS) approach in an IFR flight plan unless current weather forecasts indicate that at the ETA at the alternate airport the ceiling is at least 600 ft. and visibility is 2 SM.
Answer (B) is incorrect because the alternate airport weather minimums apply to the ETA, not 2 hr. plus or minus. Answer (C) is incorrect because 800 ft. and 2 SM are the alternate airport minimums for a nonprecision approach.

Answer (B) is correct (4760). *(FAR 91.169)*
Unless otherwise authorized, no person may include an alternate airport that has a precision (ILS) approach in an IFR flight plan unless current weather forecasts indicate that at the ETA at the alternate airport the ceiling is at least 600 ft. and visibility is 2 SM.
Answer (A) is incorrect because 400 ft. is not a standard minimum ceiling used as an alternative airport minimum. Answer (C) is incorrect because 800 ft. and 2 SM are the alternate airport minimums for nonprecision approaches.

**54.**
**4769.** An airport without an authorized IAP may be included on an IFR flight plan as an alternate, if the current weather forecast indicates that the ceiling and visibility at the ETA will

A— be at least 300 feet and 2 miles.
B— be at least 1,000 feet and 1 mile.
C— allow for a descent from the MEA approach, and a landing under basic VFR.

Answer (C) is correct (4769). *(FAR 91.169)*
Unless otherwise authorized, no person may include an alternate airport that does not have a standard instrument approach on an IFR flight plan unless current weather forecasts indicate that at the ETA at the alternate airport the ceiling and visibility will allow for a descent from the MEA, approach, and landing under basic VFR.
Answer (A) is incorrect because 600 (not 300) ft. and 2 SM are the standard alternate airport weather minimums at ETA for a precision approach procedure. Answer (B) is incorrect because 800 (not 1,000) ft. and 2 (not 1) SM are the standard alternate airport weather minimums at ETA for a nonprecision approach procedure.

## 91.171 VOR Equipment Check for IFR Operations

**55.**
**4046.** What record shall be made in the aircraft log or other permanent record by the pilot making the VOR operational check?

A— The date, place, bearing error, and signature.
B— The date, frequency of VOR or VOT, number of flight hours since last check, and signature.
C— The date, place, satisfactory or unsatisfactory, and signature.

Answer (A) is correct (4046). *(FAR 91.171)*
Each person making the VOR operational check shall enter the date, place and bearing error, and sign the aircraft log or other record.
Answer (B) is incorrect because VOR frequency and number of flight hr. since last check are not required. Answer (C) is incorrect because the bearing error rather than "satisfactory" or "unsatisfactory" is required.

**56.**
**4036.** When must an operational check on the aircraft VOR equipment be accomplished to operate under IFR?

A— Within the preceding 10 days or 10 hours of flight time.
B— Within the preceding 30 days or 30 hours of flight time.
C— Within the preceding 30 days.

Answer (C) is correct (4036). *(FAR 91.171)*
No person may operate a civil aircraft under IFR using the VOR system of radio navigation unless the VOR equipment of that aircraft is maintained, checked, and inspected under an approved procedure, or has been operationally checked within the preceding 30 days and was found to be within the limits of the permissible indicated bearing error.
Answer (A) is incorrect because it must be checked every 30 days, not 10 days or 10 hr. Answer (B) is incorrect because there is no time requirement regarding hours of flight time.

**57.**
**4044.** Which data must be recorded in the aircraft log or other appropriate log by a pilot making a VOR operational check for IFR operations?

A— VOR name or identification, date of check, amount of bearing error, and signature.
B— Place of operational check, amount of bearing error, date of check, and signature.
C— Date of check, VOR name or identification, place of operational check, and amount of bearing error.

Answer (B) is correct (4044). *(FAR 91.171)*
Each person making the VOR operational check shall enter the date, place and bearing error, and sign the aircraft log or other record.
Answer (A) is incorrect because the place of operational check rather than the VOR name or identification is required. Answer (C) is incorrect because a signature is required and the VOR name is not required.

**58.**
**4054.** When making an airborne VOR check, what is the maximum allowable tolerance between the two indicators of a dual VOR system (units independent of each other except the antenna)?

A— 4° between the two indicated bearings of a VOR.
B— Plus or minus 4° when set to identical radials of a VOR.
C— 6° between the two indicated radials of a VOR.

Answer (A) is correct (4054). *(FAR 91.171)*
If a dual VOR system (units independent of each other except the antenna) is installed in the aircraft, you may check one system against the other. You tune both systems to the same VOR station and note the indicated bearings to that station. The maximum permissible variation between the two indicated bearings is 4°.
Answer (B) is incorrect because you center the CDI and note the bearing, not set both VORs to the same radial. Answer (C) is incorrect because the maximum allowable difference between the two VORs is 4° (not 6°) of the indicated radial.

**59.**
**4048.** Which checks and inspections of flight instruments or instrument systems must be accomplished before an aircraft can be flown under IFR?

A— VOR within 30 days, altimeter systems within 24 calendar months, and transponder within 24 calendar months.
B— ELT test within 30 days, altimeter systems within 12 calendar months, and transponder within 24 calendar months.
C— VOR within 24 calendar months, transponder within 24 calendar months, and altimeter system within 12 calendar months.

Answer (A) is correct (4048). *(FARs 91.171, 91.411, and 91.413)*
No person may operate a civil aircraft under IFR using the VOR system of radio navigation unless the VOR equipment of that aircraft is maintained, checked, and inspected under an approved procedure, or has been operationally checked within the preceding 30 days and was found to be within the limits of the permissible indicated bearing error. Also, within the preceding 24 calendar months, each altimeter system and transponder must be tested, inspected, and found to comply with the regulations.
Answer (B) is incorrect because check and inspection of the altimeter system is required every 24 (not 12) months and ELTs are maintained in accordance with the manufacturer's requirements. The FARs do not require a time interval on ELT tests, only battery replacement. Answer (C) is incorrect because VORs must be checked within 30 days (not 24 months), and altimeter systems within 24 (not 12) months.

**60.**
**4372.** What is the maximum tolerance allowed for an operational VOR equipment check when using a VOT?

A— Plus or minus 4°.
B— Plus or minus 6°.
C— Plus or minus 8°.

Answer (A) is correct (4372). *(FAR 91.171)*
When using a VOT for an operational VOR equipment check, the maximum permissible indicated bearing error is plus or minus 4°.
Answer (B) is incorrect because plus or minus 6° is the maximum error allowed when using an airborne checkpoint. Answer (C) is incorrect because plus or minus 8° is not an acceptable error for any type of VOR equipment check.

## 91.173 ATC Clearance and Flight Plan Required

**61.**
**4068.** When departing from an airport located outside controlled airspace during IMC, you must file an IFR flight plan and receive a clearance before

A— takeoff.
B— entering IFR conditions.
C— entering Class E airspace.

Answer (C) is correct (4068). *(FAR 91.173)*
No person may operate an aircraft in controlled airspace under IFR unless (s)he has filed an IFR flight plan and received an appropriate ATC clearance.
Answer (A) is incorrect because an IFR flight plan and clearance are not required until you enter controlled airspace. Answer (B) is incorrect because an IFR flight plan and clearance are not required until you enter controlled airspace.

**62.**
**4065.** To operate an aircraft under IFR, a flight plan must have been filed and an ATC clearance received prior to

A— controlling the aircraft solely by use of instruments.
B— entering weather conditions in any airspace.
C— entering controlled airspace.

Answer (C) is correct (4065). *(FAR 91.173)*
No person may operate an aircraft in controlled airspace under IFR unless (s)he has filed an IFR flight plan and received an appropriate ATC clearance.
Answer (A) is incorrect because an IFR flight plan and clearance are not required until you enter controlled airspace. Answer (B) is incorrect because an IFR flight plan and clearance are not required until you enter controlled airspace.

**63.**
**4064.** To operate under IFR below 18,000 feet, a pilot must file an IFR flight plan and receive an appropriate ATC clearance prior to

A— entering controlled airspace.
B— entering weather conditions below VFR minimums.
C— takeoff.

Answer (A) is correct (4064). *(FAR 91.173)*
No person may operate an aircraft in controlled airspace under IFR unless (s)he has filed an IFR flight plan and received an appropriate ATC clearance.
Answer (B) is incorrect because an IFR flight plan and clearance are not required until you enter controlled airspace. Answer (C) is incorrect because an IFR flight plan and clearance are not required until you enter controlled airspace.

**64.**
**4063.** Prior to which operation must an IFR flight plan be filed and an appropriate ATC clearance received?

A— Flying by reference to instruments in controlled airspace.
B— Entering controlled airspace when IMC exists.
C— Takeoff when IFR weather conditions exist.

**Answer (B) is correct (4063).** *(FAR 91.173)*
No person may operate an aircraft in controlled airspace under IFR unless (s)he has filed an IFR flight plan and received an appropriate ATC clearance.
Answer (A) is incorrect because you may fly by reference to instruments with a safety pilot in VFR weather conditions without an IFR flight plan or an IFR clearance. Answer (C) is incorrect because an IFR flight plan is not required until you enter controlled airspace.

**65.**
**4427.** No person may operate an aircraft in controlled airspace under IFR unless he/she files a flight plan

A— and receives a clearance by telephone prior to takeoff.
B— prior to takeoff and requests the clearance upon arrival on an airway.
C— and receives a clearance prior to entering controlled airspace.

**Answer (C) is correct (4427).** *(FAR 91.173)*
No person may operate an aircraft in controlled airspace under IFR unless (s)he has filed an IFR flight plan and received an appropriate ATC clearance.
Answer (A) is incorrect because it does not matter how the clearance is obtained. Answer (B) is incorrect because an IFR flight plan must have been filed before operating in controlled airspace, e.g., a Federal airway.

## 91.177 Minimum Altitudes for IFR Operations

**66.**
**4006.** Except when necessary for takeoff or landing or unless otherwise authorized by the Administrator, the minimum altitude for IFR flight is

A— 3,000 feet over all terrain.
B— 3,000 feet over designated mountainous terrain; 2,000 feet over terrain elsewhere.
C— 2,000 feet above the highest obstacle over designated mountainous terrain; 1,000 feet above the highest obstacle over terrain elsewhere.

**Answer (C) is correct (4006).** *(FAR 91.177)*
Except when necessary for takeoff or landing, no person may operate an aircraft under IFR below 2,000 ft. above the highest obstacle within a horizontal distance of 4 NM from the course to be flown over designated mountainous terrain, and 1,000 ft. above the highest obstacle within a horizontal distance of 4 NM from the course to be flown over terrain elsewhere.
Answer (A) is incorrect because the minimum IFR altitude over mountainous terrain is 2,000 ft. above the highest obstacle and 1,000 ft. over the highest obstacle over terrain elsewhere, not 3,000 ft. over all terrain. Answer (B) is incorrect because the minimum IFR altitude over mountainous terrain is 2,000 (not 3,000) ft. above the highest obstacle, and 1,000 (not 2,000) ft. above the highest obstacle over terrain elsewhere.

## 91.205 Powered Civil Aircraft with Standard Category U.S. Airworthiness Certificates: Instrument and Equipment Requirements

**67.**
**4055.** What minimum navigation equipment is required for IFR flight?

A— VOR/LOC receiver, transponder, and DME.
B— VOR receiver and, if in ARTS III environment, a coded transponder equipped for altitude reporting.
C— Navigation equipment appropriate to the ground facilities to be used.

**Answer (C) is correct (4055).** *(FAR 91.205)*
The minimum navigation equipment requirement for IFR flight is that the navigation equipment is appropriate to the ground facilities to be used.
Answer (A) is incorrect because a VOR/LOC receiver and DME are only required if VORTAC stations will be used for navigation and DME fixes need to be identified. If you are using alternative means of navigation (e.g., LORAN), this equipment is not needed. A transponder is not a navigation system. Answer (B) is incorrect because a VOR is only required if using VOR stations for navigation. If using NDB stations, then a VOR is not required. A transponder is not a navigation system.

**68.**
**4050.** Where is DME required under IFR?

A— At or above 24,000 feet MSL if VOR navigational equipment is required.
B— In positive control areas.
C— Above 18,000 feet MSL.

**Answer (A) is correct (4050).** *(FAR 91.205)*
If VOR navigational equipment is required, no person may operate a U.S. registered civil aircraft within the 50 states, and the District of Columbia, at or above 24,000 ft. MSL (FL 240) unless that aircraft is equipped with approved distance measuring equipment (DME).
Answer (B) is incorrect because Class A airspace begins at 18,000 ft. MSL and a DME is required at or above FL 240, if VOR navigational equipment is required. Answer (C) is incorrect because Class A airspace begins at 18,000 ft. MSL and a DME is required at or above FL 240, if VOR navigational equipment is required.

**69.**
**4051.** An aircraft operated during IFR under FAR Part 91 is required to have which of the following?

A— Radar altimeter.
B— Dual VOR system.
C— Gyroscopic direction indicator.

**Answer (C) is correct (4051).** *(FAR 91.205)*
An aircraft operated during IFR under FAR Part 91 is required to have a gyroscopic direction indicator (directional gyro or equivalent).
Answer (A) is incorrect because only a sensitive (not radar) altimeter is required. Answer (B) is incorrect because, if VOR navigation is to be used, only one (not two) VOR is required under FAR Part 91.

### 91.211 Supplemental Oxygen

**70.**
**4053.** What is the oxygen requirement for an unpressurized aircraft at 15,000 feet?

A— All occupants must use oxygen for the entire time at this altitude.
B— Crew must start using oxygen at 12,000 feet and passengers at 15,000 feet.
C— Crew must use oxygen for the entire time above 14,000 feet and passengers must be provided supplemental oxygen only above 15,000 feet.

**Answer (C) is correct (4053).** *(FAR 91.211)*
No one may operate a U.S. civil aircraft at cabin pressure altitudes above 14,000 ft. MSL unless the required minimum flight crew is provided with and uses supplemental oxygen during the entire flight time at those altitudes. At cabin pressure altitudes above 15,000 ft. MSL, each passenger must be provided with supplemental oxygen.
Answer (A) is incorrect because required minimum flight crew must use oxygen above 14,000 ft. MSL and others must be provided with oxygen above 15,000 ft. MSL. Answer (B) is incorrect because the crew must start using oxygen at 14,000 ft. MSL or after 30 min. above 12,500 ft. MSL.

**71.**
**4052.** What is the maximum IFR altitude you may fly in an unpressurized aircraft without providing passengers with supplemental oxygen?

A— 12,500 feet.
B— 14,000 feet.
C— 15,000 feet.

**Answer (C) is correct (4052).** *(FAR 91.211)*
At cabin pressure altitudes above 15,000 ft. MSL, each occupant must be provided with supplemental oxygen.
Answer (A) is incorrect because, at cabin pressure altitudes above 12,500 ft. MSL up to and including 14,000 ft. MSL, only the minimum flight crew must use supplemental oxygen for that part of the flight at those altitudes that is more than 30 min. duration. Answer (B) is incorrect because, at cabin pressure altitudes above 14,000 ft. MSL, only the required minimum flight crew must use supplemental oxygen.

**72.**
**4045.** What is the maximum cabin pressure altitude at which a pilot can fly for longer than 30 minutes without using supplemental oxygen?

A— 10,500 feet.
B— 12,000 feet.
C— 12,500 feet.

**Answer (C) is correct (4045).** *(FAR 91.211)*
No one may operate a U.S. civil aircraft at cabin pressure altitudes above 12,500 ft. MSL up to and including 14,000 ft. MSL unless the required minimum flight crew uses supplemental oxygen for that part of the flight at those altitudes that is of more than 30 min. duration.
Answer (A) is incorrect because supplemental oxygen is not required at any time at 10,500 ft. Answer (B) is incorrect because supplemental oxygen is not required at any time at 12,000 ft.

**73.**
**4042.** If an unpressurized aircraft is operated above 12,500 feet MSL, but not more than 14,000 feet MSL, for a period of 2 hours 20 minutes, how long during that time is the minimum flightcrew required to use supplemental oxygen?

A— 2 hours 20 minutes.
B— 1 hour 20 minutes.
C— 1 hour 50 minutes.

Answer (C) is correct (4042). *(FAR 91.211)*
No one may operate a U.S. civil aircraft at cabin pressure altitudes above 12,500 ft. MSL up to and including 14,000 ft. MSL unless the required minimum flight crew uses supplemental oxygen for that part of the flight at those altitudes that is of more than 30 min. duration. If the flight lasts 2 hr. and 20 min., the crew must use supplemental oxygen for all but 30 min., or 1 hr. and 50 min.
Answer (A) is incorrect because one may fly for 30 min. without supplemental oxygen between 12,500 ft. MSL and 14,000 ft. MSL. Answer (B) is incorrect because 30 min. of flight, not 1 hr., is permitted without supplemental oxygen between 12,500 ft. MSL up to and including 14,000 ft. MSL.

## 91.215 ATC Transponder and Altitude Reporting Equipment and Use

**74.**
**4037.** In the 48 contiguous states, excluding the airspace at or below 2,500 feet AGL, an operable coded transponder equipped with Mode C capability is required in all controlled airspace at and above

A— 12,500 feet MSL.
B— 10,000 feet MSL.
C— Flight level (FL) 180.

Answer (B) is correct (4037). *(FAR 91.215)*
Unless otherwise authorized or directed by ATC, no person may operate an aircraft in the 48 contiguous states at and above 10,000 ft. MSL, excluding the airspace at or below 2,500 ft. AGL, unless the aircraft is equipped with an operable Mode C transponder.
Answer (A) is incorrect because 12,500 ft. MSL pertains to supplemental oxygen, not Mode C, requirements. Answer (C) is incorrect because FL 180 is the floor of Class A airspace.

**75.**
**4038.** A coded transponder equipped with altitude reporting capability is required in all controlled airspace

A— at and above 10,000 feet MSL, excluding at and below 2,500 feet AGL.
B— at and above 2,500 feet above the surface.
C— below 10,000 feet MSL, excluding at and below 2,500 feet AGL.

Answer (A) is correct (4038). *(FAR 91.215)*
Unless otherwise authorized or directed by ATC, no person may operate an aircraft in the 48 contiguous states at and above 10,000 ft. MSL, excluding the airspace at or below 2,500 ft. AGL, unless the aircraft is equipped with an operable Mode C transponder.
Answer (B) is incorrect because the airspace above 2,500 ft. AGL must also be at or above 10,000 ft. MSL. Answer (C) is incorrect because the limit is at and above (not below) 10,000 ft. MSL.

**76.**
**4439.** A request for a deviation from the 4096 code transponder equipment requirement, when operating in Class B airspace, must be submitted to the

A— FAA Administrator at least 24 hours before the proposed operation.
B— nearest FAA General Aviation District Office 24 hours before the proposed operation.
C— controlling ATC facility at least 1 hour before the proposed flight.

Answer (C) is correct (4439). *(FAR 91.215)*
ATC may authorize deviations on a continuing basis, or for individual flights, for operations of aircraft without a transponder. The request for a deviation must be submitted to the ATC facility having jurisdiction over the airspace concerned at least 1 hr. before the proposed operation.
Answer (A) is incorrect because the ATC facility having jurisdiction over the Class B airspace, not the FAA Administrator, authorizes deviations from the transponder requirements, and the request must be made at least 1 (not 24) hr. before the proposed operation. Answer (B) is incorrect because the ATC facility having jurisdiction over the Class B airspace (not the nearest FAA office) authorizes deviations from the transponder requirements, and the request must be made at least 1 (not 24) hr. before the proposed operation.

**77.**
**4007.** If the aircraft's transponder fails during flight within Class B airspace,

A— the pilot should immediately request clearance to depart the Class B airspace.

B— ATC may authorize deviation from the transponder requirement to allow aircraft to continue to the airport of ultimate destination.

C— aircraft must immediately descend below 1,200 feet AGL and proceed to destination.

Answer (B) is correct (4007). *(FAR 91.215)*
If an aircraft's transponder fails during flight within Class B airspace, ATC may authorize deviation from the transponder requirement to allow the aircraft to continue to the airport of ultimate destination, including any intermediate stops, or to proceed to a place where suitable repairs can be made or both.
Answer (A) is incorrect because ATC can immediately authorize a deviation from the transponder requirement without requiring the pilot to request clearance to depart the Class B airspace area. Answer (C) is incorrect because a pilot may only descend if clearance from ATC is obtained.

## 91.411  Altimeter System and Altitude Reporting Equipment Tests and Inspections

**78.**
**4047.** Your aircraft had the static pressure system and altimeter tested and inspected on January 5, of this year, and was found to comply with FAA standards. These systems must be reinspected and approved for use in controlled airspace under IFR by

A— January 5, next year.

B— January 5, 2 years hence.

C— January 31, 2 years hence.

Answer (C) is correct (4047). *(FAR 91.411)*
Within the preceding 24 calendar months, each static pressure system, each altimeter instrument, and each automatic pressure altitude reporting system must be tested, inspected, and found to comply with the regulations. The 24-calendar-month period following January of this year begins February 1, this year, and ends on January 31, 2 years hence.
Answer (A) is incorrect because it is 24 months (not 12 months). Answer (B) is incorrect because the requirement is within the preceding 24 calendar months (not within 24 months).

**79.**
**4049.** An aircraft altimeter system test and inspection must be accomplished within

A— 12 calendar months.

B— 18 calendar months.

C— 24 calendar months.

Answer (C) is correct (4049). *(FAR 91.411)*
Within the preceding 24 calendar months, each static pressure system, each altimeter instrument, and each automatic pressure altitude reporting system must be tested, inspected, and found to comply with the regulations.
Answer (A) is incorrect because an annual inspection (not the altimeter system) must be accomplished within the preceding 12 calendar months. Answer (B) is incorrect because the aircraft's altimeter system must be tested and inspected within 24 (not 18) calendar months.

## 5.3  NTSB PART 830  NOTIFICATION AND REPORTING OF AIRCRAFT ACCIDENTS OR INCIDENTS AND OVERDUE AIRCRAFT, AND PRESERVATION OF AIRCRAFT WRECKAGE, MAIL, CARGO, AND RECORDS

**80.**
**4088.** Which publication covers the procedures required for aircraft accident and incident reporting responsibilities for pilots?

A— FAR Part 61.

B— FAR Part 91.

C— NTSB Part 830.

Answer (C) is correct (4088). *(NTSB 830.1)*
NTSB Part 830 contains rules pertaining to:

1. Notification and reporting aircraft accidents and incidents and certain other occurrences in the operation of aircraft when they involve civil aircraft of the U.S. wherever they occur, or foreign civil aircraft when such events occur in the U.S., its territories, or possessions.
2. Reporting aircraft accidents and listed incidents in the operation of aircraft when they involve certain public aircraft.
3. Preservation of aircraft wreckage, mail, cargo, and records involving all civil aircraft in the U.S., its territories, or possessions.

Answer (A) is incorrect because FAR 61 concerns certification of pilots and flight instructors. Answer (B) is incorrect because FAR 91 concerns general operating and flight rules.

# END OF CHAPTER

# CHAPTER SIX
# NAVIGATION

This chapter contains outlines of major concepts tested, all FAA Instrument Rating written test questions and answers regarding instrument navigation, and an explanation of each answer. The subtopics or modules within this chapter are listed above, followed in parentheses by the number of questions from the FAA written test pertaining to that particular module. The two numbers following the parentheses are the page numbers on which the outline and questions begin for that module.

**CAUTION:** Recall that the **sole purpose** of this book is to expedite your passing the FAA written test for the instrument rating. Accordingly, all extraneous material (i.e., topics or regulations not directly tested on the FAA written test) is omitted, even though much more information and knowledge are necessary to fly safely. This additional material is presented in *Instrument Pilot FAA Practical Test Prep* and *Aviation Weather and Weather Services*, available from Gleim Publications, Inc. See the order form on page 478.

## 6.1 DISTANCE MEASURING EQUIPMENT (DME) AND LORAN  (Questions 1-6)

1. DME displays slant range distance in nautical miles.

2. Ignore slant range error if the airplane is 1 NM or more from the ground facility for each 1,000 ft. AGL.

    a. The greatest slant range error comes at high altitudes very close to the VORTAC.

    b. EXAMPLE: If you are 6,000 ft. AGL directly above a VORTAC, your DME will read 1.0 NM.

3. A pilot can check the Airplane Flight Manual Supplement to determine if a LORAN C equipped aircraft is approved for IFR operations.

## 6.2 AUTOMATIC DIRECTION FINDER (ADF)  (Questions 7-21)

1. The ADF indicator always has its needle pointing toward the NDB station (nondirectional beacon, also known as a radio beacon).

    a. If the NDB is directly in front of the airplane, the needle will point straight up.

    b. If the NDB is directly off the right wing, i.e., 3 o'clock, the needle will point directly to the right.

    c. If the NDB is directly behind the aircraft, the needle will point straight down, etc.

    d. The figure on the next page illustrates the terms that are used with the ADF.

2.    Relative bearing (RB) to the station is the number of degrees you would have to turn to the right to fly directly to the NDB.

    a.    This is shown by the head of the needle.

        1)    In the figure below, the RB to the station is 220°.

    b.    Relative bearing FROM is given by the tail of the needle.

        1)    In the figure below, the RB from the station is 40° (220 − 180).

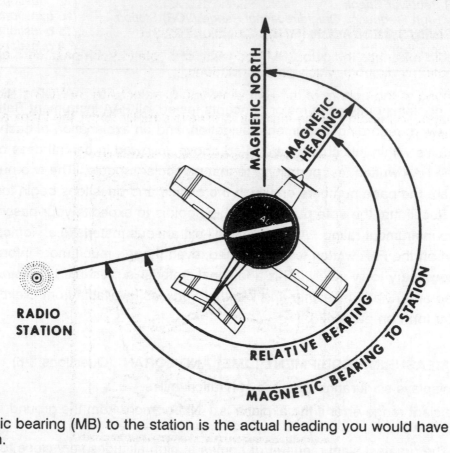

3.    Magnetic bearing (MB) to the station is the actual heading you would have to fly to the station.

    a.    If you turn right from your present heading to fly to the station, you are adding the number of degrees of turn to your heading.

    b.    Thus, magnetic heading + relative bearing = magnetic bearing to the station, or MH + RB = MB (TO).

        1)    For MB (FROM) subtract or add 180°.

        2)    EXAMPLE:  If the airplane shown above has an MH of 40° and an RB of 220°, the MB (TO) is 260° (40 + 220).  The MB (FROM) is 80° (260 − 180).

    c.    If MH and MB (TO) are known, use the formula:  RB = MB (TO) − MH.

        1)    Add or subtract 360° to obtain a figure between 0° and 360°, if needed.

4.    A fixed card ADF always shows 0° at the top.

    a.    Thus, RB may be read directly from the card and MB must be calculated using the above formula.

    b.    If the MB is given, the MH may be calculated as follows:  MB − RB = MH.

5.  A movable card ADF always shows magnetic heading (MH) at the top.

    a.  Thus, MB (TO) may be read directly from the card under the head of the needle.
    b.  MB (FROM) is indicated by the tail of the needle.
    c.  RB may be calculated as follows:  MB − MH = RB.

6.  When working ADF problems, it is often helpful to draw the information given (as illustrated on page 164) to provide a picture of the airplane's position relative to the NDB station.

## 6.3 RADIO MAGNETIC INDICATOR (RMI)  (Questions 22-31)

1.  The radio magnetic indicator (RMI) consists of a rotating compass card and one or more navigation indicators which point to stations.

2.  The knobs at the bottom of the RMI allow you to select ADF or VOR stations.

3.  The magnetic heading of the airplane is always directly under the index at the top of the instrument.

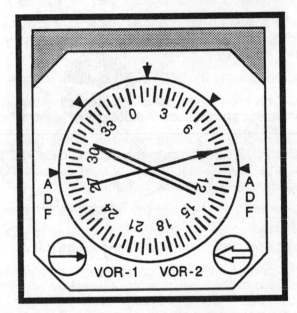

4.  The bearing pointer displays magnetic bearings to selected navigation stations.

    a.  The tail of the indicator tells you which radial you are on, or the magnetic bearing FROM the station.

5.  DME arcs with the RMI.  On right-hand arcs the RMI needle should point to the right wingtip and the left wingtip on left-hand arcs.  This assumes a no-wind situation.

    a.  Crosswind from the inside of the arc (e.g., left crosswind on a left-hand arc) -- You must turn toward the NAVAID to compensate for the crosswind and the RMI needle will point in front of the wingtip reference.

    b.  Crosswind from the outside of the arc -- Requires you to turn to the outside of the arc which puts the RMI needle behind the wingtip reference.

## 6.4  VOR RECEIVER CHECK  (Questions 32-43)

1.  The Airport/Facility Directory provides a listing of available VOR receiver ground checkpoints and VOTs (VOR Receiver Test Facilities).

    a.  VOT frequencies are also listed on En Route Low Altitude Charts.

2.  Over airborne checkpoints designated by the FAA, the maximum permissible bearing error for the VOR receiver is plus or minus 6° of the designated radial.

    a.  An alternative to a certified airborne checkpoint is to select a prominent ground reference point that is more than 20 NM from a VOR station that is along an established VOR airway.

        1)  Once over this point with the CDI needle centered, the OBS should indicate plus or minus 6° of the published radial.

3.  The maximum difference between two indicators of a dual VOR system is 4° between the two indicated bearings to the VOR.

    a.  The CDI needles should be centered and the indicated bearings checked rather than setting to identical radials and looking at the CDI needles.

4.  VOR Receiver Test Facilities (VOTs) are available at a specified frequency at certain airports.  The facility permits you to check the accuracy of your VOR receiver while you are on the ground.

    a.  The VOT transmits only the 360° radial in all directions.

    b.  Tune the VOR receiver to the specified frequency and turn the OBS (omnibearing selector) to select an omnibearing course of either 0° or 180°.

        1)  The CDI needle should be centered; if not, then center the needle.
        2)  If 0°, the TO/FROM indicator should indicate FROM.
        3)  If 180°, the TO/FROM indicator should indicate TO.
        4)  The maximum error is plus or minus 4°.

    c.  When using an RMI, the head of the needle will indicate 180°.

5.  When making a VOR receiver check and your airplane is located on the designated ground checkpoint, the designated radial should be set on the OBS.

    a.  The CDI must center within plus or minus 4° of that radial with a FROM indication.

## 6.5  VERY HIGH FREQUENCY OMNIDIRECTIONAL RANGE (VOR) STATION  (Questions 44-59)

1.  When VORs are undergoing maintenance, the coded and/or voice identification is not broadcast from the VOR.

2.  DME/TACAN coded identification is transmitted one time for each three or four times the VOR identification is transmitted.

    a.  If the VOR is out of service, the DME identification will be transmitted about once every 30 seconds at 1350 Hz.

3.  A full-scale (from the center position to either side of the dial) deflection of a VOR CDI indicates a 10° deviation from the course centerline.

    a.  About 10°-12° of change of the OBS setting should deflect the CDI from the center to the last dot.

4.  An (H) Class VORTAC facility has a range of 100 NM from 14,500 ft. AGL to 60,000 ft.

    a.  To use (H) Class VORTAC facilities to define a direct route of flight between these altitudes, they should be no farther apart than 200 NM.

5. VOR station passage is indicated by a complete reversal of the TO/FROM indicator.

   a. If after station passage the CDI shows a ½ scale deflection and remains constant for a period of time, you are flying away from the selected radial.

6. Airplane displacement from a course is approximately 200 ft. per dot per NM on VORs.

   a. At 30 NM out, one dot is 1 NM displacement, two dots 2 NM.
   b. At 60 NM out, one dot is 2 NM displacement, two dots 4 NM.

7. Time/distance to station formula. When tracking inbound, make a 90° turn and measure time and degrees of bearing change.

   a. $Min.\ to\ Station = \dfrac{60\ x\ Min.\ between\ Bearings}{Degrees\ of\ Bearing\ Change}$

   b. $Distance\ to\ Station = \dfrac{TAS\ x\ Min.\ Flown}{Degrees\ of\ Bearing\ Change}$

      1) You may also use your flight computer to calculate the distance.

## 6.6 HORIZONTAL SITUATION INDICATOR (HSI) (Questions 60-74)

1. The horizontal situation indicator (HSI) is a combination of the vertical azimuth card indicator and the VOR/ILS indicator, as illustrated and explained below.

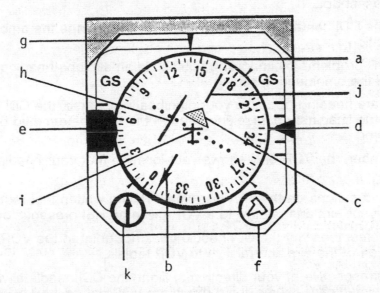

   a. The azimuth card, which rotates so that the heading is shown under the index at the top of the instrument.

      1) The azimuth card may be part of a remote indicating compass (RIC).

      2) Or the azimuth card must be checked against the magnetic compass and reset with a heading set knob.

   b. The course indicating arrow, which is the VOR (OBS) indicator.

   c. The TO/FROM indicator for the VOR.

   d. Glide slope deviation pointer. It indicates above or below the glide slope, which is the longer center line.

   e. Glide slope warning flag, which comes out when reliable signals are not received by the glide slope deviation pointer.

f.  Heading set knob, which is used to coordinate the heading indicator (directional gyro, etc.) with the actual compass.

1)  If the azimuth card is part of an RIC, this is normally a heading bug (pointer) set knob that moves a bug around the periphery of the azimuth card.

g.  Lubber line, which shows the current heading.

h.  Course deviation bar, which indicates the direction one would have to turn to intercept the desired radial if one were on the approximate heading of the OBS selection.

i.  The airplane symbol, which is fixed. It shows the airplane relative to the selected course as though you were above the airplane looking down.

j.  The tail of the course indicating arrow, which shows the reciprocal of the OBS heading.

k.  The course setting knob, which is used to adjust the OBS.

2.  Airplane displacement from a course is approximately 200 ft. per dot per NM on VORs.

a.  At 30 NM out, one dot is 1 NM displacement, two dots 2 NM.
b.  At 60 NM out, one dot is 2 NM displacement, two dots 4 NM.

3.  A full-scale deflection of a VOR CDI indicates a 10° deviation from the course centerline.

a.  About 10° to 12° of change of the OBS setting should deflect the CDI from the center to the last dot.

b.  With the CDI centered, rotate the OBS 180° to change the ambiguity (TO/FROM) indication.

4.  Solve all VOR problems by imagining yourself in an airplane heading in the general direction of the omnibearing setting.

a.  If you are heading opposite your omnibearing course, the CDI needle will point away from the imaginary course line through the VOR determined by your omnibearing selector.

b.  Remember, the VOR only shows your location (not your heading) with respect to the VOR.

5.  A few of the questions on the FAA Instrument Rating written test require you to identify the position of your airplane relative to a VOR given an HSI presentation.

a.  First, remember that the CDI needle does not point to the VOR. It indicates the position of the airplane relative to VOR radials.

1)  Irrespective of your direction of flight, the CDI needle always points toward the imaginary course line through the VOR determined by your omnibearing selector.

b.  The TO/FROM indicator operates independently of the direction (heading) of your airplane. It indicates which side of the VOR your airplane is on, based on the radial set on your omnibearing selector.

1)  Irrespective of your direction of flight, the TO/FROM indicator shows you whether you are before, on, or past a line 90° (perpendicular) to the course line determined by your omnibearing setting.

6.  The following diagram explains the TO/FROM indicator and the CDI needle.

    a.  Remember, you must "rotate" the diagram so the omnibearing direction is "pointed" in the general direction in which your omnibearing selector is set.

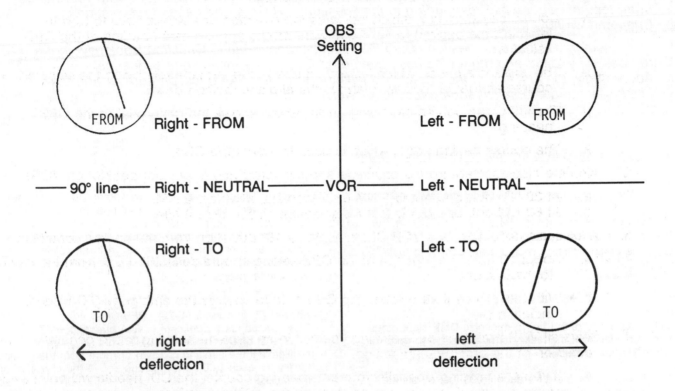

## 6.7 HSI/LOCALIZER  (Questions 75-83)

1.  When VOR is tuned to a localizer frequency (108.10 to 111.95), the OBS (course selection) setting has no impact on the indications of the VOR.

2.  When an HSI is tuned to a localizer frequency (108.10 to 111.95) the setting of the front course heading with the head of the needle will eliminate reverse sensing on back courses.

    a.  Inbound on a back course the tail of the needle will be at the top of the instrument and you will have positive sensing.

    b.  If the HSI needle is set to the front course heading, you will have normal sensing on the HSI, whether you are flying a front course or a back course approach.

    c.  If the HSI needle is set to the back course heading, you will have reverse sensing on the HSI, whether you are flying a front course or a back course approach.

3.  The localizer information is reported on the face of the HSI instrument just as VOR signals are.

    a.  That is, it is based upon position rather than heading.

4.  Similar to VORs, if one is going in the direction specified for an approach to a runway, a left deflection means one is to the right of course if one is facing in the approximate direction of the localizer.

---

**QUESTIONS AND ANSWER EXPLANATIONS**

All the FAA questions from the written test for the instrument rating relating to navigation and the material outlined previously are reproduced on the following pages in the same modules as the outlines. To the immediate right of each question are the correct answer and answer explanation. You should cover these answers and answer explanations with your hand or a piece of paper while responding to the questions. Refer to the general discussion in Chapter 1 on how to take the FAA written test.

Remember that the questions from the FAA Instrument Rating Question Book have been reordered by topic, and the topics have been organized into a meaningful sequence. Accordingly, the first line of the answer explanation gives the FAA question number and the citation of the authoritative source for the answer.

---

### 6.1 Distance Measuring Equipment (DME) and LORAN

**1.**
**4397.** Which distance is displayed by the DME indicator?

A— Slant range distance in NM.
B— Slant range distance in SM.
C— Line-of-sight direct distance from aircraft to VORTAC in SM.

Answer (A) is correct (4397). *(IFH Chap VII)*
DME (Distance Measuring Equipment) displays line-of-sight direct distance, i.e., slant range, from the aircraft to the VORTAC in nautical miles.
Answer (B) is incorrect because the measurement is in nautical miles, not statute miles. Answer (C) is incorrect because the measurement is in nautical miles, not statute miles.

**2.**
**4472.** As a rule of thumb, to minimize DME slant range error, how far from the facility should you be to consider the reading as accurate?

A— Two miles or more for each 1,000 feet of altitude above the facility.
B— One or more miles for each 1,000 feet of altitude above the facility.
C— No specific distance is specified since the reception is line-of-sight.

Answer (B) is correct (4472). *(IFH Chap VII)*
*This question is a duplicate of FAA question 4487.*
You should consider the DME slant range error negligible if the airplane is 1 NM or more from the ground facility for each 1,000 ft. of altitude above the elevation of the facility.
Answer (A) is incorrect because the accuracy is 1 NM, not 2 NM, for each 1,000 ft. AGL. Answer (C) is incorrect because a specific distance *is* required because the reception is line-of-sight.

**3.**
**4487.** As a rule of thumb, to minimize DME slant range error, how far from the facility should you be to consider the reading as accurate?

A— Two miles or more for each 1,000 feet of altitude above the facility.
B— One or more miles for each 1,000 feet of altitude above the facility.
C— No specific distance is specified since the reception is line-of-sight.

Answer (B) is correct (4487). *(IFH Chap VII)*
*This question is a duplicate of FAA question 4472.*
You should consider the DME slant range error negligible if the airplane is 1 NM or more from the ground facility for each 1,000 ft. of altitude above the elevation of the facility.
Answer (A) is incorrect because the accuracy is 1 NM, not 2 NM, for each 1,000 ft. AGL. Answer (C) is incorrect because a specific distance *is* required because the reception is line-of-sight.

**4.**
**4399.** Where does the DME indicator have the greatest error between ground distance to the VORTAC and displayed distance?

A— High altitudes far from the VORTAC.
B— High altitudes close to the VORTAC.
C— Low altitudes far from the VORTAC.

Answer (B) is correct (4399). *(IFH Chap VII)*
Because the DME reads slant range distance, its greatest error occurs at high altitudes very close to the VORTAC. For example, if one were at 12,000 ft. directly over the VOR, the DME would show a distance from the VOR of approximately 2 NM.
Answer (A) is incorrect because, as you get farther away from the station, the slant range error of the DME becomes minimal. Answer (C) is incorrect because the DME has the greatest error at high (not low) altitudes close to (not far from) the VORTAC.

**5.**
**4413.** Which DME indication should you receive when you are directly over a VORTAC site at approximately 6,000 feet AGL?

A— 0.
B— 1.
C— 1.3.

Answer (B) is correct (4413). *(IFH Chap VII)*
Because the DME indicates slant range distance, it will indicate your altitude if you are directly above the VORTAC. One nautical mile equals approximately 6,000 ft., so the DME would read 1 NM.
Answer (A) is incorrect because the DME would only indicate zero if you were at ground level next to the VORTAC. Answer (C) is incorrect because it would mean that your altitude was about 8,000 ft. AGL (6,000 x 1.3).

**6.**
**4665.** By which means may a pilot determine if a Loran C equipped aircraft is approved for IFR operations?

A— Not necessary; Loran C is not approved for IFR.
B— Check aircraft logbook.
C— Check the Airplane Flight Manual Supplement.

Answer (C) is correct (4665). *(AIM Para 1-17)*
Pilots must be aware of the authorized operational approval level (e.g., VFR or IFR) of a LORAN receiver installed in their aircraft. Approval information is contained in the Aircraft Flight Manual Supplement, on FAA Form 337, in aircraft maintenance records, or possibly by a placard installed near or on the control panel.
Answer (A) is incorrect because some LORAN C receivers are approved for IFR operations by the FAA. Answer (B) is incorrect because the operational approval level may be found in the aircraft maintenance records, not necessarily the aircraft logbook.

## 6.2 Automatic Direction Finder (ADF)

**7.**
**4578.** (Refer to figure 101 below.) What is the magnetic bearing TO the station?

A— 060°.
B— 260°.
C— 270°.

Answer (B) is correct (4578). *(IFH Chap VII)*
Magnetic bearing TO the station is equal to the sum of magnetic heading plus relative bearing. Magnetic heading is given on the heading indicator as 350° and the relative bearing is given as 270°. The sum is 620°. To obtain answers between 0° and 360°, you may have to add or subtract 360°. 620° – 360° = 260° magnetic bearing TO the station.

$$
\begin{aligned}
MH + RB &= MB \\
620° &= MB \\
620° - 360° &= MB \\
260° &= MB
\end{aligned}
$$

Answer (A) is incorrect because 060° would be the MB FROM (not TO) the station if the MH were 330°. Answer (C) is incorrect because 270° is the relative (not magnetic) bearing TO the station.

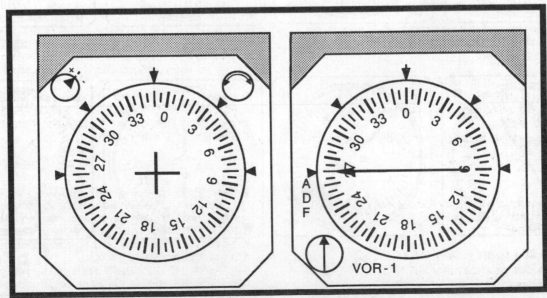

FIGURE 101.—Directional Gyro and ADF Indicator.

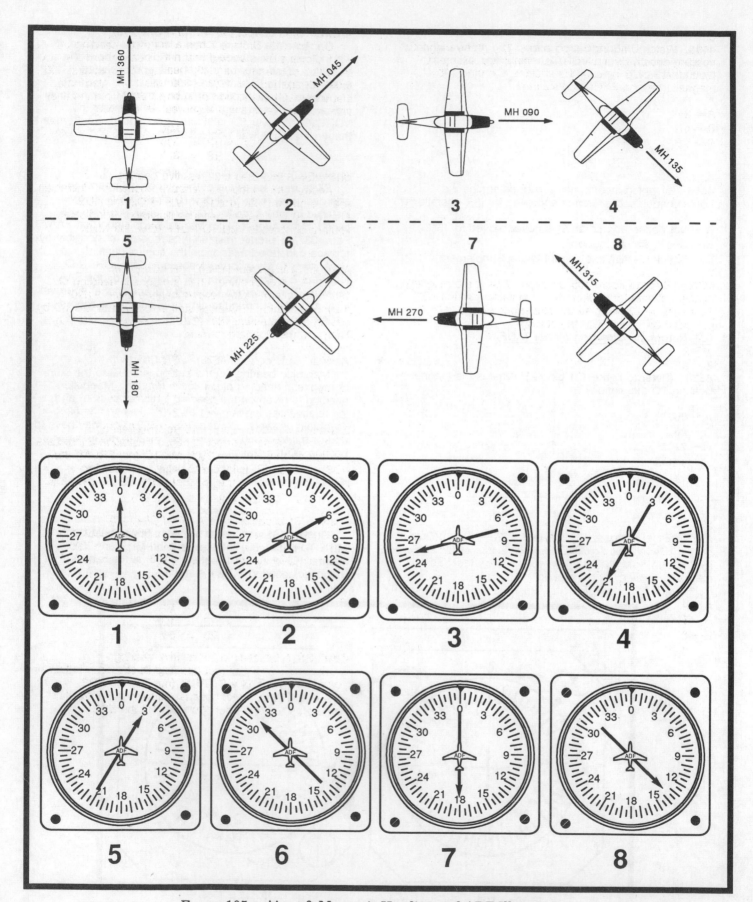

FIGURE 105.—Aircraft Magnetic Heading and ADF Illustration.

**8.**
**4591.**  (Refer to figure 105 on page 172.)  If the magnetic heading shown for airplane 7 is maintained, which ADF illustration would indicate the airplane is on the 120° magnetic bearing FROM the station?

A— 2.
B— 4.
C— 5.

**Answer (C) is correct (4591).**  *(IFH Chap VII)*
On Fig. 105, airplane 7 has a magnetic heading of 270°.  To use the standard magnetic bearing formula, you must first convert to magnetic bearing TO by adding 180° to MB FROM (120° + 180° = 300° MB TO).  Also note that you may have to add or subtract 360° from the final answer to arrive at a figure between 0° and 360°.

$$MH + RB = MB$$
$$270° + RB = 300°$$
$$RB = 30°$$

Illustration 5 indicates a 30° relative bearing.
Answer (A) is incorrect because illustration 2 indicates you are on the 150° (not 120°) MB FROM the NDB.  Answer (B) is incorrect because illustration 4 indicates you are on the 120° MB TO (not FROM) the NDB.

**9.**
**4592.**  (Refer to figure 105 on page 172.)  If the magnetic heading shown for airplane 5 is maintained, which ADF illustration would indicate the airplane is on the 210° magnetic bearing FROM the station?

A— 2.
B— 3.
C— 4.

**Answer (C) is correct (4592).**  *(IFH Chap VII)*
On Fig. 105, airplane 5 has a magnetic heading of 180°.  To determine the relative bearing given a 210° magnetic bearing FROM the station, convert to MB TO by adding or subtracting 180° (210° − 180° = 30° MB TO).  Then use the standard formula.

$$MH + RB = MB$$
$$180° + RB = 30°$$
$$RB = -150°$$
$$RB = -150° + 360°$$
$$RB = 210°$$

Illustration 4 indicates a of 210° relative bearing.
Answer (A) is incorrect because illustration 2 indicates you are on the 240° (not 210°) MB TO (not FROM) the NDB.  Answer (B) is incorrect because illustration 3 indicates you are on the 75° (not 210°) MB TO the NDB.

**10.**
**4593.**  (Refer to figure 105 on page 172.)  If the magnetic heading shown for airplane 3 is maintained, which ADF illustration would indicate the airplane is on the 120° magnetic bearing TO the station?

A— 4.
B— 5.
C— 8.

**Answer (B) is correct (4593).**  *(IFH Chap VII)*
On Fig. 105, airplane 3 has a magnetic heading of 090°.  To determine the relative bearing given a 120° magnetic bearing TO the station, use the standard magnetic bearing formula to get the bearing to the station.

$$MH + RB = MB$$
$$90° + RB = 120°$$
$$RB = 30°$$

Illustration 5 indicates a 30° relative bearing.
Answer (A) is incorrect because illustration 4 indicates you are on the 120° MB FROM (not TO) the NDB.  Answer (C) is incorrect because illustration 8 indicates you are on the 225° (not 120°) MB TO the NDB.

**11.**
**4594.** (Refer to figure 105 on page 172.) If the magnetic heading shown for airplane 1 is maintained, which ADF illustration would indicate the airplane is on the 060° magnetic bearing TO the station?

A— 2.
B— 4.
C— 5.

Answer (A) is correct (4594). *(IFH Chap VII)*
On Fig. 105, airplane 1 has a magnetic heading of 360° or 0°. To determine the relative bearing given a 060° magnetic bearing TO the station, use the standard magnetic bearing formula to get the bearing to the station.

$$MH + RB = MB$$
$$0° + RB = 60°$$
$$RB = 60°$$

Illustration 2 indicates a 60° relative bearing.
Answer (B) is incorrect because illustration 4 indicates you are on the 210° (not 060°) MB TO the NDB.
Answer (C) is incorrect because illustration 5 indicates you are on the 030° (not 060°) MB TO the NDB.

**12.**
**4595.** (Refer to figure 105 on page 172.) If the magnetic heading shown for airplane 2 is maintained, which ADF illustration would indicate the airplane is on the 255° magnetic bearing TO the station?

A— 2.
B— 4.
C— 5.

Answer (B) is correct (4595). *(IFH Chap VII)*
On Fig. 105, airplane 2 has a magnetic heading of 045°. To determine the relative bearing given a 255° magnetic bearing TO the station, use the standard magnetic bearing formula to get the bearing to the station.

$$MH + RB = MB$$
$$45° + RB = 255°$$
$$RB = 210°$$

Illustration 4 indicates a 210° relative bearing.
Answer (A) is incorrect because illustration 2 indicates you are on the 105° (not 255°) MB TO the NDB.
Answer (C) is incorrect because illustration 5 indicates you are on the 255° MB FROM (not TO) the NDB.

**13.**
**4596.** (Refer to figure 105 on page 172.) If the magnetic heading shown for airplane 4 is maintained, which ADF illustration would indicate the airplane is on the 135° magnetic bearing TO the station?

A— 1.
B— 4.
C— 8.

Answer (A) is correct (4596). *(IFH Chap VII)*
On Fig. 105, airplane 4 has a magnetic heading of 135°. To determine the relative bearing given a 135° magnetic bearing TO the station, use the standard magnetic bearing formula to get the magnetic bearing to the station.

$$MH + RB = MB$$
$$135° + RB = 135°$$
$$RB = 0°$$

Illustration 1 indicates a 0° relative bearing.
Answer (B) is incorrect because illustration 4 indicates you are on the 345° (not 135°) MB TO the NDB.
Answer (C) is incorrect because illustration 8 indicates you are on the 270° (not 135°) MB TO the NDB.

**14.**
**4597.** (Refer to figure 105 on page 172.) If the magnetic heading shown for airplane 6 is maintained, which ADF illustration would indicate the airplane is on the 255° magnetic bearing FROM the station?

A— 2.
B— 4.
C— 5.

Answer (B) is correct (4597). *(IFH Chap VII)*
On Fig. 105, airplane 6 has a magnetic heading of 225°. To determine the relative bearing given a 255° magnetic bearing FROM the station, convert to MB TO by subtracting 180° (255° − 180° = 75° MB TO). Then use the standard formula.

$$MH + RB = MB$$
$$225° + RB = 75°$$
$$RB = -150° + 360°$$
$$RB = 210°$$

Illustration 4 indicates a 210° relative bearing.
Answer (A) is incorrect because illustration 2 indicates you are on the 105° (not 255°) MB FROM the NDB.
Answer (C) is incorrect because illustration 5 indicates you are on the 255° MB TO (not FROM) the NDB.

**15.**
**4598.** (Refer to figure 105 on page 172.) If the magnetic heading shown for airplane 8 is maintained, which ADF illustration would indicate the airplane is on the 090° magnetic bearing FROM the station?

A— 3.
B— 4.
C— 6.

Answer (C) is correct (4598). *(IFH Chap VII)*
On Fig. 105, airplane 8 has a magnetic heading of 315°. To determine the relative bearing given a 090° magnetic bearing FROM the station, convert to MB TO by adding 180° (90° + 180° = 270° MB TO). Then use the standard formula.

$$
\begin{aligned}
\text{MH} + \text{RB} &= \text{MB} \\
315° + \text{RB} &= 270° \\
\text{RB} &= -45° + 360° \\
\text{RB} &= 315°
\end{aligned}
$$

Illustration 6 indicates a 315° relative bearing.
Answer (A) is incorrect because illustration 3 indicates you are on the 030° (not 090°) MB FROM the NDB. Answer (B) is incorrect because illustration 4 indicates you are on the 345° (not 090°) MB FROM the NDB.

**16.**
**4599.** (Refer to figure 105 on page 172.) If the magnetic heading shown for airplane 5 is maintained, which ADF illustration would indicate the airplane is on the 240° magnetic bearing TO the station?

A— 2.
B— 3.
C— 4.

Answer (A) is correct (4599). *(IFH Chap VII)*
On Fig. 105, airplane 5 has a magnetic heading of 180°. To determine the relative bearing given a 240° magnetic bearing TO the station, use the standard magnetic bearing formula to get the relative bearing to the station.

$$
\begin{aligned}
\text{MH} + \text{RB} &= \text{MB} \\
180° + \text{RB} &= 240° \\
\text{RB} &= 60°
\end{aligned}
$$

Illustration 2 indicates a 60° relative bearing.
Answer (B) is incorrect because illustration 3 indicates you are on the 075° (not 240°) MB TO the NDB. Answer (C) is incorrect because illustration 4 indicates you are on the 030° (not 240°) MB TO the NDB.

**17.**
**4600.** (Refer to figure 105 on page 172.) If the magnetic heading shown for airplane 8 is maintained, which ADF illustration would indicate the airplane is on the 315° magnetic bearing TO the station?

A— 3.
B— 4.
C— 1.

Answer (C) is correct (4600). *(IFH Chap VII)*
On Fig. 105, airplane 8 has a magnetic heading of 315°. To determine the relative bearing given a 060° magnetic bearing TO the station, use the standard magnetic bearing formula to get the bearing to the station.

$$
\begin{aligned}
\text{MH} + \text{RB} &= \text{MB} \\
315° + \text{RB} &= 315° \\
\text{RB TO} &= 0°
\end{aligned}
$$

Illustration 1 indicates a 0° relative bearing.
Answer (A) is incorrect because illustration 3 indicates you are on the 210° (not 060°) MB TO the NDB. Answer (B) is incorrect because illustration 4 indicates you are on the 165° (not 060°) MB TO the NDB.

**18.**
**4583.** (Refer to instruments in figure 102 below.) On the basis of this information, the magnetic bearing TO the station would be

A— 175°.
B— 255°.
C— 355°.

Answer (C) is correct (4583). *(IFH Chap VII)*
On Fig. 102, the airplane has a magnetic heading of 215° and a relative bearing of 140°. To determine the magnetic bearing TO the station, use the standard magnetic bearing formula to get the bearing TO the station.

$$MH + RB = MB$$
$$215° + 140° = MB$$
$$MB = 355°$$

Answer (A) is incorrect because 175° is the MB FROM (not TO) the NDB. Answer (B) is incorrect because 255° is not a related direction in this problem.

FIGURE 102.—Directional Gyro and ADF Indicator.

**19.**
**4584.** (Refer to instruments in figure 102 above.) On the basis of this information, the magnetic bearing FROM the station would be

A— 175°.
B— 255°.
C— 355°.

Answer (A) is correct (4584). *(IFH Chap VII)*
On Fig. 102, the airplane has a magnetic heading of 215° and a relative bearing of 140°. To determine the magnetic bearing FROM the station, use the standard magnetic bearing formula to get the magnetic bearing TO the station, and then add or subtract 180° to convert MB TO to MB FROM.

$$MH + RB = MB$$
$$215° + 140° = 355° \text{ MB TO}$$
$$MB \text{ FROM} = 355° - 180° = 175°$$

Answer (B) is incorrect because 255° is not a related direction in this problem. Answer (C) is incorrect because 355° is the MB TO (not FROM) the NDB.

**20.**
**4586.** (Refer to instruments in figure 103 below.) On the basis of this information, the magnetic bearing TO the station would be

A— 060°.
B— 240°.
C— 270°.

Answer (B) is correct (4586). *(IFH Chap VII)*
On Fig. 103, the airplane has a magnetic heading of 330° and a relative bearing of 270°. To determine the magnetic bearing TO the station, use the standard magnetic bearing formula to get the magnetic bearing TO the station.

$$MH + RB = MB$$
$$330° + 270° = MB$$
$$MB = 600°$$
$$600° - 360° = 240°$$

Answer (A) is incorrect because 060° is the MB FROM (not TO) the NDB. Answer (C) is incorrect because 270° is the RB (not MB) TO the NDB.

FIGURE 103.—Directional Gyro and ADF Indicator.

**21.**
**4585.** (Refer to instruments in figure 103 above.) On the basis of this information, the magnetic bearing FROM the station would be

A— 030°.
B— 060°.
C— 240°.

Answer (B) is correct (4585). *(IFH Chap VII)*
On Fig. 103, the airplane has a magnetic heading of 330° and a relative bearing of 270°. To determine the magnetic bearing FROM the station, use the standard magnetic bearing formula to get the magnetic bearing TO the station. Then add or subtract 180° to convert MB TO to MB FROM.

$$MH + RB = MB$$
$$330° + 270° = MB$$
$$MB = 600°$$
$$600° - 360° = 240° \text{ MB TO}$$
$$MB \text{ FROM} = 240° - 180° = 60°$$

Answer (A) is incorrect because 030° is a heading unrelated to this problem. Answer (C) is incorrect because 240° is the MB TO (not FROM) the NDB.

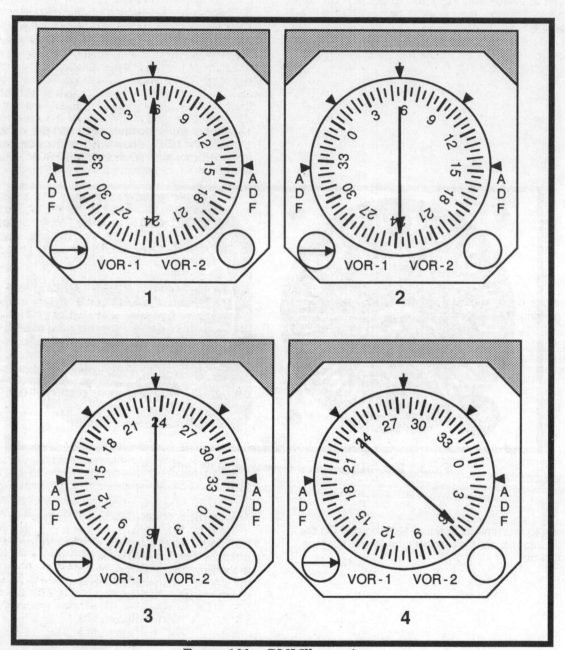

FIGURE 100.—RMI Illustrations.

## 6.3  Radio Magnetic Indicator (RMI)

**22.**
**4579.** (Refer to figure 100 on page 178.) Which RMI illustration indicates the aircraft to be flying outbound on the magnetic bearing of 235° FROM the station? (Wind 050° at 20 knots.)

A— 2.
B— 3.
C— 4.

**Answer (B) is correct (4579).** *(IFH Chap VIII)*
A Radio Magnetic Indicator (RMI) consists of a compass card which rotates as the airplane turns. The magnetic heading of the airplane is always directly under the index at the top of the instrument. The bearing pointer displays magnetic bearings TO the selected station. The tail of the indicator tells you which radial you are on or the magnetic bearing FROM the station. Thus, a magnetic bearing of 235° FROM the station is indicated when the tail of the needle as in RMI 3 is on 235°. The airplane's heading is also 235°, which indicates it is tracking outbound on the 235° MB FROM. The 20-kt. wind from 50° is a direct tailwind which would not require wind correction.
Answer (A) is incorrect because RMI 2 indicates outbound on the 235° MB TO, not FROM, the station. Answer (C) is incorrect because RMI 4 indicates a large wind correction to the right, e.g., to compensate for a strong crosswind which does not exist in this question.

**23.**
**4580.** (Refer to figure 100 on page 178.) What is the magnetic bearing TO the station as indicated by illustration 4?

A— 285°.
B— 055°.
C— 235°.

**Answer (B) is correct (4580).** *(IFH Chap VIII)*
The magnetic heading of the airplane is always directly under the index at the top of the instrument. The bearing pointer displays the magnetic bearing TO the selected station. In RMI 4, the needle is pointing to 055°, which is the magnetic bearing TO the station.
Answer (A) is incorrect because 285° is the magnetic heading (not magnetic bearing). Answer (C) is incorrect because 235° is the magnetic bearing FROM (not TO) the station.

**24.**
**4581.** (Refer to figure 100 on page 178.) Which RMI illustration indicates the aircraft is southwest of the station and moving closer TO the station?

A— 1.
B— 2.
C— 3.

**Answer (A) is correct (4581).** *(IFH Chap VIII)*
If the airplane is to the southwest of the station and moving toward it, the heading and the needle should both be indicating northeast, which is shown in RMI 1. It indicates a magnetic bearing TO the station of 055°. The magnetic heading is also 055°, which means the airplane is flying to the station.
Answer (B) is incorrect because RMI 2 shows a heading of 055° and the VOR behind the airplane, i.e., the airplane is northeast (not southwest) of the station, and moving away FROM the station. Answer (C) is incorrect because RMI 3 shows a heading of 235° and the VOR behind the airplane, i.e., the airplane moving further FROM (not TO) the station.

**25.**
**4582.** (Refer to figure 100 on page 178.) Which RMI illustration indicates the aircraft is located on the 055° radial of the station and heading away from the station?

A— 1.
B— 2.
C— 3.

**Answer (B) is correct (4582).** *(IFH Chap VIII)*
A radial, or bearing FROM, is indicated by the tail of the needle. Thus, the 055° radial is indicated when the tail of the needle is on 055°, as in RMI 2. The heading is also 055°, which means you are flying northeast, which is away from the station, and you are on the 055° radial.
Answer (A) is incorrect because RMI 1 indicates on the 235° radial flying toward the station. Answer (C) is incorrect because RMI 3 indicates flying away from the station on the 235° radial.

**26.**
**4602.** (Refer to figure 107 below.) Where should the bearing pointer be located relative to the wingtip reference to maintain the 16 DME range in a right-hand arc with a right crosswind component?

A— Behind the right wingtip reference for VOR-2.
B— Ahead of the right wingtip reference for VOR-2.
C— Behind the right wingtip reference for VOR-1.

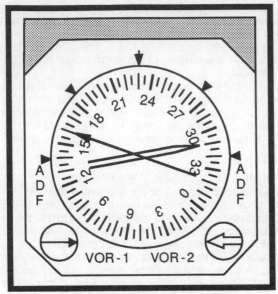

FIGURE 107.—RMI—DME—ARC
Illustration Wind Component.

Answer (B) is correct (4602). *(IFH Chap VIII)*
Normally when flying a DME arc with an RMI, the RMI needle will point directly to the VORTAC, and in a no-wind situation it will be on either a 90° or 3 o'clock (for right-hand arc) or 270° or 9 o'clock (for left-hand arc) indication. Since you are flying a right-hand arc, you should be using VOR 2, which points to the right. The right crosswind component will be blowing you away from the VORTAC. You should crab to the right so the VOR 2 bearing pointer is in front of the right wingtip reference. This indicates you are correcting back into the wind and toward the VORTAC.
Answer (A) is incorrect because the bearing pointer would be behind the wingtip reference if you were crabbed away from the VORTAC such as in a left-hand crosswind and a right-hand arc. Answer (C) is incorrect because VOR 1 is pointing toward the left which would indicate a left-hand (not right-hand) DME arc.

**27.**
**4603.** (Refer to figure 108 below.) Where should the bearing pointer be located relative to the wingtip reference to maintain the 16 DME range in a left-hand arc with a left crosswind component?

A— Ahead of the left wingtip reference for the VOR-2.
B— Ahead of the right wingtip reference for the VOR-1.
C— Behind the left wingtip reference for the VOR-2.

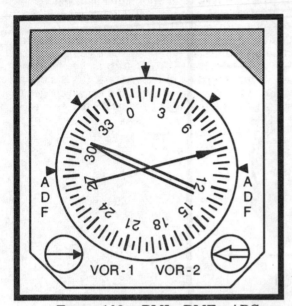

FIGURE 108.—RMI—DME—ARC
Illustration Wind Component.

Answer (A) is correct (4603). *(IFH Chap VIII)*
Since you are flying a left-hand arc, you should be using VOR 2, which points to the left. The left crosswind component will be blowing you away from the VORTAC. You should crab to the left so the VOR 2 bearing pointer is in front of the left wingtip reference. This indicates you are correcting back into the wind and toward the VORTAC.
Answer (B) is incorrect because you should use VOR 2 as you are making a left-hand (not right-hand) turn. Answer (C) is incorrect because the needle would be behind the wingtip if you were crabbed away from (not toward) the VORTAC.

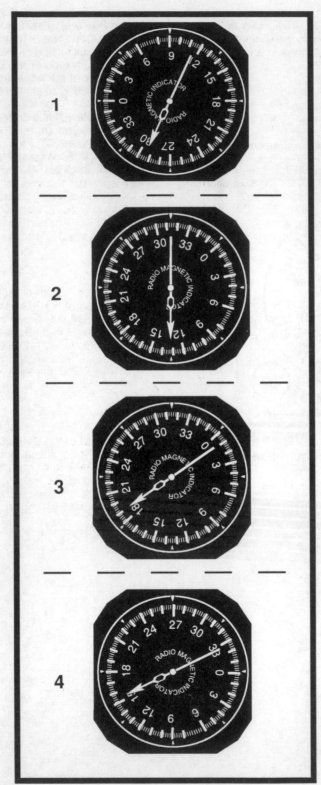

FIGURE 104.—Radio Magnetic Indicator.

**28.**
**4590.** (Refer to figure 104 on page 182.) If the radio magnetic indicator is tuned to a VOR, which illustration indicates the aircraft is on the 010° radial?

A— 1.
B— 2.
C— 3.

Answer (C) is correct (4590). (IFH Chap VIII)
A Radio Magnetic Indicator (RMI) consists of a rotating compass card and one or more indicators which point to stations. The tail of the indicator tells you what radial you are on. RMI 3 shows the tail of the indicator on 010°, which means that you are on the 010° radial.
Answer (A) is incorrect because RMI 1 indicates the 115° radial. Answer (B) is incorrect because RMI 2 indicates the 315° radial.

**29.**
**4587.** (Refer to figure 104 on page 182.) If the radio magnetic indicator is tuned to a VOR, which illustration indicates the aircraft is on the 115° radial?

A— 1.
B— 2.
C— 3.

Answer (A) is correct (4587). (IFH Chap VIII)
The tail of the RMI indicator tells you what radial you are on. RMI 1 shows the tail of the indicator on 115°, which means that you are on the 115° radial.
Answer (B) is incorrect because RMI 2 indicates the 315° radial. Answer (C) is incorrect because RMI 3 indicates the 010° radial.

**30.**
**4588.** (Refer to figure 104 on page 182.) If the radio magnetic indicator is tuned to a VOR, which illustration indicates the aircraft is on the 335° radial?

A— 2.
B— 3.
C— 4.

Answer (C) is correct (4588). (IFH Chap VIII)
The tail of the RMI indicator tells you what radial you are on. RMI 4 shows the tail of the indicator on 335°, which means that you are on the 335° radial.
Answer (A) is incorrect because RMI 2 indicates the 315° radial. Answer (B) is incorrect because RMI 3 indicates the 010° radial.

**31.**
**4589.** (Refer to figure 104 on page 182.) If the radio magnetic indicator is tuned to a VOR, which illustration indicates the aircraft is on the 315° radial?

A— 2.
B— 3.
C— 4.

Answer (A) is correct (4589). (IFH Chap VIII)
The tail of the RMI indicator tells you what radial you are on. RMI 2 shows the tail of the indicator on 315°, which means that you are on the 315° radial.
Answer (B) is incorrect because RMI 3 indicates the 010° radial. Answer (C) is incorrect because RMI 4 indicates the 335° radial.

## 6.4 VOR Receiver Check

**32.**
**4388.** In which publication can the VOR receiver ground checkpoint(s) for a particular airport be found?

A— Airman's Information Manual.
B— En Route Low Altitude Chart.
C— Airport/Facility Directory.

**Answer (C) is correct (4388).** *(AIM Para 1-4)*
The Airport/Facility Directory provides a listing of available VOR receiver ground checkpoints.
Answer (A) is incorrect because the Airman's Information Manual contains general flight information, not data concerning specific airports. Answer (B) is incorrect because En Route Low Altitude Charts do not indicate VOR receiver ground checkpoints (only VOT frequencies).

**33.**
**4389.** Which is the maximum tolerance for the VOR indication when the CDI is centered and the airplane is directly over the airborne checkpoint?

A— Plus or minus 6° of the designated radial.
B— Plus or minus 7° of the designated radial.
C— Plus or minus 8° of the designated radial.

**Answer (A) is correct (4389).** *(AIM Para 1-4)*
Airborne checkpoints consist of certified radials that should be received over specific landmarks while airborne in the immediate vicinity of an airport. The maximum tolerance when the CDI is centered is ±6°.
Answer (B) is incorrect because 6° (not 7°) is the maximum tolerance for airborne checkpoints. Answer (C) is incorrect because 6° (not 8°) is the maximum tolerance for airborne checkpoints.

**34.**
**4378.** When the CDI needle is centered during an airborne VOR check, the omnibearing selector and the TO/FROM indicator should read

A— within 4° of the selected radial.
B— within 6° of the selected radial.
C— 0° TO, only if you are due south of the VOR.

**Answer (B) is correct (4378).** *(AIM Para 1-4)*
Airborne VOR checkpoints consist of certified radials that should be received over specific landmarks. If no checkpoint is available, a prominent ground point should be selected more than 20 NM from a VOR station that is along an established VOR airway. Once over this point with the CDI centered, the OBS should indicate within 6° of the published radial.
Answer (A) is incorrect because the maximum error for a ground (not airborne) VOR check is ±4°. Answer (C) is incorrect because you should use a certified airborne checkpoint or select a ground reference that is under an established VOR airway, not a randomly selected radial.

**35.**
**4391.** When making an airborne VOR check, what is the maximum allowable tolerance between the two indicators of a dual VOR system (units independent of each other except the antenna)?

A— 4° between the two indicated radials of a VOR.
B— Plus or minus 4° when set to identical radials of a VOR.
C— 6° between the two indicated radials of a VOR.

**Answer (A) is correct (4391).** *(FAR 91.171)*
If a dual system VOR (units independent of each other except for the antenna) is installed in the airplane, one system may be checked against the other in place of other VOR check procedures. The test consists of tuning both systems to the same VOR and centering the CDI needles, then noting the bearing variation between the two VOR units. It should be less than 4°.
Answer (B) is incorrect because the CDIs are to be centered, not set to the same radials. Answer (C) is incorrect because it is a maximum tolerance of 4°, not 6°.

**36.**
**4383.** While airborne, what is the maximum permissible variation between the two indicated bearings when checking one VOR system against the other?

A— Plus or minus 4° when set to identical radials of a VOR.
B— 4° between the two indicated bearings to a VOR.
C— Plus or minus 6° when set to identical radials of a VOR.

**Answer (B) is correct (4383).** *(AIM Para 1-4)*
If a dual system VOR (units independent of each other except for the antenna) is installed in the airplane, one system may be checked against the other in place of other check procedures. The test consists of tuning both systems to the same VOR with the CDI centered and noting the bearing variation between the two VOR units. It should be less than 4°.
Answer (A) is incorrect because the CDIs must be centered, not set to identical radials. Answer (C) is incorrect because it is a maximum permissible variation of 4°, not 6°, between the indicated bearings.

**37.**
**4384.** How should the pilot make a VOR receiver check when the airplane is located on the designated checkpoint on the airport surface?

A— With the aircraft headed directly toward the VOR and the OBS set to 000°, the CDI should center within plus or minus 4° of that radial with a TO indication.

B— Set the OBS on the designated radial. The CDI must center within plus or minus 4° of that radial with a FROM indication.

C— Set the OBS on 180° plus or minus 4°; the CDI should center with a FROM indication.

Answer (B) is correct (4384). *(AIM Para 1-4)*
This question is a duplicate of FAA question 4377.
A VOR receiver check is a checkpoint on the airport surface near a VOR. When the airplane is on the checkpoint, the designated radial should be set on the OBS. The CDI must then center within 4° of the radial. Also, there will be a FROM indication.
Answer (A) is incorrect because VOR indications are given the same no matter which heading the aircraft is on. The VOR indication is based upon position, not heading. Answer (C) is incorrect because the specified radial (not 180°) should be set on the OBS.

**38.**
**4377.** How should the pilot make a VOR receiver check when the aircraft is located on the designated checkpoint on the airport surface?

A— Set the OBS on 180° plus or minus 4°; the CDI should center with a FROM indication.

B— Set the OBS on the designated radial. The CDI must center within plus or minus 4° of that radial with a FROM indication.

C— With the aircraft headed directly toward the VOR and the OBS set to 000°, the CDI should center within plus or minus 4° of that radial with a TO indication.

Answer (B) is correct (4377). *(AIM Para 1-4)*
This question is a duplicate of FAA question 4384.
A VOR receiver check is a checkpoint on the airport surface near a VOR. When the airplane is on the checkpoint, the designated radial should be set on the OBS. The CDI must then center within 4° of the radial. Also, there will be a FROM indication.
Answer (A) is incorrect because the specified radial (not 180°) should be set on the OBS. Answer (C) is incorrect because VOR indications are given the same no matter which heading the aircraft is on. The VOR indication is based upon position, not heading.

**39.**
**4386.** Where can the VOT frequency for a particular airport be found?

A— On the IAP Chart and in the Airport/Facility Directory.

B— Only in the Airport/Facility Directory.

C— In the Airport/Facility Directory and on the A/G Voice Communication Panel of the En Route Low Altitude Chart.

Answer (C) is correct (4386). *(AIM Para 1-4)*
Both the Airport/Facility Directory and the A/G Voice Communication Panel of the En Route Low Altitude Chart provide a listing of the VOT frequency for a particular airport.
Answer (A) is incorrect because VOT frequencies are not listed on approach charts. Answer (B) is incorrect because VOT frequencies are also published in En Route Low Altitude Charts.

**40.**
**4376.** When using VOT to make a VOR receiver check, the CDI should be centered and the OBS should indicate that the aircraft is on the

A— 090 radial.

B— 180 radial.

C— 360 radial.

Answer (C) is correct (4376). *(AIM Para 1-4)*
A VOT transmits only the 360° radial. Thus, with the CDI centered, the OBS should indicate 0° with a FROM indication and 180° with a TO indication.
Answer (A) is incorrect because the VOT transmits only the 360° (not 090°) radial in all directions.
Answer (B) is incorrect because the VOT transmits only the 360° (not 180°) radial in all directions.

**41.**
**4387.** Which indications are acceptable tolerances when checking both VOR receivers by use of the VOT?

A— 360° TO and 003° TO, respectively.

B— 001° FROM and 005° FROM, respectively.

C— 176° TO and 003° FROM, respectively.

Answer (C) is correct (4387). *(AIM Para 1-4)*
A VOT transmits a 360° radial in all directions. Thus, with the course deviation indicator (CDI) centered, the omnibearing selector (OBS) should read 0° with the TO-FROM indicator showing FROM or the OBS read 180° with the TO-FROM indicator showing TO with a maximum error of 4°.
Answer (A) is incorrect because at 000°, FROM, not TO, should be indicated. Answer (B) is incorrect because it exceeds the 4° maximum error limit.

**42.**
**4382.** (Refer to figure 81 below.) When checking a dual VOR system by use of a VOT, which illustration indicates the VOR's are satisfactory?

A— 1.
B— 2.
C— 4.

Answer (A) is correct (4382).  *(AIM Para 1-4)*
   A VOT transmits a 360° radial in all directions.  Thus, when using an RMI, the tail of each indicator should point to 360, ±4°.
   Answer (B) is incorrect because it shows the head (not the tail) of one indicator pointing to 360°.
   Answer (C) is incorrect because it shows the heads (not the tails) of both indicators pointing to 360°.

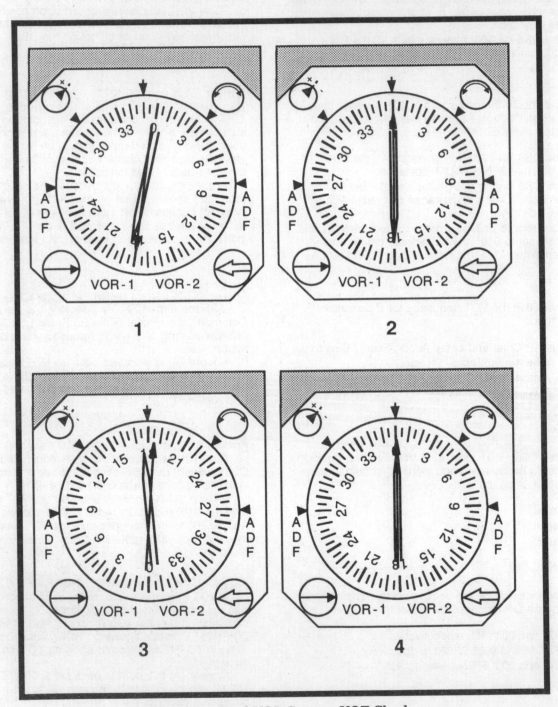

FIGURE 81.—Dual VOR System, VOT Check.

**43.**
**4385.** (Refer to figure 82 below.) Which is an acceptable range of accuracy when performing an operational check of dual VOR's using one system against the other?

A— 1.
B— 2.
C— 4.

Answer (C) is correct (4385). *(AIM Para 1-4)*
When performing an operational check of dual VORs using one system against the other, the difference between the two indicated bearings must be 4° or less. On an RMI, which has two VOR indicators, the VORs should point in the same direction, as in illustration 4 of Fig. 82.
Answer (A) is incorrect because the needles have a 180° difference. Answer (B) is incorrect because there is a 10° difference.

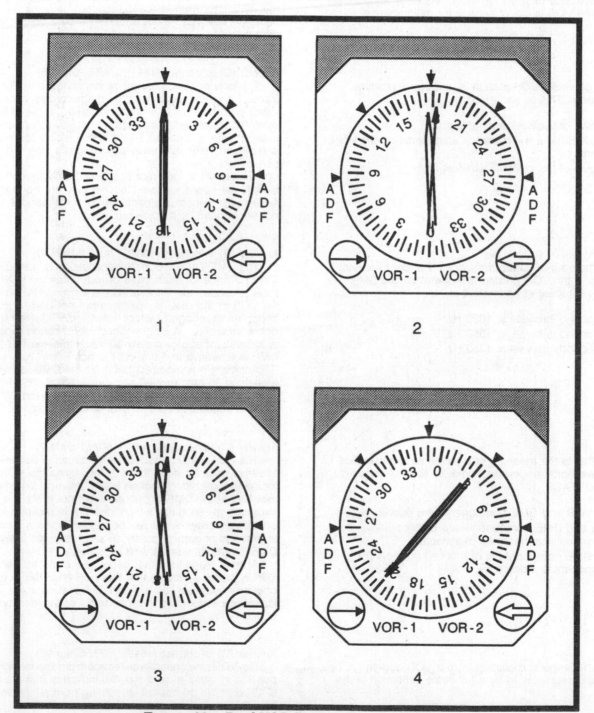

FIGURE 82.—Dual VOR System, Accuracy Check.

## 6.5  Very High Frequency Omnidirectional Range (VOR) Station

**44.**
**4410.**  What indication should a pilot receive when a VOR station is undergoing maintenance and may be considered unreliable?

A— No coded identification, but possible navigation indications.
B— Coded identification, but no navigation indications.
C— A voice recording on the VOR frequency announcing that the VOR is out of service for maintenance.

Answer (A) is correct (4410).  *(AIM Para 1-3)*
The only positive method of identifying a VOR is by Morse Code identification and/or by the recorded voice identification, which is always indicated by use of the word "VOR" following the VOR name.  During periods of maintenance, the facility identification is removed, although navigational signals may still be transmitted.
Answer (B) is incorrect because the coded identification is removed when the station is undergoing maintenance.  Answer (C) is incorrect because an out-of-service VOR is not announced by a voice recording.

**45.**
**4411.**  A particular VOR station is undergoing routine maintenance.  This is evidenced by

A— removal of the navigational feature.
B— broadcasting a maintenance alert signal on the voice channel.
C— removal of the identification feature.

Answer (C) is correct (4411).  *(AIM Para 1-3)*
The only positive method of identifying a VOR is by Morse Code identification or by the recorded voice identification, which is always indicated by use of the word "VOR" following the VOR name.  During periods of maintenance, the coded and/or voice facility identification is removed, although navigational signals may still be transmitted.
Answer (A) is incorrect because the navigational signals may continue even though they are not accurate.  Answer (B) is incorrect because an out-of-service VOR is not announced by a voice recording.

**46.**
**4663.**  When a VOR/DME is collocated under frequency pairings and the VOR portion is inoperative, the DME identifier will repeat at an interval of

A— 20 second intervals at 1020 Hz.
B— 30 second intervals at 1350 Hz.
C— 60 second intervals at 1350 Hz.

Answer (B) is correct (4663).  *(AIM Para 1-7)*
The DME/TACAN coded identification is transmitted at 1350 Hz once for each three or four times the VOR or localizer coded identification is transmitted.  When either the VOR or the DME is operative but not both, it is important to recognize which identifier is retained for the operative facility.  A single-coded identification repeated at intervals of approximately 30 sec. indicates that the DME is operative and the VOR is not.
Answer (A) is incorrect because the DME identifier repeats at 30-sec. (not 20-sec.) intervals at 1350 Hz (not 1020 Hz).  Answer (C) is incorrect because the DME identifier repeats at 30-sec. (not 60-sec.) intervals.

**47.**
**4412.**  What is the meaning of a single coded identification received only once approximately every 30 seconds from a VORTAC?

A— The VOR and DME components are operative.
B— VOR and DME components are both operative, but voice identification is out of service.
C— The DME component is operative and the VOR component is inoperative.

Answer (C) is correct (4412).  *(AIM Para 1-7)*
The DME/TACAN coded identification is transmitted at 1350 Hz once for each three or four times the VOR or localizer coded identification is transmitted.  When either the VOR or the DME is operative but not both, it is important to recognize which identifier is retained for the operative facility.  A single-coded identification repeated at intervals of approximately 30 sec. indicates that the DME is operative and the VOR is not.
Answer (A) is incorrect because a constant series of identity codes indicates that the VOR and DME are both operative.  Answer (B) is incorrect because voice identification operates independently of the identity codes.

**48.**
**4548.**  What angular deviation from a VOR course centerline is represented by a full-scale deflection of the CDI?

A— 4°.
B— 5°.
C— 10°.

Answer (C) is correct (4548).  *(IFH Chap VII)*
On VORs, full needle deflection from the center position to either side of the dial indicates that the aircraft is 10° or more off course, assuming normal needle sensitivity.
Answer (A) is incorrect because 4° is indicated by a 2-dot deflection on a 5-dot VOR scale.  Answer (B) is incorrect because 5° is indicated by a 2-dot deflection on a 4-dot VOR scale.

**49.**
**4666.** Full scale deflection of a CDI occurs when the course deviation bar or needle

A— deflects from left side of the scale to right side of the scale.
B— deflects from the center of the scale to either far side of the scale.
C— deflects from half scale left to half scale right.

**Answer (B) is correct (4666).** *(IFH Chap VII)*
Full scale deflection of a CDI occurs when the needle deflects from the center of the scale to either far side of the scale. This indicates that the aircraft is 10° or more off course, assuming normal needle sensitivity.
Answer (A) is incorrect because it indicates moving from a left full deflection to a right full deflection, i.e., 10° left of course to 10° right of course. Answer (C) is incorrect because it indicates moving from a left half deflection to a right half deflection, i.e., 5° left of course to 5° right of course.

**50.**
**4400.** For operations off established airways at 17,000 feet MSL in the contiguous U.S., (H) Class VORTAC facilities used to define a direct route of flight should be no farther apart than

A— 75 NM.
B— 100 NM.
C— 200 NM.

**Answer (C) is correct (4400).** *(AIM Para 1-8)*
(H) Class VORTAC facilities have a range of 100 NM from 14,500 ft. AGL up to and including 60,000 ft. Thus, (H) Class VORTAC facilities should be no farther apart than 200 NM.
Answer (A) is incorrect because 75 NM is the range of an (HH) Class NDB facility, not an (H) Class VORTAC. Answer (B) is incorrect because 100 NM is the range of an (H) Class VORTAC at 17,000 ft. MSL, thus the distance between two (H) Class VORTAC facilities can be 200 NM.

**51.**
**4549.** When using VOR for navigation, which of the following should be considered as station passage?

A— The first movement of the CDI as the airplane enters the zone of confusion.
B— The moment the TO-FROM indicator becomes blank.
C— The first positive, complete reversal of the TO-FROM indicator.

**Answer (C) is correct (4549).** *(IFH Chap VII)*
When approaching a VOR, the TO-FROM indicator and the CDI flicker as the airplane flies into the zone of confusion (no signal area). Station passage is shown by complete reversal of the TO-FROM indicator.
Answer (A) is incorrect because it indicates you are in the zone of confusion over the VOR (not station passage). Answer (B) is incorrect because it indicates you are in the zone of confusion over the VOR (not station passage).

**52.**
**4550.** Which of the following should be considered as station passage when using VOR?

A— The first flickering of the TO-FROM indicator and CDI as the station is approached.
B— The first full-scale deflection of the CDI.
C— The first complete reversal of the TO-FROM indicator.

**Answer (C) is correct (4550).** *(IFH Chap VII)*
When approaching a VOR, the TO-FROM indicator and the CDI flicker as the airplane flies in the zone of confusion (no signal area). Station passage is shown by complete reversal of the TO-FROM indicator.
Answer (A) is incorrect because it indicates you are in the zone of confusion over the VOR but not station passage. Answer (B) is incorrect because it indicates you are in the zone of confusion over the VOR but not station passage.

**53.**
**4551.** When checking the sensitivity of a VOR receiver, the number of degrees in course change as the OBS is rotated to move the CDI from center to the last dot on either side should be between

A— 5° and 6°.
B— 8° and 10°.
C— 10° and 12°.

**Answer (C) is correct (4551).** *(IFH Chap VIII)*
In addition to VOR receiver checks, course sensitivity may be checked by noting the number of degrees of change in the course selected as you rotate the OBS to move the CDI from center to the last dot on either side. This range should be between 10° and 12°.
Answer (A) is incorrect because 5° to 6° of course change should result in a ½ (not full) scale needle deflection. Answer (B) is incorrect because 8° to 10° of course change should result in a ¾ (not full) scale needle deflection.

**54.**
**4552.** A VOR receiver with normal five-dot course sensitivity shows a three-dot deflection at 30 NM from the station. The aircraft would be displaced approximately how far from the course centerline?

A— 2 NM.
B— 3 NM.
C— 5 NM.

**Answer (B) is correct (4552).** *(IFH Chap VIII)*
Airplane displacement from a course is approximately 200 ft. per dot per nautical mile for VORs. For example, at 30 NM from the station, a one dot deflection indicates approximately 1 NM displacement of the airplane from the course centerline. A full course deflection is 5 dots. With a 3-dot deflection, one would be about 3 NM from the course centerline.
Answer (A) is incorrect because two dots (not three) indicate 2 NM off course. Answer (C) is incorrect because five dots (not three) indicate 5 NM off course.

**55.**
**4553.** An aircraft which is located 30 miles from a VOR station and shows a ½ scale deflection on the CDI would be how far from the selected course centerline?

A— 1½ miles.
B— 2½ miles.
C— 3½ miles.

**Answer (B) is correct (4553).** *(IFH Chap VIII)*
Airplane displacement from a course is approximately 200 ft. per dot per nautical mile for VORs. For example, at 30 NM from the station, a 1-dot deflection indicates approximately 1 NM displacement of the airplane from the course centerline. A full course deflection is 5 dots. Since a ½-scale deflection on the CDI would be 2½ dots, the airplane would be about 2½ mi. from the course centerline.
Answer (A) is incorrect because 1½ mi. would be indicated by a 1½-dot deflection. Answer (C) is incorrect because 3½ mi. would be indicated by a 3½-dot deflection.

**56.**
**4554.** What angular deviation from a VOR course centerline is represented by a ½ scale deflection of the CDI?

A— 2°.
B— 4°.
C— 5°.

**Answer (C) is correct (4554).** *(IFH Chap VIII)*
A full course deflection is 5 dots, which is approximately 10°. Since rotation of the OBS to move the CDI from the center to the last dot is approximately 10°, a ½-scale deflection would be approximately 5°.
Answer (A) is incorrect because a full scale deflection is 10° (not 4°). Answer (B) is incorrect because a full scale deflection is 10° (not 8°).

**57.**
**4556.** After passing a VORTAC, the CDI shows ½ scale deflection to the right. What is indicated if the deflection remains constant for a period of time?

A— The airplane is getting closer to the radial.
B— The OBS is erroneously set on the reciprocal heading.
C— The airplane is flying away from the radial.

**Answer (C) is correct (4556).** *(IFH Chap VIII)*
If the CDI shows a ½-scale deflection to the right, the airplane is flying 5° to the left of course. If it is constant, it means the airplane is flying away from the radial because the 5° off course increases in actual distance as one gets farther away from the VORTAC.
Answer (A) is incorrect because a steady deflection would indicate the airplane is getting closer to the radial if it were flying TO (not FROM) the station. Answer (B) is incorrect because if you use the reciprocal heading you get reverse indications from the CDI.

**58.**
**4604.** Determine the approximate time and distance to a station if a 5° wingtip bearing change occurs in 1.5 minutes with a true airspeed of 95 knots.

A— 16 minutes and 14.3 NM.
B— 18 minutes and 28.5 NM.
C— 18 minutes and 33.0 NM.

**Answer (B) is correct (4604).** *(IFH Chap VIII)*
Use the following formula to compute the time to station:

$$\text{Time to Station} = \frac{60 \times \text{Minutes between Bearings}}{\text{Degrees of Bearing Change}}$$

$$= (60 \times 1.5) \div 5 = 18$$

Thus, it is 18 min. to the station, which is less than 1/3 of an hour. One-third of 95 is less than 33, and thus must be 28.5 rather than 33.0. On the computer side of your flight computer, put 95 kt. on the outer scale over 60 on the inner scale. Find 18 min. on the inner scale and 28.5 NM is on the outer scale.
Answer (A) is incorrect because the time is 18 (not 16) min. Answer (C) is incorrect because 18 min. is less than 1/3 hr., and 1/3 of 95 kt. is less than 33 NM.

**59.**
**4601.** (Refer to figure 106 below.) The course selector of each aircraft is set on 360°. Which aircraft would have a FROM indication on the ambiguity meter and the CDI pointing left of center?

A— 1.
B— 2.
C— 3.

Answer (B) is correct (4601). *(IFH Chap VIII)*
If airplane 2 were heading 360°, the course would be to the left and the airplane would fly away FROM the VOR. See discussion of VOR orientation presented at the end of the HSI outline.
Answer (A) is incorrect because, if airplane 1 were heading 360°, the course would be to the right (not left). Answer (C) is incorrect because, as airplane 3 is heading 360°, it is flying closer TO (not further FROM) the station and the CDI would be pointing right, not left, of center.

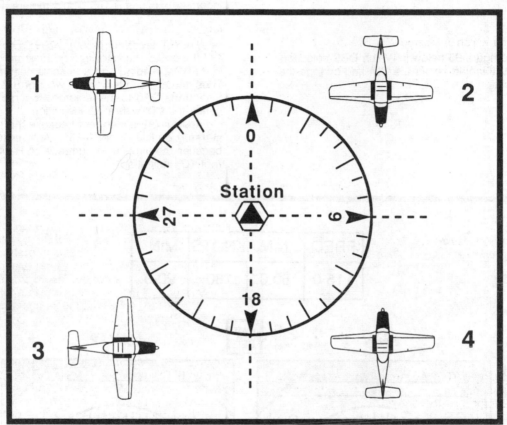

FIGURE 106.—Aircraft Location Relative to VOR.

## 6.6 Horizontal Situation Indicator (HSI)

**60.**
**4557.** (Refer to figure 95 on page 192.) What is the lateral displacement of the aircraft in NM from the radial selected on the No. 1 NAV?

A— 5.0 NM.
B— 7.5 NM.
C— 10.0 NM.

Answer (A) is correct (4557). *(IFH Chap VIII)*
On VORs, the displacement from course is approximately 200 ft. per dot per nautical mile. At 30 NM from the station, one dot deflection indicates approximately 1 NM displacement of the airplane from the course centerline. At 60 NM, it would be 2 NM for every dot of displacement. Since here displacement is 2½ dots, the airplane would be 5 NM from the centerline.
Answer (B) is incorrect because 7.5 NM would be indicated by a ¾ deflection. Answer (C) is incorrect because 10 NM would be indicated by a full deflection.

**61.**
**4558.** (Refer to figure 95 below.)  On which radial is the aircraft as indicated by the No. 1 NAV?

A— R-175.
B— R-165.
C— R-345.

Answer (C) is correct (4558).  *(IFH Chap VIII)*
    The course selector in Fig. 95 is set on 350° with a FROM reading, indicating that if the course deflection bar were centered, the airplane would be on R-350.  Since a total deflection is approximately 10° to 12°, one-half deflection is 5° to 6°.  Here, deflection is less than one-half, so it is about 5°.  The course deflection bar indicates that this airplane is to the west of R-350, which would be R-345.
    Answer (A) is incorrect because R-175 would require a TO indicator and a left deflection.  Answer (B) is incorrect because R-165 would require a TO indicator.

**62.**
**4559.** (Refer to figure 95 below.)  Which OBS selection on the No. 1 NAV would center the CDI and change the ambiguity indication to a TO?

A— 175°.
B— 165°.
C— 345°.

Answer (B) is correct (4559).  *(IFH Chap VIII)*
    The course selector in Fig. 95 is set on 350°, resulting in a FROM reading and a ½-scale needle deflection.  Thus, the airplane is 5° or 6° west of R-350, i.e., R-345.  Setting the OBS to the reciprocal course of 165° would center the CDI with a TO indication.
    Answer (A) is incorrect because the airplane is currently on R-345, not R-355.  Answer (C) is incorrect because the airplane is currently on R-345 with a FROM, (not TO) indication.

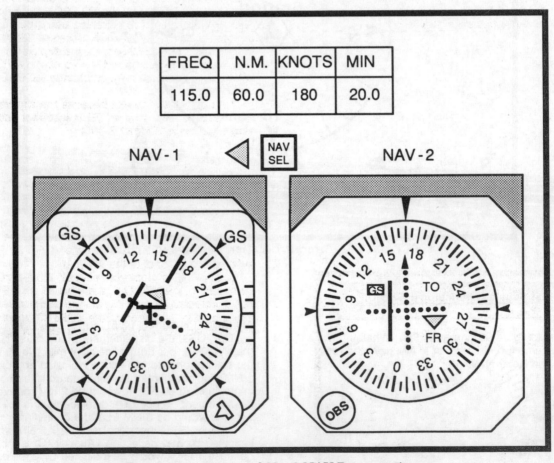

FIGURE 95.—No. 1 and No. 2 NAV Presentation.

**63.**
**4560.** (Refer to figure 95 on page 192.) What is the lateral displacement in degrees from the desired radial on the No. 2 NAV?

A— 1°.
B— 2°.
C— 4°.

Answer (C) is correct (4560). *(IFH Chap VIII)*
Since on a standard 5-dot VOR indicator a full deflection of 5 dots is about 10°, 2 dots means a 4° deflection.
Answer (A) is incorrect because each dot is 2°, not ½°. Answer (B) is incorrect because each dot is 2°, not 1°.

**64.**
**4561.** (Refer to figure 95 on page 192.) Which OBS selection on the No. 2 NAV would center the CDI?

A— 174°.
B— 166°.
C— 335°.

Answer (A) is correct (4561). *(IFH Chap VIII)*
The course selector in Fig. 95 is set to 170° (it is not an HSI; it is a VOR) and the TO-FROM indicator indicates FROM, which means the airplane would be on R-170 if the course deviation bar were centered. Since the bar indicates a left 2-dot deflection, the airplane is 4° to the west of the radial, or on R-174.
Answer (B) is incorrect because a right (not left) deflection would indicate R-166. Answer (C) is incorrect because, on R-335 with an OBS setting of 170°, there would be a TO (not FROM) indication.

**65.**
**4562.** (Refer to figure 95 on page 192.) Which OBS selection on the No. 2 NAV would center the CDI and change the ambiguity indication to a TO?

A— 166°.
B— 346°.
C— 354°.

Answer (C) is correct (4562). *(IFH Chap VIII)*
The course selector in Fig. 95 is set to 170° (it is not an HSI; it is a VOR) and the TO-FROM indicator indicates FROM, which means the airplane would be on R-170 if the course deviation bar were centered. Since the bar indicates a 2-dot left deflection, the airplane is 4° to the west of the radial, or on R-174. To obtain a TO indication, one would have to change the OBS selection by 180° from 174° to 354°.
Answer (A) is incorrect because the airplane is on R-174 (not R-346). Answer (B) is incorrect because the airplane is on R-174 (not R-166).

**66.**
**4606.** (Refer to figure 109 below.) In which general direction from the VORTAC is the aircraft located?

A— Northeast.
B— Southeast.
C— Southwest.

Answer (A) is correct (4606). *(IFH Chap VIII)*
The course indicating arrow (OBS) is set to 180°, and the TO-FROM indicator indicates TO (triangle pointing TO arrowhead), which means the airplane is north of the VORTAC. Since the course deviation bar indicates that the airplane needs to be flown to the right, the airplane is to the east of the 360° radial of the VORTAC. Thus, the airplane is northeast of the VORTAC.
Answer (B) is incorrect because, if the airplane were southwest of the VORTAC, there would be a FROM (not TO) indication. Answer (C) is incorrect because, if the airplane were southwest of the VORTAC, there would be a FROM (not TO) indication and a left (not right) bar deflection.

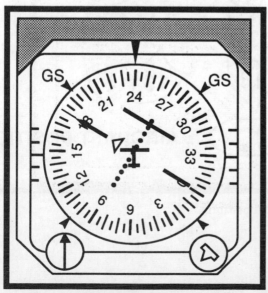

FIGURE 109.—CDI Direction from VORTAC.

**67.**
**4575.** (Refer to figure 98 below and 99 on page 195.)
To which aircraft position does HSI presentation "A"
correspond?

A— 1.
B— 8.
C— 11.

Answer (A) is correct (4575).   *(IFH Chap VIII)*
     On Figs. 98 and 99, HSI "A" has a VOR course selec-
tion of 090°, with a TO indication, meaning the airplane is
to the left of the 360/180 radials.  It has a right deflection,
which means it is north of the 270/90 radials.  The
airplane heading is 205°, which means airplane 1 is
described.
     Answer (B) is incorrect because airplane 8 is to the
right of the 360/180 radials, which would require a FROM
(not TO) indication.  Answer (C) is incorrect because
airplane 11 is to the right of the 360/180 radials and is
south of the 270/090 radials, which would require a
FROM (not TO) indication and a left (not right) bar
deflection.

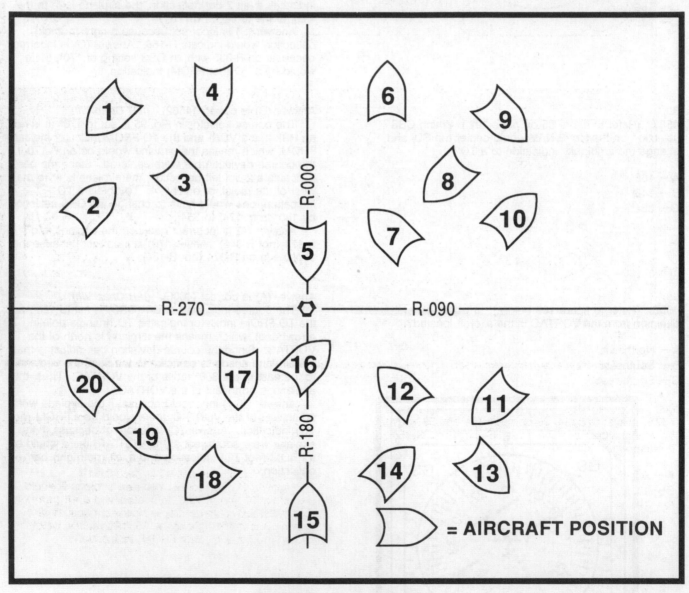

FIGURE 98.—Aircraft Position.

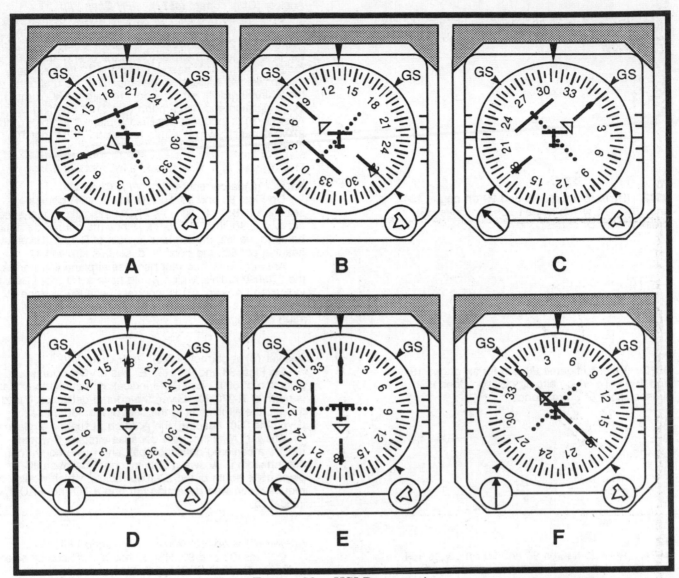

FIGURE 99.—HSI Presentation.

**68.**
**4576.** (Refer to figure 98 on page 194 and 99 above.) To which aircraft position does HSI presentation "B" correspond?

A— 9.
B— 13.
C— 19.

Answer (C) is correct (4576). *(IFH Chap VIII)*
    On Figs. 98 and 99, HSI "B" has a VOR course selection of 270° with a FROM indication, meaning that the airplane is to the left of the 360/180 radials. Since it has a right deflection, the airplane is south of R-270. Given a heading of 135°, airplane 19 is described.
    Answer (A) is incorrect because airplane 9 would require a TO (not FROM) indication and a left (not right) bar deflection. Answer (B) is incorrect because airplane 13 is to the right of the 360/180 radials, which would require a TO (not FROM) indication.

**69.**
**4577.** (Refer to figures 98 and 99 on pages 194 and 195.) To which aircraft position does HSI presentation "C" correspond?

A— 6.
B— 7.
C— 12.

Answer (C) is correct (4577). *(IFH Chap VIII)*
On Figs. 98 and 99, HSI "C" has a VOR course selection of 360° with a TO indication, meaning the airplane is south of the 270/090 radials. Since the course deflection bar is to the left, the airplane is to the east of the 180° radial. Given a 310° heading, airplane 12 is described.
Answer (A) is incorrect because airplane 6 is north of the 270/090 radials, which would require a FROM (not TO) indication and has a north (not 310°) heading. Answer (B) is incorrect because airplane 7 is north of the 270/090 radials, which would require a FROM (not TO) indication.

**70.**
**4572.** (Refer to figures 98 and 99 on pages 194 and 195.) To which aircraft position does HSI presentation "D" correspond?

A— 4.
B— 15.
C— 17.

Answer (C) is correct (4572). *(IFH Chap VIII)*
On Figs. 98 and 99, HSI "D" has a VOR course selection (OBS) of 180°. Its FROM indication means the airplane is south of R-270/90. Since the course deflection bar is to the left, the airplane is west of R-180. Given the heading of 180°, the position describes airplane 17.
Answer (A) is incorrect because airplane 4 is north of the 270/090 radials, which would have a TO (not FROM) indication. Answer (B) is incorrect because airplane 15 would have a centered deflection bar and a north (not 180°) heading.

**71.**
**4573.** (Refer to figures 98 and 99 on pages 194 and 195.) To which aircraft position does HSI presentation "E" correspond?

A— 5.
B— 6.
C— 15.

Answer (B) is correct (4573). *(IFH Chap VIII)*
On Figs. 98 and 99, HSI "E" has a VOR course selection of 360°. Its FROM indication means the airplane is north of R-270/90. Given the course deflection bar to the left, the airplane is to the east of the 360° radial. Given the 360° heading, the position describes airplane 6.
Answer (A) is incorrect because airplane 5 would require a centered deflection bar, and has a south (not 360°) heading. Answer (C) is incorrect because airplane 15 is south of the 270/090 radials, which would require a centered deflection bar and a TO (not FROM) indication.

**72.**
**4574.** (Refer to figures 98 and 99 on pages 194 and 195.) To which aircraft position does HSI presentation "F" correspond?

A— 10.
B— 14.
C— 16.

Answer (C) is correct (4574). *(IFH Chap VIII)*
On Figs. 98 and 99, HSI "F" has a VOR course selection of 180° with a FROM indication, meaning that the airplane is south of the 270/90 radials. Since the course deflection bar is centered, the airplane is on R-180. Given a heading of 045° (at the top of the HSI), airplane 16 is described.
Answer (A) is incorrect because airplane 10 is east of the 360/180 radials and north of the 270/090 radials, which would require a bar deflection (not a centered bar) and a TO (not FROM) indication. Answer (B) is incorrect because airplane 14 is east of the 360/180 radials, which would require a bar deflection (not a centered bar).

**73.**

**4607.** (Refer to figure 110 below.) In which general direction from the VORTAC is the aircraft located?

A— Southwest.
B— Northwest.
C— Northeast.

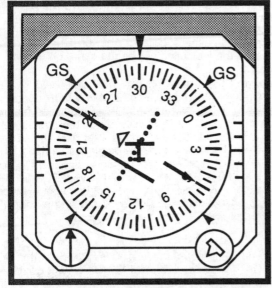

FIGURE 110.—CDI Direction from VORTAC.

**74.**

**4608.** (Refer to figure 111 below.) In which general direction from the VORTAC is the aircraft located?

A— Northeast.
B— Southeast.
C— Northwest.

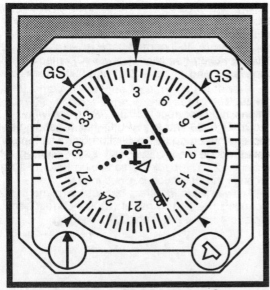

FIGURE 111.—CDI Direction from VORTAC.

Answer (C) is correct (4607). *(IFH Chap VIII)*
The course indicator arrow (OBS) is set to 60°, and the TO-FROM indicates FROM (opposite the head of the arrow), which means the airplane is northeast of the VORTAC. Since the course deviation bar indicates to the right ½ deflection, the airplane is to the north of the 60° radial by 6°, which is in the northeast.
Answer (A) is incorrect because southwest would require a TO (not FROM) indication. Answer (B) is incorrect because northwest would require a full right (not a ½-scale) deflection.

Answer (C) is correct (4608). *(IFH Chap VIII)*
The course indicator arrow (OBS) is set to 360° and the TO-FROM indicator is FROM, which means the airplane is north of the VORTAC. Since the course deviation bar is to the right, it means that the airplane is to the west of the 360° radial of the VORTAC. Accordingly, the airplane is to the northwest of the VORTAC.
Answer (A) is incorrect because a left (not right) deflection would indicate the airplane is in the northeast. Answer (B) is incorrect because a TO (not FROM) indication would indicate the airplane is south of the VORTAC.

## 6.7  HSI/Localizer

**Note:  HSI presentations B, C, D, E, and I have backcourse settings of 090°, which means there is reverse sensing irrespective of the airplane's heading.**

**75.**
**4563.** (Refer to figure 96 below and 97 on page 199.) To which aircraft position(s) does HSI presentation "A" correspond?

A— 9 and 6.
B— 9 only.
C— 6 only.

Answer (A) is correct (4563).  *(IFH Chap VII)*
On Figs. 96 and 97, HSI "A" has a heading of 360° with no localizer deviation, which means the airplane is on the localizer.  Airplanes 6 and 9 are on the localizer with a 360° heading.
Answer (B) is incorrect because the indication will be the same on either localizer.  Answer (C) is incorrect because the indication will be the same on either localizer.

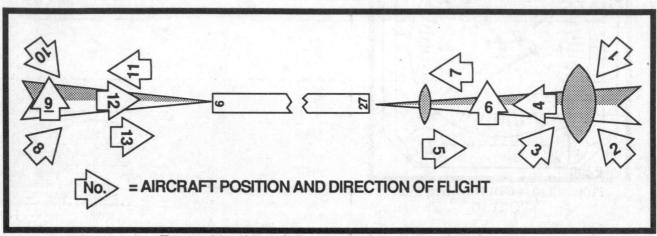

FIGURE 96.—Aircraft Position and Direction of Flight.

**76.**
**4564.** (Refer to figure 96 above and 97 on page 199.) To which aircraft position(s) does HSI presentation "B" correspond?

A— 11.
B— 5 and 13.
C— 7 and 11.

Answer (B) is correct (4564).  *(IFH Chap VII)*
On Figs. 96 and 97, HSI "B" has a heading of 090°.  It has localizer course setting of 090° with a right deflection, meaning the airplane is south of the localizer.  Both airplanes 5 and 13 are described.  Note the backcourse setting.  If the front course 270° (instead of 90°) had been set, normal (rather than reverse) sensing would be indicated.
Answer (A) is incorrect because airplane 11 has a 270° (not 090°) heading.  Answer (C) is incorrect because airplanes 7 and 11 have 270° (not 090°) headings.

**77.**
**4565.** (Refer to figure 96 above and 97 on page 199.) To which aircraft position does HSI presentation "C" correspond?

A— 9.
B— 4.
C— 12.

Answer (C) is correct (4565).  *(IFH Chap VII)*
On Figs. 96 and 97, HSI "C" has a heading of 090° with a centered course deflection bar, which means the airplane is on the localizer with a 090° heading, which is airplane 12.  The backcourse setting (090) has no effect because the deflection bar is centered.
Answer (A) is incorrect because airplane 9 has a 360° (not 090°) heading.  Answer (B) is incorrect because airplane 4 has a 270° (not 090°) heading.

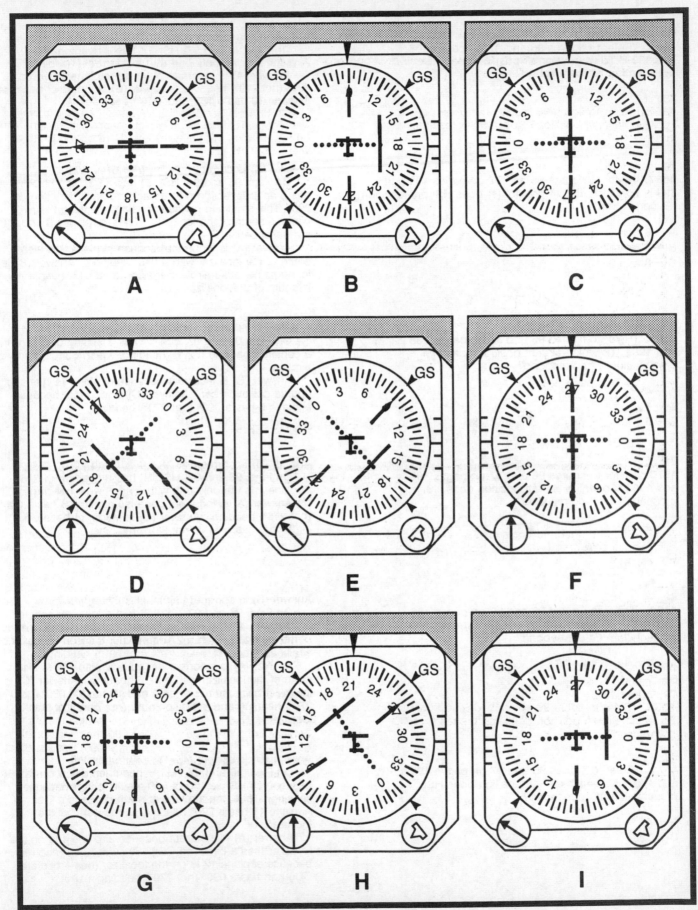

FIGURE 97.—HSI Presentation.

**78.**
**4566.**   (Refer to figures 96 and 97 on pages 198 and 199.)  To which aircraft position does HSI presentation "D" correspond?

A— 1.
B— 10.
C— 2.

Answer (C) is correct (4566).  *(IFH Chap VII)*
    On Figs. 96 and 97, HSI "D" has a heading of 310°.  Airplane 2 is the only one with a northwest heading.
    Answer (A) is incorrect because airplane 1 is on a 225° (not 310°) heading.  Answer (B) is incorrect because airplane 10 has a 135° (not 310°) heading.

**79.**
**4567.**   (Refer to figures 96 and 97 on pages 198 and 199.)  To which aircraft position(s) does HSI presentation "E" correspond?

A— 8 only.
B— 3 only.
C— 8 and 3.

Answer (C) is correct (4567).  *(IFH Chap VII)*
    On Figs. 96 and 97, HSI "E" has a heading of 045°.  It has a right deflection with a backcourse HSI setting of 090.  This results in reverse sensing, meaning the airplane is south of the localizer.  Thus, airplanes 3 and 8 are described.
    Answer (A) is incorrect because airplane 3 is also south of the localizer with a 045° heading.  Answer (B) is incorrect because airplane 8 also has a 045° heading and is south of the localizer.

**80.**
**4568.**   (Refer to figures 96 and 97 on pages 198 and 199.)  To which aircraft position does HSI presentation "F" correspond?

A— 4.
B— 11.
C— 5.

Answer (A) is correct (4568).  *(IFH Chap VII)*
    On Figs. 96 and 97, HSI "F" has a setting of 270° with a centered bar and a 270° heading, which corresponds to airplane 4.
    Answer (B) is incorrect because airplane 11 has a left course deviation bar.  Answer (C) is incorrect because airplane 5 has a 090° (not 270°) heading.

**81.**
**4570.**   (Refer to figures 96 and 97 on pages 198 and 199.)  To which aircraft position does HSI presentation "H" correspond?

A— 8.
B— 1.
C— 2.

Answer (B) is correct (4570).  *(IFH Chap VII)*
    On Figs. 96 and 97, HSI "H" has a heading of 215°.  Airplane 1 is the only one with a southwest heading.
    Answer (A) is incorrect because airplane 8 has a 045° (not 215°) heading.  Answer (C) is incorrect because airplane 2 has a 315° (not 215°) heading.

**82.**
**4569.**   (Refer to figures 96 and 97 on pages 198 and 199.)  To which aircraft position(s) does HSI presentation "G" correspond?

A— 7 only.
B— 7 and 11.
C— 5 and 13.

Answer (B) is correct (4569).  *(IFH Chap VII)*
    On Figs. 96 and 97, HSI "G" has a localizer setting at 270° with a left deviation, meaning the airplane is north of the localizer.  With a 270° heading, it corresponds to airplanes 7 and 11.
    Answer (A) is incorrect because airplane 11 is also north of the localizer with a 270° heading.  Answer (C) is incorrect because airplanes 5 and 13 have a 090° (not 270°) heading and are also south (not north) of the localizer.

**83.**
**4571.**   (Refer to figures 96 and 97 on pages 198 and 199.)  To which aircraft position does HSI presentation "I" correspond?

A— 4.
B— 12.
C— 11.

Answer (C) is correct (4571).  *(IFH Chap VII)*
    On Figs. 96 and 97, HSI "I" has a left deviation with a backcourse HSI setting of 090 resulting in reverse sensing.  Thus, the airplane is north of the localizer.  Airplane 11 has a 270° heading and is north of the localizer.
    Answer (A) is incorrect because airplane 4 is on the localizer (has a centered CDI).  Answer (B) is incorrect because airplane 12 is on the localizer (has a centered CDI) and has a 090° (not 270°) heading.

# END OF CHAPTER

# CHAPTER SEVEN
# FLIGHT PHYSIOLOGY

This chapter contains outlines of major concepts tested, all FAA test questions and answers regarding flight physiology, and an explanation of each answer. The subtopics or modules within this chapter are listed above, followed in parentheses by the number of questions from the FAA written test pertaining to that particular module. The two numbers following the parentheses are the page numbers on which the outline and questions begin for that module.

**CAUTION:** Recall that the **sole purpose** of this book is to expedite passing the instrument rating FAA written test. Accordingly, extraneous material (i.e., topics or regulations not directly tested on the FAA written test) is omitted, even though much more information and knowledge are necessary to fly safely. This additional material is presented in *Instrument Pilot FAA Practical Test Prep* and *Aviation Weather and Weather Services*, available from Gleim Publications, Inc. See the order form on page 478.

## 7.1 HYPOXIA AND HYPERVENTILATION (Questions 1-2)

1.  Hypoxia results from a lack of oxygen in the bloodstream and causes a lack of clear thinking, fatigue, euphoria, and, shortly thereafter, unconsciousness.

    a.  Symptoms of hypoxia are difficult to detect before the pilot's reactions are affected.

2.  Hyperventilation occurs when an excessive amount of air is breathed into the lungs at an excessive rate, e.g., when one becomes excited as a result of stress, fear, or anxiety.

    a.  Overcome hyperventilation symptoms by slowing the breathing rate, placing a paper bag over your nose and mouth and breathing into it, or by talking aloud.

## 7.2 SPATIAL DISORIENTATION (Questions 3-12)

1.  Spatial disorientation (sometimes called vertigo) is a state of temporary confusion resulting from misleading information sent to the brain by various sensory organs.

2.  The best way to overcome the effects of spatial disorientation is to rely on the airplane instruments and ignore body (kinesthetic) signals.

3.  The nervous system often interprets centrifugal force as vertical movement, i.e., rising or falling.

4.  Coriolis illusion is caused by an abrupt head movement in a prolonged constant-rate turn.

    a.  This can cause spatial disorientation.

5.  An abrupt change from a climb to straight and level flight can create the illusion of tumbling backwards.

6.  A rapid acceleration during takeoff can create the illusion of being in a nose-up attitude.

7.  False horizons is an illusion that is caused by a sloping cloud formation, an obscured horizon, or a dark scene spread with ground lights and stars.

## 7.3 VISION AND VISUAL ILLUSION (Questions 13-18)

1. Pilots should adapt their eyes for night flying by avoiding bright white lights for 30 min. prior to flight.

   a. Thereafter, white light must be avoided because it will cause temporary night blindness and impair night vision adaptation.

2. The most effective way to scan for other aircraft in daylight is to use a series of short, regularly-spaced eye movements that bring successive areas of the sky into your central vision field.

   a. Each movement should not exceed 10° and each area should be observed for at least 1 second to enable detection.

   b. Only a very small center area of the eye has the ability to send clear, sharply-focused messages to the brain. All other areas provide less detail.

   c. At night, however, the eyes are most effective at seeing objects off-center. Accordingly, pilots should scan slowly back and forth to facilitate off-center viewing.

3. Haze can also create the illusion of being a greater distance from the runway, resulting in the pilot flying a lower-than-normal approach.

4. A narrower-than-usual runway may create the illusion that the airplane is higher than it actually is.

   a. This results in a lower-than-normal approach.
   b. A wider-than-usual runway creates the opposite illusion and problem.

5. An upward sloping runway may create the illusion that the airplane is at a higher-than-actual altitude.

   a. This results in a lower-than-normal approach.
   b. A downward sloping runway creates the opposite illusion and problem.

---

### QUESTIONS AND ANSWER EXPLANATIONS

*All the FAA questions from the written test for the instrument rating relating to flight physiology and the material outlined previously are reproduced on the following pages in the same modules as the above outlines. To the immediate right of each question are the correct answer and answer explanation. You should cover these answers and answer explanations with your hand or a piece of paper while responding to the questions. Refer to the general discussion in Chapter 1 on how to take the examination.*

*Remember that the questions from the FAA Instrument Rating Question Book have been reordered by topic, and the topics have been organized into a meaningful sequence. The first line of the answer explanation gives the FAA question number and the citation of the authoritative source for the answer.*

## 7.1 Hypoxia and Hyperventilation

**1.**
**4809.** Why is hypoxia particularly dangerous during flights with one pilot?

A— Night vision may be so impaired that the pilot cannot see other aircraft.
B— Symptoms of hypoxia may be difficult to recognize before the pilot's reactions are affected.
C— The pilot may not be able to control the aircraft even if using oxygen.

**2.**
**4816.** What action should be taken if hyperventilation is suspected?

A— Breathe at a slower rate by taking very deep breaths.
B— Consciously breathe at a slower rate than normal.
C— Consciously force yourself to take deep breaths and breathe at a faster rate than normal.

## 7.2 Spatial Disorientation

**3.**
**4814.** A pilot is more subject to spatial disorientation if

A— kinesthetic senses are ignored.
B— eyes are moved often in the process of cross-checking the flight instruments.
C— body signals are used to interpret flight attitude.

**4.**
**4815.** Which procedure is recommended to prevent or overcome spatial disorientation?

A— Reduce head and eye movements to the extent possible.
B— Rely on the kinesthetic sense.
C— Rely on the indications of the flight instruments.

**5.**
**4810.** The sensations which lead to spatial disorientation during instrument flight conditions

A— are frequently encountered by beginning instrument pilots, but never by pilots with moderate instrument experience.
B— occur, in most instances, during the initial period of transition from visual to instrument flight.
C— must be suppressed and complete reliance placed on the indications of the flight instruments.

**Answer (B) is correct (4809).** *(AIM Para 8-2)*
Hypoxia symptoms are gradual, and a pilot may not recognize the symptoms before his/her reactions are affected. Because the symptoms of hypoxia vary with the individual, having two pilots increases the chance of detection before pilot reactions are affected.
Answer (A) is incorrect because hypoxia, which is a lack of sufficient oxygen, affects all mental and physical activity, not just night vision. Answer (C) is incorrect because hypoxia will not occur if supplemental oxygen is used properly.

**Answer (B) is correct (4816).** *(AIM Para 8-3)*
Hyperventilation occurs when abnormally large amounts of air are breathed in and out of the lungs. Early symptoms of hyperventilation and hypoxia are similar and include dizziness, drowsiness, tingling of the fingers and toes, and sensation of body heat. If hyperventilation is suspected, you should consciously breathe at a slower rate than normal.
Answer (A) is incorrect because taking deep breaths will only aggravate hyperventilation. Answer (C) is incorrect because taking deep breaths and breathing at a faster rate than normal is the cause (not cure) of hyperventilation.

**Answer (C) is correct (4814).** *(MHP Chap 14)*
Spatial disorientation is a state of temporary confusion resulting from misleading information being sent to the brain by various sensory organs. Thus, the pilot should ignore sensations of muscles and inner ear and kinesthetic senses (those which sense motion).
Answer (A) is incorrect because spatial disorientation is prevented/overcome by ignoring the kinesthetic senses. Answer (B) is incorrect because spatial disorientation is prevented/overcome by using and trusting the flight instruments.

**Answer (C) is correct (4815).** *(MHP Chap 14)*
To overcome the effect of spatial disorientation, pilots should rely entirely on the indications of the flight instruments.
Answer (A) is incorrect because although rapid head movements should be avoided, eye movement is necessary for proper scanning of the flight instruments. Answer (B) is incorrect because the kinesthetic sense is creating the problem, i.e., it should be ignored.

**Answer (C) is correct (4810).** *(PHAK Chap 8)*
In instrument flight conditions, the only way to prevent spatial disorientation is by visual reference to and reliance on the flight instruments.
Answer (A) is incorrect because pilots with moderate and even heavy instrument experience can experience spatial disorientation. Answer (B) is incorrect because spatial disorientation can occur at any time outside visual references are lost. This can happen on a clear day flying VFR or in IMC.

**6.**

**4811.** How can an instrument pilot best overcome spatial disorientation?

A— Rely on kinesthetic sense.
B— Use a very rapid cross-check.
C— Read and interpret the flight instruments, and act accordingly.

Answer (C) is correct (4811). *(IFH Chap II)*
    To overcome spatial disorientation, the IFR pilot should read and interpret the flight instruments and ignore all the body senses.
    Answer (A) is incorrect because the kinesthetic sense is what causes the problem, i.e., it should be ignored. Answer (B) is incorrect because the flight instruments should be read and understood in a deliberate manner, not in haste or panic.

**7.**

**4813.** How can an instrument pilot best overcome spatial disorientation?

A— Use a very rapid cross-check.
B— Properly interpret the flight instruments and act accordingly.
C— Avoid banking in excess of 30°.

Answer (B) is correct (4813). *(IFH Chap II)*
    To overcome spatial disorientation, the IFR pilot should read and interpret the flight instruments and ignore all the body senses.
    Answer (A) is incorrect because the flight instruments should be read and understood in a deliberate manner, not in haste or panic. Answer (C) is incorrect because spatial disorientation can also occur in bank angles less than 30°.

**8.**

**4802.** Without visual aid, a pilot often interprets centrifugal force as a sensation of

A— rising or falling.
B— turning.
C— motion reversal.

Answer (A) is correct (4802). *(IFH Chap II)*
    Nerves in tendons and muscles, including shifting of abdominal muscles, often incorrectly interpret centrifugal force as vertical movement, i.e., rising or falling.
    Answer (B) is incorrect because centrifugal force is caused by turning, but is often misinterpreted as rising or falling. Answer (C) is incorrect because centrifugal force is caused by turning, not motion reversal.

**9.**

**4805.** Abrupt head movement during a prolonged constant rate turn in IMC or simulated instrument conditions can cause

A— pilot disorientation.
B— false horizon.
C— elevator illusion.

Answer (A) is correct (4805). *(AIM Para 8-5)*
    An abrupt head movement in a prolonged constant-rate turn that has ceased stimulating the motion sensing system can create the illusion of rotation or movement in an entirely different axis. This illusion is called the Coriolis illusion and can lead to spatial disorientation.
    Answer (B) is incorrect because a false horizon is an illusion caused by sloping cloud formations, an obscured horizon, a dark scene spread with ground lights and stars, and certain geometric patterns of ground light can create an illusion of not being aligned correctly with the actual horizon. This can also lead to spatial disorientation. Answer (C) is incorrect because an elevator illusion is caused by an abrupt upward vertical acceleration, usually by an updraft. This can also lead to spatial disorientation.

**10.**

**4807.** An abrupt change from climb to straight-and-level flight can create the illusion of

A— tumbling backwards.
B— a noseup attitude.
C— a descent with the wings level.

Answer (A) is correct (4807). *(AIM Para 8-5)*
    An abrupt change from climb to straight-and-level flight can create the illusion of tumbling backwards. The disoriented pilot will push the airplane abruptly into a nose-low attitude, possibly intensifying this illusion. This is called an inversion illusion.
    Answer (B) is incorrect because a rapid acceleration during takeoff can create an illusion of being in a nose-up attitude. This is called a somatogravic illusion. Answer (C) is incorrect because an observed loss of altitude during a coordinated constant-rate turn that has ceased stimulating the motion sensing system (i.e., inner ear) can create the illusion of being in a descent with the wings level. This is called a graveyard spiral.

**11.**
**4808.** A rapid acceleration during takeoff can create the illusion of

A— spinning in the opposite direction.
B— being in a noseup attitude.
C— diving into the ground.

Answer (B) is correct (4808). *(AIM Para 8-5)*
A rapid acceleration during takeoff can create the illusion of being in a nose-up attitude. The disoriented pilot will push the airplane into a nose-low, or dive, attitude. This is called a somatogravic illusion.
Answer (A) is incorrect because a proper recovery from a spin that has ceased stimulating the motion sensing system (i.e., inner ear) can create the illusion of spinning in the opposite direction. This is known as a graveyard spin. Answer (C) is incorrect because a rapid deceleration or an abrupt downward vertical acceleration (usually caused by a downdraft) can cause the illusion of a nose-down, or dive, attitude.

**12.**
**4806.** A sloping cloud formation, an obscured horizon, and a dark scene spread with ground lights and stars can create an illusion known as

A— elevator illusions.
B— autokinesis.
C— false horizons.

Answer (C) is correct (4806). *(AIM Para 8-5)*
A sloping cloud formation, an obscured horizon, a dark scene spread with ground lights and stars, and certain geometric patterns of ground light can create an illusion known as false horizons. The disoriented pilot will place the airplane in a dangerous attitude.
Answer (A) is incorrect because elevator illusions are caused by abrupt upward or downward vertical accelerations, usually by updrafts and downdrafts. These lead to illusions of being in a climb or descent. Answer (B) is incorrect because, at night, a static light will appear to move about when stared at for many seconds, creating an illusion known as autokinesis.

## 7.3 Vision and Visual Illusion

**13.**
**4817.** Which use of cockpit lighting is correct for night flight?

A— Reducing the lighting intensity to a minimum level will eliminate blind spots.
B— The use of regular white light, such as a flashlight, will impair night adaptation.
C— Coloration shown on maps is least affected by the use of direct red lighting.

Answer (B) is correct (4817). *(AIM Para 8-6)*
*This question is a duplicate of FAA question 4812.*
After a pilot's eyes have become adapted to darkness, the pilot must avoid exposing them to any bright white light which would cause temporary night blindness and impair night adaptation.
Answer (A) is incorrect because the minimum level of cockpit lighting may be insufficient to read maps, gauges, etc. Answer (C) is incorrect because the colors on maps can be severely distorted when using a red light.

**14.**
**4812.** Which statement is correct regarding the use of cockpit lighting for night flight?

A— Reducing the lighting intensity to a minimum level will eliminate blind spots.
B— The use of regular white light, such as a flashlight, will impair night adaptation.
C— Coloration shown on maps is least affected by the use of direct red lighting.

Answer (B) is correct (4812). *(AIM Para 8-6)*
*This question is a duplicate of FAA question 4817.*
After a pilot's eyes have become adapted to darkness, the pilot must avoid exposing them to any bright white light which would cause temporary night blindness and impair night adaptation.
Answer (A) is incorrect because the minimum level of cockpit lighting may be insufficient to read maps, gauges, etc. Answer (C) is incorrect because the colors on maps can be severely distorted when using a red light.

**15.**
**4818.** Which technique should a pilot use to scan for traffic to the right and left during straight-and-level flight?

A— Systematically focus on different segments of the sky for short intervals.
B— Concentrate on relative movement detected in the peripheral vision area.
C— Continuous sweeping of the windshield from right to left.

Answer (A) is correct (4818). *(AIM Para 8-6)*
    The most effective way to scan for other aircraft during daylight is to use a series of short, regularly spaced eye movements that bring successive areas of the sky into your central vision field. Only a very small center area of the eye has the ability to send clear, sharply focused messages to the brain. All other areas provide less detail.
    Answer (B) is incorrect because the peripheral areas do not send sharply focused messages to the brain. Peripheral vision is more effective at night. Answer (C) is incorrect because concentration for at least 1 second is needed for each 10° sector.

**16.**
**4819.** What effect does haze have on the ability to see traffic or terrain features during flight?

A— Haze causes the eyes to focus at infinity, making terrain features harder to see.
B— The eyes tend to overwork in haze and do not detect relative movement easily.
C— Haze creates the illusion of being a greater distance than actual from the runway, and causes pilots to fly a lower approach.

Answer (C) is correct (4819). *(AIM Para 8-5)*
    Haze can create the illusion of being at a greater distance from the runway, and often causes pilots to fly a lower approach.
    Answer (A) is incorrect because haze may cause the condition known as empty-field myopia. This is when the pilot has nothing specific to focus on outside the airplane and the eyes relax and focus at a range of about 10 to 30 ft., not infinity. Answer (B) is incorrect because in haze the eyes tend to relax, not overwork, thus causing empty-field myopia, or looking without seeing.

**17.**
**4803.** Due to visual illusion, when landing on a narrower-than-usual runway, the aircraft will appear to be

A— higher than actual, leading to a lower-than-normal approach.
B— lower than actual, leading to a higher-than-normal approach.
C— higher than actual, leading to a higher-than-normal approach.

Answer (A) is correct (4803). *(AIM Para 8-5)*
    A narrower-than-usual runway may create the illusion that the aircraft is higher than actual, resulting in a lower-than-normal approach.
    Answer (B) is incorrect because wider (not narrower) runways give a lower-than-actual altitude illusion. Answer (C) is incorrect because a higher-than-actual altitude illusion results in a lower (not higher) than usual approach.

**18.**
**4804.** What visual illusion creates the same effect as a narrower-than-usual runway?

A— An upsloping runway.
B— A wider-than-usual runway.
C— A downsloping runway.

Answer (A) is correct (4804). *(AIM Para 8-5)*
    A narrower-than-usual runway and an upsloping runway may both create the illusion that the airplane is at a higher altitude than it actually is. The pilot will fly a lower approach and risk striking obstructions or landing short.
    Answer (B) is incorrect because a wider-than-usual runway may create the illusion that the aircraft is at a lower altitude than it actually is, and the unknowing pilot may land hard or overshoot the runway. Answer (C) is incorrect because a downsloping runway may create the illusion that the aircraft is at a lower altitude than it actually is, and the unknowing pilot may land hard or overshoot the runway.

# END OF CHAPTER

# CHAPTER EIGHT
# FLIGHT OPERATIONS

This chapter contains outlines of major concepts tested, all FAA Instrument Rating test questions and answers regarding flight operations, and an explanation of each answer. The subtopics or modules within this chapter are listed above, followed in parentheses by the number of questions from the FAA written test pertaining to that particular module. The two numbers following the parentheses are the page numbers on which the outline and questions begin for that module.

**CAUTION:** Recall that the **sole purpose** of this book is to expedite your passing the FAA written test for the instrument rating. Accordingly, all extraneous material (i.e., topics or regulations not directly tested on the FAA written test) is omitted, even though much more information and knowledge are necessary to fly safely. This additional material is presented in *Instrument Pilot FAA Practical Test Prep* and *Aviation Weather and Weather Services*, available from Gleim Publications, Inc. See the order form on page 478.

## 8.1 TURNS (Questions 1-12)

1.   An airplane requires a sideward force to make it turn.

   a.   When the airplane is banked, lift (which acts perpendicular to the wingspan) acts not only upward, but horizontally as well.

   b.   The vertical component acts upward to oppose weight.

   c.   The horizontal component acts sideward to turn the airplane, opposing centrifugal force.

   d.   The rate of turn (at a given airspeed) depends on the magnitude of the horizontal lift component, which is determined by bank angle.

2.   A turn is said to be coordinated when the horizontal lift component equals centrifugal force (the ball is centered).

   a.   Centrifugal force is greater than horizontal lift in skidding turns (the ball is on the outside of the turn).

   b.   Centrifugal force is less than horizontal lift in slipping turns (the ball is on the inside of the turn).

3.  To coordinate a turn, one should center the ball on the turn-and-slip indicator or the turn coordinator.

    a.  Center the ball by applying rudder pressure on the side where the ball is (e.g., if the ball is on the left, use left rudder).

4.  A standard rate turn is indicated when the needle is on the "doghouse" (i.e., standard rate) mark on the turn-and-slip indicator.

5.  The angle of attack must be increased in turns to maintain altitude because additional lift is required to maintain a constant amount of vertical lift.

    a.  Thus, load factor always increases in turns (assuming level flight).

6.  If airspeed is increased in a turn, the angle of bank must be increased and/or the angle of attack decreased to maintain level flight.

    a.  Conversely, if airspeed is decreased in a turn, the angle of bank must be decreased and/or the angle of attack must be increased to maintain level flight.

## 8.2 TURN RATES  (Questions 13-20)

1.  The standard rate turn is 360° in 2 min., i.e., 3°/sec.

    a.  A half-standard rate turn is 360° in 4 min., i.e., 1.5°/sec.

    b.  EXAMPLE:  A 150° heading change using a standard rate turn would take 50 sec. (150° ÷ 3°/sec. = 50 sec.)

2.  At a constant bank, an increase in airspeed decreases the rate of turn and increases the radius of the turn.

    a.  The rate of turn can be increased and the radius of turn decreased by decreasing airspeed and/or increasing the bank.

## 8.3 CLIMBS AND DESCENTS  (Questions 21-30)

1.  The three conditions which determine pitch attitude, i.e., angle of attack, required to maintain level flight are:

    a.  Airspeed
    b.  Air density
    c.  Airplane weight

2.  When leveling off from a climb or descent to a specific altitude, it is necessary to start the level-off before reaching the desired altitude.

    a.  Throughout the transition to level flight, the aircraft will continue to climb or descend at a decreasing rate.

    b.  An effective practice is to lead the altitude by 10% of the indicated vertical speed.

        1)  Since the last 1,000 ft. of a climb or descent should be made at 500 fpm, you will generally use a lead of 50 ft.

    c.  To level off from a descent at a higher airspeed than descent speed, begin adding power 100 to 150 ft. above the desired altitude, assuming a descent rate of 500 fpm.

3.   The pitch instruments are the attitude indicator, the altimeter, the vertical speed indicator, and the airspeed indicator.

   a.   The attitude indicator should be used to make a pitch correction when you have deviated from your altitude, then the altimeter and vertical speed indicator are used to monitor the result.

   b.   Altitude corrections of less than 100 ft. should be corrected by using a half-bar-width correction on the attitude indicator.

4.   To enter a constant airspeed descent from level cruise and maintain cruise airspeed, simultaneously reduce power and adjust the pitch using the attitude indicator as a reference to maintain cruise airspeed.

5.   To enter a constant airspeed climb from level cruise, increase the pitch such that the artificial horizon indicates an approximate nose-high attitude appropriate for the desired climb speed.

   a.   Then apply the desired climb power setting.

## 8.4 FUNDAMENTAL INSTRUMENT SKILLS (Questions 31-34)

1.   The three fundamental skills for attitude instrument flying are (in order)

   a.   Instrument cross-check, the continuous and logical observation of instruments for attitude and performance information.

   b.   Instrument interpretation, the understanding of each instrument's construction, operating principle, and relationship to the performance of the airplane.

   c.   Airplane control. The elements of airplane control are:

      1)   Pitch control
      2)   Bank control
      3)   Power control

## 8.5 APPROPRIATE INSTRUMENTS FOR IFR (Questions 35-53)

1.   Flight instruments are divided into the following three categories:

   a.   Pitch Instruments:

      1)   Attitude Indicator (AI)
      2)   Altimeter (ALT)
      3)   Airspeed Indicator (ASI)
      4)   Vertical-Speed Indicator (VSI)

   b.   Bank Instruments:

      1)   Attitude Indicator (AI)
      2)   Heading Indicator (HI)
      3)   Turn Coordinator (TC) or Turn-and-Slip Indicator (T&SI)
      4)   Magnetic Compass

   c.   Power Instruments:

      1)   Manifold Pressure Gauge (MP)
      2)   Tachometer (RPM)
      3)   Airspeed Indicator (ASI)

2. For any maneuver or condition of flight, the pitch, bank, and power control requirements are most clearly indicated by certain key instruments. Those instruments which provide the most pertinent and essential information will be referred to as primary instruments. Supporting instruments back up and supplement the information shown on the primary instruments.

| | PITCH | BANK | POWER |
|---|---|---|---|
| a. Straight and level | | | |
| Primary | ALT | HI | ASI |
| Supporting | AI, VSI | AI, TC | MP and/or RPM |
| b. Airspeed changes in straight and level | | | |
| Primary | ALT | HI | MP and/or RPM initially |
| Supporting | AI, VSI | AI, TC | ASI as desired air-speed is approached |
| c. Straight constant rate stabilized climb | | | |
| Primary | VSI | HI | ASI |
| Supporting | AI | AI, TC | MP and/or RPM |
| d. Establishing a level standard rate turn | | | |
| Primary | ALT | AI | ASI |
| Supporting | AI, VSI | TC | MP and/or RPM |
| e. Transitioning from straight and level to constant airspeed climb | | | |
| Primary | AI | HI | MP and/or RPM |
| Supporting | ASI, VSI | AI, TC | ASI |
| f. Stabilized standard rate turn | | | |
| Primary | ALT | TC | ASI |
| Supporting | AI, VSI | AI | MP and/or RPM |
| g. Straight constant airspeed climb | | | |
| Primary | ASI | HI | MP and/or RPM |
| Supporting | AI, VSI | AI, TC | ASI |
| h. Change of airspeed in level turn | | | |
| Primary | ALT | TC | MP and/or RPM |
| Supporting | AI, VSI | AI | ASI |
| i. As power is increased to enter a straight, constant rate climb | | | |
| Primary | ASI | HI | MP and/or RPM |
| Supporting | AI, VSI | AI, TC | -- |

3. For straight-and-level flight the magnetic compass replaces the HI as the primary bank instrument if the HI is inoperative.

4. The ball of the turn coordinator or turn-and-slip instrument indicates the quality of the turn.

## 8.6 UNUSUAL ATTITUDES  (Questions 54-59)

1. For recovery from nose-low unusual attitudes (negative VSI, increasing airspeed, decreasing altitude, airplane below horizon on attitude indicator):

   a. Reduce power to prevent excess airspeed and loss of altitude.
   b. Level the wings with coordinated rudder and aileron.
   c. Gently raise the nose to level flight attitude.

2. For recovery from nose-high unusual attitudes (positive VSI, decreasing airspeed, increasing altitude, airplane above horizon on attitude indicator):

   a. Add power.
   b. Lower the nose.
   c. Level the wings.
   d. Return to the original altitude and heading.

3. When recovering without the aid of the attitude indicator, level flight attitude is reached when the altimeter and the airspeed indicator stop prior to reversing their direction of movement and the vertical speed indicator reverses trend.

4. If the attitude indicator has exceeded its limits in an unusual attitude, nose-low or nose-high attitude can be determined by the airspeed indicator and the altimeter.

   a. The vertical speed indicator is also useful, but not as reliable in turbulent air.

## 8.7 INOPERATIVE INSTRUMENTS  (Questions 60-65)

1. To determine an inoperative instrument, analyze each instrument to determine what it is indicating and determine which instrument is in conflict with the others.

2. Also, consider grouping the instruments by the systems which power them.

   a. The heading indicator and the attitude indicator are vacuum-driven.
   b. The turn coordinator is usually electric.
   c. The airspeed indicator, altimeter, and VSI rely on the static source.

      1) The airspeed indicator also relies on the pitot tube.

         a) Remember that if the pitot tube's ram air and drain hole are clogged, the airspeed indicator acts as an altimeter; i.e., lower altitudes result in lower airspeeds and vice versa.

         b) Also remember that if only the ram air hole is clogged, the pressure in the line will vent out the drain hole, causing the airspeed indication to drop to zero.

## 8.8 WAKE TURBULENCE  (Questions 66-69)

1. The greatest vortex strength occurs behind heavy, clean, and slow aircraft.

   a. For example, during the takeoff of a jet transport, because it has a high gross weight and a high angle of attack.

2. Light quartering tailwinds prolong the hazards of wake turbulence the longest because they move the vortices of preceding aircraft forward to the touchdown zone and hold the upwind vortex on the runway.

   a. A light crosswind of 3 to 7 kt. would result in an upwind vortex tending to remain over the runway.

3. When landing behind a large aircraft on the same runway, stay at or above the other aircraft's final approach flight path and land beyond that airplane's touchdown point.

## 8.9 TURBULENCE AND WIND SHEAR (Questions 70-72)

1.  In severe turbulence, set power for the design maneuvering speed ($V_A$) and maintain a level flight attitude.

    a.  Attempting to turn or maintain altitude or airspeed may impose excessive load on the wings.

2.  Flight at or below $V_A$ means the airplane will stall before excessive loads can be imposed on the wings.

3.  When climbing or descending through an inversion or wind shear zone, the pilot should be alert for any sudden change in airspeed.

## 8.10 COLLISION AVOIDANCE (Questions 73-76)

1.  When climbing to an assigned altitude on an airway, use the centerline except to avoid other aircraft when in VFR conditions.

2.  During climbs and descents in VFR conditions, pilots should execute gentle banks left and right to permit continual scanning of surrounding airspace.

3.  When weather conditions permit, i.e., VFR, each pilot must assume the responsibility to see and avoid other aircraft, regardless of whether operating under IFR or VFR.

---

### QUESTIONS AND ANSWER EXPLANATIONS

All the FAA questions from the written test for the instrument rating relating to flight operations and the material outlined previously are reproduced on the following pages in the same modules as the outlines. To the immediate right of each question are the correct answer and answer explanation. You should cover these answers and answer explanations with your hand or a piece of paper while responding to the questions. Refer to the general discussion in Chapter 1 on how to take the FAA written test.

Remember that the questions from the FAA Instrument Rating Question Book have been reordered by topic, and the topics have been organized into a meaningful sequence. Accordingly, the first line of the answer explanation gives the FAA question number and the citation of the authoritative source for the answer.

## 8.1 Turns

**1.**
**4870.** What force causes an airplane to turn?

A— Rudder pressure or force around the vertical axis.
B— Vertical lift component.
C— Horizontal lift component.

Answer (C) is correct (4870). *(IFH Chap III)*
An airplane, like any object, requires a sideward force to make it turn. This force is supplied by banking the airplane so that lift is separated into two components at right angles to each other. The lift acting upward opposing weight is the vertical lift component, and the lift acting horizontally and opposing centrifugal force is the horizontal lift component. The horizontal lift component is the sideward force that causes an airplane to turn.
Answer (A) is incorrect because the rudder pressure only coordinates flight when the airplane is banked. Answer (B) is incorrect because the vertical component of lift counteracts weight and thus affects altitude.

**2.**
**4843.** The rate of turn at any airspeed is dependent upon

A— the horizontal lift component.
B— the vertical lift component.
C— centrifugal force.

Answer (A) is correct (4843). *(IFH Chap III)*
At a given airspeed, the rate at which an airplane turns depends upon the amount of the horizontal component of lift.
Answer (B) is incorrect because the vertical component of lift determines altitude and change in altitude. Answer (C) is incorrect because centrifugal force acts against the horizontal lift component, thus acting against turning the airplane.

**3.**
**4868.** What is the relationship between centrifugal force and the horizontal lift component in a coordinated turn?

A— Horizontal lift exceeds centrifugal force.
B— Horizontal lift and centrifugal force are equal.
C— Centrifugal force exceeds horizontal lift.

Answer (B) is correct (4868). *(IFH Chap III)*
When a turn is coordinated, horizontal lift equals centrifugal force. This is indicated when the ball on the turn coordinator or turn-and-slip indicator is centered.
Answer (A) is incorrect because when horizontal lift exceeds centrifugal force there is a slipping turn. Answer (C) is incorrect because when centrifugal force exceeds horizontal lift there is a skidding turn.

**4.**
**4915.** The primary reason the angle of attack must be increased, to maintain a constant altitude during a coordinated turn, is because the

A— thrust is acting in a different direction, causing a reduction in airspeed and loss of lift.
B— vertical component of lift has decreased as the result of the bank.
C— use of ailerons has increased the drag.

Answer (B) is correct (4915). *(IFH Chap III)*
In comparison to level flight, a bank results in the division of lift between vertical and horizontal components. To provide a vertical component of lift sufficient to maintain altitude in a level turn, an increase in the angle of attack is required.
Answer (A) is incorrect because thrust is always a forward acting force. The reduction in airspeed (assuming constant power) is due to an increase in angle of attack to compensate for the loss of vertical lift in a turn, i.e., to maintain altitude. Answer (C) is incorrect because in a coordinated turn the ailerons are streamlined and no aileron drag exists. Entering or recovering from turns, the aileron drag is counteracted by use of the rudder.

**5.**
**4931.** (Refer to figure 144 below.) What changes in control displacement should be made so that "2" would result in a coordinated standard rate turn?

A— Increase left rudder and increase rate of turn.
B— Increase left rudder and decrease rate of turn.
C— Decrease left rudder and decrease angle of bank.

Answer (A) is correct (4931). *(IFH Chap IV)*
   Illustration 2 in Fig. 144 indicates a slip, in which the rate of turn is too slow for the angle of bank, and the lack of centrifugal force causes the ball to move to the inside of the turn. To return to a coordinated standard rate turn, you should increase left rudder (i.e., step on the ball) and increase the rate of turn. A standard rate turn is indicated when the needle is on the "doghouse" (i.e., standard rate) mark. It is presently indicating a half-standard rate turn.
   Answer (B) is incorrect because the rate of turn must be increased (not decreased) to establish a standard rate turn. Answer (C) is incorrect because left rudder pressure must be increased (not decreased) in a slip to the left.

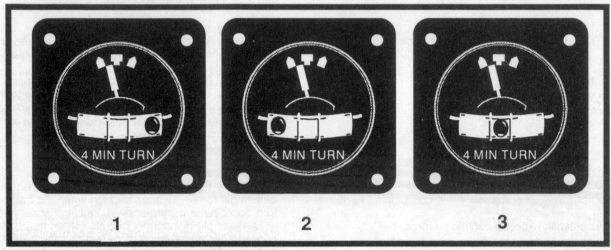

FIGURE 144.—Turn-and-Slip Indicator.

**6.**
**4932.** (Refer to figure 144 above.) Which illustration indicates a coordinated turn?

A— 3.
B— 1.
C— 2.

Answer (A) is correct (4932). *(IFH Chap IV)*
   A coordinated turn is one in which the ball is centered as indicated in illustration 3. The horizontal component of lift equals centrifugal force.
   Answer (B) is incorrect because illustration 1 shows a skidding turn, in which centrifugal force exceeds the horizontal component of lift. Answer (C) is incorrect because illustration 2 shows a slipping turn, in which centrifugal force is less than the horizontal component of lift.

**7.**
**4934.** (Refer to figure 144 above.) What changes in control displacement should be made so that "1" would result in a coordinated standard rate turn?

A— Increase right rudder and decrease rate of turn.
B— Increase right rudder and increase rate of turn.
C— Decrease right rudder and increase angle of bank.

Answer (B) is correct (4934). *(IFH Chap IV)*
   Illustration 1 in Fig. 144 indicates a skid, in which the rate of turn is too great for the angle of bank, and excessive centrifugal force causes the ball to move to the outside of the turn. To return to coordinated flight, you should increase right rudder (i.e., step on the ball) to center the ball. A standard rate turn is indicated when the needle is on the doghouse mark. Thus, the rate of turn must be increased to result in a standard rate turn.
   Answer (A) is incorrect because the rate of turn must be increased, not decreased. Answer (C) is incorrect because right rudder must be increased, not decreased.

**8.**
**4933.** (Refer to figure 144 on page 214.) Which illustration indicates a skidding turn?

A— 2.
B— 1.
C— 3.

**9.**
**4935.** (Refer to figure 144 on page 214.) Which illustration indicates a slipping turn?

A— 1.
B— 3.
C— 2.

**10.**
**4844.** During a skidding turn to the right, what is the relationship between the component of lift, centrifugal force, and load factor?

A— Centrifugal force is less than horizontal lift and the load factor is increased.
B— Centrifugal force is greater than horizontal lift and the load factor is increased.
C— Centrifugal force and horizontal lift are equal and the load factor is decreased.

**11.**
**4878.** When airspeed is increased in a turn, what must be done to maintain a constant altitude?

A— Decrease the angle of bank.
B— Increase the angle of bank and/or decrease the angle of attack.
C— Decrease the angle of attack.

**12.**
**4833.** When airspeed is decreased in a turn, what must be done to maintain level flight?

A— Decrease the angle of bank and/or increase the angle of attack.
B— Increase the angle of bank and/or decrease the angle of attack.
C— Increase the angle of attack.

Answer (B) is correct (4933). *(IFH Chap IV)*
A skidding turn occurs when centrifugal force is greater than horizontal lift. As shown by illustration 1, the ball is outside the turn.
Answer (A) is incorrect because illustration 2 shows a slipping turn. Answer (C) is incorrect because illustration 3 shows a coordinated turn.

Answer (C) is correct (4935). *(IFH Chap IV)*
A slipping turn is one in which the centrifugal force is less than horizontal lift. As shown by illustration 2, the ball is inside the turn.
Answer (A) is incorrect because illustration 1 shows a skidding turn. Answer (B) is incorrect because illustration 3 shows a coordinated turn.

Answer (B) is correct (4844). *(IFH Chap III)*
In skidding turns, centrifugal force is greater than horizontal lift. The load factor increases in level turns.
Answer (A) is incorrect because a slipping (not skidding) turn occurs when centrifugal force is less than horizontal lift. Answer (C) is incorrect because centrifugal force and horizontal lift are equal in a coordinated (not skidding) turn and in a level turn the load factor is increased (not decreased).

Answer (B) is correct (4878). *(IFH Chap III)*
To compensate for added lift, which would result if airspeed were increased during a turn, the angle of attack must be decreased and the angle of bank increased if a constant altitude is to be maintained.
Answer (A) is incorrect because the angle of bank must be increased, not decreased. Answer (C) is incorrect because, as an alternative, the angle of bank can be increased.

Answer (A) is correct (4833). *(IFH Chap III)*
To compensate for the decreased lift resulting from decreased airspeed during a turn, the angle of bank must be decreased and/or the angle of attack increased.
Answer (B) is incorrect because the increased vertical lift required must be obtained by a decrease (not increase) in angle of bank and/or increase (not decrease) in angle of attack. Answer (C) is incorrect because the angle of bank can be decreased as well as the angle of attack increased.

## 8.2  Turn Rates

**13.**
**4904.** If a standard rate turn is maintained, how much time would be required to turn to the left from a heading of 090° to a heading of 300°?

A— 30 seconds.
B— 40 seconds.
C— 50 seconds.

**Answer (C) is correct (4904).** *(IFH Chap IV)*
A standard rate turn means an airplane is turning at a rate of 3°/sec. A left turn from 090° to 300° is a total of 150° (90° to north and another 60° to 300°). Thus, at standard rate it would take 50 sec. (150° ÷ 3°/sec.).
Answer (A) is incorrect because at standard rate of turn an airplane would turn left 90° to a heading of 360° (not 300°) in 30 sec. Answer (B) is incorrect because at standard rate of turn an airplane would turn left 120° to a heading of 330° (not 300°) in 40 sec.

**14.**
**4905.** If a half-standard rate turn is maintained, how long would it take to turn 135°?

A— 1 minute.
B— 1 minute 20 seconds.
C— 1 minute 30 seconds.

**Answer (C) is correct (4905).** *(IFH Chap IV)*
A standard rate turn means an airplane is turning at a rate of 3°/sec. Thus, a half-standard rate is a turn at the rate of 1.5°/sec. To turn 135° at half-standard rate would take 90 sec. (135° ÷ 1.5°/sec.) or 1 min. 30 sec.
Answer (A) is incorrect because an airplane would turn 90° (not 135°) in 1 min. at half-standard rate. Answer (B) is incorrect because an airplane would turn 120° (not 135°) in 1 min. 20 sec. at half-standard rate.

**15.**
**4895.** If a half-standard rate turn is maintained, how long would it take to turn 360°?

A— 1 minute.
B— 2 minutes.
C— 4 minutes.

**Answer (C) is correct (4895).** *(IFH Chap IV)*
A standard rate turn (3°/sec) takes 2 min. for 360°. A half-standard rate turn (1.5°/sec.) would thus take 4 min. for 360°.
Answer (A) is incorrect because a half-standard rate turn would take 1 min. to turn 90° (not 360°). Answer (B) is incorrect because a standard (not half-standard) rate turn completes 360° in 2 min.

**16.**
**4896.** If a standard rate turn is maintained, how long would it take to turn 180°?

A— 1 minute.
B— 2 minutes.
C— 3 minutes.

**Answer (A) is correct (4896).** *(IFH Chap IV)*
A standard rate turn means an airplane is turning at a rate of 3°/sec. To turn 180° at a standard rate would take 60 sec. (180° ÷ 3°/sec.) or 1 min.
Answer (B) is incorrect because an airplane would turn 180° in 2 min. at a half-standard (not standard) rate of turn. Answer (C) is incorrect because an airplane would turn 540° in 3 min. at a standard rate (3°/sec.)

**17.**
**4897.** If a half-standard rate turn is maintained, how much time would be required to turn clockwise from a heading of 090° to a heading of 180°?

A— 30 seconds.
B— 1 minute.
C— 1 minute 30 seconds.

**Answer (B) is correct (4897).** *(IFH Chap III)*
A half-standard rate turn means an airplane is turning at a rate of 1.5°/sec. A turn clockwise from 090° to 180° is a total of 90°. Thus, at a half-standard rate it would take 60 sec. (90° ÷ 1.5°/sec.).
Answer (A) is incorrect because it would take 30 sec. to turn 90° at a standard (not half-standard) rate of turn. Answer (C) is incorrect because an airplane would turn 135° (not 90°) in 1 min. 30 sec. at a half-standard rate of turn.

**18.**
**4898.** During a constant-bank level turn, what effect would an increase in airspeed have on the rate and radius of turn?

A— Rate of turn would increase, and radius of turn would increase.
B— Rate of turn would decrease, and radius of turn would decrease.
C— Rate of turn would decrease, and radius of turn would increase.

Answer (C) is correct (4898). *(IFH Chap III)*
The radius of turn at a constant-bank level turn varies directly with the airspeed, while the rate of turn at a constant-bank level turn also varies with airspeed. If airspeed is increased during a constant-bank level turn the radius of turn would increase, and rate of turn is decreased.
Answer (A) is incorrect because the rate of turn decreases, not increases. Answer (B) is incorrect because the radius of the turn increases, not decreases.

**19.**
**4914.** Rate of turn can be increased and radius of turn decreased by

A— decreasing airspeed and shallowing the bank.
B— decreasing airspeed and increasing the bank.
C— increasing airspeed and increasing the bank.

Answer (B) is correct (4914). *(IFH Chap III)*
To increase the rate and decrease the radius of turn, you should decrease airspeed and increase the bank angle.
Answer (A) is incorrect because decreasing (shallowing) the bank decreases (not increases) the rate of turn. Answer (C) is incorrect because the airspeed should be decreased (not increased) to increase the rate of turn.

**20.**
**4903.** If a standard rate turn is maintained, how much time would be required to turn to the right from a heading of 090° to a heading of 270°?

A— 1 minute.
B— 2 minutes.
C— 3 minutes.

Answer (A) is correct (4903). *(IFH Chap IV)*
A standard rate turn means an airplane is turning at the rate of 3°/sec. A turn to the right (or left) from 090° to 270° is a total of 180°. Thus, at standard rate it would take 60 sec. (180° ÷ 3°/sec.) or 1 min.
Answer (B) is incorrect because it would take 2 min. to turn 180° at a half-standard (not standard) rate of turn. Answer (C) is incorrect because it would take 3 min. to turn 270° (not 180°) at a half-standard (not standard) rate of turn.

## 8.3 Climbs and Descents

**21.**
**4899.** The three conditions which determine pitch attitude required to maintain level flight are

A— flightpath, wind velocity, and angle of attack.
B— airspeed, air density, and aircraft weight.
C— relative wind, pressure altitude, and vertical lift component.

Answer (B) is correct (4899). *(IFH Chap III)*
Three factors affect the pitch attitude required to maintain level flight: airspeed, air density, and aircraft weight. At a constant angle of attack, any change in airspeed will vary the lift. Lift varies directly with changes in air density. To support heavier loads at a given airspeed, the angle of attack must be relatively greater to provide the necessary lift.
Answer (A) is incorrect because flight path is the direction of travel of the airplane, which in this case is level flight. Wind velocity is not considered in maintaining level flight. Angle of attack is the resultant pitch attitude to maintain level flight. Answer (C) is incorrect because relative wind is the direction of airflow produced by an airplane in flight and the vertical lift component is an aerodynamic force that acts perpendicular to the relative wind. The density (not pressure) altitude is one condition which determines the pitch attitude required to maintain level flight.

**22.**
**4906.** Approximately what percent of the indicated vertical speed should be used to determine the number of feet to lead the level-off from a climb to a specific altitude?

A— 10 percent.
B— 20 percent.
C— 25 percent.

Answer (A) is correct (4906). *(IFH Chap V)*
To level off from a climb and maintain a specific altitude, it is necessary to start the level-off before reaching the desired altitude. If your airplane is climbing at 500 fpm, it will continue to climb at a decreasing rate throughout the transition to level flight. An effective practice is to lead the altitude by 10% of the indicated vertical speed (i.e., at 500 fpm, use a 50-ft. lead).
Answer (B) is incorrect because you should begin to level off from a climb at approximately 10% (not 20%) of the indicated vertical speed. Answer (C) is incorrect because you should begin to level off from a climb at approximately 10% (not 25%) of the indicated vertical speed.

**23.**
**4907.** To level off from a descent to a specific altitude, the pilot should lead the level-off by approximately

A— 10 percent of the vertical speed.
B— 30 percent of the vertical speed.
C— 50 percent of the vertical speed.

Answer (A) is correct (4907). *(IFH Chap V)*
To level off from a descent to a specific altitude, it is necessary to start the level-off before reaching the desired altitude. If your airplane is descending at 500 fpm, it will continue to descend at a decreasing rate throughout the transition to level flight. An effective practice is to lead the desired altitude by 10% of the indicated vertical speed (i.e., at 500 fpm, use a 50-ft. lead).
Answer (B) is incorrect because you should begin to level off from a descent at approximately 10% (not 30%) of the indicated vertical speed. Answer (C) is incorrect because you should begin to level off from a descent at approximately 10% (not 50%) of the indicated vertical speed.

**24.**
**4876.** Which instruments should be used to make a pitch correction when you have deviated from your assigned altitude?

A— Altimeter and VSI.
B— Manifold pressure gauge and VSI.
C— Attitude indicator, altimeter, and VSI.

Answer (C) is correct (4876). *(IFH Chap V)*
The pitch instruments are the attitude indicator, the altimeter, the vertical speed indicator, and the airspeed indicator. The attitude indicator gives you a direct indication of changes in pitch attitude when correcting for altitude variations. The rate and direction of the altimeter and vertical speed indicator confirm the correct pitch adjustment was made and the altimeter is used to determine when you have reached your assigned altitude.
Answer (A) is incorrect because the question implies you have all instruments available. Without an attitude indicator, you would use the altimeter and vertical speed indicator to make pitch corrections. Answer (B) is incorrect because the manifold pressure gauge is a power (not pitch) instrument.

**25.**
**4820.** As a rule of thumb, altitude corrections of less than 100 feet should be corrected by using a

A— full bar width on the attitude indicator.
B— half bar width on the attitude indicator.
C— two bar width on the attitude indicator.

Answer (B) is correct (4820). *(IFH Chap V)*
As a rule of thumb, altitude corrections of less than 100 ft. should be corrected by using a half-bar-width correction on the attitude indicator.
Answer (A) is incorrect because as a rule of thumb, altitude corrections in excess of (not less than) 100 ft. should be corrected by an initial full-bar-width correction on the attitude indicator. Answer (C) is incorrect because altitude corrections of less than 100 ft. should be corrected by using a half-bar- (not two-bar-) width correction on the attitude indicator.

**26.**
**4924.** To enter a constant-airspeed descent from level-cruising flight, and maintain cruising airspeed, the pilot should

A— first adjust the pitch attitude to a descent using the attitude indicator as a reference, then adjust the power to maintain the cruising airspeed.
B— first reduce power, then adjust the pitch using the attitude indicator as a reference to establish a specific rate on the VSI.
C— simultaneously reduce power and adjust the pitch using the attitude indicator as a reference to maintain the cruising airspeed.

**27.**
**4925.** To level off at an airspeed higher than the descent speed, the addition of power should be made, assuming a 500 FPM rate of descent, at approximately

A— 50 to 100 feet above the desired altitude.
B— 100 to 150 feet above the desired altitude.
C— 150 to 200 feet above the desired altitude.

**28.**
**4926.** To level off from a descent maintaining the descending airspeed, the pilot should lead the desired altitude by approximately

A— 20 feet.
B— 50 feet.
C— 60 feet.

**29.**
**4928.** While cruising at 160 knots, you wish to establish a climb at 130 knots. When entering the climb (full panel), it is proper to make the initial pitch change by increasing back elevator pressure until the

A— attitude indicator, airspeed, and vertical speed indicate a climb.
B— vertical speed indication reaches the predetermined rate of climb.
C— attitude indicator shows the approximate pitch attitude appropriate for the 130-knot climb.

Answer (C) is correct (4924). *(IFH Chap V)*
To enter a constant airspeed descent from level cruising flight, and maintain cruising airspeed, you should simultaneously reduce the power smoothly to the desired setting and reduce the pitch attitude slightly by using the attitude indicator as a reference to maintain the cruising airspeed.
Answer (A) is incorrect because airspeed will increase if you adjust the pitch attitude first. Answer (B) is incorrect because airspeed will decrease if you first reduce power. You use the airspeed (not vertical speed) indicator to maintain a constant airspeed.

Answer (B) is correct (4925). *(IFH Chap V)*
To level off from a descent at an airspeed higher than the descent speed, it is necessary to start the level-off before reaching the desired altitude. At 500 fpm an effective practice is to lead the desired altitude by approximately 100 to 150 ft. above the desired altitude. At this point, add power to the appropriate level flight cruise setting.
Answer (A) is incorrect because, to level off at descent airspeed (not a higher airspeed), lead the desired altitude by approximately 50 to 100 ft. Answer (C) is incorrect because 150 to 200 ft. above the desired altitude is not a lead point when descending at 500 fpm.

Answer (B) is correct (4926). *(IFH Chap V)*
To level off from a descent at descent airspeed, lead the desired altitude by approximately 50 ft., simultaneously adjusting the pitch attitude to level flight and adding power to a setting that will hold airspeed constant. Trim off the control pressures and continue with the normal straight-and-level flight cross-check.
Answer (A) is incorrect because you should lead the desired altitude by approximately 50 (not 20) ft. when leveling off from a descent at descent airspeed. Answer (C) is incorrect because you should lead the desired altitude by approximately 50 (not 60) ft. when leveling off from a descent at descent airspeed.

Answer (C) is correct (4928). *(IFH Chap V)*
To enter a constant airspeed climb from cruising airspeed, raise the miniature aircraft in the attitude indicator to the approximate nose-high indication appropriate to the predetermined climb speed. The attitude will vary according to the type of airplane you are flying. Apply light elevator back pressure to initiate and maintain the climb attitude. The amount of back pressure will increase as the airplane decelerates.
Answer (A) is incorrect because the adjustment should be to the climb attitude for the predetermined climb speed, not just a climb indication on the instruments. Answer (B) is incorrect because the airspeed is predetermined, i.e., constant climb speed, not constant climb rate.

**30.**
**4929.** While cruising at 190 knots, you wish to establish a climb at 160 knots. When entering the climb (full panel), it would be proper to make the initial pitch change by increasing back elevator pressure until the

A— attitude indicator shows the approximate pitch attitude appropriate for the 160-knot climb.

B— attitude indicator, airspeed, and vertical speed indicate a climb.

C— airspeed indication reaches 160 knots.

Answer (A) is correct (4929). *(IFH Chap V)*
    To enter a constant airspeed climb from cruising airspeed, raise the miniature aircraft in the attitude indicator to the approximate nose-high indication appropriate to the predetermined climb speed. The attitude will vary according to the type of airplane you are flying. Apply light elevator back pressure to initiate and maintain the climb attitude. The required back pressure will increase as the airplane decelerates.
    Answer (B) is incorrect because you make the adjustment to the climb attitude for the predetermined climb speed, not just a climb indication on the instruments. Answer (C) is incorrect because you make an initial pitch adjustment, not an increasing adjustment, i.e., airspeed will decrease gradually.

## 8.4 Fundamental Instrument Skills

**31.**
**4862.** What is the first fundamental skill in attitude instrument flying?

A— Aircraft control.

B— Instrument cross-check.

C— Instrument interpretation.

Answer (B) is correct (4862). *(IFH Chap V)*
    The first fundamental skill in attitude instrument flying is instrument cross-check. Cross-checking is the continuous and logical observation of instruments for attitude and performance information.
    Answer (A) is incorrect because the third (not first) fundamental skill in attitude instrument flying is aircraft control. Aircraft control is composed of three components: pitch, bank, and power control.
    Answer (C) is incorrect because the second (not first) fundamental skill in attitude instrument flying is instrument interpretation. For each maneuver, you must know what performance to expect and the combination of instruments that you must interpret in order to control airplane attitude during the maneuver.

**32.**
**4855.** What are the three fundamental skills involved in attitude instrument flying?

A— Instrument interpretation, trim application, and aircraft control.

B— Cross-check, instrument interpretation, and aircraft control.

C— Cross-check, emphasis, and aircraft control.

Answer (B) is correct (4855). *(IFH Chap V)*
    The three fundamental skills involved in all instrument flight maneuvers are instrument cross-check, instrument interpretation, and aircraft control. Cross-checking is the continuous and logical observation of the instruments for attitude and performance information. Instrument interpretation requires you to understand each instrument's construction, operating principle, and relationship to the performance of your airplane. Aircraft control requires you to substitute instruments for outside references.
    Answer (A) is incorrect because trim application is only one aspect of aircraft control. Answer (C) is incorrect because emphasis (along with fixation and omission) are common errors in instrument cross-checking.

**33.**
**4859.** What is the third fundamental skill in attitude instrument flying?

A— Instrument cross-check.

B— Power control.

C— Aircraft control.

Answer (C) is correct (4859). *(IFH Chap V)*
    The third fundamental skill in instrument flying is aircraft control. It consists of pitch, bank, and power control.
    Answer (A) is incorrect because instrument cross-check is the first (not third) fundamental skill in attitude instrument flying. Cross-checking is the continuous and logical observation of instruments for attitude and performance information. Answer (B) is incorrect because power control is only one component of aircraft control.

**34.**
**4840.** What is the correct sequence in which to use the three skills used in instrument flying?

A— Aircraft control, cross-check, and instrument interpretation.
B— Instrument interpretation, cross-check, and aircraft control.
C— Cross-check, instrument interpretation, and aircraft control.

Answer (C) is correct (4840). *(IFH Chap V)*
The correct sequence in which to use the three fundamental skills of instrument flying is cross-check, instrument interpretation, and aircraft control. Although you learn these skills separately and in deliberate sequence, a measure of your proficiency in precision flying will be your ability to integrate these skills into unified, smooth, positive control responses to maintain any desired flight path.
Answer (A) is incorrect because aircraft control is the third (not first) skill used in instrument flying. Answer (B) is incorrect because instrument interpretation is the second (not first) skill and cross-check is the first (not second) skill used in instrument flying.

## 8.5 Appropriate Instruments for IFR

**35.**
**4863.** As power is reduced to change airspeed from high to low cruise in level flight, which instruments are primary for pitch, bank, and power, respectively?

A— Attitude indicator, heading indicator, and manifold pressure gauge or tachometer.
B— Altimeter, attitude indicator, and airspeed indicator.
C— Altimeter, heading indicator, and manifold pressure gauge or tachometer.

Answer (C) is correct (4863). *(IFH Chap V)*
In straight-and-level flight, when reducing airspeed from high to low cruise, the primary instrument for pitch is the altimeter; the primary instrument for bank is the heading indicator; and the primary instrument for power is the manifold pressure gauge or tachometer.
Answer (A) is incorrect because the primary pitch instrument is the altimeter, not attitude indicator. Answer (B) is incorrect because the primary bank instrument is the heading indicator, not attitude indicator; and the primary power instrument is the manifold pressure gauge or tachometer, not airspeed indicator.

**36.**
**4836.** What instruments are considered supporting bank instruments during a straight, stabilized climb at a constant rate?

A— Attitude indicator and turn coordinator.
B— Heading indicator and attitude indicator.
C— Heading indicator and turn coordinator.

Answer (A) is correct (4836). *(IFH Chap V)*
During a straight, stabilized climb at a constant rate, the heading indicator is the primary instrument for bank. The supporting bank instruments are the turn coordinator and the attitude indicator.
Answer (B) is incorrect because the heading indicator is the primary, not supporting, bank instrument in a straight climb. Answer (C) is incorrect because the heading indicator is the primary, not supporting, bank instrument in a straight climb.

**37.**
**4866.** Which instruments are considered primary and supporting for bank, respectively, when establishing a level standard rate turn?

A— Turn coordinator and attitude indicator.
B— Attitude indicator and turn coordinator.
C— Turn coordinator and heading indicator.

Answer (B) is correct (4866). *(IFH Chap V)*
When establishing a level standard rate turn, the attitude indicator is the primary bank instrument and is used to establish the approximate angle of bank. While doing this, the turn coordinator is the supporting bank instrument as you check for the standard-rate turn indication.
Answer (A) is incorrect because the turn coordinator is primary bank and the attitude indicator is supporting bank only after the standard rate turn is established, not while entering the turn. Answer (C) is incorrect because the turn coordinator is supporting (not primary) bank instrument and the heading indicator is neither primary nor supporting bank instrument when establishing a standard rate turn.

**38.**
**4865.** Which instrument provides the most pertinent information (primary) for bank control in straight-and-level flight?

A— Turn-and-slip indicator.
B— Attitude indicator.
C— Heading indicator.

Answer (C) is correct (4865).  *(IFH Chap V)*
The primary instrument for bank control in straight-and-level flight is the heading indicator.
Answer (A) is incorrect because the turn-and-slip indicator is supporting (not primary) bank instrument in straight-and-level flight.  Answer (B) is incorrect because the attitude indicator is supporting (not primary) bank and pitch instrument in straight-and-level flight.

**39.**
**4869.** Which instruments, in addition to the attitude indicator, are pitch instruments?

A— Altimeter and airspeed only.
B— Altimeter and VSI only.
C— Altimeter, airspeed indicator, and vertical speed indicator.

Answer (C) is correct (4869).  *(IFH Chap V)*
The pitch control instruments are the attitude indicator, altimeter, vertical speed indicator, and airspeed indicator.
Answer (A) is incorrect because it omits the vertical speed indicator and the airspeed indicator.  Answer (B) is incorrect because it omits the airspeed indicator.

**40.**
**4871.** Which instrument provides the most pertinent information (primary) for pitch control in straight-and-level flight?

A— Attitude indicator.
B— Airspeed indicator.
C— Altimeter.

Answer (C) is correct (4871).  *(IFH Chap V)*
The primary pitch instrument for straight-and-level flight is the altimeter.
Answer (A) is incorrect because the attitude indicator is a supporting (not primary) pitch instrument in straight-and-level flight.  Answer (B) is incorrect because the airspeed indicator is the primary power (not pitch) control instrument in straight-and-level flight.

**41.**
**4920.** For maintaining level flight at constant thrust, which instrument would be the least appropriate for determining the need for a pitch change?

A— Altimeter.
B— VSI.
C— Attitude indicator.

Answer (C) is correct (4920).  *(IFH Chap V)*
To maintain level flight at constant thrust, the attitude indicator is the least appropriate for determining the need for pitch change.  Until you have established and identified the level flight attitude for that airspeed, you have no way of knowing whether level flight as indicated on the attitude indicator is resulting in level flight as shown on the altimeter, vertical speed indicator, and airspeed indicator.
Answer (A) is incorrect because, since level flight means a constant altitude, the altimeter is the primary pitch instrument in level flight.  Answer (B) is incorrect because the vertical speed indicator (as a trend instrument) shows immediately the initial vertical movement of the airplane, which, disregarding turbulence, can be a reflection of pitch change at a constant thrust.

**42.**
**4832.** The gyroscopic heading indicator is inoperative. What is the primary bank instrument in unaccelerated straight-and-level flight?

A— Magnetic compass.
B— Attitude indicator.
C— Miniature aircraft of turn coordinator.

Answer (A) is correct (4832).  *(IFH Chap V)*
With the gyroscopic heading indicator inoperative, the primary bank instrument in unaccelerated straight-and-level flight is the magnetic compass.  Since any banking results in a turn and change in heading, the magnetic compass is the only other instrument that indicates direction.
Answer (B) is incorrect because, although the attitude indicator shows any change in bank, it does not provide information (i.e., heading) needed to maintain straight flight.  Answer (C) is incorrect because the miniature aircraft of the turn coordinator is the primary bank instrument in established standard rate turns, not in straight flight.

**43.**

**4837.** What instruments are primary for pitch, bank, and power, respectively, when transitioning into a constant airspeed climb from straight-and-level flight?

A— Attitude indicator, heading indicator, and manifold pressure gauge or tachometer.
B— Attitude indicator for both pitch and bank; airspeed indicator for power.
C— Vertical speed, attitude indicator, and manifold pressure or tachometer.

Answer (A) is correct (4837). *(IFH Chap V)*
When entering a constant airspeed climb, the attitude indicator is the primary pitch instrument, the heading indicator is the primary bank instrument, and the tachometer or manifold pressure gauge is the primary power instrument.
Answer (B) is incorrect because the heading indicator (not attitude indicator) is primary for bank, and the manifold pressure gauge (not airspeed indicator) is primary for power. Answer (C) is incorrect because the attitude indicator (not vertical speed indicator) is the primary instrument for pitch, and the heading indicator (not attitude indicator) is primary for bank.

**44.**

**4838.** What is the primary bank instrument once a standard rate turn is established?

A— Attitude indicator.
B— Turn coordinator.
C— Heading indicator.

Answer (B) is correct (4838). *(IFH Chap V)*
After a standard rate turn is established, the turn coordinator is the primary bank instrument.
Answer (A) is incorrect because the attitude indicator is the primary bank instrument in establishing a standard rate turn but not for maintaining the turn once established. Answer (C) is incorrect because the heading indicator is the primary bank instrument for straight flight.

**45.**

**4850.** What is the primary pitch instrument when establishing a constant altitude standard rate turn?

A— Altimeter.
B— VSI.
C— Airspeed indicator.

Answer (A) is correct (4850). *(IFH Chap V)*
The primary pitch instrument in level flight, either straight or turns, is the altimeter.
Answer (B) is incorrect because the vertical speed indicator is a supporting (not primary) pitch instrument for establishing a level standard rate turn. Answer (C) is incorrect because the airspeed indicator is the primary power (not pitch) instrument when establishing a constant altitude standard rate turn.

**46.**

**4851.** What is the initial primary bank instrument when establishing a level standard rate turn?

A— Turn coordinator.
B— Heading indicator.
C— Attitude indicator.

Answer (C) is correct (4851). *(IFH Chap V)*
The initial primary bank instrument when establishing a level standard rate turn is the attitude indicator.
Answer (A) is incorrect because only after the turn is established does the turn coordinator become the primary bank instrument. Answer (B) is incorrect because the heading indicator is the primary bank instrument for straight flight.

**47.**

**4858.** What is the primary bank instrument while transitioning from straight-and-level flight to a standard rate turn to the left?

A— Attitude indicator.
B— Heading indicator.
C— Turn coordinator (miniature aircraft).

Answer (A) is correct (4858). *(IFH Chap V)*
The initial primary bank instrument when establishing a level standard rate of turn is the attitude indicator.
Answer (B) is incorrect because the heading indicator is the primary bank instrument for straight flight. Answer (C) is incorrect because only after the turn is established does the turn coordinator become the primary bank instrument.

**48.**

**4853.** What instrument(s) is(are) supporting bank instrument when entering a constant airspeed climb from straight-and-level flight?

A— Heading indicator.
B— Attitude indicator and turn coordinator.
C— Turn coordinator and heading indicator.

Answer (B) is correct (4853). *(IFH Chap V)*
When entering a constant airspeed climb from straight-and-level flight, the primary bank instrument is the heading indicator. Supporting bank instruments are the turn coordinator and the attitude indicator.
Answer (A) is incorrect because the heading indicator is the primary (not supporting) bank instrument for straight flight. Answer (C) is incorrect because the heading indicator is the primary (not supporting) bank instrument for straight flight.

**49.**
**4848.**  What is the primary pitch instrument during a stabilized climbing left turn at cruise climb airspeed?

A— Attitude indicator.
B— VSI.
C— Airspeed indicator.

**50.**
**4872.**  Which instruments are considered to be supporting instruments for pitch during change of airspeed in a level turn?

A— Airspeed indicator and VSI.
B— Altimeter and attitude indicator.
C— Attitude indicator and VSI.

**51.**
**4874.**  Which instrument is considered primary for power as the airspeed reaches the desired value during change of airspeed in a level turn?

A— Airspeed indicator.
B— Attitude indicator.
C— Altimeter.

**52.**
**4884.**  Which instrument indicates the quality of a turn?

A— Attitude indicator.
B— Heading indicator or magnetic compass.
C— Ball of the turn coordinator.

**53.**
**4845.**  As power is increased to enter a 500 feet per minute rate of climb in straight flight, which instruments are primary for pitch, bank, and power respectively?

A— Airspeed indicator, heading indicator, and manifold pressure gauge or tachometer.
B— VSI, attitude indicator, and airspeed indicator.
C— Airspeed indicator, attitude indicator, and manifold pressure gauge or tachometer.

Answer (C) is correct (4848). *(IFH Chap V)*
In a climbing left turn at a constant airspeed, the airspeed indicator is the primary instrument for pitch once the climb is established.
Answer (A) is incorrect because the attitude indicator is a supporting (not primary) pitch instrument in a stabilized climb. Answer (B) is incorrect because the vertical speed indicator is a supporting (not primary) pitch instrument in a stabilized climb.

Answer (C) is correct (4872). *(IFH Chap V)*
The supporting instruments for pitch during a change of airspeed in a level turn are the attitude indicator and the vertical speed indicator. The primary instrument is the altimeter.
Answer (A) is incorrect because the airspeed indicator is a supporting power (not pitch) instrument during a change of airspeed in a level turn. It becomes the primary power instrument as the desired airspeed is reached. Answer (B) is incorrect because the altimeter is the primary (not supporting) pitch instrument in level flight.

Answer (A) is correct (4874). *(IFH Chap V)*
The airspeed indicator is the primary power instrument as the airspeed reaches the desired value during a change of airspeed in a level turn.
Answer (B) is incorrect because the attitude indicator is supporting pitch and bank instrument. Answer (C) is incorrect because the altimeter is primary pitch instrument.

Answer (C) is correct (4884). *(IFH Chap V)*
The quality (coordination) of a turn relates to whether the horizontal component of lift balances the centrifugal force. It is indicated by the ball of the turn coordinator or the ball in a turn-and-slip indicator. The airplane is neither slipping nor skidding when the ball is centered, indicating the desired quality of a turn.
Answer (A) is incorrect because the attitude indicator provides both pitch and bank information. Answer (B) is incorrect because the heading indicator and/or magnetic compass show current direction and changes in direction, not quality of a turn.

Answer (A) is correct (4845). *(IFH Chap V)*
As the power is increased to enter a constant rate climb in straight flight, the primary pitch instrument is the airspeed indicator until the vertical speed indicator stabilizes at the desired rate of climb (then the vertical speed indicator becomes primary). The primary bank instrument is the heading indicator. The primary power instrument is the manifold pressure gauge or tachometer.
Answer (B) is incorrect because the vertical speed indicator is the primary pitch instrument once the constant rate climb is established. Also, the manifold pressure gauge, not the airspeed indicator, is primary for power. Answer (C) is incorrect because the heading indicator, not the attitude indicator, is primary for bank in straight flight.

## 8.6 Unusual Attitudes

**54.**
**4936.** (Refer to figure 145 below.) What is the correct sequence for recovery from the unusual attitude indicated?

A— Reduce power, increase back elevator pressure, and level the wings.
B— Reduce power, level the wings, bring pitch attitude to level flight.
C— Level the wings, raise the nose of the aircraft to level flight attitude, and obtain desired airspeed.

Answer (B) is correct (4936). *(IFH Chap V)*
In Fig. 145, a nose-low attitude is indicated by a negative vertical speed indicator, high airspeed (i.e., near $V_{NE}$, and the airplane below the horizon on the attitude indicator. For nose-low unusual attitudes, the correct sequence for recovery is to reduce power to prevent excessive airspeed and loss of altitude; level the wings with coordinated aileron and rudder pressure to straight flight by referring to the turn coordinator; and raise the nose to level flight attitude by smooth back elevator pressure.
Answer (A) is incorrect because the wings should be level before you increase back pressure to decrease the load factor during leveling off. Answer (C) is incorrect because the power should be reduced first.

FIGURE 145.—Instrument Sequence (Unusual Attitude).

**55.**
**4867.** While recovering from an unusual flight attitude without the aid of the attitude indicator, approximate level pitch attitude is reached when the

A— airspeed and altimeter stop their movement and the VSI reverses its trend.
B— airspeed arrives at cruising speed, the altimeter reverses its trend, and the vertical speed stops its movement.
C— altimeter and vertical speed reverse their trend and the airspeed stops its movement.

**56.**
**4938.** (Refer to figure 147 below.) Which is the correct sequence for recovery from the unusual attitude indicated?

A— Level wings, add power, lower nose, descend to original attitude, and heading.
B— Add power, lower nose, level wings, return to original attitude and heading.
C— Stop turn by raising right wing and add power at the same time, lower the nose, and return to original attitude and heading.

Answer (A) is correct (4867).  *(IFH Chap V)*
As the rate of movement of the altimeter and airspeed indicator needles decreases, the attitude is approaching level flight.  When the needles stop and reverse direction, the aircraft is passing through level flight.
Answer (B) is incorrect because the vertical speed indicator will be lagging, i.e., showing a decrease in vertical movement when vertical movement has stopped.  Answer (C) is incorrect because the rate is only slowing and has not stabilized when the altimeter reverses its trend, i.e., it must stop to indicate level flight.

Answer (B) is correct (4938).  *(IFH Chap V)*
In Fig. 147, a nose-high attitude is indicated by the increasing altitude, the rate-of-climb indication on the vertical speed indicator, and the decreasing airspeed.  The correct sequence for recovery is to add power, apply forward elevator pressure to lower the nose and prevent a stall, level the wings with coordinated aileron and rudder pressure to straight flight, and return to original altitude and heading.
Answer (A) is incorrect because you should both add power and lower the nose before you level the wings.  Answer (C) is incorrect because you should both add power and lower the nose before you level the wings.

FIGURE 147.—Instrument Sequence (Unusual Attitude).

**57.**
**4873.** If an airplane is in an unusual flight attitude and the attitude indicator has exceeded its limits, which instruments should be relied on to determine pitch attitude before starting recovery?

A— Turn indicator and VSI.
B— Airspeed and altimeter.
C— VSI and airspeed to detect approaching VSI or VMO.

Answer (B) is correct (4873). *(IFH Chap V)*
If the attitude indicator is inoperative, a nose-low or nose-high attitude can be determined by the airspeed and altimeter. In a nose-high attitude, airspeed is decreasing and altimeter is increasing, and vice versa for nose-low attitudes.
Answer (A) is incorrect because the turn indicator indicates nothing about pitch attitude. Answer (C) is incorrect because the altimeter, not the VSI, is the primary pitch instrument. Note the FAA answer selection has VSI and VMO, which should be $V_{S1}$ and $V_{MO}$, respectively.

**58.**
**4875.** Which is the correct sequence for recovery from a spiraling, nose-low, increasing airspeed, unusual flight attitude?

A— Increase pitch attitude, reduce power, and level wings.
B— Reduce power, correct the bank attitude, and raise the nose to a level attitude.
C— Reduce power, raise the nose to level attitude, and correct the bank attitude.

Answer (B) is correct (4875). *(IFH Chap V)*
For nose-low unusual attitudes, one should reduce the power, level the wings, and then increase the pitch to raise the nose to a level attitude.
Answer (A) is incorrect because the power should be decreased first, then the wings leveled. Answer (C) is incorrect because the wings should be leveled before the nose is raised to minimize the load factor.

**59.**
**4927.** During recoveries from unusual attitudes, level flight is attained the instant

A— the horizon bar on the attitude indicator is exactly overlapped with the miniature airplane.
B— a zero rate of climb is indicated on the VSI.
C— the altimeter and airspeed needles stop prior to reversing their direction of movement.

Answer (C) is correct (4927). *(IFH Chap V)*
In unusual attitudes, you can determine the attainment of level flight (not vertical movement) when the altimeter and airspeed needles stop prior to reversing their direction of movement.
Answer (A) is incorrect because the attitude indicator has a tendency to precess during an unusual attitude and may not be reliable. Answer (B) is incorrect because there is a lag or delay in the vertical speed indicator. It cannot be relied on for determining the instant level flight is attained.

## 8.7 Inoperative Instruments

**60.**
**4937.** (Refer to figure 146 below.) Identify the system that has failed and determine a corrective action to return the airplane to straight-and-level flight.

A— Static/pitot system is blocked; lower the nose and level the wings to level-fight attitude by use of attitude indicator.
B— Vacuum system has failed; reduce power, roll left to level wings, and pitchup to reduce airspeed.
C— Electrical system has failed; reduce power, roll left to level wings, and raise the nose to reduce airspeed.

**Answer (A) is correct (4937).** *(IFH Chap IV)*
In Fig. 146, the airplane is in a right turn as indicated by the attitude indicator, the heading indicator, and the turn coordinator, thus the vacuum and electrical instruments are consistent with each other. Since the attitude indicator indicates a climb, which is consistent with the altimeter and the VSI, the airspeed should not be increasing. Thus, the pitot tube ram air and drain holes are blocked, causing the airspeed indicator to react like an altimeter. To return the airplane to straight-and-level flight you should lower the nose and level the wings to level-flight attitude by use of the attitude indicator.
Answer (B) is incorrect because the attitude indicator and heading indicator are consistent with the turn coordinator. Answer (C) is incorrect because the turn coordinator, which is normally electric, is consistent with the attitude indicator, which is normally a vacuum system instrument.

FIGURE 146.—Instrument Sequence (System Failed).

**61.**
**4939.** (Refer to figure 148 below.) What is the flight attitude? One system which transmits information to the instruments has malfunctioned.

A— Climbing turn to left.
B— Climbing turn to right.
C— Level turn to left.

Answer (B) is correct (4939). *(IFH Chap IV)*
Fig. 148 illustrates a climbing turn to the right. Note that the attitude indicator shows a climbing turn to the right, the heading indicator shows a turn to the right, and both the altimeter and vertical speed indicator indicate a climb. The turn coordinator shows no turn and is malfunctioning.
Answer (A) is incorrect because the turn is to the right, not left. Answer (C) is incorrect because the attitude indicator, altimeter, and vertical speed indicator all indicate a climb, and the turn is to the right, not left.

FIGURE 148.—Instrument Interpretation (System Malfunction).

**62.**

**4940.** (Refer to figure 149 below.) What is the flight attitude? One system which transmits information to the instruments has malfunctioned.

A— Level turn to the right.
B— Level turn to the left.
C— Straight-and-level flight.

Answer (C) is correct (4940). *(IFH Chap IV)*

In Fig. 149, the vertical speed indicator, altimeter, and turn coordinator all indicate straight-and-level flight. The heading indicator indicates a turn to the south from west, which is a turn to the left. The attitude indicator indicates a turn to the right, i.e., the attitude indicator and heading indicator are in conflict. Thus, the vacuum system must be malfunctioning, and the airplane must be in straight-and-level flight.

Answer (A) is incorrect because the vacuum system is inoperative (i.e., the attitude and heading indicators), and the airplane is in straight flight, not a right turn. Answer (B) is incorrect because the vacuum system is inoperative (i.e., the attitude and heading indicators), and the airplane is in straight flight, not a left turn.

FIGURE 149.—Instrument Interpretation (System Malfunction).

**63.**

**4941.** (Refer to figure 150 below.) What is the flight attitude? One instrument has malfunctioned.

A— Climbing turn to the right.
B— Climbing turn to the left.
C— Descending turn to the right.

Answer (A) is correct (4941). *(IFH Chap IV)*

In Fig. 150, the airplane is in a climb as evidenced by the vertical speed indicator, altimeter, and airspeed indicator. The heading indicator indicates a turn from west to north, which is a turn to the right. The turn coordinator also indicates a turn to the right. Thus, the airplane is in a climbing turn to the right. The attitude indicator is the instrument that is malfunctioning, since it indicates a level turn to the left.

Answer (B) is incorrect because the attitude indicator is inoperative; thus, the airplane is turning to the right, not left. Answer (C) is incorrect because the airspeed indicator, altimeter, and vertical speed indicator all show that the airplane is climbing, not descending.

FIGURE 150.—Instrument Interpretation (Instrument Malfunction).

**64.**
**4942.** (Refer to figure 151 below.)  What is the flight attitude?  One instrument has malfunctioned.

A— Climbing turn to the right.
B— Level turn to the right.
C— Level turn to the left.

Answer (B) is correct (4942).  *(IFH Chap IV)*
The vertical speed indicator and altimeter indicate level flight as does the attitude indicator.  The turn coordinator, attitude indicator, and heading indicator each indicate a turn to the right.  Accordingly, there is a level turn to the right, and the airspeed should not be near the stall speed.  Thus, the ram air inlet of the pitot tube is clogged, while the drain hole is open, causing the pressure in the line to vent out and the indicator to drop to zero.

Answer (A) is incorrect because flight is level (not climbing) according to the vertical speed indicator, altimeter, and attitude indicator.  Answer (C) is incorrect because the turn is to the right, not left.

FIGURE 151.—Instrument Interpretation (Instrument Malfunction).

**65.**

**4943.** (Refer to figure 152 below.)  What is the flight attitude?  One system which transmits information to the instruments has failed.

A— Climbing turn to right.
B— Level turn to left.
C— Descending turn to right.

Answer (C) is correct (4943).  *(IFH Chap IV)*

In Fig. 152, the attitude indicator, turn coordinator, and heading indicator each indicate a turn to the right.  The vertical speed indicator and altimeter each indicate a descent, which means the airplane is in a descending turn to the right.  Since the airplane is in a descent, the airspeed indicator should not be indicating less than stall speed.  Thus, the pitot tube's ram air and drain holes may be blocked, causing the airspeed indicator to react like an altimeter.  Note the FAA has failed to put an arrow next to the airspeed indicator to indicate a decrease since altitude is decreasing.

Answer (A) is incorrect because the altimeter and vertical speed indicator each indicate a descent, not a climb.  Answer (B) is incorrect because the attitude indicator, heading indicator, and turn coordinator each indicate a turn to the right, not left, and the altimeter and vertical speed indicator each indicate a descent, not level flight.

FIGURE 152.—Instrument Interpretation (System Failed).

## 8.8  Wake Turbulence

**66.**
**4707.** What wind condition prolongs the hazards of wake turbulence on a landing runway for the longest period of time?

A— Direct headwind.
B— Direct tailwind.
C— Light quartering tailwind.

**Answer (C) is correct (4707).** *(AIM Para 7-44)*
Light quartering tailwinds require maximum caution because they can move the vortices of preceding aircraft forward into the touchdown zone and hold the upwind vortex on the runway.
Answer (A) is incorrect because a direct headwind will permit the vortices to move away from each side of the runway. Answer (B) is incorrect because a direct tailwind will permit the vortices to move away from each side of the runway.

**67.**
**4708.** Wake turbulence is near maximum behind a jet transport just after takeoff because

A— the engines are at maximum thrust output at slow airspeed.
B— the gear and flap configuration increases the turbulence to maximum.
C— of the high angle of attack and high gross weight.

**Answer (C) is correct (4708).** *(AIM Para 7-43)*
The greatest vortex strength occurs when the generating aircraft is heavy, clean, and slow, such as in takeoff climbout. At this time there is a high gross weight and also a high angle of attack.
Answer (A) is incorrect because vortices have to do with airflows about the wingtips, not the engines. Answer (B) is incorrect because the gear and flap configuration will change the characteristics of the vortex.

**68.**
**4709.** What effect would a light crosswind of approximately 7 knots have on vortex behavior?

A— The light crosswind would rapidly dissipate vortex strength.
B— The upwind vortex would tend to remain over the runway.
C— The downwind vortex would tend to remain over the runway.

**Answer (B) is correct (4709).** *(AIM Para 7-44)*
A light crosswind of 1 to 7 kt. could result in the upwind vortex of a preceding aircraft remaining in the touchdown zone for a period of time. Also, it could hasten the drift of the downwind vortex toward another runway.
Answer (A) is incorrect because strong (not light) winds would help rapidly dissipate vortex strength. Answer (C) is incorrect because the upwind (not downwind) vortex would tend to remain over the runway in a light crosswind.

**69.**
**4710.** When landing behind a large jet aircraft, at which point on the runway should you plan to land?

A— If any crosswind, land on the windward side of the runway and prior to the jet's touchdown point.
B— At least 1,000 feet beyond the jet's touchdown point.
C— Beyond the jet's touchdown point.

**Answer (C) is correct (4710).** *(AIM Para 7-46)*
When landing behind a large aircraft on the same runway, stay at or above the large aircraft's final approach flight path, and land beyond its touchdown point.
Answer (A) is incorrect because you must land beyond, not prior to, the touchdown point. Answer (B) is incorrect because there is no minimum distance (i.e., 1,000 ft.) that you should land beyond the jet's touchdown point.

## 8.9  Turbulence and Wind Shear

**70.**
**4160.** If you fly into severe turbulence, which flight condition should you attempt to maintain?

A— Constant airspeed ($V_A$).
B— Level flight attitude.
C— Constant altitude and constant airspeed.

**Answer (B) is correct (4160).** *(AvW Chap 11)*
In severe turbulence, you should attempt to maintain a level flight attitude. You will not be able to maintain a constant altitude and/or airspeed, but you should fly at or below design maneuvering speed ($V_A$) and attempt to maintain a level-flight attitude.
Answer (A) is incorrect because you want to maintain an airspeed at or below $V_A$, but in severe turbulence there will be large variations in airspeed, and you will not be able to keep it constant. Answer (C) is incorrect because in severe turbulence you will not be able to maintain a constant altitude and/or constant airspeed.

**71.**
**4916.** If severe turbulence is encountered during your IFR flight, the airplane should be slowed to the design maneuvering speed because the

A— maneuverability of the airplane will be increased.
B— amount of excess load that can be imposed on the wing will be decreased.
C— airplane will stall at a lower angle of attack, giving an increased margin of safety.

**Answer (B) is correct (4916).** *(AvW Chap 11)*
Flight at or below the design maneuvering speed ($V_A$) means that the airplane will stall before excess loads can be imposed on the wings.
Answer (A) is incorrect because you should slow the airspeed to reduce excessive loads, not because the airplane will be more maneuverable at a slow airspeed. Answer (C) is incorrect because an airplane will always stall when the critical angle of attack is exceeded.

**72.**
**4917.** When a climb or descent through an inversion or wind-shear zone is being performed, the pilot should be alert for which of the following change in airplane performance?

A— A fast rate of climb and a slow rate of descent.
B— A sudden change in airspeed.
C— A sudden surge of thrust.

**Answer (B) is correct (4917).** *(AvW Chap 10)*
When climbing through an inversion or wind-shear zone, the danger is a sudden change in airspeed. If the airplane were to move abruptly from a headwind to a tailwind, the airspeed would slow dramatically, and a stall or rapid descent could be induced.
Answer (A) is incorrect because a fast rate of climb and a slow rate of descent are usually not a safety problem, as the reverse could be. Answer (C) is incorrect because the amount of thrust does not change as a result of wind shears.

## 8.10 Collision Avoidance

**73.**
**4441.** Which procedure is recommended while climbing to an assigned altitude on the airway?

A— Climb on the centerline of the airway except when maneuvering to avoid other air traffic in VFR conditions.
B— Climb slightly on the right side of the airway when in VFR conditions.
C— Climb far enough to the right side of the airway to avoid climbing or descending traffic coming from the opposite direction if in VFR conditions.

**Answer (A) is correct (4441).** *(FAR 91.181)*
When climbing to an assigned altitude on an airway, one should use the centerline except to avoid other aircraft when in VFR conditions. This procedure is specified in FAR 91.181, which requires aircraft to operate along the centerline of Federal airways.
Answer (B) is incorrect because you are required to maintain the centerline (not remain on the right side) while operating on a Federal airway. Answer (C) is incorrect because you are required to maintain the centerline (not remain on the right side) while operating on a Federal airway.

**74.**
**4634.** What is expected of you as pilot on an IFR flight plan if you are descending or climbing in VFR conditions?

A— If on an airway, climb or descend to the right of the centerline.
B— Advise ATC you are in visual conditions and will remain a short distance to the right of the centerline while climbing.
C— Execute gentle banks, left and right, at a frequency which permits continuous visual scanning of the airspace about you.

**Answer (C) is correct (4634).** *(AIM Para 4-94)*
During climbs and descents in VFR conditions, pilots should execute gentle banks left and right to permit continual scanning of surrounding airspace.
Answer (A) is incorrect because you are required to maintain (not remain to the right of) the centerline while operating on a Federal airway, except when maneuvering to avoid other traffic in VFR conditions. Answer (B) is incorrect because you are not required to advise ATC that you are in visual conditions, but you are required to maintain (not remain to the right of) the centerline while operating on a Federal airway, except when maneuvering to avoid other traffic in VFR conditions.

**75.**
**4373.** When is a pilot on an IFR flight plan responsible for avoiding other aircraft?

A— At all times when not in radar contact with ATC.
B— When weather conditions permit, regardless of whether operating under IFR or VFR.
C— Only when advised by ATC.

Answer (B) is correct (4373).  *(FAR 91.113)*
 When weather conditions permit, regardless of whether an operation is conducted under IFR or VFR, vigilance shall be maintained by each pilot so as to see and avoid other aircraft.
 Answer (A) is incorrect because, if weather conditions permit, each pilot is responsible for avoiding other aircraft, regardless if in radar contact or not.  Answer (C) is incorrect because, if weather conditions permit, each pilot (not ATC) is responsible for avoiding other aircraft.

**76.**
**4471.** What responsibility does the pilot in command of an IFR flight assume upon entering VFR conditions?

A— Report VFR conditions to ARTCC so that an amended clearance may be issued.
B— Use VFR operating procedures.
C— To see and avoid other traffic.

Answer (C) is correct (4471).  *(FAR 91.113)*
 When weather conditions permit, regardless of whether an operation is conducted under IFR or VFR, vigilance shall be maintained by each pilot so as to see and avoid other aircraft.
 Answer (A) is incorrect because VFR conditions are not reported unless so requested by ATC.  Answer (B) is incorrect because IFR operating procedures are to be followed on an IFR flight.

# END OF CHAPTER

# CHAPTER NINE
# INSTRUMENT APPROACHES

This chapter contains outlines of major concepts tested, all FAA test questions and answers regarding instrument approaches, and an explanation of each answer. The subtopics or modules within this chapter are listed above, followed in parentheses by the number of questions from the FAA written test pertaining to that particular module. The two numbers following the parentheses are the page numbers on which the outline and questions begin for that module.

Most of the charts herein contain old airspace terminology. Memory aid: list A down to G (no F) and match old airspace classifications based on height from highest to lowest: A = PCA, B = TCA, C= ARSA, D = ATA, E = general controlled, and G = uncontrolled.

**CAUTION:** Recall that the **sole purpose** of this book is to expedite your passing the FAA written test for the instrument rating. Accordingly, all extraneous material (i.e., topics or regulations not directly tested on the FAA written test) is omitted, even though much more information and knowledge are necessary to fly safely. This additional material is presented in *Instrument Pilot FAA Practical Test Prep* and *Aviation Weather and Weather Services*, available from Gleim Publications, Inc. See the order form on page 478.

## 9.1 CONTACT AND VISUAL APPROACHES (Questions 1-6)

1. A contact approach may be requested by the pilot if there is 1 SM flight visibility and the pilot can operate clear of clouds to the destination airport.

    a. It is an alternative to a standard instrument approach procedure (SIAP).
    b. It cannot be assigned by ATC.

2. ATC may assign a visual approach to an airport or authorize you to follow other airplanes for a landing if it can be accomplished in VFR.

    a. The pilot must have the airport or the preceding aircraft in sight.

    b. Visual approaches can be assigned by ATC; contact approaches cannot.

    c. On visual approaches, radar service is automatically terminated when the aircraft is instructed to contact the tower.

## 9.2 SDF AND LDA APPROACHES  (Questions 7-10)

1.  LDA (localizer-type directional aid) is as useful and accurate as a localizer (3° to 6° course width).

    a.  The LDA is very similar to an ILS but it usually does not have a glide slope, i.e., only a localizer, and is **not** aligned with the runway.

2.  SDF (simplified directional facility) has a course width of either 6° or 12°.

    a.  SDF approaches may or may not be aligned with a runway (and their courses are wider).  SDF does not have a glide slope.

## 9.3 RUNWAY VISUAL RANGE (RVR)  (Questions 11-15)

1.  RVR is an instrumentally derived value that represents the horizontal distance the pilot can see down the runway from the approach end.

    a.  It is based on the measurement of a transmissometer near the touchdown point of the instrument runway and is reported in hundreds of feet.

2.  If RVR is inoperative and cannot be reported, convert the RVR minimum to ground visibility and use that as the visibility minimums for takeoffs and landings.

    a.  See Legend 13 on page 246 for a chart of RVR/visibility comparable values.

3.  The normal ILS visibility minimum is ½ SM, which is 2400 RVR.

## 9.4 MISSED APPROACHES  (Questions 16-17)

1.  When executing a missed approach prior to the missed approach point (MAP), continue the approach to the MAP at or above the MDA or DH before executing any turns.

2.  If you lose visual reference in a circle to land from an instrument approach, you should make a climbing turn toward your landing runway to become established on the missed approach course.

## 9.5 ILS SPECIFICATIONS  (Questions 18-27)

1.  The ILS missed approach should be executed upon arrival at the decision height (DH) on the glide slope if the visual reference requirements are not met.

2.  The normal decision height for ILS is 200 ft. AGL.

    a.  This is the height of the glide slope centerline at the middle marker.

3.  The amount of deflection and distance from the localizer and the glide slope for an ILS is presented as Fig. 139 on page 265.

    a.  A series of questions asks how far you are from the localizer or glide slope centerlines given certain types of deflection on your glide slope indicator.  This requires interpreting Fig. 139.

4.  Compass locators, when used for the outer marker (OM) and middle marker (MM) of an ILS, transmit two-letter identification groups.

    a.  The outer compass locator (LOM) transmits the first two letters of the localizer identification group.

    b.  The middle compass locator (LMM) transmits the last two letters of the localizer identification group.

    c.  If the OM and/or MM are not compass locators, there is no two-letter identification transmission.

5. An inner marker (IM) is identified by continuous dots at the rate of 6 per second and a flashing white marker beacon.

6. If DME is available on an ILS or localizer approach, the DME/TACAN channel will be indicated in the localizer frequency box on the instrument approach chart.

7. Legend 28 below contains the ILS standard characteristics and terminology.

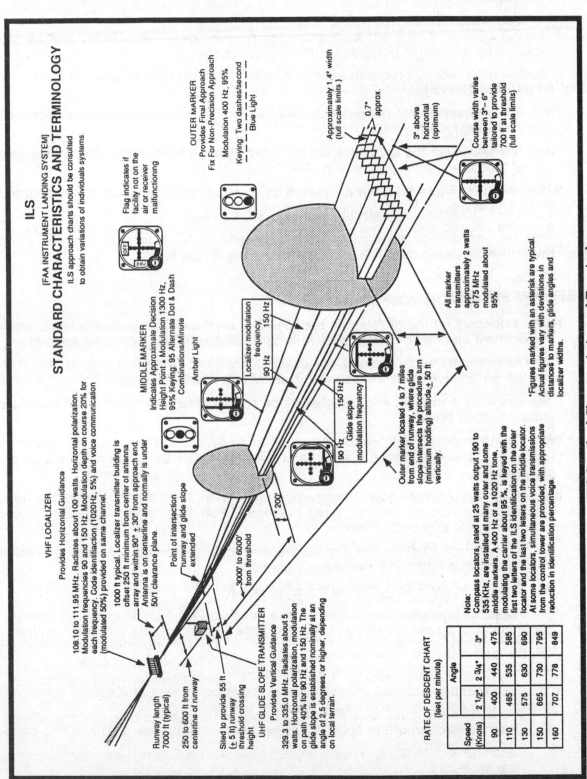

LEGEND 28.—ILS Standard Characteristics and Terminology.

## 9.6  UNUSABLE ILS COMPONENTS  (Questions 28-35)

1.    ILS components include

    a.    Localizer
    b.    Glide slope
    c.    Outer marker
    d.    Middle marker
    e.    Approach lights

2.    If more than one component is unusable, each minimum is raised to the highest minimum required by any single component that is inoperative.

3.    A compass locator or precision approach radar (PAR) may be substituted for an inoperative OM or MM.

    a.    An inoperative MM does not change the landing minimums, thus no substitution is necessary.

4.    When installed with the ILS and specified in the approach procedure, DME may be used in lieu of the OM.

5.    When the glide slope fails, the ILS reverts to a nonprecision localizer (LOC) approach.

    a.    The LOC MDA and visibility minimums will be used.

6.    If you are on the glide slope when the ILS fails and a VASI is in sight, you should continue the approach using the VASI and report the malfunction to ATC.

## 9.7  FLYING THE APPROACH  (Questions 36-47)

1.    Rate of descent on the glide slope is dependent on the airplane groundspeed because the descent must be constant relative to the distance traveled over the ground.

    a.    As groundspeed increases, the descent rate must increase.
    b.    As groundspeed decreases, the descent rate must decrease.

2.    If the airspeed is too fast and the glide slope and localizer are centered, you should initially reduce power.

3.    When being vectored at ILS and you are about to fly through the localizer, you should maintain your last assigned heading and question ATC rather than deviate from a clearance.

4.    If a wind shear changes from a headwind to a tailwind, the airspeed drops, the nose pitches down, and the vertical speed increases.  You must initially increase power to resume normal approach speed.

    a.    Then power must be reduced as airspeed stabilizes so you can maintain the glide slope due to the increased groundspeed.

    b.    The tendency is to go below the glide slope.

5.    If a wind shear changes from a tailwind to a headwind (or even to calm), you must decrease your power initially, and then increase it once you are through the shear to maintain the glide slope.

    a.    The tendency is to go above the glide slope.

6.    In tracking the localizer, you should have your drift correction established to maintain the localizer centerline before reaching the outer marker.

    a.    Then completion of the approach should be accomplished with heading corrections no greater than 2°.

## 9.8 ASR APPROACHES (Questions 48-52)

1. During airport surveillance radar (ASR) approaches, ATC provides headings, when to commence descent to MDA, the airplane's position each mile on final from the runway, and arrival at the MAP.

2. Surveillance approaches may be used at airports for which civil radar instrument approach minimums have been published.

3. ATC radar, when approved for approach control service, may be used for course guidance to the final approach, ASR and PAR approaches, and monitoring of nonradar approaches.

4. During a no-gyro approach (i.e., when your gyroscopic instruments have failed), all turns prior to final approach should be made at the standard rate.

    a. After being handed off to the final approach controller, all turns should be at one-half the standard rate.

## 9.9 SIDE-STEP APPROACHES (Questions 53-54)

1. A side-step approach is an instrument approach to one runway until you can see a parallel runway and "side step" to land on the parallel runway.

2. Side-step approaches are used when a pilot executes an approach procedure serving one of parallel runways that are separated by 1,200 ft. or less, and this is followed by a straight-in approach to a parallel runway.

3. Execute a side-step procedure as soon as possible after the runway environment is in sight.

## 9.10 TIMED APPROACHES FROM HOLDING FIXES (Questions 55-58)

1. A timed approach is one in which you are cleared to leave the final approach fix or outer marker at a specified future time.

2. Timed approaches from a holding fix may be executed only

    a. When a tower is in operation.

    b. Direct communication is maintained between pilot and approach control or center until switching to tower.

    c. If more than one missed approach procedure is available, none may require a course reversal, i.e., the missed approach procedure must not take you back to the final approach fix.

    d. If only one missed approach procedure is available, the reported ceiling and visibility must be greater than the highest circling minimum for the IAP.

3. When making a timed approach from a holding fix at the outer marker, the pilot should adjust the holding pattern to leave the final approach fix inbound at the assigned time.

4. Author's note: These are primarily used in nonradar environments.

## 9.11 HOLDING (Questions 59-79)

1. Holding patterns are specified by ATC to slow traffic flow. They are race track-shaped patterns based on a fix which is a radio navigation facility (VOR, ADF, or other NAVAID), an intersection of NAVAID bearings, radials, or a DME fix.

    a. Right turns are standard unless ATC specifies left turns.

2. Holding patterns consist of the following components (note that the fix is always at the end of the inbound leg):

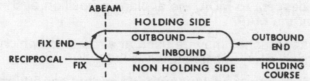

3. You enter a holding pattern using one of three procedures as illustrated in the figure below. This illustrates a standard pattern; the same concept is used in a nonstandard pattern.

    a. Parallel procedure -- fly parallel holding course as in (a). Turn left and return to holding fix or intercept holding course.

    b. Teardrop procedure -- proceed on outbound track of 30° or less to holding course, turn right to intercept holding courses, as in (b).

    c. Direct entry procedure -- turn right and fly the pattern, as in (c).

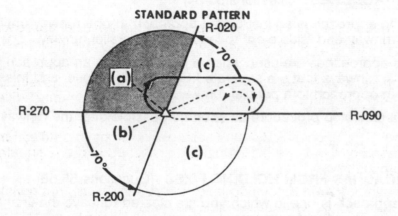

4. The best way to determine the entry method is to draw a holding pattern complete with the fix and inbound leg.

    a. Through the fix, draw the 70° angle such that it intersects the outbound leg at about 1/3 of the outbound leg length.

    b. Then slightly shade the (a) area (110°), which means parallel entry, as shown.

    c. The (b) area is the 70° angle between the 70° line and the extension of the inbound leg.

    d. EXAMPLE: In the above illustration, the inbound leg to the fix is 270°.

       R-200 to R-270    teardrop
       R-270 to R-020    parallel
       R-020 to R-200    direct

5. The timing of the outbound leg begins over or abeam the fix, whichever occurs later.

    a. If the abeam position cannot be determined, start timing when the turn to outbound is complete (i.e., wings level).

    b. At an NDB (nondirectional beacon), the timing for the outbound leg should be when abeam the fix.

6. Maximum holding pattern speeds:

    a. For turbojets from the minimum holding altitude (MHA) through 14,000 ft. is 230 kt.
    b. For turbojets above 14,000 ft. is 265 kt.

7. When a holding pattern is used in lieu of a procedure turn, the holding maneuver must still be executed within the 1-min. time limitation or published leg length.

8. When more than one circuit of the holding pattern is needed to lose altitude or become better established on course, additional circuits can be made at the pilot's discretion only if the pilot advises ATC and ATC approves.

## 9.12 INSTRUMENT APPROACH CHARTS (Questions 80-138)

1. The questions on the FAA written test in this module are wide ranging. They are best prepared for by studying the Approach Chart Legends on pages 246 through 253. These legends are found in the FAA's question book in Appendix 2 after the questions and subject matter codes and before the figures. The questions will not refer you to these legends, but you should use them when needed. Remember, approach charts consist of several parts:

   a. Top and bottom margin identification
   b. Planview
   c. Profile view
   d. Minimums section
   e. Airport diagram

2. Initial approach fixes (IAF) identify the beginning of an initial approach segment of an instrument approach procedure and are identified by the letters IAF on the planview of approach charts.

3. Aircraft approach categories are listed as A, B, C, D, and E based upon 1.3 times the stall speed of the aircraft in the landing configuration at maximum certified gross landing weight (1.3 $V_{so}$).

4. The symbol "T" in a point-down black triangle indicates that takeoff minimums are not standard and/or departure minimums are published and one should consult alternative takeoff procedures.

   a. The symbol "A" in a point-up black triangle indicates that nonstandard minimums exist to list the airport as an IFR alternate.

      1) Standard alternate minimums are 800-2 for a nonprecision approach and 600-2 for a precision approach.

5. The absence of the procedure turn barb on the planview on an approach chart indicates that a procedure turn is not authorized for that approach.

   a. The term NoPT means that there is no procedure turn.

6. A course reversal (procedure turn) is not required (or authorized) when radar vectors are being provided.

7. Minimum safe sector altitudes are depicted on approach charts. These provide at least 1,000 ft. of obstacle clearance within a 25-NM radius of the VOR or NDB but do not necessarily assure acceptable navigational signal coverage.

8. Published landing minimums apply when making an instrument approach to an airport.

9. A pilot adhering to the minimum altitudes depicted on the IAP is assured of terrain and obstacle clearance.

10. When being radar vectored to an instrument approach, you should comply with the last assigned altitude until the airplane is established on a segment of a published route or IAP and you have been cleared for the approach, after which you should continue descents to the listed minimum altitudes.

11. When simultaneous approaches are in progress, each pilot will be advised to monitor the tower frequency to receive advisories and instructions.

12. When straight-in minima are not published, you can make a straight-in landing if the active runway is in sight and there is sufficient time to make a normal landing and has been cleared to land.

13. If you are doing an approach in a category B airplane but maintaining a speed faster than the maximum specified for that category, you should use category C minimums.

14. When an instrument approach procedure involves a procedure turn, the maximum allowable indicated airspeed is 250 kt.

15. When a DME is inoperative, there will be no code tone (identifier) broadcast.

16. On instrument approach segments, the minimum altitudes are indicated on the planview and profile view, which YOU are expected to be able to interpret and specify on the FAA written test.

17. When holding patterns exist in lieu of outbound procedure turns, the length of the outbound leg may be indicated in terms of nautical miles (NM) in terms of a navigational aid with a perpendicular line through the end of the outbound leg with the distance indicated.

18. On RNAV approaches, the MAP is identified when the TO/FROM indicator changes, which indicates station passage at the MAP waypoint.

19. RNAV waypoints when used for an instrument approach contain boxes in which the latitude and longitude are listed on the first line and the VOR direction and distance on the second line.

20. RNAV approaches require an approved RNAV receiver; no other navigation equipment is specifically required.

21. LDA (localizer-type directional aid) is as useful and accurate as an ILS localizer but is not part of a complete ILS.

    a. The LDA is not aligned with the runway.

22. On procedure turns, there may be a distance limitation from a NAVAID, and procedural turns should be made entirely on the side of the inbound radial or bearing to which the procedural turn arrow points.

    a. If a teardrop turn is depicted, only a teardrop course reversal can be executed.

23. If you are not able to identify a NAVAID marking a descent to a lower altitude on a nonprecision approach, you cannot descend to the next lower altitude.

24. The MAP of a precision approach is arrival at the decision height (DH) on the glide slope.

25. The appropriate approach and tower frequencies are indicated at the top of the planview.

26. When a marker beacon receiver becomes inoperative and you cannot identify the MM during an ILS approach, you should use the published minimums.

27. A second VOR receiver may be needed when doing a localizer approach with a final step-down fix to be identified by a VOR radial.

28. Some nonprecision approaches will allow descents to a lower altitude at specified DME distances.

    a. The advantage of DME can be determined by comparing the two MDA values.

29. Use the recommended entry into holding patterns as discussed in the previous module.

30. The minimum navigation equipment required for a VOR/DME approach is one VOR receiver and DME.

31. Restrictions to circle to land procedures are found below the minimums section of an NOS IAP and in the circling minimums table of a JEPP IAP.

32. The height above touchdown (HAT) is the height of the MDA or DH above the touchdown zone. It is the smaller numbers that appear after the MDA or DH.

    a. The numbers in parentheses are military minimums.

33. The minimums section of the approach chart provides the MDA or DH and the visibility (expressed as RVR or SM).

34. When making an LOC approach to the primary airport of the Class B airspace, the aircraft must be equipped with

    a. Two-way radio communication,
    b. Mode C transponder, and
    c. VOR.

35. When the glide slope becomes inoperative during an ILS approach, the approach becomes a nonprecision LOC approach.

    a. The LOC minimums then apply.

36. The final approach fix (FAF) for a precision approach is identified on the approach chart by a lightning bolt ($\mathbf{\xi}$).

    a. The intercept altitude is indicated next to the symbol.

37. On a nonprecision approach, the distance from the FAF to the MAP is indicated below the airport diagram.

38. A category C aircraft must use category C minimums, even if using category B approach speed.

39. Legends 13 through 21 (except 18) from Appendix 2 of the FAA question book concern instrument approaches, and are presented on pages 246 through 253.

## 9.13 SIDs AND STARs (Questions 139-151)

1. SIDs (Standard Instrument Departures), STARs (Standard Terminal Arrival Routes), and visual approaches are all routinely assigned by ATC as appropriate.

2. SIDs and STARs are issued to simplify clearance delivery procedures when ATC deems it appropriate unless the pilot has requested "no SID" or "no STAR" in the remarks section of the flight plan.

    a. Less desirably, pilots may refuse SIDs and STARs when they are part of a clearance.

3. When a SID requires a minimum climb rate of a specified number of ft. per NM, you may be requested to convert the climb rate into feet per minute.

    a. Use the Rate of Climb Table in Legend 18 on page 258.

    b. Another method is first to divide the groundspeed by 60 to get the NM per min. Then multiply NM per min. times the required climb rate per NM to determine climb rate in feet per minute (fpm).

        1) EXAMPLE: If 200 ft. per NM were required to a specified altitude and your groundspeed is 120 kt., you would be traveling 2 NM/min. (120 NM/60 min.), which would require a minimum climb rate of 400 fpm (200 required ft./NM x 2 NM/min.).

4. To accept a SID, you must have at least a textual description of it.

5. Preferred IFR routes are correlated with SIDs and STARs and may be defined by airways, jet routes, and direct routes between NAVAIDs.

6. The Departure Route Description explains the departure procedures. It also explains the route to be used if communication is lost.

7. You will be asked to interpret VOR indication to determine your position relative to a fix.

8. A STAR's purpose is to simplify clearance delivery procedures.

9. Legends 9 through 12 and 18 from Appendix 2 of the FAA question book concern SIDs and STARs, and are presented on pages 254 through 258.

## INSTRUMENT APPROACH PROCEDURES EXPLANATION OF TERMS

The United States Standard for Terminal Instrument Procedures (TERPS) is the approved criteria for formulating instrument approach procedures.

### AIRCRAFT APPROACH CATEGORIES

Speeds are based on 1.3 times the stall speed in the landing configuration at maximum gross landing weight. An aircraft shall fit in only one category. If it is necessary to maneuver at speeds in excess of the upper limit of a speed range for a category, the minimums for the next higher category should be used. For example, an aircraft which falls in Category A, but is circling to land at a speed in excess of 91 knots, should use the approach Category B minimums when circling to land. See following category limits:

### MANEUVERING TABLE

| Approach Category | A | B | C | D | E |
|---|---|---|---|---|---|
| Speed (Knots) | 0-90 | 91-120 | 121-140 | 141-165 | Abv 165 |

### RVR/Meteorological Visibility Comparable Values

The following table shall be used for converting RVR to meteorlogical visibility when RVR is not reported for the runway of intended operation. Adjustment of landing minima may be required – see Inoperative Components Table.

| RVR (feet) | Visibility (statute miles) | RVR (feet) | Visibility (statute miles) |
|---|---|---|---|
| 1600 | $\frac{1}{4}$ | 4500 | $\frac{7}{8}$ |
| 2400 | $\frac{1}{2}$ | 5000 | 1 |
| 3200 | $\frac{5}{8}$ | 6000 | $1\frac{1}{4}$ |
| 4000 | $\frac{3}{4}$ | | |

### LANDING MINIMA FORMAT

In this example airport elevation is 1179, and runway touchdown zone elevation is 1152.

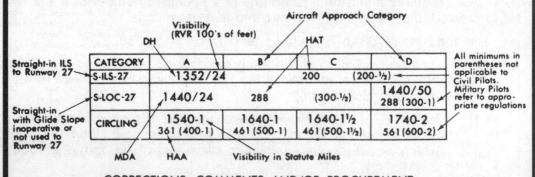

### CORRECTIONS, COMMENTS AND/OR PROCUREMENT

FOR CHARTING ERRORS:

Contact National Ocean Service
NOAA, N/CG31
6010 Executive Blvd.
Rockville, MD. 20852
Telephone Toll -Free 800-626-3677

FOR CHANGES, ADDITIONS, OR
RECOMMENDATIONS ON PROCEDURAL ASPECTS:

Contact Federal Aviation Administration, ATO-258
800 Independence Avenue, S.W.
Washington, D.C. 20591
Telephone (202) 267-9297

PROCURE FROM:

National Ocean Service
NOAA, N/CG33
Distribution Branch
Riverdale, MD. 20737
Telephone (301) 436-6993

**LEGEND 13.—Instrument Approach Procedures Explanation of Terms**

87295   Julian Date of Last Revision   **GENERAL INFORMATION & ABBREVIATIONS**

★ Indicates control tower or ATIS operates non-continuously, or non-standard Pilot Controlled Lighting.
Distances in nautical miles (except visibility in statute miles and Runway Visual Range in hundreds of feet).
Runway Dimensions in feet. Elevations in feet Mean Sea Level (MSL). Ceilings in feet above airport elevation.
Radials/bearings/headings/courses are magnetic
\# Indicates control tower temporarily closed UFN.

| | |
|---|---|
| ADF | Automatic Direction Finder |
| ALS | Approach Light System |
| ALSF | Approach Light System with Sequenced Flashing Lights |
| APP CON | Approach Control |
| ARR | Arrival |
| ASR/PAR | Published Radar Minimums at this Airport |
| ATIS | Automatic Terminal Information Service |
| AWOS | Automated Weather Observing System |
| AZ | Azimuth |
| BC | Back Course |
| C | Circling |
| CAT | Category |
| CCW | Counter Clockwise |
| Chan | Channel |
| CLNC DEL | Clearance Delivery |
| CTAF | Common Traffic Advisory Frequency |
| CW | Clockwise |
| DH | Decision Heights |
| DME | Distance Measuring Equipment |
| DR | Dead Reckoning |
| ELEV | Elevation |
| FAF | Final Approach Fix |
| FM | Fan Marker |
| GPI | Ground Point of Interception |
| GS | Glide Slope |
| HAA | Height Above Airport |
| HAL | Height Above Landing |
| HAT | Height Above Touchdown |
| HIRL | High Intensity Runway Lights |
| IAF | Initial Approach Fix |
| ICAO | International Civil Aviation Organization |
| IM | Inner Marker |
| Intcp | Intercept |
| INT | Intersection |
| LDA | Localizer Type Directional Aid |
| Ldg | Landing |
| LDIN | Lead in Light System |
| LIRL | Low Intensity Runway Lights |
| LOC | Localizer |
| LR | Lead Radial. Provides at least 2 NM (Copter 1 NM) of lead to assist in turning onto the intermediate/final course |
| MALS | Medium Intensity Approach Light System |

| | |
|---|---|
| MALSR | Medium Intensity Approach Light Systems with RAIL |
| MAP | Missed Approach Point |
| MDA | Minimum Descent Altitude |
| MIRL | Medium Intensity Runway Lights |
| MLS | Microwave Landing System |
| MM | Middle Marker |
| NA | Not Authorized |
| NDB | Non-directional Radio Beacon |
| NM | Nautical Miles |
| NoPT | No Procedure Turn Required (Procedure Turn shall not be executed without ATC clearance) |
| ODALS | Omnidirectional Approach Light System |
| OM | Outer Marker |
| R | Radial |
| RA | Radio Altimeter setting height |
| Radar Required | Radar vectoring required for this approach |
| RAIL | Runway Alignment Indicator Lights |
| RBn | Radio Beacon |
| RCLS | Runway Centerline Light System |
| REIL | Runway End Identifier Lights |
| RNAV | Area Navigation |
| RPI | Runway Point of Intercept(ion) |
| RRL | Runway Remaining Lights |
| Runway Touchdown Zone | First 3000' of Runway |
| Rwy | Runway |
| RVR | Runway Visual Range |
| S | Straight-in |
| SALS | Short Approach Light System |
| SSALR | Simplified Short Approach Light System with RAIL |
| SDF | Simplified Directional Facility |
| TA | Transition Altitude |
| TAC | TACAN |
| TCH | Threshold Crossing Height (height in feet Above Ground Level) |
| TDZ | Touchdown Zone |
| TDZE | Touchdown Zone Elevation |
| TDZ/CL | Touchdown Zone and Runway Centerline Lighting |
| TDZL | Touchdown Zone Lights |
| TLv | Transition Level |
| VASI | Visual Approach Slope Indicator |
| VDP | Visual Descent Point |
| WPT | Waypoint (RNAV) |
| X | Radar Only Frequency |

## PILOT CONTROLLED AIRPORT LIGHTING SYSTEMS

Available pilot controlled lighting (PCL) systems are indicated as follows:
1. Approach lighting systems that bear a system identification are symbolized using negative symbology, e.g., (A), (V), ☆
2. Approach lighting systems that do not bear a system identification are indicated with a negative " (L) " beside the name.
A star (★) indicates non-standard PCL, consult Directory/Supplement, e.g., (L)★
To activate lights use frequency indicated in the communication section of the chart with a (L) or the appropriate lighting system identification e.g., UNICOM 122.8 (L), (A), (V)

| KEY MIKE | FUNCTION |
|---|---|
| 7 times within 5 seconds | Highest intensity available |
| 5 times within 5 seconds | Medium or lower intensity (Lower REIL or REIL-off) |
| 3 times within 5 seconds | Lowest intensity available (Lower REIL or REIL-off) |

**LEGEND 14.—General Information and Abbreviations**

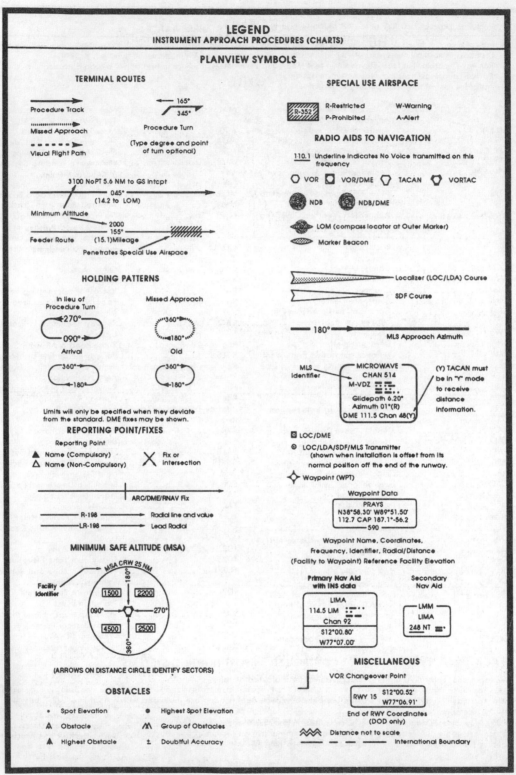

LEGEND 15.—Instrument Approach Procedures (Planview).

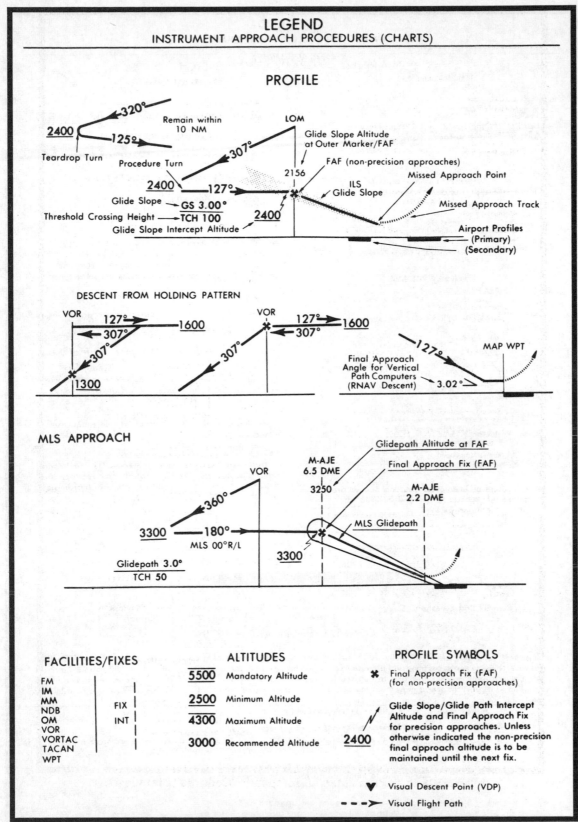

## LEGEND
### INSTRUMENT APPROACH PROCEDURES (CHARTS)

#### PROFILE

320°
2400
125°
Teardrop Turn
Remain within 10 NM
Procedure Turn

LOM
307°
Glide Slope Altitude at Outer Marker/FAF
2156
FAF (non-precision approaches)
Missed Approach Point
ILS Glide Slope
Missed Approach Track

2400
127°
Glide Slope — GS 3.00°
Threshold Crossing Height — TCH 100
Glide Slope Intercept Altitude
2400

Airport Profiles
(Primary)
(Secondary)

#### DESCENT FROM HOLDING PATTERN

VOR
127° — 1600
307°
307°
1300

VOR
127° — 1600
307°
307°

127°
Final Approach Angle for Vertical Path Computers (RNAV Descent)
3.02°
MAP WPT

#### MLS APPROACH

Glidepath Altitude at FAF
M-AJE 6.5 DME
Final Approach Fix (FAF)
3250
M-AJE 2.2 DME
VOR
360°
MLS Glidepath
3300 — 180°
MLS 00°R/L
3300
Glidepath 3.0°
TCH 50

#### FACILITIES/FIXES

| | |
|---|---|
| FM | |
| IM | |
| MM | FIX |
| NDB | |
| OM | INT |
| VOR | |
| VORTAC | |
| TACAN | |
| WPT | |

#### ALTITUDES

5500 Mandatory Altitude

2500 Minimum Altitude

4300 Maximum Altitude

3000 Recommended Altitude

#### PROFILE SYMBOLS

✖ Final Approach Fix (FAF) (for non-precision approaches)

Glide Slope/Glide Path Intercept Altitude and Final Approach Fix for precision approaches. Unless otherwise indicated the non-precision final approach altitude is to be maintained until the next fix.
2400

▼ Visual Descent Point (VDP)

- - -► Visual Flight Path

**LEGEND 16.—Instrument Approach Procedures (Profile)**

## LEGEND
### INSTRUMENT APPROACH PROCEDURES (CHARTS)

### AIRPORT DIAGRAM/AIRPORT SKETCH

**Runways**

Hard Surface    Other Than Hard Surface    Overruns, Taxiways, Parking Areas    Displaced Threshold

Helicopter Alighting Areas    (H) ✳ H ⚠ ⊞

Negative Symbols used to identify Copter Procedure landing point............ H ⊞ H ⚠ ⊞

Closed Runways    Closed Taxiways    Under Construction    Metal Surface    Runway Centerline Lighting

Runway TDZ elevation ....... TDZE 123

Total Runway Gradient ....... 0.8%→UP
    (shown when runway gradient exceeds 0.3%)

**Arresting Gear**

uni-directional    bi-directional    Jet Barrier

⊠ U.S. Navy Optical Landing System (OLS) "OLS" location is shown because of its height of approximately 7 feet and proximity to edge of runway may create on obstruction for some types of aircraft.

### REFERENCE FEATURES

Buildings ................................ ■

Tanks ................................ ●

Obstruction ................................ ∧

Airport Beacon # ................................ ☆

Runway Radar Reflectors ........................ ⧓

Control Tower # ........................ ▪

\# When Control Tower and Rotating Beacon are co-located, Beacon symbol will be used and further identified as TWR.

Approach light symbols are shown on a separate legend.

Airport diagram scales are variable.

True/magnetic North orientation may vary from diagram to diagram.

Coordinate values are shown in 1 or ½ minute increments. They are further broken down into 6 second ticks, within each 1 minute increment.

Positional accuracy within ±600 feet unless otherwise noted on the chart.

NOTE:
Airport diagrams that are referenced to the World Geodetic System (WGS) (noted on appropriate diagram), may not be compatible with local coordinates published in FLIP.

Runway Gradient    FIELD ELEV 174    Runway Identification

0.7% UP→

20    9000 X 200    ←023.2° 1000 X 200

Runway End Elevation —ELEV 164    Runway Dimensions (in feet)    Runway Heading (Magnetic)    Overrun Dimensions (in feet)

### GENERAL INFORMATION (NOS)
#### SCOPE

Airport diagrams are specifically designed to assist in the movement of ground traffic at locations with complex runway/taxiway configurations and provide information for updating Inertial Navigation Systems (INS) aboard aircraft. Airport diagrams are not intended to be used for approach and landing or departure operations. Requisition for the creation of airport diagrams must meet the above criteria and will be approved by the FAA or DOD on a case-by-case basis.

### MINIMA DATA

⚠ Alternate Minimums not standard.
Civil users refer to tabulation.
USA/USN/USAF pilots refer to appropriate regulations.

⚠ NA Alternate minimums are Not Authorized due to unmonitored facility or absence of weather reporting service.

▽ Take-off Minimums not standard and/or Departure Procedures are published. Refer to tabulation.

**LEGEND 17.—Instrument Approach Procedures (Airport Diagram/Sketch)**

## INSTRUMENT APPROACH PROCEDURE CHARTS
### RATE OF DESCENT TABLE
#### (ft. per min.)

A rate of descent table is provided for use in planning and executing precision descents under known or approximate ground speed conditions. It will be especially useful for approaches when the localizer only is used for course guidance. A best speed, power, attitude combination can be programmed which will result in a stable glide rate and attitude favorable for executing a landing if minimums exist upon breakout. Care should always be exercised so that the minimum descent altitude and missed approach point are not exceeded.

| ANGLE OF DESCENT (degrees and tenths) | GROUND SPEED (knots) | | | | | | | | | | |
|---|---|---|---|---|---|---|---|---|---|---|---|
| | 30 | 45 | 60 | 75 | 90 | 105 | 120 | 135 | 150 | 165 | 180 |
| 2.0 | 105 | 160 | 210 | 265 | 320 | 370 | 425 | 475 | 530 | 585 | 635 |
| 2.5 | 130 | 200 | 265 | 330 | 395 | 465 | 530 | 595 | 665 | 730 | 795 |
| 3.0 | 160 | 240 | 320 | 395 | 480 | 555 | 635 | 715 | 795 | 875 | 955 |
| 3.5 | 185 | 280 | 370 | 465 | 555 | 650 | 740 | 835 | 925 | 1020 | 1110 |
| 4.0 | 210 | 315 | 425 | 530 | 635 | 740 | 845 | 955 | 1060 | 1165 | 1270 |
| 4.5 | 240 | 355 | 475 | 595 | 715 | 835 | 955 | 1075 | 1190 | 1310 | 1430 |
| 5.0 | 265 | 395 | 530 | 660 | 795 | 925 | 1060 | 1190 | 1325 | 1455 | 1590 |
| 5.5 | 290 | 435 | 580 | 730 | 875 | 1020 | 1165 | 1310 | 1455 | 1600 | 1745 |
| 6.0 | 315 | 475 | 635 | 795 | 955 | 1110 | 1270 | 1430 | 1590 | 1745 | 1905 |
| 6.5 | 345 | 515 | 690 | 860 | 1030 | 1205 | 1375 | 1550 | 1720 | 1890 | 2065 |
| 7.0 | 370 | 555 | 740 | 925 | 1110 | 1295 | 1480 | 1665 | 1850 | 2035 | 2220 |
| 7.5 | 395 | 595 | 795 | 990 | 1190 | 1390 | 1585 | 1785 | 1985 | 2180 | 2380 |
| 8.0 | 425 | 635 | 845 | 1055 | 1270 | 1480 | 1690 | 1905 | 2115 | 2325 | 2540 |
| 8.5 | 450 | 675 | 900 | 1120 | 1345 | 1570 | 1795 | 2020 | 2245 | 2470 | 2695 |
| 9.0 | 475 | 715 | 950 | 1190 | 1425 | 1665 | 1900 | 2140 | 2375 | 2615 | 2855 |
| 9.5 | 500 | 750 | 1005 | 1255 | 1505 | 1755 | 2005 | 2255 | 2510 | 2760 | 3010 |
| 10.0 | 530 | 790 | 1055 | 1320 | 1585 | 1845 | 2110 | 2375 | 2640 | 2900 | 3165 |
| 10.5 | 555 | 830 | 1105 | 1385 | 1660 | 1940 | 2215 | 2490 | 2770 | 3045 | 3320 |
| 11.0 | 580 | 870 | 1160 | 1450 | 1740 | 2030 | 2320 | 2610 | 2900 | 3190 | 3480 |
| 11.5 | 605 | 910 | 1210 | 1515 | 1820 | 2120 | 2425 | 2725 | 3030 | 3335 | 3635 |
| 12.0 | 630 | 945 | 1260 | 1575 | 1890 | 2205 | 2520 | 2835 | 3150 | 3465 | 3780 |

LEGEND 19.—Instrument Approach Procedure Charts, Rate-of-Descent Table.

# INOPERATIVE COMPONENTS OR VISUAL AIDS TABLE

Landing minimums published on instrument approach procedure charts are based upon full operation of all components and visual aids associated with the particular instrument approach chart being used. Higher minimums are required with inoperative components or visual aids as indicated below. If more than one component is inoperative, each minimum is raised to the highest minimum required by any single component that is inoperative. ILS glide slope inoperative minimums are published on instrument approach charts as localizer minimums. This table may be amended by notes on the approach chart. Such notes apply only to the particular approach category(ies) as stated. See legend page for description of components indicated below.

(1) ILS, MLS, and PAR

| Inoperative Component or Aid | Approach Category | Increase Visibility |
|---|---|---|
| ALSF 1 & 2, MALSR, & SSALR | ABCD | 1/4 mile |

(2) ILS with visibility minimum of 1,800 RVR.

| | | |
|---|---|---|
| ALSF 1 & 2, MALSR, &SSALR | ABCD | To 4000 RVR |
| TDZI RCLS | ABCD | To 2400 RVR |
| RVR | ABCD | To 1/2 mile |

(3) VOR, VOR/DME, VORTAC, VOR (TAC), VOR/DME (TAC), LOC, LOC/DME, LDA, LDA/DME, SDF, SDF/DME, RNAV, and ASR

| Inoperative Visual Aid | Approach Category | Increase Visibility |
|---|---|---|
| ALSF 1 & 2, MALSR, & SSALR | ABCD | 1/2 mile |
| SSALS, MALS, & ODALS | ABC | 1/4 mile |

(4) NDB

| | | |
|---|---|---|
| ALSF 1 & 2, MALSR & SSALR | C | 1/2 mile |
| | ABD | 1/4 mile |
| MALS, SSALS, ODALS | ABC | 1/4 mile |

LEGEND 20.—Inoperative Components or Visual Aids Table.

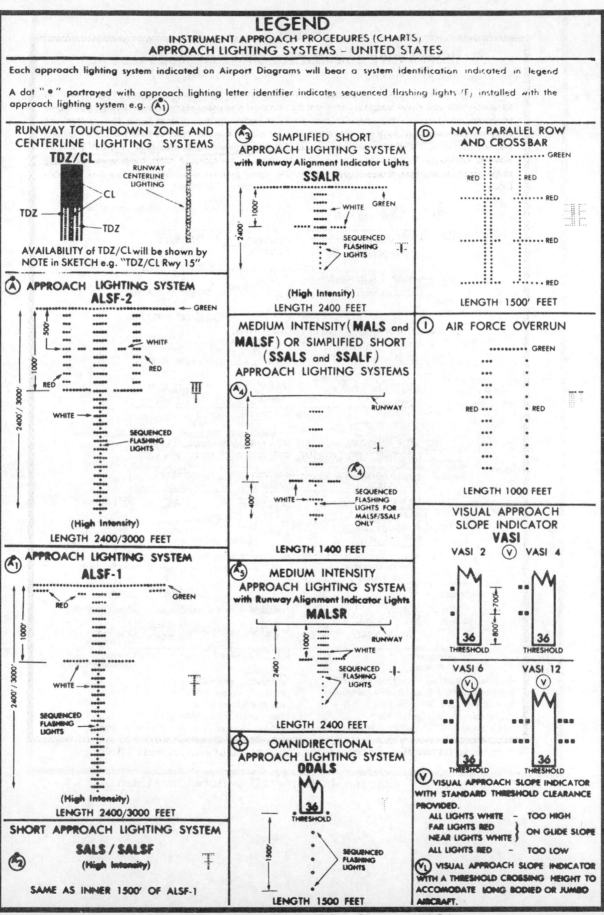

## LEGEND
### INSTRUMENT APPROACH PROCEDURES (CHARTS)
### APPROACH LIGHTING SYSTEMS – UNITED STATES

Each approach lighting system indicated on Airport Diagrams will bear a system identification indicated in legend

A dot " • " portrayed with approach lighting letter identifier indicates sequenced flashing lights (F) installed with the approach lighting system e.g. (A₁)

### RUNWAY TOUCHDOWN ZONE AND CENTERLINE LIGHTING SYSTEMS
**TDZ/CL**

RUNWAY CENTERLINE LIGHTING

CL
TDZ
TDZ

AVAILABILITY of TDZ/CL will be shown by NOTE in SKETCH e.g. "TDZ/CL Rwy 15"

### Ⓐ APPROACH LIGHTING SYSTEM
**ALSF-2**

GREEN
500'
WHITE
RED
1000'
RED
WHITE
SEQUENCED FLASHING LIGHTS
2400'/3000'

(High Intensity)
LENGTH 2400/3000 FEET

### (A₁) APPROACH LIGHTING SYSTEM
**ALSF-1**

GREEN
RED
1000'
WHITE
SEQUENCED FLASHING LIGHTS
2400'/3000'

(High Intensity)
LENGTH 2400/3000 FEET

### SHORT APPROACH LIGHTING SYSTEM
**SALS / SALSF**
(A₂)
(High Intensity)

SAME AS INNER 1500' of ALSF-1

### (A₃) SIMPLIFIED SHORT APPROACH LIGHTING SYSTEM
with Runway Alignment Indicator Lights
**SSALR**

1000'
WHITE
GREEN
SEQUENCED FLASHING LIGHTS
2400'

(High Intensity)
LENGTH 2400 FEET

### MEDIUM INTENSITY (**MALS** and **MALSF**) OR SIMPLIFIED SHORT (**SSALS** and **SSALF**) APPROACH LIGHTING SYSTEMS
(A₄)

RUNWAY
1000'
(A₄)
400'
WHITE
SEQUENCED FLASHING LIGHTS FOR MALSF/SSALF ONLY

LENGTH 1400 FEET

### (A₅) MEDIUM INTENSITY APPROACH LIGHTING SYSTEM
with Runway Alignment Indicator Lights
**MALSR**

1000'
RUNWAY
WHITE
SEQUENCED FLASHING LIGHTS
2400'

LENGTH 2400 FEET

### OMNIDIRECTIONAL APPROACH LIGHTING SYSTEM
**ODALS**

36
THRESHOLD
1500'
SEQUENCED FLASHING LIGHTS

LENGTH 1500 FEET

### Ⓓ NAVY PARALLEL ROW AND CROSS BAR

GREEN
RED          RED
RED
RED
RED

LENGTH 1500' FEET

### Ⓘ AIR FORCE OVERRUN

GREEN
RED          RED

LENGTH 1000 FEET

### VISUAL APPROACH SLOPE INDICATOR
**VASI**

VASI 2     Ⓥ     VASI 4

36          36
THRESHOLD   THRESHOLD
800'—700'

VASI 6          VASI 12

(VL)            Ⓥ

36              36
THRESHOLD       THRESHOLD

Ⓥ VISUAL APPROACH SLOPE INDICATOR WITH STANDARD THRESHOLD CLEARANCE PROVIDED.

ALL LIGHTS WHITE — TOO HIGH
FAR LIGHTS RED } ON GLIDE SLOPE
NEAR LIGHTS WHITE }
ALL LIGHTS RED — TOO LOW

(VL) VISUAL APPROACH SLOPE INDICATOR WITH A THRESHOLD CROSSING HEIGHT TO ACCOMODATE LONG BODIED OR JUMBO AIRCRAFT.

LEGEND 21.—Approach Lighting Systems (U.S.)

# LEGEND
## STANDARD INSTRUMENT DEPARTURE (SID) CHARTS

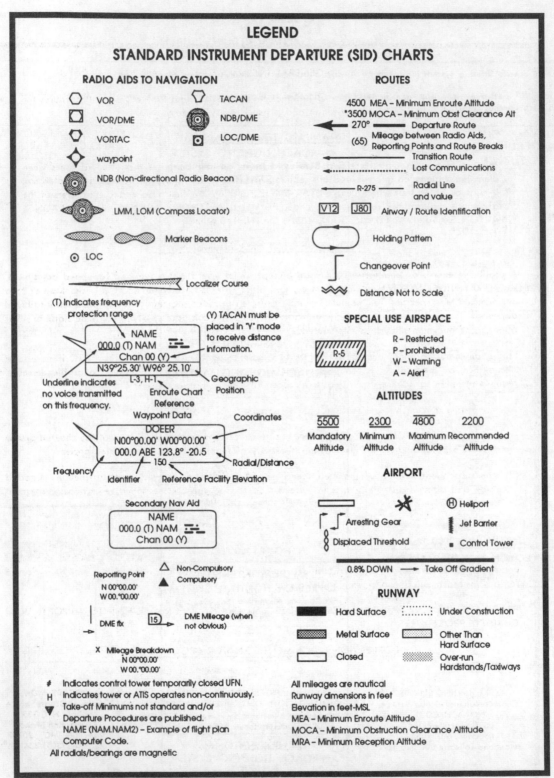

**RADIO AIDS TO NAVIGATION**

⬡ VOR
▢ VOR/DME
⬠ VORTAC
◇ waypoint
◎ NDB (Non-directional Radio Beacon
LMM, LOM (Compass Locator)
Marker Beacons
⊙ LOC

⬠ TACAN
◉ NDB/DME
▣ LOC/DME

Localizer Course

(T) Indicates frequency protection range

(Y) TACAN must be placed in "Y" mode to receive distance information.

NAME
000.0 (T) NAM ▄▄
Chan 00 (Y)
N39°25.30' W96° 25.10'
L-3, H-1

Underline indicates no voice transmitted on this frequency.

Enroute Chart Reference

Geographic Position

Waypoint Data

Coordinates

DOEER
N00°00.00' W00°00.00'
000.0 ABE 123.8° -20.5
150

Frequency    Identifier    Reference Facility Elevation

Radial/Distance

Secondary Nav Aid

NAME
000.0 (T) NAM ▄▄
Chan 00 (Y)

△ Non-Compulsory
▲ Compulsory

Reporting Point
N 00°00.00'
W 00.°00.00'

DME fix

[15] DME Mileage (when not obvious)

X   Mileage Breakdown
N 00°00.00'
W 00.°00.00'

\# Indicates control tower temporarily closed UFN.
H Indicates tower or ATIS operates non-continuously.
▼ Take-off Minimums not standard and/or Departure Procedures are published.
NAME (NAM.NAM2) – Example of flight plan Computer Code.
All radials/bearings are magnetic

**ROUTES**

4500  MEA – Minimum Enroute Altitude
*3500 MOCA – Minimum Obst Clearance Alt
◄━━━ 270° ━━━ Departure Route
(65)  Mileage between Radio Aids, Reporting Points and Route Breaks
━━━ Transition Route
┄┄┄ Lost Communications
━ R-275 ━ Radial Line and value
[V12] [J80] Airway / Route Identification
⬭ Holding Pattern
⌐ Changeover Point
〰〰 Distance Not to Scale

**SPECIAL USE AIRSPACE**

▨ R-5

R – Restricted
P – prohibited
W – Warning
A – Alert

**ALTITUDES**

5500̲    2̲300    4̲800    2200
Mandatory Altitude    Minimum Altitude    Maximum Altitude    Recommended Altitude

**AIRPORT**

▭  ✳    Ⓗ Heliport
⌐ Arresting Gear    Jet Barrier
Displaced Threshold    ■ Control Tower

0.8% DOWN ━► Take Off Gradient

**RUNWAY**

■ Hard Surface    ⋯ Under Construction
▨ Metal Surface    ▨ Other Than Hard Surface
▭ Closed    ▨ Over-run Hardstands/Taxiways

All mileages are nautical
Runway dimensions in feet
Elevation in feet-MSL
MEA – Minimum Enroute Altitude
MOCA – Minimum Obstruction Clearance Altitude
MRA – Minimum Reception Altitude

LEGEND 9.—Standard Instrument Departure Chart (SID).

## GENERAL INFORMATION

This publication consists of Standard Terminal Arrivals (STAR) and Profile Descent Procedures for use by both civil and military aviation and is issued every 56 days.

### STANDARD TERMINAL ARRIVAL

The use of the associated codified STAR and transition identifiers are requested of users when filing flight plans via teletype and are required for users filing flight plans via computer interface. It must be noted that when filing a STAR with a transition, the first three coded characters of the STAR are replaced by the transition code. Examples: ACTON SIX ARRIVAL, file (AQN.AQN6); ACTON SIX ARRIVAL EDNAS TRANSITION, file (EDNAS.AQN6).

### PROFILE DESCENT PROCEDURAL NOTE

A profile descent is an uninterrupted descent (except where level flight is required for speed adjustment, e.g., 250 knots at 10,000 feet MSL) from cruising altitude/level to interception of a glide slope or to a minimum altitude specified for the initial or intermediate approach segment of a non-precision instrument approach. The profile descent normally terminates at the approach gate or where the glide slope or other appropriate minimum altitude is intercepted.

Profile descent clearances are subject to traffic conditions and may be altered by ATC if necessary. Acceptance, by the pilot, of a profile descent clearance; i.e., "cleared for Runway 28 profile descent," requires the pilot to adhere to all depicted procedures on the profile descent chart.

After a profile descent has been issued and accepted:

(1) Any subsequent ATC revision of altitude or route cancels the remaining portion of the charted profile descent procedure. ATC will then assign necessary altitude, route, and speed clearances.

(2) Any subsequent revision of depicted speed restriction voids all charted speed restrictions. Charted route and altitude restrictions are not affected by revision to depicted speed restrictions. If the pilot cannot comply with charted route and/or altitude restrictions because of revised speed, he is expected to so advise ATC.

THE PROFILE DESCENT CLEARANCES DOES NOT CONSTITUTE CLEARANCE TO FLY AN INSTRUMENT APPROACH PROCEDURE (IAP). The last "maintain altitude" specified in the PROFILE DESCENT procedure constitutes that the last ATC assigned altitude and the pilot must maintain such altitude until he is cleared for an approach unless another altitude is assigned by ATC.

PILOTS SHOULD REVIEW RUNWAY PROFILE DESCENT CHARTS BEFORE FLIGHT INTO AIRPORTS WITH CHARTED PROCEDURES.

### CORRECTIONS, COMMENTS AND/OR PROCUREMENT

#### CIVIL

FOR CHARTING ERRORS:
Contact National Ocean Service
NOAA, N/CG31
6010 Executive Blvd.
Rockville, MD. 20852
Telephone Toll-Free 800-626-3677

FOR CHANGES, ADDITIONS, OR
RECOMMENDATIONS ON PROCEDURAL ASPECTS:
Contact Federal Aviation Administration, ATO-258
800 — Independence Avenue, S.W.
Washington, D.C., 20591
Telephone (202) 267-9297

PROCURE FROM:
National Ocean Service
NOAA, N/CG33
Distribution Branch
Riverdale, MD 20737
Telephone (301) 436-6993

#### MILITARY

For Corrections Information, see Chapter 11 of General Planning (GP). For Procurement refer to DOD Catalog of Aeronautical Charts and Flight Information Publications.

**LEGEND 10.—General Information, Standard Terminal Arrival (STAR)**

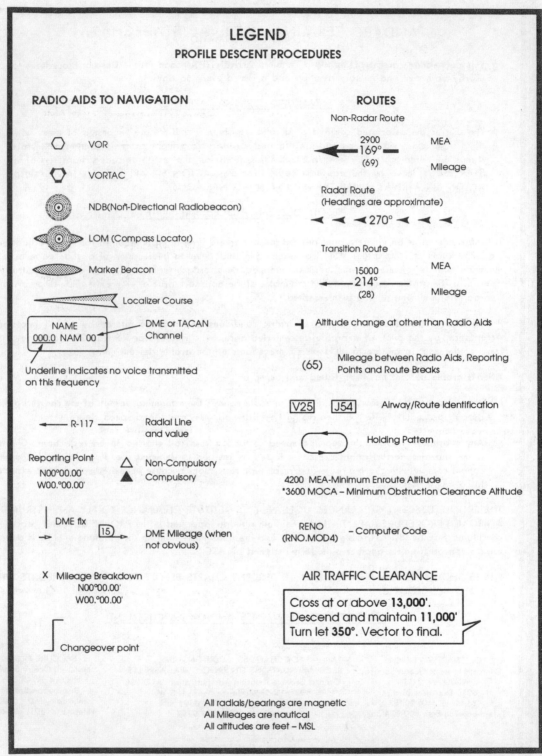

# LEGEND
## PROFILE DESCENT PROCEDURES

### RADIO AIDS TO NAVIGATION

⬡ VOR

⬡ VORTAC

◎ NDB(Non-Directional Radiobeacon)

LOM (Compass Locator)

Marker Beacon

Localizer Course

| NAME |
| 000.0 NAM 00 | → DME or TACAN Channel

Underline indicates no voice transmitted on this frequency

← R-117 — Radial Line and value

Reporting Point
N00°00.00'
W00.°00.00'

△ Non-Compulsory
▲ Compulsory

| DME fix

→  15  DME Mileage (when not obvious)

X  Mileage Breakdown
N00°00.00'
W00.°00.00'

Changeover point

### ROUTES

Non-Radar Route

◄——— 2900
169°
(69)

MEA

Mileage

Radar Route
(Headings are approximate)

◄ ◄ ◄270° ◄ ◄ ◄

Transition Route

←——— 15000
214°
(28)

MEA

Mileage

⊣ Altitude change at other than Radio Aids

(65)  Mileage between Radio Aids, Reporting Points and Route Breaks

V25   J54   Airway/Route Identification

⬭ Holding Pattern

4200  MEA-Minimum Enroute Altitude
*3600 MOCA – Minimum Obstruction Clearance Altitude

RENO
(RNO.MOD4)  – Computer Code

### AIR TRAFFIC CLEARANCE

> Cross at or above **13,000'**.
> Descend and maintain **11,000'**
> Turn let **350°**. Vector to final.

All radials/bearings are magnetic
All Mileages are nautical
All altitudes are feet – MSL

LEGEND 11.— Profile Descent Procedures.

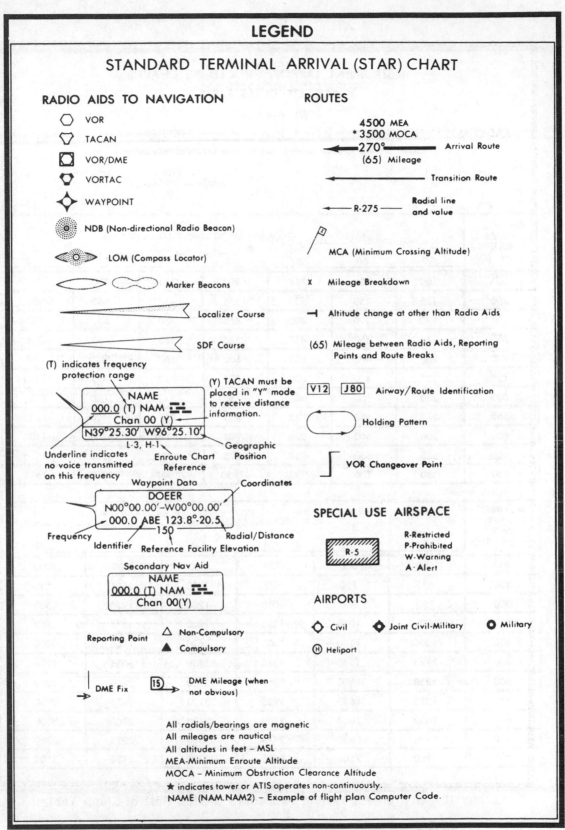

# LEGEND

## STANDARD TERMINAL ARRIVAL (STAR) CHART

### RADIO AIDS TO NAVIGATION

- VOR
- TACAN
- VOR/DME
- VORTAC
- WAYPOINT
- NDB (Non-directional Radio Beacon)
- LOM (Compass Locator)
- Marker Beacons
- Localizer Course
- SDF Course

(T) indicates frequency protection range

(Y) TACAN must be placed in "Y" mode to receive distance information.

NAME
000.0 (T) NAM
Chan 00 (Y)
N39°25.30' W96°25.10'
L-3, H-1

Underline indicates no voice transmitted on this frequency

Enroute Chart Reference

Geographic Position

Waypoint Data
DOEER
N00°00.00'–W00°00.00'
000.0 ABE 123.8°-20.5
150

Coordinates

Frequency

Identifier      Reference Facility Elevation

Radial/Distance

Secondary Nav Aid
NAME
000.0 (T) NAM
Chan 00(Y)

Reporting Point
△ Non-Compulsory
▲ Compulsory

DME Fix

15  DME Mileage (when not obvious)

### ROUTES

4500 MEA
* 3500 MOCA
270°         Arrival Route
(65) Mileage

Transition Route

R-275     Radial line and value

MCA (Minimum Crossing Altitude)

X   Mileage Breakdown

Altitude change at other than Radio Aids

(65) Mileage between Radio Aids, Reporting Points and Route Breaks

V12   J80   Airway/Route Identification

Holding Pattern

VOR Changeover Point

### SPECIAL USE AIRSPACE

R-5
R-Restricted
P-Prohibited
W-Warning
A-Alert

### AIRPORTS

◇ Civil      ◆ Joint Civil-Military      ● Military
Ⓗ Heliport

All radials/bearings are magnetic
All mileages are nautical
All altitudes in feet – MSL
MEA-Minimum Enroute Altitude
MOCA – Minimum Obstruction Clearance Altitude
★ indicates tower or ATIS operates non-continuously.
NAME (NAM.NAM2) – Example of flight plan Computer Code.

LEGEND 12.—Standard Terminal Arrival Chart (STAR)

# INSTRUMENT TAKEOFF PROCEDURE CHARTS
## RATE OF CLIMB TABLE
### (ft. per min.)

A rate of climb table is provided for use in planning and executing
takeoff procedures under known or approximate ground speed conditions.

| REQUIRED CLIMB RATE (ft. per NM) | GROUND SPEED (KNOTS) 30 | 60 | 80 | 90 | 100 | 120 | 140 |
|---|---|---|---|---|---|---|---|
| 200 | 100 | 200 | 267 | 300 | 333 | 400 | 467 |
| 250 | 125 | 250 | 333 | 375 | 417 | 500 | 583 |
| 300 | 150 | 300 | 400 | 450 | 500 | 600 | 700 |
| 350 | 175 | 350 | 467 | 525 | 583 | 700 | 816 |
| 400 | 200 | 400 | 533 | 600 | 667 | 800 | 933 |
| 450 | 225 | 450 | 600 | 675 | 750 | 900 | 1050 |
| 500 | 250 | 500 | 667 | 750 | 833 | 1000 | 1167 |
| 550 | 275 | 550 | 733 | 825 | 917 | 1100 | 1283 |
| 600 | 300 | 600 | 800 | 900 | 1000 | 1200 | 1400 |
| 650 | 325 | 650 | 867 | 975 | 1083 | 1300 | 1516 |
| 700 | 350 | 700 | 933 | 1050 | 1167 | 1400 | 1633 |

| REQUIRED CLIMB RATE (ft. per NM) | GROUND SPEED (KNOTS) 150 | 180 | 210 | 240 | 270 | 300 |
|---|---|---|---|---|---|---|
| 200 | 500 | 600 | 700 | 800 | 900 | 1000 |
| 250 | 625 | 750 | 875 | 1000 | 1125 | 1250 |
| 300 | 750 | 900 | 1050 | 1200 | 1350 | 1500 |
| 350 | 875 | 1050 | 1225 | 1400 | 1575 | 1750 |
| 400 | 1000 | 1200 | 1400 | 1600 | 1700 | 2000 |
| 450 | 1125 | 1350 | 1575 | 1800 | 2025 | 2250 |
| 500 | 1250 | 1500 | 1750 | 2000 | 2250 | 2500 |
| 550 | 1375 | 1650 | 1925 | 2200 | 2475 | 2750 |
| 600 | 1500 | 1800 | 2100 | 2400 | 2700 | 3000 |
| 650 | 1625 | 1950 | 2275 | 2600 | 2925 | 3250 |
| 700 | 1750 | 2100 | 2450 | 2800 | 3150 | 3500 |

LEGEND 18.—Instrument Takeoff Procedure Charts, Rate-of-Climb Table

## 9.14 MICROWAVE LANDING SYSTEM (Questions 152-155)

1. Microwave landing systems consist of five parts:

    a. Approach azimuth angle guidance
    b. Back azimuth angle guidance
    c. Approach elevation angle guidance
    d. Range guidance
    e. Data communications

2. MLS identification is a four-character alphabetical designation starting with the letter M transmitted in Morse Code at least 6 times per min.

3. The approach azimuth angle coverage on an MLS extends up to 20,000 ft. AGL.

4. The lateral approach azimuth angle limits are at least 40° on each side of the runway.

5. The range limits on an MLS are

    a. At least 20 NM for front azimuth angle guidance.
    b. At least 7 NM for back azimuth angle guidance.

6. See Legend 27 below for MLS coverage volumes.

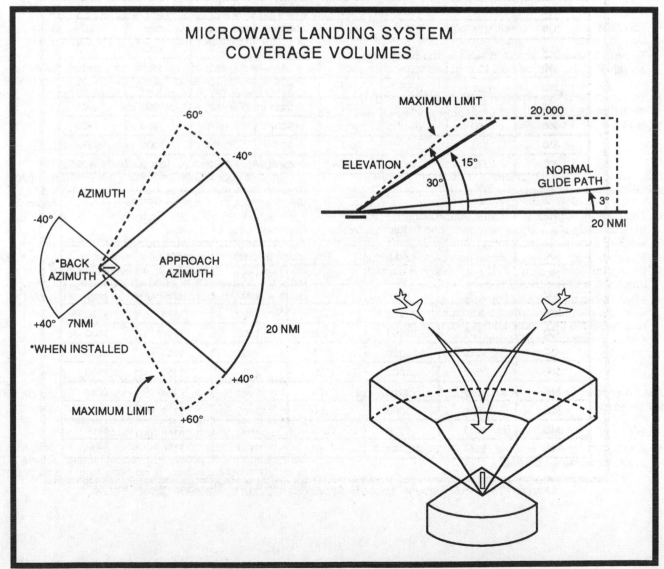

LEGEND 27.—Microwave Landing System, Coverage Volumes.

---

## QUESTIONS AND ANSWER EXPLANATIONS

    *All the FAA questions from the written test for the instrument rating relating to instrument approaches and the material outlined previously are reproduced on the following pages in the same modules as the outlines.  To the immediate right of each question are the correct answer and answer explanation.  You should cover these answers and answer explanations with your hand or a piece of paper while responding to the questions.  Refer to the general discussion in Chapter 1 on how to take the test.*

    *Remember that the questions from the FAA Instrument Rating Question Book have been reordered by topic, and the topics have been organized into a meaningful sequence.  Accordingly, the first line of the answer explanation gives the FAA question number and the citation of the authoritative source for the answer.*

---

## 9.1  Contact and Visual Approaches

**1.**
**4743.**  What conditions are necessary before ATC can authorize a visual approach?

A— You must have the preceding aircraft in sight, and be able to remain in VFR weather conditions.

B— You must have the airport in sight or the preceding aircraft in sight, and be able to proceed to, and land in IFR conditions.

C— You must have the airport in sight or a preceding aircraft to be followed, and be able to proceed to the airport in VFR conditions.

Answer (C) is correct (4743).  *(AIM Para 5-58)*
ATC may authorize airplanes to conduct visual approaches to an airport or to follow another airplane when flight to and landing at the airport can be accomplished in VFR weather.  You must have the airport or preceding aircraft in sight before the clearance is issued.
Answer (A) is incorrect because you can have the airport in sight instead of having the preceding aircraft in sight.  Answer (B) is incorrect because you must be able to land in VFR, not IFR, conditions.

**2.**
**4718.**  What are the main differences between a visual approach and a contact approach?

A— The pilot must request a contact approach; the pilot may be assigned a visual approach and higher weather minimums must exist.

B— The pilot must request a visual approach and report having the field in sight; ATC may assign a contact approach if VFR conditions exist.

C— Anytime the pilot reports the field in sight, ATC may clear the pilot for a contact approach; for a visual approach, the pilot must advise that the approach can be made under VFR conditions.

Answer (A) is correct (4718).  *(AIM Para 5-60)*
Contact approaches can only be issued upon pilot request, but visual approaches may be assigned by ATC.  Visual approaches require VFR conditions.  Contact approaches require 1 SM flight visibility and the ability to remain clear of clouds.
Answer (B) is incorrect because ATC may assign visual approaches without pilot request, and ATC cannot issue a contact approach clearance without the pilot's request.  Answer (C) is incorrect because ATC cannot issue a contact approach clearance without the pilot's request.

**3.**
**4750.**  A contact approach is an approach procedure that may be used

A— in lieu of conducting a SIAP.

B— if assigned by ATC and will facilitate the approach.

C— in lieu of a visual approach.

Answer (A) is correct (4750).  *(AIM Para 5-60)*
A contact approach may be requested by the pilot if there is 1 SM flight visibility and the pilot can operate clear of clouds.  It is an alternative to a standard instrument approach procedure (SIAP).
Answer (B) is incorrect because ATC cannot assign a contact approach; pilots must request them.  Answer (C) is incorrect because there is no need to utilize a contact approach if a visual approach is possible.

**4.**
**4735.** What are the requirements for a contact approach to an airport that has an approved IAP, if the pilot is on an instrument flight plan and clear of clouds?

A— The controller must determine that the pilot can see the airport at the altitude flown and can remain clear of clouds.

B— The pilot must agree to the approach when given by ATC and the controller must have determined that the visibility was at least 1 mile and be reasonably sure the pilot can remain clear of clouds.

C— The pilot must request the approach, have at least 1-mile visibility, and be reasonably sure of remaining clear of clouds.

**5.**
**4736.** When is radar service terminated during a visual approach?

A— Automatically when ATC instructs the pilot to contact the tower.

B— Immediately upon acceptance of the approach by the pilot.

C— When ATC advises, "Radar service terminated; resume own navigation."

**6.**
**4737.** When may you obtain a contact approach?

A— ATC may assign a contact approach if VFR conditions exist or you report the runway in sight and are clear of clouds.

B— ATC may assign a contact approach if you are below the clouds and the visibility is at least 1 mile.

C— ATC will assign a contact approach only upon request if the reported visibility is at least 1 mile.

**9.2 SDF and LDA Approaches**

**7.**
**4705.** What are the main differences between the SDF and the localizer of an ILS?

A— The useable off-course indications are limited to 35° for the localizer and up to 90° for the SDF.

B— The SDF course may not be aligned with the runway and the course may be wider.

C— The course width for the localizer will always be 5° while the SDF course will be between 6° and 12°.

**8.**
**4703.** What is the difference between a Localizer-Type Directional Aid (LDA) and the ILS localizer?

A— The LDA is not aligned with the runway.

B— The LDA uses a course width of 6° or 12°, while an ILS uses only 5°.

C— The LDA signal is generated from a VOR-type facility and has no glide slope.

Answer (C) is correct (4735). *(AIM Para 5-60)*
Pilots operating in accordance with an IFR flight plan, provided they are clear of clouds, have at least 1 SM flight visibility, and can reasonably expect to continue to the destination airport in those conditions, may request ATC authorization for a contact approach.
Answer (A) is incorrect because the pilot must determine whether (s)he can reasonably expect to continue to the airport in at least 1 SM flight visibility and clear of clouds, not the controller. Answer (B) is incorrect because the pilot must request a contact approach; ATC does not solicit or assign contact approaches.

Answer (A) is correct (4736). *(AIM Para 5-58)*
Radar service is automatically terminated without advising the pilot once the pilot has been instructed to contact the tower.
Answer (B) is incorrect because approach clearance is given well before radar service is terminated. Answer (C) is incorrect because "resume own navigation" is generally an en route instruction and is not applicable to approaches.

Answer (C) is correct (4737). *(AIM Para 5-60)*
ATC will only assign a contact approach upon pilot request if the pilot is operating clear of clouds, has at least 1 SM flight visibility, and expects to reach the airport and land in those conditions.
Answer (A) is incorrect because ATC may assign a visual (not a contact) approach if VFR conditions exist. ATC may not assign a contact approach. Answer (B) is incorrect because ATC may not assign a contact approach. The pilot must request one.

Answer (B) is correct (4705). *(AIM Para 1-11)*
The approach techniques and procedures used in performance of an SDF instrument approach are essentially identical to those employed to execute a standard localizer approach, except that the SDF course may not be aligned with the runway and the course may be wider, resulting in less precision.
Answer (A) is incorrect because the off-course indications are limited to 35° for both types of approach. Answer (C) is incorrect because the course width for the localizer is usually between 3° and 6°, and SDF is either 6° or 12° (not between).

Answer (A) is correct (4703). *(AIM Para 1-10)*
The localizer-type directional aid (LDA) is similar to a localizer but is not part of a complete ILS, and it is not aligned with the runway.
Answer (B) is incorrect because the LDA uses the same course width as the ILS, i.e., 3° to 6°. The SDF uses 6° or 12°. Answer (C) is incorrect because the LDA is a localizer-type (not VOR-type) signal.

**9.**
**4704.**  How wide is an SDF course?

A— Either 3° or 6°.
B— Either 6° or 12°.
C— Varies from 5° to 10°.

Answer (B) is correct (4704).  *(AIM Para 1-11)*
The simplified directional facility (SDF) signal is fixed at either 6° or 12° as necessary to provide maximum fly-ability and optimum course quality.
Answer (A) is incorrect because either 3° or 6° is half the course width of an SDF.  Answer (C) is incorrect because a course 5° to 10° wide does not relate to ILS, LDA, or SDF.

**10.**
**4702.**  What is a difference between an SDF and an LDA facility?

A— The SDF course width is either 6° or 12° while the LDA course width is approximately 5°.
B— The SDF course has no glide slope guidance while the LDA does.
C— The SDF has no marker beacons while the LDA has at least an OM.

Answer (A) is correct (4702).  *(AIM Para 1-10)*
The localizer-type directional aid (LDA) is of comparable utility and accuracy as a localizer but is not part of a complete ILS.  The LDA usually provides a more precise approach course than the simplified directional facility (SDF) installation, which has a course width of 6° or 12°.  The LDA course widths are from 3° to 6°.
Answer (B) is incorrect because neither the SDF or LDA has glide slope guidance.  Answer (C) is incorrect because both SDF and LDA may have marker beacons.

## 9.3  Runway Visual Range (RVR)

**11.**
**4401.**  What does the Runway Visual Range (RVR) value, depicted on certain straight-in IAP Charts, represent?

A— The slant range distance the pilot can see down the runway while crossing the threshold on glide slope.
B— The horizontal distance a pilot should see down the runway from the approach end of the runway.
C— The slant visual range a pilot should see down the final approach and during landing.

Answer (B) is correct (4401).  *(AWS Sect 2)*
RVR is an instrumentally derived value that represents the horizontal distance the pilot will see down the runway from the approach end.  It is based on the measurement of a transmissometer near the touchdown point of the instrument runway and is reported in hundreds of feet.
Answer (A) is incorrect because RVR is the horizontal (not slant range) distance the pilot will see down the runway.  Answer (C) is incorrect because RVR is the horizontal (not slant) distance the pilot will see down the runway (not the final approach).

**12.**
**4759.**  The RVR minimums for takeoff or landing are published in an IAP, but RVR is inoperative and cannot be reported for the runway at the time.  Which of the following would apply?

A— RVR minimums which are specified in the procedure should be converted and applied as ground visibility.
B— RVR minimums may be disregarded, providing the runway has an operative HIRL system.
C— RVR minimums may be disregarded, providing all other components of the ILS system are operative.

Answer (A) is correct (4759).  *(FAR 91.175)*
*This question is a duplicate of FAA question 4716.*
If RVR minimums for takeoff or landing are prescribed in an instrument approach procedure, but RVR is inoperative and cannot be reported for the runway of intended operation, the RVR minimum shall be converted to ground visibility and shall be the visibility minimum for takeoff or landing on that runway.
Answer (B) is incorrect because RVR minimums must be converted to ground visibility (not disregarded).  Answer (C) is incorrect because RVR minimums must be converted to ground visibility (not disregarded).

**13.**
**4716.**  RVR minimums for landing are prescribed in an IAP, but RVR is inoperative and cannot be reported for the intended runway at the time.  Which of the following would be an operational consideration?

A— RVR minimums which are specified in the procedures should be converted and applied as ground visibility.
B— RVR minimums may be disregarded, providing the runway has an operative HIRL system.
C— RVR minimums may be disregarded, providing all other components of the ILS system are operative.

Answer (A) is correct (4716).  *(FAR 91.175)*
*This question is a duplicate of FAA question 4759.*
If RVR minimums for takeoff or landing are prescribed in an instrument approach procedure, but RVR is inoperative and cannot be reported for the runway of intended operation, the RVR minimum shall be converted to ground visibility and shall be the visibility minimum for takeoff or landing on that runway.
Answer (B) is incorrect because RVR minimums must be converted to ground visibility (not disregarded).  Answer (C) is incorrect because RVR minimums must be converted to ground visibility (not disregarded).

**14.**
**4762.** If the RVR equipment is inoperative for an IAP that requires a visibility of 2400 RVR, how should the pilot expect the visibility requirement to be reported in lieu of the published RVR?

A— As a slant range visibility of 2,400 feet.
B— As an RVR of 2,400 feet.
C— As a ground visibility of ½ SM.

Answer (C) is correct (4762). *(FAR 91.175)*
Refer to Legend 13 on page 246 for a chart of RVR/visibility comparable values. An RVR of 2,400 ft. may be converted to ½ SM visibility when the RVR is not reported.
Answer (A) is incorrect because RVR is a horizontal (not slant range) visibility. Answer (B) is incorrect because RVR cannot be reported if the RVR equipment is inoperative. It must be converted to ground visibility.

**15.**
**4754.** If the RVR is not reported, what meteorological value should you substitute for 2400 RVR?

A— A ground visibility of ½ NM.
B— A slant range visibility of 2,400 feet for the final approach segment of the published approach procedure.
C— A ground visibility of ½ SM.

Answer (C) is correct (4754). *(FAR 91.175)*
Refer to Legend 13 on page 246 for a chart of RVR/visibility comparable values. An RVR of 2,400 ft. may be converted to ½ SM visibility when the RVR is not reported.
Answer (A) is incorrect because RVR is converted into statute (not nautical) miles. Answer (B) is incorrect because when RVR is not reported, ground visibility (not slant range visibility on approach) is substituted.

## 9.4 Missed Approaches

**16.**
**4667.** If an early missed approach is initiated before reaching the MAP, the following procedure should be used unless otherwise cleared by ATC.

A— Proceed to the missed approach point at or above the MDA or DH before executing a turning maneuver.
B— Begin a climbing turn immediately and follow missed approach procedures.
C— Maintain altitude and continue past MAP for 1 minute or 1 mile whichever occurs first.

Answer (A) is correct (4667). *(AIM Para 5-57)*
When an early missed approach is executed, the pilot should, unless otherwise directed by ATC, fly the IAP as specified on the approach plate to the missed approach point at or above the MDA or DH before executing a turning maneuver.
Answer (B) is incorrect because one should continue to the MAP before executing any turns. Answer (C) is incorrect because one need only continue to (not past) the MAP.

**17.**
**4631.** If the pilot loses visual reference while circling to land from an instrument approach and ATC radar service is not available, the missed approach action should be to

A— execute a climbing turn to parallel the published final approach course and climb to the initial approach altitude.
B— climb to the published circling minimums then proceed direct to the final approach fix.
C— make a climbing turn toward the landing runway and continue the turn until established on the missed approach course.

Answer (C) is correct (4631). *(AIM Para 5-57)*
If visual reference is lost while circling to land, the missed approach specified for that particular procedure must be followed. To become established on the prescribed missed approach course, the pilot should make an initial climbing turn toward the landing runway and continue the turn until established on the missed approach course.
Answer (A) is incorrect because the climbing turn should be toward the landing runway and then execute the published missed approach procedures. Answer (B) is incorrect because there should be a climbing turn toward the landing runway.

## 9.5 ILS Specifications

**18.**
**4744.** If all ILS components are operating and the required visual references are not established, the missed approach should be initiated upon

A— arrival at the DH on the glide slope.
B— arrival at the middle marker.
C— expiration of the time listed on the approach chart for missed approach.

Answer (A) is correct (4744). *(FAR 91.175)*
The missed approach procedure should be executed upon arrival at the decision height (DH) on the glide slope if the visual reference requirements are not met. Thus, DH on an ILS is the MAP.
Answer (B) is incorrect because the DH rather than the middle marker is the MAP. Answer (C) is incorrect because the time listed on the approach chart for missed approaches is used in conjunction with the localizer for a timed approach if the glide slope fails during the ILS approach; i.e., it is not the primary indicator.

**19.**
**4763.** If during an ILS approach in IFR conditions, the approach lights are not visible upon arrival at the DH, the pilot is

A— required to immediately execute the missed approach procedure.
B— permitted to continue the approach and descend to the localizer MDA.
C— permitted to continue the approach to the approach threshold of the ILS runway.

Answer (A) is correct (4763).  *(FAR 91.175)*
The missed approach procedure should be executed upon arrival at the decision height (DH) on the glide slope if the visual reference requirements are not met. Thus, the DH on an ILS is the MAP.
Answer (B) is incorrect because the DH is the MAP on an ILS, which is lower than the localizer MDA. Answer (C) is incorrect because the pilot may only continue the approach below the DH if the required visual references (e.g., approach lights) are established.

**20.**
**4669.** How does a pilot determine if DME is available on an ILS/LOC?

A— IAP indicate DME\TACAN channel in LOC frequency box.
B— LOC\DME are indicated on en route low altitude frequency box.
C— LOC\DME frequencies available in the Airman's Information Manual.

Answer (A) is correct (4669).  *(IFH Chap X)*
If DME is available on an ILS or localizer approach, the DME/TACAN channel will be indicated in the localizer frequency box on the approach plate.
Answer (B) is incorrect because LOC/DME frequencies are available on approach plates (not en route charts).  Answer (C) is incorrect because the AIM gives general information (not specific frequencies).

**21.**
**4753.** Approximately what height is the glide slope centerline at the MM of a typical ILS?

A— 100 feet.
B— 200 feet.
C— 300 feet.

Answer (B) is correct (4753).  *(AIM Para 1-10)*
The ILS glide path projection angle is normally 3° above horizontal so it intersects the middle marker (MM) at 200 ft. and the outer marker (OM) at about 1,400 ft. above the touchdown zone elevation (TDZE).
Answer (A) is incorrect because the glide slope centerline at the inner (not middle) marker on a Category II ILS is at 100 ft. above the TDZE.  Answer (C) is incorrect because the glide slope centerline at the MM is usually 200 ft. AGL (not 300 ft).

**22.**
**4824.** (Refer to figures 139 and 140 on page 265.) Which displacement from the localizer and glide slope at the 1.9 NM point is indicated?

A— 710 feet to the left of the localizer centerline and 140 feet below the glide slope.
B— 710 feet to the right of the localizer centerline and 140 feet above the glide slope.
C— 430 feet to the right of the localizer centerline and 28 feet above the glide slope.

Answer (B) is correct (4824).  *(AIM Para 1-10)*
The airplane is to the right of the localizer and above the glide slope each by 2 dots at 1.9 NM out.  Per Fig. 139, 2 dots at 1.9 NM are 140 ft. above the glide slope and 710 ft. to the right of the localizer.
Answer (A) is incorrect because the airplane is to the right (not left) of the localizer and above (not below) the glide slope.  Answer (C) is incorrect because the 430 ft. and 28 ft. deviations are at 1,300 ft., not 1.9 NM.

**23.**
**4825.** (Refer to figures 139 and 141 on page 265.) Which displacement from the localizer centerline and glide slope at the 1,300-foot point from the runway is indicated?

A— 21 feet below the glide slope and approximately 320 feet to the right of the runway centerline.
B— 28 feet above the glide slope and approximately 250 feet to the left of the runway centerline.
C— 21 feet above the glide slope and approximately 320 feet to the left of the runway centerline.

Answer (C) is correct (4825).  *(AIM Para 1-10)*
The airplane is above the glide slope and to the left of the localizer by 1½ dots each at 1,300 ft. out.  Per extrapolation and Fig. 139, this is 21 ft. above the glide slope and about 320 ft. to the left of the localizer.
Answer (A) is incorrect because the airplane is above (not below) the glide slope, and to the left (not right) of the localizer.  Answer (B) is incorrect because 28 ft. is 2 dots, and 250 ft. is less than 1¼ dots.

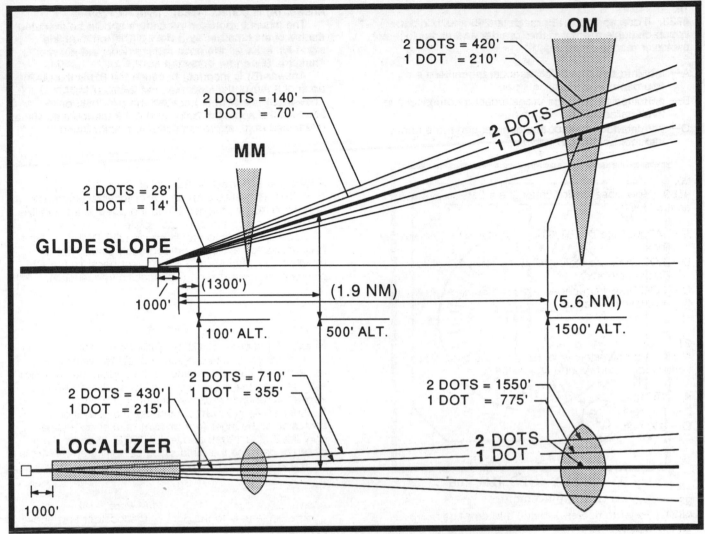

FIGURE 139.—Glide Slope and Localizer Illustration.

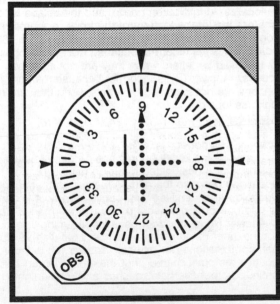

FIGURE 140.—OBS, ILS, and
GS Displacement.

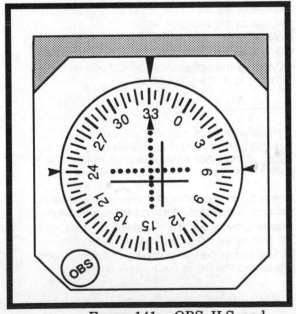

FIGURE 141.—OBS, ILS, and
GS Displacement.

**24.**
**4826.** (Refer to figure 139 on page 265 and 142 below.) Which displacement from the localizer and glide slope at the outer marker is indicated?

A— 1,550 feet to the left of the localizer centerline and 210 feet below the glide slope.
B— 1,550 feet to the right of the localizer centerline and 210 feet above the glide slope.
C— 775 feet to the left of the localizer centerline and 420 feet below the glide slope.

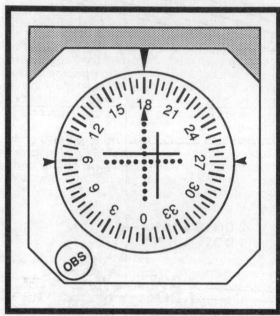

FIGURE 142.—OBS, ILS, and GS Displacement.

**25.**
**4729.** Which range facility associated with the ILS is identified by the last two letters of the localizer identification group?

A— Inner marker.
B— Outer marker.
C— Middle compass locator.

**26.**
**4747.** Which indications will a pilot receive where an IM is installed on a front course ILS approach?

A— One dot per second and a steady amber light.
B— Six dots per second and a flashing white light.
C— Alternate dashes and a blue light.

Answer (A) is correct (4826). *(AIM Para 1-10)*
The airplane is below the glide slope by 1 dot and to the left of the localizer by 2 dots at the outer marker. Per Fig. 139, 1 dot on the glide slope is 210 ft. at the outer marker (OM), and 2 dots on the localizer is 1,550 ft.
Answer (B) is incorrect because the airplane is to the left (not right) of the localizer, and below (not above) the glide slope. Answer (C) is incorrect because at the OM 775 ft. is 1 dot on the localizer, not the glide slope, and 420 ft. is 2 dots on the glide slope, not the localizer.

Answer (C) is correct (4729). *(AIM Para 1-10)*
Compass locators transmit two letter identification groups. The outer locator transmits the first two letters of the localizer identification group, and the middle locator transmits the last two letters of the localizer identification group.
Answer (A) is incorrect because marker beacons are not identified by letters when they are not compass locators. Answer (B) is incorrect because marker beacons are not identified by letters when they are not compass locators.

Answer (B) is correct (4747). *(AIM Para 1-10)*
The inner marker (IM) indicates a point at which an airplane is at a designated decision height (DH) on the glide slope between the middle marker and the landing threshold. It is identified with continuous dots keyed at the rate of 6 dots per second and a white marker beacon.
Answer (A) is incorrect because the middle marker (not the inner marker) has an amber light with 95 dot-dash combinations per minute. Answer (C) is incorrect because the outer marker (not the inner marker) has continuous (not alternate) dashes and a blue light.

**27.**
**4730.** Which range facility associated with the ILS can be identified by a two-letter coded signal?

A— Middle marker.
B— Outer marker.
C— Compass locator.

Answer (C) is correct (4730). (AIM Para 1-10)
Each compass locator (middle and outer) is identified by a two-letter coded signal.
Answer (A) is incorrect because marker beacons are not identified by letters when they are not a compass locator. Answer (B) is incorrect because marker beacons are not identified by letters when they are not a compass locator.

### 9.6 Unusable ILS Components

**28.**
**4731.** Which pilot action is appropriate if more than one component of an ILS is unusable?

A— Use the highest minimum required by any single component that is unusable.
B— Request another approach appropriate to the equipment that is useable.
C— Raise the minimums a total of that required by each component that is unusable.

Answer (A) is correct (4731). (AIM Para 1-10)
Landing minimums published on instrument approach procedure charts are based upon full operation of all components and the use of visual aids associated with the particular instrument approach chart. Higher visibility minimums are required with inoperative components or visual aids as specified in FAA tables. If more than one component is inoperative, each minimum is raised to the highest minimum required by any single component that is inoperative.
Answer (B) is incorrect because an ILS has many components, one or more of which may be inoperative and the approach is still usable. Answer (C) is incorrect because it is not cumulative; you need only use the highest minimum required as a result of any one component's being unusable.

**29.**
**4732.** Which substitution is permitted when an ILS component is inoperative?

A— A compass locator or precision radar may be substituted for the ILS outer or middle marker.
B— ADF or VOR bearings which cross either the outer or middle marker sites may be substituted for these markers.
C— DME, when located at the localizer antenna site, should be substituted for the outer or middle marker.

Answer (A) is correct (4732). (FAR 91.175)
A compass locator or precision radar may be substituted for an inoperative outer or middle marker. Compass locators, precision radar, DME, VOR, or nondirectional fixes authorized in the standard instrument approach or surveillance radar may be substituted for an inoperative outer marker.
Answer (B) is incorrect because ADF and VOR bearings can be substituted for the outer marker but not the middle marker. Answer (C) is incorrect because DME can be substituted for the outer marker but not the middle marker.

**30.**
**4733.** What facilities, if any, may be substituted for an inoperative middle marker during an ILS approach without affecting the straight-in minimums?

A— ASR.
B— Substitution not necessary, minimums do not change.
C— Compass locator, PAR, and ASR.

Answer (B) is correct (4733). (FAR 91.175)
Refer to Legend 20, Inoperative Components or Visual Aids Table, on page 252. Note that an inoperative middle marker (MM) is not listed as an inoperative ILS component that would require an increase in the visibility minimum. While a compass locator or PAR may be substituted for an inoperative MM, no substitution is necessary since the landing minimums are not changed.
Answer (A) is incorrect because no substitution is necessary for an inoperative MM since the landing minimums do not change. Answer (C) is incorrect because no substitution is necessary for an inoperative MM since the landing minimums do not change.

**31.**
**4742.** Which of these facilities may be substituted for an MM during a complete ILS IAP?

A— Surveillance and precision radar.
B— Compass locator and precision radar.
C— A VOR/DME fix.

Answer (B) is correct (4742). (FAR 91.175)
Compass locators or precision radar may be substituted for the outer or middle marker.
Answer (A) is incorrect because airport surveillance radar may be substituted for the outer marker but not the middle marker. Answer (C) is incorrect because a VOR/DME fix authorized in the standard instrument approach may only be substituted for the outer marker.

**32.**

**4664.** When installed with the ILS and specified in the approach procedures, DME may be used

A— in lieu of the OM.
B— in lieu of visibility requirements.
C— to determine distance from TDZ.

Answer (A) is correct (4664). *(AIM Para 1-10)*
When installed with the ILS and specified in the approach procedure, DME may be used in lieu of the outer marker (OM).
Answer (B) is incorrect because DME has no effect on visibility requirements. Answer (C) is incorrect because touchdown zone (TDZ) is the first 3,000 ft. of the runway, not a specific point.

**33.**

**4770.** Which substitution is appropriate during an ILS approach?

A— A VOR radial crossing the outer marker site may be substituted for the outer marker.
B— LOC minimums should be substituted for ILS minimums whenever the glide slope becomes inoperative.
C— DME, when located at the localizer antenna site, should be substituted for either the outer or middle marker.

Answer (B) is correct (4770). *(AIM Para 1-10)*
When the glide slope becomes inoperative, the approach becomes a localizer approach and the LOC minimums apply.
Answer (A) is incorrect because a VOR radial must be authorized in the standard approach procedure to be used as a substitute. Answer (C) is incorrect because DME can be substituted for the outer marker, but not the middle marker.

**34.**

**4764.** Immediately after passing the final approach fix inbound during an ILS approach in IFR conditions, the glide slope warning flag appears. The pilot is

A— permitted to continue the approach and descend to the DH.
B— permitted to continue the approach and descend to the localizer MDA.
C— required to immediately begin the prescribed missed approach procedure.

Answer (B) is correct (4764). *(AIM Para 1-10)*
When the glide slope fails, the ILS reverts to a nonprecision localizer approach. Accordingly, if the glide slope fails on an ILS approach, the pilot may switch to the localizer approach and descend to the localizer MDA (minimum descent altitude).
Answer (A) is incorrect because, once the glide slope is inoperative, the localizer may only be used for a nonprecision approach which has MDA, not DH. Answer (C) is incorrect because one should execute the missed approach procedure only after reaching the missed approach point.

**35.**

**4706.** A pilot is making an ILS approach and is past the OM to a runway which has a VASI. What action should the pilot take if an electronic glide slope malfunction occurs and the pilot has the VASI in sight?

A— The pilot should inform ATC of the malfunction and then descend immediately to the localizer DH and make a localizer approach.
B— The pilot may continue the approach and use the VASI glide slope in place of the electronic glide slope.
C— The pilot must request an LOC approach, and may descend below the VASI at the pilot's discretion.

Answer (B) is correct (4706). *(FAR 91.175)*
Once the necessary specified visual requirements, e.g., the VASI, are attained for the intended runway, the pilot may continue the approach and use the VASI in place of the electronic glide slope.
Answer (A) is incorrect because, once the pilot has the necessary visual references, the approach may be continued visually. Answer (C) is incorrect because, once the pilot has the necessary visual references, the approach may be continued visually. Descent below the VASI glide path shall only occur when necessary for a safe landing.

## 9.7 Flying the Approach

**36.**

**4752.** The rate of descent on the glide slope is dependent upon

A— true airspeed.
B— calibrated airspeed.
C— groundspeed.

Answer (C) is correct (4752). *(IFH Chap VIII)*
The rate of descent required to stay on the ILS glide slope depends on the groundspeed because the descent must be constant relative to the distance traveled over the ground. Thus, the descent must be decreased if groundspeed is decreased.
Answer (A) is incorrect because the rate of descent is based on groundspeed (not true airspeed). Answer (B) is incorrect because the rate of descent is based on groundspeed (not calibrated airspeed).

**37.**
**4745.** The rate of descent required to stay on the ILS glide slope

A— must be increased if the groundspeed is decreased.
B— will remain constant if the indicated airspeed remains constant.
C— must be decreased if the groundspeed is decreased.

Answer (C) is correct (4745). *(IFH Chap VIII)*
The rate of descent required to stay on the ILS glide slope is dependent on the groundspeed because the descent must be constant relative to the distance traveled over the ground. Thus, the descent must be decreased if groundspeed is decreased.
Answer (A) is incorrect because, if groundspeed decreases and descent increases, the airplane will go below the glide slope. Answer (B) is incorrect because groundspeed rather than airspeed determines the rate of descent.

**38.**
**4748.** To remain on the ILS glidepath, the rate of descent must be

A— decreased if the airspeed is increased.
B— decreased if the groundspeed is increased.
C— increased if the groundspeed is increased.

Answer (C) is correct (4748). *(IFH Chap VIII)*
The rate of descent required to stay on the ILS glide slope depends on the groundspeed because the descent must be constant relative to the distance traveled over the ground. Thus, the descent must be increased if groundspeed is increased.
Answer (A) is incorrect because the rate of descent must be based upon groundspeed, not airspeed, while on the glide slope. Answer (B) is incorrect because, if one decreases the rate of descent with groundspeed increasing, the airplane will rise above the glide slope.

**39.**
**4720.** When passing through an abrupt wind shear which involves a shift from a tailwind to a headwind, what power management would normally be required to maintain a constant indicated airspeed and ILS glide slope?

A— Higher than normal power initially, followed by a further increase as the wind shear is encountered, then a decrease.
B— Lower than normal power initially, followed by a further decrease as the wind shear is encountered, then an increase.
C— Higher than normal power initially, followed by a decrease as the shear is encountered, then an increase.

Answer (B) is correct (4720). *(AC 00-54)*
When on the ILS and there is a change from a tailwind to a headwind, the groundspeed will decrease. During the tailwind, lower than normal power will be required. When the wind shear is encountered, even lower power will be required to decrease the spurt in airspeed. Once into the headwind, an increase in power is required to maintain the necessary groundspeed to stay on the glide slope.
Answer (A) is incorrect because initially there is lower (not higher) than normal power with a tailwind, and when the headwind is encountered, a decrease (not an increase) in power is required. Answer (C) is incorrect because initially there is lower (not higher) than normal power with a tailwind.

**40.**
**4721.** What effect will a change in wind direction have upon maintaining a 3° glide slope at a constant true airspeed?

A— When groundspeed decreases, rate of descent must increase.
B— When groundspeed increases, rate of descent must increase.
C— Rate of descent must be constant to remain on the glide slope.

Answer (B) is correct (4721). *(IFH Chap VIII)*
The rate of descent required to stay on the ILS glide slope is dependent on the groundspeed because the descent must be constant relative to the distance traveled over the ground. Thus, the descent must be increased if groundspeed is increased.
Answer (A) is incorrect because, if you increase the rate of descent when the groundspeed decreases, you will fly below the glide slope. Answer (C) is incorrect because the rate of descent must change with changes in groundspeed.

**41.**
**4756.** The glide slope and localizer are centered, but the airspeed is too fast. Which should be adjusted initially?

A— Pitch and power.
B— Power only.
C— Pitch only.

Answer (B) is correct (4756). *(IFH Chap VIII)*
If the glide slope and localizer are centered but the airspeed is too fast, you should reduce power initially. Almost immediately, you will then have to make pitch adjustments to compensate for the power adjustment to maintain the glidepath.
Answer (A) is incorrect because, although the pitch and power adjustments must be closely coordinated, the power is actually adjusted first. Answer (C) is incorrect because adjusting pitch initially would cause you to fly above the glide path.

**42.**
**4757.** While being vectored, if crossing the ILS final approach course becomes imminent and an approach clearance has not been issued, what action should be taken by the pilot?

A— Turn outbound on the final approach course, execute a procedure turn, and inform ATC.
B— Turn inbound and execute the missed approach procedure at the outer marker if approach clearance has not been received.
C— Maintain the last assigned heading and query ATC.

Answer (C) is correct (4757). *(AIM Para 5-43)*
While being vectored, if you determine that crossing the final approach course is imminent and you have not been informed that you will be vectored across it, you should question the controller. You should not turn inbound on the final approach course unless you have received an approach clearance.
Answer (A) is incorrect because you should maintain the last assigned heading until you receive an amended clearance. When in doubt, query ATC. Answer (B) is incorrect because you should maintain the last assigned heading until you receive an amended clearance. When in doubt, query ATC.

**43.**
**4739.** Thrust is managed to maintain IAS, and glide slope is being flown. What characteristics should be observed when a headwind shears to be a constant tailwind?

A— PITCH ATTITUDE: Increases; REQUIRED THRUST: Increased, then reduced; VERTICAL SPEED: Increases; IAS: Increases, then decreases to approach speed.
B— PITCH ATTITUDE: Decreases; REQUIRED THRUST: Increased, then reduced; VERTICAL SPEED: Increases; IAS: Decreases, then increases to approach speed.
C— PITCH ATTITUDE: Increases; REQUIRED THRUST: Reduced, then increased; VERTICAL SPEED: Decreases; IAS: Decreases, then increases to approach speed.

Answer (B) is correct (4739). *(AC 00-54)*
When a headwind shears to a tailwind, the airspeed drops, the nose pitches down, and the vertical speed increases. The power must be increased initially to resume normal approach speed, then reduced as airspeed stabilizes to maintain the glide slope due to the increased groundspeed.
Answer (A) is incorrect because the airspeed decreases (not increases) initially as the headwind shears to a tailwind, causing the pitch to decrease (not increase). Answer (C) is incorrect because the pitch attitude decreases (not increases) due to the decreased airspeed, causing the vertical speed to increase (not decrease). The thrust must be increased (not decreased) initially to maintain approach airspeed.

**44.**
**4727.** While flying a 3° glide slope, a constant tailwind shears to a calm wind. Which conditions should the pilot expect?

A— Airspeed and pitch attitude decrease and there is a tendency to go below glide slope.
B— Airspeed and pitch attitude increase and there is a tendency to go below glide slope.
C— Airspeed and pitch attitude increase and there is a tendency to go above glide slope.

Answer (C) is correct (4727). *(AC 00-54)*
When a constant tailwind shears to a calm wind, the airspeed increases, the nose pitches up, and there is a tendency to go above the glide slope. The nose pitches up due to the increased lift from the increased airspeed.
Answer (A) is incorrect because the airspeed and pitch increase (not decrease) and there is a tendency to go above (not below) the glide slope. Answer (B) is incorrect because the tendency is to go above (not below) the glide slope.

**45.**
**4755.** While flying a 3° glide slope, a headwind shears to a tailwind. Which conditions should the pilot expect on the glide slope?

A— Airspeed and pitch attitude decrease and there is a tendency to go below glide slope.
B— Airspeed and pitch attitude increase and there is a tendency to go above glide slope.
C— Airspeed and pitch attitude decrease and there is a tendency to remain on the glide slope.

Answer (A) is correct (4755). *(AC 00-54)*
When a headwind shears to a tailwind, the airspeed drops, the nose pitches down, and the aircraft will begin to drop below the glide slope. The aircraft will be both slow and power deficient.
Answer (B) is incorrect because airspeed and pitch decrease (not increase) and there is a tendency to go below (not above) the glide slope. Answer (C) is incorrect because there is a tendency to go below (not remain on) the glide slope.

**46.**
**4772.** During a precision radar or ILS approach, the rate of descent required to remain on the glide slope will

A— remain the same regardless of groundspeed.
B— increase as the groundspeed increases.
C— decrease as the groundspeed increases.

Answer (B) is correct (4772). *(IFH Chap VIII)*
The rate of descent required to stay on the ILS glide slope is dependent on the groundspeed because the descent must be constant relative to the distance traveled over the ground. Thus, the descent must be increased if groundspeed is increased.
Answer (A) is incorrect because the descent rate varies with the groundspeed. Answer (C) is incorrect because the descent rate must increase (not decrease) as groundspeed increases.

**47.**
**4773.** When tracking inbound on the localizer, which of the following is the proper procedure regarding drift corrections?

A— Drift corrections should be accurately established before reaching the outer marker and completion of the approach should be accomplished with heading corrections no greater than 2°.
B— Drift corrections should be made in 5° increments after passing the outer marker.
C— Drift corrections should be made in 10° increments after passing the outer marker.

Answer (A) is correct (4773). *(IFH Chap VIII)*
When tracking inbound on the localizer, drift correction should be small and reduced proportionately as the course narrows. By the time you reach the outer marker, your drift correction should be established accurately enough to permit completion of the approach with heading corrections no greater than 2°.
Answer (B) is incorrect because, after passing the outer marker, drift corrections should be no greater than 2° (not 5°). Answer (C) is incorrect because, after passing the outer marker, drift corrections should be no greater than 2° (not 10°).

## 9.8 ASR Approaches

**48.**
**4741.** Which information, in addition to headings, does the radar controller provide without request during an ASR approach?

A— The recommended altitude for each mile from the runway.
B— When reaching the MDA.
C— When to commence descent to MDA, the aircraft's position each mile on final from the runway, and arrival at the MAP.

Answer (C) is correct (4741). *(AIM Para 5-50)*
A surveillance approach (ASR) provides navigation guidance in azimuths (direction) only. The pilot is furnished headings to align the airplane with the extended centerline of the landing runway and will be advised when to commence descent to the MDA and the MAP. In addition, the pilot will be advised of the airplane's position each mile on the final approach from the runway or MAP as appropriate.
Answer (A) is incorrect because the recommended altitude for each mile from the runway is only provided upon request. Answer (B) is incorrect because the controller does not have precise altitude capability.

**49.**
**4711.** Where may you use a surveillance approach?

A— At any airport that has an approach control.
B— At any airport which has radar service.
C— At airports for which civil radar instrument approach minimums have been published.

Answer (C) is correct (4711). *(AIM Para 5-50)*
ASR (surveillance) approaches are available at airports for which radar instrument approach minimums have been published and a separate approach chart is available. That is, a surveillance approach must have previously been authorized and established by the FAA for a particular runway at a particular airport prior to its availability.
Answer (A) is incorrect because specific procedures, minimums, missed approach points, etc., must be established before a surveillance approach can be conducted by ATC. Answer (B) is incorrect because specific procedures, minimums, missed approach points, etc., must be established before a surveillance approach can be conducted by ATC.

**50.**
**4728.** How is ATC radar used for instrument approaches when the facility is approved for approach control service?

A— Precision approaches, weather surveillance, and as a substitute for any inoperative component of a navigation aid used for approaches.

B— ASR approaches, weather surveillance, and course guidance by approach control.

C— Course guidance to the final approach course, ASR and PAR approaches, and the monitoring of nonradar approaches.

**51.**
**4822.** During a "no-gyro" approach and prior to being handed off to the final approach controller, the pilot should make all turns

A— one-half standard rate unless otherwise advised.

B— any rate not exceeding a 30° bank.

C— standard rate unless otherwise advised.

**52.**
**4823.** After being handed off to the final approach controller during a "no-gyro" surveillance or precision approach, the pilot should make all turns

A— one-half standard rate.

B— based upon the groundspeed of the aircraft.

C— standard rate.

## 9.9 Side-Step Approaches

**53.**
**4740.** When cleared to execute a published sidestep maneuver for a specific approach and landing on the parallel runway, at what point is the pilot expected to commence this maneuver?

A— At the published minimum altitude for a circling approach.

B— As soon as possible after the runway or runway environment is in sight.

C— At the localizer MDA minimum and when the runway is in sight.

Answer (C) is correct (4728). *(AIM Para 5-43)*
Where radar is approved for approach control service, it is used not only for radar approaches but also to provide vectors in conjunction with published nonradar approaches based on radio NAVAIDs.
Answer (A) is incorrect because approach control radar is not designed for weather surveillance.
Answer (B) is incorrect because approach control radar is not designed for weather surveillance.

Answer (C) is correct (4822). *(AIM Para 5-50)*
During "no-gyro" approaches prior to the final approach, all turns should be made at the standard rate unless otherwise advised by ATC.
Answer (A) is incorrect because a one-half standard rate turn should be used in conjunction with the final approach controller. Answer (B) is incorrect because the turn should be at the standard rate unless otherwise advised.

Answer (A) is correct (4823). *(AIM Para 5-50)*
After being handed off to the final approach controller on a "no-gyro" surveillance or precision approach, all turns should be at one-half standard rate.
Answer (B) is incorrect because the established procedure is one-half standard rate turns regardless of groundspeed. Answer (C) is incorrect because a standard rate turn should be used on "no-gyro" approaches prior to working with the final approach controller.

Answer (B) is correct (4740). *(AIM Para 5-55)*
Pilots are expected to commence the side-step maneuver as soon as possible after the runway or runway environment is in sight.
Answer (A) is incorrect because the side-step maneuver should be performed only when the runway environment is in sight. Answer (C) is incorrect because the side-step maneuver should be performed as soon as the runway environment is in sight, which may be before reaching the MDA.

**54.**
**4771.** Assume this clearance is received:

"CLEARED FOR ILS RUNWAY 07 LEFT APPROACH, SIDE-STEP TO RUNWAY 07 RIGHT."

When would the pilot be expected to commence the side-step maneuver?

A— As soon as possible after the runway environment is in sight.
B— Any time after becoming aligned with the final approach course of Runway 07 left, and after passing the final approach fix.
C— After reaching the circling minimums for Runway 07 right.

### 9.10 Timed Approaches from Holding Fixes

**55.**
**4768.** Which of the following conditions is required before "timed approaches from a holding fix" may be conducted?

A— If more than one missed approach procedure is available, only one may require a course reversal.
B— If more than one missed approach procedure is available, none may require a course reversal.
C— Direct communication between the pilot and the tower must be established prior to beginning the approach.

**56.**
**4627.** If only one missed approach procedure is available, which of the following conditions is required when conducting "timed approaches from a holding fix"?

A— The pilot must contact the airport control tower prior to departing the holding fix inbound.
B— The reported ceiling and visibility minimums must be equal to or greater than the highest prescribed circling minimums for the IAP.
C— The reported ceiling and visibility minimums must be equal to or greater than the highest prescribed straight-in MDA minimums for the IAP.

**57.**
**4628.** Prior to conducting "timed approaches from a holding fix," which one of the following is required?

A— The time required to fly from the primary facility to the field boundary must be determined by a reliable means.
B— The airport where the approach is to be conducted must have a control tower in operation.
C— The pilot must have established two-way communications with the tower before departing the holding fix.

Answer (A) is correct (4771). *(AIM Para 5-55)*
Pilots are expected to commence the side-step maneuver as soon as possible after the runway or runway environment is in sight.
Answer (B) is incorrect because the side-step maneuver can only be performed and should be performed as soon as possible after the runway or runway environment is in sight. Answer (C) is incorrect because the side-step maneuver can only be performed and should be performed as soon as possible after the runway or runway environment is in sight.

Answer (B) is correct (4768). *(AIM Para 5-49)*
Timed approaches from a holding fix may be conducted when a control tower is in operation at the airport of intended landing and direct communications are maintained between the pilot and center approach until switching to the tower. Course reversals are not permitted when more than one missed approach procedure exists.
Answer (A) is incorrect because no course reversals are permitted on missed approach procedure if more than one missed approach procedure is available. Answer (C) is incorrect because, prior to beginning the approach, the pilot must be in contact with approach, not the tower.

Answer (B) is correct (4627). *(AIM Para 5-49)*
If only one missed approach procedure is available, the reported ceiling and visibility must be equal to or greater than the highest prescribed circling minimums for the IAP.
Answer (A) is incorrect because the pilot contacts the tower when so directed by approach or center.
Answer (C) is incorrect because the ceiling and visibility minimums must exceed the highest circling (not straight-in) minimums.

Answer (B) is correct (4628). *(AIM Para 5-49)*
One requirement for timed approaches is that the airport where the approach is to be conducted must have a control tower in operation.
Answer (A) is incorrect because the times to fly from the holding fix to the runway at various groundspeeds are provided on approach plates. Answer (C) is incorrect because the pilot must be in communication with approach or center until told to switch to the tower.

**58.**
**4629.** When making a "timed approach" from a holding fix at the outer marker, the pilot should adjust the

A— holding pattern to start the procedure turn at the assigned time.

B— airspeed at the final approach fix in order to arrive at the missed approach point at the assigned time.

C— holding pattern to leave the final approach fix inbound at the assigned time.

Answer (C) is correct (4629).  *(AIM Para 5-49)*
The pilot should adjust the holding pattern to leave the final approach fix inbound at the assigned time.
Answer (A) is incorrect because, in timed approaches, the pilot will not execute a procedure turn unless cleared to do so by ATC.  Answer (B) is incorrect because the assigned time is the departure time from the final approach fix, not the arrival time at the MAP.

### 9.11  Holding

**59.**
**4620.** At what point should the timing begin for the first leg outbound in a nonstandard holding pattern?

A— Abeam the holding fix, or wings level, whichever occurs last.

B— When the wings are level at the completion of the 180° turn outbound.

C— When abeam the holding fix.

Answer (C) is correct (4620).  *(IFH Chap XII)*
Outbound leg timing begins over/abeam the fix, whichever occurs later.  If the abeam position cannot be determined, start timing when the turn to outbound is completed (i.e., wings return to level).
Answer (A) is incorrect because timing begins on the outbound leg when the wings are level only if the abeam position cannot be determined.  Answer (B) is incorrect because the wings may be level before you are abeam the fix.

**60.**
**4618.** (Refer to figure 115 below.)  You receive this ATC clearance:

"...HOLD WEST OF THE ONE FIVE DME FIX ON THE ZERO EIGHT SIX RADIAL OF ABC VORTAC, FIVE MILE LEGS, LEFT TURNS..."

You arrive at the 15 DME fix on a heading of 350°.  Which holding pattern correctly complies with these instructions, and what is the recommended entry procedure?

A— 1; teardrop.

B— 2; direct.

C— 1; direct.

Answer (C) is correct (4618).  *(AIM Para 5-37)*
Holding pattern 1 is correct because the holding fix is always at the end of the inbound leg.  Draw the 70° line through the fix such that it intersects the outbound leg 1/3 of the leg length from abeam the fix.

| Heading | Entry |
| --- | --- |
| 336° to 156° | Direct |
| 156° to 266° | Parallel |
| 266° to 336° | Teardrop |

A 350° heading to the fix requires a direct entry, which requires a standard rate left turn to 266° beginning over the holding fix.
Answer (A) is incorrect because approaching the fix on a heading of 350° requires a direct (not teardrop) entry.  Answer (B) is incorrect because holding pattern 2 does not show the holding fix at the end of the inbound leg.

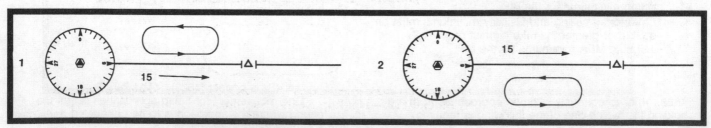

FIGURE 115.—DME Fix with Holding Pattern.

**61.**
**4609.** (Refer to figure 112 below.) You arrive at the 15 DME fix on a heading of 350°. Which holding pattern correctly complies with the ATC clearance below, and what is the recommended entry procedure?

"...HOLD WEST OF THE ONE FIVE DME FIX ON THE ZERO EIGHT SIX RADIAL OF THE ABC VORTAC, FIVE MILE LEGS, LEFT TURNS..."

A— 1; teardrop entry.
B— 1; direct entry.
C— 2; direct entry.

Answer (B) is correct (4609). *(AIM Para 5-57)*
Holding pattern 1 is correct because the holding fix is always at the end of the inbound leg. Draw the 70° line through the fix such that it intersects the outbound leg 1/3 of the leg length from abeam the fix.

| Heading | Entry |
|---|---|
| 336° to 156° | Direct |
| 156° to 266° | Parallel |
| 266° to 336° | Teardrop |

A 350° heading to the fix requires a direct entry, which requires a standard rate left turn to 266° beginning over the holding fix.
Answer (A) is incorrect because approaching the fix on a heading of 350° requires a direct (not teardrop) entry. Answer (C) is incorrect because holding pattern 2 does not show the holding fix at the end of the inbound leg.

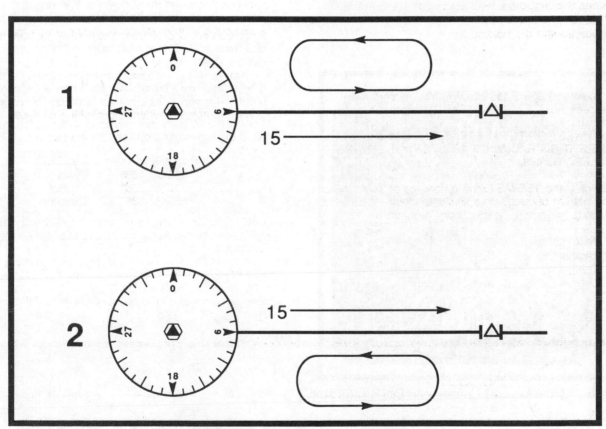

FIGURE 112.—Holding Entry Procedure.

**62.**
**4617.** To ensure proper airspace protection while in a holding pattern, what is the recommended maximum airspeed above 14,000 feet?

A— 220 knots.
B— 265 knots.
C— 200 knots.

Answer (B) is correct (4617). *(AIM Para 5-37)*
*This question is a duplicate of FAA question 4766.*
The maximum airspeed above 14,000 ft. MSL for holding patterns is 265 kt. indicated in civil turbojets. For all propeller planes, it is 175 kt. maximum.
Answer (A) is incorrect because 220 kt. is not a maximum holding airspeed. Answer (C) is incorrect because 200 kt. is not a maximum holding airspeed.

**63.**
**4766.** To ensure proper airspace protection while in a holding pattern, what is the recommended maximum indicated airspeed above 14,000 feet?

A— 220 knots.
B— 265 knots.
C— 200 knots.

**64.**
**4614.** (Refer to figure 114 below.) A pilot receives this ATC clearance:

"...CLEARED TO THE ABC VORTAC. HOLD WEST ON THE TWO SEVEN ZERO RADIAL..."

What is the recommended procedure to enter the holding pattern?

A— Parallel or teardrop.
B— Parallel only.
C— Direct only.

Figure 114.—Aircraft Course and DME Indicator.

**65.**
**4615.** (Refer to figure 114 above.) A pilot receives this ATC clearance:

"...CLEARED TO THE XYZ VORTAC. HOLD NORTH ON THE THREE SIX ZERO RADIAL, LEFT TURNS..."

What is the recommended procedure to enter the holding pattern?

A— Teardrop only.
B— Parallel only.
C— Direct only.

Answer (B) is correct (4766). *(AIM Para 5-37)*
*This question is a duplicate of FAA question 4617.*
The maximum airspeed above 14,000 ft. MSL for holding patterns is 265 kt. indicated in civil turbojets. For all propeller planes, it is 175 kt. maximum.
Answer (A) is incorrect because 220 kt. is not a maximum holding airspeed. Answer (C) is incorrect because 200 kt. is not a maximum holding airspeed.

Answer (C) is correct (4614). *(AIM Para 5-37)*
When holding west on the 270° radial, use right turns because left turns were not stated in the clearance. The holding pattern will be to the south of the 270° radial, so the VORTAC (the fix) is at the end of the inbound leg. To determine entry procedures, draw a 70° line through the holding fix such that there is the 70° line cross through the outbound leg 1/3 of the leg length from abeam the fix.

| | |
|---|---|
| R-020 to R-090 | Teardrop |
| R-090 to R-200 | Parallel |
| R-200 to R-020 | Direct |

Since you are approaching the holding fix from the northwest on R-330 of ABC VORTAC (Fig. 114), you will make a direct entry.
Answer (A) is incorrect because the parallel or teardrop entries are alternatives only when approaching on R-090. Answer (B) is incorrect because the parallel entry is only appropriate when approaching on R-090 to R-200.

Answer (C) is correct (4615). *(AIM Para 5-37)*
Visualize a 360° radial with left turns. The pattern will be to the east of the radial with the holding fix being the VORTAC. Since you are approaching from the northwest R-330 of XYZ VORTAC (see Fig. 114.), you will be able to make a direct entry.

| | |
|---|---|
| R-180 to R-250 | Teardrop |
| R-250 to R-070 | Direct |
| R-070 to R-180 | Parallel |

Answer (A) is incorrect because if you were approaching on R-180 to R-250, you would make a teardrop entry. Answer (B) is incorrect because if you were approaching on R-070 to R-180, you would fly through the VOR, parallel the holding course, turn right to the holding course, and make an entry.

**66.**
**4616.** (Refer to figure 114 on page 276.) A pilot receives this ATC clearance:

"...CLEARED TO THE ABC VORTAC. HOLD SOUTH ON THE ONE EIGHT ZERO RADIAL..."

What is the recommended procedure to enter the holding pattern?

A— Teardrop only.
B— Parallel only.
C— Direct only.

**67.**
**4619.** (Refer to figure 116 below.) You arrive over the 15 DME fix on a heading of 350°. Which holding pattern correctly complies with the ATC clearance below, and what is the recommended entry procedure?

"...HOLD WEST OF THE ONE FIVE DME FIX ON THE TWO SIX EIGHT RADIAL OF THE ABC VORTAC, FIVE MILE LEGS, LEFT TURNS..."

A— 1; teardrop entry.
B— 2; direct entry.
C— 1; direct entry.

**Answer (A) is correct (4616).** *(AIM Para 5-37)*
If you are holding south on the 180° radial, you will have right turns because left turns are not specified and you will be on the east side of the radial (to cross the VORTAC at the end of your inbound leg). Draw the 70° line through the VORTAC on R-110/R-290. Since you are inbound on R-330 (Fig. 114), you would make a teardrop entry.

| | |
|---|---|
| R-290 to R-360 | Teardrop |
| R-360 to R-110 | Parallel |
| R-110 to R-290 | Direct |

Answer (B) is incorrect because a parallel entry is appropriate from R-360 to R-110. Answer (C) is incorrect because a direct entry is appropriate from R-110 to R-290.

**Answer (B) is correct (4619).** *(AIM Para 5-37)*
Alternative 2 is acceptable and 1 is not because the holding fix is always at the end of the inbound leg. Draw in the 70° line through the fix such that it intersects the outbound leg 1/3 of the length from abeam the fix. Direct entry is used with a heading of 338° to 158°.

| Heading | Entry |
|---|---|
| 338° to 158° | Direct |
| 158° to 268° | Parallel |
| 268° to 338° | Teardrop |

Answer (A) is incorrect because the fix is always at the end of the inbound leg. Answer (C) is incorrect because the fix is always at the end of the inbound leg.

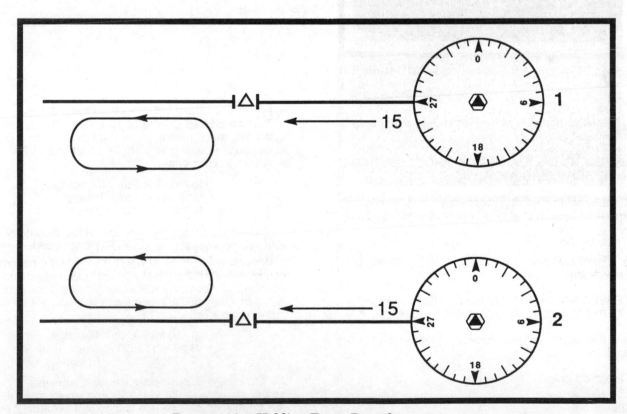

FIGURE 116.—Holding Entry Procedure.

**68.**
**4610.** (Refer to figure 113 below.) You receive this ATC clearance:

"...HOLD EAST OF THE ABC VORTAC ON THE ZERO NINER ZERO RADIAL, LEFT TURNS..."

What is the recommended procedure to enter the holding pattern?

A— Parallel only.
B— Direct only.
C— Teardrop only.

FIGURE 113.—Aircraft Course and DME Indicator.

Answer (A) is correct (4610). *(AIM Para 5-37)*
     You are cleared to hold east of the ABC VORTAC with left turns on R-090. The holding side will be south of R-090, with the holding fix being the VORTAC. Draw the 70° line through the VORTAC on R-340/R-160.

| | |
|---|---|
| R-270 to R-340 | Teardrop |
| R-340 to R-160 | Direct |
| R-160 to R-270 | Parallel |

Since you are approaching the VORTAC from the southwest on R-240 (see Fig. 113), you will make a parallel entry.
     Answer (B) is incorrect because a direct entry would be appropriate if you were coming in on R-340 to R-160. Answer (C) is incorrect because a teardrop entry would be appropriate if you were coming in from R-270 to R-340.

**69.**
**4611.** (Refer to figure 113 above.) You receive this ATC clearance:

"...CLEARED TO THE ABC VORTAC. HOLD SOUTH ON THE ONE EIGHT ZERO RADIAL..."

What is the recommended procedure to enter the holding pattern?

A— Teardrop only.
B— Direct only.
C— Parallel only.

Answer (B) is correct (4611). *(AIM Para 5-37)*
     You are cleared to hold south on the 180° radial with right turns, which means you will be to the east of R-180. Since you are coming in from the southwest (R-240), you can make a direct entry.

| | |
|---|---|
| R-290 to R-360 | Teardrop |
| R-360 to R-110 | Parallel |
| R-110 to R-290 | Direct |

     Answer (A) is incorrect because a teardrop entry would be appropriate only from R-290 to R-360. Answer (C) is incorrect because a parallel entry would only be appropriate from R-360 to R-110.

**70.**

**4612.** (Refer to figure 113 on page 278.) You receive this ATC clearance:

"...CLEARED TO THE XYZ VORTAC. HOLD NORTH ON THE THREE SIX ZERO RADIAL, LEFT TURNS..."

What is the recommended procedure to enter the holding pattern.

A— Parallel only.
B— Direct only.
C— Teardrop only.

**71.**

**4613.** (Refer to figure 113 on page 278.) You receive this ATC clearance:

"...CLEARED TO THE ABC VORTAC. HOLD WEST ON THE TWO SEVEN ZERO RADIAL..."

What is the recommended procedure to enter the holding pattern?

A— Parallel only.
B— Direct only.
C— Teardrop only.

**72.**

**4624.** What timing procedure should be used when performing a holding pattern at a VOR?

A— Timing for the outbound leg begins over or abeam the VOR, whichever occurs later.
B— Timing for the inbound leg begins when initiating the turn inbound.
C— Adjustments in timing of each pattern should be made on the inbound leg.

**73.**

**4621.** (Refer to figure 117 on page 280.) You receive this ATC clearance:

"...CLEARED TO THE ABC NDB. HOLD SOUTHEAST ON THE ONE FOUR ZERO DEGREE BEARING FROM THE NDB. LEFT TURNS..."

At station passage you note the indications in figure 117. What is the recommended procedure to enter the holding pattern?

A— Direct only.
B— Teardrop only.
C— Parallel only.

**Answer (C) is correct (4612).** *(AIM Para 5-37)*
Holding north of the XYZ VORTAC with left turns on R-360 means you are on the east side of the radial. Since you are coming in from the southwest (R-240), you will be making a teardrop entry.

| | |
|---|---|
| R-180 to R-250 | Teardrop |
| R-250 to R-070 | Direct |
| R-070 to R-110 | Parallel |

Answer (A) is incorrect because a parallel approach would only be appropriate if coming in between R-070 and R-180. Answer (B) is incorrect because a direct entry is only appropriate between R-250 and R-070.

**Answer (B) is correct (4613).** *(AIM Para 5-37)*
You are cleared to hold west on R-270 with right turns, so you will be south of R-270. Since you are coming in on R-240, you need to make a direct entry.

| | |
|---|---|
| R-020 to R-090 | Teardrop |
| R-090 to R-200 | Parallel |
| R-200 to R-020 | Direct |

Answer (A) is incorrect because a parallel entry is only appropriate on R-090 to R-200. Answer (C) is incorrect because a teardrop entry is only appropriate when coming in on R-020 to R-090.

**Answer (A) is correct (4624).** *(AIM Para 5-37)*
Outbound leg timing begins over or abeam the fix, whichever occurs later. If abeam the position cannot be determined, start timing when the turn to outbound is completed.
Answer (B) is incorrect because the timing for the inbound leg begins when the inbound turn is completed, not when it is initiated. Answer (C) is incorrect because the timing of the pattern is adjusted by varying the length of the outbound leg. Once inbound, one must fly to the holding fix and cannot adjust the length of the leg.

**Answer (C) is correct (4621).** *(AIM Para 5-37)*
Holding southeast on the 140° bearing means that you are south and to the west of the 140° and 320° bearings from the NDB with left turns. Since you are entering from the southwest on a 055° heading, you must make a parallel entry.

| Heading | Entry |
|---|---|
| 210° to 030° | Direct |
| 030° to 140° | Parallel |
| 140° to 210° | Teardrop |

Answer (A) is incorrect because a direct entry would be appropriate if approaching from a heading of 210° to 030°. Answer (B) is incorrect because a teardrop entry would be appropriate if approaching from a heading of 140° to 210°.

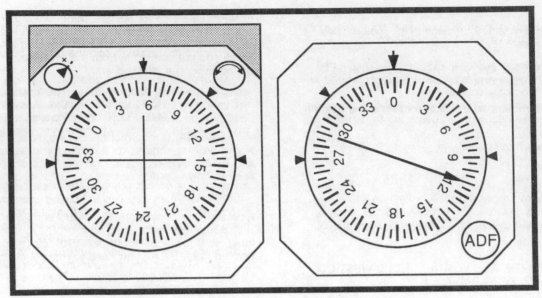

FIGURE 117.—Heading and ADF Indicators.

**74.**
**4622.** (Refer to figure 117 above.) You receive this ATC clearance:

"...CLEARED TO THE XYZ NDB. HOLD NORTHEAST ON THE ZERO FOUR ZERO DEGREE BEARING FROM THE NDB. LEFT TURNS..."

At station passage you note the indications in figure 117. What is the recommended procedure to enter the holding pattern?

A— Direct only.
B— Teardrop only.
C— Parallel only.

**75.**
**4623.** (Refer to figure 117 above.) You receive this ATC clearance:

"...CLEARED TO THE ABC NDB. HOLD SOUTHWEST ON THE TWO THREE ZERO DEGREE BEARING FROM THE NDB..."

At station passage you note the indications in figure 117. What is the recommended procedure to enter the holding pattern?

A— Direct only.
B— Teardrop only.
C— Parallel only.

Answer (B) is correct (4622). *(AIM Para 5-37)*
You are holding northeast on the 040° bearing with left turns. This means you are to the east and south of 040° bearing from the NDB. Since you are entering from a 055° heading, you will make a teardrop entry.

| Heading | Entry |
|---|---|
| 110° to 290° | Direct |
| 290° to 040° | Parallel |
| 040° to 110° | Teardrop |

Answer (A) is incorrect because a direct entry would be appropriate when approaching from a heading of 110° to 290°. Answer (C) is incorrect because you would use a parallel entry only if approaching on a heading from 290° to 040°.

Answer (A) is correct (4623). *(AIM Para 5-37)*
You are holding southwest on the 230° bearing from the NDB but you will be on the southeast side of the inbound leg. Since you are approaching from the southwest on a 055° heading, you will make a direct entry.

| Heading | Entry |
|---|---|
| 340° to 160° | Direct |
| 160° to 230° | Teardrop |
| 230° to 340° | Parallel |

Answer (B) is incorrect because a teardrop entry would only be appropriate if you were approaching the NDB on a heading from 160° to 230°. Answer (C) is incorrect because a parallel entry would only be appropriate if approaching the NDB on a heading from 230° to 340°.

**76.**
**4625.** When holding at an NDB, at what point should the timing begin for the second leg outbound?

A— When the wings are level and the wind drift correction angle is established after completing the turn to the outbound heading.
B— When the wings are level after completing the turn to the outbound heading, or abeam the fix, whichever occurs first.
C— When abeam the holding fix.

**77.**
**4626.** To ensure proper airspace protection while holding at 5,000 feet in a civil turbojet airplane, what is the recommended maximum indicated airspeed a pilot should use?

A— 230 knots.
B— 200 knots.
C— 210 knots.

**78.**
**4767.** Where a holding pattern is specified in lieu of a procedure turn, the holding maneuver must be executed within

A— the 1 minute time limitation or published leg length.
B— a radius of 5 miles from the holding fix.
C— 10 knots of the specified holding speed.

**79.**
**4668.** When more than one circuit of the holding pattern is needed to lose altitude or become better established on course, the additional circuits can be made

A— at pilot's discretion.
B— only in an emergency.
C— only if pilot advises ATC and ATC approves.

**9.12 Instrument Approach Charts**

**80.**
**4715.** How can an IAF be identified on a Standard Instrument Approach Procedure (SIAP) Chart?

A— The procedure turn and the fixes labeled IAF where no procedure turn is authorized.
B— Any fix illustrated within the 10-mile ring other than the FAF or stepdown fix.
C— The procedure turn and the fixes on the feeder facility ring.

Answer (C) is correct (4625). *(AIM Para 5-37)*
Outbound timing begins over or abeam the fix, whichever occurs later. If the abeam position cannot be determined, start timing when the turn to outbound is completed.
Answer (A) is incorrect because only when one cannot determine position abeam the fix should one start the timing when the turn is complete. Answer (B) is incorrect because timing of the outbound leg begins when abeam the fix, not when the wings are level.

Answer (A) is correct (4626). *(AIM Para 5-37)*
The maximum airspeed in holding patterns for a civil turbojet is 230 kt. below 14,000 ft. MSL. The maximum holding airspeed for propeller-driven aircraft is 175 kt.
Answer (B) is incorrect because 200 kt. is not a maximum holding airspeed. Answer (C) is incorrect because 210 kt. is not a maximum holding airspeed.

Answer (A) is correct (4767). *(AIM Para 5-37)*
Holding patterns should always be executed within the 1-min. time limitation or published leg length.
Answer (B) is incorrect because a radius of 5 mi. for a procedure turn can only be specified for category A or helicopter aircraft. Answer (C) is incorrect because ATC does not specify a holding speed. You need only remain below the maximum allowable holding speed.

Answer (C) is the best answer (4668). *(AIM Para 5-48)*
If you are cleared for the approach while in a holding pattern, ATC will not expect you to make any additional circuits in the hold. If you do elect to make additional circuits to lose altitude or become better established on course, it is your responsibility to so advise ATC when you receive your approach clearance.
Answer (A) is incorrect because, while you may elect to make additional circuits in the holding pattern, you are required to advise ATC of your intentions. Answer (B) is incorrect because additional circuits may be made at your discretion (declaring an emergency is not necessary).

Answer (A) is correct (4715). *(AIM P/C Glossary)*
The fixes depicted on Instrument Approach Procedure Charts that identify the beginning of an initial approach segment are the initial approach fixes (IAF). Initial approach fixes are identified by the letters IAF on instrument approach charts. There may be more than one for any given approach. Additionally, initial approach fixes requiring a procedural turn are not labeled with IAF.
Answer (B) is incorrect because IAF are specifically identified with "IAF" except for the procedure turn approach pattern. Answer (C) is incorrect because IAF are specifically identified with "IAF" except for the procedure turn approach pattern.

**81.**
**4746.** Which fixes on the IAP Charts are initial approach fixes?

A— Any fix on the en route facilities ring, the feeder facilities ring, and those at the start of arc approaches.
B— Only the fixes at the start of arc approaches and those on either the feeder facilities ring or en route facilities ring that have a transition course shown to the approach procedure.
C— Any fix that is identified by the letters IAF.

**Answer (C) is correct (4746).** *(AIM P/C Glossary)*
The fixes depicted on Instrument Approach Procedure Charts that identify the beginning of an initial approach segment are the initial approach fixes (IAF). Initial approach fixes are identified by the letters IAF on instrument approach charts. There may be more than one for any given approach.
Answer (A) is incorrect because IAF are specifically identified with "IAF" except for the procedure turn approach pattern. Answer (B) is incorrect because IAF are specifically identified with "IAF" except for the procedure turn approach pattern.

**82.**
**4717.** Aircraft approach categories are based on

A— certificated approach speed at maximum gross weight.
B— 1.3 times the stall speed in landing configuration at maximum gross landing weight.
C— 1.3 times the stall speed at maximum gross weight.

**Answer (B) is correct (4717).** *(IFH Chap X)*
IFR approach minimums are specified for various aircraft speed/weight combinations. Speeds are based upon the value of 1.3 times the stall speed of the aircraft in the landing configuration at maximum certified gross landing weight.
Answer (A) is incorrect because aircraft do not have certificated approach speeds. Answer (C) is incorrect because it is 1.3 times the stall speed in landing configuration at maximum gross landing weight, not just maximum gross weight.

**83.**
**4470.** What does the symbol T within a black triangle in the minimums section of the IAP for a particular airport indicate?

A— Takeoff minimums are 1 mile for aircraft having two engines or less and ½ mile for those with more than two engines.
B— Instrument takeoffs are not authorized.
C— Takeoff minimums are not standard and/or departure procedures are published.

**Answer (C) is correct (4470).** *(ACL)*
The symbol in the question indicates that takeoff minimums are not standard and/or departure procedures are published, and one should consult the alternate takeoff procedures. Takeoff minimums apply to commercial operations, i.e., operations other than Part 91.
Answer (A) is incorrect because it gives the standard minimums for takeoff when there is a published instrument approach. Answer (B) is incorrect because the alternate takeoff procedures will indicate if instrument takeoffs are not authorized.

**84.**
**4636.** What does the absence of the procedure turn barb on the planview on an approach chart indicate?

A— A procedure turn is not authorized.
B— Teardrop-type procedure turn is authorized.
C— Racetrack-type procedure turn is authorized.

**Answer (A) is correct (4636).** *(AIM Para 5-48)*
The absence of the procedure turn barb in the plan view indicates that a procedure turn is not authorized for that approach.
Answer (B) is incorrect because the absence of a procedure turn barb indicates that all (not just teardrop-type) procedure turns are not authorized. Answer (C) is incorrect because the absence of a procedure turn barb indicates that all (not just racetrack-type) procedure turns are not authorized.

**85.**
**4671.** During an instrument approach, under what conditions, if any, is the holding pattern course reversal not required?

A— When radar vectors are provided.
B— When cleared for the approach.
C— None, since it is always mandatory.

**Answer (A) is correct (4671).** *(AIM Para 5-48)*
A course reversal (procedure turn) is not required when radar vectors are being provided.
Answer (B) is incorrect because a course reversal may be required when cleared for a full approach. Answer (C) is incorrect because a course reversal is not mandatory when radar vectors are provided.

**86.**
**4637.** When making an instrument approach at the selected alternate airport, what landing minimums apply?

A— Standard alternate minimums (600-2 or 800-2).
B— The IFR alternate minimums listed for that airport.
C— The landing minimums published for the type of procedure selected.

Answer (C) is correct (4637). *(FAR 91.175)*
Published landing minimums always apply when making an instrument approach to an airport.
Answer (A) is incorrect because alternate minimums refer to the minimum forecast weather allowable to list an airport as an alternate on the flight plan. Answer (B) is incorrect because alternate minimums refer to the minimum forecast weather allowable to list an airport as an alternate on the flight plan.

**87.**
**4632.** When the approach procedure involves a procedure turn, the maximum speed should not be greater than

A— 180 knots IAS.
B— 200 knots IAS.
C— 250 knots IAS.

Answer (C) is correct (4632). *(AIM Para 5-48)*
When the approach procedure involves a procedure turn, a maximum speed of not greater than 250 kt. IAS should be observed, and the turn should be executed within the distance specified in the profile view.
Answer (A) is incorrect because the maximum speed that should be used is 250 kt. (not 180 kt.). Answer (B) is incorrect because the maximum speed that should be used is 250 kt. (not 200 kt.).

**88.**
**4540.** What obstacle clearance and navigation signal coverage is a pilot assured with the Minimum Sector Altitudes depicted on the IAP charts?

A— 1,000 feet and acceptable navigation signal coverage within a 25 NM radius of the navigation facility.
B— 1,000 feet within a 25 NM radius of the navigation facility but not acceptable navigation signal coverage.
C— 500 feet and acceptable navigation signal coverage within a 10 NM radius of the navigation facility.

Answer (B) is correct (4540). *(AIM Para 5-45)*
Minimum sector altitudes are depicted on approach charts and provide at least 1,000 ft. of obstacle clearance within a 25-NM radius of the navigation facility upon which the procedure is predicated. These altitudes are for emergency use only and do not necessarily assure acceptable navigational signal coverage.
Answer (A) is incorrect because minimum sector altitudes do not guarantee acceptable signal coverage. Answer (C) is incorrect because minimum sector altitudes do not guarantee acceptable signal coverage, and they provide 1,000 ft. (not 500 ft.) of obstacle clearance.

**89.**
**4672.** During an instrument precision approach, terrain and obstacle clearance depends on adherence to

A— minimum altitude shown on the IAP.
B— terrain contour information.
C— natural and man-made reference point information.

Answer (A) is correct (4672). *(AIM Para 5-45)*
A pilot adhering to the altitudes, flight paths, and weather minimums depicted on the IAP chart is assured of terrain and obstruction clearance.
Answer (B) is incorrect because the design of IAPs takes terrain and obstacle clearance into account. Answer (C) is incorrect because, during instrument approaches, instrument (not visual) reference points are used to assure terrain and obstacle clearance.

**90.**
**4734.** When being radar vectored for an ILS approach, at what point may you start a descent from your last assigned altitude to a lower minimum altitude if cleared for the approach?

A— When established on a segment of a published route or IAP.
B— You may descend immediately to published glide slope interception altitude.
C— Only after you are established on the final approach unless informed otherwise by ATC.

Answer (A) is correct (4734). *(AIM Para 5-47)*
While being radar vectored and you are cleared for the approach, you must maintain your last assigned altitude until the airplane is established on a segment of a published route or IAP. Then use the published altitude to descend within each succeeding route or approach segment.
Answer (B) is incorrect because you must wait until you are on part of the published procedure to descend. Answer (C) is incorrect because you should follow prescribed altitudes whenever you are on a segment of a published route or IAP.

**91.**
**4641.** While being radar vectored, an approach clearance is received. The last assigned altitude should be maintained until

A— reaching the FAF.
B— advised to begin descent.
C— established on a segment of a published route or IAP.

Answer (C) is correct (4641). *(AIM Para 5-47)*
When an approach clearance is received, the last assigned altitude should be maintained until the aircraft is established on a segment of a published route or IAP. Then published altitudes apply.
Answer (A) is incorrect because published altitudes may be used as soon as the aircraft is on a published route, which should be before the FAF. Answer (B) is incorrect because when ATC issues an approach clearance, descent to published altitudes is left to the discretion of the pilot.

**92.**
**4670.** When simultaneous approaches are in progress, how does each pilot receive radar advisories?

A— On tower frequency.
B— On approach control frequency.
C— One pilot on tower frequency and the other on approach control frequency.

Answer (A) is correct (4670). *(AIM Para 5-52)*
When simultaneous approaches are in progress, each pilot will be advised to monitor the tower frequency to receive advisories and instructions.
Answer (B) is incorrect because pilots will receive radar advisories on tower (not approach control) frequency. Answer (C) is incorrect because both pilots will receive radar advisories on tower frequency.

**93.**
**4749.** When may a pilot make a straight-in landing, if using an IAP having only circling minimums?

A— A straight-in landing may not be made, but the pilot may continue to the runway at MDA and then circle to land on the runway.
B— The pilot may land straight-in if the runway is the active runway and (s)he has been cleared to land.
C— A straight-in landing may be made if the pilot has the runway in sight in sufficient time to make a normal approach for landing, and has been cleared to land.

Answer (C) is correct (4749). *(IFH Chap X)*
When the normal rate of descent or the runway alignment factor of 30° is exceeded, a straight-in minimum is not published and a circling minimum applies. Even without published straight-in minimums, the pilot may land straight-in if (s)he has the active runway in sight and sufficient time to make a normal landing, and has been cleared to land.
Answer (A) is incorrect because a straight-in landing may be made if it is the appropriate runway. Answer (B) is incorrect because the pilot must also have sufficient time to make a normal approach for a landing.

**94.**
**4714.** Which procedure should be followed by a pilot who is circling to land in a Category B airplane, but is maintaining a speed 5 knots faster than the maximum specified for that category?

A— Use the approach minimums appropriate for Category C.
B— Use Category B minimums.
C— Use Category D minimums since they apply to all circling approaches.

Answer (A) is correct (4714). *(IFH Chap X)*
If it is necessary to maneuver at speeds in excess of the upper limit of the speed range for any category, the minimums for the next higher category should be used.
Answer (B) is incorrect because a pilot should use minimums for the category appropriate to the approach speed being used. Answer (C) is incorrect because Category D minimums do not necessarily apply to all circling approaches.

**95.**
**4662.** (Refer to figure 127 or 127A on pages 285 and 286.) If cleared for NDB RWY 28 approach (Lancaster/Fairfield) over ZZV VOR, the flight would be expected to

Category A Aircraft
Last assigned altitude 3,000 feet

A— proceed straight in from CRISY to the S-28 minimums of 1620-1.
B— proceed to CRISY, then execute the teardrop procedure as depicted on the approach chart.
C— proceed direct to CASER, then straight in to S-28 minimums of 1620-1.

Answer (A) is correct (4662). *(IFH Chap X)*
From ZZV VOR (which is an IAF), there is a NoPT transition published through CRISY INT. Thus, the teardrop procedure turn is not authorized (or necessary). The straight-in minimums for a Category A aircraft are an MDA of 1,620 ft. MSL and visibility of 1 SM.
Answer (B) is incorrect because the NoPT symbol just under ZZV VOR indicates that the procedure turn is not authorized when approaching from ZZV. Answer (C) is incorrect because the arrow southwest of ZZV VOR indicates the route to CRISY (not CASER) and then straight in.

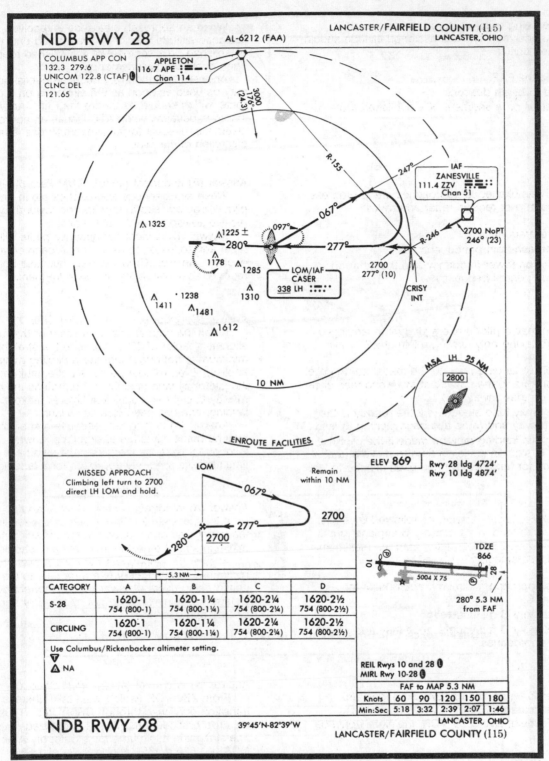

FIGURE 127.—NDB RWY 28, Lancaster/Fairfield County.

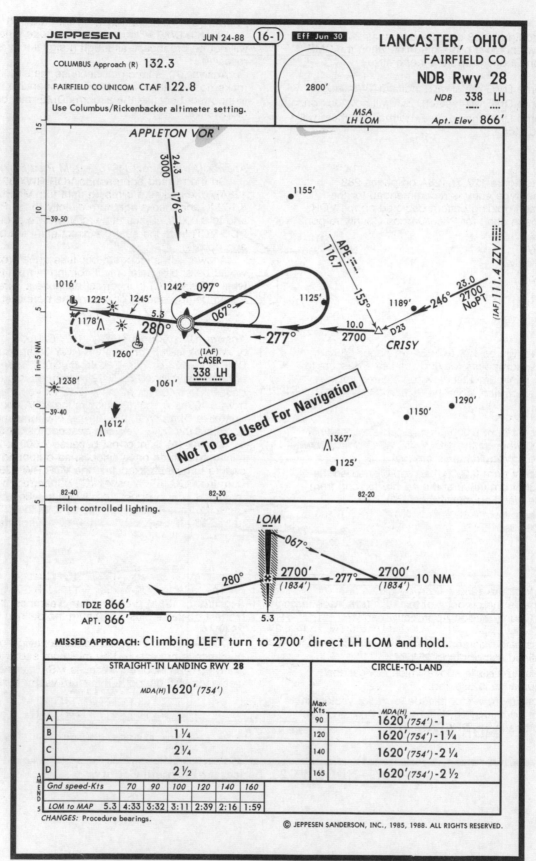

FIGURE  127A.—NDB RWY 28, Lancaster, Ohio.

**96.**
**4674.** (Refer to figure 128 or 128A on pages 288 and 289.) How should a pilot determine when the DME at Price/Carbon County Airport is inoperative?

A— The airborne DME will always indicate "0" mileage.
B— The airborne DME will "search," but will not "lock on."
C— The airborne DME may appear normal, but there will be no code tone.

**97.**
**4675.** (Refer to figure 128 or 128A on pages 288 and 289.) What type entry is recommended for the missed approach holding pattern depicted on the VOR RWY 36 approach chart for Price/Carbon County Airport?

A— Direct only.
B— Teardrop only.
C— Parallel only.

**98.**
**4677.** (Refer to figures 128 or 128A on pages 288 and 289.) At which points may you initiate a descent to the next lower minimum altitude when cleared for the VOR RWY 36 approach, from the PUC R-095 IAF (DME operative)?

A— Start descent from 8,000 when established on final, from 7,500 when at the 4 DME fix, and from 6,180 when landing requirements are met.
B— Start descent from 8,000 when established on the PUC R-186, from 6,400 at the 4 DME fix, and from 6,180 when landing requirements are met.
C— Start descent from 8,000 at the R-127, from 6,400 at the LR-127, from 6,180 at the 4 DME fix.

**99.**
**4678.** (Refer to figure 128 or 128A on pages 288 and 289.) What is the purpose of the 10,300 MSA on the Price/Carbon County Airport Approach Chart?

A— It provides safe clearance above the highest obstacle in the defined sector out to 25 NM.
B— It provides an altitude above which navigational course guidance is assured.
C— It is the minimum vector altitude for radar vectors in the sector southeast of PUC between 020° and 290° magnetic bearing to PUC VOR.

Answer (C) is correct (4674). *(AIM Para 1-7)*
When a DME is inoperative, the code tone (identifier) will not be broadcast, although a signal may still be received.
Answer (A) is incorrect because the airborne DME will make no indication if the DME is inoperative. Answer (B) is incorrect because the airborne DME may be inoperative.

Answer (A) is correct (4675). *(AIM Para 5-37)*
On the missed approach to VOR RWY 36 (Fig. 128 or 128A), one makes a climbing right turn via PUC R-127 to 8,100 ft. and then a right turn directly to the PUC VOR and to 9,000 ft. Since the aircraft will be approaching PUC VOR from the south, a direct entry will be appropriate.
Answer (B) is incorrect because a teardrop entry would be appropriate only if coming in from the northwest. Answer (C) is incorrect because a parallel entry would be appropriate only from the northeast.

Answer (B) is correct (4677). *(IFH Chap X)*
When cleared for the VOR RWY 36 approach with DME (Fig. 128 or 128A), maintain 8,000 ft. on the 10 DME arc until established on R-186 when you may begin descent to 6,400 ft. At the 4 DME fix you may descend from 6,400 to 6,180 ft., which is the MDA with an operative DME. With the runway environment in sight, at or before the MAP, you can descend below 6,180 ft.
Answer (A) is incorrect because 7,500 ft. is the minimum altitude once established outbound on the procedure turn when executing the VOR RWY 36 approach from the PUC IAF. Answer (C) is incorrect because you may start your descent from 8,000 ft. when established on R-186 (not R-127), from 6,400 ft. at the 4 DME fix, and from 6,180 ft. only with the runway environment in sight, at or before the MAP.

Answer (A) is correct (4678). *(IFH Chap X)*
The MSA in PUC sector R-110 to R-200 at 10,300 ft. (Fig. 128 or 128A) provides safe clearance above the highest obstacle plus 1,000 ft. in the defined sector out to 25 NM.
Answer (B) is incorrect because navigational course guidance is not assured by minimum sector altitudes. Answer (C) is incorrect because MSA gives a safe clearance altitude, not a minimum vector altitude.

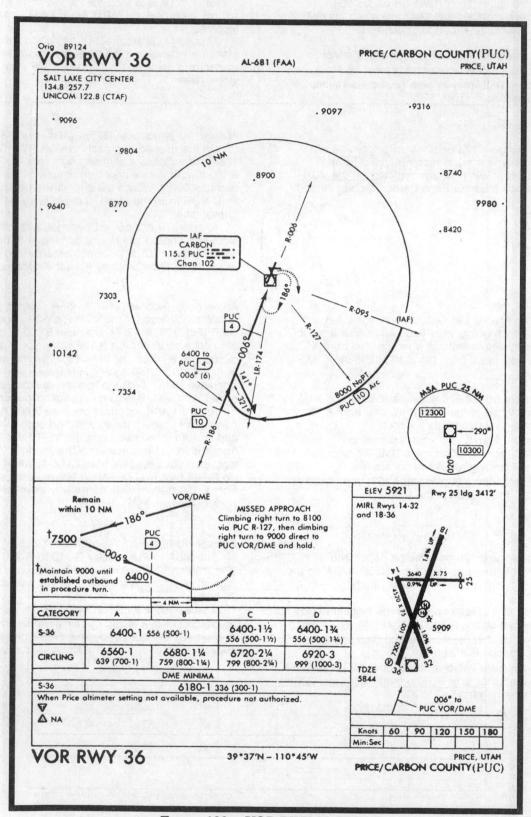

FIGURE 128.—VOR RWY 36 (PUC).

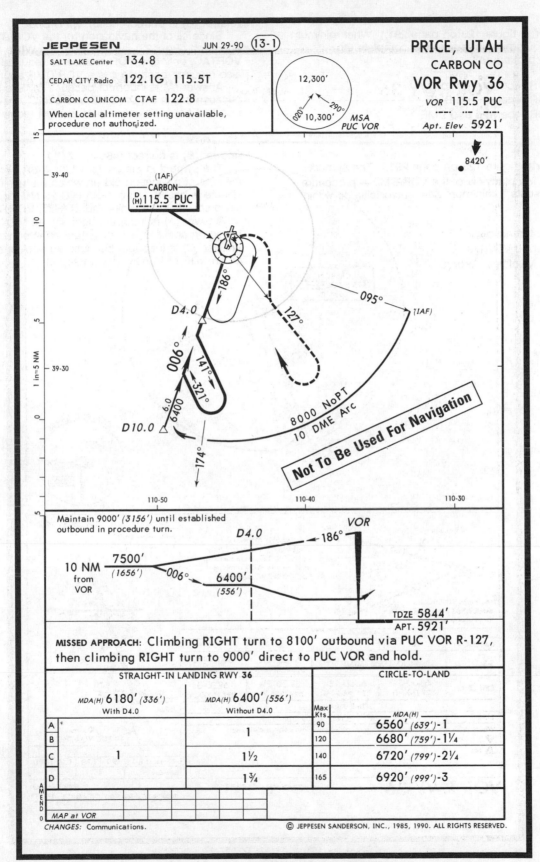

**JEPPESEN** JUN 29-90 (13-1)

SALT LAKE Center **134.8**

CEDAR CITY Radio **122.1G 115.5T**

CARBON CO UNICOM CTAF **122.8**

When Local altimeter setting unavailable, procedure not authorized.

12,300'

020° 290°
10,300' MSA
PUC VOR

**PRICE, UTAH**
CARBON CO
**VOR Rwy 36**
VOR 115.5 PUC
·--· ··-·· -·-·
Apt. Elev **5921'**

8420'

(IAF)
CARBON
D(H) 115.5 PUC

186°

D4.0

006°  141°  321°

6400'  6.0

D10.0

095°  (IAF)

127°

8000 NoPT
10 DME Arc

174°

110-50   110-40   110-30

Maintain 9000' (3156') until established outbound in procedure turn.

VOR

D4.0  186°

10 NM from VOR  7500' (1656')  006°  6400' (556')

TDZE 5844'
APT. 5921'

**MISSED APPROACH:** Climbing RIGHT turn to 8100' outbound via PUC VOR R-127, then climbing RIGHT turn to 9000' direct to PUC VOR and hold.

| | STRAIGHT-IN LANDING RWY 36 | | | CIRCLE-TO-LAND | |
|---|---|---|---|---|---|
| | MDA(H) 6180' (336') With D4.0 | MDA(H) 6400' (556') Without D4.0 | Max Kts | MDA(H) | |
| A | | 1 | 90 | 6560' (639')-1 | |
| B | | 1 | 120 | 6680' (759')-1¼ | |
| C | 1 | 1½ | 140 | 6720' (799')-2¼ | |
| D | | 1¾ | 165 | 6920' (999')-3 | |

AMEND 0

MAP at VOR

CHANGES: Communications.

FIGURE 128A.—VOR RWY 36 (PUC).

**100.**
**4653.** (Refer to figure 123 on page 291.) What minimum navigation equipment is required to complete the VOR/DME-A procedure?

A— One VOR receiver.
B— One VOR receiver and DME.
C— Two VOR receivers and DME.

Answer (B) is correct (4653). *(IFH Chap X)*
Since all of the navigation for the VOR/DME-A approach (Fig. 123) is done from the White Cloud VORTAC, only one VOR receiver is required. DME is also required because it is a VOR/DME approach.
Answer (A) is incorrect because DME is also required because this is a VOR/DME approach. Answer (C) is incorrect because only 1 (not 2) VOR receiver is required.

**101.**
**4654.** (Refer to figure 123 on page 291.) The symbol ⬛ 2800 ⬛ on the planview of the VOR/DME-A procedure at 7D3 represents a minimum safe sector altitude within 25 NM of

A— DEANI intersection.
B— White Cloud VORTAC.
C— Baldwin Municipal Airport.

Answer (B) is correct (4654). *(ACL)*
The symbol in the center of the MSA circle identifies the type of navigation aid on which the minimum safe altitude is based. Also, MSA HIC 25 NM on top of the circle specifies the White Cloud (HIC) VORTAC.
Answer (A) is incorrect because an MSA is always based on an NDB or a VOR (not an intersection). Answer (C) is incorrect because an MSA is always based on an NDB or a VOR (not an airport).

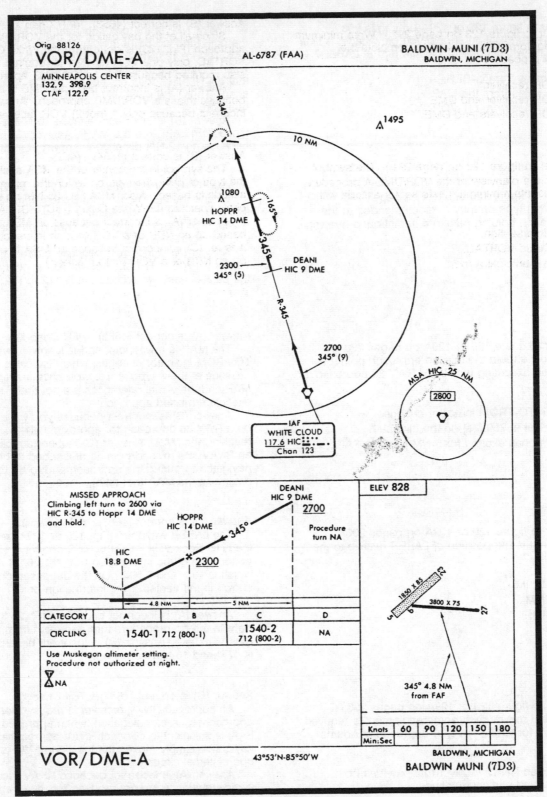

FIGURE 123.—VOR/DME-A (7D3).

**102.**
**4680.** (Refer to figure 129 or 129A on pages 293 and 294.) What indication should you get when it is time to turn inbound while in the procedure turn at LABER?

A— 4 DME miles from LABER.
B— 10 DME miles from the MAP.
C— 12 DME miles from LIT VORTAC.

Answer (A) is correct (4680). *(AIM Para 5-37)*
The "4 NM" at the perpendicular line across the end of the outbound leg of the holding pattern southeast of LABER (Fig. 129) means the turn inbound should begin when 4 DME are indicated from LABER waypoint. Note that a 4-NM line does not appear on the Jeppesen IAP chart. Thus, you must use the NOS chart to answer this question.
Answer (B) is incorrect because 10 NM is the distance from LABER to the MAP. Answer (C) is incorrect because no 12-NM distance is shown from LIT.

**103.**
**4681.** (Refer to figure 129 or 129A on pages 293 and 294.) What type of entry is recommended to the missed approach holding pattern if the inbound heading is 050°?

A— Direct.
B— Parallel.
C— Teardrop.

Answer (C) is correct (4681). *(AIM Para 5-37)*
Extend the 222° radial from Bendy (Fig. 129 or 129A). If you are coming in on a 050° heading, you would be on R-230. The teardrop approach should be used because you are north of R-222.
Answer (A) is incorrect because a direct entry would be from R-292 to R-112. Answer (B) is incorrect because the parallel entry would be from R-112 to R-222.

**104.**
**4682.** (Refer to figure 129 or 129A on pages 293 and 294.) How should the missed approach point be identified when executing the RNAV RWY 36 approach at Adams Field?

A— When the TO-FROM indicator changes.
B— Upon arrival at 760 feet on the glidepath.
C— When time has expired for 5 NM past the FAF.

Answer (A) is correct (4682). *(IFH Chap X)*
The MAP is a waypoint and is identified when the TO-FROM indicator changes, which indicates station passage at the waypoint; i.e., you have arrived at the MAP and the visual references are not there, so you must execute a missed approach.
Answer (B) is incorrect because you will be at 760 ft. on a RWY 36 approach for approximately 1½ NM before reaching the MAP. Answer (C) is incorrect because, on an RNAV, the missed point is prescribed to be used and navigated to during the approach and to be used to determine the MAP (not time).

**105.**
**4683.** (Refer to figure 129 or 129A on pages 293 and 294.) What is the position of LABER relative to the reference facility?

A— 316°, 24.3 NM.
B— 177°, 10 NM.
C— 198°, 8 NM.

Answer (C) is correct (4683). *(IFH Chap X)*
The LABER waypoint (Fig. 129 or 129A) is based on the Little Rock VOR. On the NOS chart it is shown in the bottom line of the information box, "113.9 LIT 198.0°-8," which is 198° and 8 NM. On the Jeppesen chart it is shown in the center of the information box, "LIT 198.3°/7.9."
Answer (A) is incorrect because 316°, 24.3 NM has to do with the no procedure turn approach from the Pine Bluff VORTAC. Answer (B) is incorrect because LABER is 177° and 10 NM from the MAP.

**106.**
**4684.** (Refer to figure 129 or 129A on pages 293 and 294.) What minimum airborne equipment is required to be operative for RNAV RWY 36 approach at Adams Field?

A— An approved RNAV receiver that provides both horizontal and vertical guidance.
B— A transponder and an approved RNAV receiver that provides both horizontal and vertical guidance.
C— Any approved RNAV receiver.

Answer (C) is correct (4684). *(IFH Chap X)*
An approved RNAV receiver is required for RNAV approaches. Area navigation, when approved by the FAA, is sufficient to conduct RNAV approaches. Area navigation simply moves the location of VORs based upon internal circuitry.
Answer (A) is incorrect because RNAV receivers with vertical guidance are not required for RNAV approaches. Answer (B) is incorrect because RNAV receivers with vertical guidance are not required for RNAV approaches.

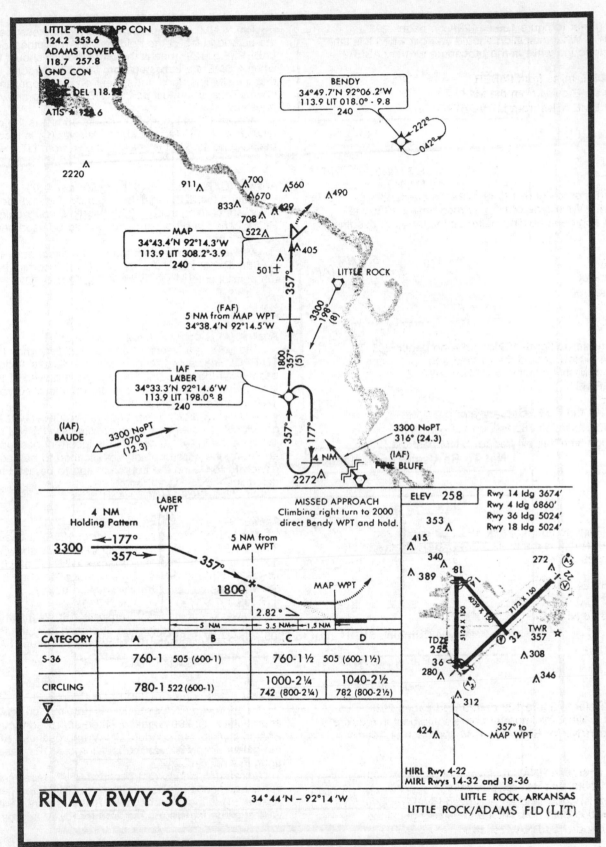

FIGURE 129.—RNAV RWY 36 (LIT).

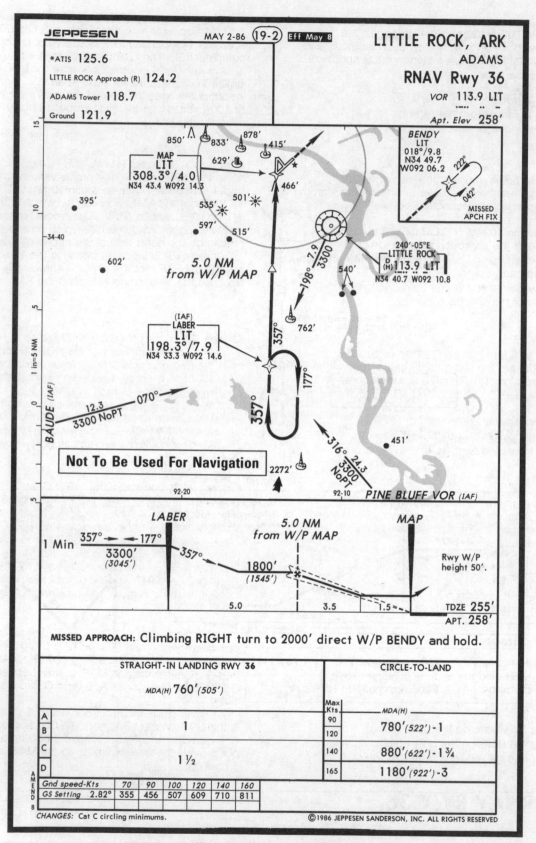

FIGURE 129A.—RNAV RWY 36 (LIT).

**107.**
**4685.** (Refer to figure 130 or 130A on pages 296 and 297.) How does an LDA facility, such as the one at Roanoke Regional, differ from a standard ILS approach facility?

A— The LOC is wider.
B— The LOC is offset from the runway.
C— The GS is unusable beyond the MM.

**108.**
**4686.** (Refer to figure 130 or 130A on pages 296 and 297.) What are the procedure turn restrictions on the LDA RWY 6 approach at Roanoke Regional?

A— Remain within 10 NM of CLAMM INT and on the north side of the approach course.
B— Remain within 10 NM of the airport on the north side of the approach course.
C— Remain within 10 NM of the outer marker on the north side of the approach course.

**109.**
**4687.** (Refer to figure 130 or 130A on pages 296 and 297.) What are the restrictions regarding circle to land procedures for LDA RWY/GS 6 approach at Roanoke Regional?

A— Circling to runway 24 not authorized.
B— Circling not authorized NW of RWY 6-24.
C— Visibility increased ½ mile for circling approach.

**110.**
**4688.** (Refer to figure 130 or 130A on pages 296 and 297.) At what minimum altitude should you cross CLAMM intersection during the S-LDA 6 approach at Roanoke Regional?

A— 4,200 MSL.
B— 4,182 MSL.
C— 2,800 MSL.

**111.**
**4689.** (Refer to figure 130 or 130A on pages 296 and 297.) How should the pilot identify the missed approach point for the S-LDA GS 6 approach to Roanoke Regional?

A— Arrival at 1,540 feet on the glide slope.
B— Arrival at 1.0 DME on the LDA course.
C— Time expired for distance from OM to MAP.

Answer (B) is correct (4685). *(AIM Para 1-10)*
LDA (localizer-type directional aid) has utility and accuracy comparable to a localizer but is not part of a complete ILS. The LDA is not aligned with the runway.
Answer (A) is incorrect because the LOC in an LDA is similar in width to the localizer in an ILS. Answer (C) is incorrect because the note in the profile view of Fig. 130 or 130A states that the glide slope is unusable inside (not beyond) the MM.

Answer (A) is correct (4686). *(IFH Chap X)*
In Fig. 130 or 130A, the profile view indicates in its upper left corner: "remain within 10 NM." That means 10 NM from the final approach fix, which is the CLAMM INT on the Callahan NDB. The procedure turn also indicates right turn outbound, which means that one must remain on the north side of the approach course.
Answer (B) is incorrect because the 10-NM ring is around the FAF, not the airport. Answer (C) is incorrect because the 10-NM ring is around the FAF, not the outer marker.

Answer (B) is correct (4687). *(IFH Chap X)*
In the remarks section of the NOS IAP chart (Fig. 130) or in the circling minimums table on the Jeppesen Chart (Fig. 130A), it is noted that circling is not authorized (NA) northwest of RWY 6-24 and to RWY 15.
Answer (A) is incorrect because circling to runway 15 (not 24) is not authorized. Answer (C) is incorrect because the minimum circling visibility goes up 1/4 to 3/4 SM, depending on aircraft category.

Answer (A) is correct (4688). *(IFH Chap X)*
On the final approach using the S-LDA 6 approach (Fig. 130 or 130A), you presumably do not have glide slope capability (otherwise you will use S-LDA/GS 6). Thus, the minimum altitude at CLAMM is 4,200 ft. MSL (see the note at 4,500 glide slope interception altitude).
Answer (B) is incorrect because 4,182 ft. is the GS altitude at CLAMM. Answer (C) is incorrect because 2,800 ft. is the minimum altitude after CLAMM and prior to SKIRT OM.

Answer (A) is correct (4689). *(IFH Chap X)*
Since the S-LDA GS 6 (Fig. 130 or 130A) is a precision approach, the MAP is arrival at decision height (1,540 ft. for Categories A, B, and C aircraft) on the glide slope.
Answer (B) is incorrect because 1.3 (not 1.0) DME is the MAP on the LDA (not LDA GS) approach. Answer (C) is incorrect because precision approaches do not provide for time expiration to the MAP (other than as a backup).

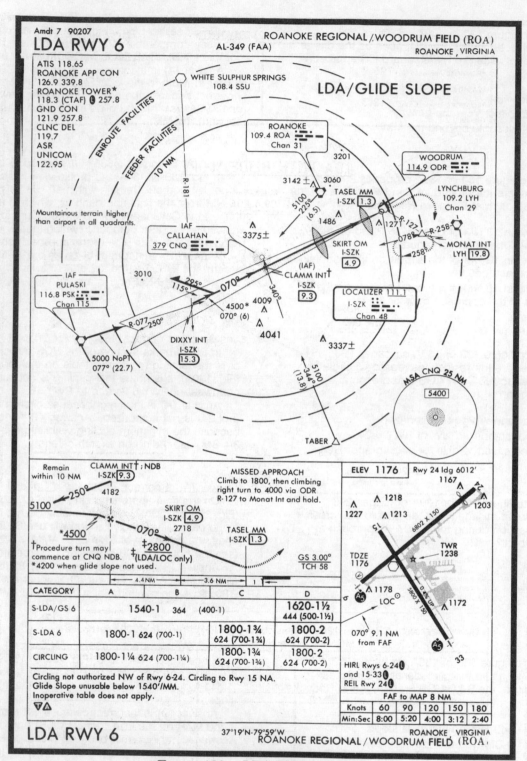

FIGURE 130.—LDA RWY 6 (ROA).

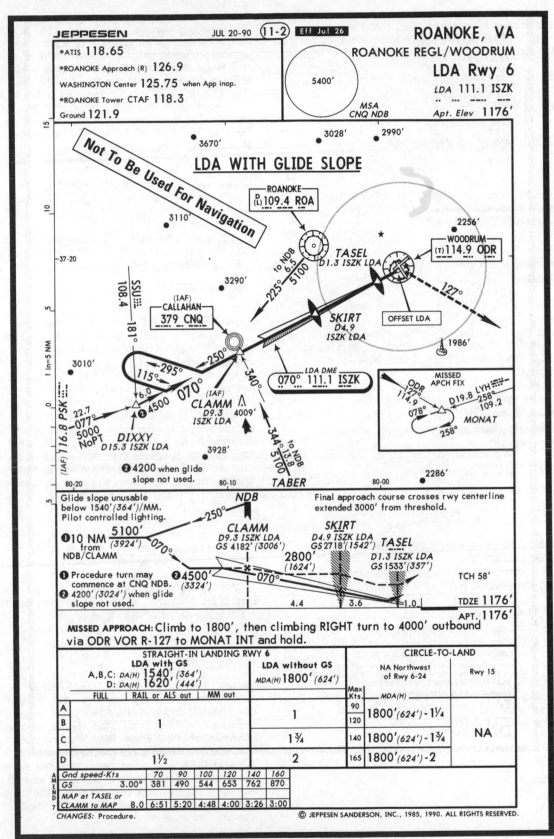

FIGURE 130A.—LDA RWY 6 (ROA).

**112.**
**4691.** (Refer to figure 131 on page 299.) What is the Category B HAT for the LOC RWY S-18 approach at Stapleton International?

A— 300 AGL.
B— 547 AGL.
C— 319 AGL.

Answer (C) is correct (4691). *(IFH Chap X)*
HAT (height above touchdown) is the height of the MDA above the touchdown zone. This is published on the approach plate in conjunction with the minimums. The HAT is the smaller numbers that appear after the MDA and RVR (or visibility). Thus, for the LOC RWY S-18 approach (Fig. 131), the HAT for all categories is 319 ft. AGL.
Answer (A) is incorrect because the 300-1 in parentheses refers to military minimums. Answer (B) is incorrect because 547 is the HAA (height above airport) which is the MDA which is used in circling.

**113.**
**4690.** (Refer to figure 131 on page 299.) What is the landing minimum if you are cleared for the LOC RWY S-18 approach at Stapleton International?

A— 5,000 RVR.
B— 300-foot ceiling and 1 mile visibility.
C— 1 mile visibility.

Answer (A) is correct (4690). *(IFH Chap X)*
The landing minimum on any approach is the RVR or visibility. The LOC RWY S-18 (Fig. 131) shows an RVR minimum of 5,000 ft.
Answer (B) is incorrect because 300 ft. and 1 SM are the military minimums. Answer (C) is incorrect because 1 SM is the circling (not straight-in) minimum.

**114.**
**4695.** (Refer to figure 131 on page 299.) What minimum equipment, in addition to voice communications, is required to make the LOC RWY 18 approach at Stapleton International Airport?

A— VOR/LOC, transponder with altitude/encoding.
B— VOR/LOC, ADF, and DME.
C— DME, transponder with altitude encoding, VOR/LOC, and Marker Beacon.

Answer (A) is correct (4695). *(IFH Chap X)*
A VOR/LOC is required because this is a localizer approach. Since Stapleton International is in Class B airspace (see Fig. 132 on page 300), a transponder with altitude encoding is also required. The various fixes on the approach may be identified by DME or radar, so as long as ATC's radar is operational, no DME is required.
Answer (B) is incorrect because a transponder with altitude encoding is required in Class B airspace. ADF is not required for this approach, and DME is not required as long as radar is operational. Answer (C) is incorrect because DME is not required as long as radar is operational, and no marker beacons are used in this approach.

**115.**
**4693.** (Refer to figure 131 on page 299.) Which approach and tower frequencies are appropriate if you are approaching Stapleton International Airport from the north and are cleared for the LOC RWY 18 approach?

A— 120.8 and 119.5.
B— 127.4 and 118.3.
C— 125.6 and 119.5.

Answer (B) is correct (4693). *(IFH Chap X)*
In the upper left of the plan view in Fig. 131, Denver Approach Control when approaching from the north is 127.4. The tower frequency is 118.3 or 119.5.
Answer (A) is incorrect because 120.8 is approach control for the south. Answer (C) is incorrect because 125.6 is the arrival ATIS frequency.

**116.**
**4694.** (Refer to figure 131 on page 299.) What are the alternate minimums for the LOC RWY 18 approach at Stapleton International Airport?

A— 800-2.
B— 600-2.
C— Nonstandard.

Answer (A) is correct (4694). *(IFH Chap X)*
In the minimums section (Fig. 131), there is no solid black triangle with an A reversed out to indicate that alternate minimums exist. Thus, the standard nonprecision minimums of 800-2 apply. Note that the question specifies LOC RWY 18 which is nonprecision.
Answer (B) is incorrect because 600-2 are the standard alternate minimums for airports with a precision approach. Answer (C) is incorrect because the black triangle with a T reversed out indicates there are nonstandard takeoff, not alternate, minimums.

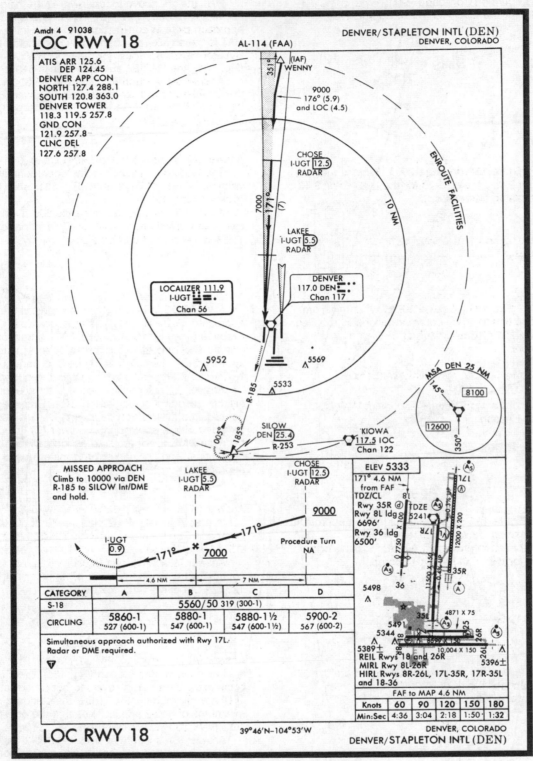

FIGURE 131.—LOC RWY 18 (DEN).

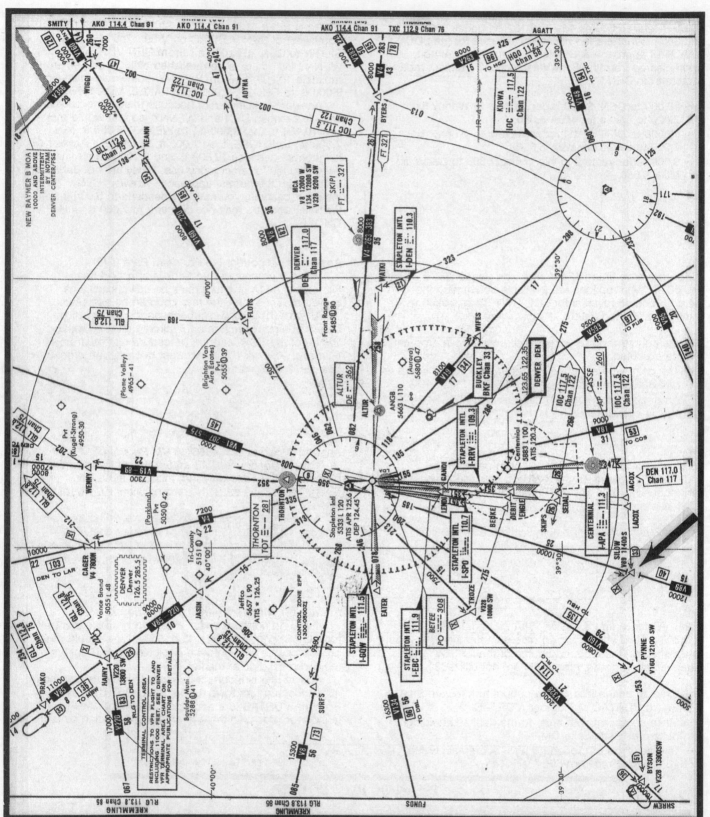

FIGURE 132.—Terminal Area Chart.

**117.**
**4692.** (Refer to figures 131 and 132 on pages 299 and 300.) What are the minimum altitudes for the LOC RWY S-18 approach at Stapleton International Airport, when cleared from the Silow intersection? (Expect radar vectors from DEN VOR).

A— 10,000 to DEN; 9,000 radar vectors to Wenny fix; 7,000 to Lakee fix; MDA 5,560.

B— 12,600 to DEN; 8,100 radar vectors to Wenny fix; 7,000 to Lakee fix; MDA 5,560.

C— 9,000 radar vectors to Wenny fix; 7,000 to Lakee fix; MDA 5,560.

**No answer is correct (4692).** *(IFH Chap X)*
Refer to Fig. 131 and 132. SILOW INT is 25 NM southwest of DEN VORTAC on V-89. The MEA from SILOW to DEN is 10,000 ft. From DEN VORTAC to WENNY INT, there is no published altitude, so you would maintain 10,000 ft. From WENNY, you would maintain 9,000 ft. to CHOSE, 7,000 ft. to LAKEE, MDA 5,560 ft.
Answer (A) is incorrect because there is no published altitude between DEN and WENNY, so you would maintain 10,000 ft. (not 9,000 ft.) to WENNY, 9,000 ft. (not 7,000 ft.) to CHOSE, then 7,000 ft. to LAKEE. Answer (B) is incorrect because 12,600 ft. and 8,100 ft. are minimum safe altitudes for emergency use. They are not published altitudes for the normal approach. Answer (C) is incorrect because you may not descend to 9,000 ft. until WENNY, and you may not descend to 7,000 ft. until CHOSE.

**118.**
**4655.** (Refer to figure 124 or 124A on pages 302 and 303.) What options are available concerning the teardrop course reversal for LOC RWY 35 approach to Duncan/Halliburton Field?

A— If a course reversal is required, only the teardrop can be executed.

B— The point where the turn is begun and the type and rate of turn are optional.

C— A normal procedure turn may be made if the 10 DME limit is not exceeded.

**Answer (A) is correct (4655).** *(AIM Para 5-48)*
When a procedure turn track is specified as in Fig. 124 or 124A, the turn must be flown exactly as depicted. Thus, only the teardrop can be executed.
Answer (B) is incorrect because the turn must be begun at a point such that the aircraft remains within 10 NM of the VOR, and the procedure turn must be a teardrop. Answer (C) is incorrect because the procedure turn must be a teardrop.

**119.**
**4656.** (Refer to figure 124 or 124A on pages 302 and 303.) The point on the teardrop procedure where the turn inbound (LOC RWY 35) Duncan/Halliburton, is initiated is determined by

A— DME and timing to remain within the 10-NM limit.

B— Timing for a 2 minute maximum.

C— Estimating groundspeed and radius of turn.

**Answer (A) is correct (4656).** *(AIM Para 5-48)*
The pilot may use DME and/or timing to determine his/her position, and may turn inbound at his/her discretion as long as (s)he remains within 10 NM of Duncan VOR.
Answer (B) is incorrect because the only maximum limit on the procedure turn is 10 NM from the VOR. Answer (C) is incorrect because estimating groundspeed and radius of turn is only part of what is required, i.e., also remain within 10 NM.

**120.**
**4696.** (Refer to figure 133 or 133A on pages 305 and 306.) How should a pilot reverse course to get established on the inbound course of the ILS RWY 9, if radar vectoring or the three IAF's are not utilized?

A— Execute a standard 45° procedure turn toward Seal Beach VORTAC or Pomona VORTAC.

B— Make an appropriate entry to the depicted holding pattern at Swan Lake OM/INT.

C— Use any type of procedure turn, but remain within 10 NM of Riverside VOR.

**Answer (B) is correct (4696).** *(IFH Chap X)*
If you do not have radar vectoring or utilize the 3 IAFs for the ILS RWY 9 in Fig. 133 or 133A, you should make an appropriate entry into the depicted holding pattern at the Swan Lake outer marker.
Answer (A) is incorrect because to execute a standard 45° procedure turn toward Seal Beach VORTAC or Pomona VORTAC is a nonsense statement. Answer (C) is incorrect because there is a depicted holding pattern.

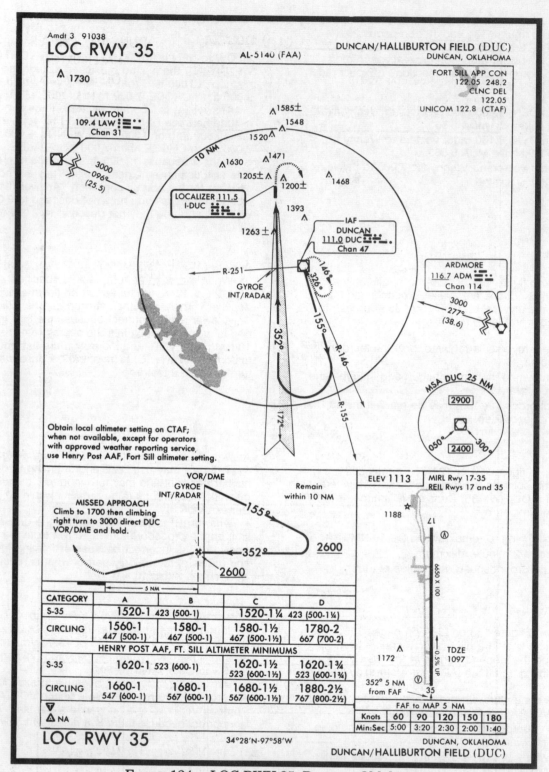

Amdt 3  91038
## LOC RWY 35
AL-5140 (FAA)

DUNCAN/HALLIBURTON FIELD (DUC)
DUNCAN, OKLAHOMA

FORT SILL APP CON
122.05  248.2
CLNC DEL
122.05
UNICOM 122.8 (CTAF)

△ 1730

LAWTON
109.4 LAW
Chan 31

3000
096°
(25.5)

△1585±
1548
1520△
△1471
△1630  △  1205±  △  1200±  △ 1468
LOCALIZER 111.5
I-DUC
1393
△
IAF
DUNCAN
111.0 DUC
Chan 47
1263±
R-251
GYROE
INT/RADAR
326°
146°
155°
R-146
352°
R-155
172°
10 NM

ARDMORE
116.7 ADM
Chan 114

3000
277°
(38.6)

MSA DUC 25 NM
2900
050°  300°
2400

Obtain local altimeter setting on CTAF;
when not available, except for operators
with approved weather reporting service,
use Henry Post AAF, Fort Sill altimeter setting.

VOR/DME
GYROE
INT/RADAR

MISSED APPROACH
Climb to 1700 then climbing
right turn to 3000 direct DUC
VOR/DME and hold.

Remain
within 10 NM

155°
352°
2600
2600

5 NM

ELEV 1113

MIRL Rwy 17-35
REIL Rwys 17 and 35

1188
☆
17
1172  △
6650 X 100
0.5% UP
TDZE
1097
352° 5 NM
from FAF
35

| CATEGORY | A | B | C | D |
|---|---|---|---|---|
| S-35 | 1520-1 | 423 (500-1) | 1520-1¼ | 423 (500-1¼) |
| CIRCLING | 1560-1 447 (500-1) | 1580-1 467 (500-1) | 1580-1½ 467 (500-1½) | 1780-2 667 (700-2) |
| HENRY POST AAF, FT. SILL ALTIMETER MINIMUMS | | | | |
| S-35 | 1620-1 | 523 (600-1) | 1620-1½ 523 (600-1½) | 1620-1¾ 523 (600-1¾) |
| CIRCLING | 1660-1 547 (600-1) | 1680-1 567 (600-1) | 1680-1½ 567 (600-1½) | 1880-2½ 767 (800-2½) |

▽
△ NA

| FAF to MAP 5 NM | | | | | |
|---|---|---|---|---|---|
| Knots | 60 | 90 | 120 | 150 | 180 |
| Min:Sec | 5:00 | 3:20 | 2:30 | 2:00 | 1:40 |

## LOC RWY 35
34°28'N-97°58'W

DUNCAN, OKLAHOMA
DUNCAN/HALLIBURTON FIELD (DUC)

FIGURE 124.—LOC RWY 35, Duncan, Oklahoma.

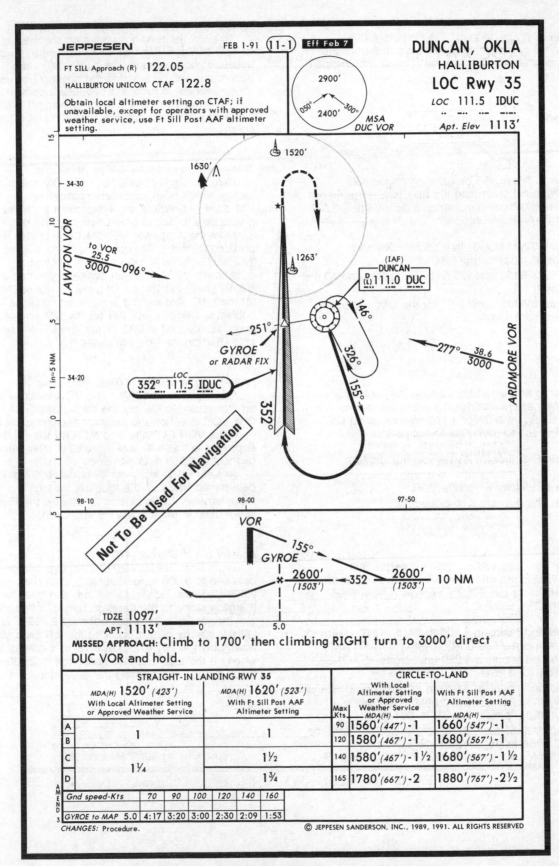

FIGURE 124A.—LOC RWY 35, Duncan, Oklahoma.

**121.**
**4698.** (Refer to figure 133 or 133A on pages 305 and 306.) What type of entry is recommended for the missed approach holding pattern at Riverside Municipal?

A— Direct.
B— Parallel.
C— Teardrop.

Answer (A) is correct (4698). *(IFH Chap X)*
To enter the holding pattern on the missed approach for ILS RWY 9 in Fig. 133 or 133A, use a direct entry because you come into the back side of the holding pattern and will be entering the holding pattern on R-078.
Answer (B) is incorrect because a parallel entry would be made from the northwest. Answer (C) is incorrect because a teardrop entry would be made from the southwest.

**122.**
**4699.** (Refer to figure 133 or 133A on pages 305 and 306.) What action should the pilot take if the marker beacon receiver becomes inoperative during the S-ILS 9 approach at Riverside Municipal?

A— Substitute SWAN LAKE INT. for the OM and surveillance radar for the MM.
B— Raise the DH 100 feet (50 feet for the OM and 50 feet for the MM).
C— Substitute SWAN LAKE INT. for the OM and use published minimums.

Answer (C) is correct (4699). *(IFH Chap X)*
Refer to Fig. 133 or 133A. The OM has a compass locator which is an acceptable substitute. An inoperative MM does not require any adjustment to be made to the published minimums (see Legend 20 on page 252).
Note the Jeppesen IAP chart (Fig. 133A) was not updated for this edition of the test and still has an "MM out" column in the minimum section.
Answer (A) is incorrect because you can substitute SWAN LAKE INT for the OM, but no substitute is required for the MM. Answer (B) is incorrect because you can substitute SWAN LAKE INT for the OM and no substitute is necessary for the MM. Thus, the DH will be as published on the IAP, not raised 100 ft.

**123.**
**4700.** (Refer to figure 133 or 133A on pages 305 and 306.) Why are two VOR/LOC receivers recommended to obtain an MDA of 1,160 when making an S-LOC 9 approach to Riverside Municipal?

A— To obtain R-327 of PDZ when on the localizer course.
B— In order to identify Riverside VOR.
C— To utilize the published stepdown fix.

Answer (C) is correct (4700). *(IFH Chap X)*
See Fig. 133 or 133A. Two VOR/localizer receivers are necessary to identify the step-down fix at Agnes INT. One VOR is set on the localizer and the other is set to Paradise VOR (R-032). The MDA for the S-LOC 9 approach is 1,260 ft. until Agnes INT after which a descent to 1,160 ft. is permitted.
Answer (A) is incorrect because R-327 of PDZ can be determined when on the localizer through the Swan Lake NDB. Answer (B) is incorrect because the Riverside VOR is not used in the ILS RWY 9 approach.

**124.**
**4701.** (Refer to figure 133 or 133A on pages 305 and 306.) What is the minimum altitude descent procedure if cleared for the S-ILS 9 approach from Seal Beach VORTAC?

A— Descend and maintain 3,000 to JASER INT, descend to and maintain 2,500 until crossing SWAN LAKE, descend and maintain 1,260 until crossing AGNES, and to 991 (DH) after passing AGNES.
B— Descend and maintain 3,000 to JASER INT, descend to 2,800 when established on the LOC course, intercept and maintain the GS to 991 (DH).
C— Descend and maintain 3,000 to JASER INT, descend to 2,500 while established on the LOC course inbound, intercept and maintain the GS to 991 (DH).

Answer (C) is correct (4701). *(IFH Chap X)*
From Seal Beach VORTAC on Fig. 133 or 133A, descend to 3,000 ft. to Jaser INT, then descend to 2,500 ft. on the localizer inbound, and then descend on the glide slope to the decision height of 991 ft.
Answer (A) is incorrect because 2,500 ft. is maintained until the glide slope and the ILS glide slope is flown down to 991 ft. Answer (B) is incorrect because, when on the localizer, one descends to 2,500 ft. (not 2,800 ft.) until intercepting the glide slope.

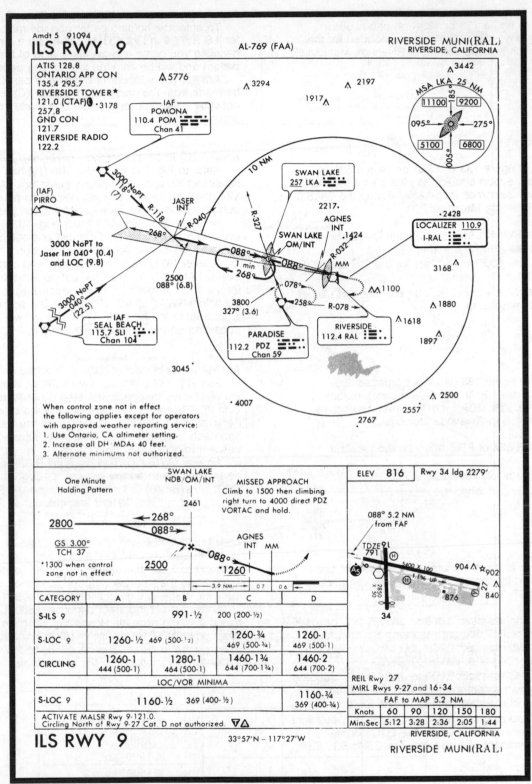

FIGURE 133.—ILS RWY 9 (RAL).

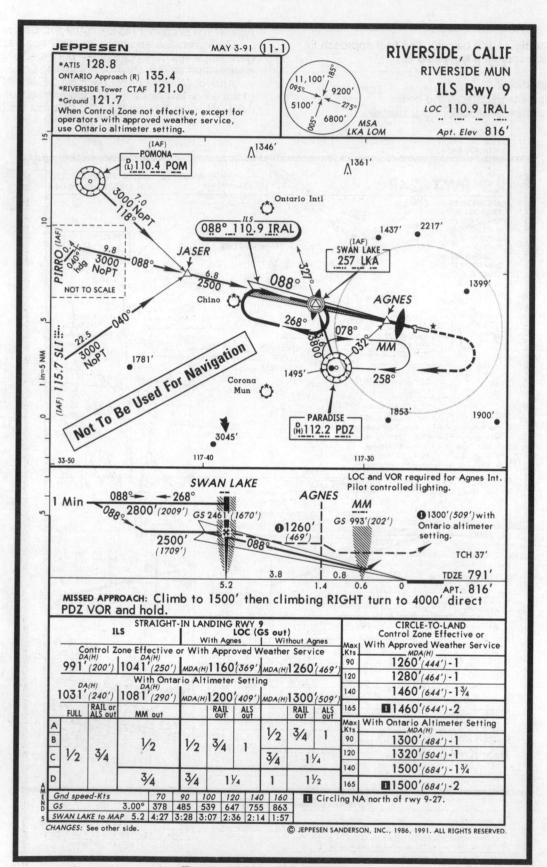

FIGURE 133A.—ILS RWY 9.

**125.**
**4642.** (Refer to figure 119 below.) The final approach fix for the precision approach is located at

A— DENAY intersection.
B— Glide slope intercept (lightning bolt).
C— ROMEN intersection/locator outer marker.

Answer (B) is correct (4642). *(AIM P/C Glossary)*
On a precision approach, the final approach fix is the glide slope intercept point at the published altitude. It is identified on an IAP chart by a lightning bolt.
Answer (A) is incorrect because DENAY INT is an IAF (not the FAF). Answer (C) is incorrect because ROMEN INT/LOM is the FAF on the LOC 24R (not the ILS).

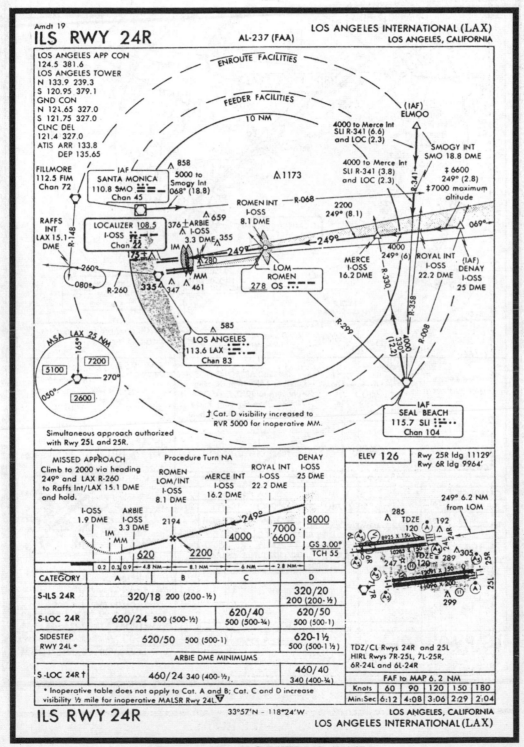

FIGURE 119.—ILS RWY 24R (LAX).

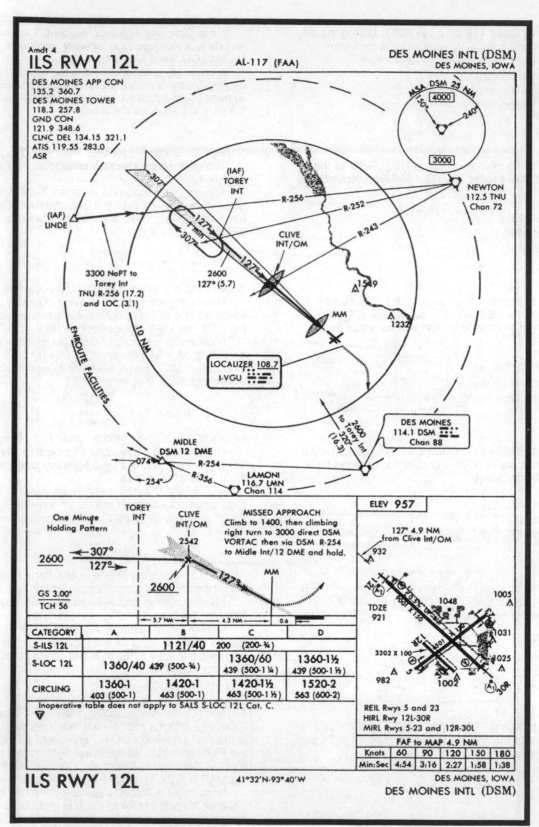

FIGURE 118.—ILS RWY 12L (DSM).

**126.**
**4635.** (Refer to figure 118 on page 308.) During the ILS RWY 12L procedure at DSM, what altitude minimum applies if the glide slope becomes inoperative?

A— 1,420 feet.
B— 1,360 feet.
C— 1,121 feet.

Answer (B) is correct (4635). (AIM Para 1-10)
If the glide slope fails during an ILS approach, the ILS reverts to a nonprecision localizer approach. The MDA for the LOC RWY 12L is 1,360 ft.
Answer (A) is incorrect because 1,420 ft. is the circling (not straight-in) MDA for Categories B and C. Answer (C) is incorrect because 1,121 ft. is the DH for the ILS (not the MDA for the localizer).

**127.**
**4648.** (Refer to figure 120 on page 310.) Refer to the DEN ILS RWY 35R procedure. The FAF intercept altitude is

A— 7,488 feet MSL.
B— 7,500 feet MSL.
C— 9,000 feet MSL.

Answer (B) is correct (4648). (AIM P/C Glossary)
The glide slope intercept altitude at the FAF (lightning bolt) is 7,500 ft. MSL.
Answer (A) is incorrect because 7,488 ft. MSL is the glide slope altitude over the OM. Answer (C) is incorrect because 9,000 ft. MSL is a minimum altitude between SEDAL and ENGLE INTs.

**128.**
**4649.** (Refer to figure 120 on page 310.) The symbol on the planview of the ILS RWY 35R procedure at DEN represents a minimum safe sector altitude within 25 NM of

A— Denver VORTAC.
B— Gandi outer marker.
C— Denver/Stapleton International Airport.

Answer (A) is correct (4649). (AIM Para 5-45)
Minimum safe altitudes provide obstacle clearance within 25 NM of the specified navigational facility. In Fig. 120, the MSA circle specifies DEN VORTAC.
Answer (B) is incorrect because an MSA will always be based on a VOR or an NDB (not an OM). Answer (C) is incorrect because an MSA will always be based on a VOR or an NDB (not an airport).

**129.**
**4650.** (Refer to figure 121 on page 311.) During the ILS RWY 30R procedure at DSM, the minimum altitude for glide slope interception is

A— 2,365 feet MSL.
B— 2,500 feet MSL.
C— 3,000 feet MSL.

Answer (B) is correct (4650). (AIM P/C Glossary)
The minimum glide slope interception altitude for an ILS is the FAF (marked by a lightning bolt). In Fig. 121, the FAF is 2,500 ft. MSL.
Answer (A) is incorrect because 2,365 ft. MSL is the glide slope altitude over the LOM. Answer (C) is incorrect because 3,000 ft. MSL is the MSA when south of the LOM.

**130.**
**4651.** (Refer to figure 121 on page 311.) During the ILS RWY 30R procedure at DSM, what MDA applies should the glide slope become inoperative?

A— 1,157 feet.
B— 1,320 feet.
C— 1,360 feet.

Answer (B) is correct (4651). (AIM Para 1-10)
When the glide slope fails on an ILS approach, the ILS reverts to a nonprecision localizer approach. The MDA for the LOC 30R (Fig. 121) is 1,320 ft.
Answer (A) is incorrect because 1,157 ft. is the DH for the ILS (not the MDA for the localizer). Answer (C) is incorrect because 1,360 ft. is the circling (not straight-in) MDA for Category A.

**131.**
**4652.** (Refer to figure 122 on page 312.) The missed approach point of the ATL S-LOC 8L procedure is located how far from the LOM?

A— 4.8 NM.
B— 5.1 NM.
C— 5.2 NM.

Answer (C) is correct (4652). (AIM P/C Glossary)
In Fig. 122 the profile view indicates that CATTA LOM is the FAF for the S-LOC 8L approach, as indicated by the Maltese cross. At the lower right corner of the IAP chart, it indicates that from the FAF (i.e., CATTA LOM) to the MAP is 5.2 NM, for the S-LOC 8L approach.
Answer (A) is incorrect because 4.8 NM is the distance from the LOM to the MM, not the MAP. Answer (B) is incorrect because 5.1 NM is the distance from the LOM to the IM, not the MAP.

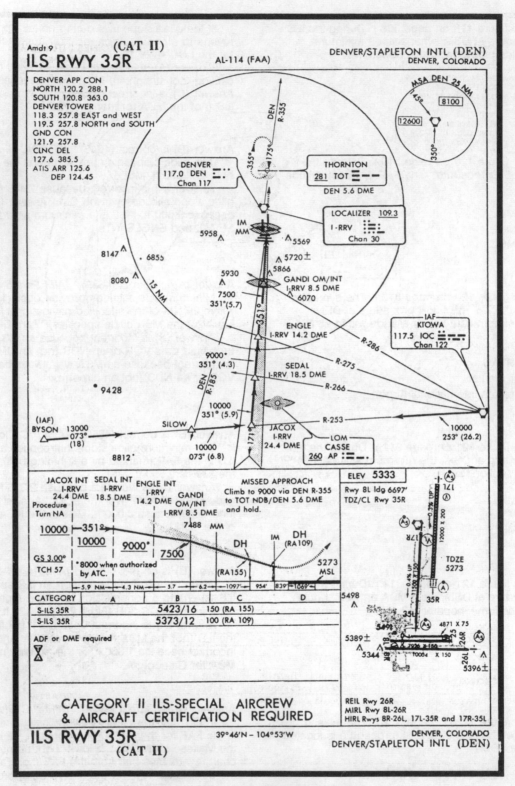

FIGURE 120.—ILS RWY 35R (DEN).

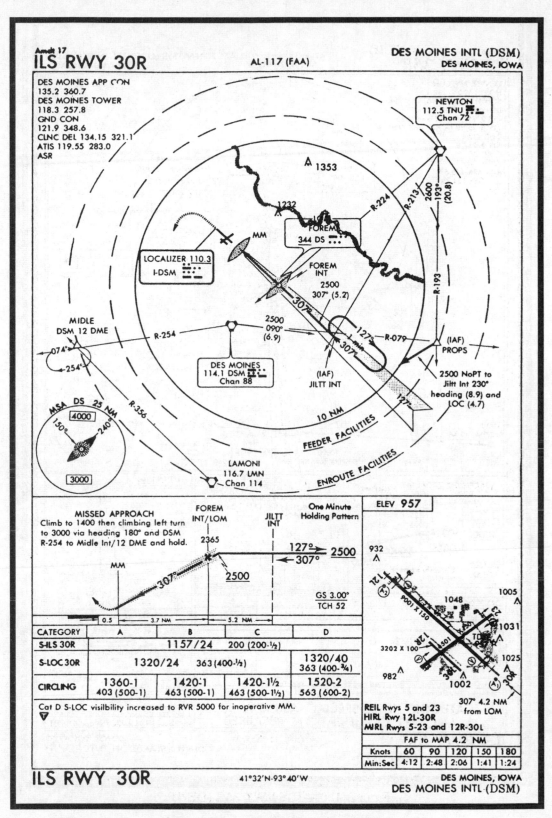

FIGURE 121.—ILS RWY 30R (DSM).

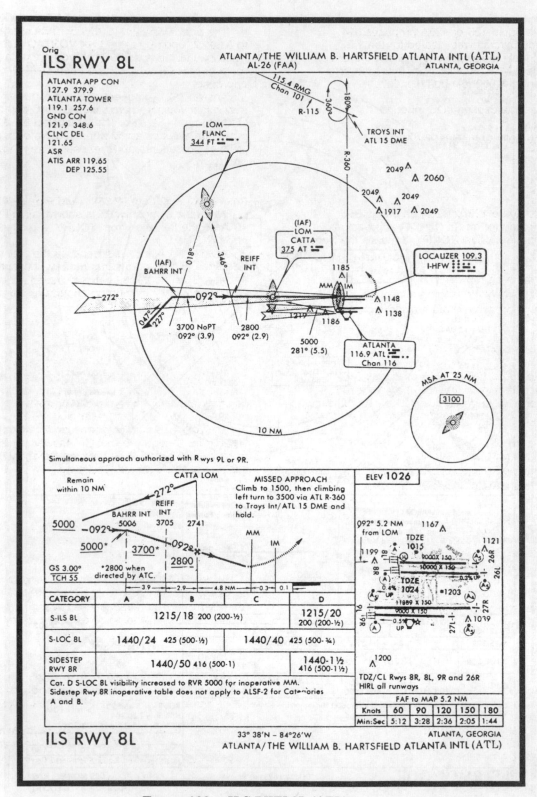

FIGURE 122.—ILS RWY 8L (ATL).

**132.**
**4657.** (Refer to figure 125 or 125A on pages 314 and 315.) If your aircraft was cleared for the ILS RWY 17R at Lincoln Municipal and crossed the Lincoln VOR at 5,000 feet MSL, at what point in the teardrop could a descent to 3,000 feet commence?

A— As soon as intercepting LOC inbound.
B— Immediately.
C— Only at the point authorized by ATC.

**133.**
**4658.** (Refer to figure 125 or 125A on pages 314 and 315.) If cleared for an S-LOC 17R approach at Lincoln Municipal from over TOUHY, it means the flight should

A— land straight in on runway 17R.
B— comply with straight-in landing minimums.
C— begin final approach without making a procedure turn.

**134.**
**4659.** (Refer to figure 126 or 126A on pages 316 and 317.) What landing minimums apply for a FAR part 91 operator at Dothan, AL using a category C aircraft during a circling LOC 31 approach at 120 knots? (DME available.)

A— MDA 860 feet MSL and visibility 2 SM.
B— MDA 860 feet MSL and visibility 1 and ½ SM.
C— MDA 720 feet MSL and visibility 3/4 SM.

**135.**
**4660.** (Refer to figure 126 or 126A on pages 316 and 317.) If cleared for a straight-in LOC approach from over OALDY, it means the flight should

A— land straight in on runway 31.
B— comply with straight-in landing minimums.
C— begin final approach without making a procedure turn.

**136.**
**4661.** (Refer to figure 126 or 126A on pages 316 and 317.) What is the ability to identify the RRS 2.5 stepdown fix worth in terms of localizer circle-to-land minimums for a category C aircraft?

A— Decreases MDA by 20 feet.
B— Decreases visibility by ½ SM.
C— Without the stepdown fix, a circling approach is not available.

Answer (B) is correct (4657). *(AIM Para 5-47)*
The profile view in Fig. 125 or 125A shows a descent to 3,000 ft. upon crossing LNK VORTAC outbound. Published altitudes apply when you are on a published route or procedure, and have been cleared for the approach.
Answer (A) is incorrect because a descent to 3,000 ft. may begin when you are LNK VORTAC outbound (not LOC inbound). Answer (C) is incorrect because published altitudes apply when you are on a published route or procedure and have been cleared for the approach.

Answer (C) is correct (4658). *(AIM Para 5-48)*
When the symbol NoPT is shown, as in Fig. 125 or 125A on the transition from TOUHY, a procedure turn is not authorized.
Answer (A) is incorrect because the pilot may request clearance to land on another runway, if desired. Answer (B) is incorrect because circling minimums should be used if landing on another runway is desired.

Answer (B) is correct (4659). *(IFH Chap X)*
Although the aircraft is circling at 120 kt. (which is Category B), it is a Category C aircraft, and the higher category applies. Thus, the circling minimums (with an operative DME) are 860 ft. MSL and 1½ SM.
Answer (A) is incorrect because 2 SM is the minimum visibility for Category D, not C. Answer (C) is incorrect because 720 ft. and ¾ SM are the Category D straight-in minimums, not Category C circling.

Answer (C) is correct (4660). *(AIM Para 5-48)*
When the symbol NoPT is shown, as in Fig. 126 or 126A on the transition from OALDY, a procedure turn is not authorized.
Answer (A) is incorrect because the pilot may request clearance to land on another runway, if desired. Answer (B) is incorrect because circling minimums should be used if landing on another runway is desired.

Answer (A) is correct (4661). *(IFH Chap X)*
The MDA without DME is 880 ft. and with DME is 860 ft. (refer to Fig. 126 or 126A). Thus, DME decreases MDA by 20 ft.
Answer (B) is incorrect because visibility minima remain the same, regardless of DME. Answer (C) is incorrect because circling is authorized without DME.

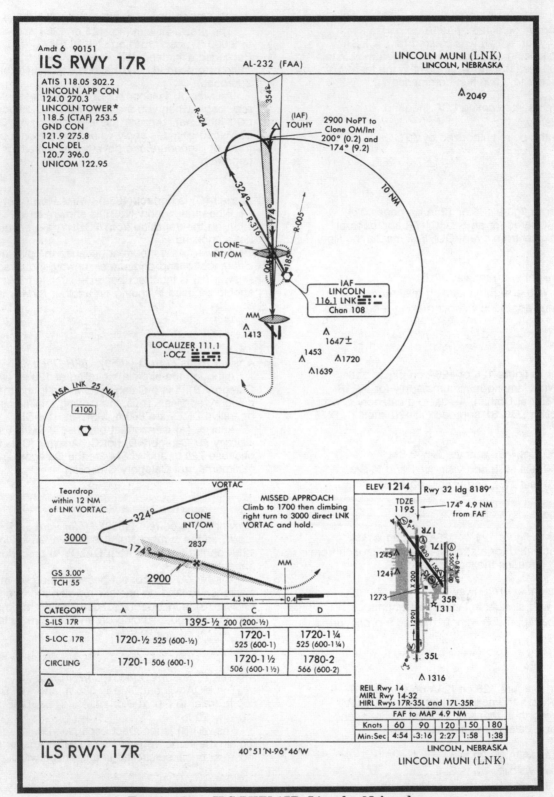

FIGURE 125.—ILS RWY 17R, Lincoln, Nebraska.

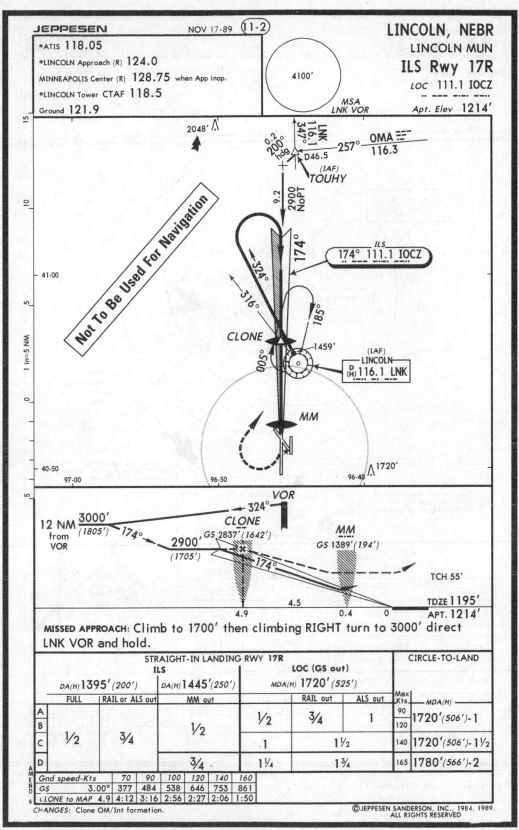

FIGURE 125A.—ILS RWY 17R, Lincoln, Nebraska.

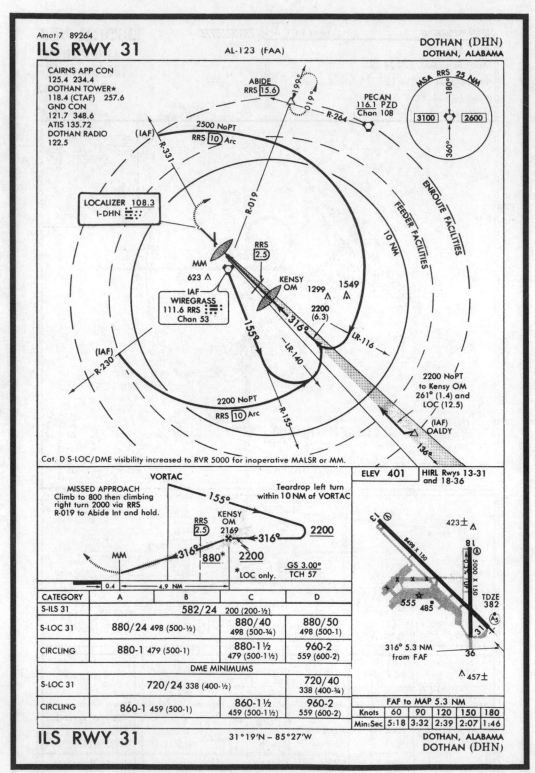

FIGURE 126.—ILS RWY 31, Dothan, Alabama.

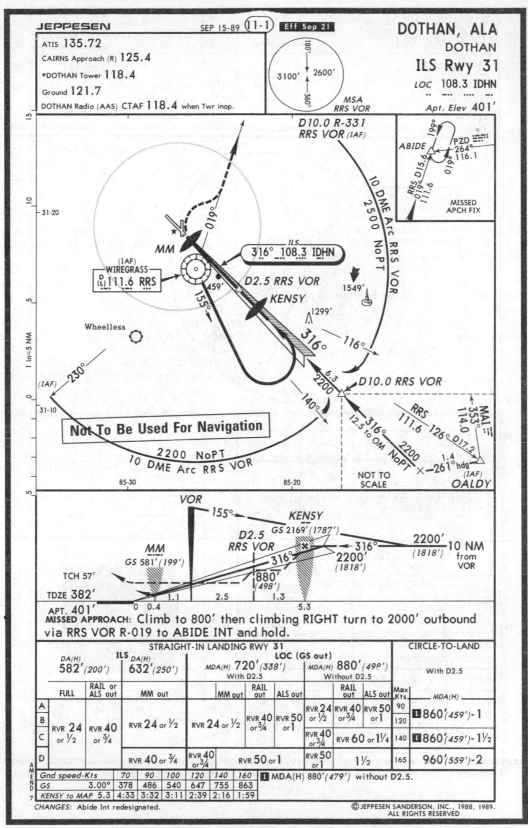

FIGURE 126A.—ILS RWY 31, Dothan, Alabama.

**137.**
**4332.** (Refer to figures 60A and 60B on pages 319 and 320.)  What is the elevation of the TDZE for RWY 4?

A— 70 feet MSL.
B— 54 feet MSL.
C— 46 feet MSL.

Answer (C) is correct (4332).  *(IFH Chap X)*
The TDZE (Touch Down Zone Elevation) is the highest elevation in the first 3,000 ft. of the runway on a straight-in landing approach.  On an NOS chart, it is marked in the airport diagram near the approach end of the runway.  On a Jeppesen Chart, it is marked in the profile view next to the runway.  Thus, the TDZE for RWY 4 is 46 ft. MSL.
Answer (A) is incorrect because 70 ft. MSL is the elevation of a tower near the approach end of RWY 4.  Answer (B) is incorrect because 54 ft. MSL is the TCH (Threshold Crossing Height) on the ILS RWY 4 approach, i.e., the height at which the airplane's glide slope antenna should cross the runway's threshold on the glide slope.

**138.**
**4331.** (Refer to figures 60A and 60B on pages 319 and 320, and 61 below.)  What is your position relative to the PLATS intersection, glide slope, and the localizer course?

A— Past PLATS, below the glide slope, and right of the localizer course.
B— Approaching PLATS, above the glide slope, and left of the localizer course.
C— Past PLATS, above the glide slope, and right of the localizer course.

Answer (C) is correct (4331).  *(IFH Chap VIII)*
The VOR in Fig. 61 is tuned to the localizer.  The CDI and glide slope needles show your position as above glide slope and right of the localizer course.  The RMI #2 indicator is tuned to the Scholes VORTAC and shows your position as R-300 (tail of the double needle).  Since PLATS Intersection is on R-291, you are northeast of PLATS, or past it on the inbound course.
Answer (A) is incorrect because the glide slope needle is below center, indicating above (not below) glide slope.  Answer (B) is incorrect because R-300 of Scholes VORTAC is northeast (not southwest) of PLATS, and the CDI is left of center, indicating right (not left) of course.

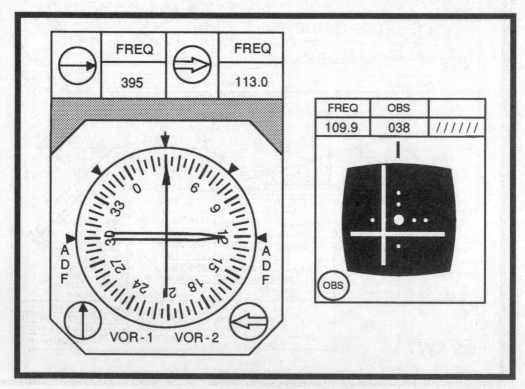

FIGURE 61.—RMI and CDI Indicators.

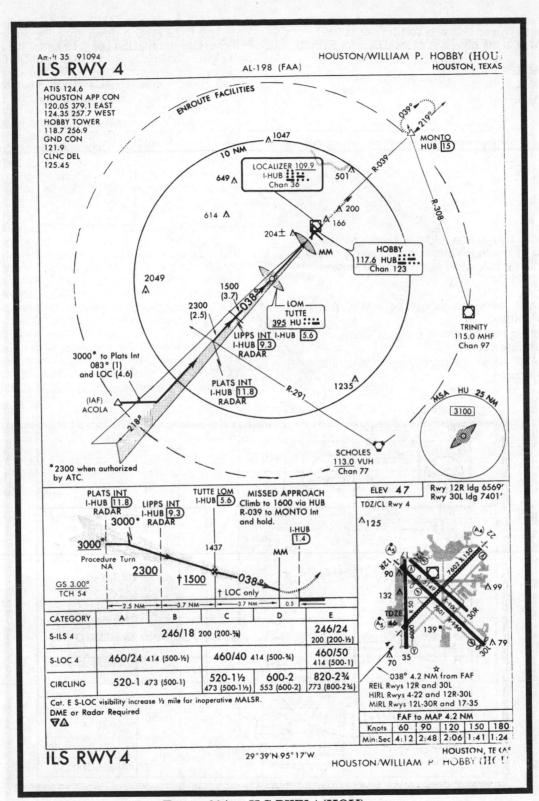

FIGURE 60A.—ILS RWY 4 (HOU).

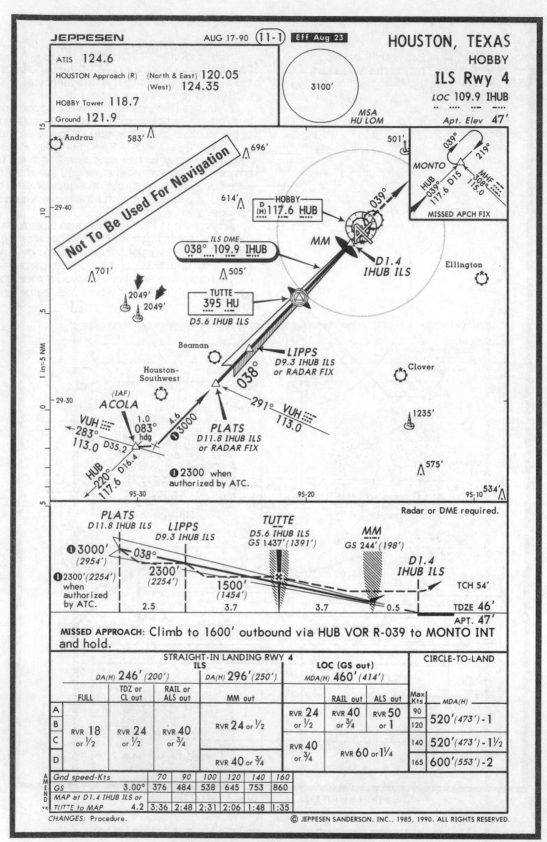

FIGURE 60B.— ILS RWY 4 (HOU).

## 9.13 SIDs and STARs

**139.**
**4488.** (Refer to figure 85 on page 323 and 86 below.) Which combination of indications confirm that you are approaching WAGGE intersection slightly to the right of the LOC centerline on departure?

A— 1 and 3.
B— 1 and 4.
C— 2 and 3.

Answer (C) is the best answer (4488). *(IFH Chap VIII)*

Note that in VOR indications 3 and 4 in Fig. 86 the FAA erroneously indicates VOR frequencies of 112.8 and 115.9, not the SWR VORTAC frequency of 113.2. The OBS is set to the proper radial.

If you are flying out on the back course you have front course indications. Therefore, if you are to the right of the localizer centerline, you will get a left indication, such as in 2 (see Figs. 85 and 86). Since answer (C) is the only choice that has indication 2, it is the best answer. To determine whether you are at WAGGE INT, visualize yourself flying out on Squaw Valley R-062 (113.2). If you were north of the radial, you would get a right deviation such as in 3.

Answer (A) is incorrect because illustration 1 would mean you are left (not right) of the localizer centerline. Answer (B) is incorrect because illustration 1 would mean you are left (not right) of the localizer centerline. Also, a left deviation on 113.2 (as in 4) would mean that you were south of R-062 and would thus be beyond WAGGE INT.

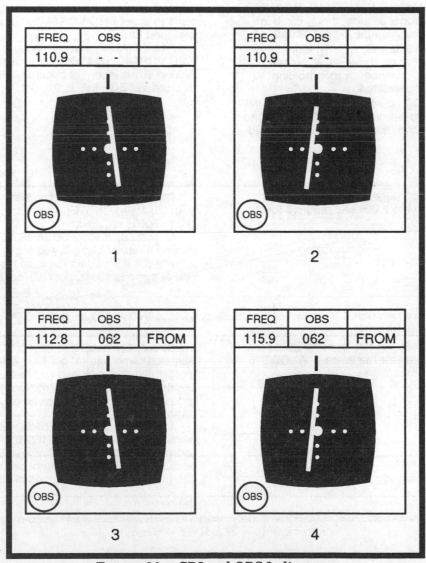

FIGURE 86.—CDI and OBS Indicators.

**140.**
**4489.** (Refer to figure 85 on page 323.) What route should you take if cleared for the Washoe Two Departure and your assigned route is V6?

A— Climb on the LOC south course to WAGGE where you will be vectored to V6.
B— Climb on the LOC south course to cross WAGGE at 9,000, turn left and fly direct to FMG VORTAC and cross at or above 10,000, and proceed on FMG R-241.
C— Climb on the LOC south course to WAGGE, turn left and fly direct to FMG VORTAC. If at 10,000 turn left and proceed on FMG R-241; if not at 10,000 enter depicted holding pattern and climb to 10,000 before proceeding on FMG R-241.

Answer (A) is correct (4489). *(AIM Para 5-23)*
The instructions on Fig. 85 for the Washoe Two Departure are to "climb via Reno localizer south course to WAGGE INT for radar vector to assigned route."
Answer (B) is incorrect because it describes the lost communication procedure. Answer (C) is incorrect because it describes the lost communication procedure.

**141.**
**4490.** (Refer to figure 85 on page 323.) What procedure should be followed if communications are lost before reaching 9,000 feet?

A— At 9,000, turn left direct to FMG VORTAC, then via assigned route if at proper altitude; if not, climb in holding pattern until reaching the proper altitude.
B— Continue climb to WAGGE INT, turn left direct to FMG VORTAC, then if at or above MCA, proceed on assigned route; if not, continue climb in holding pattern until at the proper altitude.
C— Continue climb on LOC course to cross WAGGE INT at or above 9,000, turn left direct to FMG VORTAC to cross at 10,000 or above, and continue on assigned course.

Answer (B) is correct (4490). *(AIM Para 5-23)*
Per Fig. 85, "If not in contact with departure control within 1 min. after takeoff or if communications are lost before 9,000 ft., continue climbing to WAGGE INT, turn left, proceed directly to FMG VORTAC, then via (assigned route) or climb in holding pattern northeast on R-041, left turns to cross FMG VORTAC at or above MCA for assigned route.
Answer (A) is incorrect because you are to turn left to FMG VORTAC at WAGGE, irrespective of altitude. Answer (C) is incorrect because there is no requirement to cross WAGGE INT at 9,000 ft.

**142.**
**4491.** (Refer to figure 85 on page 323.) What is the minimum rate climb per NM to 9,000 feet required for the WASH2 WAGGE Departure?

A— 400 feet.
B— 750 feet.
C— 875 feet.

Answer (A) is correct (4491). *(AIM Para 5-23)*
The right-hand side of the Washoe Two Departure (Fig. 85) states, "NOTE: Minimum climb rate of 400' per NM to 9000' required."
Answer (B) is incorrect because the required minimum rate of climb is 400 ft. per NM (not 750 ft.). Answer (C) is incorrect because the required minimum rate of climb is 400 ft. per NM (not 875 ft.).

**143.**
**4492.** (Refer to figure 85 on page 323.) Of the following, which is the minimum acceptable rate of climb (feet per minute) to 9,000 feet required for the WASH2 WAGGE departure at a GS of 150 knots?

A— 750 feet per minute.
B— 825 feet per minute.
C— 1,000 feet per minute.

Answer (C) is correct (4492). *(ACL)*
The required climb rate is 400 ft./NM (Fig. 85). Use the Rate of Climb table in Legend 18 on page 258. Required climb rate (ft. per NM) is found on the left margin and groundspeed (kt.) is found on the top. Locate 400 ft. per NM and move right to the 150-kt. groundspeed column to determine a 1,000-fpm rate of climb.
Answer (A) is incorrect because 750 fpm is the rate of climb at a groundspeed of 150 kt. that requires a climb of 300 (not 400) ft. per NM. Answer (B) is incorrect because 825 fpm is the rate of climb at approximately 125 (not 150) kt. for a required climb of 400 ft. per NM.

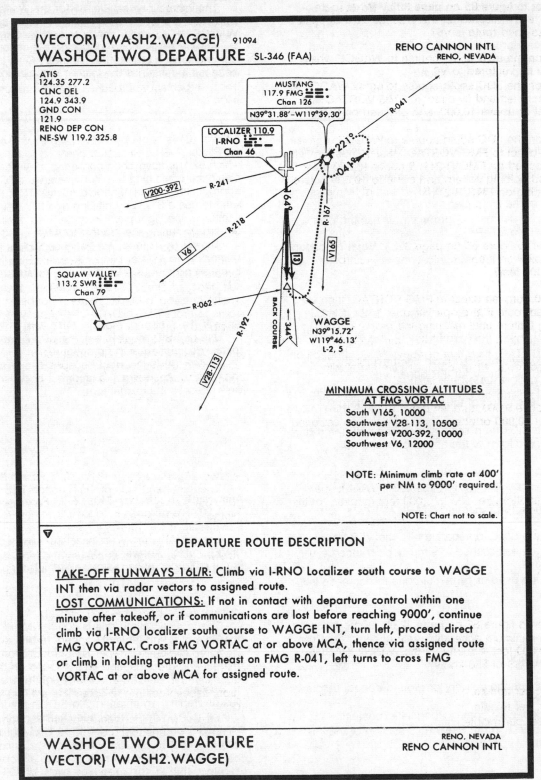

FIGURE 85.—WASHOE TWO DEPARTURE.

**144.**
**4442.** Which clearance procedures may be issued by ATC without prior pilot request?

A— SID's, standard terminal arrival route (STAR), and contact approaches.

B— Contact and visual approaches.

C— SID's, STAR's, and visual approaches.

Answer (C) is correct (4442). *(AIM Para 5-73)*
SIDs, STARs, and visual approaches are all routinely assigned by ATC as appropriate. Contact approaches must be requested by the pilot and made in lieu of a standard or special instrument approach.
Answer (A) is incorrect because contact approaches must be requested by the pilot. Answer (B) is incorrect because contact approaches must be requested by the pilot.

**145.**
**4751.** Under which condition does ATC issue a STAR?

A— To all pilots wherever STAR's are available.

B— Only if the pilot requests a STAR in the "Remarks" section of the flight plan.

C— When ATC deems it appropriate, unless the pilot requests "No STAR."

Answer (C) is correct (4751). *(AIM Para 5-41)*
Pilots of IFR civil aircraft destined to locations for which STARs have been published may be issued a clearance containing a STAR whenever ATC deems it appropriate. The pilot should notify ATC if (s)he does not wish to use a STAR by placing "No STAR" in the remarks section of the flight plan or by the less desirable method of verbally stating the request to ATC.
Answer (A) is incorrect because STARs are not mandatory to ATC or pilots. Answer (B) is incorrect because pilot request is necessary to avoid, not obtain, STARs.

**146.**
**4638.** Which is true regarding the use of a SID chart?

A— At airfields where SID's have been established, SID usage is mandatory for IFR departures.

B— To use a SID, the pilot must possess at least the textual description of the approved standard departure.

C— To use a SID, the pilot must possess both the textual and graphic form of the approved standard departure.

Answer (B) is correct (4638). *(AIM Para 5-26)*
Use of a SID requires that the pilot have at least the textual description of the procedure.
Answer (A) is incorrect because use of a SID is never mandatory. Answer (C) is incorrect because a pilot need only possess the textual form.

**147.**
**4640.** Which is true regarding STAR's?

A— STAR's are used to separate IFR and VFR traffic.

B— STAR's are established to simplify clearance delivery procedures.

C— STAR's are used at certain airports to decrease traffic congestion.

Answer (B) is correct (4640). *(AIM Para 5-41)*
A STAR's purpose is to simplify clearance delivery procedures.
Answer (A) is incorrect because STARs do not pertain to VFR traffic. Answer (C) is incorrect because STARs are used to decrease radio (not traffic) congestion.

**148.**
**4417.** What action is recommended if a pilot does not wish to use a SID?

A— Advise clearance delivery or ground control before departure.

B— Advise departure control upon initial contact.

C— Enter "No SID" in the REMARKS section of the IFR flight plan.

Answer (C) is correct (4417). *(AIM Para 5-26)*
A pilot who does not possess SID charts or does not wish to use SIDs should advise ATC by indicating "No SID" in the remarks section of the flight plan.
Answer (A) is incorrect because verbal requests are less desirable than entering "No SID" in the flight plan. Answer (B) is incorrect because verbal requests are less desirable than entering "No SID" in the flight plan.

**149.**
**4418.** A particular SID requires a minimum climb rate of 210 feet per NM to 8,000 feet. If you climb with a groundspeed of 140 knots, what is the rate of climb required in feet per minute?

A— 210.
B— 450.
C— 490.

Answer (C) is correct (4418). *(ACL)*
Use the Rate of Climb table in Legend 18 on page 258. Required climb rate (ft. per NM) is found on the left margin and groundspeed (kt.) is found on the top. Since 210 ft. per NM is not on the chart, you must interpolate between 200 and 250 ft. per NM at 140 kt. At 200 ft. per NM the climb rate is 467 fpm, and at 250 ft. per NM it is 583 fpm. Interpolate for 210 ft. per NM to determine a rate of climb of 490 fpm.
Answer (A) is incorrect because 210 is the required ft. per NM (not fpm). Answer (B) is incorrect because the required climb rate is 490 (not 450) fpm.

**150.**
**4419.** Which procedure applies to SID's?

A— SID clearances will not be issued unless requested by the pilot.
B— The pilot in command must accept a SID when issued by ATC.
C— If a SID is accepted, the pilot must possess at least a textual description.

Answer (C) is correct (4419). *(AIM Para 5-26)*
Once a SID is accepted, the presumption by ATC is that the pilot possesses a textual description of the SID.
Answer (A) is incorrect because pilots operating from locations with SID procedures may expect ATC clearances containing a SID. Answer (B) is incorrect because you must reject a SID clearance if you do not have a text of the SID or if it is otherwise unacceptable.

**151.**
**4070.** Preferred IFR routes beginning with a fix indicate that departing aircraft will normally be routed to the fix via

A— the established airway(s) between the departure airport and the fix.
B— a standard instrument departure (SID), or radar vectors.
C— direct route only.

Answer (B) is correct (4070). *(P/C Glossary)*
Preferred IFR routes are correlated with SIDs and STARs and may be defined by airways, jet routes, and direct routes between NAVAIDs. Thus, preferred routes beginning with a fix indicate that the departing traffic will normally be routed to the fix via a SID or radar vectors.
Answer (A) is incorrect because established airways may not exist between the airport and the fix, and other methods may be more efficient and effective. Answer (C) is incorrect because a direct route may not be appropriate due to obstructions or traffic flows.

### 9.14 Microwave Landing System

**152.**
**4798.** What international Morse Code identifier is used to identify a specific interim standard microwave landing system?

A— A two letter Morse Code identifier preceded by the Morse Code for the letters "IM".
B— A three letter Morse Code identifier preceded by the Morse Code for the letter "M".
C— A three letter Morse Code identifier preceded by the Morse Code for the letters "ML".

Answer (B) is correct (4798). *(AIM Para 1-12)*
MLS identification is a 4-character alphabetic designation starting with the letter "M", transmitted in international Morse Code at least 6 times per minute.
Answer (A) is incorrect because the identifier letter is the single character "M" and followed by three other letters. Answer (C) is incorrect because the identifier letter is the single character "M" and followed by three other letters.

**153.**
**4799.** To at least which altitude AGL is the approach azimuth guidance angle coverage of an MLS?

A— 20,000 feet.
B— 10,000 feet.
C— 8,000 feet.

Answer (A) is correct (4799). *(AIM Para 1-12)*
The approach azimuth guidance angle coverage of an MLS extends in elevation to an angle of 15° and to at least 20,000 ft.
Answer (B) is incorrect because an MSL provides coverage to at least 20,000 ft. (not 10,000 ft.).
Answer (C) is incorrect because an MSL provides coverage to at least 20,000 ft. (not 8,000 ft.).

**154.**
**4800.** What are the lateral approach azimuth angle limits, referenced to either side of the landing runway, of an MLS?

A— At least 15°.
B— 20°.
C— At least 40°.

Answer (C) is correct (4800).  *(AIM Para 1-12)*
The lateral approach azimuth angle limits are at least 40° on each side of the runway.
Answer (A) is incorrect because vertical (not lateral) coverage extends to 15°.  Answer (B) is incorrect because lateral limits are 40° (not 20°).

**155.**
**4801.** What are the respective range limits for the front and back guidance of an MLS?

A— 10 NM and 10 NM.
B— 15 NM and 10 NM.
C— 20 NM and 7 NM.

Answer (C) is correct (4801).  *(AIM Para 1-12)*
The range limit for the front (approach) azimuth angle guidance of an MLS is at least 20 NM.  The range limit for the back azimuth angle guidance is at least 7 NM.
Answer (A) is incorrect because the front and back limits, respectively, are 20 NM and 7 NM (not 10 NM and 10 NM).  Answer (B) is incorrect because the front and back limits, respectively, are 20 NM and 7 NM (not 15 NM and 10 NM).

# END OF CHAPTER

# CHAPTER TEN
# IFR EN ROUTE

This chapter contains outlines of major concepts tested, all FAA test questions and answers regarding IFR en route, and an explanation of each answer. The subtopics or modules within this chapter are listed above, followed in parentheses by the number of questions from the FAA written test pertaining to that particular module. The two numbers following the parentheses are the page numbers on which the outline and questions begin for that module.

Most of the charts herein contain old airspace terminology. Memory aid: list A down to G (no F) and match old airspace classifications based on height from highest to lowest: A = PCA, B = TCA, C = ARSA, D = ATA, E = general controlled, and G = uncontrolled.

**CAUTION:** Recall that the **sole purpose** of this book is to expedite your passing the FAA written test for the instrument rating. Accordingly, all extraneous material (i.e., topics or regulations not directly tested on the FAA written test) is omitted, even though much more information and knowledge are necessary to fly safely. This additional material is presented in *Instrument Pilot FAA Practical Test Prep* and *Aviation Weather and Weather Services*, available from Gleim Publications, Inc. See the order form on page 478.

## 10.1 MINIMUM EN ROUTE ALTITUDE (Questions 1-13)

1. MRA (minimum reception altitude) is the lowest altitude at which an intersection can be determined.

2. MOCA (minimum obstruction clearance altitude) assures acceptable navigational signal coverage only within 22 NM (25 SM) of a VOR.

   a. ATC may assign the MOCA as an assigned altitude when certain special conditions exist, and when within 22 NM of a VOR.

3. MEA (minimum en route altitude) is the lowest published altitude between radio fixes which assures acceptable navigational signal coverage and meets obstacle clearance requirements between those fixes.

   a. It is the minimum altitude to cross a fix beyond which a higher minimum applies.

4. Obstruction clearance in nonmountainous areas is guaranteed for the MOCA and all other minimum IFR altitudes providing at least 1,000 ft. of vertical distance from the highest obstruction 4 NM either side of the center of the airway to be flown.

   a. In mountainous areas, 2,000 ft. of vertical distance is provided.

5. Routes designed to serve aircraft operating from 18,000 ft. MSL up to and including FL 450 are referred to as jet routes or "J" routes.

## 10.2 VFR-on-Top (Questions 14-27)

1. VFR-on-Top can be conducted only after a pilot has received a VFR-on-Top clearance to operate in VFR conditions.

   a. Note: The pilot must request a VFR-on-Top clearance.

2. VFR-on-Top must comply with the appropriate VFR cruising altitudes as prescribed in FAR 91.159, which is based upon magnetic courses.

   a. 000°-179° -- odd 1,000 ft. plus 500 ft.
   b. 180°-359° -- even 1,000 ft. plus 500 ft.

3. VFR-on-Top must be conducted at an altitude above the minimum IFR altitude.

4. VFR-on-Top is conducted such that both VFR and IFR rules apply.

5. A clearance "to VFR-on-Top" is to fly through cloud layers to VFR conditions on top.

6. VFR-on-Top operations are specifically prohibited in Class A airspace.

7. In VFR-on-Top clearances, you must provide the same reports to ATC that are required for any other IFR flight.

## 10.3 IFR EN ROUTE CHART INTERPRETATION (Questions 28-59)

1. The FAA written test questions in this module are wide ranging. They are best prepared for by studying the Legend for En Route Low Altitude Charts through page 330. These legends are reprinted from the FAA Instrument Rating Written Test Book.

   a. Some questions require application of previously covered topics such as interpretation of VOR indicators.

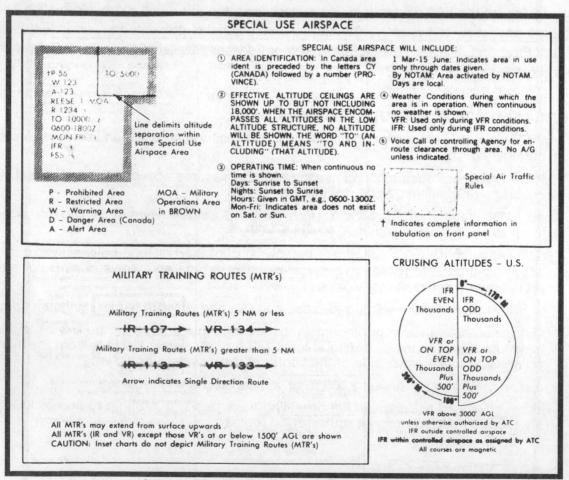

LEGEND 24.—En Route Low Altitude Charts

# UNITED STATES GOVERNMENT
## FLIGHT INFORMATION PUBLICATION
# ENROUTE LOW ALTITUDE – U. S.
### For use up to but not including 18,000' MSL
### HORIZONTAL DATUM: NORTH AMERICAN DATUM OF 1927

# L E G E N D

## AIRPORTS

Airports/Seaplane bases shown in BLUE have an approved Low Altitude Instrument Approach Procedure published. Those shown in DARK BLUE have an approved DOD Low Altitude Instrument Approach Procedure and/or DOD RADAR MINIMA published in DOD FLIPS, Alaska Supplement or Alaska Terminal. Airports/Seaplane bases shown in BROWN do not have a published Instrument Approach Procedure.

**LAND**      **SEA**

◇ ◈    Civil    ⊕ ⬥

◈ ◈    Civil-Military    ◈ ◈

◎ ●    Military    ⊕ ●

Ⓗ Ⓗ    Heliport

### RELATED FACILITIES

Pilot to Metro Service (PMSV)

●━●    Continuous Operation

○━○    Less than Continuous

◇    Weather Radar (WXR)

◆▷    PMSV and WXR Combined

Published ILS and/or Localizer Procedure available

Published SDF Procedure available

1. Parentheses around airport name indicate military landing rights not available
2. Airport elevation given in feet above or below mean sea level
3. Length of longest runway given to nearest 100 feet with 70 feet as the dividing point (Add 00)
4. Airport symbol may be offset for enroute navigation aids
5. Pvt – Private use, not available to general public
6. A box enclosing the airport name indicates FAR 93 Special Requirements – See Directory/Supplement

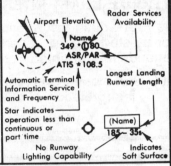

Night Landing Capability. Asterisk indicates lighting on request or operating part of night only. Circle indicates Pilot Controlled Lighting (PCL). For information consult Directory or FLIP IFR Supplement.

Airport Elevation — 349 *①80

Radar Services Availability — ASR/PAR

Automatic Terminal Information Service and Frequency — ATIS *108.5

Longest Landing Runway Length

Star indicates operation less than continuous or part time

No Runway Lighting Capability

(Name) 185– 35ᴸ

Indicates Soft Surface

## RADIO AIDS TO NAVIGATION AND COMMUNICATION BOXES

### RADIO AIDS TO NAVIGATION

VHF/UHF Data is depicted in BLUE
LF/MF Data is depicted in BROWN

**COMPASS ROSE** Oriented to magnetic north. Size of compass rose has no significance. Smaller sizes are used in congested areas.

⬡ VOR    ▽ TACAN    ⬡ VORTAC

▢ VOR/DME    ◉ NDB/DME

LF/MF Non-directional Radiobeacon or Marine Radiobeacon with magnetic north indicator

UHF Non-directional Radiobeacon

Compass Locator Beacon

◉ Consolan Station

Ⓖ Ground Control Intercept (GCI)

ILS Localizer Course with ATC function. Feathered side indicates Blue Sector.

SDF Localizer Course with ATC function.

### RADIO AIDS TO NAVIGATION DATA BOXES

Abnormal Status Underprint for affected data, e.g., SHUT DOWN, MAY BE COMSN, etc.

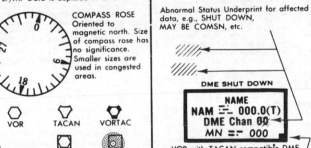

**DME SHUT DOWN**

```
       NAME
NAM  ⋮⋮  000.0(T)
DME Chan 00
MN  ⋮⋮  000
```

**VOR with TACAN compatible DME**
A solid square indicates information available. Enroute weather, when available, is broadcasted on the associated NAVAID frequency. For terminal weather frequencies see A/G Frequency Tab under associated airport.

**(T)** Frequency protection Usable range at 12,000' – 25 NM

**(Y)** TACAN must be placed in "Y" mode to receive distance information

*Operates less than continuous or On-Request

```
      NAME
NAM  ⋮⋮  *000
DME Chan 00
```

**NDB with DME**
Underline indicates No Voice Transmitted on this frequency
TACAN channels are without voice but are not underlined

Norfolk Weather Radio    ○   U.S. Weather Station with Voice Communication

IDENT 000    ⊙   Commercial Broadcast Station

### AIR/GROUND COMMUNICATION BOXES

HEAVY LINE BOXES indicate Flight Service Stations (FSS). Frequencies 255.4, 122.2, and emerg. 243.0 and 121.5 are normally available at all FSS's and are not shown above boxes. All other frequencies available at FSS's are shown.
Frequencies transmit and receive except those followed by R or T: R – receive only T – transmit only

```
123.6   122.6
   122.1R
```

Airport Advisory Service (AAS) 123.6

Frequencies positioned above thin line NAVAID boxes are remoted to the NAVAID site
Other frequencies at the controlling FSS named are available, however, altitude and terrain may determine their reception

**FAYETTEVILLE FYV**

Name and identifier for FSS not associated with NAVAID

122.1R

**WASHINGTON**

Controlling FSS Name

Thin line box, without frequencies and controlling FSS name indicates no FSS frequencies available.

⊙ Flight Service Station (FSS)
Remote Communications Outlet (RCO)

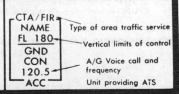

```
CTA/FIR
  NAME
 FL 180
  GND
  CON
  120.5
  ACC
```

Type of area traffic service

Vertical limits of control

A/G Voice call and frequency

Unit providing ATS

**LEGEND 22.—En Route Low Altitude Charts**

## AIR TRAFFIC SERVICES AND AIRSPACE INFORMATION

### AIR TRAFFIC SERVICE ROUTE DATA

VHF/UHF Data is depicted in BLUE
LF/MF Data is depicted in BROWN

V4 — VOR Airway and identification

G3 — LF/MF Airway and identification

BR 25 — Uncontrolled LF/MF Airway and identification

BR 57V — Bahama Route and identification

BR 10L — Bahama Route and identification

AR1 — Atlantic Route and identification

A15 ROUTE — Oceanic Route and identification

B509 — ATS Route and identification

⊢⊢⊢⊢  ⊢⊢⊢⊢ — Military IFR Route

+ + + +  + + + — Flight Planning Route

o-o-o-o-o-o-o — Substitute Route
See Notams or Appropriate publication for specific information

/\/\/\/\/\ — Unusable or Closed Segment

V5 ▶ — Preferred Single Direction Airway

NME 000.0 — Facility Locators used in formation of reporting points
NAM 000

—036→ — Radial outbound from a UHF/VHF Radio Aid

←036— — Bearing inbound to a LF/MF Radio Aid

123 — Total Mileage between Compulsory Reporting Points and/or Radio Aids

(123)

23 — Mileage between other Reporting Points, Radio Aids and/or Mileage Breakdown
23

### (Center column)

1734 — Overall Mileage (Flight Planning and Military IFR Routes)

x    x — Mileage Breakdown

42
26 — VOR Changeover Point giving mileage to Radio Aids (Not shown at mid-point locations)

#### TACAN Fix Data

ident    Chan
EDF 84
Radial from TACAN  180° 52  Distance from TACAN

◀EVEN — Direction of Flight Indicator (Canada only)

3500
3500 — Minimum Enroute Altitude (MEA)

* 2000
* 2000 — Minimum Obstruction Clearance Altitude (MOCA)

MAA-15500 — Maximum Authorized Altitude (MAA)

—⊢— — MEA, MAA and/or MOCA change at other than Radio Aids to navigation

R  R — Minimum Reception Altitude (MRA)

X  X — Minimum Crossing Altitude (MCA)

#### REPORTING POINTS

▲  ▲ — Compulsory Reporting Point

△  △ — Non-compulsory Reporting Point

▲  ▲ — Off-set arrows indicate facility forming a reporting point (toward LF/MF, away from VHF/UHF)

→ — Denotes DME fix (distance same as airway mileage)

15 → — Denotes DME fix (encircled mileage shown when not otherwise obvious)

### BOUNDARIES

Ⓐ — Altimeter Setting Change

↔ A ↔ — Altimeter Setting Change when not otherwise defined

Air Route Traffic Control Center (ARTCC)

NAME
Name
134.3  269.5 — ARTCC Remoted Sites with discrete VHF and UHF frequencies

Oceanic Control Area (CTA)/ Flight Information Region (FIR)

Air Defense Identification Zone (ADIZ)

Combined ADIZ and FIR

Oceanic Control

Control Zone (effective 24 hours unless otherwise noted)

Canadian Class "C" Control Zone

Canadian Aerodrome Traffic Zone

ΤΤΤΤΤ — Control Zones within which fixed-wing special VFR flight is prohibited

▮▮▮▮ — Non-Free Flying Area (teeth point to area)

▲▲▲▲ — Buffer Zone (teeth point to area)

International Boundary (omitted when coincident with ARTCC or FIR)

U.S. - Russia Convention Line of 1867

Area of Enlargement (contains only data for through flights) See Area Charts for complete data

.......... Official Time Zone

### AIRSPACE INFORMATION

Open area (white) indicates controlled airspace

Shaded area (brown) indicates uncontrolled airspace

In Alaska – indicates designated controlled airspace outside the continental control area above 14,500'

In Canada – indicates designated controlled airspace above 12,500'

TCA Area

Mode C Area
See FAR 91.24

### MISCELLANEOUS

7° E  1985 Isogonic Line and Value

ALL MILEAGES ARE NAUTICAL EXCEPT AS NOTED

ALL RADIALS AND BEARINGS ARE MAGNETIC

ALL ALTITUDES ARE MSL UNLESS OTHERWISE STATED

ALL TIME IS COORDINATED UNIVERSAL TIME (UTC)

‡ DURING PERIODS OF DAYLIGHT SAVING TIME (DT) EFFECTIVE HOURS WILL BE ONE HOUR EARLIER THAN SHOWN. ALL STATES OBSERVE DT EXCEPT ARIZONA AND THAT PORTION OF INDIANA IN THE EASTERN TIME ZONE.

---

#### EXAMPLE OF GROUPING

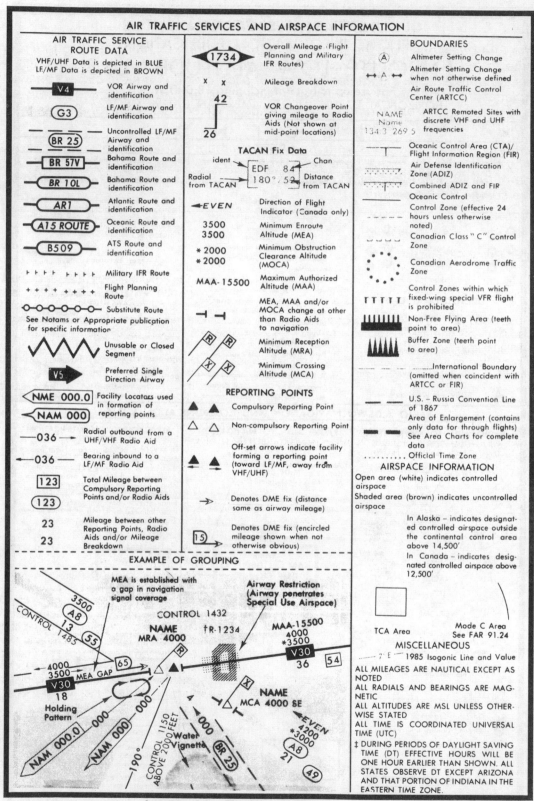

**LEGEND 23.—En Route Altitude Charts**

---

### QUESTIONS AND ANSWER EXPLANATIONS

All the FAA questions from the written test for the instrument rating relating to IFR en route flight and the material outlined previously are reproduced on the following pages in the same modules as the outlines. To the immediate right of each question are the correct answer and answer explanation. You should cover these answers and answer explanations with your hand or a piece of paper while responding to the questions. Refer to the general discussion in Chapter 1 on how to take the examination.

Remember that the questions from the FAA Instrument Rating Question Book have been reordered by topic, and the topics have been organized into a meaningful sequence. Accordingly, the first line of the answer explanation gives the FAA question number and the citation of the authoritative source for the answer.

---

## 10.1 Minimum En Route Altitude

**1.**
**4429.** What is the definition of MEA?

A— The lowest published altitude which meets obstacle clearance requirements and assures acceptable navigational signal coverage.
B— The lowest published altitude which meets obstacle requirements, assures acceptable navigational signal coverage, two-way radio communications, and provides adequate radar coverage.
C— An altitude which meets obstacle clearance requirements, assures acceptable navigation signal coverage, two-way radio communications, adequate radar coverage, and accurate DME mileage.

Answer (A) is correct (4429). *(AIM P/C Glossary)*
The minimum en route altitude (MEA) is the lowest published altitude between radio fixes which assures acceptable navigational signal coverage and meets the obstacle clearance requirements between those fixes.
Answer (B) is incorrect because, by definition, the MEA does not assure either two-way radio communications or adequate radar coverage. Answer (C) is incorrect because, by definition, the MEA is the lowest published (not any) altitude that meets obstacle clearance and assures acceptable navigation signal coverage. It does not provide for either two-way radio communications or adequate radar coverage.

**2.**
**4435.** Reception of signals from an off-airway radio facility may be inadequate to identify the fix at the designated MEA. In this case, which altitude is designated for the fix?

A— MRA.
B— MCA.
C— MOCA.

Answer (A) is correct (4435). *(AIM P/C Glossary)*
MRA (minimum reception altitude) is the lowest altitude at which an intersection can be determined. It is the altitude assigned for a fix when the MEA will not provide adequate reception of an off-airway radio facility (NAVAID) identifying the fix.
Answer (B) is incorrect because MCA (minimum crossing altitude) is the lowest altitude at a fix at which an aircraft must cross when proceeding in the direction of a higher MEA. Answer (C) is incorrect because the MOCA (minimum obstruction clearance altitude) is the lowest published altitude in effect between radio fixes on VOR airways, off-airway routes, or route segments which meets obstacle clearance requirements for the entire route segment and which assures acceptable navigation signal coverage only within 22 NM of a VOR.

**3.**

**4544.** Reception of signals from a radio facility, located off the airway being flown, may be inadequate at the designated MEA to identify the fix. In this case, which altitude is designated for the fix?

A— MOCA.
B— MRA.
C— MCA.

**Answer (B) is correct (4544).** *(AIM P/C Glossary)*
MRA (minimum reception altitude) is the lowest altitude at which an intersection can be determined. It is the altitude assigned for a fix when the MEA will not provide adequate reception of an off-airway radio facility (NAVAID) identifying the fix.

Answer (A) is incorrect because the MOCA (minimum obstruction clearance altitude) is the lowest published altitude in effect between radio fixes on VOR airways, off-airway routes, or route segments which meets obstacle clearance requirements for the entire route segment and which assures acceptable navigation signal coverage only within 22 NM of a VOR. Answer (C) is incorrect because MCA (minimum crossing altitude) is the lowest altitude at a fix at which an aircraft must cross when proceeding in the direction of a higher MEA.

**4.**

**4545.** ATC may assign the MOCA when certain special conditions exist, and when within

A— 22 NM of a VOR.
B— 25 NM of a VOR.
C— 30 NM of a VOR.

**Answer (A) is correct (4545).** *(AIM P/C Glossary)*
MOCA (minimum obstruction clearance altitude) is the lowest published altitude in effect between radio fixes on VOR airways, off-airway routes, or route segments which meets obstacle clearance requirements for the entire route segment and which assures acceptable navigational signal coverage only within 22 NM of a VOR. Thus, ATC may assign the MOCA as an assigned altitude, but only within 22 NM of a VOR.

Answer (B) is incorrect because the MOCA provides acceptable navigational signal coverage only within 25 SM (not NM) of a VOR. Answer (C) is incorrect because ATC may only assign the MOCA as an assigned altitude only within 22 (not 30) NM.

**5.**

**4547.** Acceptable navigational signal coverage at the MOCA is assured for a distance from the VOR of only

A— 12 NM.
B— 22 NM.
C— 25 NM.

**Answer (B) is correct (4547).** *(AIM P/C Glossary)*
MOCA (minimum obstruction clearance altitude) is the lowest published altitude in effect between radio fixes on VOR airways, off-airway routes, or route segments which meets obstacle clearance requirements for the entire route segment and which assures acceptable navigational signal coverage only within 22 NM of a VOR. Thus, ATC may assign the MOCA as an assigned altitude, but only within 22 NM of a VOR.

Answer (A) is incorrect because it is 22 (not 12) NM. Answer (C) is incorrect because it is 25 SM (not NM).

**6.**

**4546.** If no MCA is specified, what is the lowest altitude for crossing a radio fix, beyond which a higher minimum applies?

A— The MOCA for the route segment beyond the fix.
B— The MEA at which the fix is approached.
C— The MRA at which the fix is approached.

**Answer (B) is correct (4546).** *(FAR 91.177)*
*This question is a duplicate of FAA question 4437.*
If no MCA (minimum crossing altitude) is specified, the lowest altitude for crossing a radio fix beyond which a higher minimum IFR altitude exists is the MEA at which the fix is approached. A climb must be initiated to a higher minimum immediately after passing the point beyond which that minimum altitude applies.

Answer (A) is incorrect because, if there is no MCA, the higher minimum altitude does not apply until immediately after passing the fix. Answer (C) is incorrect because, if a higher minimum altitude exists after the fix and a higher altitude is needed to identify a fix, usually an MCA (not an MRA) is established at that fix.

**7.**
**4432.** The MEA assures acceptable navigational signal coverage and

A— DME response.
B— radar coverage.
C— meets obstacle clearance requirements.

Answer (C) is correct (4432). *(AIM P/C Glossary)*
MEA (minimum en route altitude) is the lowest published altitude between radio fixes which assures acceptable navigational signal coverage and meets obstacle clearance requirements between those fixes.
Answer (A) is incorrect because there may not be a DME response when there is acceptable VOR coverage. Answer (B) is incorrect because radar coverage is entirely different from navigational signal coverage and obstruction requirements.

**8.**
**4436.** Which condition is guaranteed for all of the following altitude limits: MAA, MCA, MRA, MOCA, and MEA? (Non-mountainous area.)

A— Adequate navigation signals.
B— Adequate communications.
C— 1,000-foot obstacle clearance.

Answer (C) is correct (4436). *(AIM P/C Glossary)*
The MAA, MCA, MRA, MOCA, and MEA meet the minimum obstacle clearance requirements. In non-mountainous areas, 1,000 ft. above the highest obstacle is guaranteed within a horizontal distance of 4 NM from the course to be flown.
Answer (A) is incorrect because the MOCA only assures acceptable navigational signals within 22 NM of a VOR. Answer (B) is incorrect because the minimum IFR altitudes do not guarantee adequate communications coverage.

**9.**
**4437.** If no MCA is specified, what is the lowest altitude for crossing a radio fix, beyond which a higher minimum applies?

A— The MEA at which the fix is approached.
B— The MRA at which the fix is approached.
C— The MOCA for the route segment beyond the fix.

Answer (A) is correct (4437). *(FAR 91.177)*
*This question is a duplicate of FAA question 4546.*
If no MCA (minimum crossing altitude) is specified, the lowest altitude for crossing a radio fix beyond which a higher minimum IFR altitude exists is the MEA at which the fix is approached. A climb must be initiated to a higher minimum immediately after passing the point beyond which that minimum altitude applies.
Answer (B) is incorrect because, if a higher minimum altitude exists after the fix and a higher altitude is needed to identify a fix, usually an MCA (not an MRA) is established at that fix. Answer (C) is incorrect because, if there is no MCA, the higher minimum altitude does not apply until immediately after passing the fix.

**10.**
**4765.** In the case of operations over an area designated as a mountainous area, no person may operate an aircraft under IFR below 2,000 feet above the highest obstacle within a horizontal distance of

A— 3 SM from the course flown.
B— 4 SM from the course flown.
C— 4 NM from the course flown.

Answer (C) is correct (4765). *(FAR 91.177)*
In the case of operations over an area designated as a mountainous area where no other minimum altitude is prescribed, no person may operate an aircraft under IFR below 2,000 ft. above the highest obstacle within a horizontal distance of 4 NM from the course to be flown.
Answer (A) is incorrect because the horizontal distance is 4 NM (not 3 SM) from the course flown. Answer (B) is incorrect because the horizontal distance is 4 NM (not SM) from the course flown.

**11.**
**4541.** In the case of operations over an area designated as a mountainous area where no other minimum altitude is prescribed, no person may operate an aircraft under IFR below an altitude of

A— 500 feet above the highest obstacle.
B— 1,000 feet above the highest obstacle.
C— 2,000 feet above the highest obstacle.

Answer (C) is correct (4541). *(FAR 91.177)*
In the case of operations over an area designated as a mountainous area where no other minimum altitude is prescribed, no person may operate an aircraft under IFR below 2,000 ft. above the highest obstacle within a horizontal distance of 4 NM from the course to be flown.
Answer (A) is incorrect because no person may operate an aircraft under IFR below an altitude of 2,000 (not 500) ft. above the highest obstacle in a mountainous area. Answer (B) is incorrect because no person may operate an aircraft under IFR below an altitude of 1,000 ft. above the highest obstacle in a non-mountainous (not mountainous) area.

**12.**
**4542.** The MEA is an altitude which assures

A— obstacle clearance, accurate navigational signals from more than one VORTAC, and accurate DME mileage.
B— a 1,000-foot obstacle clearance within 2 miles of an airway and assures accurate DME mileage.
C— acceptable navigational signal coverage and meets obstruction clearance requirements.

Answer (C) is correct (4542). *(AIM P/C Glossary)*
The minimum en route altitude (MEA) is the lowest published altitude between radio fixes which assures acceptable navigational signal coverage and meets the obstacle clearance requirements between those fixes.
Answer (A) is incorrect because only one VORTAC is needed at a time to provide acceptable coverage, and DME is not a required navigational signal. Answer (B) is incorrect because the clearance is within 4 NM, not 2 mi., and there is no assurance of DME coverage.

**13.**
**4485.** Unless otherwise specified on the chart, the minimum en route altitude along a jet route is

A— 18,000 feet MSL.
B— 24,000 feet MSL.
C— 10,000 feet MSL.

Answer (A) is correct (4485). *(FAR 71.603)*
Each designated jet route consists of a direct course for navigating from 18,000 ft. MSL up to and including FL 450, between the navigational aids and intersections specified for that route. Thus, the MEA along a jet route is 18,000 ft. MSL.
Answer (B) is incorrect because 24,000 ft. MSL (FL 240) is the minimum altitude at which DME is required when navigating by VOR, not the MEA for a jet route. Answer (C) is incorrect because 10,000 ft. MSL is the minimum altitude at which aircraft are required to operate the transponder on Mode C, not the MEA for a jet route.

## 10.2 VFR-on-Top

**14.**
**4633.** Under which of the following circumstances will ATC issue a VFR restriction to an IFR flight?

A— Whenever the pilot reports the loss of any navigational aid.
B— When it is necessary to provide separation between IFR and special VFR traffic.
C— When the pilot requests it.

Answer (C) is correct (4633). *(AIM Para 4-87)*
VFR-on-Top is an ATC authorization for an IFR aircraft to operate in VFR conditions at any appropriate VFR altitude. ATC may not authorize VFR-on-Top operations unless the pilot requests the clearance to operate in VFR conditions.
Answer (A) is incorrect because a pilot would only report a malfunction of navigation equipment (not a loss of any navigational aid) to ATC. Answer (B) is incorrect because special VFR traffic would be found near an airport in Class B, C, or D airspace or Class E airspace designated for an airport that is currently experiencing IMC. Thus, ATC would not issue a VFR restriction to an IFR flight.

**15.**
**4430.** What altitude may a pilot select upon receiving a VFR-on-Top clearance?

A— Any altitude at least 1,000 feet above the meteorological condition.
B— Any appropriate VFR altitude at or above the MEA in VFR weather conditions.
C— Any VFR altitude appropriate for the direction of flight at least 1,000 feet above the meteorological condition.

Answer (B) is correct (4430). *(AIM Para 4-87)*
When operating in VMC with an ATC authorization to "maintain VFR-on-Top/maintain VFR conditions," pilots on IFR flight plans must:

1. Fly at the appropriate VFR altitude;
2. Comply with the VFR visibility and distance from clouds criteria; and
3. Comply with instrument flight rules that are applicable to the flight, i.e., minimum IFR altitudes, position reporting, course to be flown, adherence to ATC clearances, etc.

Answer (A) is incorrect because, after receiving a VFR-on-Top clearance, the pilot may select any appropriate VFR altitude at or above the minimum IFR altitude in VMC, not only 1,000 ft. above the meteorological condition. This may be above, below, between layers, or in areas where there is no meteorological obscuration. Answer (C) is incorrect because, after receiving a VFR-on-Top clearance, the pilot may select any appropriate VFR altitude at or above the minimum IFR altitude in VMC, not only 1,000 ft. above the meteorological condition. This may be above, below, between layers, or in areas where there is no meteorological obscuration.

**16.**
**4449.** Which rules apply to the pilot in command when operating on a VFR-on-Top clearance?

A— VFR only.
B— VFR and IFR.
C— VFR when "in the clear" and IFR when "in the clouds."

Answer (B) is correct (4449). *(AIM Para 4-87)*
When operating in VMC with an ATC authorization to "maintain VFR-on-Top/maintain VFR conditions," pilots on IFR flight plans must:

1. Fly at the appropriate VFR altitude;
2. Comply with the VFR visibility and distance from clouds criteria; and
3. Comply with instrument flight rules that are applicable to the flight, i.e., minimum IFR altitudes, position reporting, course to be flown, adherence to ATC clearances, etc.

Answer (A) is incorrect because an ATC clearance to operate VFR-on-Top does not imply cancellation of the IFR flight plan. Answer (C) is incorrect because a VFR-on-Top clearance is issued when the pilot is in VMC and must remain in VMC unless the VFR-on-Top clearance is canceled. It does not allow a pilot to fly in IMC.

**17.**
**4451.** Which ATC clearance should instrument-rated pilots request in order to climb through a cloud layer or an area of reduced visibility and then continue the flight VFR?

A— To VFR on Top.
B— Special VFR to VFR Over-the-Top.
C— VFR Over-the-Top.

Answer (A) is correct (4451). *(AIM Para 4-87)*
Pilots desiring to climb through a cloud, haze, smoke, or other meteorological formation and then either cancel their IFR flight plan or operate VFR-on-Top may request an ATC clearance to climb to VFR-on-Top.
Answer (B) is incorrect because a special VFR clearance is issued only in Class B, C, or D airspace or Class E airspace designated for an airport and the pilot must remain clear of clouds, not climb through them. Answer (C) is incorrect because it is VFR-on-Top, not VFR-over-the-Top.

**18.**
**4450.** When can a VFR-on-Top clearance be assigned by ATC?

A— Only upon request of the pilot when conditions are indicated to be suitable.
B— Any time suitable conditions exist and ATC wishes to expedite traffic flow.
C— When VFR conditions exist, but there is a layer of clouds below the MEA.

Answer (A) is correct (4450). *(AIM Para 4-87)*
ATC may assign a VFR-on-Top clearance only when the pilot requests such a clearance, and the flight must be conducted in VFR weather conditions.
Answer (B) is incorrect because ATC can issue a VFR-on-Top clearance only upon a pilot's (not ATC's) request. Answer (C) is incorrect because ATC can issue a VFR-on-Top clearance only upon a pilot's request, not based only on the meteorological conditions.

**19.**
**4452.** When on a VFR-on-Top clearance, the cruising altitude is based on

A— true course.
B— magnetic course.
C— magnetic heading.

Answer (B) is correct (4452). *(FAR 91.159)*
While operating under a VFR-on-Top clearance, you must fly at the appropriate VFR altitude, which is based on magnetic course.
Answer (A) is incorrect because VFR cruising altitudes are based on magnetic (not true) course. Answer (C) is incorrect because VFR cruising altitudes are based on magnetic course (not heading).

**20.**
**4431.** When must a pilot fly at a cardinal altitude plus 500 feet on an IFR flight plan?

A— When flying above 18,000 feet in VFR conditions.
B— When flying in VFR conditions above clouds.
C— When assigned a VFR-on-Top clearance.

Answer (C) is correct (4431). *(AIM Para 4-87)*
VFR-on-Top clearances are flown at VFR altitudes, which are even or odd thousand-foot intervals plus 500 ft. This is in contrast to IFR altitudes that are at even or odd thousand-foot intervals. Cardinal altitude means 1,000-ft. intervals, e.g., 3,000, 4,000, etc.
Answer (A) is incorrect because VFR-on-Top is not permitted in Class A airspace, which is from 18,000 ft. MSL to and including FL 600. Answer (B) is incorrect because a pilot on an IFR flight plan only uses VFR altitudes when assigned a VFR-on-Top clearance.

**21.**
**4447.** Where are VFR-on-Top operations prohibited?

A— In Class A airspace.
B— During off-airways direct flights.
C— When flying through Class B airspace.

**22.**
**4433.** You have filed an IFR flight plan with a VFR-on-Top clearance in lieu of an assigned altitude. If you receive this clearance and fly a course of 180°, at what altitude should you fly? (Assume VFR conditions.)

A— Any IFR altitude which will enable you to remain in VFR conditions.
B— An odd thousand-foot MSL altitude plus 500 feet.
C— An even thousand-foot MSL altitude plus 500 feet.

**23.**
**4457.** What minimums must be considered in selecting an altitude when operating with a VFR-on-Top clearance?

A— At least 500 feet above the lowest MEA, or appropriate MOCA, and at least 1,000 feet above the existing meteorological condition.
B— At least 1,000 feet above the lowest MEA, appropriate MOCA, or existing meteorological condition.
C— Minimum IFR altitude, minimum distance from clouds, and visibility appropriate to altitude selected.

**24.**
**4543.** If, while in controlled airspace, a clearance is received to "maintain VFR conditions on top," the pilot should maintain a VFR cruising altitude based on the direction of the

A— true course.
B— magnetic heading.
C— magnetic course.

**25.**
**4453.** In which airspace is VFR-on-Top operation prohibited?

A— Class B airspace.
B— Class E airspace.
C— Class A airspace.

Answer (A) is correct (4447). *(AIM Para 4-87)*
ATC will not authorize VFR or VFR-on-Top operations in Class A airspace.
Answer (B) is incorrect because VFR-on-Top operations during off-airway direct flights are not prohibited.
Answer (C) is incorrect because VFR-on-Top operations within Class B airspace are permitted.

Answer (C) is correct (4433). *(FAR 91.159)*
When operating in VMC with a VFR-on-Top clearance, you must fly at the appropriate VFR cruising altitude. On a magnetic course of 180° through 359°, an even thousand-foot MSL altitude plus 500 ft. must be flown.
Answer (A) is incorrect because, on VFR-on-Top, one uses VFR (not IFR) altitudes. Answer (B) is incorrect because odd thousand-foot altitudes plus 500 ft. are for a magnetic course of 0° through 179°, not 180°.

Answer (C) is correct (4457). *(AIM Para 4-87)*
When operating in VMC with an ATC authorization to "maintain VFR-on-Top/maintain VFR conditions," pilots on IFR flight plans must:

1. Fly at the appropriate VFR altitude;
2. Comply with the VFR visibility and distance from clouds criteria; and
3. Comply with instrument flight rules that are applicable to the flight, i.e., minimum IFR altitudes, position reporting, course to be flown, adherence to ATC clearances, etc.

Answer (A) is incorrect because you must be at or above (not a specified distance from) the minimum IFR altitude and while on a VFR-on-Top clearance you may operate above, below, or between layers (not only above) of the existing meteorological condition. Answer (B) is incorrect because you must be at or above (not a specified distance from) the minimum IFR altitude and while on a VFR-on-Top clearance you may operate above, below, or between layers (not only above) of the existing meteorological condition.

Answer (C) is correct (4543). *(FAR 91.159)*
While operating under a VFR-on-Top clearance, you must fly at the appropriate VFR cruising altitude which is based on magnetic course.
Answer (A) is incorrect because VFR cruising altitudes are based on magnetic (not true) course. Answer (B) is incorrect because VFR cruising altitudes are based on magnetic course (not heading).

Answer (C) is correct (4453). *(AIM Para 4-87)*
ATC will not authorize VFR or VFR-on-Top operations in Class A airspace.
Answer (A) is incorrect because VFR-on-Top operations are permitted, not prohibited, in Class B airspace. Answer (B) is incorrect because VFR-on-Top operations are permitted, not prohibited, in Class E airspace.

**26.**
**4454.** What cruising altitude is appropriate for VFR on Top on a westbound flight below 18,000 feet?

A— Even thousand-foot levels.
B— Even thousand-foot levels plus 500 feet, but not below MEA.
C— Odd thousand-foot levels plus 500 feet, but not below MEA.

Answer (B) is correct (4454). *(FAR 91.159)*
When operating in VMC with a VFR-on-Top clearance, you must fly at the appropriate VFR cruising altitude but not below the minimum IFR altitude (e.g., MEA). On a magnetic course of 180° through 359° (i.e., westbound), an even thousand-foot MSL altitude plus 500 ft. must be flown.
Answer (A) is incorrect because an even thousand-foot level is an IFR (not VFR) cruising altitude for a westbound flight. VFR-on-Top clearances must maintain VFR altitudes. Answer (C) is incorrect because an odd thousand-foot level plus 500 ft. is for eastbound (not westbound) flight or a magnetic course from 0° to 179°.

**27.**
**4455.** What reports are required of a flight operating on an IFR clearance specifying VFR on Top in a nonradar environment?

A— The same reports that are required for any IFR flight.
B— All normal IFR reports except vacating altitudes.
C— Only the reporting of any unforecast weather.

Answer (A) is correct (4455). *(AIM Para 4-87)*
When on a VFR-on-Top Clearance, you must comply with instrument flight rules that are applicable to the flight, e.g., minimum flight altitudes, position reporting, radio communications, course to be flown, adherence to ATC communications, etc.
Answer (B) is incorrect because all normal IFR reports are required when operating on a VFR-on-Top clearance. You should advise ATC prior to any altitude change to ensure the exchange of accurate traffic information. Answer (C) is incorrect because all IFR reports, not only unforecast weather, must be made while operating on a VFR-on-Top clearance.

## 10.3 IFR En Route Chart Interpretation

**28.**
**4493.** (Refer to figure 87 on page 339.) Where is the VOR changeover point when flying east on V306 from Daisetta (a) to Lake Charles (d)?

A— At OFERS intersection.
B— At SILBE intersection.
C— 30 miles east of Daisetta.

Answer (C) is correct (4493). *(AIM Para 5-36)*
On Fig. 87, when flying east on V306 from Daisetta (area A) to Lake Charles (area D), the VOR changeover point (COP) is indicated by the symbol " ⌠ " and the mileages are given to each VORTAC station. The COP is 30 NM east of Daisetta or 50 NM west of Lake Charles.
Answer (A) is incorrect because OFERS INT is about 22 NM east of the changeover point. Answer (B) is incorrect because SILBE INT is about 2 NM west of the changeover point.

**29.**
**4494.** (Refer to figure 87 on page 339.) At STRUT intersection (b) headed eastbound, ATC instructs you to hold west on the 10 DME fix LCH (c) on V306, standard turns, what entry procedure is recommended?

A— Direct.
B— Teardrop.
C— Parallel.

Answer (A) is correct (4494). *(AIM Para 5-37)*
Note the FAA question incorrectly locates STRUT INT and LCH VORTAC. STRUT INT is located south of area D, not area B, and LCH VORTAC is located southeast of area D, not area C, in Fig. 87.
You are instructed to hold west of the 10 DME fix from LCH VORTAC on V306. Since you are at STRUT INT, flying eastbound on V306, you would make a direct entry and turn right (standard turn) to the outbound heading of 265°.
Answer (B) is incorrect because a teardrop entry may be used if you were instructed to hold east, not west, of the holding fix. Answer (C) is incorrect because a parallel entry may be used if you were instructed to hold east, not west, of the holding fix.

**30.**
**4496.** (Refer to figure 87 on page 339.) What is indicated by the localizer course symbol at Scholes Field (b)?

A— The airport has a Category II ILS approach procedure.
B— The airport has an LDA approach procedure.
C— An ILS localizer course with an ATC function.

Answer (C) is the best answer (4496). *(ACL)*
Scholes Field (west of B) has an arrow-shaped symbol which has shading on one side. This symbol indicates that there is a published ILS and/or LOC IAP available at Scholes Field. A large arrow-shaped symbol would have specifically indicated that the LOC has an ATC function. See Legend 22 on page 329.
Answer (A) is incorrect because the symbol only indicates an ILS and/or LOC IAP and does not specify the category of ILS approach. Answer (B) is incorrect because an airport with a published SDF, not LDA, IAP is shown by an arrow symbol without any shading.

**31.**
**4497.** (Refer to figure 87 on page 339.) Which VHF frequencies, other than 121.5, can be used to receive Lake Charles FSS (d) during the day in the Lake Charles area?

A— 121.1, 126.4.
B— 121.1, 122.3.
C— 122.2, 122.3.

Answer (C) is the best answer (4497). *(ACL)*
Note: In this edition of the test, a new chart is used showing that the controlling FSS in the Lake Charles area is De Ridder FSS, not Lake Charles FSS.
The Lake Charles VORTAC communication box is located at area D in Fig. 87. The available frequencies are shown above the box and the controlling FSS (De Ridder) is shown below the box. All FSSs normally use frequency 122.2 and emergency 121.5 and are not shown. Note the thin line box indicates that other frequencies at the controlling FSS are available, however, altitude and terrain may determine their reception. Thus, you can receive De Ridder FSS on the VHF frequencies (other than 121.5) of 122.2 and 122.3.
Answer (A) is incorrect because neither 121.1 nor 126.4 is not an available frequency to receive De Ridder FSS. Answer (B) is incorrect because 121.1 is not an available frequency to receive De Ridder FSS.

**32.**
**4498.** (Refer to figure 87 on page 339.) Why is the BC localizer course at Jefferson County (e) depicted with a large symbol?

A— Both the front and back courses are not aligned with a runway.
B— Both the front and back courses have a glide slope.
C— Both the front and back courses have ATC functions.

Answer (C) is the best answer (4498). *(ACL)*
Jefferson County (point E) has two arrow-shaped symbols, one long and one short, and each has shading on one side. These symbols indicate that there is a published ILS and/or LOC IAP available. The long arrow is further identified (on the chart) as the back course. Additionally, the back course has an assigned ATC function to identify both PORTZ and MARSA intersections. See Legend 22 on page 329.
Answer (A) is incorrect because the back course symbol indicates a localizer course, which is always aligned with the runway. Answer (B) is incorrect because the symbol only indicates an ILS and/or LOC, not that it is an ILS.

**33.**
**4499.** (Refer to figure 87 on page 339.) Where is the VOR changeover point between Beaumont (e) and Hobby (c)?

A— Halfway point.
B— MOCKS intersection.
C— Anahuac Beacon.

Answer (A) is correct (4499). *(AIM Para 5-36)*
In Fig. 87, V20 connects Beaumont (BPT) VORTAC (area E) and Hobby (HUB) VORTAC. Note that HUB VORTAC is southwest of area C and is not shown on the chart. The changeover point (COP) is located midway between the BPT and HUB, which is 34 NM. When the COP is not located at the MIDWAY point, the symbol " ∫ " is used and the mileage to the NAVAIDs are given (see Legend 23 on page 330).
Answer (B) is incorrect because MOCKS INT is 25 NM from BPT, and the halfway point is 34 NM. Answer (C) is incorrect because Anahuac Beacon is not on the airway.

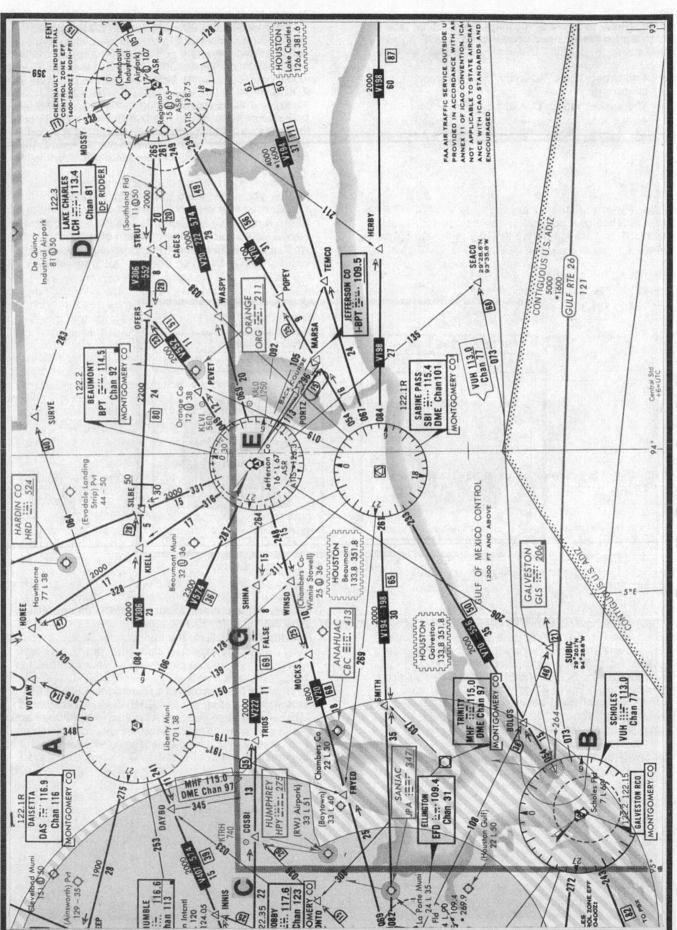

FIGURE 87.—En Route Chart Segment.

**34.**
**4495.** (Refer to figure 87 on page 339 and 88 below.) What is your position with reference to FALSE intersection (g) if your VOR receivers indicate as shown?

A— Southeast.
B— Northeast.
C— Northwest.

Answer (A) is correct (4495). *(IFH Chap VIII)*
Your No. 1 VOR (Fig. 88) is tuned to the BPT VORTAC (area E), Fig. 87, with an OBS setting of 264. If you are flying outbound (FROM) BPT on V222 (R-264), a right deflection indicates that V222 is to the right of your location. Thus, you are to the south of V222. Your No. 2 VOR is tuned to the DAS VORTAC (area A) with an OBS setting of 139. If you are flying outbound (FROM) DAS on R-139, a right deflection would mean that R-139 is to the right of your location. Thus, you are to the east of R-139. FALSE INT (g) is the intersection of V222 (BPT R-264) and DAS R-139; you are presently to the southeast of FALSE INT.

Answer (B) is incorrect because to be northeast of FALSE, you would need to be north of V222, which would result in a left (not right) CDI deflection in the No. 1 VOR. Answer (C) is incorrect because to be northwest of FALSE you would need to be north of V222 and to the west of DAS R-139, which would be indicated by a left (not right) CDI deflection on both No. 1 and No. 2 VORs.

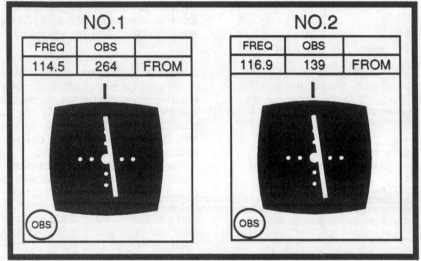

FIGURE 88.—CDI and OBS Indicators.

**35.**
**4500.** While holding at the 10 DME fix east of LCH for an ILS approach to Rwy 15 at Lake Charles Muni Airport, ATC advises you to expect clearance for the approach at 1015. At 1000 you experience two-way radio communications failure. Which procedure should be followed?

A— Squawk 7600 and listen on the LOM frequency for instructions from ATC. If no instructions are received, start your approach at 1015.
B— Squawk 7700 for 1 minute, then 7600. After 1 minute, descend to the minimum final approach fix altitude. Start your approach at 1015.
C— Squawk 7600; plan to begin your approach at 1015.

Answer (C) is correct (4500). *(FAR 91.185 and AIM Para 6-32)*
Upon radio failure, the transponder should be set to 7600. Since the expected clearance for the approach was 1015, you should plan to begin your approach at 1015.

Answer (A) is incorrect because there is no LOM shown on the chart at Lake Charles Muni. Answer (B) is incorrect because you should not squawk 7700 unless you are in an emergency situation and you should hold at your altitude until the time necessary to begin your approach at 1015.

**36.**

**4501.** (Refer to figure 89 on page 343.) When flying from Milford Municipal (c) to Bryce Canyon (a) via V235 and V293, what minimum altitude should you be at when crossing Cedar City VOR (d)?

A— 11,400 feet.

B— 12,000 feet.

C— 13,000 feet.

**Answer (B) is correct (4501).** *(ACL)*

In Fig. 89, CDC VOR (area D) has a flag with an "X" inside to indicate an MCA (minimum crossing altitude). The MCA is indicated above the CDC communication box. When flying east on V293 to Bryce Canyon, you must cross CDC at a minimum altitude of 12,000 ft. (V293 12000E).

Answer (A) is incorrect because 11,400 ft. is the MCA when flying south on V21E. Answer (C) is incorrect because 13,000 ft. is the MEA for V293.

**37.**

**4502.** (Refer to figure 89 on page 343.) What VHF frequencies are available for communications with Cedar City FSS (a)?

A— 123.6, 121.5, 108.6, and 112.8.

B— 122.2, 121.5, 122.6, and 112.1.

C— 122.2, 121.5, 122.0, and 123.6.

**Answer (B) is the best answer (4502).** *(ACL)*

Cedar City FSS is located at point D, not point A, in Fig. 89. Point A is Bryce Canyon. Cedar City FSS has VHF frequencies 122.2 and 121.5, which are available at all FSSs. Additionally, near point D you may use 122.6, and near point C the FSS transmits on 112.1 (MLF VORTAC) and you will transmit on 122.1.

Answer (A) is incorrect because 123.6 is not listed above any communication boxes controlled by Cedar City FSS and BCE VORTAC is underlined, which means there is no voice on that frequency. Answer (C) is incorrect because 122.0 and 123.6 are not listed above any communication boxes controlled by Cedar City FSS.

**38.**

**4503.** (Refer to figure 89 on page 343.) What are the oxygen requirements for an IFR flight northeast bound on V8 at 17,000 feet altitude from Bryce Canyon (a) in an unpressurized aircraft?

A— The required minimum crew must be provided and use supplemental oxygen for that part of the flight of more than 30 minutes.

B— The required minimum crew must be provided and use supplemental oxygen for that part of the flight of more than 30 minutes, and the passengers must be provided supplemental oxygen.

C— The required minimum crew must be provided and use supplemental oxygen, and all occupants must be provided supplemental oxygen for the entire flight upon reaching the assigned altitude.

**Answer (C) is correct (4503).** *(FAR 91.211)*

At cabin pressure altitudes above 14,000 ft. MSL, the required minimum flight crew must be provided with and use supplemental oxygen during the entire flight time at those altitudes. Additionally, each occupant must be provided with supplemental oxygen at cabin pressure altitudes above 15,000 ft. MSL.

Answer (A) is incorrect because the required minimum crew must be provided with and use supplemental oxygen for that part of the flight of more than 30 minutes is the oxygen requirements when at cabin pressure altitudes above 12,500 ft. MSL up to and including 14,000 ft. MSL, not at 17,000 ft. MSL. Answer (B) is incorrect because the required minimum crew must be provided with and use supplemental oxygen for that part of the flight of more than 30 minutes is the oxygen requirements when at cabin pressure altitudes above 12,500 ft. MSL up to and including 14,000 ft. MSL, not at 17,000 ft. MSL.

**39.**

**4505.** (Refer to figure 89 on page 343.) In the event of two-way radio communications failure while operating on an IFR clearance in VFR conditions over HVE(b), the pilot should continue

A— by the route assigned in the last ATC clearance received.

B— the flight under VFR, if possible, and land as soon as practical.

C— the flight by the most direct route to the fix specified in the last clearance.

**Answer (B) is correct (4505).** *(FAR 91.185)*

If two-way radio communications fail while operating in VFR conditions, or if VFR conditions are encountered after the failure, each pilot shall continue the flight under VFR and land as soon as practicable.

Answer (A) is incorrect because, if the failure occurs in IFR (not VFR) conditions, and VFR conditions are not encountered after the failure, each pilot shall continue the flight by the route assigned in the last ATC clearance received. Answer (C) is incorrect because one continues the last route assigned by ATC if in IFR, not just directly to the next fix.

**40.**
**4504.**  On what frequency should you obtain En Route Flight Advisory Service below FL 180?

A— 122.1T/112.8R.
B— 123.6.
C— 122.0.

Answer (C) is correct (4504).  *(AIM Para 7-4)*
    En Route Flight Advisory Service (EFAS) is a service specifically designed to provide en route aircraft with timely and meaningful weather advisories pertinent to the type of flight intended, route of flight, and altitude.  EFAS is normally available from 6:00 a.m. to 10:00 p.m.  EFAS provides communications capabilities for aircraft flying at 5,000 ft. AGL to 17,500 ft. MSL on a common frequency of 122.0 MHz.
    Answer (A) is incorrect because 122.1T/112.8R is an example of communicating with an FSS through a VOR, not the EFAS frequency below FL 180.  Answer (B) is incorrect because you would use 122.0, not 123.6, to contact EFAS below FL 180.

**41.**
**4506.**  (Refer to figure 89 on page 343.)  What is the ARTCC discrete frequency from the COP on V8 southwest bound to Bryce Canyon VORTAC (a)?

A— 127.8.
B— 124.2.
C— 133.6.

Answer (C) is correct (4506).  *(ACL)*
    The COP on V8 southwest bound to BCE VORTAC (area A) from HVE VORTAC (area B) is at the midpoint, or 44 NM.  Notice the ragged line (see Legend 23 on page 330) south of HVE VORTAC which is the symbol that divides Salt Lake City ARTCC to the north and Denver ARTCC to the south.  Thus, the COP is in Salt Lake City ARTCC airspace.  Just below and to the right of HVE VORTAC is a box indicating that Salt Lake City ARTCC uses an RCO at Hanksville on a discrete frequency of 133.6.
    Answer (A) is incorrect because 127.8 MHz is not listed on the en route chart in Fig. 89.  Answer (B) is incorrect because 124.2 is the Los Angeles ARTCC discrete frequency on V8 southwest from, not to, BCE VORTAC (i.e., between OZN VORTAC and BCE VORTAC).

**42.**
**4508.**  (Refer to figure 89 on page 343.)  What type airspace exists above Bryce Canyon Airport (a) from the surface to 700 feet AGL?

A— Class D airspace.
B— Class E airspace.
C— Class G airspace.

Answer (C) is correct (4508).  *(ACL)*
    Notice that Fig. 89 is in color when you take the written test.  Bryce Canyon Airport (area A) symbol is blue in color which means that it has an approved IAP.  The airport is not indicated to be in Class B, C, D, or E airspace.  Since an IAP exists at the airport, the floor of Class E airspace is at 700 ft. in conjunction with the IAP.  Thus, from the surface to 700 ft. AGL is Class G airspace.
    Answer (A) is incorrect because Class D airspace normally extends from the surface to 2,500 ft. AGL, not 700 ft. AGL.  Answer (B) is incorrect because Class E airspace begins at 700 ft. AGL, not the surface.

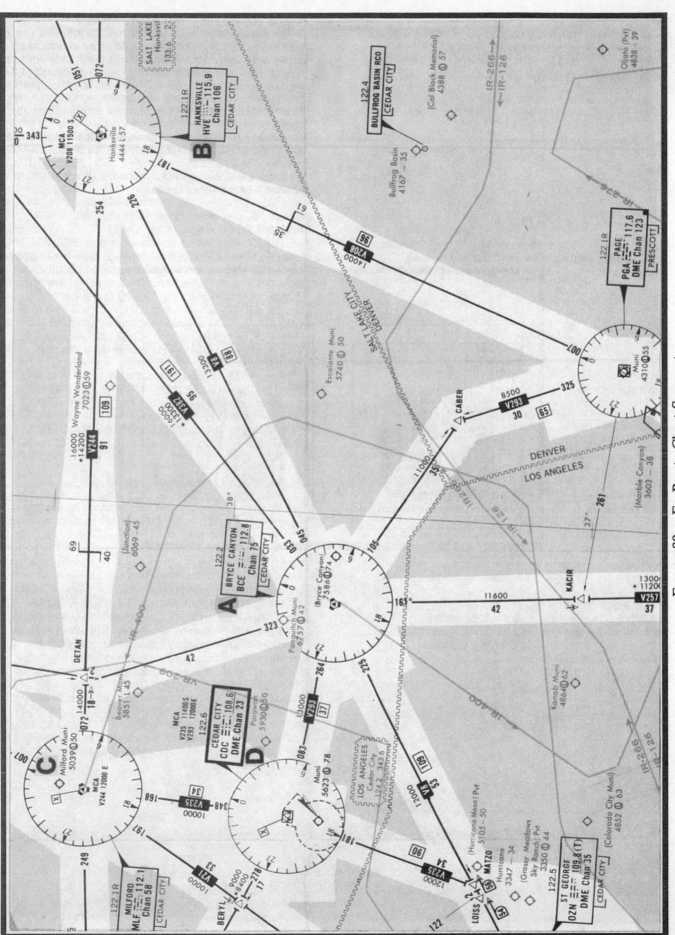

FIGURE 89.—En Route Chart Segment.

**43.**

**4507.** (Refer to figures 89 on page 343 and 90 below.) What is your relationship to the airway while en route from BCE VORTAC (a) to HVE VORTAC (b) on V8?

A— Left of course on V8.
B— Left of course on V382.
C— Right of course on V8.

Answer (A) is correct (4507). *(IFH Chap VIII)*

Your No. 1 VOR (Fig. 90) is tuned to the BCE VORTAC with a OBS setting of 033° FROM the station. This is the course for V382, which is north of V8 in Fig. 89. The CDI is deflected to the left which indicates you are to the right of V382. Your No. 2 VOR is tuned to the HVE VORTAC with an OBS setting of 046° TO the station, which is the inbound course on V8. The CDI is deflected to the right which means you are to the left of course on V8. Thus, you are located to the right of V382 and to the left of V8 while en route from BCE VORTAC to HVE VORTAC.

Answer (B) is incorrect because, if you were left of V382, you would have a right, not left, CDI deflection on NAV No. 1. Answer (C) is incorrect because, if you were right of V8, you would have a left, not right, CDI deflection on NAV No. 2.

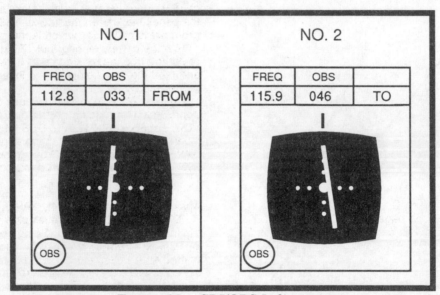

FIGURE 90.—CDI/OBS Indicators.

**44.**

**4510.** (Refer to figure 91 on page 347.) What are the two limiting cruising altitudes useable for a VFR-on-Top flight from BZN VOR to DBS VORTAC?

A— 13,200 and 18,000 feet.
B— 14,000 and 18,000 feet.
C— 14,500 and 16,500 feet.

Answer (C) is correct (4510). *(FAR 91.159)*

In Fig. 91, a flight from BZN VOR south to DBS VORTAC will be on V343 which has an MEA of 14,000 ft. A flight with a clearance of VFR-on-Top will operate at appropriate VFR cruising altitudes, at or above the minimum IFR altitude. On a magnetic course of 186°, you must be at an even thousand-foot altitude plus 500 ft. Thus, a VFR-on-Top flight is limited to only 14,500 ft. and 16,500 ft. You cannot operate VFR in Class A airspace, i.e., 18,000 ft. MSL to FL 600.

Answer (A) is incorrect because VFR-on-Top altitudes are cardinal (1,000, 2,000, etc.) plus 500 ft. Answer (B) is incorrect because VFR-on-Top altitudes are cardinal (1,000, 2,000, etc.) plus 500 ft.

**45.**
**4509.** (Refer to figure 91 on page 347.) What is the minimum crossing altitude at DBS VORTAC for a northbound IFR flight on V257?

A— 7,500 feet.
B— 8,600 feet.
C— 11,100 feet.

Answer (B) is correct (4509). *(ACL)*
DBS VORTAC is at the center of the large compass rose in the lower left of Fig. 91. At DBS VORTAC, there is a flag with an "X" inside that indicates an MCA. The MCA is indicated next to the VORTAC symbol. When flying north on V257, you must cross DBS VORTAC at a minimum altitude of 8,600 ft. (V21-257 8600N).
Answer (A) is incorrect because 7,500 ft. is the MEA on V257 south of DBS VORTAC. Answer (C) is incorrect because 11,100 ft. is the MOCA on V21-257 northwest of DBS VORTAC.

**46.**
**4511.** (Refer to figure 91 on page 347.) What should be the approximate elapsed time from BZN VOR to DBS VORTAC, if the wind is 24 knots from 260° and your intended TAS is 185 knots? (VAR 17 °E.)

A— 33 minutes.
B— 37 minutes.
C— 39 minutes.

Answer (C) is correct (4511). *(PHAK Chap VII)*
First convert your wind from 260° true to 243° magnetic because of the 17°E variation. Then place the 243 below the true index on the wind side of your flight computer and mark the wind speed of 24 kt. up from the grommet (center hole). Then place your magnetic course of 186° under the true index. Next, slide the scale so that the pencil mark is on the 185-kt. TAS and note that the grommet is at 171 kt., which is the groundspeed.
On the computer side, put 171 kt. on the outer scale under the true index. Locate 111 NM on the outer scale and read the time below on the inner scale, which is approximately 39 min.
Answer (A) is incorrect because 33 min. is the approximate time going north from DBS VORTAC to BZN VOR, not from BZN VOR to DBS VORTAC. Answer (B) is incorrect because 37 min. is the approximate time from BZN VOR to DBS VORTAC using the wind direction of 260°, not the magnetic wind direction of 243°.

**47.**
**4514.** (Refer to figure 91 on page 347.) Southbound on V257, at what time should you arrive at DBS VORTAC if you crossed over CPN VORTAC at 0850 and over DIVID intersection at 0854?

A— 0939.
B— 0943.
C— 0947.

Answer (B) is correct (4514). *(PHAK Chap VII)*
CPN VORTAC is on the left side of the chart about 1½ in. down from the top. Going south on V257, DIVID INT is 9 NM from CPN VORTAC. Use your flight computer to determine the groundspeed. Locate 9 on the outer scale and place 4 on the min. scale under the 9. The groundspeed is read over the index, which is 135 kt.
From DIVID to DLN VORTAC is 39 NM, then from DLN VORTAC to DBS VORTAC is 71 NM, or a total of 110 NM. To determine the time, place 135 kt. over the index of your flight computer and locate 110 NM on the outer scale, and the time is read below on the min. scale, which is 49 min. from DIVID INT to DBS VORTAC. Thus, your ETA at DBS VORTAC is 0943 (0854 + 49).
Answer (A) is incorrect because the 49 min. is added to the time you crossed DIVID INT (0854), not the time you crossed CPN VORTAC (0850). Answer (C) is incorrect because the distance from CPN VORTAC to DIVID INT (9 NM) must be subtracted from the 48 NM between CPN VORTAC and DLN VORTAC.

**48.**
**4513.** (Refer to figure 91 on page 347.) What are the oxygen requirements for an IFR flight eastbound on V520 from DBS VORTAC in an unpressurized aircraft at the MEA?

A— The required minimum crew must be provided and use supplemental oxygen for that part of the flight of more than 30 minutes.

B— The required minimum crew must be provided and use supplemental oxygen for that part of the flight of more than 30 minutes, and the passengers must be provided supplemental oxygen.

C— The required minimum crew must be provided and use supplemental oxygen.

**Answer (C) is correct (4513).** *(FAR 91.211)*
On Fig. 91, when going eastbound from DBS VORTAC on V520, the MEA is 15,000 ft. MSL. At cabin pressure altitudes above 14,000 ft. MSL, the flight crew must be provided and use supplemental oxygen for the entire flight. At cabin pressure altitudes above 15,000 ft. MSL, the passengers must be provided with supplemental oxygen.
Answer (A) is incorrect because the required minimum crew must be provided and use supplemental oxygen for that part of the flight of more than 30 min. at cabin pressure altitudes above 12,500 ft. MSL up to and including 14,000 ft. MSL. Answer (B) is incorrect because the required minimum crew must be provided and use supplemental oxygen at all times (not only that part of more than 30 min.) at cabin pressure altitudes above 14,000 ft. MSL. Passengers must be provided supplemental oxygen at cabin pressure altitudes above (not at) 15,000 ft. MSL.

**49.**
**4515.** (Refer to figure 91 on page 347.) What is the function of the Yellowstone RCO?

A— Long range communications outlet for Idaho Falls Center.

B— Remote communications outlet for Idaho Falls FSS.

C— Satellite FSS controlled by Idaho Falls FSS with limited service.

**Answer (B) is correct (4515).** *(ACL)*
The Yellowstone RCO communication box is located in the center of the chart, in Fig. 91, just above the DBS VORTAC box. An arrow points to a symbol ⊙, which indicates an FSS remote communications outlet (see Legend 22 on page 329). The name of the controlling FSS is listed underneath the communication box and the frequency is on top. Thus, Yellowstone RCO is a remote communications outlet for Idaho Falls FSS on 122.45 MHz.
Answer (A) is incorrect because the center for that area is Salt Lake City (not Idaho Falls) as indicated by the ARTCC RCO box above the Yellowstone RCO box. The ARTCC remote site is Ashton, not Yellowstone. Answer (C) is incorrect because Yellowstone RCO is just an antenna site, not an FSS, that extends the communication range for the controlling FSS (e.g., Idaho Falls FSS). FSS services are not limited when communicating through an RCO.

**50.**
**4516.** (Refer to figure 91 on page 347.) Where should you change VOR frequencies when en route from DBS VORTAC to DNW VORTAC on V298?

A— 41 and ½ NM (halfway).

B— 68 NM from DBS VORTAC.

C— QUIRT intersection.

**Answer (B) is the best answer (4516).** *(AIM Para 5-36)*
Note that the FAA incorrectly used CPN VORTAC instead of DBS VORTAC. Your author has changed answer (B) to correct this error; however, it may not be corrected on your FAA written exam. The FAA will probably make this correction on the computer test.
When flying from DBS VORTAC to DNW VORTAC on V298 (Fig. 91), notice that very close to the DNW VORTAC is a VOR changeover point symbol (∫), which is 68 NM from the DBS VORTAC.
Answer (A) is incorrect because when the changeover point (COP) is not located at the midway point, the COP is marked by the symbol " ∫ " and mileage is given to the VORs. Answer (C) is incorrect because QUIRT INT is located 3 NM to the east of the changeover point.

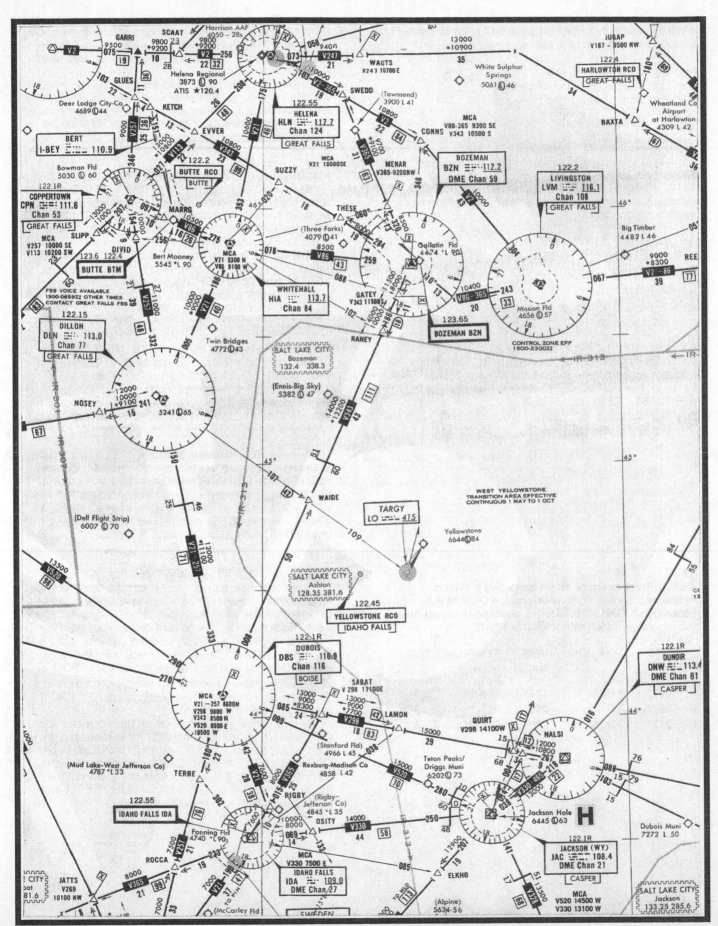

FIGURE 91.—En Route Chart Segment.

**51.**
**4512.** (Refer to figure 91 on page 347.) What lighting is indicated on the chart for Jackson Hole Airport (h)?

A— Lights on prior request.
B— Lights temporarily out of service.
C— Pilot controlled lighting.

**Answer (C) is correct (4512). *(ACL)***
The Jackson Hole Airport is located at the lower right of Fig. 91. The "L" indicates that Jackson Hole Airport has night lighting. The circle indicates pilot controlled lighting.
Answer (A) is incorrect because an asterisk would indicate lighting on request or operating part of the night only. Answer (B) is incorrect because lights temporarily out of service would be indicated in a NOTAM or the Airport/Facility Directory.

**52.**
**4517.** (Refer to figure 91 on page 347.) What is the minimum crossing altitude at SABAT intersection when eastbound on V298?

A— 8,500 feet.
B— 11,100 feet.
C— 13,000 feet.

**Answer (B) is correct (4517). *(ACL)***
SABAT INT is located east of DBS VORTAC on V298 at the lower middle area in Fig. 91. There is a flag with an "X" in it which indicates an MCA at SABAT. Underneath the SABAT is the MCA which is 11,100 ft. when eastbound on V298 (V298 11100E).
Answer (A) is incorrect because 8,500 ft. is not an indicated minimum IFR altitude on V298 between DBS VORTAC and DNW VORTAC. Answer (C) is incorrect because 13,000 ft. is the MEA when eastbound on V298 between DBS VORTAC and SABAT INT.

**53.**
**4325.** (Refer to figure 58 on page 349.) On which frequencies could you receive the College Station FSS?

A— 122.65, 122.2, 122.1, 113.3.
B— 122.65, 122.2.
C— 118.5, 122.65, 122.2.

**Answer (B) is correct (4325). *(A/FD)***
Fig. 58 is an excerpt from an A/FD for Easterwood Field located at College Station, TX. Locate the "Communications" heading for information on frequencies. The FSS name is Montgomery County (not College Station). There is a College Station RCO to communicate with the FSS on frequencies 122.65 and 122.2 only.
Answer (A) is incorrect because 122.1 is not available at College Station to contact the Montgomery County FSS. College Station VORTAC operates on frequency 113.3, but under Radio Aids to Navigation, the "W" after VORTAC means that no voice is transmitted on this frequency. Answer (C) is incorrect because 118.5 is the tower/CTAF, not FSS, frequency.

**54.**
**4326.** (Refer to figure 58 on page 349.) Which indications on the VOR receivers and DME at the Easterwood Field VOR receiver checkpoint would meet the regulatory requirement for this flight?

| VOR No. 1 | TO/FROM | VOR No. 2 | TO/FROM | DME |
|---|---|---|---|---|
| A— 097° | FROM | 101° | FROM | 3.3 |
| B— 097° | TO | 096° | TO | 3.2 |
| C— 277° | FROM | 280° | FROM | 3.3 |

**Answer (A) is correct (4326). *(FAR 91.171)***
The bottom portion of Fig. 58 lists the VOR receiver checkpoints. Locate College Station (Easterwood Field) to determine that the checkpoint is on the ground (on west edge of parking ramp) and the azimuth from the VORTAC is 097° (i.e., R-097) and the distance is 3.2 NM from the VORTAC. On the R-097 you want the CDI needle centered with an OBS setting of 097° FROM or 277° TO the station, with the acceptable error of ±4°. Thus, the acceptable VOR indications are 097° FROM and 101° FROM the station.
Answer (B) is incorrect because the magnetic azimuth (i.e., radial) from the station at the ground checkpoint is 097°, which results in a FROM (not TO) indication with the OBS set to 097°. Answer (C) is incorrect because the magnetic azimuth (i.e., radial) from the station at the ground checkpoint is 097°, which results in a TO (not FROM) indication with the OBS set to 277°.

140                                    **TEXAS**

**COLLEGE STATION**
  **EASTERWOOD FLD**    (CLL)    3 SW    UTC–6(–5DT)    30°35'18"N 96°21'49"W                    HOUSTON
    320   B   S4   **FUEL** 100LL, JET A   OX 2   ARFF Index A                                   H-2K, 5B, L-17A
    **RWY 16-34:** H7000X150 (ASPH–GRVD)    S-70, D-90, DT-150   MIRL                            IAP
      **RWY 16:** VASI(V4R)—GA 3.0°TCH 51'. Tree.        **RWY 34:** MALSR.
    **RWY 10-28:** H5160X150 (CONC)    S-27, D-50, DT-87   MIRL
      **RWY 10:** VASI(V4L)—GA 3.0°TCH 50'. Tree.        **RWY 28:** REIL VASI(V4L)—GA 3.0° TCH 54'. Tree.
    **RWY 04-22:** H5149X150 (CONC)    S-27, D-50, DT-87
      **RWY 04:** Tree.        **RWY 22:** Tree.
    **AIRPORT REMARKS:** Attended 1200-0500Z‡. CAUTION: deer on rwys. CAUTION: Rwy 10-28 taxiway B and taxiway E
      have uneven surfaces. Birds on and in vicinity of arpt. MIRL Rwy 10–28 preset medium ints when twr clsd, to
      increase ints and ACTIVATE MIRL Rwy 16–34 and MALSR Rwy 34—CTAF. CLOSED to unscheduled air carrier
      ops with more than 30 passenger seats except 24 hours PPR call, arpt manager 409–845–4811. Rwy 04–22
      day VFR ops only. Itinerant acft park North of twr, overnight parking fee. Ldg fee scheduled FAR 135 and all FAR
      121 ops. For fuel after hours PPR call 409–845–4811/823 –0690 or ctc Texas A and M University police
      409–845–2345; late ngt fee. Rwy 16–34 grvd except south 200'. Rwy 04–22 deteriorating and vegetation
      growing through cracks. NOTE: See SPECIAL NOTICE—Simultaneous Operations on Intersecting Runways.
    **COMMUNICATIONS:** CTAF 118.5    ATIS 126.85 (1200–0400Z‡)    UNICOM 122.95
      MONTGOMERY COUNTY FSS (CXO) TF 1–800–WX–BRIEF. NOTAM FILE CLL.
      COLLEGE STATION RCO 122.65 122.2 (MONTGOMERY COUNTY FSS).
      ®HOUSTON CENTER APP/DEP CON: 120.4
        **TOWER:** 118.5 (1200–0400Z‡) (VFR only)    **GND CON:** 121.7
    **RADIO AIDS TO NAVIGATION:** NOTAM FILE CLL. VHF/DF ctc FSS
      COLLEGE STATION (L) VORTACW 113.3    CLL    Chan 80    30°36'17"N 96°25'13"W    100° 3.1 NM to fld.
        370/08E. HIWAS.
      ROWDY NDB (LOM) 260    CL    30°29'36"N 96°20'16"W    341° 5.9 NM to fld.
      ILS 111.7 I-CLL Rwy 34 LOM ROWDY NDB. ILS unmonitored when twr closed.

**COLLEGE STATION**    30°36'17"N 96°25'13"W    NOTAM FILE CLL.                                HOUSTON
  (L) VORTACW 113.3    CLL    Chan 80    100° 3.1 NM to Easterwood Fld. 370/08E. **HIWAS.**     H-2K, 5B, L-17A
  RCO 122.65 122.2 (MONTGOMERY COUNTY FSS)

## VOR RECEIVER CHECK                                                                         259

### TEXAS

#### VOR RECEIVER CHECK POINTS

| Facility Name (Arpt Name) | Freq/Ident | Type Check Pt. Gnd. AB/ALT | Azimuth from Fac. Mag | Dist. from Fac. N.M. | Check Point Description |
|---|---|---|---|---|---|
| **Abilene** (Abilene Regional) | 113.7/ABI | A/2800 | 047 | 10.1 | Over silos in center of Ft Phantom Lake. |
| **Alice** (Alice International) | 114.5/ALI | G | 270 | 0.5 | On twy N of hangar. |
| **Amarillo** (Amarillo Internationl) | 117.2/AMA | G | 210 | 4.5 | On east runup pad Rwy 22. |
| **Austin** (Robert Mueller Muni) | 114.6/AUS | G | 118 | 0.6 | On runup area on twy to Rwy 31L. |
| **Beaumont** (Jefferson County) | 114.5/BPT | G | 310 | 1.0 | On runup area for Rwy 12. |
| **Big Spring** (Big Spring McMahon-Wrinkle) | 114.3/BGS | A/3500 | 107 | 10.5 | Over red and white water tank. |
| **Borger** (Hutchinson Co) | 108.6/BGD | G | 175 | 6.7 | On intersecting twy in front of terminal. |
| **Brownsville** (Brownsville/South Padre Island Intl) | 116.3/BRO | G | 248 | 3.2 | On NE corner of parking ramp. |
| **Brownwood** (Brownwood Muni) | 108.6/BWD | A/2600 | 169 | 6.2 | Over rotating bcn. |
| **Childress** (Childress Muni) | 117.6/CDS | G | 353 | 3.7 | At intersection of edge of ramp at center twy. |
| **College Station** (Easterwood Field) | 113.3/CLL | G | 097 | 3.2 | On W edge of parking ramp. |
| **Corpus Christi** (Corpus Christi Intl) | 115.5/CRP | A/1100 | 187 | 7.5 | Over grain elevator. |
| **Corpus Christi** (San Patricio County) | 115.5/CRP | A/1000 | 318 | 9.5 | Over rotating beacon on arpt. |
| **Daisetta** (Liberty Muni) | 116.9/DAS | A/1200 | 195 | 7.5 | Over hangar S of arpt. |
| **Dalhart** (Dalhart Muni) | 112.0/DHT | G | 170 | 3.9 | On SE corner of main ramp. |
| **Eagle Lake** (Eagle Lake) | 116.4/ELA | A/1200 | 180 | 4.5 | Over water tank 0.4 NM SW |

FIGURE 58.—Excerpts from Airport/Facility Directory.

**55.**
**4327.**  (Refer to figure 59 on page 351 and 60 on page 352.)  What are the operating hours (local standard time) of the Houston EFAS?

A— 0600 to 2400.
B— 0700 to 2300.
C— 1800 to 1000.

Answer (A) may be correct (4327).  *(AIM Para 7-4)*
    EFAS is specifically designed to provide en route aircraft with timely and meaningful weather advisories pertinent to the type of flight intended, route of flight, and altitude.  EFAS is provided by specialists in selected AFSSs/FSSs controlling multiple RCOs covering a large geographic area.
    The bottom of Fig. 60 shows the EFAS outlets and indicates that the Houston EFAS is operated by Montgomery Co. FSS.  The hours of operation are from 1200Z to 0400Z.  Convert Z time to local time by subtracting 6 hr. as indicated in the time conversion in the first line of the A/FD.  Thus the hours of operation (local standard time) are from 0600 to 2200.
    Note:  The FAA may change answer (A) to indicate 0600 to 2200 on the computer test.
    Answer (B) is incorrect because to convert Z time to local standard time you must subtract 6 hr. not 5 hr.  Answer (C) is incorrect because to convert Z time to local standard time you must subtract, not add, 6 hr.

**56.**
**4337.**  (Refer to figure 64 on page 353.)  The course deviation indicator (CDI) are centered.  Which indications on the No. 1 and No. 2 VOR receivers over the Lafayette Regional Airport would meet the requirements for the VOR receiver check?

| VOR No. 1 | TO/FROM | VOR No. 2 | TO/FROM |
|-----------|---------|-----------|---------|
| A— 162°   | TO      | 346°      | FROM    |
| B— 160°   | FROM    | 162°      | FROM    |
| C— 341°   | FROM    | 330°      | FROM    |

Answer (A) is correct (4337).  *(FAR 91.171)*
    The top portion of Fig. 64 lists the VOR receiver checkpoints.  Locate Lafayette (Lafayette Regional) to determine that the checkpoint is an airborne checkpoint at 1,000 ft. over the rotating beacon and the azimuth from the VORTAC is 340° (i.e., R-340).  On the R-340 you want the CDI needle centered with an OBS setting of 340° FROM or 160° TO the station, with an acceptable error of ±6°.  Thus, acceptable VOR indications are 162° TO and 346° FROM the station.
    Answer (B) is incorrect because the magnetic azimuth (i.e., radial) from the station at the checkpoint is 340°, which results in a TO (not FROM) indication with the OBS set to 160° and 162°.  Answer (C) is incorrect because the No. 2 VOR OBS of 330° is greater than 6° difference from the 340° azimuth from the VORTAC.

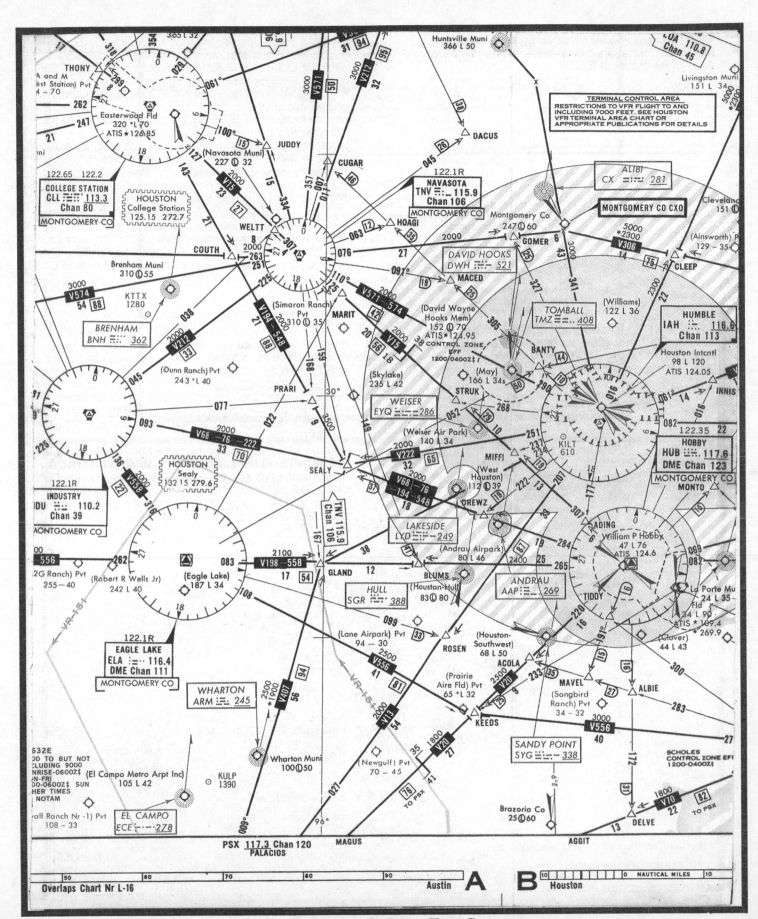

FIGURE 59.—En Route Chart Segment.

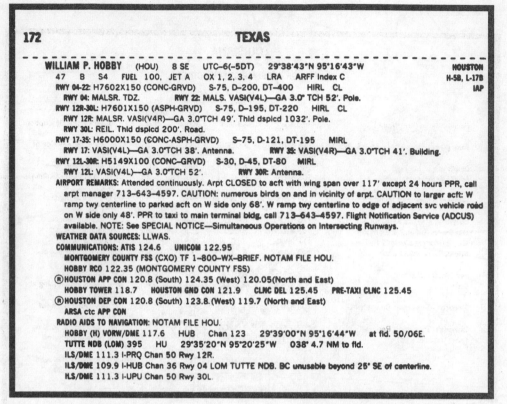

172                                    TEXAS                                  HOUSTON

WILLIAM P. HOBBY   (HOU)   8 SE   UTC–6(–5DT)   29°38'43"N 95°16'43"W                H-5B, L-17B
47   B   S4   FUEL 100, JET A   OX 1, 2, 3, 4   LRA   ARFF Index C                        IAP
RWY 04-22: H7602X150 (CONC-GRVD)   S-75, D-200, DT-400   HIRL CL
   RWY 04: MALSR. TDZ.          RWY 22: MALS. VASI(V4L)—GA 3.0° TCH 52'. Pole.
RWY 12R-30L: H7601X150 (ASPH-GRVD)   S-75, D-195, DT-220   HIRL CL
   RWY 12R: MALSR. VASI(V4R)—GA 3.0°TCH 49'. Thld dsplcd 1032'. Pole.
   RWY 30L: REIL. Thld dsplcd 200'. Road.
RWY 17-35: H6000X150 (CONC-ASPH-GRVD)   S-75, D-121, DT-195   MIRL
   RWY 17: VASI(V4L)—GA 3.0°TCH 38'. Antenna.   RWY 35: VASI(V4R)—GA 3.0°TCH 41'. Building.
RWY 12L-30R: H5149X100 (CONC-GRVD)   S-30, D-45, DT-80   MIRL
   RWY 12L: VASI(V4L)—GA 3.0°TCH 52'.          RWY 30R: Antenna.
AIRPORT REMARKS: Attended continuously. Arpt CLOSED to acft with wing span over 117' except 24 hours PPR, call
   arpt manager 713–643–4597. CAUTION: numerous birds on and in vicinity of arpt. CAUTION to larger acft: W
   ramp twy centerline to parked acft on W side only 68'. W ramp twy centerline to edge of adjacent svc vehicle road
   on W side only 48'. PPR to taxi to main terminal bldg, call 713–643–4597. Flight Notification Service (ADCUS)
   available. NOTE: See SPECIAL NOTICE—Simultaneous Operations on Intersecting Runways.
WEATHER DATA SOURCES: LLWAS.
COMMUNICATIONS: ATIS 124.6   UNICOM 122.95
   MONTGOMERY COUNTY FSS (CXO) TF 1–800–WX–BRIEF. NOTAM FILE HOU.
   HOBBY RCO 122.35 (MONTGOMERY COUNTY FSS)
®HOUSTON APP CON 120.8 (South) 124.35 (West) 120.05(North and East)
   HOBBY TOWER 118.7   HOUSTON GND CON 121.9   CLNC DEL 125.45   PRE-TAXI CLNC 125.45
®HOUSTON DEP CON 120.8 (South) 123.8 (West) 119.7 (North and East)
   ARSA ctc APP CON
RADIO AIDS TO NAVIGATION: NOTAM FILE HOU.
   HOBBY (H) VORW/DME 117.6   HUB   Chan 123   29°39'00"N 95°16'44"W   at fld. 50/06E.
   TUTTE NDB (LOM) 395   HU   29°35'20"N 95°20'25"W   038° 4.7 NM to fld.
   ILS/DME 111.3 I-PRQ Chan 50 Rwy 12R
   ILS/DME 109.9 I-HUB Chan 36 Rwy 04 LOM TUTTE NDB. BC unusable beyond 25° SE of centerline.
   ILS/DME 111.3 I-UPU Chan 50 Rwy 30L.

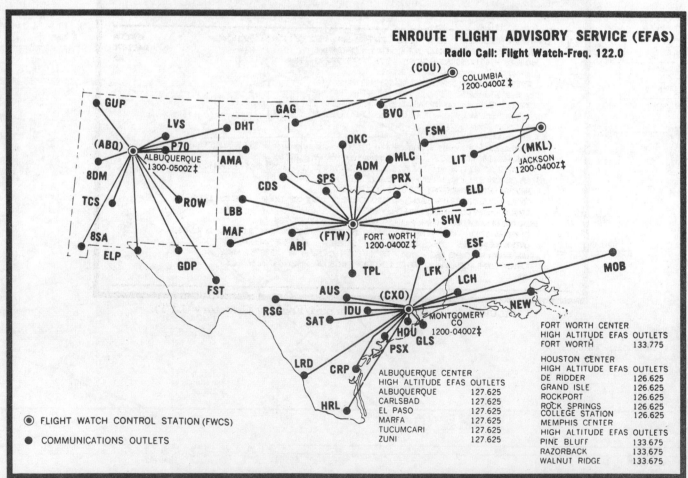

ENROUTE FLIGHT ADVISORY SERVICE (EFAS)
Radio Call: Flight Watch-Freq. 122.0

◉ FLIGHT WATCH CONTROL STATION (FWCS)
● COMMUNICATIONS OUTLETS

ALBUQUERQUE CENTER
HIGH ALTITUDE EFAS OUTLETS
ALBUQUERQUE        127.625
CARLSBAD           127.625
EL PASO            127.625
MARFA              127.625
TUCUMCARI          127.625
ZUNI               127.625

FORT WORTH CENTER
HIGH ALTITUDE EFAS OUTLETS
FORT WORTH         133.775

HOUSTON CENTER
HIGH ALTITUDE EFAS OUTLETS
DE RIDDER          126.625
GRAND ISLE         126.625
ROCKPORT           126.625
ROCK SPRINGS       126.625
COLLEGE STATION    126.625
MEMPHIS CENTER
HIGH ALTITUDE EFAS OUTLETS
PINE BLUFF         133.675
RAZORBACK          133.675
WALNUT RIDGE       133.675

FIGURE 60.—Airport/Facilty Directory and Enroute Flight Advisory Service (EFAS).

## LOUISIANA

### VOR RECEIVER CHECK POINTS

| Facility Name (Arpt Name) | Freq/Ident | Type Check Pt. Gnd. AB/ALT | Azimuth from Fac. Mag | Dist. from Fac. N.M. | Check Point Description |
|---|---|---|---|---|---|
| Baton Rouge (Baton Rouge Metro, Ryan)... | 116.5/BTR | A/1500 | 063 | 7.7 | Over water tank W side of arpt. |
| Downtown................. | 108.6/DTN | A/1500 | 290 | 10 | Over white water tower. |
| Esler (Esler Regional) ............. | 108.8/ESF | G | 151 | 3.5 | On ramp in front of admin bldg. |
| Hammond (Hammond Muni) .......... | 109.6/HMU | G | 342 | .6 | On twy W side app end Rwy 18. |
| Lafayette (Lafayette Regional) ......... | 110.8/LFT | A/1000 | 340 | 25 | Over rotating beacon. |
| Lake Charles (Lake Charles Muni) ....... | 113.4/LCH | A/1000 | 253 | 6.2 | Over rotg bcn on atct. |
| Monroe (Monroe Muni) ........... | 117.2/MLU | G | 209 | 0.9 | On ramp SE of atct. |
| Natchez (Concordia Parish)  ......... | 110.0/HEZ | A/1000 | 247 | 10.5 | Over hangar NW end of field. |
| New Orleans (Lakefront) .............. | 113.2/MSY | A/1000 | 081 | 7.7 | Over lakefront atct. |
| Ruston ........................ | 112.8/RSN | A/2000 | 343 | 14 | Over hwy & RR crossing at Dubash. |
| Shreveport (Shreveport Downtown) ...... | 108.6/DTN | G | 307 | .5 | On runup area N side of rwy 14. |
| Shreveport (Shreveport Regional) ........ | 117.4/SHV | A/1200 | 175 | 19.3 | Over old terminal building. |
| Tibby (Thibodaux Muni) ............. | 112.0/TBD | A/1000 | 006 | 5.0 | Over railroad bridge off apch end rwy 26. |
|  | 112.0/TBD | A/1000 | 117 | 10.0 | Over intersection of rwys 17-35 and 12-30. |

§ **LAFAYETTE REGIONAL**    (LFT)   2 SE   GMT-6(-5DT)   30°12′14″N 91°59′16″W          **HOUSTON**
42.  B   S4   **FUEL** 100LL, JET A   OX 1   CFR Index B                                **H-4F, L-17C**
RWY 03-21: H7651X150 (ASPH-GRVD)   S-75, D-170, DT-290   HIRL                           **IAP**
  RWY 03: REIL. VASI(V4L)—GA 3.0°TCH 35′. Tree.
  RWY 21: MALSR. VASI(V4L)—GA 3.0°TCH 44′. Tree.
RWY 10-28: H5401X150 (ASPH)   S-85, D-110, DT-175   MIRL
  RWY 10: REIL (out of svc indefinitely). VASI(V4L)—GA 3.0° TCH 35.33′. Tree.
  RWY 28: REIL. VASI(V4L)—GA 3.0° TCH 55′. Thld dsplcd 202′. Tree.
RWY 01-19: H5069X150 (ASPH)   S-25, D-45
  RWY 01: VASI(V4R)—GA 3.0°TCH 50′. Tree.
AIRPORT REMARKS: Attended continuously. Rwy 01-19 closed to air carriers. ACTIVATE MALSR Rwy 21—118.5.
COMMUNICATIONS: CTAF 118.5   ATIS 120.5 Opr 1200-0500Z‡   UNICOM 122.95
  LAFAYETTE FSS (LFT) on arpt. 122.35, 122.2, 122.1R, 110.8T LD 318-233-4952 NOTAM FILE LFT.
Ⓡ APP/DEP CON 121.1 (011°-190°) 124.0 (191°-010°) (1200-0400Z‡)
  HOUSTON CENTER APP/DEP CON 133.65 (0400-1200Z‡)
  TOWER 118.5, 121.35 (Helicopter ops) (1200-0400Z‡)     GND CON 121.8     CLNC DEL 125.55
  STAGE III ctc APP CON within 25 NM below 7000′
RADIO AIDS TO NAVIGATION: NOTAM FILE LFT. VHF/DF ctc LAFAYETTE FSS
  (L) VORTAC 110.8   LFT   Chan 45   30°08′45″N 91°59′00″W   344°3.0 NM to fld. 40/06E
  LAFFS NDB (LOM) 375   LF   30°17′21″N 91°54′29″W   215° 5.8 NM to fld
  LAKE MARTIN NDB (MHW) 362   LKM   30°11′33″N 91°52′58″W   270° 5.2 NM to fld
  ILS/DME 109.5 I-LFT Chan 32 Rwy 21 LOM LAFFS NDB. Unmonitored when twr clsd.
ASR

FIGURE 64.—Excerpt from Airport/Facility Directory (LFT).

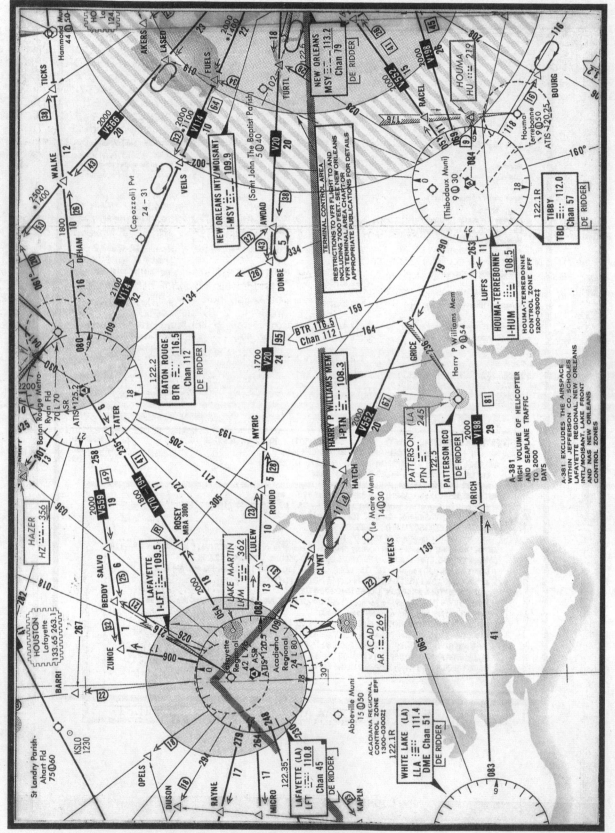

FIGURE 65.—En Route Chart Segment.

**57.**
**4336.** (Refer to figure 65 on page 354.)  Which point would be the appropriate VOR COP on V552 from the LFT to the TBD VORTACs?

A— CLYNT intersection.
B— HATCH intersection.
C— 33 DME from the LFT VORTAC.

Answer (C) is correct (4336).  *(AIM Para 5-36)*
The changeover point (COP) is located midway between the navigation facilities for straight route segments, unless the COP symbol ( ⌐ ) is depicted on the route, in which case that is the COP.  Since no COP symbol appears on V552 from LFT VORTAC (middle left) to TBD VORTAC (lower right), in Fig. 65, the COP is at the midway point.  Since the leg is 67 NM, the COP would be approximately at 33 DME from LFT VORTAC.
Answer (A) is incorrect because CLYNT INT is only about 1/4, not 1/2, the distance from LFT to TBD VORTACs.  Answer (B) is incorrect because HATCH INT is 5 NM before the COP at 33 NM (i.e., midway point between the LFT and TBD VORTACs).

**58.**
**4338.** (Refer to figure 65 on page 354 and 66 below.)  What is your position relative to GRICE intersection?

A— Right of V552 and approaching GRICE intersection.
B— Right of V552 and past GRICE intersection.
C— Left of V552 and approaching GRICE intersection.

Answer (A) is correct (4338).  *(IFH Chap VIII)*
GRICE INT is located at the lower middle portion of Fig. 65 along V552, and is the intersection of V552 and the localizer course to Harry P. Williams Mem. Airport.  Your No. 1 VOR (Fig. 66) is tuned to the TBD VORTAC with an OBS setting of 110° TO the station.  If you are flying toward TBD VORTAC on V552 (R-290), a left CDI deflection indicates that you are to the right of V552.  Your No. 2 VOR is tuned to the I-PTN localizer course.  If you are flying inbound on the localizer, a left CDI needle deflection indicates that you are to the right of the localizer course.  Thus, you are right of V552 and approaching GRICE INT.
Answer (B) is incorrect because if you were past GRICE INT you would be to the left of the localizer; thus, the CDI needle would have a right (not left) deflection.  Answer (C) is incorrect because if you were to the left of V552 the CDI needle would have a right (not left) deflection.

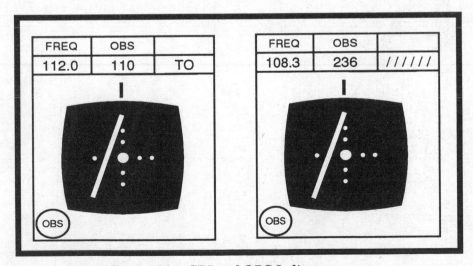

FIGURE 66.—CDI and OBS Indicators.

**59.**

**4339.**   (Refer to figure 65 on page 354 and 67 below.) What is the significance of the symbol at GRICE intersection?

A— It signifies a localizer-only approach is available at Harry P. Williams Memorial.

B— The localizer has an ATC function in addition to course guidance.

C— GRICE intersection also serves as the FAF for the ILS approach procedure to Harry P. Williams Memorial.

Answer (B) is correct (4339).   *(ACL)*
   The large localizer symbol from Harry P. Williams Memorial to GRICE INT (Fig. 65) indicates that the localizer has an ATC function in addition to course guidance.   In this case, the localizer ATC's function is to identify GRICE INT.
   Answer (A) is incorrect because the localizer symbol indicates the availability of an ILS (not an LOC only) approach.   Answer (C) is incorrect because GRICE INT is identified by the localizer course.   The FAF on an ILS is the interception of the glide slope, not an intersection.

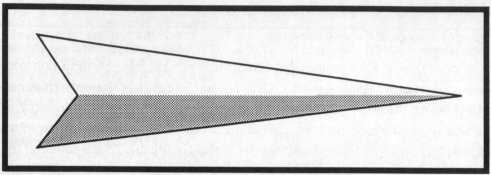

FIGURE 67.—Localizer Symbol.

# END OF CHAPTER

# CHAPTER ELEVEN
# COMPREHENSIVE IFR TRIP REVIEW

This chapter contains all FAA Instrument Rating test questions regarding comprehensive IFR trip reviews and an explanation of each answer. **CAUTION:** Recall that the **sole purpose** of this book is to expedite your passing the FAA written test for the instrument rating. Accordingly, all extraneous material (i.e., topics or regulations not directly tested on the FAA written test) is omitted, even though much more information and knowledge are necessary to fly safely. This additional material is presented in *Instrument Pilot FAA Practical Test Prep* and *Aviation Weather and Weather Services*, available from Gleim Publications, Inc. See the order form on page 478.

Most of the charts herein contain old airspace terminology. Memory aid: list A down to G (no F) and match old airspace classifications based on height from highest to lowest: A = PCA, B = TCA, C = ARSA, D = ATA, E = general controlled, and G = uncontrolled.

Note there are two helicopter trips in the FAA book. We do not believe it is appropriate to ask helicopter questions on an airplane written test. However, nine of the questions included in these two helicopter trips are generic to IFR flight, i.e., could apply to you in an airplane. Examples are questions regarding en route charts and the A/FD. These questions will appear in other chapters as appropriate, e.g., IFR En Route.

This chapter consists of 94 questions relating to eight IFR trips. The trips are from

1. Grand Junction, CO to Durango, CO  (Questions 1-7)
2. Medford, OR to Eugene, OR  (Questions 8-18)
3. Yakima, WA to Portland, OR  (Questions 19-33)
4. Santa Barbara, CA to Paso Robles, CA  (Questions 34-43)
5. Hot Springs, AR to Dallas, TX  (Questions 44-54)
6. Big Spring, TX to Dallas, TX  (Questions 55-66)
7. W. Milford, NJ to Windsor Locks, CT  (Questions 67-80)
8. Helena, MT to Billings, MT  (Questions 81-94)

Each trip provides you with the following types of data:

1. Partially completed IFR flight plan
2. Aircraft model and equipment status sheet
3. Partially completed flight log
4. SIDs and STARs
5. Appropriate Airport/Facility Directory excerpts
6. Instrument approach chart(s)
7. Low Altitude En Route Chart

The general sequence of questions includes

1.  Equipment code to put in Block 3 of your IFR flight plan (the Legend below is also provided in Appendix 2 at the back of the FAA Instrument Rating Question Book):

---

### AIRCRAFT EQUIPMENT CODE

/X—NO TRANSPONDER
/T—TRANSPONDER WITH NO ALTITUDE ENCODING CAPABILITY
/U—TRANSPONDER WITH ALTITUDE ENCODING CAPABILITY
/D—DME, BUT NO TRANSPONDER
/B—DME AND TRANSPONDER, BUT NO ALTITUDE ENCODING CAPABILITY
/A—DME AND TRANSPONDER WITH ALTITUDE ENCODING CAPABILITY
/M—TACAN ONLY, BUT NO TRANSPONDER
/N—TACAN ONLY AND TRANSPONDER, BUT WITH NO ALTITUDE ENCODING CAPABILITY
/P—TACAN ONLY AND TRANSPONDER WITH ALTITUDE ENCODING CAPABILITY
/C—RNAV AND TRANSPONDER, BUT WITH NO ALTITUDE ENCODING CAPABILITY
/R—RNAV AND TRANSPONDER WITH ALTITUDE ENCODING CAPABILITY
/W—RNAV BUT NO TRANSPONDER
/G—FLIGHT MANAGEMENT SYSTEM (FMS) AND ELECTRONIC FLIGHT INSTRUMENT SYSTEM (EFIS) EQUIPPED AIRCRAFT WITH /R CAPABILITY HAVING A "SPECIAL AIRCRAFT AND AIRCREW AUTHORIZATION" ISSUED BY THE FAA.

---

LEGEND 25.—Aircraft Equipment Codes.

2.  Calibrated airspeed (CAS) to maintain true airspeed (TAS) indicated in flight plan.

    a.  On your flight computer, put air temperature (given in question) over the flight altitude (given in the IFR flight plan).  Then on outer scale find TAS, and CAS is on inner scale.

3.  Time to complete the flight (time en route for Block 10 of the IFR flight plan).

    a.  This requires you to complete the flight log, which involves wind triangle computations (on your manual or electronic flight computer).

4.  Interpret ADF, VOR, RMI, HSI, and GS/LOC indicators to determine position relative to a position specified on a particular approach, SID, STAR, or en route chart.

    a.  These interpretations are covered in Chapter 6, Navigation.

5.  Interpret appropriate procedures, minimum altitude, and other restrictions on instrument approach charts.

    a.  See the instrument approach chart legends (on pages 246 through 253) in Chapter 9, Instrument Approaches.

6.  Interpret appropriate procedures, minimum altitude, and other restrictions on low altitude en route charts.

    a.  See the IFR en route chart legends (on pages 328 through 330) in Chapter 10, IFR En Route.

7.  Interpret SIDs and STARs.

    a.  A careful reading of the SID or STAR usually provides the correct answer, especially in conjunction with the SID/STAR legends which are reproduced on pages 254 through 258 in Chapter 9, Instrument Approaches.

## 11.1  GJT to DRO

Questions 1 through 7 (FAA Nos. 4259 through 4265) (pages 360 and 361) pertain to an IFR flight from Walker Field, Grand Junction, Colorado to Durango-La Plata County Airport, Durango, Colorado, and return to Grand Junction.

The route of flight is given in Block 8 on the flight plan portion of Figs. 21 and 21A on pages 362 and 363. Information which pertains to your aircraft is given on the bottom portion of Figs. 21 and 21A. The partially completed flight planning log is given in Figs. 22 and 22A on pages 364 and 365.

The following figures provided for this flight are listed below, which we have grouped and presented together after the sequence of questions. Note that not all are needed to answer these seven questions.

## 11.1 GJT to DRO

**1.**
**4260.** (Refer to FD excerpt below, and use the wind entry closest to the flight planned altitude.) Determine the time to be entered in block 10 of the flight from GJT to DRO.

Route of flight . . . . . . . . . . . . . . . . . . . . . . . Figure 21
Flight log & MAG VAR . . . . . . . . . . . . . . . . Figure 22
En route chart . . . . . . . . . . . . . . . . . . . . . . Figure 24

| FT | 12,000 | 18,000 |
|---|---|---|
| FNM | 2408–05 | 2208–21 |

A— 1 hour 08 minutes.
B— 1 hour 03 minutes.
C— 58 minutes.

**2.**
**4259.** (Refer to figures 21, 21A, 22, 22A, 23, 23A, 24, 25, 25A, 26 and 26A on pages 362 through 372.) After departing GJT and arriving at Durango Co., La Plata Co. Airport, you are unable to land because of weather. How long can you hold over DRO before departing for return flight to the alternate, Grand Junction Co., Walker Field Airport?

Total useable fuel on board, 68 gallons.
Average fuel consumption 15 GPH.
Wind and velocity at 16,000, 2308–16°.

A— 1 hour 33 minutes.
B— 1 hour 37 minutes.
C— 1 hour 42 minutes.

**Answer (A) is correct (4260).** *(IFH Chap XIII)*
Complete the flight log for GJT to DRO (Fig. 22). Note that the wind has been interpolated for you from the figures for 12,000 and 18,000 ft. Calculate groundspeed for the cruise portion of the trip using the wind side of the flight computer. Remember to convert wind direction to magnetic direction first, i.e., 230° – 14° E var. = 216° at 8 kt. Then compute ETE for each leg.

| | Distance | MC | Wind (Mag) | Ground-speed | Time |
|---|---|---|---|---|---|
| HERRM INT. | X | 151°G | 216/8G | X | :24:00G |
| MANCA INT. | 75 | 151°G | 216/8G | 172 | :26:10 |
| Approach and Landing | X | 92°G | 216/8G | X | :18:30G |
| | | | | | 1:08:40 |

G = Given

Answer (B) is incorrect because the total time en route is 1 hr. 8 min. (not 1 hr. 3 min.). Answer (C) is incorrect because the total time en route is 1 hr. 8 min. (not 58 min.).

**Answer (A) is correct (4259).** *(IFH Chap XIII)*
To solve this problem, you must calculate times en route and fuel consumption for both trips, GJT-DRO and DRO-GJT, add 45 min. reserve, and subtract the total fuel used from 68 gal.

First, complete the flight log for each trip (Figs. 22 and 22A). Calculate groundspeed for the cruise portions of each trip using the wind side of the flight computer. Remember to convert wind direction to magnetic direction first, i.e., 230° – 14°E var. = 216° at 8 kt. Then compute ETE for each leg and fuel consumption for each trip using the slide rule side of the computer.

### GJT to DRO

| | Distance | MC | Ground-speed | Time | Fuel (gal.) |
|---|---|---|---|---|---|
| HERRM INT. | X | X | X | :24:00G | 6.0 |
| MANCA INT. | 75 | 151° | 172 | :26:10 | 6.5 |
| Approach and Landing | X | X | X | :18:30G | 4.6 |
| | | | | 1:08:40 | 17.1 |

G = Given

### DRO to GJT

| | Distance | MC | Ground-speed | Time | Fuel (gal.) |
|---|---|---|---|---|---|
| MANCA INT. | X | X | X | :14:30G | 3.6 |
| HERRM INT. | 75 | 333° | 177 | :25:21 | 6.3 |
| JNC | 35 | 331° | 177 | :11:52 | 3.0 |
| Approach and Landing | X | X | X | 12:00G | 3.0 |
| | | | | 1:03:43 | 15.9 |

G = Given

| | Fuel (gal.) |
|---|---|
| GJT-DRO | 17.1 |
| DRO-GJT | 15.9 |
| 45 min. reserve | 11.3 |
| Total | 44.3 |

With 68 gal. usable fuel there would be 23.7 gal. (68 – 44.3) available to hold at DRO. At 15-GPH fuel consumption, this would be approximately 1 hr. 34 min. of fuel.

Answer (B) is incorrect because there is only 1 hr. 34 min. (not 1 hr. 37 min.) of fuel available for holding. Answer (C) is incorrect because there is only 1 hr. 34 min. (not 1 hr. 42 min.) of fuel available for holding.

**3.**
**4265.** (Refer to figures 21, 22, and 24 on pages 362, 364, and 368.) What fuel would be consumed on the flight between Grand Junction Co. and Durango, Co. if the average fuel consumption is 15 GPH?

A— 17 gallons.
B— 20 gallons.
C— 25 gallons.

**4.**
**4261.** (Refer to figure 24 on page 368.) Using the L-6 chart, proceeding southbound on V187, 50 NM north of FMN VOR (vicinity of Cortez) contact is lost with Denver Center. What frequency should be used to contact Denver Center?

A— 134.15.
B— 108.4.
C— 122.2.

**5.**
**4262.** (Refer to figures 22 and 24 on pages 364 and 368.) For planning purposes, what would the highest MEA be on the flight planned between Grand Junction, Walker Airport, and Durango, La Plata Co. Airport?

A— 12,000 feet.
B— 15,000 feet.
C— 16,000 feet.

**6.**
**4263.** (Refer to figure 24 on page 368.) At what point should a VOR changeover be made from JNC VOR to FMN VOR southbound on V187?

A— 36 NM south of JNC.
B— 52 NM south of JNC.
C— 74 NM south of JNC.

**7.**
**4264.** (Refer to figure 24 on page 368.) What is the MOCA between JNC and MANCA intersection on V187?

A— 10,900 feet MSL.
B— 12,000 feet MSL.
C— 13,700 feet MSL.

Answer (A) is correct (4265). *(IFH Chap XIII)*
Complete the flight log by computing the fuel consumption at 15 GPH.

|  | Time | Fuel (gal.) |
|---|---|---|
| HERRM INT. | :24:00G | 6.0 |
| MANCA INT. | :26:10 | 6.5 |
| Approach and landing | :18:30G | 4.6 |
| Total | 1:08:40 | 17.1 |

G = Given

Answer (B) is incorrect because 20 gal. of fuel would require an average fuel consumption of 18 (not 15) GPH. Answer (C) is incorrect because 25 gal. of fuel would require an average fuel consumption of 22 (not 15) GPH.

Answer (A) is correct (4261). *(ACL)*
To the northwest of the Cortez VOR and south of Dove Creek VORTAC is a box with serrated edges. This box shows the frequency for Denver Center in the Cortez area as 134.15.
Answer (B) is incorrect because 108.4 is the frequency for the Cortez VOR (not Denver Center). Answer (C) is incorrect because 122.2 is a universal FSS (not Denver Center) frequency.

Answer (B) is correct (4262). *(ACL)*
The highest MEA along the route is 15,000 ft. MSL along V187 between HERRM INT. and MANCA INT.
Answer (A) is incorrect because 12,000 ft. MSL is the MEA between JNC and HERRM INT., but is not the highest. Answer (C) is incorrect because 16,000 ft. MSL is not an MEA along any part of this route.

Answer (B) is correct (4263). *(AIM Para 5-36)*
The VOR changeover point is depicted on V187, south of HERRM INT. and depicts the mileage between the VORTAC stations. It shows the COP as being 52 NM south of JNC.
Answer (A) is incorrect because the COP is depicted as 52 NM (not 36 NM) south of JNC. Answer (C) is incorrect because the COP is depicted as 52 NM (not 74 NM) south of JNC.

Answer (C) is correct (4264). *(ACL)*
The MOCA (Minimum Obstruction Clearance Altitude) appears with an asterisk under the MEA on V187. It is 13,700 ft. MSL.
Answer (A) is incorrect because 10,900 ft. MSL is the MEA (not MOCA) between MANCA and MARKE intersections. Answer (B) is incorrect because 12,000 ft. MSL is the MEA (not MOCA) between JNC and HERRM INT.

Form Approved: OMB No 2120-0034

| U.S. DEPARTMENT OF TRANSPORTATION FEDERAL AVIATION ADMINISTRATION **FLIGHT PLAN** | (FAA USE ONLY) ☐ PILOT BRIEFING ☐ VNR ☐ STOPOVER | | TIME STARTED | SPECIALIST INITIALS |
|---|---|---|---|---|

| 1 TYPE | 2 AIRCRAFT IDENTIFICATION | 3 AIRCRAFT TYPE/ SPECIAL EQUIPMENT | 4 TRUE AIRSPEED | 5 DEPARTURE POINT | 6 DEPARTURE TIME | | 7 CRUISING ALTITUDE |
|---|---|---|---|---|---|---|---|
| ☐ VFR X IFR ☐ DVFR | N 123RC | T210N/ | 175 | GJT | PROPOSED (Z) | ACTUAL (Z) | 15,000 |

**8 ROUTE OF FLIGHT**

JNC9,  JNC,  V187,  MANCA,  V211

| 9 DESTINATION (Name of airport and city) | 10 EST TIME ENROUTE | | 11 REMARKS |
|---|---|---|---|
| DRO | HOURS | MINUTES | |

| 12 FUEL ON BOARD | | 13 ALTERNATE AIRPORT(S) | 14 PILOTS NAME, ADDRESS & TELEPHONE NUMBER & AIRCRAFT HOME BASE | 15 NUMBER ABOARD |
|---|---|---|---|---|
| HOURS | MINUTES | GJT | 17 DESTINATION CONTACT/TELEPHONE (OPTIONAL) | 2 |
| 4 | 30 | | | |

| 16 COLOR OF AIRCRAFT | CIVIL AIRCRAFT PILOTS. FAR Part 91 requires you file an IFR flight plan to operate under instrument flight rules in controlled airspace. Failure to file could result in a civil penalty not to exceed $1,000 for each violation (Section 901 of the Federal Aviation Act of 1958. as amended; Filing of a VFR flight plan is recommended as a good operating practice. See also Part 99 for requirements concerning DVFR flight plans. |
|---|---|
| RED, WHITE, BLUE | |

FAA Form 7233-1 (8-82)     CLOSE VFR FLIGHT PLAN WITH _____ FSS ON ARRIVAL

---

## AIRCRAFT INFORMATION

MAKE CESSNA          MODEL T210N

N 123RC          Vso 58 ___

---

## AIRCRAFT EQUIPMENT/STATUS**

**NOTE:  X= OPERATIVE   INOP= INOPERATIVE     N/A= NOT APPLICABLE
TRANSPONDER: X (MODE C ) X ILS: (LOCALIZER) X (GLIDE SLOPE) X
VOR NO.1 X (NO 2) X ADF: X RNAV: X
VERTICAL PATH COMPUTER: NA   DME: X
MARKER BEACON: X (AUDIO) X (VISUAL) X

FIGURE 21.—Flight Plan and Aircraft Information.

Form Approved: OMB No. 2120-0034

| | | (FAA USE ONLY) | ☐ PILOT BRIEFING | ☐ VNR | TIME STARTED | SPECIALIST INITIALS |
|---|---|---|---|---|---|---|

**U.S. DEPARTMENT OF TRANSPORTATION**
**FEDERAL AVIATION ADMINISTRATION**

# FLIGHT PLAN

☐ STOPOVER

| 1. TYPE | 2. AIRCRAFT IDENTIFICATION | 3. AIRCRAFT TYPE/ SPECIAL EQUIPMENT | 4. TRUE AIRSPEED | 5. DEPARTURE POINT | 6. DEPARTURE TIME | | 7. CRUISING ALTITUDE |
|---|---|---|---|---|---|---|---|
| | | | | | PROPOSED (Z) | ACTUAL (Z) | |
| VFR | | | | | | | |
| X IFR | N 123RC | T210N/ | 175 KTS | DRO | | | 16,000 |
| DVFR | | | | | | | |

**8. ROUTE OF FLIGHT**

V211, MANCA, V187, HERRM, V187, JNC

| 9. DESTINATION (Name of airport and city) | 10. EST. TIME ENROUTE | | 11. REMARKS |
|---|---|---|---|
| | HOURS | MINUTES | |
| GJT | | | |

| 12. FUEL ON BOARD | | 13. ALTERNATE AIRPORT(S) | 14. PILOT'S NAME, ADDRESS & TELEPHONE NUMBER & AIRCRAFT HOME BASE | 15. NUMBER ABOARD |
|---|---|---|---|---|
| HOURS | MINUTES | | | |
| | | | 17. DESTINATION CONTACT/TELEPHONE (OPTIONAL) | 2 |

| 16. COLOR OF AIRCRAFT | CIVIL AIRCRAFT PILOTS. FAR Part 91 requires you file an IFR flight plan to operate under instrument flight rules in controlled airspace. Failure to file could result in a civil penalty not to exceed $1,000 for each violation (Section 901 of the Federal Aviation Act of 1958, as amended). Filing of a VFR flight plan is recommended as a good operating practice. See also Part 99 for requirements concerning DVFR flight plans. |
|---|---|
| RED/WHITE/BLUE | |

FAA Form 7233-1 (8-82)    CLOSE VFR FLIGHT PLAN WITH_____FSS ON ARRIVAL

---

## AIRCRAFT INFORMATION

MAKE  Cessna          MODEL  T210N

N 123RC             Vso 58 ___

---

## AIRCRAFT EQUIPMENT/STATUS**

**NOTE: X= OPERATIVE   INOP= INOPERATIVE   N/A= NOT APPLICABLE
TRANSPONDER: X (MODE C) X  ILS: (LOCALIZER) X  (GLIDE SLOPE) X
VOR NO. 1 X (NO. 2) X  ADF: X  RNAV: X
VERTICAL PATH COMPUTER: N/A  DME: X
MARKER BEACON: X (AUDIO) X (VISUAL) X

FIGURE 21A.—Flight Plan and Aircraft Information.

# FLIGHT LOG

GRAND JUNCTION (GJT) TO WALKER FIELD, DURANGO (DRO)

| CHECK POINTS | | ROUTE | COURSE | WIND | SPEED-KTS | | DIST | TIME | | FUEL | |
|---|---|---|---|---|---|---|---|---|---|---|---|
| FROM | TO | ALTITUDE | | TEMP | TAS | GS | NM | LEG | TOT | LEG | TOT |
| GJT | JNC | JNC9.JNC CLIMB | | 230 08 | | | | ✕ | | | |
| | HERRM | V187 15.000 | 151° | | 175 | | | :24:0 | | | |
| | MANCA | V187 | 151° | | | | | | | | |
| APPROACH & LANDING | | V211 DESCENT | 092° | | | | | :18:30 | | | |
| | DRO | | | | | | | | | | |
| | | | | | | | | | | | |
| | | | | | | | | | | | |
| | | | | | | | | | | | |
| | | | | | | | | | | | |
| | | | | | | | | | | | |

OTHER DATA:
NOTE:   TAKEOFF RUNWAY 29.
MAG. VAR. 14° E.

### FLIGHT SUMMARY

| TIME | FUEL (LBS) | |
|---|---|---|
| | | EN ROUTE |
| | | RESERVE |
| | | MISSED APPR. |
| | | TOTAL |

FIGURE 22.—Flight Planning Log.

# FLIGHT LOG

DURANGO (DRO) TO GRAND JUNCTI0N, WALKER FIELD (GJT)

| CHECK POINTS | | ROUTE | COURSE | WIND | SPEED-KTS | | DIST | TIME | | FUEL | |
|---|---|---|---|---|---|---|---|---|---|---|---|
| FROM | TO | ALTITUDE | | TEMP | TAS | GS | NM | LEG | TOT | LEG | TOT |
| DRO | MANCA | V211 CLIMB | 272° | 230 08 | | | | :14:30 | | | |
| | HERRM | V187 16.000 | 333° | | 174 | | | | | | |
| | JNC | V187 | 331° | | | | | | | | |
| APPROACH & LANDING | | DESCENT | | | | | | :12:00 | | | |
| | GJT | | | | | | | | | | |
| | | | | | | | | | | | |
| | | | | | | | | | | | |
| | | | | | | | | | | | |
| | | | | | | | | | | | |
| | | | | | | | | | | | |

OTHER DATA:

    NOTE:  MAG. VAR. 14° E.

### FLIGHT SUMMARY

| TIME | FUEL (LBS) | |
|---|---|---|
| | | EN ROUTE |
| | | RESERVE |
| | | MISSED APPR. |
| | | TOTAL |

FIGURE 22A.—Flight Planning Log.

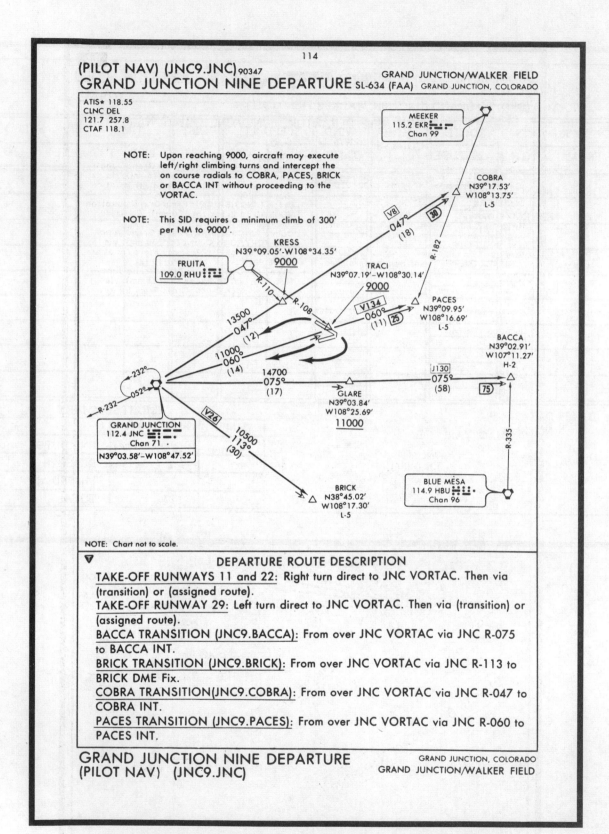

FIGURE 23.— Grand Junction Nine Departure (JNC9.JNC).

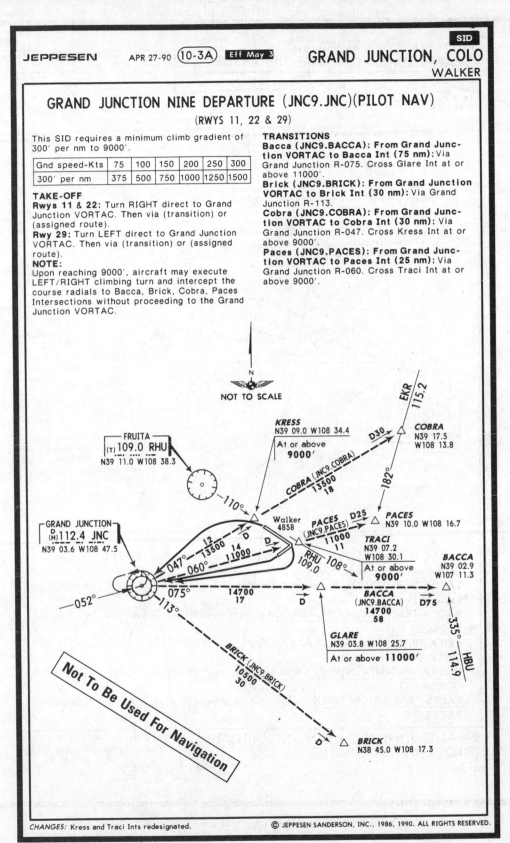

## GRAND JUNCTION NINE DEPARTURE (JNC9.JNC)(PILOT NAV)
### (RWYS 11, 22 & 29)

This SID requires a minimum climb gradient of 300' per nm to 9000'.

| Gnd speed-Kts | 75 | 100 | 150 | 200 | 250 | 300 |
|---|---|---|---|---|---|---|
| 300' per nm | 375 | 500 | 750 | 1000 | 1250 | 1500 |

**TAKE-OFF**
**Rwys 11 & 22:** Turn RIGHT direct to Grand Junction VORTAC. Then via (transition) or (assigned route).
**Rwy 29:** Turn LEFT direct to Grand Junction VORTAC. Then via (transition) or (assigned route).
**NOTE:**
Upon reaching 9000', aircraft may execute LEFT/RIGHT climbing turn and intercept the course radials to Bacca, Brick, Cobra, Paces Intersections without proceeding to the Grand Junction VORTAC.

**TRANSITIONS**
**Bacca (JNC9.BACCA): From Grand Junction VORTAC to Bacca Int (75 nm):** Via Grand Junction R-075. Cross Glare Int at or above 11000'.
**Brick (JNC9.BRICK): From Grand Junction VORTAC to Brick Int (30 nm):** Via Grand Junction R-113.
**Cobra (JNC9.COBRA): From Grand Junction VORTAC to Cobra Int (30 nm):** Via Grand Junction R-047. Cross Kress Int at or above 9000'.
**Paces (JNC9.PACES): From Grand Junction VORTAC to Paces Int (25 nm):** Via Grand Junction R-060. Cross Traci Int at or above 9000'.

FIGURE 23A.—Grand Junction Nine Departure (JNC9.JNC).

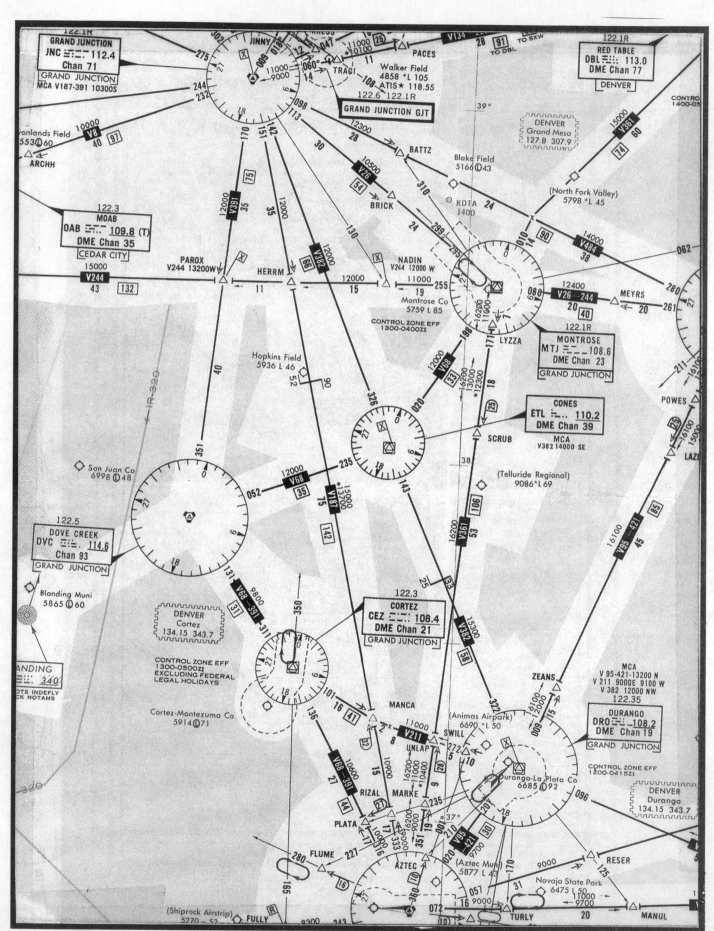

FIGURE 24.—En Route Low-Altitude Chart Segment.

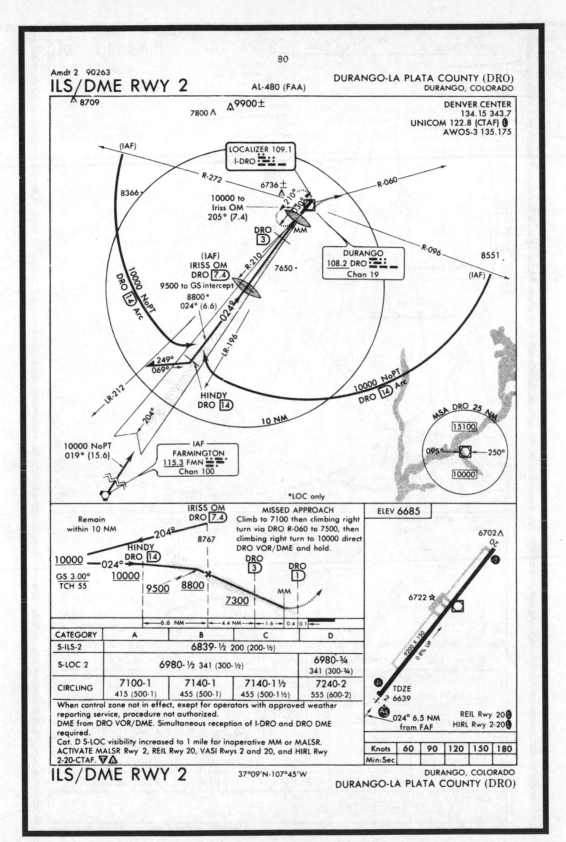

FIGURE 25.—ILS/DME RWY 2.

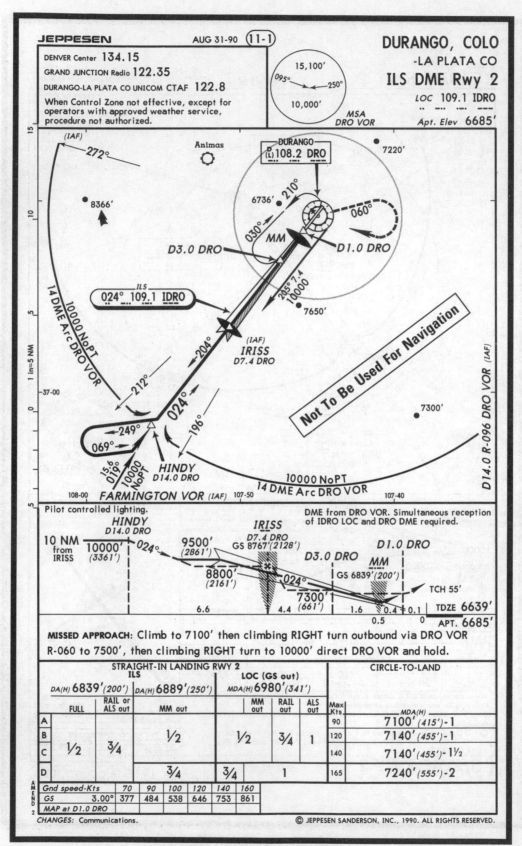

FIGURE 25A.—ILS/DME RWY 2.

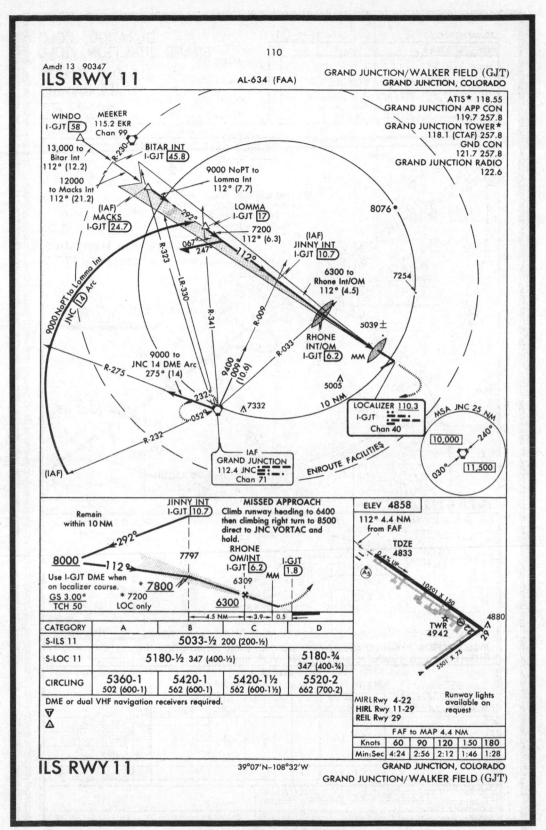

FIGURE 26.— ILS RWY 11.

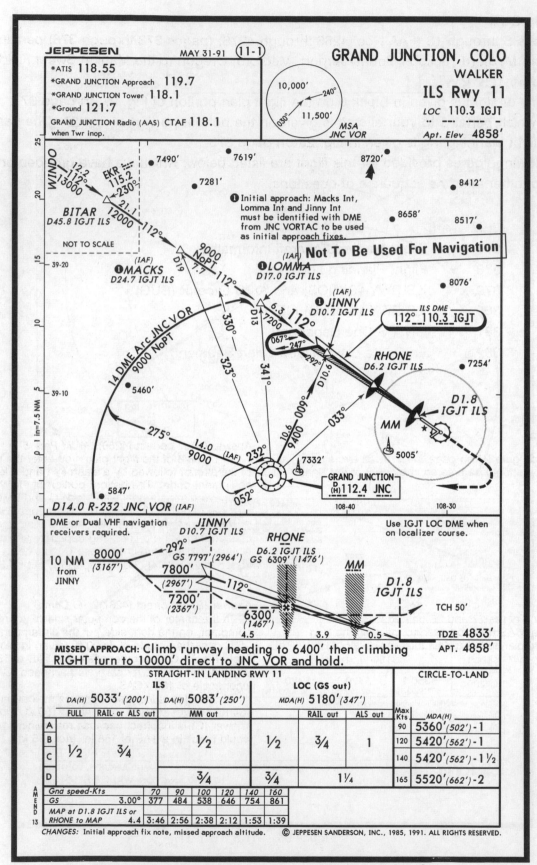

FIGURE 26A.—ILS RWY 11, Grand Junction, Colorado.

## 11.2 MFR to EUG

Questions 8 through 18 (FAA Nos. 4266 through 4276) (pages 373 through 376) pertain to an IFR flight from Medford-Jackson County Airport, Medford, Oregon to the Mahlon Sweet Field, Eugene, Oregon.

The route of flight is given in Block 8 on the flight plan portion of Fig. 27 on page 377. Information which pertains to your aircraft is given on the bottom portion of Fig. 27. The partially completed flight planning log is given in Fig. 28 on page 378.

The following figures provided for this flight are listed below, which we have grouped and presented together after the sequence of questions.

| Fig. | Page | |
|---|---|---|
| 27 | 377 | Flight Plan and Aircraft Information |
| 28 | 378 | Flight Planning Log |
| 29 | 379 | ILS RWY 16 (NOS) and A/FD Excerpt (EUG) |
| 29A | 380 | ILS RWY 16 (EUG) (JEPP) |
| 30 | 381 | GNATS One Departure |
| 31 | 382 | En Route Low-Altitude Chart Segment |

### 11.2 MFR to EUG

**8.**
**4266.** (Refer to figure 27 on page 377.) What aircraft equipment code should be entered in block 3 of the flight plan?

A— T.
B— U.
C— A.

Answer (C) is correct (4266). *(AIM Para 5-7)*
In Block 3 of the flight plan, you enter the designation of the aircraft followed by a slash ( / ) and a letter for the equipment code. The bottom portion of Fig. 27 indicates you have a transponder with Mode C and DME, which requires code A. (See Legend 25 on page 358.)
Answer (A) is incorrect because T indicates only a transponder with no encoding capability and no DME. Answer (B) is incorrect because U indicates a transponder with encoding capability, but no DME.

**9.**
**4267.** (Refer to figures 27 and 28 on pages 377 and 378.) What CAS must be used to maintain the filed TAS at the flight planned altitude if the outside air temperature is −5 °C?

A— 134 KCAS.
B— 139 KCAS.
C— 142 KCAS.

Answer (B) is correct (4267). *(Fl Comp)*
In the center of the computer side of your flight computer, on the right side put the air temperature of −5°C over the altitude of 8,000 ft. (given in Block 7 of the Flight Plan). On the outer scale find TAS of 155 (from Block 4), which is over calibrated airspeed (CAS) on the inner scale of 139 KCAS.
Answer (A) is incorrect because maintaining 134 KCAS would result in a TAS of 150 kt. (not 155 kt.). Answer (C) is incorrect because maintaining 142 KCAS would result in a TAS of 158 kt. (not 155 kt.).

**10.**
**4268.** (Refer to figures 27, 28, 29, 29A, 30, and 31 on pages 377 through 382.) (Refer to the FD excerpt below, and use the wind entry closest to the flight planned altitude.) Determine the time to be entered in block 10 of the flight plan.

Route of flight . . . . . . . Figures 27, 28, 29, 29A, 30, & 31
Flight log & MAG VAR . . . . . . . . . . . . . . . . . Figure 28
GNATS ONE DEPARTURE
  and Excerpt from AFD  . . . . . . . . . . . . . . . Figure 30

| FT | 3000 | 6000 | 9000 |
|-----|------|--------|--------|
| OTH | 0507 | 2006+03 | 2215−05 |

A— 1 hour 10 minutes.
B— 1 hour 15 minutes.
C— 1 hour 20 minutes.

Answer (C) is correct (4268). *(IFH Chap XIII)*
To determine the estimated time en route to be entered in Block 10, you must complete the flight planning log in Fig. 28.

Compute the distance from MERLI intersection to MOURN intersection. First, compute the distance traveled on the OED 15 DME from R-251 (MERLI) to R-333. The number of degrees of the arc is 82° (333-251). Use the following formula:

$$\text{Dist. of arc} = \frac{\text{\# of deg. x DME arc}}{60}$$

$$\text{Dist. of arc} = \frac{82 \times 15}{60} = 20.5 \text{ NM}$$

Next, add the 16 NM on R-333 from the 15 DME arc to MOURN, which is 36.5 (20.5 + 16). Given an average groundspeed of 135 kt., the time is 16 min. 13 sec.

For the next three legs you need to compute the wind triangle on either your flight computer or your electronic computer to determine the groundspeed as given in the table below.

Remember that winds are given in true direction and must be converted to magnetic. Fig. 28 shows a variation of 20°E. Use the wind at 9,000 ft. because that is closest to the flight planned altitude of 8,000 ft. 220° − 20°E var. = 200° at 15 kt.

|  | Distance | MC | Wind (Mag) | Ground-speed | Time |
|--------------|----------|------|------------|-----------|---------|
| MERLI INT. | X | X | X | X | :11:00G |
| MOURN INT. | 37 | X | X | 135G | :16:13 |
| RBG VOR | 19 | 287° | 200/15 | 153 | :07:26 |
| OTH VORTAC | 38 | 271° | 200/15 | 149 | :15:15 |
| EUG VORTAC | 59 | 024° | 200/15 | 170 | :20:50 |
| Approach and Landing | X | X | X | X | :10:00G |
|  |  |  |  |  | 1:20:44 |

G = Given

Answer (A) is incorrect because the total time en route is 1 hr. 20 min. (not 1 hr. 13 min.). Answer (B) is incorrect because the total time en route is 1 hr. 20 min. (not 1 hr. 15 min.).

**11.**
**4269.** (Refer to figure 30 on page 381.) During the arc portion of the SID, a left crosswind is encountered (see GNATS ONE). Where should the bearing pointer of an RMI be referenced relative to the wingtip to compensate for wind drift and maintain the 15 DME arc?

A— Behind the right wingtip reference point.
B— On the right wingtip reference point.
C— Behind the left wingtip reference point.

Answer (A) is correct (4269). *(IFH Chap VII)*
Normally when flying a DME arc, the RMI needle will point exactly to 090° or 270° in wind-free conditions. Given a crosswind from the left, you will have to make a correction to the left, which will mean that the needle is behind the right wing while on an arc to the right.

Answer (B) is incorrect because it will only be on the right wingtip when there is no wind. Answer (C) is incorrect because the VOR is to the right and the RMI points directly to the VOR.

**12.**
**4270.** (Refer to figure 30 on page 381.) Using an average groundspeed of 120 knots, what minimum rate of climb must be maintained to meet the required climb rate (feet per NM) to 4,100 feet as specified on the SID?

A— 400 feet per minute.
B— 500 feet per minute.
C— 800 feet per minute.

Answer (C) is correct (4270). *(ACL)*
The SID in Fig. 30 has a note which indicates a minimum climb of 400 ft. per NM to 4,100 ft. To convert this to a rate of climb (fpm), use Legend 18 on page 258. Find the 400 ft. per NM column on the left margin and move right to the 120-kt. groundspeed column to determine a rate of climb of 800 fpm.

Answer (A) is incorrect because 400 ft. per min. would require an average groundspeed of 60 kt. (not 120 kt.). Answer (B) is incorrect because 500 ft. per min. would require an average groundspeed of 75 kt. (not 120 kt.).

**13.**
**4271.** (Refer to figure 30 on page 381.) Which restriction to the use of the OED VORTAC would be applicable?

A— R-333 beyond 30 NM below 6,500 feet.
B— R-210 beyond 35 NM below 8,500 feet.
C— R-251 within 15 NM below 6,100 feet.

Answer (A) is correct (4271). *(ACL)*
On Fig. 30, in the A/FD under the "Radio Aids to Navigation" for the OED VORTAC, the VORTAC is listed as being unusable in certain segments. For example, it indicates that radials 280° to 345° are not usable below 6,500 ft. beyond 30 NM. This includes R-333.
Answer (B) is incorrect because there is no restriction to R-210. Answer (C) is incorrect because the restriction to R-251 is beyond 25 NM (not within 15 NM).

**14.**
**4273.** (Refer to figures 27 and 30 on pages 377 and 381.) To which maximum service volume distance from the OED VORTAC should you expect to receive adequate signal coverage for navigation at the flight planned altitude?

A— 100 NM.
B— 80 NM.
C— 40 NM.

Answer (C) is correct (4273). *(AIM Para 1-8)*
The flight plan in Fig. 27 shows a planned altitude of 8,000 ft. OED VORTAC is an H-type (high altitude) VORTAC as indicated in the A/FD in Fig. 30 by (H) ABVORTAC in the first line of "Radio Aids to Navigation." For such VORTACs, the altitude and range boundaries are from 1,000 ft. AGL up to and including 14,500 ft. AGL at distances out to 40 NM.
Answer (A) is incorrect because 100 NM applies to 14,000 ft. AGL up to 60,000 ft. AGL. Answer (B) is incorrect because 80 NM is not given as a range for VORs.

**15.**
**4272.** (Refer to figure 30 on page 381 and 30A below.) What is your position relative to GNATS intersection and the SID departure routing?

A— On departure course and past GNATS.
B— Right of departure course and past GNATS.
C— Left of departure course and have not passed GNATS.

Answer (B) is correct (4272). *(IFH Chap VII)*
On the RMI, the fat needle is tuned to the OED VOR (113.6). The tail of the needle is on 224°, which means that the airplane is on R-224. Accordingly, the airplane is past GNATS (which is on R-216). The thin needle is tuned to the VIOLE LMM (356). The tail of the needle is on 280°, which means that the airplane is on the 280° MB FROM. Thus, the airplane is to the right of the departure course (which is the 270° MB FROM).
Answer (A) is incorrect because the ADF needle indicates the 280° MB FROM which is right of (not on) the departure course. Answer (C) is incorrect because the ADF needle indicates the 280° MB FROM which is right (not left) of the departure course, and the VOR needle indicates R-224 which is past (not approaching) GNATS.

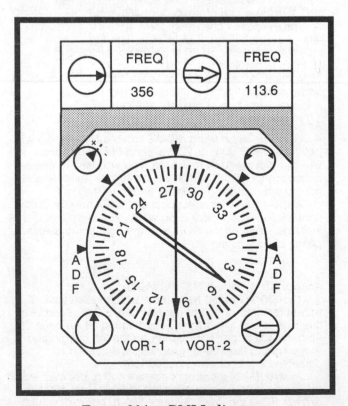

FIGURE 30A.—RMI Indicator.

**16.**
**4274.** (Refer to figures 29 and 29A on pages 379 and 380.) What is the TDZ elevation for RWY 16 on Eugene/Mahlon Sweet Field?

A— 363 feet MSL.
B— 365 feet MSL.
C— 396 feet MSL.

Answer (A) is correct (4274). (ACL)
The NOS chart (Fig. 29) shows the TDZE in the airport diagram near the approach end of the landing runway. The JEPP chart (Fig. 29A) shows the TDZE in the profile view next to the landing runway.
Answer (B) is incorrect because 365 ft. MSL is the airport elevation. Answer (C) is incorrect because 396 ft. MSL is the height of an obstacle to the right of the approach end of RWY 16.

**17.**
**4275.** (Refer to figure 29 on page 379.) What are the hours of operation (local standard time) of the control tower at Eugene/Mahlon Sweet Field?

A— 0800 - 2300.
B— 0600 - 0000.
C— 0700 - 0100.

Answer (B) is correct (4275). (IFH Chap X)
The hours of operation of the control tower at Eugene/Mahlon Sweet Field are listed on Fig. 29 in the A/FD under Eugene tower. It operates from 1400Z to 0800Z. To convert to local standard time, use the conversion code on the first line of the A/FD: GMT-8(-7DT). This means that to adjust Greenwich Mean Time (GMT) to local standard time you subtract 8 hr. which is 0600 - 0000.
Answer (A) is incorrect because 0800 - 2300 are not related hours at this airport. Answer (C) is incorrect because 0700 - 0100 are the hours of operation converted to daylight (not standard) time. Note the symbol (‡) indicates that during periods of Daylight Saving Time, effective hours will be 1 hr. earlier than shown (i.e., Standard Time).

**18.**
**4276.** (Refer to figure 29 on page 379.) Using a groundspeed of 90 knots on the ILS final approach course, what rate of descent should be used as a reference to maintain the ILS glide slope?

A— 415 feet per minute.
B— 480 feet per minute.
C— 555 feet per minute.

Answer (B) is correct (4276). (IFH Chap X)
The profile view of the NOS chart (Fig. 29) shows a glide slope angle of 3.00°. Legend 19 on page 251 gives rates of descent based on various glide slope angles and groundspeeds. Find the 3.0° glide slope at the left margin and move right to the 90-kt. groundspeed column to determine a rate of descent of 480 fpm.
The Jeppesen chart (Fig. 29A) shows the required rate of descent in the FAF to MAP time table below the minimums section. At 90 kt., a rate of descent of 486 fpm is required.
Answer (A) is incorrect because 415 fpm is not found on either chart. Answer (C) is incorrect because 555 fpm is the required rate of descent at 90 kt. on a 3.5° (not 3.0°) glide slope.

Form Approved: OMB No.2120-0034

## FLIGHT PLAN

U. S. DEPARTMENT OF TRANSPORTATION
FEDERAL AVIATION ADMINSTRANTION

| (FAA USE ONLY) | ☐ PILOT BRIEFING | ☐ VNR | TIME STARTED | SPECIALIST INITIALS |
|---|---|---|---|---|
| | ☐ STOPOVER | | | |

| 1 TYPE | 2 AIRCRAFT IDENTIFICATION | 3 AIRCRAFT TYPE/ SPECIAL EQUIPMENT | 4 TRUE AIRSPEED | 5 DEPARTURE POINT | 6 DEPARTURE TIME | | 7 CRUISING ALTITUDE |
|---|---|---|---|---|---|---|---|
| VFR | | | | | PROPOSED (Z) | ACTUAL (Z) | |
| X IFR | N132SM | C 182/ | 155 | MFR | | | 8,000 |
| DVFR | | | | | | | |

8 ROUTE OF FLIGHT

GNATS 1, MOURN, V121 EUG

| 9 DESTINATION (Name of airport and city) | 10 EST TIME ENROUTE | | 11 REMARKS |
|---|---|---|---|
| MAHLON/SWEET FIELD, EUGENE, OR. | HOURS | MINUTES | INSTRUMENT TRAINING FLIGHT |

| 12 FUEL ON BOARD | | 13 ALTERNATE AIRPORT(S) | 14 PILOTS NAME, ADDRESS & TELEPHONE NUMBER & AIRCRAFT HOME BASE | 15 NUMBER ABOARD |
|---|---|---|---|---|
| HOURS | MINUTES | N/R | 17 DESTINATION CONTACT/TELEPHONE (OPTIONAL) | |

| 16 COLOR OF AIRCRAFT | CIVIL AIRCRAFT PILOTS. FAR Part 91 requires you file an IFR flight plan to operate under instrument flight rules in controlled airspace. Failure to file could result in a civil penalty not to exceed $1,000 for each violation (Section 901 of the Federal Aviation Act of 1958. as amended; Filing of a VFR flight plan is recommended as a good operating practice. See also Part 99 for requirements concerning DVFR flight plans. |
|---|---|

FAA Form 7233-1 (8-82)          CLOSE VFR FLIGHT PLAN WITH _____ FSS ON ARRIVAL

---

## AIRCRAFT INFORMATION

MAKE CESSNA          MODEL 182

N 132SM          Vso 57

---

## AIRCRAFT EQUIPMENT/STATUS**

**NOTE:  X= OPERATIVE   INOP= INOPERATIVE     N/A= NOT APPLICABLE
TRANSPONDER: X (MODE C ) X ILS: (LOCALIZER) X (GLIDE SLOPE) N/A
VOR NO.1 X (NO 2) X ADF: X RNAV: N/A
VERTICAL PATH COMPUTER: NA  DME: X
MARKER BEACON:  (AUDIO) Inop. (VISUAL) Inop.

FIGURE 27.—Flight Plan and Aircraft Information.

# FLIGHT LOG

MEDFORD - JACKSON CO. AIRPORT TO HAHLON/SWEET FIELD, EUGENE, OR.

| CHECK POINTS | | ROUTE | COURSE | WIND | SPEED-KTS | | DIST | TIME | | FUEL | |
| FROM | TO | ALTITUDE | | TEMP | TAS | GS | NM | LEG | TOT | LEG | TOT |
|---|---|---|---|---|---|---|---|---|---|---|---|
| MFR | MERLI | GNATS 1 CLIMB | 333° | | 155 | | | :11:0 | | | |
| | MOURN | V121 8000 | 287° | | | AVER. 135 | | | | | |
| | RBG | V121 8000 | 272° | | | | | | | | |
| | OTH | V121 8000 | 024° | | | | | | | | |
| | EUG | APPROACH | | | | | | | | | |
| APPROACH & LANDING | | DESCENT | | | | | | :10:0 | | | |
| | SWEET FIELD | | | | | | | | | | |
| | | | | | | | | | | | |
| | | | | | | | | | | | |

OTHER DATA:
NOTE:  MAG. VAR. 20° E.
AVERAGE G.S. 135 KTS. FOR GNATS 1
DEPARTURE CLIMB.

FLIGHT SUMMARY

| TIME | FUEL (LB) | |
|---|---|---|
| | | EN ROUTE |
| | | RESERVE |
| | | MISSED APPR. |
| | | TOTAL |

FIGURE 28.—Flight Planning Log.

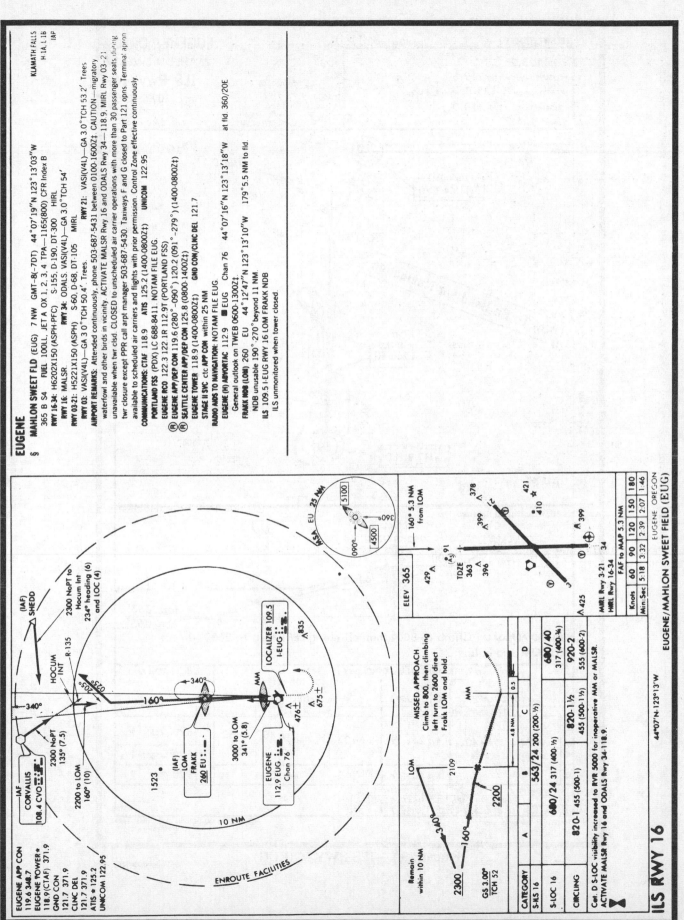

FIGURE 29.—ILS RWY 16 (EUG) and Excerpt from Airport/Facility Directory.

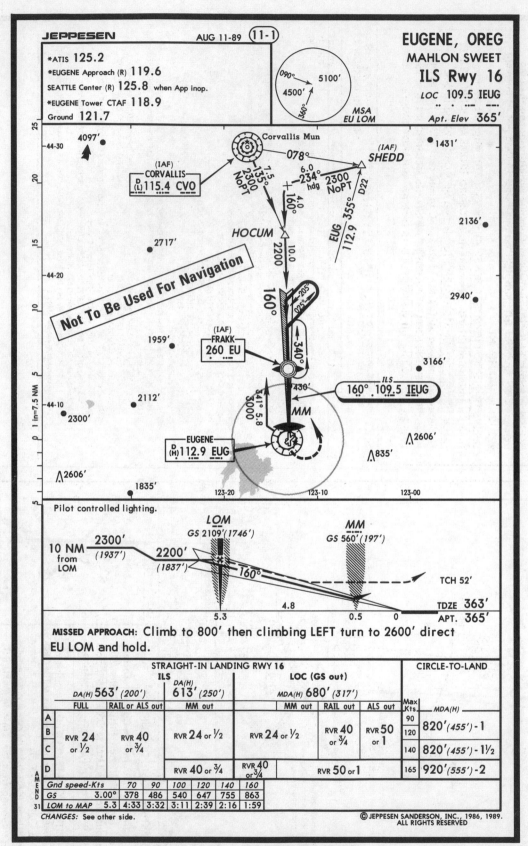

FIGURE 29A.—ILS RWY 16 (EUG).

## GNATS ONE DEPARTURE (GNATS1.GNATS)

MEDFORD-JACKSON CO
MEDFORD, OREGON

### DEPARTURE ROUTE DESCRIPTION
(Continued)

MOURN TRANSITION (GNATS1.MOURN): Continue via 270° magnetic bearing from the LMM to MERLI INT, turn right via MEDFORD 15 DME ARC to intercept V23-121 to MOURN INT.

DREWS TRANSITION (GNATS1.DREWS): Continue via 270° magnetic bearing from the LMM to MERLI INT, turn right via MEDFORD 15 DME ARC to DREWS INT.

TALEM TRANSITION (GNATS1.TALEM): Turn left via MEDFORD R-216 to 15 DME Fix thence turn left via MEDFORD 15 DME ARC to intercept V23 to TALEM INT.

HANDY TRANSITION (GNATS1.HANDY): Turn left via MEDFORD R-216 to 15 DME Fix, thence turn left via MEDFORD 15 DME Arc to HANDY DME Fix.

## GNATS ONE DEPARTURE (GNATS1.GNATS)

MEDFORD, OREGON
MEDFORD-JACKSON CO

§ **MEDFORD-JACKSON CO** (MFR)   3 N   GMT−8(−7DT)   42°22'21"N 122°52'17"W   KLAMATH FALLS   H-1A, L-1A
1331   B   S4   FUEL 80, 100, 100LL, JET A1 +   OX 1, 3   CFR Index B   IAP
RWY 14-32: H6700X150 (ASPH-PFC)   S-200, D-200, DT-400   HIRL   .5% up S
RWY 14: MALSR. Trees.   RWY 32: REIL VASI(V4L)—GA 3.0° TCH 49'. Road.
RWY 09-27: H3145X150 (ASPH)   S-50, D-70, DT-108   MIRL
RWY 27: Road.
**AIRPORT REMARKS:** Attended continuously. CLOSED to unscheduled Part 121 air carriers operation, without prior approval, call 503-776-7222. Night refueling delay sunset-1500Z‡, ctc TOWER. Rwy 09-27 clsd to acft over 12,500 lbs GWT. Rwy 09/27 CLOSED when tower clsd. Rwy lgts 14/32 operate med ints when tower closed. ACTIVATE MALSR 14—119.4. Flocks of large waterfowl in vicinity Nov-May
**COMMUNICATIONS:** CTAF 119.4   ATIS 125.75   UNICOM 122.95
**NORTH BEND FSS** (OTH) LC 773-3256. NOTAM FILE MFR.
RCO 122.65 122.1R 113.6T (NORTH BEND FSS)
**APP CON** 124.3 (1400-0800Z‡)   **DEP CON** 124.3 (1400-0800Z‡)
**SEATTLE CENTER APP/DEP CON** 125.3 (0800-1400Z‡)
**TOWER** 119.4 (1400-0800Z‡)   **GND CON** 121.7
**VFR ADVSY SVC** ctc TOWER
**RADIO AIDS TO NAVIGATION:** NOTAM FILE OTH.   VHF/DF ctc Medford TOWER
   (V)ABVORTAC 113.6   ■ OED   Chan 83   42°28'47"N 122°54'43"W   146°/6.1 NM to fld. 2080'/19E
      VORTAC unusable:
         160°-165° beyond 35 NM below 8900'   280°-345° beyond 30 NM below 6500'
         198°-205° beyond 35 NM below 8500'   345°-360° beyond 35 NM below 6800'
         250°-280° beyond 25 NM below 6100'
   PUMIE NDB (LOM) 373   MF   42°27'04"N 122°54'44"W   140°/4.5 NM to fld. NOTAM FILE MFR
      LOM unusable 150°-165° and 260°-265° beyond 5 miles.
   VIOLE NDB (LMM) 356   FR   42°23'22"N 122°52'47"W   140°/0.5 NM to fld. NOTAM FILE MFR
      LMM unusable 305°-335° beyond 10 NM. all altitudes
   ILS/DME 110.3 I-MFR Chan 40 Rwy 14 LOM PUMIE NDB. LMM VIOLE NDB. ILS unmonitored when tower closed.
      Localizer unusable inside threshold.

MEDFORD GND CON 121.7
MEDFORD DEP CON 124.3 257.8
ATIS 125.75
CTAF 119.4

NOTE: This SID requires a minimum climb rate of 400' per NM to 4100' for obstacle clearance.

NOTE: Chart not to scale.

### DEPARTURE ROUTE DESCRIPTION

Climb direct to the VIOLE ILS Middle Compass Locator (south take-off turn right), then climb on the 270° magnetic bearing from the LMM to GNATS INT, cross GNATS INT at or above 4100; thence via (transition) or (route).

COPPO TRANSITION (GNATS1.COPPO): Turn left via R-216 to 15 DME Fix, thence turn left via MEDFORD 15 DME Arc to COPPO DME Fix.

KOLER TRANSITION (GNATS1.KOLER): Continue via 270° magnetic bearing from the LMM to MERLI INT, turn right via ROSEBURG R-154 to KOLER INT.

(Continued on next page)

## GNATS ONE DEPARTURE (GNATS1.GNATS)

MEDFORD, OREGON
MEDFORD-JACKSON CO

FIGURE 30.—GNATS One Departure and Excerpt from Airport/Facility Directory.

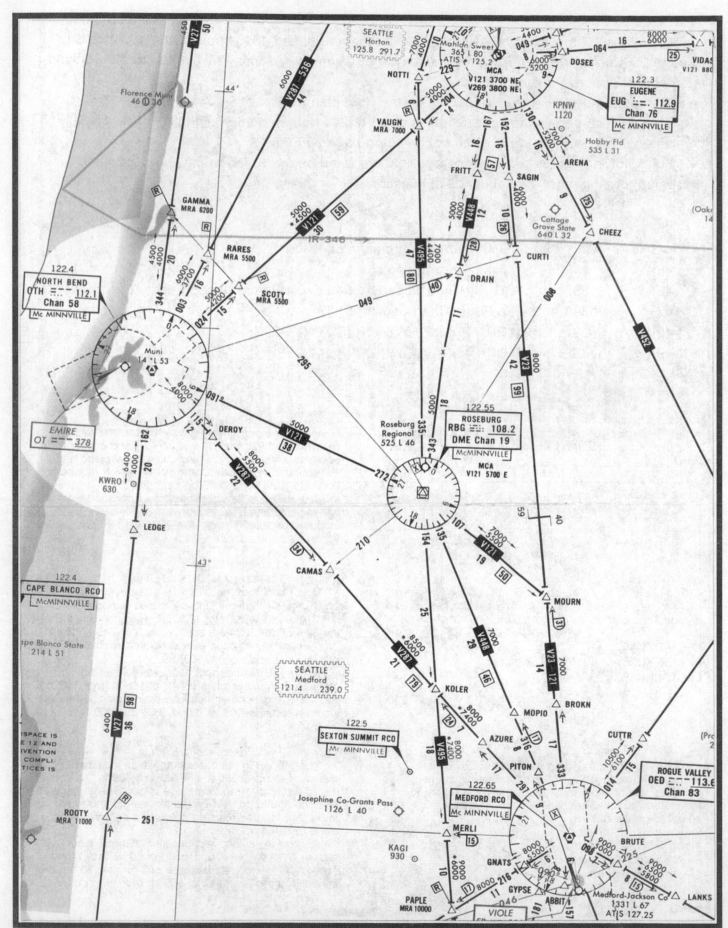

FIGURE 31.—En Route Low-Altitude Chart Segment.

## 11.3  YKM to PDX

Questions 19 through 33 (FAA Nos. 4300 through 4311 and 4645 through 4647) (pages 383 through 386) pertain to an IFR flight from Yakima Air Terminal, Yakima, Washington to the Portland International Airport, Portland, Oregon.

The route of flight is given in Block 8 on the flight plan portion of Fig. 44 on page 387. Information which pertains to your aircraft is given on the bottom portion of Fig. 44. The partially completed flight planning log is given in Fig. 45 on page 388.

The following figures provided for this flight are listed below, which we have grouped and presented together after the sequence of questions.

| Fig. | Page | |
| --- | --- | --- |
| 44 | 387 | Flight Plan and Aircraft Information |
| 45 | 388 | Flight Planning Log |
| 46 | 389 | GROMO Two Departure and Excerpt from Airport/Facility Directory (YKM) |
| 47 | 390 | En Route Chart Segment |
| 49 | 391 | LORAN RNAV RWY 10R (PDX) (NOS) |
| 49A | 392 | LORAN RNAV RWY 10R (PDX) (JEPP) |

## 11.3  YKM to PDX

**19.**
**4300.** (Refer to figure 44 on page 387.) What aircraft equipment code should be entered in block 3 of the flight plan?

A— A.
B— C.
C— R.

Answer (C) is correct (4300). *(AIM Para 5-7)*
In Block 3 of the flight plan you enter the designation of the aircraft followed by a slash ( / ) and a letter for an equipment mode. Fig. 44 indicates the airplane has a transponder with Mode C and RNAV, which requires code R. (See Legend 25 on page 358.)
Answer (A) is incorrect because A means Mode C transponder and DME, but no RNAV. Answer (B) is incorrect because C indicates RNAV and a transponder with no altitude encoding capability.

**20.**
**4301.** (Refer to figure 44 on page 387.) What CAS must be used to maintain the filed TAS at the flight planned altitude if the outside air temperature is +5 °C?

A— 147 KCAS.
B— 150 KCAS.
C— 154 KCAS.

Answer (A) is correct (4301). *(Fl Comp)*
In the center of the slide rule side of your flight computer, on the right side put the air temperature of +5°C over the altitude of 12,000 ft. (given in Block 7 of the Flight Plan). On the outer scale find TAS of 180 kt. (from Block 4), which is over calibrated airspeed (CAS) on the inner scale of 147 KCAS.
Answer (B) is incorrect because maintaining 150 KCAS would result in a TAS of 185 kt. (not 180 kt.). Answer (C) is incorrect because maintaining 154 KCAS would result in a TAS of 190 kt. TAS (not 180 kt.).

**21.**
**4303.** (Refer to figure 46 on page 389.) Using an average groundspeed of 140 knots, what minimum indicated rate of climb must be maintained to meet the required climb rate (feet per NM) to 6,300 feet as specified on the SID?

A— 350 feet per minute.
B— 583 feet per minute.
C— 816 feet per minute.

Answer (C) is correct (4303). *(ACL)*
The SID in Fig. 46 has a note which indicates a minimum climb of 350 ft. per NM to 6,300 ft. To convert this to a rate of climb (fpm), use Legend 18 on page 258. Find the 350 ft. per NM on the left margin and move right to the 140-kt. groundspeed column to determine a rate of climb of 816 fpm.
Answer (A) is incorrect because 350 fpm would require an average groundspeed of 60 kt. (not 140 kt.). Answer (B) is incorrect because 583 fpm would require an average groundspeed of 100 kt. (not 140 kt.).

**22.**
**4302.** (Refer to figures 44, 45, 46, and 47 on pages 387 through 390.) Determine the time to be entered in block 10 of the flight plan. (Refer to the FD excerpt below, and use the wind entry closest to the flight planned altitude.)

Route of flight . . . . . . . . . . . . Figures 44, 45, 46, and 47
Flight log & MAG VAR . . . . . . . . . . . . . . . . . Figure 45
GROMO TWO DEPARTURE
    and Excerpt from AFD . . . . . . . . . . . . . Figure 46

| FT  | 3000 | 6000    | 9000    | 12000   |
|-----|------|---------|---------|---------|
| YKM | 1615 | 1926+12 | 2032+08 | 2035+05 |

A— 54 minutes.
B— 1 hour 02 minutes.
C— 1 hour 07 minutes.

Answer (B) is correct (4302). *(IFH Chap XIII)*
To determine estimated time en route to be entered in Block 10, you must complete the flight planning log in Fig. 45. Using the wind side of your flight computer, determine groundspeeds as given in the table below.

Remember that winds are given in true direction and must be converted to magnetic. Fig. 45 indicates a variation of 20°E. 200° – 20°E var. = 180° at 35 kt.

The distance from BTG VORTAC to PDX VOR is not given. It may be estimated at 10 NM by comparing it to other airway segments of similar length.

|               | Distance | MC   | Wind (Mag) | Ground-speed | Time     |
|---------------|----------|------|------------|--------------|----------|
| HITCH INT     | X        | X    | X          | X            | :10:00G  |
| VOR COP       | 37       | 206° | 180/35     | 148          | :15:00   |
| BTG VORTAC    | 53       | 234° | 180/35     | 157          | :20:15   |
| PDX VOR       | 10       | 160° | 180/35     | 147          | :04:05   |
| Approach and  |          |      |            |              |          |
| Landing       | X        | X    | X          | X            | :13:00G  |
|               |          |      |            |              | 1:02:20  |

G = Given

Answer (A) is incorrect because the total time en route is 1 hr. 2 min. (not 54 min.). Answer (C) is incorrect because the total time en route is 1 hr. 2 min. (not 1 hr. 7 min.).

**23.**
**4304.** (Refer to figure 46 on page 389 and 48 below.) What is your position relative to the 9 DME ARC and the 206° radial of the SID?

A— On the 9 DME arc and approaching R-206.
B— Outside the 9 DME arc and past R-206.
C— Inside the 9 DME arc and approaching R-206.

Answer (A) is correct (4304). *(IFH Chap VII)*
The HSI shows that you are currently on a 130° heading, thus flying in a southeasterly direction. The OBS selector is set on R-206, and a left deflection is indicated. This means you are west and north of R-206. (If you were flying out the R-206 with a left deflection, you would turn left to intercept.) You are approaching R-206 because you are flying in a southeasterly direction. The DME indicates 9 NM out, so you are on the 9 DME arc.

Answer (B) is incorrect because you are on (not outside) the arc and approaching (not past) R-206. Answer (C) is incorrect because you are on (not inside) the arc.

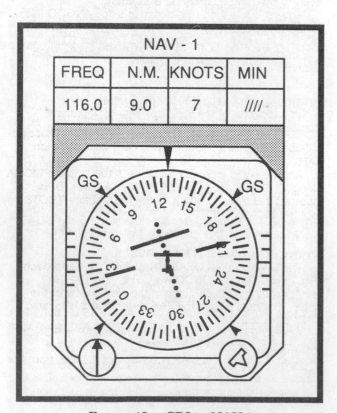

FIGURE 48.—CDI — NAV 1.

**24.**
**4305.** (Refer to figure 46 on page 389.) What are the hours of operation (local time) of the ATIS for the Yakima Air Terminal when daylight savings time is in effect?

A— 0500 to 2100 local.
B— 0600 to 2200 local.
C— 0700 to 2300 local.

**Answer (B) is correct (4305).** *(ACL)*
The hours of operation of the ATIS at Yakima Air Terminal are listed on Fig. 46 in the A/FD on the Communications line at ATIS. It operates from 1400Z to 0600Z. Note that the ‡ symbol indicates that during periods of Daylight Saving Time, effective hours of operation are 1 hr. earlier than those shown (i.e., Standard Time). For example, the ATIS will begin operation at 6:00 a.m. local time, regardless of whether daylight savings time is in effect. Thus, you should always use the standard conversion, e.g., GMT-8 = 0600-2200 local.
Answer (A) is incorrect because you must subtract 8 (not 9) from Zulu to convert to local time. Answer (C) is incorrect because you must always use the standard (not daylight) conversion.

**25.**
**4645.** (Refer to figure 47 on page 390.) En route on V112 from BTG VORTAC to DLS VORTAC, the minimum altitude crossing Gymme intersection is

A— 6,400 feet.
B— 6,500 feet.
C— 7,000 feet.

**Answer (C) is correct (4645).** *(FAR 91.177)*
When no Minimum Crossing Altitude (MCA) is specified, e.g., at GYMME intersection, the intersection may be crossed at or above the preceding MEA. Since the MEA along V112 eastbound is 7,000 ft., GYMME may be crossed no lower than 7,000 ft.
Answer (A) is incorrect because 6,400 ft. is the MOCA (not MEA) along V112. Answer (B) is incorrect because 6,500 ft. is the MEA west of GYMME when westbound (not eastbound).

**26.**
**4646.** (Refer to figure 47 on page 390.) When en route on V448 from YKM VORTAC to BTG VORTAC, what minimum navigation equipment is required to identify ANGOO intersection?

A— One VOR receiver.
B— One VOR receiver and DME.
C— Two VOR receivers.

**Answer (A) is correct (4646).** *(IFH VIII)*
To identify ANGOO INT only one VOR receiver is required. It is important to establish yourself on V448 and maintain heading while you orient yourself to DLS VORTAC R-330. Your position checks and tuning will need to be done quickly and accurately.
Answer (B) is incorrect because since ANGOO INT can be determined by cross radials, only one VOR receiver is required and not a DME. Answer (C) is incorrect because only one (not two) VOR receiver is required to identify ANGOO INT.

**27.**
**4647.** (Refer to figure 47 on page 390.) En route on V468 from BTG VORTAC to YKM VORTAC, the minimum altitude at TROTS intersection is

A— 7,100 feet.
B— 10,000 feet.
C— 11,500 feet.

**Answer (C) is correct (4647).** *(FAR 91.177)*
TROTS intersection (45 NM northeast of BTG VORTAC on V468 in Fig. 47) shows a Minimum Crossing Altitude (MCA) of 11,500 ft. when northeastbound on V468.
Answer (A) is incorrect because 7,100 ft. is the MOCA along V468 (not the MCA at TROTS). Answer (B) is incorrect because 10,000 ft. is the MEA before TROTS (not the MCA at TROTS).

**28.**
**4306.** (Refer to figures 49 and 49A on pages 391 and 392.) What should be used to establish the MAP on the LORAN RNAV RWY 10 approach at Portland International Airport?

A— 6 NM from FAF.
B— 3.5 NM from PONCO waypoint.
C— 2.5 NM from FAF.

**Answer (A) is correct (4306).** *(ACL)*
The MAP on the LORAN RNAV RWY 10R approach (Fig. 49 or 49A) is PONCO waypoint. The FAF is identified by a maltese cross in the profile view of the chart. The note above the FAF states that it is located 6 NM from the MAP.
Answer (B) is incorrect because the MAP is PONCO waypoint, not 3.5 NM from PONCO. Answer (C) is incorrect because the MAP is 6 NM, not 2.5 NM, from the FAF.

**29.**
**4307.** (Refer to figures 44, 49, and 49A on pages 387, 391, and 392.) What is the MDA and visibility criteria during the LORAN RNAV RWY 10 approach at Portland International?

A— 900 MSL; visibility RVR/24.
B— 900 MSL; visibility RVR/40.
C— 900 MSL; visibility 1 and ¼ SM.

Answer (B) is correct (4307). *(ACL)*
Refer to Fig. 44 to determine the aircraft category. $V_{S0}$ is 77 kt., thus 1.3 $V_{S0}$ is 100.1 kt., which puts the airplane in Category B (91-120). The minimums for the LORAN RNAV RWY 10R approach, Category B, are 900 ft. MSL and RVR/40.
Answer (A) is incorrect because RVR/24 is the minimum for Category A (not B). Answer (C) is incorrect because 1¼ SM is the minimum visibility when the ALS is out or for a circling-to-land approach.

**30.**
**4308.** (Refer to figures 49 and 49A on pages 391 and 392.) How many waypoints are required to fly the complete LORAN RNAV RWY 10 (Portland International) approach procedure, including the missed approach procedure?

A— 2.
B— 3.
C— 4.

Answer (C) is correct (4308). *(ACL)*
The IAP chart for the LORAN RNAV RWY 10R approach (Fig. 49 or 49A) shows 4 waypoints are required to fly the approach and the missed approach procedures. The waypoints are: SCAPO, WETTR, PONCO, and BATTLE GROUND.
Answer (A) is incorrect because 4 (not 2) waypoints are required. Answer (B) is incorrect because 4 (not 3) waypoints are required.

**31.**
**4309.** (Refer to figures 49 and 49A on pages 391 and 392.) What is the TDZE for RWY 10R at Portland International Airport?

A— 900 feet MSL.
B— 26 feet MSL.
C— 20 feet MSL.

Answer (C) is correct (4309). *(ACL)*
The NOS chart (Fig. 49) shows the TDZE in the airport diagram near the approach end of RWY 10R. The JEPP chart (Fig. 49A) shows the TDZE in the profile view next to the runway. Both indicate a TDZE of 20 ft. MSL.
Answer (A) is incorrect because 900 ft. MSL is the MDA for the approach (not the TDZE). Answer (B) is incorrect because 26 ft. MSL is the airport elevation (not the TDZE).

**32.**
**4310.** (Refer to figures 49 and 49A on pages 391 and 392.) The aircraft used on this flight has vertical guidance capability with the RNAV equipment. What is the angle of the glidepath from the FAF to the 2.5 DME from the MAP waypoint?

A— 2.88°.
B— 3.00°.
C— 3.20°.

Answer (C) is correct (4310). *(ACL)*
The NOS chart (Fig. 49) shows the glidepath angle in the profile view just below the glidepath itself. The JEPP chart (Fig. 49A) shows the glidepath angle (GS setting) below the minimums section in the FAF to MAP time table.
Answer (A) is incorrect because the glidepath angle is 3.20° (not 2.88°). Answer (B) is incorrect because the glidepath angle is 3.20° (not 3.00°).

**33.**
**4311.** (Refer to figures 49 and 49A on pages 391 and 392.) At which point or fix may descent be initiated to the MDA on the LORAN RNAV RWY 10R approach (Portland International)?

A— WETTR waypoint.
B— 3.5 NM from PONCO waypoint.
C— 6 NM from the MAP waypoint.

Answer (C) is correct (4311). *(ACL)*
On a nonprecision approach, descent to the MDA is initiated at the FAF when inbound on the final approach course. On the LORAN RNAV RWY 10R approach chart (Fig. 49 or 49A), the FAF is identified as 6 NM from the MAP waypoint (which is PONCO).
Answer (A) is incorrect because descent to 2,100 ft. (not the MDA) may be initiated at WETTR. Answer (B) is incorrect because 3.5 NM from PONCO is not an applicable fix in this approach.

Form Approved: OMB No.2120-0034

| U.S. DEPARTMENT OF TRANSPORTATION FEDERAL AVIATION ADMINISTRATION **FLIGHT PLAN** | (FAA USE ONLY) | □ PILOT BRIEFING | □ VNR | TIME STARTED | SPECIALIST INITIALS |
|---|---|---|---|---|---|
| | | □ STOPOVER | | | |

| 1 TYPE | 2 AIRCRAFT IDENTIFICATION | 3 AIRCRAFT TYPE/ SPECIAL EQUIPMENT | 4 TRUE AIRSPEED | 5 DEPARTURE POINT | 6 DEPARTURE TIME | | 7 CRUISING ALTITUDE |
|---|---|---|---|---|---|---|---|
| VFR | | | | | PROPOSED (Z) | ACTUAL (Z) | |
| X IFR DVFR | N3678A | PA31/ | 180 | YKM | | | 12000 |

**8** ROUTE OF FLIGHT

GROMO 2, HITCH, V468 BTG, DIRECT

| 9 DESTINATION (Name of airport and city) | 10 EST TIME ENROUTE | | 11 REMARKS |
|---|---|---|---|
| PORTLAND INTL. AIRPORT    PDX | HOURS | MINUTES | INSTRUMENT TRAINING FLIGHT |

| 12 FUEL ON BOARD | | 13 ALTERNATE AIRPORT(S) | 14 PILOTS NAME, ADDRESS & TELEPHONE NUMBER & AIRCRAFT HOME BASE | 15 NUMBER ABOARD |
|---|---|---|---|---|
| HOURS | MINUTES | | 17 DESTINATION CONTACT/TELEPHONE (OPTIONAL) | 2 |
| | | N/R | | |

| 16 COLOR OF AIRCRAFT | CIVIL AIRCRAFT PILOTS. FAR Part 91 requires you file an IFR flight plan to operate under instrument flight rules in controlled airspace. Failure to file could result in a civil penalty not to exceed $1,000 for each violation (Section 901 of the Federal Aviation Act of 1958. as amended; Filing of a VFR flight plan is recommended as a good operating practice. See also Part 99 for requirements concerning DVFR flight plans. |
|---|---|
| GOLD/WHITE | |

FAA Form 7233-1 (8-82)          CLOSE VFR FLIGHT PLAN WITH _____ FSS ON ARRIVAL

---

## AIRCRAFT INFORMATION

MAKE  Piper          MODEL PA-31

N 3678A               Vso  77

---

## AIRCRAFT EQUIPMENT/STATUS**

**NOTE: X= OPERATIVE   INOP= INOPERATIVE   N/A= NOT APPLICABLE
TRANSPONDER: X (MODE C ) X  ILS: (LOCALIZER) X  (GLIDE SLOPE) X
VOR NO.1 X (NO 2) X  ADF: X  RNAV: X
VERTICAL PATH COMPUTER:  NA  DME: X
MARKER BEACON: X (AUDIO) Inop. (VISUAL) X

FIGURE 44.—Flight Plan and Aircraft Information.

# FLIGHT LOG

YAKIMA AIR TERMINAL TO PORTLAND, INTL.

| CHECK POINTS | | ROUTE | | WIND | SPEED-KTS | | DIST | TIME | | FUEL | |
| FROM | TO | ALTITUDE | COURSE | TEMP | TAS | GS | NM | LEG | TOT | LEG | TOT |
|---|---|---|---|---|---|---|---|---|---|---|---|
| YKM | HITCH | GROMO 2 CLIMB | 206° | | | | | :10. | | | |
| | VOR C.O.P. | V468 12,000 | 206° | | 180 | | | | | | |
| | BTG | V468 12,000 | 234° | | | | | | | | |
| | PDX | DIRECT | 160° | | | | | | | | |
| APPROACH & LANDING | | | | | | | | :13. | | | |
| | PDX AIRPORT | | | | | | | | | | |

OTHER DATA:
NOTE: MAG. VAR. 20° E.

FLIGHT SUMMARY

| TIME | FUEL (LB) | |
|---|---|---|
| | | EN ROUTE |
| | | RESERVE |
| | | MISSED APPR. |
| | | TOTAL |

FIGURE 45.—Flight Planning Log.

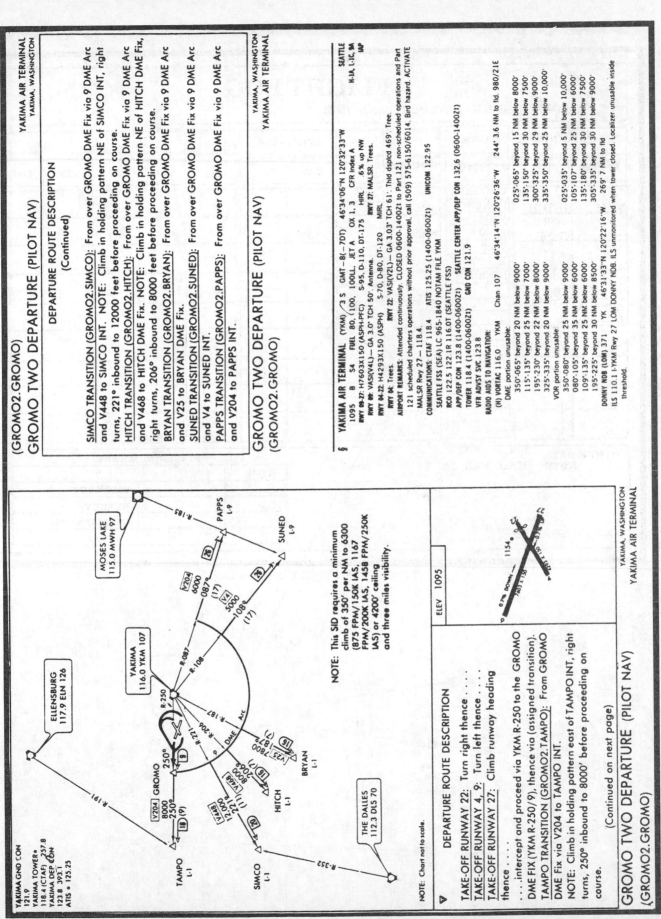

FIGURE 46.—GROMO Two Departure and Excerpt from Airport/Facility Directory.

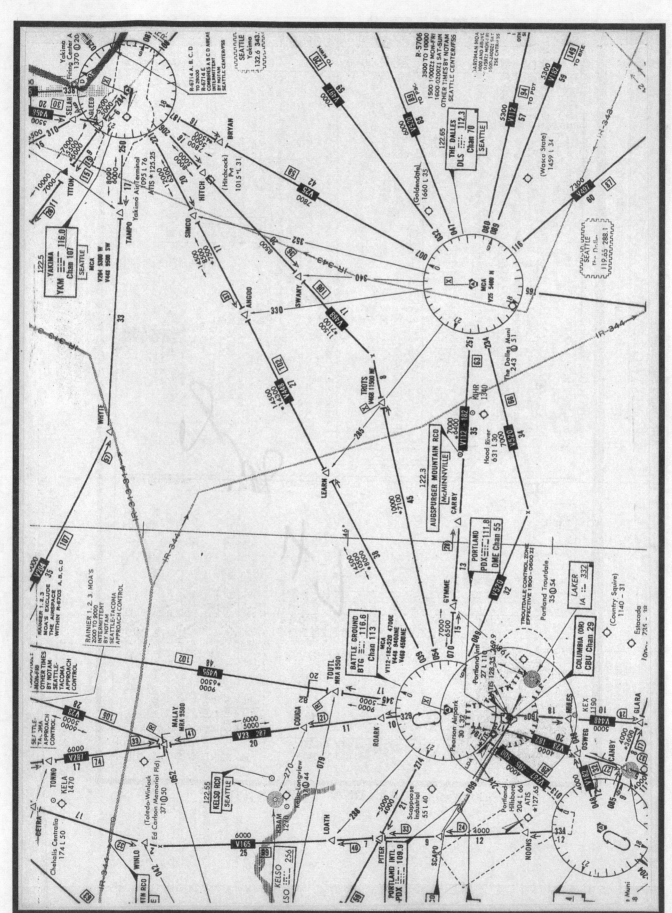

FIGURE 47.—En Route Chart Segment.

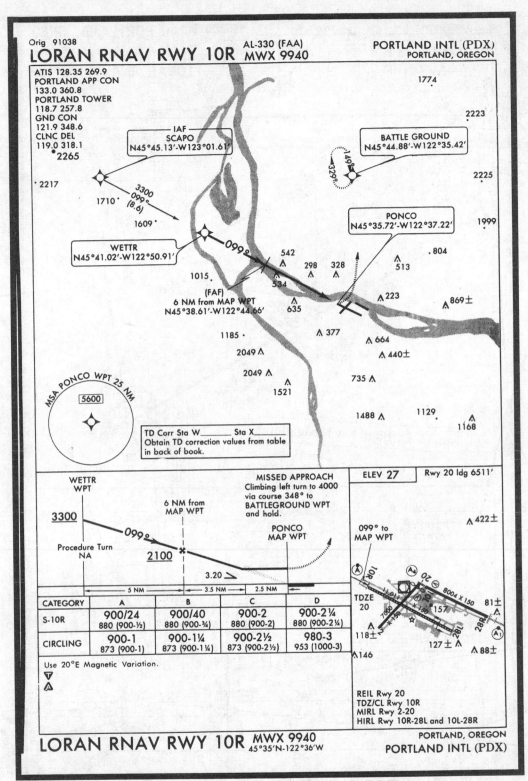

FIGURE 49.—LORAN RNAV RWY 10R (PDX).

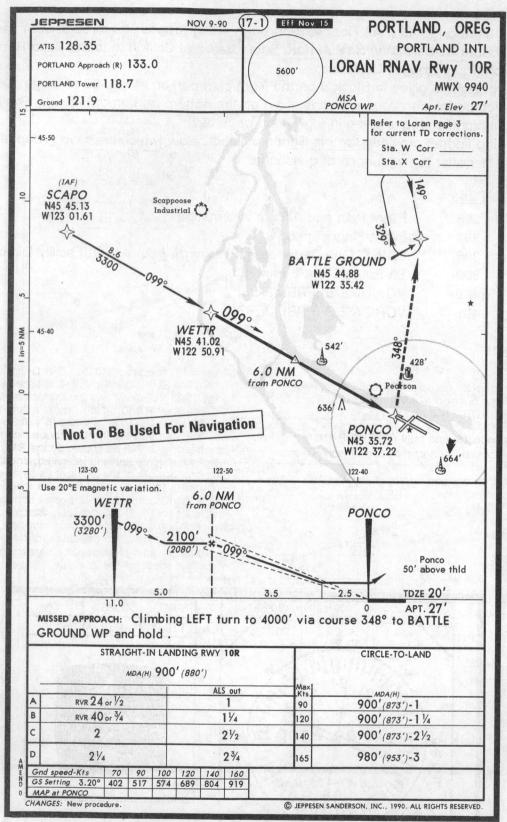

FIGURE 49A.—LORAN RNAV RWY 10R.

## 11.4 SBA to PRB

Questions 34 through 43 (FAA Nos. 4312 through 4321) (pages 393 through 395) pertain to an IFR flight from Santa Barbara Municipal Airport, Santa Barbara, California to the Paso Robles Municipal Airport, Paso Robles, California.

The route of flight is given in Block 8 on the flight plan portion of Fig. 50 on page 396. Information which pertains to your aircraft is given on the bottom portion of Fig. 50. The partially completed flight planning log is given in Fig. 51 on page 397.

The following figures provided for this flight are listed below, which we have grouped and presented together after the sequence of questions.

### 11.4 SBA to PRB

**34.**
**4315.** (Refer to figure 52 on page 398 and 54 below.) What is the aircraft's position relative to the HABUT intersection? (The VOR-2 is tuned to 116.5.)

A— South of the localizer and past the GVO R-163.
B— North of the localizer and approaching the GVO R-163.
C— South of the localizer and approaching the GVO R-163.

Answer (B) is correct (4315). *(IFH Chap VII)*
On the RMI (Fig. 54), VOR-2 is tuned to 116.5, which is the GVO VORTAC, and the tail indicates that the airplane is on R-130, which means it is to the east of HABUT INT. The VOR is tuned to 110.3 which is the localizer, and you are flying outbound on the front course (our heading is 240 as shown by the RMI). This means there is a reverse sensing indicated, and the airplane is to the north or right of the localizer as flying outbound.

Answer (A) is incorrect because when flying outbound on the front course there is reverse sensing, so you are north, not south, of the localizer. Since you are on R-130 from GVO, you are approaching, not past, R-163. Answer (C) is incorrect because when flying outbound on the front course there is reverse sensing, so you are north, not south, of the localizer.

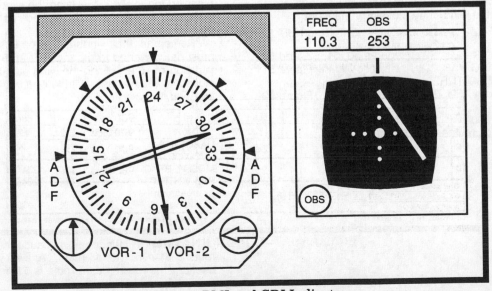

FIGURE 54.—RMI and CDI Indicators.

**35.**
**4316.** (Refer to figure 52 on page 398.) Using an average groundspeed of 100 knots, what minimum rate of climb would meet the required minimum climb rate per NM as specified by the SID?

A— 425 feet per minute.
B— 580 feet per minute.
C— 642 feet per minute.

Answer (C) is correct (4316). *(ACL)*
   The SID on Fig. 52 has a note which indicates a minimum climb rate of 385 ft. per NM to 6,000 ft. To convert this to a rate of climb (fpm), use Legend 18 on page 258. Since there is no 385 ft. per NM listed on the left margin, use 350 and 400 and interpolate between them. Move right to the 100-kt. groundspeed column to see a rate of climb between 583 and 667 fpm, but closer to 667. By interpolation, the minimum rate of climb required would be 642 fpm.
   Answer (A) is incorrect because 425 fpm would require an average groundspeed of 66 kt. (not 100 kt.). Answer (B) is incorrect because 580 fpm would require an average groundspeed of 90 kt. (not 100 kt.).

**36.**
**4312.** (Refer to figure 50 on page 396.) What aircraft equipment code should be entered in block 3 of the flight plan?

A— R.
B— T.
C— U.

Answer (A) is correct (4312). *(AIM Para 5-7)*
   In Block 3 of the flight plan you enter the designation of the aircraft followed by a slash ( / ) and a letter for the equipment code. Fig. 50 indicates the airplane has a transponder with Mode C and RNAV, which requires Code R. (See Legend 25 on page 358.)
   Answer (B) is incorrect because a T indicates only a transponder with no Mode C. Answer (C) is incorrect because a U indicates a transponder with Mode C, but no DME.

**37.**
**4313.** (Refer to figure 50 on page 396.) What CAS must be used to maintain the filed TAS at the flight planned altitude? (Temperature 0 °C.)

A— 136 KCAS.
B— 140 KCAS.
C— 147 KCAS.

Answer (B) is correct (4313). *(FI Comp)*
   In the center of the slide rule side of your flight computer, on the right side, put the air temperature of 0°C over the altitude of 8,000 ft. (given in Block 7 of flight plan). On the outer scale find TAS of 158 kt. (from Block 4), which is over CAS on the inner scale of 140 KCAS.
   Answer (A) is incorrect because maintaining 136 KCAS would result in a TAS of 154 kt. (not 158 kt.). Answer (C) is incorrect because maintaining 147 KCAS would result in a TAS of 168 kt. (not 158 kt.).

**38.**
**4314.** (Refer to figures 50, 51, 52, and 53 on pages 396 through 399.) Determine the time to be entered in block 10 of the flight plan. (Refer to the FD excerpt below, and use the wind entry closest to the flight planned altitude.)

Route of flight . . . . . . . . . . . . Figures 50, 51, 52, and 53
Flight log and MAG VAR . . . . . . . . . . . . . . . . Figure 51
HABUT ONE DEPARTURE
   and Excerpt from AFD . . . . . . . . . . . . . . Figure 52

| FT | 3000 | 6000 | 9000 |
|----|------|------|------|
| SBA | 0610 | 2115+05 | 2525+00 |

A— 43 minutes.
B— 46 minutes.
C— 51 minutes.

Answer (C) is correct (4314). *(IFH Chap XIII)*
   To determine the estimated time en route to be entered in Block 10, you must complete the flight planning log in Fig. 51. Using the wind side of your flight computer, determine groundspeeds as given in the table below.
   Remember that winds are given in true direction and must be converted to magnetic. Fig. 51 shows a variation of 16°E. Using the wind at 9,000 ft. (which is closest to the planned altitude of 8,000 ft.): 250° – 16°E var. = 234° at 25 kt.

| | Distance | MC | Wind (Mag) | Ground-speed | Time |
|---|----------|-----|------------|--------------|------|
| HABUT INT | X | X | X | X | :08:00G |
| GVO VORTAC | 6.4 | 343° | 234/25 | 164 | :02:20 |
| MQO VORTAC | 54 | 307° | 234/25 | 149 | :21:45 |
| PRB VORTAC | 26 | 358° | 234/25 | 171 | :09:07 |
| Approach and Landing | X | X | X | X | :10:00G |
| | | | | | :51:12 |

G = Given

   Answer (A) is incorrect because the total time en route is 51 min. (not 43 min.). Answer (B) is incorrect because the total time en route is 51 min. (not 46 min.).

**39.**
**4317.** (Refer to figure 53 on page 399.) Where is the VOR COP on V27 between the GVO and MQO VORTACs?

A— 20 DME from GVO VORTAC.
B— 20 DME from MQO VORTAC.
C— 30 DME from SBA VORTAC.

Answer (A) is correct (4317). *(ACL)*
When going north from GVO VORTAC to MQO VORTAC, there is a VOR changeover point (COP) 20 NM northwest of GVO VORTAC and 34 NM southeast of MQO VORTAC.
Answer (B) is incorrect because the COP is 20 NM from GVO (not MQO). Answer (C) is incorrect because SBA is Santa Barbara localizer, which is not on V27.

**40.**
**4318.** (Refer to figure 53 on page 399.) What service is indicated by the solid square in the radio aids to navigation box for PRB VORTAC?

A— VOR with TACAN compatible DME.
B— Availability of TWEB.
C— En Route Flight Advisory Service available.

Answer (B) is correct (4318). *(ACL)*
See also Legend 22 on page 329. The small square in the lower right corner of the VOR identifier box indicates the availability of TWEB (Transcribed Weather Broadcast).
Answer (A) is incorrect because the VORTAC symbol itself indicates TACAN compatible DME. Answer (C) is incorrect because En Route Flight Advisory Service (Flight Watch) is available nationwide on 122.0.

**41.**
**4319.** (Refer to figures 55 and 55A on pages 400 and 401.) Using an average groundspeed of 90 knots, what constant rate of descent from 2,400 feet MSL at the 6 DME fix would enable the aircraft to arrive at 2,000 feet MSL at the FAF?

A— 200 feet per minute.
B— 400 feet per minute.
C— 600 feet per minute.

Answer (A) is correct (4319). *(ACL)*
The profile view of the IAP chart (Fig. 55 or 55A) shows the distance from the 6 DME fix to the FAF to be 3 NM. At 90 kt. (1½ NM per min.), this distance would be traveled in 2 min. To descend from 2,400 ft. to 2,000 ft. in 2 min. would require a descent rate of 200 fpm.
Answer (B) is incorrect because 400 fpm would require an average groundspeed of 180 kt. (not 90 kt.). Answer (C) is incorrect because 600 fpm would require an average groundspeed of 270 kt. (not 90 kt.).

**42.**
**4320.** (Refer to figures 55 and 55A on pages 400 and 401.) As a guide in making range corrections, how many degrees of relative bearing change should be used for each one-half mile deviation from the desired arc?

A— 2° to 3°.
B— 5° maximum.
C— 10° to 20°.

Answer (C) is correct (4320). *(IFH Chap VIII)*
As a guide in making corrections when tracking DME arcs, turn 10° to 20° toward the arc for each ½-NM that you are off the desired arc.
Answer (A) is incorrect because 10° to 20° corrections (not 2° to 3°) should be made for each ½-NM deviation. Answer (B) is incorrect because there is no maximum; the amount of correction should be proportional to the amount of error.

**43.**
**4321.** (Refer to figures 55 and 55A on pages 400 and 401.) Under which condition should a missed approach procedure be initiated if the runway environment (Paso Robles Municipal Airport) is not in sight?

A— After descending to 1,440 feet MSL.
B— After descent to 1,440 feet or reaching the 1 NM DME, whichever occurs first.
C— When you reach the established missed approach point and determine the visibility is less than 1 mile.

Answer (C) is correct (4321). *(FAR 91.175)*
The missed approach point is the point prescribed in each instrument approach procedure at which a missed approach procedure shall be executed if the required visual reference has not been sighted or the flight visibility is less than visibility prescribed in the IAP. The MAP for VOR/DME-B (Fig. 55 or 55A) is the PRB VORTAC. Thus, when you reach the VORTAC and you determine the visibility is less than 1 SM, you must execute the missed approach procedure.
Answer (A) is incorrect because the MAP is PRB VORTAC, not arrival at the MDA. Answer (B) is incorrect because the MAP is PRB VORTAC, not arrival at the MDA or the 1 DME fix.

Form Approved: OMB No.2120-0034

| U.S. DEPARTMENT OF TRANSPORTATION FEDERAL AVIATION ADMINISTRATION **FLIGHT PLAN** | (FAA USE ONLY) ☐ PILOT BRIEFING   ☐ VNR ☐ STOPOVER | | TIME STARTED | SPECIALIST INITIALS |
|---|---|---|---|---|

| 1 TYPE | 2 AIRCRAFT IDENTIFICATION | 3 AIRCRAFT TYPE/ SPECIAL EQUIPMENT | 4 TRUE AIRSPEED | 5 DEPARTURE POINT | 6 DEPARTURE TIME | | 7 CRUISING ALTITUDE |
|---|---|---|---|---|---|---|---|
| | | | | | PROPOSED (Z) | ACTUAL (Z) | |
| X IFR (VFR / DVFR) | N2468 | A36/ | 158 | SBA | | | 8000 |

**8 ROUTE OF FLIGHT**

HABUTI GVO, V27 MQO, V113 PRB

| 9 DESTINATION (Name of airport and city) PASO ROBLES MUNI PRB | 10 EST TIME ENROUTE | | 11 REMARKS |
|---|---|---|---|
| | HOURS | MINUTES | |
| | | | IFR TRAINING FLIGHT |

| 12 FUEL ON BOARD | | 13 ALTERNATE AIRPORT(S) | 14 PILOTS NAME, ADDRESS & TELEPHONE NUMBER & AIRCRAFT HOME BASE | 15 NUMBER ABOARD |
|---|---|---|---|---|
| HOURS | MINUTES | N/R | 17 DESTINATION CONTACT/TELEPHONE (OPTIONAL) | 2 |

| 16 COLOR OF AIRCRAFT GOLD/WHITE | CIVIL AIRCRAFT PILOTS. FAR Part 91 requires you file an IFR flight plan to operate under instrument flight rules in controlled airspace. Failure to file could result in a civil penalty not to exceed $1,000 for each violation (Section 901 of the Federal Aviation Act of 1958. as amended; Filing of a VFR flight plan is recommended as a good operating practice. See also Part 99 for requirements concerning DVFR flight plans. |
|---|---|

FAA Form 7233-1 (8-82)          CLOSE VFR FLIGHT PLAN WITH _____ FSS ON ARRIVAL

---

## AIRCRAFT INFORMATION

MAKE  Beechcraft          MODEL  A-36

N  2468                   Vso  52

---

## AIRCRAFT EQUIPMENT/STATUS**

**NOTE:  X= OPERATIVE   INOP= INOPERATIVE     N/A= NOT APPLICABLE
TRANSPONDER: X (MODE C ) X ILS: (LOCALIZER) X (GLIDE SLOPE) X
VOR NO.1 X (NO 2) X ADF: X RNAV: X
VERTICAL PATH COMPUTER:  NA  DME: X
MARKER BEACON:  X (AUDIO) X (VISUAL) Inop.

FIGURE 50.—Flight Plan and Aircraft Information.

# FLIGHT LOG

SANTA BARBARA MUNI TO PASO ROBLES MUNI

| CHECK POINTS | | ROUTE | COURSE | WIND | SPEED-KTS | | DIST | TIME | | FUEL | |
|---|---|---|---|---|---|---|---|---|---|---|---|
| FROM | TO | ALTITUDE | | TEMP | TAS | GS | NM | LEG | TOT | LEG | TOT |
| SBA | HABUT | HABUT 1 CLIMB | 253° | | | | | :08:00 | | | |
| | GVO | 163°R 8000 | 343° | | 158 | | | | | | |
| | MQO | V27 8000 | 306° | | | | | | | | |
| | PRB | V113 | 358° | | | | | | | | |
| APPROACH & LANDING | | DESCENT | | | | | | :10:00 | | | |
| | PRB AIRPORT | | | | | | | | | | |
| | | | | | | | | | | | |
| | | | | | | | | | | | |
| | | | | | | | | | | | |
| | | | | | | | | | | | |

OTHER DATA:

NOTE:  MAG. VAR. 16° E.

FLIGHT SUMMARY

| TIME | FUEL (LBS) | |
|---|---|---|
| | | EN ROUTE |
| | | RESERVE |
| | | MISSED APPR. |
| | | TOTAL |

FIGURE 51.—Flight Planning Log.

## HABUT ONE DEPARTURE (HABUT1.GVO)

SANTA BARBARA MUNI
SANTA BARBARA, CALIFORNIA

SANTA BARBARA GND CON
121.7
SANTA BARBARA TOWER *
119.7 242.4
SANTA BARBARA DEP CON
120.55 321.4
ATIS * 125.1

SANTA BARBARA
114.9 SBA 96

LOCALIZER
110.3 I-SBA 40

GAVIOTA
116.5 GVO 112
L-3

R-249

6000
253°
(13)

Aprx dist
fr T/off area

6000

343°
(6.4)

073°

HABUT
INT

R-163

NOTE: This departure requires
a minimum climb rate of
385' per NM to 6000

NOTE: IFR departure Rwys 33L/R
not authorized.

NOTE: Chart not to scale

### DEPARTURE ROUTE DESCRIPTION

TAKE-OFF RUNWAY 7: Maintain runway heading to at
least 650', then turn right, thence intercept and climb
westbound via I-SBA localizer west course to HABUT INT,
thence via GVO R-163 to GVO VORTAC. Cross SBA R-249
at or above 6000'.

TAKE-OFF RUNWAY 15: Maintain runway heading to at
least 310', then turn right, thence intercept and climb
westbound via I-SBA localizer west course to HABUT INT,
thence via GVO R-163 to GVO VORTAC. Cross SBA R-249
at or above 6000'.

(Continued on next page)

HABUT ONE DEPARTURE (HABUT1.GVO)

---

## HABUT ONE DEPARTURE (HABUT1.GVO)

SANTA BARBARA MUNI
SANTA BARBARA, CALIFORNIA

### DEPARTURE ROUTE DESCRIPTION
(Continued)

TAKE-OFF RUNWAY 25: Climb westbound via I-SBA localizer west course to HABUT
INT, thence via GVO R-163 to GVO VORTAC. Cross SBA R-249 at or above 6000'.

## HABUT ONE DEPARTURE (HABUT1.GVO)

SANTA BARBARA, CALIFORNIA
SANTA BARBARA MUNI

§ **SANTA BARBARA MUNI** (SBA)  7 W  GMT-8(-7DT)  34°25'34"N 119°50'22"W    LOS ANGELES
10  B  S4  FUEL  80, 100, 100LL, JET A  OX 1, 2, 3, 4  TPA—See Remarks    H-2F, L-3B
CFR Index C    IAP
RWY 07-25: H6049X150 (ASPH-GRVD)  S-110, D-160, DT-245  HIRL
RWY 07: MALSR. Tree. Rgt tfc.    RWY 25: VASI(V4L)—GA 3.0°TCH 46'. Thld dsplcd 324'. Road.
RWY 15R-33L: H4183X100 (ASPH)  S-48, D-63, DT-100  MIRL
RWY 15R: REIL. Pole.    RWY 33L: Road. Rgt tfc.
RWY 15L-33R: H4179X75 (ASPH)  S-35, D-41, DT-63
RWY 15L: Thld dsplcd 225'. Tree.    RWY 33R: Pole. Rgt tfc.
AIRPORT REMARKS: Attended 1330-0600Z‡. Fee after hours. Numerous flocks of birds on and in vicinity of arpt.
TPA—1000(990) small acft, 1500(1490) large acft. Pure jet touch/go or low approaches prohibited.
COMMUNICATIONS: CTAF 119.7    ATIS 125.1 (1430-0600Z‡)  UNICOM 122.95
SANTA BARBARA FSS (SBA) on arpt 123.65, 122.3, 122.2, 122.1R, 116.5T LD (805) 967-2305. DL NOTAM FILE
    SBA.
® APP CON 125.4 (1430-0600Z‡)    ® DEP CON 120.55 (1430-0600Z‡)
® LOS ANGELES CENTER APP/DEP CON 128.05 (0600-1430Z‡)
TOWER 119.7 (1430-0600Z‡)    GND CON 121.7
VFR ADVSY SVC ctc TOWER
RADIO AIDS TO NAVIGATION: NOTAM FILE SBA. VHF/DF ctc SANTA BARBARA FSS
(H) ABVORTAC 114.9  ■ SBA  Chan 96  34°30'34"N 119°46'12"W  198°5.6 NM to fld. 3620/16E.
GAVIOTA (L) VORTAC 116.5  GVO  Chan 112  34°31'53"N 120°05'24"W  099°14.0 NM to fld. 2620/16E
ILS/DME 110.3 I-SBA Chan 40 Rwy 07

### CALIFORNIA

#### VOR RECEIVER CHECK POINTS

| Facility Name (Arpt Name) | Freq/Ident | Type Check Pt. Gnd. AB/ALT | Azimuth from Fac. Mag | Dist. from Fac. N.M. | Check Point Description |
|---|---|---|---|---|---|
| Sacramento (Sacramento Executive) | 115.2/SAC | A/1000 | 015 | | Over apch end rwy 02. |
| Salinas (Salinas Muni) | 117.3/SNS | G | 247 | | 0.4 NM on Compass rose. |
| Santa Ana (John Wayne Airport/Orange County) | 109.4/SNA | G | 186 | | On runup pad rwy 01R. |
| Santa Barbara | 114.9/SBA | A/2000 | 277 | 11 | Over Lake Cachuma Dam spillway. |
| Santa Barbara (Santa Barbara Muni) | 114.9/SBA | G | 200 | 5.9 | On runup area end rwy 15. |

---

SANTA BARBARA MUNI
SANTA BARBARA, CALIFORNIA

ELEV 10

25
4179 X 75
15R
103
4183 X 100
33L 33R
600 X 150

SANTA BARBARA, CALIFORNIA
SANTA BARBARA MUNI

FIGURE 52.—HABUT One Departure and Excerpt from Airport/Facility Directory.

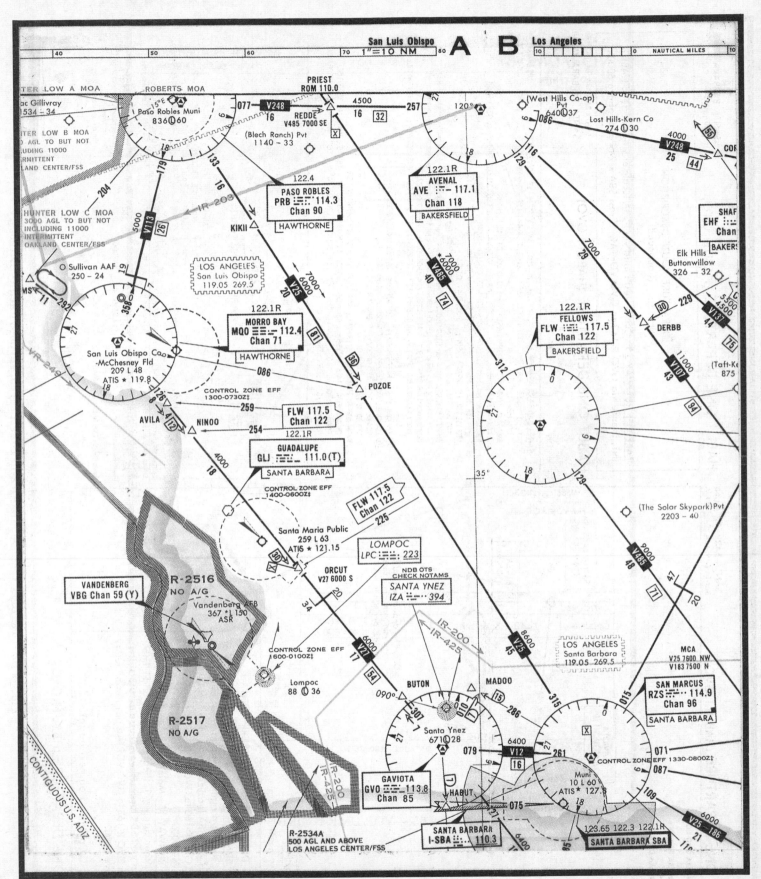

FIGURE 53.—En Route Chart Segment.

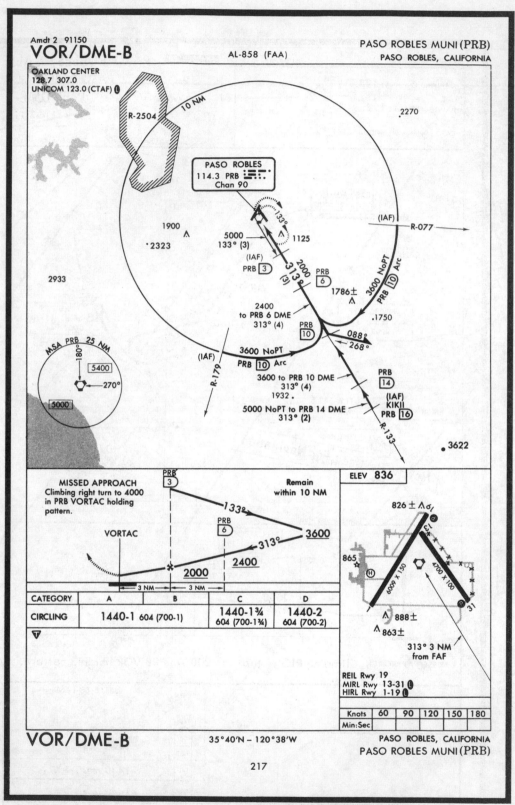

FIGURE 55.—VOR/DME-B (PRB).

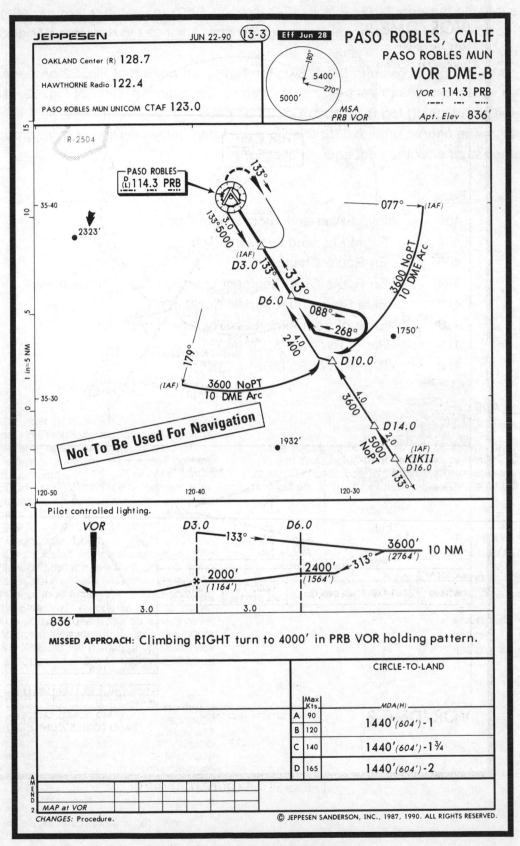

FIGURE 55A.—VOR/DME-B (PRB).

## 11.5  HOT to ADS

Questions 44 through 54 (FAA Nos. 4277 through 4287) (pages 402 through 405) pertain to an IFR flight from Hot Springs Memorial Field, Hot Springs, Arkansas to the Dallas/Addison Airport, Dallas, Texas.

The route of flight is given in Block 8 on the flight plan portion of Fig. 32 on page 406. Information which pertains to your aircraft is given on the bottom portion of Fig. 32. The partially completed flight planning log is given in Fig. 33 on page 407.

The following figures provided for this flight are listed below, which we have grouped and presented together after the sequence of questions.

### 11.5  HOT to ADS

**44.**
**4279.** (Refer to figures 32, 33, 34, and 36 on pages 406 through 410.) (Refer to the FD excerpt below, and use the wind entry closest to the flight planned altitude.) Determine the time to be entered in block 10 of the flight plan.

Route of flight . . . . . . . . . . . . . Figures 32, 33, 34, & 36
Flight log & MAG VAR . . . . . . . . . . . . . . . . . Figure 33
RNAV RWY 33 & Excerpt from AFD . . . . . . . . Figure 36

| FT | 3000 | 6000 | 9000 | 12000 |
| --- | --- | --- | --- | --- |
| DAL | 2027 | 2239+13 | 2240+08 | 2248+05 |

A— 1 hour 35 minutes.
B— 1 hour 41 minutes.
C— 1 hour 46 minutes.

Answer (A) is correct (4279). *(IFH Chap XIII)*
To determine the estimated time en route to be entered in Block 20, you must complete the flight planning log in Fig. 33. Comparing the flight log with the en route and arrival charts (Figs. 34, 35, and 35A) it becomes apparent that some alterations of the flight log are necessary. On V573 (Fig. 34) there is a bend in the airway (COP) 10 NM southwest of MARKI INT., so an additional leg is required to accurately compute groundspeeds. Also, the check points in the STAR (Figs. 35 and 35A) are not labeled well in the flight log.

Having corrected the flight log as shown below, use the wind side of your flight computer to determine groundspeeds as shown. Remember that winds are given in true direction and must be converted to magnetic. Fig. 33 shows a variation of 4°E. Using the wind at 9,000 ft. (which is closest to the planned altitude of 8,000 ft.): 220° − 4°E var. = 216° at 40 kt.

| | Distance | MC | Wind (Mag) | Ground-speed | Time |
| --- | --- | --- | --- | --- | --- |
| MARKI INT | X | X | X | X | :12:00G |
| VOR COP | 10 | 221° | 216/40 | 140 | :04:17 |
| TXK VORTAC | 45 | 210° | 216/40 | 140 | :19:17 |
| CONNY INT | 61 | 272° | 216/40 | 154 | :23:46 |
| BUJ VORTAC | 59 | 239° | 216/40 | 142 | :24:56 |
| Approach and Landing | X | X | X | X | :10:00G |
| | | | | | 1:34:16 |

G = Given

Answer (B) is incorrect because the total time en route is 1 hr. 35 min. (not 1 hr. 41 min.). Answer (C) is incorrect because the total time en route is 1 hr. 35 min. (not 1 hr. 46 min.).

**45.**
**4277.** (Refer to figure 32 on page 406.) What aircraft equipment code should be entered in block 3 of the flight plan?

A— A.
B— C.
C— R.

Answer (C) is correct (4277). *(AIM Para 5-7)*
In Block 3 of the flight plan, you enter the designation of the aircraft followed by a slash ( / ) and a letter for the equipment code. Fig. 32 indicates a transponder with Mode C and RNAV. Thus, Code R is required. (See Legend 25 on page 358.)
Answer (A) is incorrect because A indicates DME and transponder with Mode C, but no RNAV. Answer (B) is incorrect because C indicates RNAV and transponder, but with no Mode C.

**46.**
**4278.** (Refer to figure 32 on page 406.) What CAS must be used to maintain the filed TAS at the flight planned altitude if the outside air temperature is +8 °C?

A— 154 KCAS.
B— 157 KCAS.
C— 163 KCAS.

Answer (B) is correct (4278). *(FI Comp)*
In the center of the slide rule side of your flight computer, on the right side, put the air temperature of +8°C over the altitude of 8,000 ft. (see Block 7 of the Flight Plan in Fig. 32). On the outer scale find TAS of 180 (from Block 4), which is over calibrated airspeed on the inner scale of 157 KCAS.
Answer (A) is incorrect because maintaining 154 KCAS would result in a TAS of 176 kt. (not 180 kt.). Answer (C) is incorrect because maintaining 163 KCAS would result in a TAS of 187 kt. (not 180 kt.).

**47.**
**4280.** (Refer to figure 34 on page 408 and 34A below.) At which altitude and location on V573 would you expect the navigational signal of the HOT VORTAC to be unusable?

A— Below 3,500 feet at MARKI intersection.
B— Above 3,500 feet at MARKI intersection.
C— At 3,500 feet at APINE intersection.

Answer (A) is the best answer (4280). *(ACL)*
The A/FD in Fig. 34A, under "Radio Aids to Navigation," does not indicate that the HOT VOR/DME is unusable in any quadrants. At MARKI (21 NM from HOT) the MEA is 3,500 ft. and the MOCA is 2,500 ft. (Fig. 34). A usable navigational signal exists between the MOCA of 2,500 ft. and the MEA of 3,500 ft. Since MARKI is near the 22-NM boundary of usable navigational signals at the MOCA, the best answer is to expect the navigational signal of HOT VOR/DME to be unusable below 3,500 ft. at MARKI. The FAA may change an answer to make it clearly a correct answer on the computer test.
Answer (B) is incorrect because you can expect the navigational signal to be unusable below, not above, 3,500 ft. at MARKI. Answer (C) is incorrect because you can expect the navigational signal to be unusable below, not at, 3,500 ft. at APINE. The MEA at APINE is 3,500 ft.

---

**ARKANSAS**

**HOT SPRINGS**
**MEMORIAL FLD** (HOT) 3 SW UTC–6(–5DT) 34°28'41"N 93°05'46"W                    **MEMPHIS**
540 B S4 FUEL 100LL, JET A ARFF Index Ltd.                                       **H-4G, L-14E**
RWY 05-23: H6595X150 (ASPH-GRVD) S-75, D-125, DT-210, DDT-400. HIRL 0.6% up NE   **IAP**
    RWY 05: MALSR. Tree.        RWY 23: REIL. Thld dsplcd 490'. Tree.
RWY 13-31: H4099X150 (ASPH) S-28, D-36, DT-63 MIRL
    RWY 13: REIL. Road/Trees.        RWY 31: Pole.
AIRPORT REMARKS: Attended 1130-0400Z‡. CLOSED to unscheduled air carrier ops with more than 30 passenger
    seats except PPR, call arpt manager 501–624–3306. Last 500' Rwy 05 CLOSED to takeoffs. Rwy 13-31 fair
    with extensive loose grvl-pavement debris. ACTIVATE HIRL Rwy 05–23 and MALSR Rwy 05—CTAF. Rwy 23 REIL
    out of svc indefinitely. Control Zone effective 1200–0400Z‡.
COMMUNICATIONS: CTAF/UNICOM 123.0
    JONESBORO FSS (JBR) TF 1–800–WX–BRIEF. NOTAM FILE HOT.
    HOT SPRINGS RCO 122.1R 110.0T (LITTLE ROCK FSS)
    MEMPHIS CENTER APP/DEP CON: 118.85
RADIO AIDS TO NAVIGATION: NOTAM FILE HOT.
    HOT SPRINGS (L) VOR/DME 110.0 HOT Chan 37 34°28'43"N 93°05'26"W at fld. 530/4E.
    HOSSY NDB (HW/LOM) 385 HO 34°25'21"N 93°11'22"W 050° 5.7 NM to fld.
    ILS/DME 111.5 I-HOT Chan 52 Rwy 05 LOM HOSSY NDB Unmonitored.

FIGURE 34A.—Airport/Facility Directory (HOT).

**48.**
**4281.** (Refer to figure 35 on page 409 and 37 below). What is your position relative to the CONNY intersection on the BUJ.BUJ3 transition?

A— Left of the TXK R-272 and approaching the BUJ R-059°.
B— Left of the TXK R-266 and past the BUJ R-065.
C— Right of the TXK R-270 and approaching the BUJ R-245.

Answer (A) is correct (4281). *(IFH Chap VIII)*
Note the STAR has changed from the previous edition and the FAA updated the HSI illustration but kept the same RMI illustration. This is why the HSI indicates a heading of 270° and the RMI incorrectly indicates a heading of 255° instead of 270°.
Refer to Figs. 35 and 35A and note that this is actually the TXK.BUJ3 transition (to the BUJ.BUJ3 arrival). In Fig. 37, NAV 1 (an HSI) is tuned to 114.9 (BUJ VORTAC) and set to 239°. Since the bar is deflected to the northwest, you are southeast of the BUJ R-059, and thus approaching it (note the 270° heading). NAV 2 (an RMI) has the fat needle tuned to 116.3 (TXK VORTAC). The tail of the needle indicates R-270 which is south of R-272, and thus to the left.
Answer (B) is incorrect because the R-270 of TXK is right not left of the TXK R-266 and you are on (not past) the BUJ R-065. Answer (C) is incorrect because you are on (not right of) the R-270 of TXK and approaching R-244 of LIT (not BUJ).

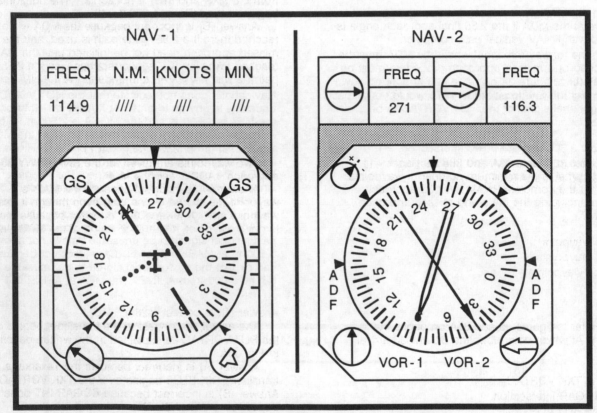

FIGURE 37.—CDI and RMI — NAV 1 and NAV 2.

**49.**
**4282.** (Refer to figures 36A and 36B on pages 411 and 412.) Under which condition should the missed approach procedure for the RNAV RWY 33 approach be initiated?

A— Immediately upon reaching the 5.0 DME from the FAF.
B— When passage of the MAP waypoint is shown on the ambiguity indicator.
C— After the MDA is reached and 1.8 DME fix from the MAP waypoint.

Answer (B) is correct (4282). *(FAR 91.175)*
The missed approach point (MAP) is the point prescribed in each instrument approach procedure at which a missed approach procedure shall be executed if the required visual reference has not been sighted. The MAP on the RNAV RWY 33 approach (Fig. 36A or 36B) is arrival at the indicated MAP waypoint. Passage of the MAP waypoint is shown on the ambiguity indicator (TO-FROM flag).
Answer (A) is incorrect because the FAF is identified as 5.0 DME from the MAP (not vice versa). Answer (C) is incorrect because 1.8 DME from the MAP waypoint is where you would arrive at MDA, assuming a 2.85° glide path.

**50.**

**4283.** (Refer to figures 32 on page 406, 36 on page 410, and 36A and 36B on pages 411 and 412.) What is the MDA and visibility criteria respectively for the S-33 approach procedure?

A— 1,240 feet MSL; 1 SM.

B— 1,280 feet MSL; 1 and ¼ SM.

C— 1,300 feet MSL; 1 SM.

Answer (A) is correct (4283). *(ACL)*

Refer to Fig. 32 to determine the aircraft category. V$_{SO}$ is 74 kt., thus 1.3 V$_{SO}$ is 96.2 kt., which puts the airplane in Category B (91-120). The minimums for the RNAV RWY 33 approach, Category B, are 1,220 ft. MSL and 1 SM on the NOS chart (Fig. 36A). The JEPP chart shows an MDA of 1,240 ft. Thus, use the JEPP minimums to answer this question.

Answer (B) is incorrect because 1,280 ft. is the MDA for circling Category D on the JEPP chart (but not the NOS chart) and 1¼ SM is not an applicable minimum. Answer (C) is incorrect because 1,300 ft. is not an applicable MDA.

**51.**

**4284.** (Refer to figures 36, 36A, and 36B on pages 410, 411, and 412.) The distance of 1.8 NM shown prior to the runway in the profile view of the RNAV RWY 33 approach procedure is the distance

A— from the MAP waypoint at which an aircraft would arrive at the MDA if the 2.85 final approach angle is used with RNAV vertical path computer.

B— from the runway threshold where the MDA must be reached or a missed approach procedure must be initiated.

C— from the runway threshold where the 2.85° VDP begins.

Answer (A) is correct (4284). *(IFH Chap X)*

The profile section of the approach plate for RNAV RWY 33, Fig. 36A or 36B, indicates that the glide slope is 2.85° as shown by the 2.85° after the angle sign. Note that the glide slope on the profile goes down to 1.8 NM from the MAP and then is horizontal. The horizontal line begins at the MDA of 1,220 ft. MSL.

Answer (B) is incorrect because the MDA will only be reached there if a 2.85° glide path is used, and the missed approach need not be initiated until the MAP is reached. Answer (C) is incorrect because the 2.85° glide path begins at the FAF and ends at the 1.8 NM point.

**52.**

**4285.** (Refer to figures 36A and 36B on pages 411 and 412.) What is the minimum number of waypoints required for the complete RNAV RWY 33 approach procedure including the IAF's and missed approach procedure?

A— One waypoint.

B— Two waypoints.

C— Three waypoints.

Answer (B) is correct (4285). *(ACL)*

Two waypoints are given for the RNAV RWY 33 approach: ADDIS and the MAP.

Answer (A) is incorrect because the MAP is a waypoint (as shown by the box) even though it has no waypoint star. Answer (C) is incorrect because the FAF is not a waypoint, it is a DME fix off of the MAP waypoint.

**53.**

**4286.** (Refer to figures 35 and 35A on pages 409 and 410.) At which point does the BUJ.BUJ3 arrival begin?

A— At the TXK VORTAC.

B— At BOGAR intersection.

C— At the BUJ VORTAC.

Answer (C) is correct (4286). *(ACL)*

The arrival, in contrast to the transition, begins over the BUJ VORTAC as explained in the written description in Fig. 35A.

Answer (A) is incorrect because the Texarkana transition, TXK BUJ8 begins over the TXK VORTAC. Answer (B) is incorrect because BOGAR INT does not appear on the BUJ.BUJ3 arrival chart.

**54.**

**4287.** (Refer to figure 34 on page 408.) For planning purposes, what is the highest useable altitude for an IFR flight on V573 from the HOT VORTAC to the TXK VORTAC?

A— 16,000 feet MSL.

B— 14,500 feet MSL.

C— 13,999 feet MSL.

Answer (A) is correct (4287). *(AIM Para 5-34)*

The VOR airway system consists of airways designated from 1,200 ft. AGL up to, but not including, 18,000 ft. MSL. Flying on V573 from HOT to TXK is a generally westerly course which requires an even-thousands altitude. Thus, 16,000 ft. MSL is the highest usable altitude.

Answer (B) is incorrect because 14,500 ft. MSL is a VFR (not IFR) cruising altitude from 180° to 359°. Answer (C) is incorrect because IFR altitudes are even or odd thousands of feet.

Form Approved: OMB No.2120-0034

| U.S. DEPARTMENT OF TRANSPORTATION FEDERAL AVIATION ADMINISTRATION **FLIGHT PLAN** | (FAA USE ONLY) | ☐ PILOT BRIEFING ☐ STOPOVER | ☐ VNR | TIME STARTED | SPECIALIST INITIALS |
|---|---|---|---|---|---|

| 1 TYPE | 2 AIRCRAFT IDENTIFICATION | 3 AIRCRAFT TYPE/ SPECIAL EQUIPMENT | 4 TRUE AIRSPEED | 5 DEPARTURE POINT | 6 DEPARTURE TIME | | 7 CRUISING ALTITUDE |
|---|---|---|---|---|---|---|---|
| | | | | | PROPOSED (Z) | ACTUAL (Z) | |
| VFR | | | | | | | |
| X IFR | N4078A | PA 31/ | 180 | HOT | | | 8,000 |
| DVFR | | | | | | | |

**8 ROUTE OF FLIGHT**

HOT V573, TXK, TXK.BUJ3

| 9 DESTINATION (Name of airport and city) DALLAS ADDISON AIRPORT DALLAS, TX | 10 EST TIME ENROUTE HOURS / MINUTES | 11 REMARKS |
|---|---|---|

| 12 FUEL ON BOARD HOURS / MINUTES | 13 ALTERNATE AIRPORT(S) N/A | 14 PILOTS NAME, ADDRESS & TELEPHONE NUMBER & AIRCRAFT HOME BASE | 15 NUMBER ABOARD |
|---|---|---|---|
| | | 17 DESTINATION CONTACT/TELEPHONE (OPTIONAL) | 2 |

| 16 COLOR OF AIRCRAFT TAN/WHITE | CIVIL AIRCRAFT PILOTS. FAR Part 91 requires you file an IFR flight plan to operate under instrument flight rules in controlled airspace. Failure to file could result in a civil penalty not to exceed $1,000 for each violation (Section 901 of the Federal Aviation Act of 1958. as amended; Filing of a VFR flight plan is recommended as a good operating practice. See also Part 99 for requirements concerning DVFR flight plans. |
|---|---|

FAA Form 7233-1 (8-82)        CLOSE VFR FLIGHT PLAN WITH _____ FSS ON ARRIVAL

---

## AIRCRAFT INFORMATION

MAKE  Piper            MODEL  PA-31

N 4078A                Vso 74

---

## AIRCRAFT EQUIPMENT/STATUS**

**NOTE: X= OPERATIVE   INOP= INOPERATIVE    N/A= NOT APPLICABLE
TRANSPONDER: X (MODE C ) X ILS: (LOCALIZER) X  (GLIDE SLOPE) X
VOR NO.1 X (NO 2) X ADF: X RNAV: X
VERTICAL PATH COMPUTER: NA DME: X
MARKER BEACON: X (AUDIO) X (VISUAL) X

FIGURE 32.—Flight Plan and Aircraft Information.

# FLIGHT LOG

HOT SPRINGS, MEMORIAL FIELD TO DALLAS, ADDISON, TX..

| CHECK POINTS | | ROUTE | COURSE | WIND | SPEED-KTS | | DIST | TIME | | FUEL | |
|---|---|---|---|---|---|---|---|---|---|---|---|
| FROM | TO | ALTITUDE | | TEMP | TAS | GS | NM | LEG | TOT | LEG | TOT |
| HOT | MARKI | V573 CLIMB | 221° | | | | | :12:00 | | | |
| | TXK | V573 8000 | 210° | | 180 | | | | | | |
| TXK | BUJ3 | BUJ3 8000 | 272° | | | | | | | | |
| | BUJ3 | BUJ3 DESCENT | 239° | | | | | | | | |
| APPROACH & LANDING | | | | | | | | :10:00 | | | |
| | DALLAS ADDISON | | | | | | | | | | |
| | | | | | | | | | | | |
| | | | | | | | | | | | |
| | | | | | | | | | | | |

OTHER DATA:

NOTE: MAG. VAR. 4° E.

FLIGHT SUMMARY

| TIME | FUEL (LBS) | |
|---|---|---|
| | | EN ROUTE |
| | | RESERVE |
| | | MISSED APPR. |
| | | TOTAL |

FIGURE 33.—Flight Planning Log.

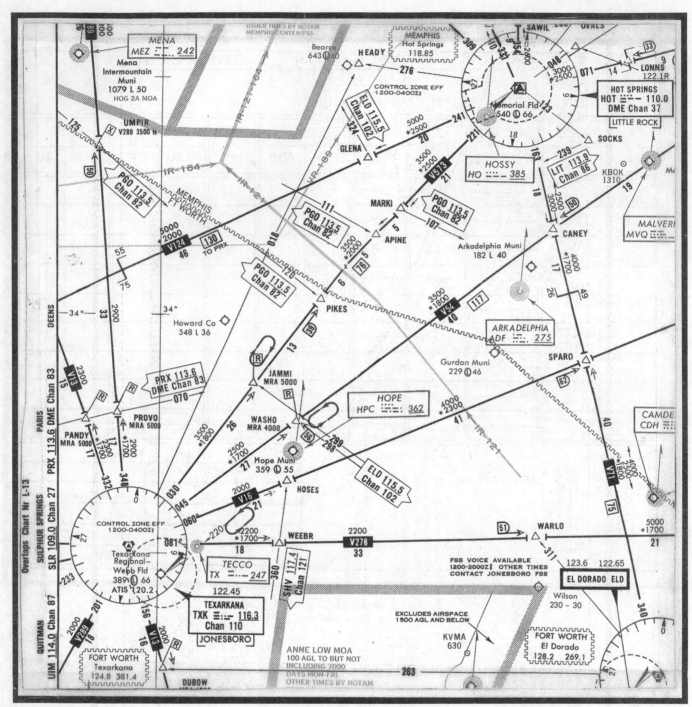

FIGURE 34.—En Route Chart.

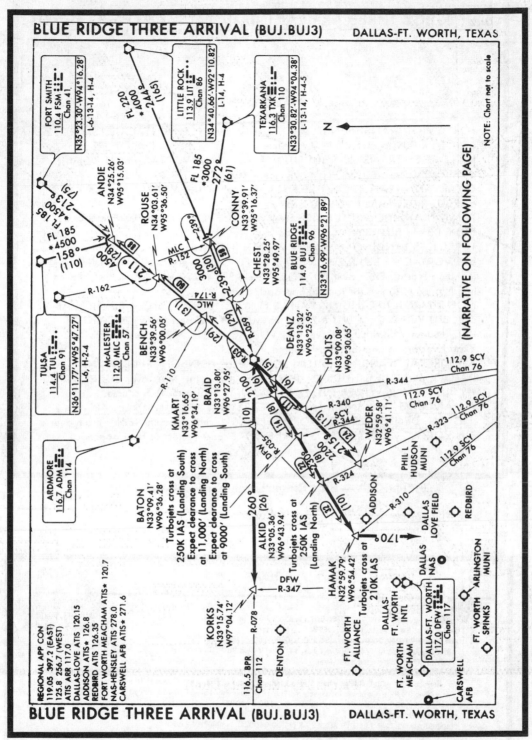

FIGURE 35.—En Route Chart Segment and Blue Ridge Three Arrival.

91094
SL-6039 (FAA)

# BLUE RIDGE THREE ARRIVAL (BUJ.BUJ3)    DALLAS-FT. WORTH, TEXAS

## ARRIVAL DESCRIPTION

FORT SMITH TRANSITION (FSM.BUJ3): From over FSM VORTAC via FSM R-213 and BUJ R-031 to BUJ VORTAC. Thence . . . .

LITTLE ROCK TRANSITION (LIT.BUJ3): From over LIT VORTAC via LIT R-244 and BUJ R-059 to BUJ VORTAC. Thence . . . .

TEXARKANA TRANSITION (TXK.BUJ3): From over TXK VORTAC via TXK R-272 and BUJ R-059 to BUJ VORTAC. Thence . . . .

TULSA TRANSITION (TUL.BUJ3): From over TUL VORTAC via TUL R-158 and BUJ R-031 to BUJ VORTAC. Thence . . . .

TURBOJETS LANDING DALLAS-FT WORTH INTL: (Landing South): From over BUJ VORTAC via BUJ R-230 to HAMAK INT. Expect vectors at BATON INT. (Landing North): From over BUJ VORTAC via BUJ R-230 to HAMAK INT, thence heading 170° for vector to final approach course.

NON-TURBOJETS LANDING DALLAS-FT WORTH INTL: (Landing South): From over BUJ VORTAC via BUJ R-230 to HAMAK INT. Expect vectors at BATON INT. (Landing North): From over BUJ VORTAC via BUJ R-215 to WEDER INT. Expect vectors to final approach course.

ALL AIRCRAFT LANDING DALLAS-LOVE FIELD, ADDISON, REDBIRD, NAS DALLAS, and PHIL L. HUDSON: (Landing South/North): From over BUJ VORTAC via BUJ R-215 to WEDER INT. Expect vectors to final approach course.

ALL AIRCRAFT LANDING MEACHAM, CARSWELL AFB, ALLIANCE, ARLINGTON, DENTON and FT. WORTH SPINKS: (Landing South/North): From over BUJ VORTAC via BUJ R-260 to KORKS INT. Expect vectors to final approach course.

FIGURE 35A.—Blue Ridge Three Arrival Description.

---

**TEXAS**    145

## DALLAS

**ADDISON** (ADS)    9 N    UTC–6(–5DT)    32°58'06"N 96°50'10"W    DALLAS-FT. WORTH
643    B    S4    FUEL 100LL, JET A    H-2K, 4F, 5B, L-13C, A
    IAP
RWY 15-33: H7201X100 (ASPH)    S-80, D-100, DT-160    MIRL
    RWY 15: MALSR. VASI(V4R)—GA 3.0°TCH 51'. Thld dsplcd 980'. Ground.
    RWY 33: REIL. Thld dsplcd 468'. Road.
AIRPORT REMARKS: Attended continuously. Numerous flocks of birds on and in vicinity of arpt. Use extreme care: numerous 200' AGL buildings within 1 mile East, and South of arpt, transmission towers and water tanks West of arpt. Rwy 33 REIL out of svc indefinitely. ACTIVATE MALSR Rwy 15—CTAF. Rwy limited to maximum gross weight 120,000 pounds. Control Zone effective 1200-0400Z‡.
WEATHER DATA SOURCES: LAWRS
COMMUNICATIONS: CTAF 121.1    ATIS 126.8 (1200-0400Z‡)    UNICOM 122.95
    FORT WORTH FSS (FTW) TF 1–800–WX–BRIEF. NOTAM FILE ADS.
Ⓡ REGIONAL APP CON 123.9    Ⓡ REGIONAL DEP CON 124.3
    TOWER 121.1 (1200-0400Z‡)    GND CON 121.6    CLNC DEL 119.55
RADIO AIDS TO NAVIGATION: NOTAM FILE DAL.
    LOVE (L) VORW/DME 114.3    LUE    Chan 90    32°50'51"N 96°51'42"W    002° 7.4 NM to fld. 490/08E.
    BRONS NDB (LOM) 407    AD    33°02'40"N 96°52'13"W    153° 4.9 NM to fld.
    ILS/DME 110.1 I-ADS Chan 38 Rwy 15. LOM BRONS NDB. Unmonitored when tower closed.
    ILS 110.1 I-TBQ Rwy 33 LOC only. Unmonitored when twr clsd.

FIGURE 36.—Excerpt from Airport/Facility Directory.

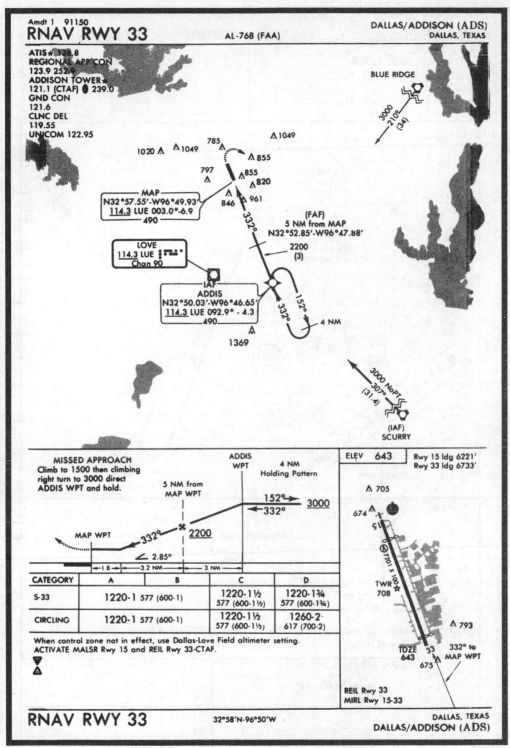

FIGURE 36A. — RNAV RWY 33 (ADS).

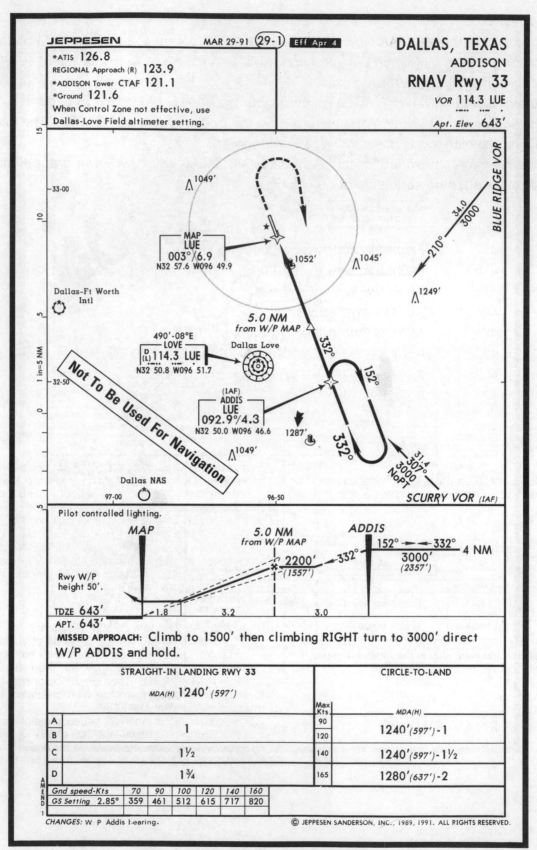

FIGURE 36B.— RNAV RWY 33 (ADS).

## 11.6  21XS to DFW

Questions 55 through 66 (FAA Nos. 4288 through 4299) (pages 413 through 416) pertain to an IFR flight from Big Spring McMahon-Wrinkle Airport, Big Spring, Texas to the Dallas-Ft. Worth International Airport, Dallas-Ft. Worth, Texas.

The route of flight is given in Block 8 on the flight plan portion of Fig. 38 on page 417. Information which pertains to your aircraft is given on the bottom portion of Fig. 38.  The partially completed flight planning log is given in Fig. 39 on page 418.

The following figures provided for this flight are listed below, which we have grouped and presented together after the sequence of questions.

| Fig. | Page | |
| --- | --- | --- |
| 38 | 417 | Flight Plan and Aircraft Information |
| 39 | 418 | Flight Log and Excerpt from Airport/Facility Directory (21XS) |
| 40 | 419 | En Route Chart Segment |
| 41 | 420 | ACTON Two Arrival |
| 41A | 421 | ACTON Two Arrival Description |
| 42 | 422 | ILS-1 RWY 36L, Dallas-Fort Worth Intl. (A/FD Excerpt) |
| 42A | 423 | ILS-1 RWY 36L (DFW) (NOS) |
| 42B | 424 | ILS-1 RWY 36L (DFW) (JEPP) |

### 11.6  21XS to DFW

**55.**
**4288.** (Refer to figure 38 on page 417.)  What aircraft equipment code should be entered in block 3 of the flight plan?

A— C.
B— R.
C— A.

Answer (B) is correct (4288).  *(AIM Para 5-7)*
In Block 3 of the flight plan, you enter the designation of the aircraft followed by a slash ( / ) and a letter for the equipment code.  Fig. 38 indicates there is a transponder with Mode C and RNAV.  Thus, you need Code R.  (See Legend 25 on page 358.)
Answer (A) is incorrect because C indicates RNAV and transponder, but with no Mode C.  Answer (C) is incorrect because A indicates DME and transponder with Mode C, but no RNAV.

**56.**
**4289.** (Refer to figure 38 on page 417.)  What CAS must be used to maintain the filed TAS at the flight planned altitude if the outside air temperature is +05 °C?

A— 129 KCAS.
B— 133 KCAS.
C— 139 KCAS.

Answer (A) is correct (4289).  *(Fl Comp)*
In the center of the slide rule side of your flight computer, on the right side, put the air temperature of +5°C over the altitude of 11,000 ft. (from Block 7 of the Flight Plan, Fig. 38).  Then on the outer scale find TAS of 156 (from Block 4), which is over calibrated airspeed on the inner scale of 129 KCAS.
Answer (B) is incorrect because maintaining 133 KCAS would result in a TAS of 161 kt. (not 156 kt.).  Answer (C) is incorrect because maintaining 139 KCAS would result in a TAS of 168 kt. (not 156 kt.).

**57.**
**4290.** (Refer to figures 38, 39, 40, and 41 on pages 417 through 420.)  (Refer to the FD excerpt below, and use the wind entry closest to the flight planned altitude.) Determine the time to be entered in block 10 of the flight plan.

Route of flight . . . . . . . . . . . . . . . Figures 38, 39, and 40
Flight log & MAG VAR . . . . . . . . . . . . . . . . . Figure 39
ACTON TWO ARRIVAL . . . . . . . . . . . . . . . Figure 41

| FT | 3000 | 6000 | 9000 | 12000 |
|----|------|------|------|-------|
| ABI | | 2033+13 | 2141+09 | 2142+05 |

A— 1 hour 24 minutes.
B— 1 hour 26 minutes.
C— 1 hour 31 minutes.

**Answer (C) is correct (4290).**  *(IFH Chap XIII)*
To determine the estimated time en route to be entered in Block 10, you must complete the flight planning log in Fig. 39.  Using the wind side of your flight computer, determine groundspeeds as shown in the table below.
Remember that winds are given in true direction and must be converted to magnetic.  Fig. 39 shows a variation of 11°E.  Using the wind at 12,000 ft. (which is closest to the planned altitude of 11,000 ft.):  210° – 11°E var. = 199° at 42 kt.

| | Distance | MC | Wind (Mag) | Ground-speed | Time |
|---|---|---|---|---|---|
| BGS VORTAC | X | X | X | X | :06:00G |
| LORAN INT | 42 | 075° | 199/42 | 176 | :14:19 |
| ABI VORTAC | 40 | 076° | 199/42 | 175 | :13:43 |
| COTTN INT | 63 | 087° | 199/42 | 167 | :22:38 |
| AQN VORTAC | 50 | 075° | 199/42 | 176 | :17:03 |
| CREEK INT | 32 | 040° | 199/42 | 194 | :09:54 |
| Approach and Landing | X | X | X | X | :08:00G |
| | | | | | 1:31:37 |

G = Given

Answer (A) is incorrect because the total time en route is 1 hr. 31 min. (not 1 hr. 24 min.).  Answer (B) is incorrect because the total time en route is 1 hr. 31 min. (not 1 hr. 26 min.).

**58.**
**4291.** (Refer to figure 40 on page 419.)  For planning purposes, what is the highest useable altitude for an IFR flight on V16 between the BGS and ABI VORTACs?

A— 17,000 feet MSL.
B— 18,000 feet MSL.
C— 6,500 feet MSL.

**Answer (A) is correct (4291).**  *(AIM Para 5-34)*
The VOR airway system consists of airways designated from 1,200 ft. AGL up to, but not including, 18,000 ft. MSL.
Answer (B) is incorrect because victor airways go up through 17,999 ft., but do not include 18,000 ft.
Answer (C) is incorrect because 6,500 ft. is the MRA at LORAN intersection.

**59.**
**4292.** (Refer to figures 41 and 41A on pages 420 and 421.)  At which point does the AQN.AQN2 arrival begin?

A— ABI VORTAC.
B— ACTON VORTAC.
C— CREEK intersection.

**Answer (B) is correct (4292).**  *(ACL)*
The arrival, in contrast to the transition, begins over the AQN VORTAC, as explained in the written description in Fig. 41A.
Answer (A) is incorrect because the ABI VORTAC is the beginning of the Abilene transition.  Answer (C) is incorrect because CREEK intersection is part (not the beginning) of the AQN.AQN8 arrival.

**60.**
**4293.** (Refer to figures 41 and 41A on pages 420 and 421.)  Which frequency would you anticipate using to contact Regional Approach Control?  (ACTON TWO ARRIVAL).

A— 119.05.
B— 124.15.
C— 125.8.

**Answer (C) is correct (4293).**  *(ACL)*
The upper left-hand corner of the STAR chart (Fig. 41) shows the pertinent frequencies to be used.  Since aircraft using this arrival are approaching from the west, the appropriate approach frequency is 125.8.
Answer (A) is incorrect because 119.05 is for aircraft approaching from an easterly direction.  Answer (B) is incorrect because 124.15 is the DFW tower (not approach control) frequency for aircraft approaching from the west.

Chapter 11: Comprehensive IFR Trip Review

415

**61.**
**4294.** (Refer to figures 41 and 41A on pages 420 and 421.) On which heading should you plan to depart CREEK intersection?

A— 010°.
B— 040°.
C— 350°.

Answer (C) is correct (4294). *(ACL)*
Presumably, you should assume that you are flying a jet aircraft since non-jet aircraft (such as the C-402 in this flight) do not fly to CREEK INT (refer to Fig. 41A). The turbojet arrival indicates that you should maintain a heading of 350° after CREEK. Non-turbojet aircraft will proceed from AQN VORTAC via AQN R-040 to CREEK INT and should expect radar vectors at BRYAR INT (i.e., before CREEK INT).
Answer (A) is incorrect because 010° is not an applicable heading in this STAR. Answer (B) is incorrect because 040° is the course from AQN to CREEK INT (not after CREEK INT).

**62.**
**4295.** (Refer to figures 41, 42, 42A, and 42B on pages 420, 422, 423, and 424.) Which frequency should you expect to use for Regional Approach Control, control tower, and ground control respectively at DFW?

A— 119.05; 126.55; 121.65.
B— 119.05; 124.15; 121.8.
C— 125.8; 124.15; 121.8.

Answer (C) is correct (4295). *(A/FD)*
Refer to the Communications section of the A/FD in Fig. 42. Since the ACTON two arrival approaches from the west, approach control uses 125.8 or 132.1, tower uses 124.15, and ground uses 121.65 or 121.8.
Answer (A) is incorrect because 119.05 is for approach control from the east (not west), and 126.55 is for tower from the east (not west). Answer (B) is incorrect because 119.05 is for approach control from the east (not west).

**63.**
**4296.** (Refer to figures 42A and 42B on pages 423 and 424.) Which navigational information and services would be available to the pilot when using the localizer frequency?

A— Localizer and glide slope, DME, TACAN with no voice capability.
B— Localizer information only, ATIS and DME are available.
C— Localizer and glide slope, DME, and no voice capability.

Answer (C) is correct (4296). *(ACL)*
On Figs. 42A and 42B, ILS RWY 36L is an ILS (localizer and glide slope). On the NOS chart a channel number indicates DME, while on the JEPP chart it states in the frequency box ILS DME. The line under the I-BXN frequency 111.9 (Fig. 42A) means no voice capability.
Answer (A) is incorrect because there is no TACAN indicated in Fig. 42A or 42B. TACAN is the military version of VOR/DME. Answer (B) is incorrect because it is an ILS approach with glide slope.

**64.**
**4297.** (Refer to figures 42, 42A and 42B on pages 422 through 424.) What is the difference in elevation (in feet MSL) between the airport elevation and the TDZE for RWY 36L?

A— 15 feet.
B— 18 feet.
C— 22 feet.

Answer (A) is correct (4297). *(ACL)*
The NOS chart (Fig. 42A) shows the airport elevation (603 ft.) in the upper left corner of the airport diagram, and the TDZE (588 ft.) to the left of the approach end of 36L. The Jeppesen chart (Fig. 42B) shows the airport elevation and the TDZE for RWY 36L in the profile view by the runway. The difference between the two is 603 − 588 = 15 ft.
Answer (B) is incorrect because 603 − 588 = 15 ft. (not 18 ft.). Answer (C) is incorrect because 22 ft. is the difference between airport elevation and the TDZE for 36R (not 36L).

**65.**
**4298.** (Refer to figures 42A and 42B on pages 423 and 424.) What rate of descent should you plan to use initially to establish the glidepath for the ILS RWY 36L approach? (Use 120 knots groundspeed.)

A— 425 feet per minute.
B— 530 feet per minute.
C— 635 feet per minute.

Answer (C) is correct (4298). *(ACL)*
    The profile view of the NOS chart (Fig. 42A) shows a glide slope angle of 3.00°. Legend 19 on page 251 gives rates of descent based on various glide slope angles and groundspeeds. Find the 3.0° on the left margin and move right to the 120-kt. groundspeed column to determine a rate of descent of 635 fpm.
    The JEPP chart (Fig. 42B) shows the required rate of descent in the FAF to MAP time table below the minimums section. At 120 kt., a rate of descent of 646 fpm is required.
    Answer (A) is incorrect because 425 fpm is the required rate of descent at 120-kt. groundspeed on a 2.0° (not 3.0°) glide slope. Answer (B) is incorrect because 530 fpm is the required rate of descent at 120-kt. groundspeed on a 2.5° (not 3.0°) glide slope.

**66.**
**4299.** (Refer to figures 42A and 42B on pages 423 and 424, and 43 below.) What is your position relative to CHARR intersection? The aircraft is level at 3,000 feet MSL.

A— Right of the localizer course approaching CHARR intersection and approaching the glide slope.
B— Left of the localizer course approaching CHARR intersection and below the glide slope.
C— Right of the localizer course, past CHARR intersection and above the glide slope.

Answer (A) is correct (4299). *(IFH Chap VIII)*
    NAV-1 (111.9) is on the I-BXN localizer indicating right of course because of the left deviation. Also, you are outside (approaching) CHARR intersection since the DME readout is 7.5 DME (CHARR is 7.2 DME). The glide slope is 3,000 ft. MSL at CHARR and thus you are beneath and approaching the glide slope. On NAV-2, the ADF frequency 233 does not appear on the approach chart. The VOR (114.3) is LOVE VOR, indicating R-230, and CHARR is R-233, which confirms you are south of CHARR position.
    Answer (B) is incorrect because the left localizer deviation means right, not left, of course. Answer (C) is incorrect because you are below, not above, the glide slope and have not passed CHARR intersection.

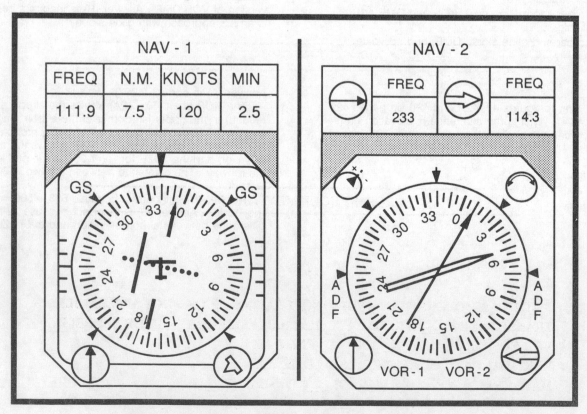

FIGURE 43.—CDI and RMI — NAV 1 and NAV 2.

Form Approved: OMB No.2120-0034

## FLIGHT PLAN

| U.S. DEPARTMENT OF TRANSPORTATION FEDERAL AVIATION ADMINISTRATION | (FAA USE ONLY) | ☐ PILOT BRIEFING | ☐ VNR | TIME STARTED | SPECIALIST INITIALS |
|---|---|---|---|---|---|
| **FLIGHT PLAN** | | ☐ STOPOVER | | | |

| 1 TYPE | 2 AIRCRAFT IDENTIFICATION | 3 AIRCRAFT TYPE/ SPECIAL EQUIPMENT | 4 TRUE AIRSPEED | 5 DEPARTURE POINT | 6 DEPARTURE TIME | | 7 CRUISING ALTITUDE |
|---|---|---|---|---|---|---|---|
| VFR | | | | | PROPOSED (Z) | ACTUAL (Z) | |
| X IFR DVFR | N4321P | C402/ | 156 | BGS | | | 110 |

8 ROUTE OF FLIGHT

DIRECT BGS, V16 ABI, ABI.AQN2

| 9 DESTINATION (Name of airport and city) | 10 EST TIME ENROUTE | | 11 REMARKS |
|---|---|---|---|
| DALLAS FT. WORTH DFW | HOURS | MINUTES | |

| 12 FUEL ON BOARD | | 13 ALTERNATE AIRPORT(S) | 14 PILOTS NAME, ADDRESS & TELEPHONE NUMBER & AIRCRAFT HOME BASE | 15 NUMBER ABOARD |
|---|---|---|---|---|
| HOURS | MINUTES | N/A | 17 DESTINATION CONTACT/TELEPHONE (OPTIONAL) | 2 |

| 16 COLOR OF AIRCRAFT | CIVIL AIRCRAFT PILOTS. FAR Part 91 requires you file an IFR flight plan to operate under instrument flight rules in controlled airspace. Failure to file could result in a civil penalty not to exceed $1,000 for each violation (Section 901 of the Federal Aviation Act of 1958. as amended; Filing of a VFR flight plan is recommended as a good operating practice. See also Part 99 for requirements concerning DVFR flight plans. |
|---|---|
| RED/BLUE/WHITE | |

FAA Form 7233-1 (8-82)　　CLOSE VFR FLIGHT PLAN WITH _____ FSS ON ARRIVAL

---

## AIRCRAFT INFORMATION

MAKE  Cessna　　　　　MODEL  402C

N 4321P　　　　　　　Vso 71

---

## AIRCRAFT EQUIPMENT/STATUS**

**NOTE:  X= OPERATIVE  INOP= INOPERATIVE　  N/A= NOT APPLICABLE

TRANSPONDER: X (MODE C ) X  ILS: (LOCALIZER) X (GLIDE SLOPE) X

VOR NO.1 X (NO 2) X  ADF: X  RNAV: X

VERTICAL PATH COMPUTER:  NA  DME: X

MARKER BEACON: X (AUDIO) X (VISUAL) X

FIGURE 38.—Flight Plan and Aircraft Information.

# FLIGHT LOG

### BIG SPRING McMAHON-WRINKLE TO DALLAS FT. WORTH (DFW)

| CHECK POINTS | | ROUTE | | WIND | SPEED-KTS | | DIST | TIME | | FUEL | |
|---|---|---|---|---|---|---|---|---|---|---|---|
| FROM | TO | ALTITUDE | COURSE | TEMP | TAS | GS | NM | LEG | TOT | LEG | TOT |
| 21XS | BGS | DIRECT CLIMB | DIRECT | | | | | :06:0 | | | |
| | LORAN | V16 11,000 | 075° | | | | | | | | |
| | ABI | V16 11,000 | 076° | | 156 | | | | | | |
| | COTTN | DIRECT 11,000 | 087° | | | | | | | | |
| | AQN | AQN2 | 075° | | | | | | | | |
| | CREEK | AQN2 | 040° | | | | | | | | |
| APPROACH & LANDING | | RADAR VEC- | | | | | | :08:0 | | | |
| | DFW AIRPORT | DESCENT | | | | | | | | | |
| | | | | | | | | | | | |
| | | | | | | | | | | | |

**OTHER DATA:**
   NOTE:   MAG. VAR. 11° E.
          (STAR) ACTON TWO ARRIVAL (AQN2)

**FLIGHT SUMMARY**

| TIME | FUEL (LB) | |
|---|---|---|
| | | EN ROUTE |
| | | RESERVE |
| | | MISSED APPR. |
| | | TOTAL |

**BIG SPRING McMAHON-WRINKLE**     (21XS) 2SW UTC-6(-5DT).         DALLAS-FT. WORTH
   32°12'45"N101°31'17"W                                            H-21, 5A, L-13A, 15B
   2572 B S4FUEL 100LL, JET A                                       IAP
   RWY 17-35: H8803X100 (ASPH-CONC) S-44, D-62, DDT-101 MIRL
   RWY 17:SSALS.PVASI(ASPH)-GA3.0°TCH 41'.
   RWY 06-24:H4600X75(ASPH) MIRL
   RWY 24:PVASI(PSIL)-GA3.55°TCH31'. P-line.
   AIRPORT REMARKS: Attended 1400-2300Z  . For fuel after hours call 915-263-3958. ACTIVATE MIRL Rwy 06-24
      and Rwy 17-35, SSALS Rwy 17 and PVASI Rwy 17 and 24-CTAF.
   COMMUNICATIONS:CTAF/UNICOM 122.8
      SAN ANGELOSFSS (SJT) TF 1-800-WX-BRIEF. NOTAM FILE SJT.
      RCO 122.4(SAN ANGELOFSS)
      FORT WORTH CENTER APP/DEP CON 133.7
   RADIO AIDS TO NAVIGATION: NOTAM FILE SJT.
      (L) VORTACW 144.3 BGS Chan 90 32°23'08"N 101°10.5NM to fld. 2670/11E.

**EXCERPT FROM AIRPORT/FACILITY DIRECTORY (21 XS)**

FIGURE 39.—Flight Log and Excerpt from Airport/Facility Directory (21 XS).

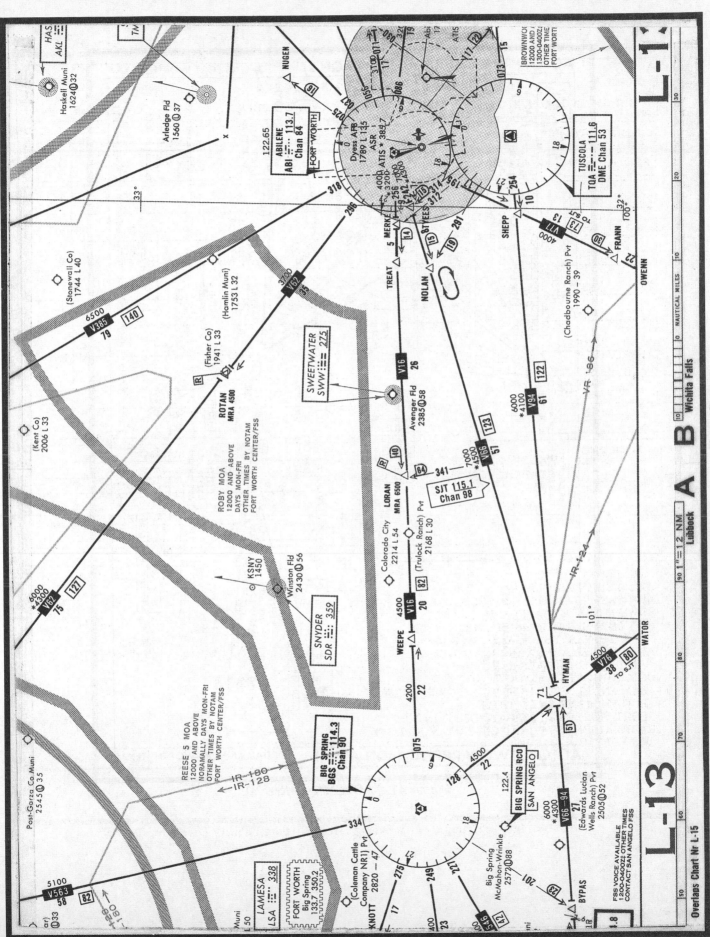

FIGURE 40.—En Route Chart Segment.

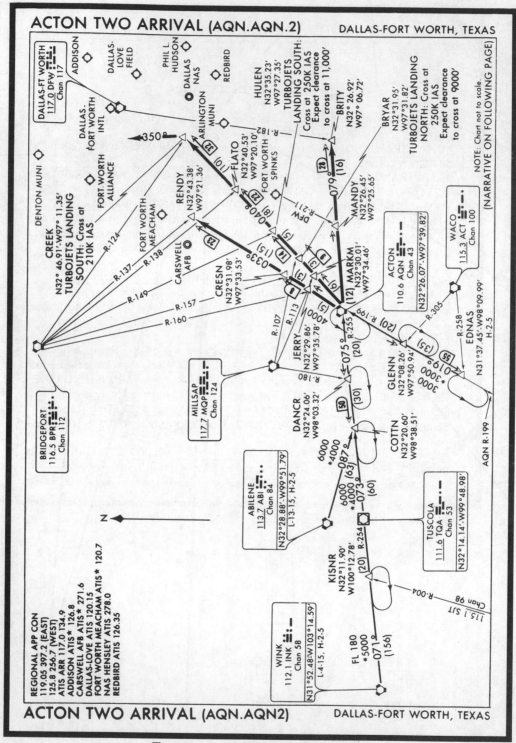

FIGURE 41.—ACTON Two Arrival.

## ACTON TWO ARRIVAL (AQN.AQN2)          DALLAS-FORT WORTH, TEXAS

### ARRIVAL DESCRIPTION

ABILENE TRANSITION (ABI.AQN2): From over ABI VORTAC via ABI R-087 and AQN R-255 to AQN VORTAC. Thence . . . .

EDNAS TRANSITION (EDNAS.AQN2): From over EDNAS INT via AQN R-199 to AQN VORTAC. Thence . . . .

WINK TRANSITION (INK.AQN2): From over INK VORTAC via INK R-071, TQA R-254, TQA R-073 and AQN R-255 to AQN VORTAC. Thence . . . .

TURBOJETS LANDING DALLAS-FT. WORTH INTL, MEACHAM, CARSWELL AFB, DENTON, ALLIANCE: (Landing South): From over AQN VORTAC via AQN R-040 to CREEK INT, thence heading 350° for vector to final approach course. (Landing North): From over AQN VORTAC via AQN R-040 to CREEK INT. Expect vectors at BRYAR INT.

NON-TURBOJETS LANDING DALLAS-FT. WORTH INTL, MEACHAM, CARSWELL AFB, DENTON, ALLIANCE: (Landing South): From over AQN VORTAC via AQN R-033 to RENDY INT. Expect vectors to final approach course. (Landing North): From over AQN VORTAC via AQN R-040 to CREEK INT. Expect vector at BRYAR INT.

TURBOJETS LANDING DALLAS-LOVE FIELD and ADDISON: (Landing South): From over AQN VORTAC via AQN R-040 to CREEK INT, thence heading 350° for vector to final approach course. (Landing North): From over AQN VORTAC via AQN R-079 to BRITY INT. Expect vector to final approach course.

NON-TURBOJETS LANDING DALLAS-LOVE FIELD and ADDISON: (Landing South/North): From over AQN VORTAC via AQN R-079 to BRITY INT. Expect vector to final approach course.

ALL AIRCRAFT LANDING FORT WORTH SPINKS, ARLINGTON, NAS DALLAS, REDBIRD, and PHIL L. HUDSON: (Landing South/North): From over AQN VORTAC via AQN R-079 to BRITY INT. Expect vectors to final approach course.

FIGURE 41A.—ACTON Two Arrival Description.

## TEXAS

- - - - - - - - - - - - - - - - - - - - - - - - - - - - - - - - - - - - - - - - - - - -

**DALLAS-FORT WORTH INTL**   (DFW)   12 NW   UTC-6(-5DT)32°53′47″N 97°02′28″W       `DALLAS-FT. WORTH
603   B   FUEL   100LL, JET A   OX 1, 3   LRA   ARFF Index E                       H-2K, 4F, 5B, L-13C, A
RWY 17L-35R: H11,388X150 (CONC-GRVD)   S-120, D-200, DT-600, DDT-850   HIRL CL          IAP
 RWY 17L: ALSF2. TDZ.      RWY 35R: MALSR. TDZ.
RWY 17R-35L: H11,388X200 (CONC-GRVD)   S-120, D-200, DT-600, DDT-850   HIRL CL
 RWY 17R: MALSR. TDZ.      RWY 35L: TDZ. VASI(V6L).
RWY 18R-36L: H11,388X150(CONC-GRVD)   S-120, D-200, DT-600, DDT-850   HIRL CL
 RWY 18R: ALSF2. TDZ      RWY 36L: MALSR. TDZ
RWY 18L-36R: H11,387X200 (CONC-GRVD)   S-120, D-200, DT-600, DDT-850   HIRL CL
 RWY 18L: MALSR. TDZ.      RWY 36R: TDZ. VASI(V6L).
RWY 13R-31L: H9300X150(CONC-GRVD)   S-120, D-220, DT-600, DDT-850   HIRL CL
 RWY 13R: MALSR. TDZ.      RWY 31L: TDZ.
RWY 13L-31R: H9000X200 (CONC-GRVD)   S-120, D-200, DT-600, DDT-850   HIRL CL   0.5% up NW
 RWY 13L: TDZ. VASI(V6L)—Upper GA 3.25° TCH 93′. Lower GA 3.0° TCH 47′.       RWY 31R: MALSR. TDZ.
RWY 18S-36S: H4000X100 (CONC)
**AIRPORT REMARKS:** Attended continuously. Rwy 18S–36S CLOSED indefinitely. Arpt under construction, men and
   equipment in movement areas. Partial outages of arpt lgt circuits will occur daily. Prior Permission Required from
   arpt ops for General Aviation acft to proceed to airline terminal gate except to General Aviation Facility. Rwy
   18S-36S located on taxiway G, 4000′ long 100′ wide restricted to prop acft 12,500 lbs. & below and stol acft
   daylight VFR plus IFR departures. Prior permission required from the primary tenant airlines to operate within
   central terminal area, CAUTION: proper minimum clearance may not be maintained within the central terminal
   area. Landing fee. Helipad H1 on apt 104X104 (CONC) Heliport located at Twy G and Twy 24 intersection,
   daylight VFR. Clearways 500X1000 each end Rwy 17L–35R, Rwy 17R–35L, Rwy 18L–36R and Rwy 18R–36L.
   Flight Notification Service (ADCUS) available.
**WEATHER DATA SOURCES:** LLWAS.
**COMMUNICATIONS:** ATIS 117.0 134.9 (ARR) 135.5 (DEP)   **UNICOM** 122.95
   FORT WORTH FSS (FTW) LC 429–6434, TF 1–800–WX–BRIEF. NOTAM FILE DFW
Ⓡ **REGIONAL APP CON** 119.05(E) 119.4(E) 125.8(W) 132.1(W)
   **REGIONAL TOWER** 126.55 (E) 124.15 (W)   **GND CON** 121.65 133.15(E) 121.8 (W)   **CLNC DEL** 128.25 127.5
Ⓡ **REGIONAL DEP CON** 118.55 (E) 124.25 (WEST) 127.75 (NORTH–SOUTH)
   **TCA:** See VFR Terminal Area chart.
**RADIO AIDS TO NAVIGATION:** NOTAM FILE DFW.
   **(H) VORTACW** 117.0   DFW   Chan 117   32°51′57″N 97°01′40″W   at fld. 560/08E.
      VOR Portion unusable 045°-050° all altitudes and distances, 350–100° beyond 30 NM below 2100′.
   **ISSUE NDB (LOM)** 233   PK   32°47′35″N 97°01′49″W   348° 6.2 NM to fld.
   **JIFFY NDB (LOM)** 219   FL   32°59′44″N 97°01′46″W   179° 6.0 NM to fld.
   **ILS/DME** 109.5 I-LWN Chan 32 Rwy 13R.
   **ILS/DME** 109.1 I-FLQ Chan 28 Rwy 17L. LOM JIFFY NDB.
   **ILS** 111.5 I-JHZ Rwy 17R. LOM JIFFY NDB.
   **ILS** 111.3 I-CIX Rwy 18L.
   **ILS/DME** 111.9 I-VYN Chan 56 Rwy 18R.
   **ILS** 110.9 I-RRA Rwy 31R.
   **ILS/DME** 109.1 I-PKQ Chan 28 Rwy 35R. LOM ISSUE NDB.
   **ILS/DME** 111.9 I-BXN Chan 56 Rwy 36L.

FIGURE 42.—ILS-1 RWY 36L, Dallas-Fort Worth Intl.

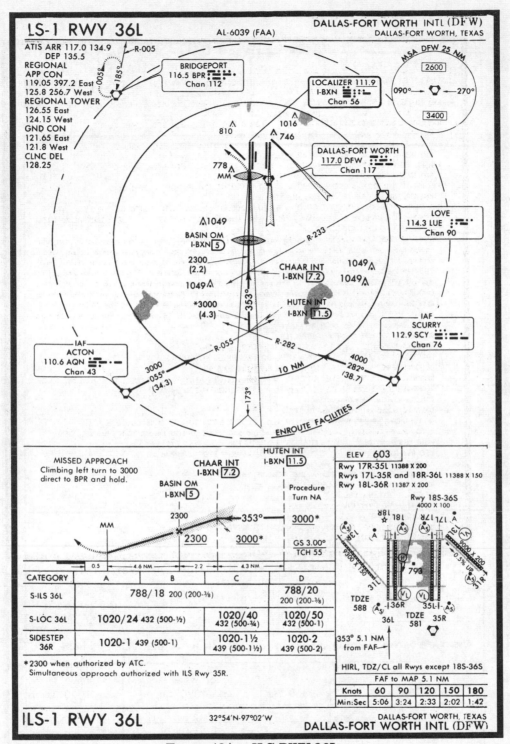

FIGURE 42A.—ILS RWY 36L.

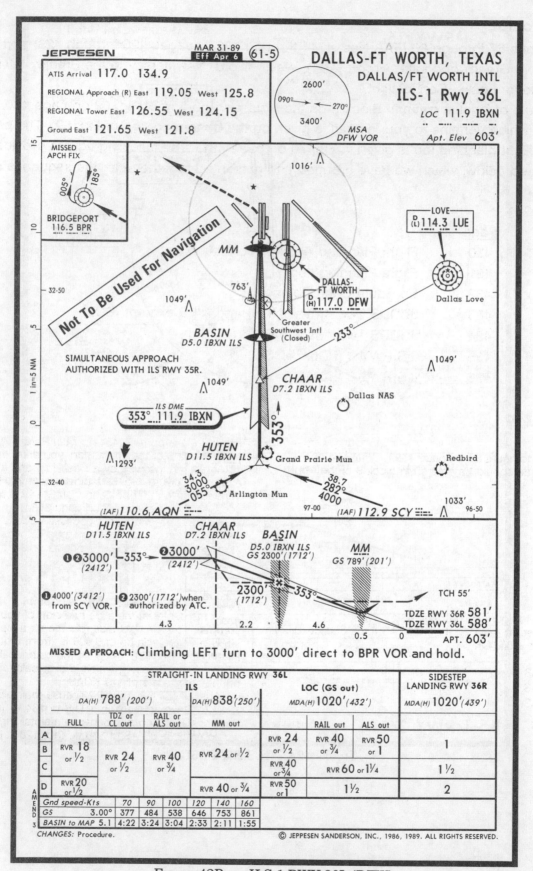

FIGURE 42B. — ILS-1 RWY 36L (DFW).

## 11.7  4N1 to BDL

Questions 67 through 80 (FAA Nos. 4344 through 4357) (pages 425 through 429) pertain to an IFR flight from Greenwood Lake Airport (4N1), West Milford, New Jersey to the Bradley International Airport, Windsor Locks, Connecticut.

The route of flight is given in Block 8 on the flight plan portion of Fig. 69 on page 430. Information which pertains to your aircraft is given on the bottom portion of Fig. 69. The partially completed flight planning log is given in Fig. 70 on page 431. The following figures provided for this flight are listed below, which we have grouped and presented together after the sequence of questions.

## 11.7  4N1 to BDL

**67.**
**4344.** (Refer to figure 69 on page 430.) What aircraft equipment code should be entered in block 3 of the flight plan?

A— A.
B— B.
C— U.

Answer (A) is correct (4344). *(AIM Para 5-7)*
In Block 3 of the Flight Plan, you enter the designation of the aircraft followed by a slash ( / ) and a letter for the equipment code. Fig. 69 indicates that you have a transponder with Mode C and DME, which requires code A. (See Legend 25 on page 358.)
Answer (B) is incorrect because code B indicates DME and transponder but no Mode C. Answer (C) is incorrect because code U indicates only a transponder with Mode C.

**68.**
**4345.** (Refer to figure 69 on page 430.) What CAS should be used to maintain the filed TAS if the outside air temperature is +05 °C?

A— 119 KCAS.
B— 124 KCAS.
C— 126 KCAS.

Answer (A) is correct (4345). *(FI Comp)*
In the center of the slide rule side of your flight computer, on the right side, put the air temperature of +5°C over the altitude of 5,000 ft. (from Block 7 of the Flight Plan, Fig. 69). Then on the outer scale find TAS of 128 kt. (from Block 4), which is over calibrated airspeed on the inner scale of 119 KCAS.
Answer (B) is incorrect because maintaining 124 KCAS would result in a TAS of 134 kt. (not 128 kt.). Answer (C) is incorrect because maintaining 126 KCAS would result in a TAS of 136 kt. (not 128 kt.).

**69.**
**4346.** (Refer to figures 69, 70, 71, 72, and 72A on pages 430 through 434.) Determine the time to be entered in block 10 of the flight plan. (Refer to the FD excerpt below, and use the wind entry closest to the flight planned altitude.)

Route of flight . . . . . . . . . . . . . . . Figures 69, 70, and 71
Flight log and MAG VAR . . . . . . . . . . . . . . . Figure 70
JUDDS TWO ARRIVAL
   and Excerpt from AFD . . . . . . . . Figures 72 and 72A

| FT | 3000 | 6000 | 9000 |
|----|------|------|------|
| BDL | 3320 | 3425+05 | 3430+00 |

A— 1 hour 14 minutes.
B— 57 minutes.
C— 50 minutes.

Answer (B) is the best answer (4346). *(IFH Chap XIII)*
   To determine the estimated time en route to be entered in Block 10, you must complete the flight planning log in Fig. 70. Using the wind side of your flight computer, determine groundspeeds as shown in the table below. The arrow in Fig. 71 points to the departure airport.
   Remember that winds are given in true direction, and must be converted to magnetic. Fig. 70 shows a variation of 14°W. Using the wind at 6,000 ft. (which is closest to the planned altitude of 5,000 ft.): 340° + 14°W var. = 354° at 25 kt.

| | Distance | MC | Wind (Mag) | Ground-speed | Time |
|---|---|---|---|---|---|
| SHAFF INT | X | X | X | X | :08:00G |
| HELON INT | 24 | 029° | 354/25 | 106 | :13:35 |
| IGN VORTAC | 21 | 102° | 354/25 | 133 | :09:28 |
| VOR COP | 15 | 112° | 354/25 | 138 | :06:31 |
| JUDDS INT | 17 | 100° | 354/25 | 132 | :07:44 |
| BRISS INT | 6 | 057° | 354/25 | 115 | :03:08 |
| Approach and Landing | X | X | X | X | :12:00G |
| | | | | | 1:00:26 |

G = Given

Note: The FAA may change answer (A) to 1 hr. on the computer test, which would be correct.
   Answer (A) is incorrect because the total time en route is 1 hr., not 1 hr. 14 min. Answer (C) is incorrect because the total time en route is 1 hr., not 50 min.

**70.**
**4347.** (Refer to figures 71 and 71A on pages 432 and 427.) What is your position relative to the V213 airway?

A— Left of the SAX R-034 and approaching the IGN R-268.
B— Right of the SAX R-214 and approaching the IGN R-088
C— Left of the SAX R-029 and past the IGN R-268.

Answer (A) is correct (4347). *(IFH Chap VII)*
   VOR-1 is tuned to IGN VORTAC (117.6) with an OBS setting of 268°. The FROM indication and right needle deflection indicates you are south of the IGN R-268 and thus approaching it (assuming you are flying northeast per the flight plan). VOR-2 is tuned to SAX VORTAC (115.7) with an OBS setting of 034°. The FROM indication and right needle deflection indicates you are to the left of the SAX R-034. Note, however, that SAX R-034 does not define V213.
   Answer (B) is incorrect because a TO (not FROM) indication and a left (not right) needle deflection in VOR-2 would indicate right of the SAX R-214. Also, a TO (not FROM) indication in VOR-1 would indicate approaching the IGN R-088. Answer (C) is incorrect because the half-scale needle deflection in VOR-2 indicates you are 5° to 6° north of R-034, i.e., on (not left of) R-029. Also, the right needle deflection in VOR-1 indicates you are approaching (not past) the IGN R-268.

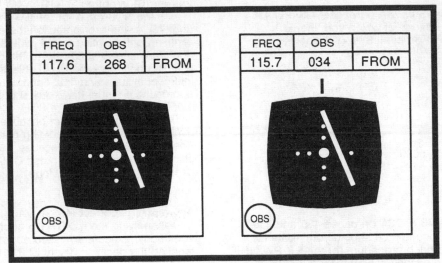

| FREQ | OBS | |
|---|---|---|
| 117.6 | 268 | FROM |

| FREQ | OBS | |
|---|---|---|
| 115.7 | 034 | FROM |

FIGURE 71A.—CDI and OBS Indicators.

**71.**
**4348.** (Refer to figures 70 and 71 on pages 431 and 432.) Which VORTAC navigational facility along the proposed route of flight could provide you with TWEB information?

A— SPARTA VORTAC.
B— HUGUENOT VORTAC.
C— KINGSTON VORTAC.

Answer (C) is correct (4348). *(ACL)*
The Kingston VORTAC (IGN) Identification Box contains a small square in the lower right-hand corner indicating TWEB information.
Answer (A) is incorrect because the Sparta (SAX) VORTAC has no small, dark square. Answer (B) is incorrect because the Huguenot VORTAC Identification Box is not shown.

**72.**
**4349.** (Refer to figure 72 or 72A on pages 433 and 434.) At which location or condition does the IGN.JUDDS2 arrival begin?

A— JUDDS intersection.
B— IGN VORTAC.
C— BRISS intersection.

Answer (B) is correct (4349). *(ACL)*
The IGN.JUDDS2 arrival on Fig. 72 or 72A indicates "from over Kingston VORTAC via R-112 ...." Thus, the JUDDS2 arrival begins over the Kingston (IGN) VORTAC.
Answer (A) is incorrect because the JUDDS INT is in the middle of the arrival route. Answer (C) is incorrect because the BRISS INT is in the middle of the arrival route.

**73.**
**4350.** (Refer to figure 72 on page 433.) How many precision approach procedures are published for Bradley International Airport?

A— One.
B— Three.
C— Four.

Answer (B) is correct (4350). *(A/FD)*
To determine the number of precision approaches at Bradley International Airport, check the appropriate Airport/Facility Directory, which is reproduced in Fig. 72. At the end of the A/FD, note ILS/DMEs for RWY 6, RWY 33, and RWY 24.
Answer (A) is incorrect because there are three (not one) ILSs. Answer (C) is incorrect because there are three (not four) ILSs.

**74.**
**4351.** (Refer to figure 73 or 73A on pages 435 and 436.) What is the minimum altitude at which you should intercept the glide slope on the ILS RWY 6 approach procedure?

A— 3,000 feet MSL.
B— 1,800 feet MSL.
C— 1,690 feet MSL.

Answer (B) is correct (4351). *(ACL)*
On the NOS chart for the ILS RWY 6 approach (Fig. 73), in the profile section there is an <u>1800</u> with a lightning bolt pointing to the glide slope. The JEPP chart (Fig. 73A) shows 1800 next to the glide slope with no lightning bolt. In either case, this is the glide slope intercept altitude and final approach fix for precision approaches. Thus, here, one should not intercept below 1,800 ft. MSL.
Answer (A) is incorrect because 3,000 ft. MSL is the minimum altitude in the holding pattern at PENNA INT. Answer (C) is incorrect because 1,690 ft. MSL is the altitude at which you will cross CHUPP LOM when descending on the glide slope.

**75.**
**4352.** (Refer to figure 73 or 73A on pages 435 and 436.) At which indication or occurrence should you initiate the published missed approach procedure for the ILS RWY 6 approach provided the runway environment is not in sight?

A— When reaching 374 feet MSL indicated altitude.
B— When 3 minutes (at 90 knots groundspeed) have expired or reaching 374 feet MSL, whichever occurs first.
C— Upon reaching 374 feet AGL.

Answer (A) is correct (4352). *(ACL)*
When flying the ILS RWY 6 approach (Fig. 73 or 73A), you should execute a missed approach when you have reached the decision height of 374 ft. MSL.
Answer (B) is incorrect because the ILS is a precision approach and timing is only for the backup localizer approach. Answer (C) is incorrect because the decision height is 374 ft. MSL (not AGL).

**76.**
**4353.** (Refer to figure 73 or 73A on pages 435 and 436.) Which sequence of marker beacon indicator lights, and their respective codes, will you receive on the ILS RWY 6 approach procedure to the MAP?

A— Blue – alternate dots and dashes; amber – dashes.
B— Amber – alternate dots and dashes; blue – dashes.
C— Blue – dashes; amber – alternate dots and dashes.

Answer (C) is correct (4353). *(AIM Para 1-10)*
The outer marker is identified with continuous dashes at the rate of two dashes per sec. and a blue marker beacon light. The middle marker is identified with alternate dots and dashes keyed at the rate of 95 dot/dash combinations per min. and an amber marker beacon light. Note that the inner marker, which is identified with continuous dots at the rate of six dots per sec. and a white marker beacon light, is crossed after (not before) the MAP.
Answer (A) is incorrect because the outer marker has dashes (not dots and dashes), and the middle marker has dots and dashes (not just dashes). Answer (B) is incorrect because the outer marker is blue with dashes and the middle marker is amber with dots and dashes (not vice versa).

**77.**
**4354.** (Refer to figure 73 or 73A on pages 435 and 436.) Using an average groundspeed of 90 knots on the final approach segment, what rate of descent should be used initially to establish the glidepath for the ILS RWY 6 approach procedure?

A— 395 feet per minute.
B— 480 feet per minute.
C— 555 feet per minute.

Answer (B) is correct (4354). *(ACL)*
The profile view of the NOS chart (Fig. 73) shows a glide slope angle of 3.00°. Legend 19 on page 251 gives rates of descent based on various glide slope angles and groundspeeds. Find the 3.0° angle of descent on the left margin and move right to the 90-kt. groundspeed column to determine a rate of descent of 480 fpm.
The JEPP chart (Fig. 73A) shows the required rate of descent in the FAF to MAP time table below the minimums section. At 90 kt., a rate of descent of 484 fpm is required.
Answer (A) is incorrect because 395 fpm is the required rate of descent at a groundspeed of 75 kt., not 90 kt. Answer (C) is incorrect because 555 fpm is the required rate of descent at a groundspeed of 105 kt., not 90 kt.

**78.**
**4355.** (Refer to figure 73 or 73A on pages 435 and 436.) What is the touchdown zone elevation for RWY 6?

A— 174 feet MSL.
B— 200 feet AGL.
C— 270 feet MSL.

**Answer (A) is correct (4355).** *(ACL)*
The NOS chart (Fig. 73) shows the TDZE in the airport diagram near the approach end of the landing runway. The JEPP chart shows the TDZE in the profile view next to the runway. The TDZE is 174 ft. MSL.
Answer (B) is incorrect because 200 ft. AGL is the HAT (Height Above Touchdown) at the DH on the ILS. Answer (C) is incorrect because 270 ft. MSL is the height of an obstruction near the approach end of RWY 6.

**79.**
**4356.** (Refer to figure 73 or 73A on pages 435 and 436.) After passing the OM, Bradley Approach Control advises you that the MM on the ILS RWY 6 approach is inoperative. Under these circumstances, what adjustments, if any, are required to be made to the DH and visibility?

A— DH 424/24.
B— No adjustments are required.
C— DH 374/24.

**Answer (B) is correct (4356).** *(ACL)*
Refer to Legend 20 on page 252, Inoperative Components or Visual Aids Table. Since the MM is not listed in the table, no adjustments are required.
Note that the JEPP chart (Fig. 73A) has a column for an inoperative MM. This is because the date of the chart is August 17, 1990 and the FAA removed the MM from the Inoperative Component Table on October 15, 1992.
Answer (A) is incorrect because there are no adjustments required due to an inoperative MM. Answer (C) is incorrect because there are no adjustments required due to an inoperative MM.

**80.**
**4357.** (Refer to figure 73 or 73A on pages 435 and 436.) Which runway and landing environment lighting is available for approach and landing on RWY 6 at Bradley International?

A— HIRL, REIL, and VASI.
B— HIRL and VASI.
C— ALSF2 and HIRL.

**Answer (C) is correct (4357).** *(ACL)*
The airport diagram in Fig. 73 has a circle enclosing the letter "A" with a dot above it, near the approach end of RWY 6. Legend 21 on page 253 indicates this means ALSF-2 approach lighting. At the bottom left corner of the airport diagram (Fig. 73), it indicates that RWY 6-24 has high intensity runway lights (HIRL).
Answer (A) is incorrect because REIL and VASI are not indicated for RWY 6. Answer (B) is incorrect because VASI is not indicated for RWY 6.

Form Approved: OMB No.2120-0034

| U.S. DEPARTMENT OF TRANSPORTATION FEDERAL AVIATION ADMINISTRATION **FLIGHT PLAN** | (FAA USE ONLY)  ☐PILOT BRIEFING   ☐VNR  ☐ STOPOVER | | TIME STARTED | SPECIALIST INITIALS |
|---|---|---|---|---|

| 1 TYPE | 2 AIRCRAFT IDENTIFICATION | 3 AIRCRAFT TYPE/ SPECIAL EQUIPMENT | 4 TRUE AIRSPEED | 5 DEPARTURE POINT | 6 DEPARTURE TIME | | 7 CRUISING ALTITUDE |
|---|---|---|---|---|---|---|---|
| VFR | | | | | PROPOSED (Z) | ACTUAL (Z) | |
| X IFR DVFR | N2142S | C172/ | 128 | GREENWOOD LAKE 4N1 | | | 5000 |

**8** ROUTE OF FLIGHT

DIRECT SHAFF INT., V213 HELON INT., V58 JUDDS INT., JUDDS2

| 9 DESTINATION (Name of airport and city) BRADLEY INTL. BDL | 10 EST TIME ENROUTE | | 11 REMARKS |
|---|---|---|---|
| | HOURS | MINUTES | |
| | | | INSTURMENT TRAINING FLIGHT |

| 12 FUEL ON BOARD | | 13 ALTERNATE AIRPORT(S) | 14 PILOTS NAME, ADDRESS & TELEPHONE NUMBER & AIRCRAFT HOME BASE | 15 NUMBER ABOARD |
|---|---|---|---|---|
| HOURS | MINUTES | | | |
| | | N/A | 17 DESTINATION CONTACT/TELEPHONE (OPTIONAL) | 2 |

| 16 COLOR OF AIRCRAFT BROWN/TAN/WHITE | CIVIL AIRCRAFT PILOTS. FAR Part 91 requires you file an IFR flight plan to operate under instrument flight rules in controlled airspace. Failure to file could result in a civil penalty not to exceed $1,000 for each violation (Section 901 of the Federal Aviation Act of 1958. as amended; Filing of a VFR flight plan is recommended as a good operating practice. See also Part 99 for requirements concerning DVFR flight plans. |
|---|---|

FAA Form 7233-1 (8-82)      CLOSE VFR FLIGHT PLAN WITH _____ FSS ON ARRIVAL

---

### AIRCRAFT INFORMATION

MAKE Cessna            MODEL  172

N 2142S                Vso 33

---

### AIRCRAFT EQUIPMENT/STATUS**

**NOTE:  X= OPERATIVE   INOP= INOPERATIVE     N/A= NOT APPLICABLE
TRANSPONDER: _X_ (MODE C ) _X_ ILS: (LOCALIZER) _X_  (GLIDE SLOPE) _X_
VOR NO.1 _X_ (NO 2) _X_ ADF: _X_ RNAV: _NA_
VERTICAL PATH COMPUTER:  NA   DME: _X_
MARKER BEACON: _X_ (AUDIO) Inop. (VISUAL) _X_

FIGURE 69.—Flight Plan and Aircraft Information.

# FLIGHT LOG

GREENWOOD LAKE (4N1) TO BRADLEY INTL. (BDL)

| CHECK POINTS | | ROUTE | | WIND | SPEED-KTS | | DIST | TIME | | FUEL | |
|---|---|---|---|---|---|---|---|---|---|---|---|
| FROM | TO | ALTITUDE | COURSE | TEMP | TAS | GS | NM | LEG | TOT | LEG | TOT |
| 4N1 | SHAFF | DIRECT CLIMB | 350° | | | | | :08:0 | | | |
| | HELON | V213 5000 | 029° | | 128 | | | | | | |
| | IGN | V58 5000 | 102° | | | | | | | | |
| | | JUDDS2 | 112° | | | | | | | | |
| | JUDDS | JUDDS2 | 100° | | | | | | | | |
| | BRISS | JUDDS2 | 057° | | | | | | | | |
| APPROACH & LANDING | BDL INTL | | | | | | | :12:0 | | | |
| | | | | | | | | | | | |

OTHER DATA:
  NOTE:  MAG. VAR. 14° W.

| FLIGHT SUMMARY | | |
|---|---|---|
| TIME | FUEL (LB) | |
| | | EN ROUTE |
| | | RESERVE |
| | | MISSED APPR. |
| | | TOTAL |

FIGURE 70.—Flight Planning Log.

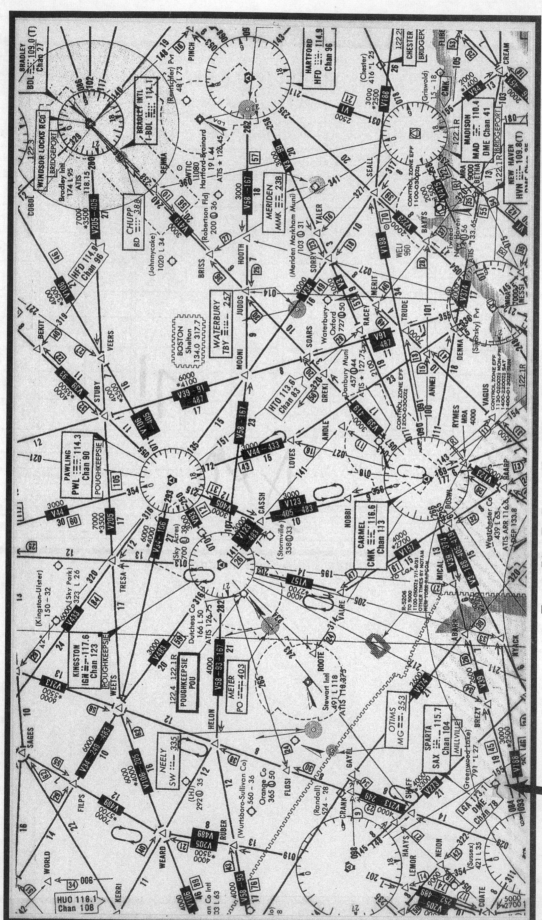

FIGURE 71.—En Route Chart Segment.

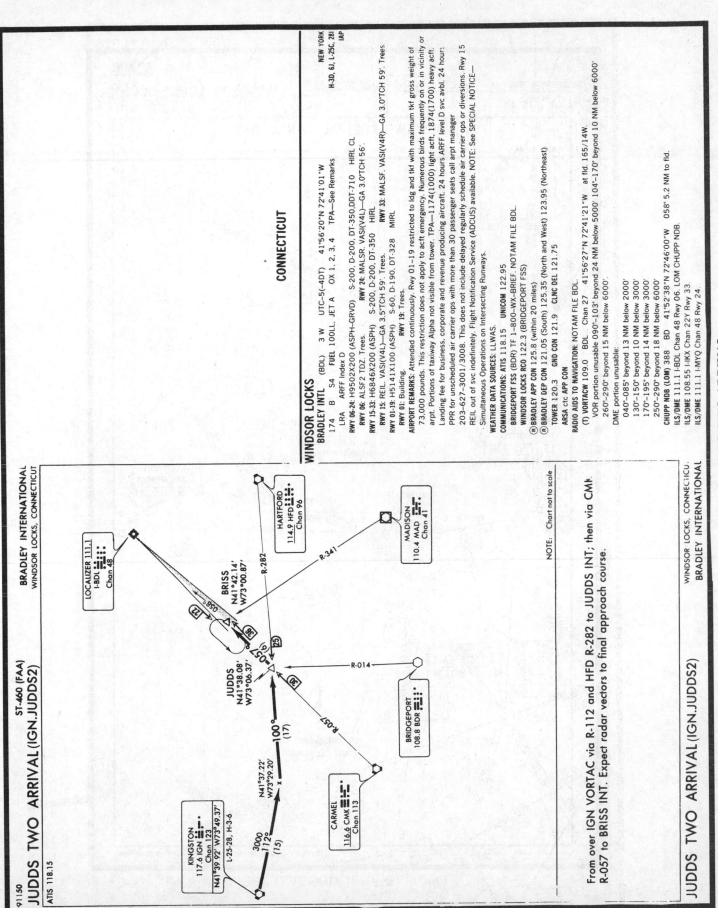

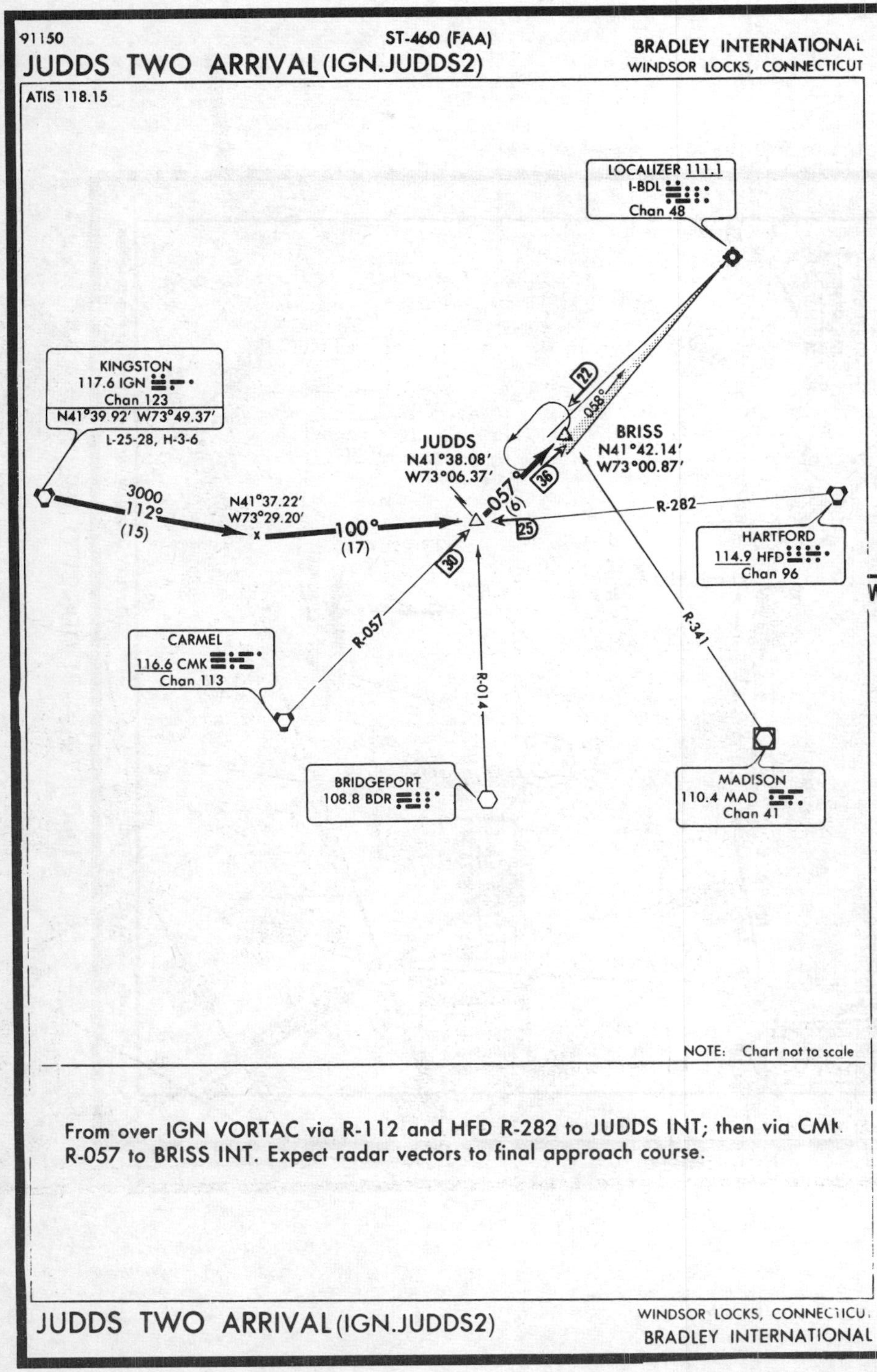
91150
ST-460 (FAA)
JUDDS TWO ARRIVAL (IGN.JUDDS2)
BRADLEY INTERNATIONAL
WINDSOR LOCKS, CONNECTICUT
ATIS 118.15
LOCALIZER 111.1
I-BDL
Chan 48
KINGSTON
117.6 IGN
Chan 123
N41°39.92′ W73°49.37′
L-25-28, H-3-6
3000
112°
(15)
N41°37.22′
W73°29.20′
100°
(17)
JUDDS
N41°38.08′
W73°06.37′
057°
(6)
BRISS
N41°42.14′
W73°00.87′
058°
R-282
HARTFORD
114.9 HFD
Chan 96
CARMEL
116.6 CMK
Chan 113
R-057
R-014
R-341
BRIDGEPORT
108.8 BDR
MADISON
110.4 MAD
Chan 41
NOTE: Chart not to scale
From over IGN VORTAC via R-112 and HFD R-282 to JUDDS INT; then via CMK R-057 to BRISS INT. Expect radar vectors to final approach course.
JUDDS TWO ARRIVAL (IGN.JUDDS2)
WINDSOR LOCKS, CONNECTICUT
BRADLEY INTERNATIONAL

## CONNECTICUT

### WINDSOR LOCKS

**BRADLEY INTL** (BDL) 3 W UTC–5(–4DT) 41°56′20″N 72°41′01″W **NEW YORK**
174 B S4 **FUEL** 100LL, JET A OX 1, 2, 3, 4 TPA—See Remarks **H-3D, 6J, L-25C, 28I**
LRA ARFF Index D **IAP**

**RWY 06-24:** H9502X200 (ASPH–GRVD) S-200, D-200, DT-350,DDT-710 HIRL CL
**RWY 06:** ALSF2 TDZ. Trees. **RWY 24:** MALSR. VASI(V4L)—GA 3.0°TCH 56′.
**RWY 15-33:** H6846X200 (ASPH) S-200, D-200, DT-350 HIRL
**RWY 15:** REIL. VASI(V4L)—GA 3.5°TCH 59′. Trees. **RWY 33:** MALSF. VASI(V4R)—GA 3.0°TCH 59′. Trees.
**RWY 01-19:** H5141X100 (ASPH) S-60, D-190, DT-328 MIRL
**RWY 01:** Building. **RWY 19:** Trees.

**AIRPORT REMARKS:** Attended continuously. Rwy 01–19 restricted to ldg and tkf with maximum tkf gross weight of 73,000 pounds. This restriction does not apply to acft emergency. Numerous birds frequently on or in vicinity or arpt. Portions of taxiway Alpha not visible from tower. TPA—1174(1000) light acft, 1874(1700) heavy acft. Landing fee for business, corporate and revenue producing aircraft. 24 hours ARFF level D svc avbl. 24 hours PPR for unscheduled air carrier ops with more than 30 passenger seats call arpt manager 203–627–3001/3008. This does not include delayed regularly schedule air carrier ops or diversions. Rwy 15 REIL out of svc indefinitely. Flight Notification Service (ADCUS) available. NOTE: See SPECIAL NOTICE—Simultaneous Operations on Intersecting Runways.

**WEATHER DATA SOURCES:** LLWAS.

**COMMUNICATIONS: ATIS** 118.15 **UNICOM** 122.95
**BRIDGEPORT FSS** (BDR) TF 1–800–WX–BRIEF. NOTAM FILE BDL.
**WINDSOR LOCKS RCO** 122.3 (BRIDGEPORT FSS)
Ⓡ **BRADLEY APP CON** 125.8 (within 20 miles)
Ⓡ **BRADLEY DEP CON** 121.05 (South) 125.35 (North and West) 123.95 (Northeast)
**TOWER** 120.3 **GND CON** 121.9 **CLNC DEL** 121.75
**ARSA** ctc **APP CON**

**RADIO AIDS TO NAVIGATION:** NOTAM FILE BDL.
(T) **VORTACW** 109.0 BDL Chan 27 41°56′27″N 72°41′21″W at fld. 165/14W.
VOR portion unusable 090°–103° beyond 24 NM below 5000′ 104°–170° beyond 10 NM below 6000′ 260°–290° beyond 15 NM below 6000′.
DME portion unusable:
040°–085° beyond 13 NM below 2000′
130°–150° beyond 10 NM below 3000′
170°–195° beyond 14 NM below 3000′
250°–290° beyond 18 NM below 6000′
**CHUPP NDB (LOM)** 388 BD 41°52′38″N 72°46′00″W 058° 5.2 NM to fld.
**ILS/DME** 111.1 I-BDL Chan 48 Rwy 06. LOM CHUPP NDB.
**ILS/DME** 108.55 I-IKX Chan 22Y Rwy 33.
**ILS/DME** 111.1 I-MYQ Chan 48 Rwy 24.

FIGURE 72.— JUDDS TWO ARRIVAL.

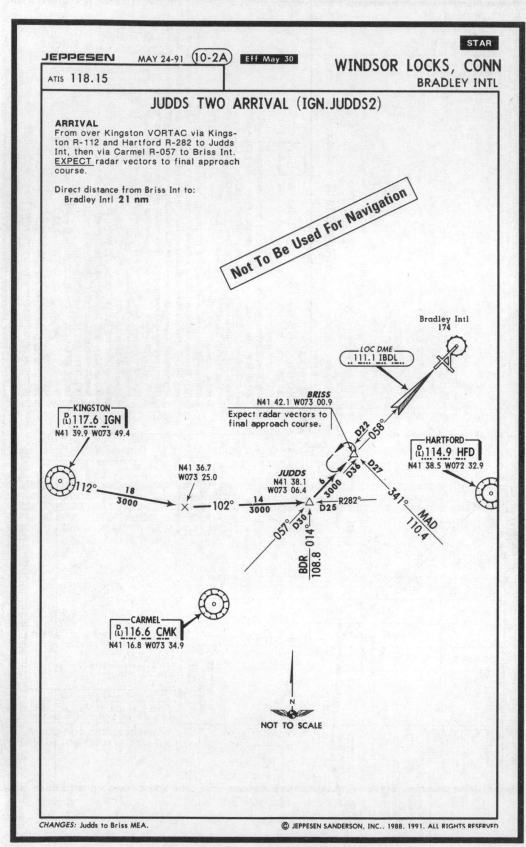

## JUDDS TWO ARRIVAL (IGN.JUDDS2)

**ARRIVAL**
From over Kingston VORTAC via Kingston R-112 and Hartford R-282 to Judds Int, then via Carmel R-057 to Briss Int. EXPECT radar vectors to final approach course.

Direct distance from Briss Int to:
  Bradley Intl **21 nm**

*Not To Be Used For Navigation*

Bradley Intl
174

LOC DME
..-- ---- .. 111.1 IBDL

BRISS
N41 42.1 W073 00.9
Expect radar vectors to
final approach course.

D22
058°

KINGSTON
D(L) 117.6 IGN
N41 39.9 W073 49.4

HARTFORD
D(L) 114.9 HFD
N41 38.5 W072 32.9

N41 36.7
W073 25.0

JUDDS
N41 38.1
W073 06.4

D36   D27
D25   R282°

112°   18   102°   14
3000         3000

6
3000

341°
MAD
110.4

057°  D30
014°

BDR
108.8

CARMEL
D(L) 116.6 CMK
N41 16.8 W073 34.9

N

NOT TO SCALE

FIGURE 72A.— JUDDS TWO ARRIVAL.

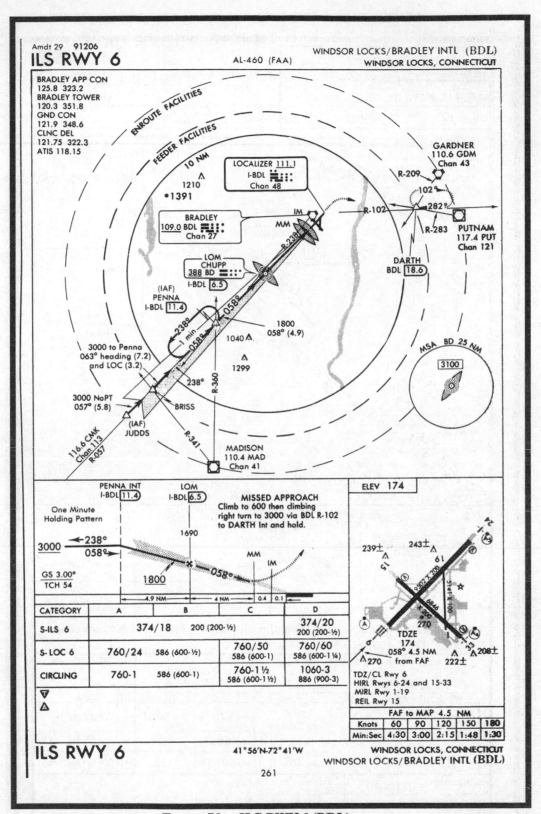

FIGURE 73.—ILS RWY 6 (BDL).

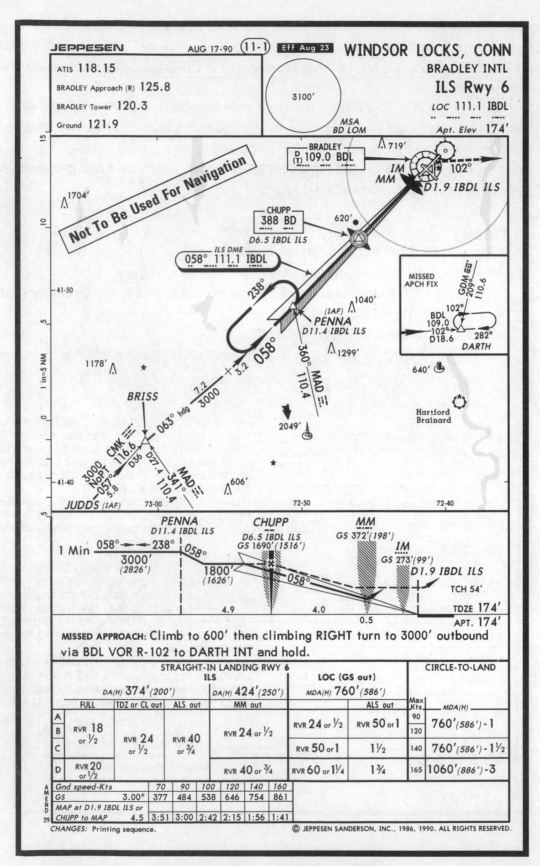

FIGURE 73A.—ILS RWY 6 (BDL).

## 11.8  HLN to BIL

Questions 81 through 94 (FAA Nos. 4358 through 4371) (pages 437 through 440) pertain to an IFR flight from Helena Regional Airport, Helena, Montana to the Billings Logan International Airport, Billings, Montana.

The route of flight is given in Block 8 on the flight plan portion of Fig. 74 on page 441. Information which pertains to your aircraft is given on the bottom portion of Fig. 74.  The partially completed flight planning log is given in Fig. 75 on page 442.

The following figures provided for this flight are listed below, which we have grouped and presented together after the sequence of questions.

| Fig. | Page | |
|------|------|---|
| 74 | 441 | Flight Plan and Aircraft Information |
| 75 | 442 | Flight Planning Log |
| 76 | 443 | VOR Indications and Excerpts from Airport/Facility Directory (HLN) |
| 77 | 444 | STAKK Two Departure |
| 78 | 445 | En Route Chart Segment |
| 80 | 446 | VOR/DME RWY 27R and Airport/Facility Directory (BIL) |

## 11.8  HLN to BIL

**81.**
**4358.** (Refer to figure 74 on page 441.)  What aircraft equipment code should be entered in block 3 of the flight plan?

A— T.
B— U.
C— A.

Answer (C) is correct (4358).  *(AIM Para 5-7)*
In Block 3 of the flight plan you enter the designation of the aircraft followed by a slash ( / ) and a letter for the equipment code.  Fig. 74 indicates that you have a DME and transponder with Mode C, which requires code A. (See Legend 25 on page 358.)
Answer (A) is incorrect because T indicates only a transponder with no Mode C.  Answer (B) is incorrect because U indicates only a transponder with Mode C.

**82.**
**4359.** (Refer to figure 74 on page 441.)  What CAS should be used to maintain the filed TAS at the flight planned altitude if the outside air temperature is +5 °C?

A— 129 KCAS.
B— 133 KCAS.
C— 139 KCAS.

Answer (B) is correct (4359).  *(Fl Comp)*
In the center of the slide rule side of your flight computer, on the right side, put the air temperature of +5°C over the altitude of 11,000 ft. (from Block 7 of the Flight Plan, Fig. 74).  On the outer scale find TAS of 160 (from Block 4), which is over calibrated airspeed on the inner scale of 133 KCAS.
Answer (A) is incorrect because maintaining 129 KCAS would result in a TAS of 156 kt. (not 133 kt.). Answer (C) is incorrect because maintaining 139 KCAS would result in a TAS of 168 kt. (not 133 kt.).

**83.**
**4360.** (Refer to figures 74, 75, 76, 77, and 78 on pages 441 through 445.) Determine the time to be entered in block 10 of the flight plan. (Refer to the FD excerpt below, and use the wind entry closest to the flight planned altitude.)

Route of flight . . . . . . . . . Figures 74, 75, 76, 77, and 78
Flight log & MAG VAR . . . . . . . . . . . . . . . . . . Figure 75
VOR indications
    and Excerpts from AFD . . . . . . . . . . . . . . Figure 76

| FT | 6000 | 9000 | 12000 | 18000 |
|---|---|---|---|---|
| BIL | 2414 | 2422+11 | 2324+05 | 2126−11 |

A— 1 hour 15 minutes.
B— 1 hour 20 minutes.
C— 1 hour 25 minutes.

Answer (C) is correct (4360). *(IFH Chap XIII)*
    To determine the estimated time en route to be entered in Block 10, you must complete the flight planning log in Fig. 75. Using the wind side of your flight computer, determine groundspeeds as shown in the table below.
    Remember that winds are given in true direction, and must be converted to magnetic. Fig. 75 shows a variation of 18°E. Using the wind at 12,000 ft. (which is closest to the planned altitude of 11,000 ft.): 230° − 18°E var. = 212° at 24 kt.

| | Distance | MC | Wind (Mag) | Ground-speed | Time |
|---|---|---|---|---|---|
| VESTS INT | X | X | X | X | :15:00G |
| BZN VOR/DME | 44 | 140° | 212/24 | 151 | :17:29 |
| VOR COP | | | | | |
| VORTAC | 13 | 110° | 212/24 | 163 | :04:47 |
| LVM VORTAC | 20 | 063° | 212/24 | 180 | :06:40 |
| REEPO INT | 39 | 067° | 212/24 | 179 | :13:04 |
| BIL VORTAC | 38 | 069° | 212/24 | 178 | :12:49 |
| Approach and | | | | | |
| Landing | X | X | X | X | :15:00G |
| | | | | | 1:24:49 |

G = Given

Answer (A) is incorrect because an ETE of 1 hr. 15 min. assumes a faster TAS or a greater tailwind. Answer (B) is incorrect because an ETE of 1 hr. 20 min. assumes a faster TAS or a greater tailwind.

**84.**
**4361.** (Refer to figure 77 on page 444.) At which point does the basic SID terminate?

A— When Helena Departure Control establishes radar contact.
B— At STAKK intersection.
C— Over the BOZEMAN VOR.

Answer (B) is correct (4361). *(ACL)*
    On the STAKK Two Departure in Fig. 77, the departure route description at the bottom indicates that for takeoffs from RWY 9 and RWY 27 one climbs eastbound on HLN R-087 to cross STAKK INT at or above 10,200 ft. "Thence via transition."
    Answer (A) is incorrect because Helena Departure Control will establish contact shortly after you get off the runway. Answer (C) is incorrect because the BOZEMAN VOR is the end of the BOZEMAN transition (not the basic SID).

**85.**
**4362.** (Refer to figure 76 on page 443.) Which indication would be an acceptable accuracy check of both VOR receivers when the airplane is located on the VOR receiver checkpoint at the Helena Regional Airport?

A— A.
B— B.
C— C.

Answer (C) is correct (4362). *(ACL)*
    To determine the VOR receiver check point at the Helena Regional Airport, consult the VOR receiver check table on Fig. 76. The checkpoint is on TWY (taxiway) E midway between TWY C and RWY 27, and is on R-237 of Helena VORTAC. Thus, the RMI should show the tails of both needles on 237°, ± 4°.
    Answer (A) is incorrect because R-180 ±4° would be the expected indication when using a VOT (not a ground VOR checkpoint). Answer (B) is incorrect because the tail (not the head) of the RMI needle indicates the radial.

**86.**

**4363.** (Refer to figure 77 on page 444.) At which minimum altitude should you cross the STAKK intersection?

A— 6,500 feet MSL.
B— 1,400 feet MSL.
C— 10,200 feet MSL.

**87.**

**4364.** (Refer to figure 77 on page 444.) Using an average groundspeed of 140 knots, what minimum rate of climb would meet the required minimum climb rate per NM as specified on the SID?

A— 350 feet per minute.
B— 475 feet per minute.
C— 700 feet per minute.

**88.**

**4365.** (Refer to figures 76 and 78 on pages 443 and 445.) Which en route low altitude navigation chart would cover the proposed routing at the BOZEMAN VORTAC?

A—L-2.
B—L-7.
C—L-9.

**89.**

**4366.** (Refer to figure 78 on page 445.) What is the maximum altitude that you may flight plan an IFR flight on V-86 EASTBOUND between BOZEMAN and BILLINGS VORTACs?

A— 14,500 feet MSL.
B— 17,000 feet MSL.
C— 18,000 feet MSL.

**90.**

**4370.** (Refer to figure 78 on page 445.) What is the minimum crossing altitude over the BOZEMAN VORTAC for a flight southeast bound on V86?

A— 8,500 feet MSL.
B— 9,300 feet MSL.
C— 9,700 feet MSL.

Answer (C) is correct (4363). *(ACL)*
On the STAKK Two Departure (Fig. 77), the departure route description for either runway states, "Cross STAKK at or above 10,200'." Thus, the minimum altitude you should cross the STAKK INT is 10,200 ft. MSL.
Answer (A) is incorrect because 6,500 ft. MSL is not a pertinent altitude in this SID. Answer (B) is incorrect because 1,400 ft. MSL is not a pertinent altitude in this SID.

Answer (C) is correct (4364). *(ACL)*
On Fig. 77 on the SID the note to the left indicates a minimum climb rate of 300 ft. per NM. To convert this to a climb rate (fpm), use Legend 18 on page 258. Find the required climb rate of 300 ft. per NM on the left margin and move right to the 140-kt. groundspeed column to determine a rate of climb of 700 fpm.
Answer (A) is incorrect because 350 fpm would require an average groundspeed of 70 kt. (not 140 kt.). Answer (B) is incorrect because 475 fpm would require an average groundspeed of 95 kt. (not 140 kt.).

Answer (C) is correct (4365). *(ACL)*
On Fig. 77 (not 76 and 78 as indicated in the question), Bozeman VOR/DME is in the planview in the lower right corner. Below the frequency box, the notation L-9 is the number of the appropriate en route low altitude navigation chart.
Answer (A) is incorrect because Bozeman VOR/DME is found on L-9 (not L-2). Answer (B) is incorrect because Bozeman VOR/DME is found on L-9 (not L-7).

Answer (B) is correct (4366). *(ACL)*
Victor airways consist of altitudes from 1,200 ft. AGL up to but not including 18,000 ft. MSL. The jet route is from 18,000 ft. MSL through FL 450. Thus, the maximum altitude on an airway is 17,000 ft. MSL, because IFR flight is conducted at cardinal altitudes, odd numbers for eastbound and even for westbound.
Answer (A) is incorrect because 14,500 ft. MSL (i.e., thousand-foot plus 500 ft.) is a VFR (not IFR) cruising altitude. Answer (C) is incorrect because Victor airways extend up to, but not including, 18,000 ft. MSL. Jet routes begin at 18,000 ft. MSL (FL 180).

Answer (B) is correct (4370). *(ACL)*
On Fig. 78, the Bozeman (BZN) VOR/DME (it is not a VORTAC) has a flag with an X, indicating a minimum crossing altitude (MCA). Near the center of the page, above the BZN VOR/DME Communications Box, is MCA V86-365 9300 SE. Thus, the minimum crossing altitude over the BZN VOR/DME for a flight southeast bound on V86 is 9,300 ft. MSL.
Answer (A) is incorrect because 8,500 ft. MSL is the MEA on V86 prior to BZN VOR/DME. The MEA is not the MCA when an MCA is specified. Answer (C) is incorrect because 9,700 ft. MSL is the MEA on V365 (not the MCA at BZN VOR/DME).

**91.**
**4367.** (Refer to figure 78 on page 445 and 79 below.) What is your position relative to the VOR COP on V86 between the BOZEMAN and LIVINGSTON VORTACs? The No. 1 VOR is tuned to 116.1 and the No. 2 VOR is tuned to 112.2.

A— Past the LVM R-243 and right of the BZN R-110.
B— Approaching the LVM R-243 and right of the BZN R-110.
C— Past the LVM R-243 and left of the BZN R-110.

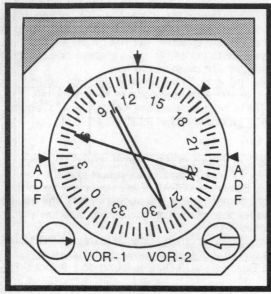

FIGURE 79.—RMI Indicator.

**92.**
**4371.** (Refer to figure 80 on page 446.) What is the TDZE for landing on RWY 27R?

A— 3,649 feet MSL.
B— 3,514 feet MSL.
C— 3,450 feet MSL.

**93.**
**4368.** (Refer to figures 74 and 80 on pages 441 and 446.) Which aircraft approach category should be used for a circling approach for a landing on RWY 25?

A— A.
B— B.
C— C.

**94.**
**4369.** (Refer to figure 80 on page 446.) How many initial approach fixes serve the VOR/DME RWY 27R (Billings Logan) approach procedure?

A— Three.
B— Four.
C— Five.

Answer (C) is correct (4367). (IFH Chap VII)
The tail of an RMI indicates the radial. You are on a 130° heading, so you are southeast bound. VOR-2 indicates R-105 of BZN (112.2). VOR-1 indicates on R-239 of LVM (116.1). Because you are on R-105 of BZN, you are to the left of BZN R-110. Because you are on R-239 of LVM, you have passed the LVM R-243.
Answer (A) is incorrect because you are left (not right) of the BZN R-110. Answer (B) is incorrect because you are past (not approaching) the LVM R-243, and left (not right) of the BZN R-110.

Answer (B) is correct (4371). (ACL)
Fig. 80 (an NOS chart) shows the TDZE in the airport diagram near the approach end of the landing runway as 3,514 ft. MSL.
Answer (A) is incorrect because 3,649 ft. MSL is the airport elevation (not the TDZE). Answer (C) is incorrect because 3,450 ft. MSL is not a relevant altitude at an airport with a 3,649 ft. MSL elevation.

Answer (B) is correct (4368). (ACL)
Approach categories are based upon 1.3 $V_{S0}$ and weight. Fig. 74 indicates $V_{S0}$ of the Cessna 310 is 72. Using the rule of thumb, 1.3 $V_{S0}$ is 93.6, which is Category B (91 to 120 kt.).
Answer (A) is incorrect because Category A is for approach speeds less than 91 kt. Answer (C) is incorrect because Category C is for approach speeds from 121 to 140 kt.

Answer (B) is correct (4369). (ACL)
Initial approach fixes are indicated by the designation "(IAF)" on instrument approach charts (Fig. 80). Note that there is an IAF at the 16 DME arc at R-157 INT and also at the R-040 INT. The Billings VORTAC is also indicated as an IAF, as is MUSTY INT.
Answer (A) is incorrect because the VOR/DME RWY 27R approach has 4 (not 3) IAFs. Answer (C) is incorrect because the VOR/DME RWY 27R approach has 4 (not 5) IAFs.

Form Approved: OMB No. 2120-0034

| U.S. DEPARTMENT OF TRANSPORTATION FEDERAL AVIATION ADMINISTRATION **FLIGHT PLAN** | (FAA USE ONLY) | ☐ PILOT BRIEFING ☐ STOPOVER | ☐ VNR | TIME STARTED | SPECIALIST INITIALS |
|---|---|---|---|---|---|

| 1. TYPE | 2. AIRCRAFT IDENTIFICATION | 3. AIRCRAFT TYPE/ SPECIAL EQUIPMENT | 4. TRUE AIRSPEED | 5. DEPARTURE POINT | 6. DEPARTURE TIME | | 7. CRUISING ALTITUDE |
|---|---|---|---|---|---|---|---|
| | | | | | PROPOSED (Z) | ACTUAL (Z) | |
| VFR | | | | | | | |
| X IFR | N242T | C310/ | 160 KTS | HLN | | | 11000 |
| DVFR | | | | | | | |

**8. ROUTE OF FLIGHT**

STAKK2, V365 BZN, V86

| 9. DESTINATION (Name of airport and city) | 10. EST. TIME ENROUTE | | 11. REMARKS |
|---|---|---|---|
| | HOURS | MINUTES | |
| LOGAN INTL. AIRPORT (BIL) | | | |

| 12. FUEL ON BOARD | | 13. ALTERNATE AIRPORT(S) | 14. PILOT'S NAME, ADDRESS & TELEPHONE NUMBER & AIRCRAFT HOME BASE | 15. NUMBER ABOARD |
|---|---|---|---|---|
| HOURS | MINUTES | | | |
| | | | 17. DESTINATION CONTACT/TELEPHONE (OPTIONAL) | 2 |
| | | N/A | | |

| 16. COLOR OF AIRCRAFT | CIVIL AIRCRAFT PILOTS. FAR Part 91 requires you file an IFR flight plan to operate under instrument flight rules in controlled airspace. Failure to file could result in a civil penalty not to exceed $1,000 for each violation (Section 901 of the Federal Aviation Act of 1958, as amended). Filing of a VFR flight plan is recommended as a good operating practice. See also Part 99 for requirements concerning DVFR flight plans. |
|---|---|
| RED/BLACK/WHITE | |

FAA Form 7233-1 (8-82)          CLOSE VFR FLIGHT PLAN WITH _____ FSS ON ARRIVAL

---

### AIRCRAFT INFORMATION

MAKE   Cessna            MODEL   310R

N 242T                   Vso 72

---

### AIRCRAFT EQUIPMENT/STATUS**

**NOTE: X= OPERATIVE   INOP= INOPERATIVE   N/A= NOT APPLICABLE
TRANSPONDER: X (MODE C) X ILS: (LOCALIZER) X (GLIDE SLOPE) INOP
VOR NO. 1 X (NO. 2) X ADF: X RNAV: N/A
VERTICAL PATH COMPUTER: N/A DME: X
MARKER BEACON: X (AUDIO) X (VISUAL) X

FIGURE 74.—Flight Plan and Aircraft Information.

# FLIGHT LOG
### HELENA REGIONAL AIRPORT TO BILLINGS LOGAN INTL.

| CHECK POINTS | | ROUTE | COURSE | WIND | SPEED-KTS | | DIST | TIME | | FUEL | |
|---|---|---|---|---|---|---|---|---|---|---|---|
| FROM | TO | ALTITUDE | | TEMP | TAS | GS | NM | LEG | TOT. | LEG | TOT |
| HLN | VESTS | STAKK2 CLIMB | 103° | | | | | :15:0 | | | |
| | BZN | V365 11000 | 140° | | 160 | | | | | | |
| | LVM | V86 11000 | 110° / 063° | | | | | | | | |
| | REEPO | V86 11000 | 067° | | | | | | | | |
| | BIL | V86 | 069° | | | | | | | | |
| APPROACH & LANDING | | | | | | | | :15:0 | | | |
| | LOGAN INTL | | | | | | | | | | |
| | | | | | | | | | | | |
| | | | | | | | | | | | |

**OTHER DATA:**
**NOTE:** MAG. VAR. 18° E.

**FLIGHT SUMMARY**

| TIME | FUEL (LB) | |
|---|---|---|
| | | EN ROUTE |
| | | RESERVE |
| | | MISSED APPR. |
| | | TOTAL |

FIGURE 75.—Flight Planning Log.

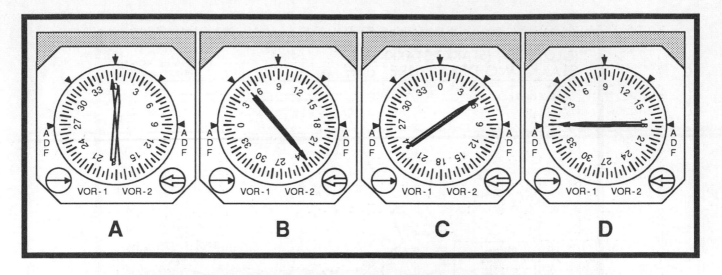

HELENA REGIONAL    (HLN)   2 NE   UTC–7(–6DT)   46°36'25"N 111°58'55"W          GREAT FALLS
  3873   B   S4   FUEL 100LL, JET A   OX 1,3   AOE   ARFF Index B                H-1C, L-9B
  RWY 09-27: H9000X150 (ASPH-PFC)   S-100, D-160, DT-250   HIRL                          IAP
    RWY 09: VASI(V4L)—GA 3.0°TCH 45'. Ground.        RWY 27: MALSR. VASI(V4L)—GA 3.0°TCH 55'. Rgt tfc.
  RWY 05-23: H4599X75 (ASPH-PFC)   S-21, D-30
    RWY 05: Road.        RWY 23: Fence. Rgt tfc.
  RWY 16-34: H2979X75 (ASPH)   S-21, D-30   MIRL
    RWY 34: Ground. Rgt tfc.
  AIRPORT REMARKS: Attended 1200-0800Z‡. East 2400' Taxiway C and first 900' Rwy 27 not visible from tower.
    Prior permission for unscheduled FAR 121 operations, Call 406-442-2821. AOE, 1 hour prior notice required,
    phone 449–1569 1500–0000Z‡; 0000–1500Z‡ 449–1024. Twys A;B; high speed and C (between A and D)
    not available for air carrier use by acft with greater than 30 passenger seats. Rwy 16–34 and Rwy 05–23 (except
    between Rwy 09–27 and Twy D) not available for air carrier use by acft with greater than 30 passenger seats.
    When tower closed, ACTIVATE HIRL Rwy 09–27 and MALSR Rwy 27—CTAF, when twr closed MIRL Rwy 16–34
    are off. Ldg fee for all acft over 12,500 lbs. NOTE: See SPECIAL NOTICE—Simultaneous Operations on
    Intersecting Runways.
  COMMUNICATIONS: CTAF 118.3        ATIS 120.4 (Mon-Fri 1300–0700Z‡, Sat-Sun 1300–0500Z‡)
    UNICOM 122.95
    GREAT FALLS FSS (GTF) TF 1-800-WX-BRIEF. NOTAM FILE HLN.
    RCO 122.2 122.1R 117.7T (GREAT FALLS FSS)
    APP/DEP CON 119.5 (Mon–Fri 1300–0700Z‡, Sat-Sun 1300–0500Z‡)
    SALT LAKE CENTER APP/DEP CON 133.4 (Mon–Fri 0700–1300Z‡, Sat-Sun 0500–1300Z‡)
    TOWER 118.3 (Mon–Fri 1300–0700Z‡, Sat–Sun 1300–0500Z‡)   GND CON 121.9
  RADIO AIDS TO NAVIGATION: NOTAM FILE HLN.
    (H) VORTAC 117.7   HLN   Chan 124   46°36'25"N 111°57'10"W   254° 1.2 NM to fld. 3810/16E.
      VORTAC unusable:
        006°-090° beyond 25 NM below 11,000'            091°-120° beyond 20 NM below 16,000'
        121°-240° beyond 25 NM below 10,000'            355°-006° beyond 15 NM below 17,500'
        241°-320° beyond 25 NM below 10,000'
    CAPITOL NDB (HW) 317   CVP   46°36'24"N 111°56'11"W   254° 1.9 NM to fld.
      NDB unmonitored when tower closed.
    HAUSER NDB (MHW) 386   HAU   46°34'08"N 111°45'26"W   268° 9.6 NM to fld.
    ILS 110.1 I-HLN Rwy 27 ILS unmonitored when tower closed.

## VOR RECEIVER CHECK

| Facility Name (Arpt Name) | Freq/Ident | Type Check Pt. Gnd. AB/ALT | Azimuth from Fac. Mag | Dist. from Fac. N.M. | Check Point Description |
|---|---|---|---|---|---|
| Helena (Helena Regional) | 117.7/HLN | G | 237 | 0.7 | On Twy E midway between Twy C and Rwy 27. |
| Kalispell (Glacier Park Intl) | 108.4/FCA | A/4000 | 316 | 6.4 | Over apch end Rwy 29. |
| Lewistown (Lewistown Muni) | 112.0/LWT | A/5200 | 072 | 5.4 | Over apch end Rwy 07. |
| Livingston | 116.1/LVM | A/6500 | 234 | 5.5 | Over northern most radio twr NE of city. |
| Miles City (Frank Wiley Field) | 112.1/MLS | G | 036 | 4.2 | On twy leading to Rwy 30. |
| Missoula (Missoula Intl) | 112.8/MSO | G | 340 | 0.6 | On edge of ramp in front of Admin Building. |

FIGURE 76.— VOR Indications and Excerpts from Airport/Facility Directory (HLN).

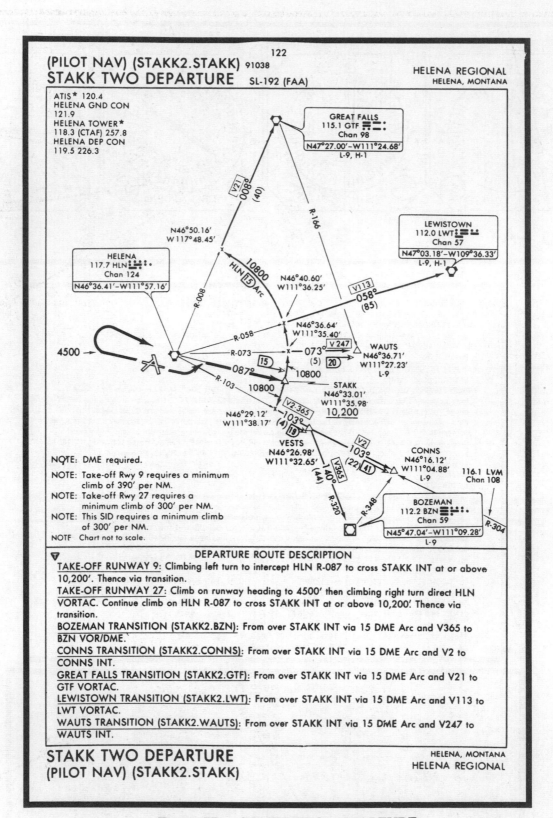

FIGURE 77.— STAKK TWO DEPARTURE.

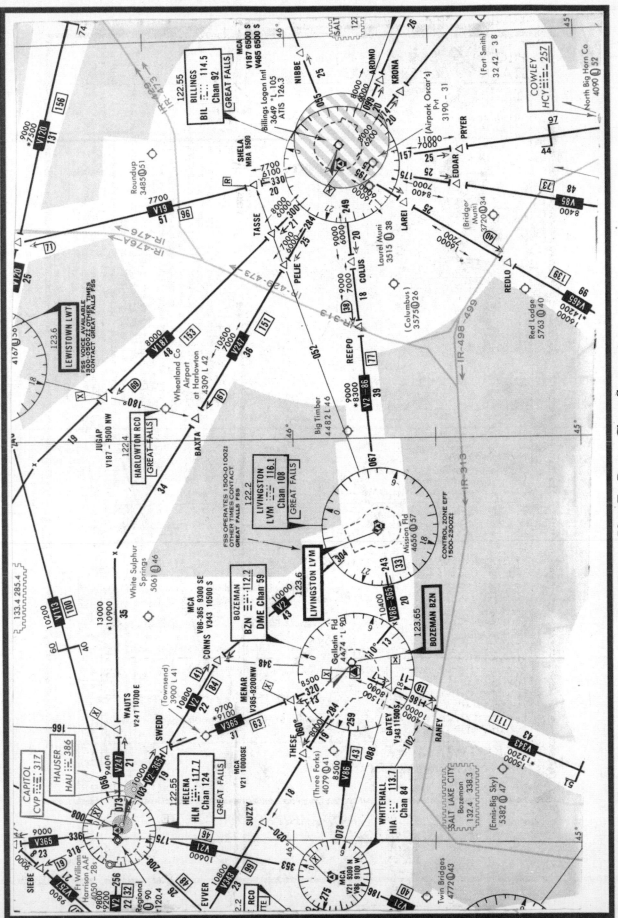

FIGURE 78.—En Route Chart Segment.

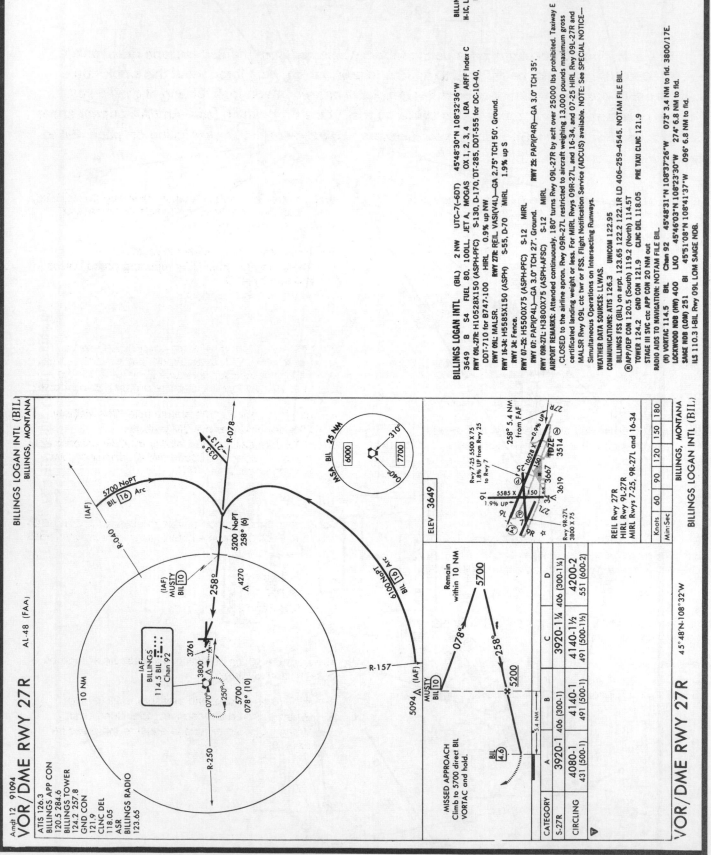

FIGURE 80.—VOR/DME RWY 27R and Airport/Facility Directory (BIL).

# APPENDIX A
# INSTRUMENT RATING PRACTICE TEST

The following 60 questions have been randomly selected from the 898 airplane questions in FAA-T-8080-20A. You will be referred to figures (charts, tables, etc.) throughout this book. Be careful not to consult the answers or answer explanations when you look for and at the figures. Topical coverage in this practice test is similar to that of the FAA written test. An FAA answer sheet is reproduced on page 453 to record your answers. Use the correct answer listing on page 454 to grade your practice test.

**1.**
**4035.** To carry passengers for hire in an airplane on cross-country flights of more than 50 NM from the departure airport, the pilot in command is required to hold at least

A— a Category II pilot authorization.
B— a First-Class Medical certificate.
C— a Commercial Pilot Certificate with an instrument rating.

**2.**
**4063.** Prior to which operation must an IFR flight plan be filed and an appropriate ATC clearance received?

A— Flying by reference to instruments in controlled airspace.
B— Entering controlled airspace when IMC exists.
C— Takeoff when IFR weather conditions exist.

**3.**
**4066.** When is an IFR clearance required during VFR weather conditions?

A— When operating in the Class E airspace.
B— When operating in a Class A airspace.
C— When operating in airspace above 14,500 feet.

**4.**
**4076.** When may a pilot cancel the IFR flight plan prior to completing the flight?

A— Any time.
B— Only if an emergency occurs.
C— Only in VFR conditions outside positive controlled airspace.

**5.**
**4078.** Where are the compulsory reporting points, if any, on a direct flight not flown on radials or courses of established airways or routes?

A— Fixes selected to define the route.
B— There are no compulsory reporting points unless advised by ATC.
C— At the changeover points.

**6.**
**4081.** What minimum weather conditions must be forecast for your ETA at an airport that has only a VOR approach with standard alternate minimums, for the airport to be listed as an alternate on the IFR flight plan?

A— 800-foot ceiling and 1 statute mile (SM) visibility.
B— 800-foot ceiling and 2 SM visibility.
C— 1,000-foot ceiling and visibility to allow descent from minimum en route altitude (MEA), approach, and landing under basic VFR.

**7.**
**4088.** Which publication covers the procedures required for aircraft accident and incident reporting responsibilities for pilots?

A— FAR Part 61.
B— FAR Part 91.
C— NTSB Part 830.

**8.**
**4090.** Under which condition will pressure altitude be equal to true altitude?

A— When the atmospheric pressure is 29.92" Hg.
B— When standard atmospheric conditions exist.
C— When indicated altitude is equal to the pressure altitude.

**9.**

**4108.** Which force, in the Northern Hemisphere, acts at a right angle to the wind and deflects it to the right until parallel to the isobars?

A— Centrifugal.
B— Pressure gradient.
C— Coriolis.

**10.**

**4118.** What type clouds can be expected when an unstable air mass is forced to ascend a mountain slope?

A— Layered clouds with little vertical development.
B— Stratified clouds with considerable associated turbulence.
C— Clouds with extensive vertical development.

**11.**

**4130.** Standing lenticular clouds, in mountainous areas, indicate

A— an inversion.
B— unstable air.
C— turbulence.

**12.**

**4161.** Which precipitation type normally indicates freezing rain at higher altitudes?

A— Snow.
B— Hail.
C— Ice pellets.

**13.**

**4167.** What situation is most conducive to the formation of radiation fog?

A— Warm, moist air over low, flatland areas on clear, calm nights.
B— Moist, tropical air moving over cold, offshore water.
C— The movement of cold air over much warmer water.

**14.**

**4193.** (Refer to figure 2 on page 117.) What approximate wind direction, speed, and temperature (relative to ISA) should a pilot expect when planning for a flight over ALB at FL 270?

A— 270° magnetic at 97 knots; ISA –4 °C.
B— 260° true at 110 knots; ISA +5 °C.
C— 275° true at 97 knots; ISA +4 °C.

**15.**

**4217.** (Refer to figure 6 on page 121.) The 12-Hour Significant Weather Prognosis Chart indicates that West Virginia will likely experience

A— continuous or showery precipitation covering half or more of the area.
B— thunderstorms and rain showers covering half or more of the area.
C— continuous rain covering less than half of the area.

**16.**

**4234.** (Refer to figure 8 on page 112.) What weather conditions are depicted in the area indicated by arrow E on the Radar Summary Chart?

A— Highest echo tops 30,000 feet MSL, weak to moderate echoes, thunderstorms and rain showers, and cell movement toward northwest at 15 knots.
B— Echo bases 29,000 to 30,000 feet MSL, strong echoes, rain showers increasing in intensity, and area movement toward northwest at 15 knots.
C— Thundershowers decreasing in intensity; area movement toward northwest at 15 knots; echo bases 30,000 feet MSL.

**17.**

**4241.** If you hear a SIGMET alert, how can you obtain the information in the SIGMET?

A— ATC will announce the hazard and advise you when to listen to an FSS broadcast.
B— Contact a weather watch station.
C— Contact the nearest FSS and ascertain whether the advisory is pertinent to your flight.

**18.**

**4249.** (Refer to figure 12 on page 132.) What is the approximate wind direction and velocity at CVG at 34,000 feet (see arrow A)?

A— 040°/35 knots.
B— 097°/40 knots.
C— 230°/35 knots.

**19.**

**4312.** (Refer to figure 50 on page 396.) What aircraft equipment code should be entered in block 3 of the flight plan?

A— R.
B— T.
C— U.

**20.**

**4313.** (Refer to figure 50 on page 396.) What CAS must be used to maintain the filed TAS at the flight planned altitude? (Temperature 0 °C.)

A— 136 KCAS.
B— 140 KCAS.
C— 147 KCAS.

**21.**

**4314.** (Refer to figures 50, 51, 52, and 53 on pages 396 through 399.) Determine the time to be entered in block 10 of the flight plan. (Refer to the FD excerpt below, and use the wind entry closest to the flight planned altitude.)

Route of flight . . . . . . . . . . . . Figures 50, 51, 52, and 53
Flight log and MAG VAR . . . . . . . . . . . . . . . . Figure 51
HABUT ONE DEPARTURE
  and Excerpt from AFD . . . . . . . . . . . . . . . Figure 52

| FT  | 3000 | 6000    | 9000    |
|-----|------|---------|---------|
| SBA | 0610 | 2115+05 | 2525+00 |

A— 43 minutes.
B— 46 minutes.
C— 51 minutes.

**22.**

**4315.** (Refer to figure 52 on page 398 and 54 on page 393.) What is the aircraft's position relative to the HABUT intersection? (The VOR-2 is tuned to 116.5.)

A— South of the localizer and past the GVO R-163.
B— North of the localizer and approaching the GVO R-163.
C— South of the localizer and approaching the GVO R-163.

**23.**

**4316.** (Refer to figure 52 on page 398.) Using an average groundspeed of 100 knots, what minimum rate of climb would meet the required minimum climb rate per NM as specified by the SID?

A— 425 feet per minute.
B— 580 feet per minute.
C— 642 feet per minute.

**24.**

**4318.** (Refer to figure 53 on page 399.) What service is indicated by the solid square in the radio aids to navigation box for PRB VORTAC?

A— VOR with TACAN compatible DME.
B— Availability of TWEB.
C— En Route Flight Advisory Service available.

**25.**

**4320.** (Refer to figures 55 and 55A on pages 400 and 401.) As a guide in making range corrections, how many degrees of relative bearing change should be used for each one-half mile deviation from the desired arc?

A— 2° to 3°.
B— 5° maximum.
C— 10° to 20°.

**26.**

**4321.** (Refer to figures 55 and 55A on pages 400 and 401.) Under which condition should a missed approach procedure be initiated if the runway environment (Paso Robles Municipal Airport) is not in sight?

A— After descending to 1,440 feet MSL.
B— After descent to 1,440 feet or reaching the 1 NM DME, whichever occurs first.
C— When you reach the established missed approach point and determine the visibility is less than 1 mile.

**27.**

**4339.** (Refer to figure 65 on page 354 and 67 on page 356.) What is the significance of the symbol at GRICE intersection?

A— It signifies a localizer-only approach is available at Harry P. Williams Memorial.
B— The localizer has an ATC function in addition to course guidance.
C— GRICE intersection also serves as the FAF for the ILS approach procedure to Harry P. Williams Memorial.

**28.**

**4410.** What indication should a pilot receive when a VOR station is undergoing maintenance and may be considered unreliable?

A— No coded identification, but possible navigation indications.
B— Coded identification, but no navigation indications.
C— A voice recording on the VOR frequency announcing that the VOR is out of service for maintenance.

**29.**

**4419.** Which procedure applies to SID's?

A— SID clearances will not be issued unless requested by the pilot.
B— The pilot in command must accept a SID when issued by ATC.
C— If a SID is accepted, the pilot must possess at least a textual description.

**30.**
**4437.** If no MCA is specified, what is the lowest altitude for crossing a radio fix, beyond which a higher minimum applies?

A— The MEA at which the fix is approached.
B— The MRA at which the fix is approached.
C— The MOCA for the route segment beyond the fix.

**31.**
**4452.** When on a VFR-on-Top clearance, the cruising altitude is based on

A— true course.
B— magnetic course.
C— magnetic heading.

**32.**
**4463.** Which procedure should you follow if you experience two-way communications failure while holding at a holding fix with an EFC time? (The holding fix is not the same as the approach fix.)

A— Depart the holding fix to arrive at the approach fix as close as possible to the EFC time.
B— Depart the holding fix at the EFC time.
C— Proceed immediately to the approach fix and hold until EFC.

**33.**
**4494.** (Refer to figure 87 on page 339.) At STRUT intersection (b) headed eastbound, ATC instructs you to hold west on the 10 DME fix LCH (c) on V306, standard turns, what entry procedure is recommended?

A— Direct.
B— Teardrop.
C— Parallel.

**34.**
**4505.** (Refer to figure 89 on page 343.) In the event of two-way radio communications failure while operating on an IFR clearance in VFR conditions over HVE(b), the pilot should continue

A— by the route assigned in the last ATC clearance received.
B— the flight under VFR, if possible, and land as soon as practical.
C— the flight by the most direct route to the fix specified in the last clearance.

**35.**
**4515.** (Refer to figure 91 on page 347.) What is the function of the Yellowstone RCO?

A— Long range communications outlet for Idaho Falls Center.
B— Remote communications outlet for Idaho Falls FSS.
C— Satellite FSS controlled by Idaho Falls FSS with limited service.

**36.**
**4530.** (Refer to figure 93 on page 69.) What is the maximum altitude that Class G airspace will exist? (Does not include airspace less than 1,500 feet AGL.)

A— 18,000 feet MSL.
B— 14,500 feet MSL.
C— 14,000 feet MSL.

**37.**
**4558.** (Refer to figure 95 on page 192.) On which radial is the aircraft as indicated by the No. 1 NAV?

A— R-175.
B— R-165.
C— R-345.

**38.**
**4566.** (Refer to figures 96 and 97 on pages 198 and 199.) To which aircraft position does HSI presentation "D" correspond?

A— 1.
B— 10.
C— 2.

**39.**
**4593.** (Refer to figure 105 on page 172.) If the magnetic heading shown for airplane 3 is maintained, which ADF illustration would indicate the airplane is on the 120° magnetic bearing TO the station?

A— 4.
B— 5.
C— 8.

**40.**
**4603.** (Refer to figure 108 on page 181.) Where should the bearing pointer be located relative to the wingtip reference to maintain the 16 DME range in a left-hand arc with a left crosswind component?

A— Ahead of the left wingtip reference for the VOR-2.
B— Ahead of the right wingtip reference for the VOR-1.
C— Behind the left wingtip reference for the VOR-2.

**41.**
**4612.** (Refer to figure 113 on page 278.) You receive this ATC clearance:

"...CLEARED TO THE XYZ VORTAC. HOLD NORTH ON THE THREE SIX ZERO RADIAL, LEFT TURNS..."

What is the recommended procedure to enter the holding pattern.

A— Parallel only.
B— Direct only.
C— Teardrop only.

**42.**
**4637.** When making an instrument approach at the selected alternate airport, what landing minimums apply?

A— Standard alternate minimums (600-2 or 800-2).
B— The IFR alternate minimums listed for that airport.
C— The landing minimums published for the type of procedure selected.

**43.**
**4655.** (Refer to figure 124 or 124A on pages 302 and 303.) What options are available concerning the teardrop course reversal for LOC RWY 35 approach to Duncan/Halliburton Field?

A— If a course reversal is required, only the teardrop can be executed.
B— The point where the turn is begun and the type and rate of turn are optional.
C— A normal procedure turn may be made if the 10 DME limit is not exceeded.

**44.**
**4659.** (Refer to figure 126 or 126A on pages 316 and 317.) What landing minimums apply for a FAR part 91 operator at Dothan, AL using a category C aircraft during a circling LOC 31 approach at 120 knots? (DME available.)

A— MDA 860 feet MSL and visibility 2 SM.
B— MDA 860 feet MSL and visibility 1 and ½ SM.
C— MDA 720 feet MSL and visibility 3/4 SM.

**45.**
**4680.** (Refer to figure 129 or 129A on pages 293 and 294.) What indication should you get when it is time to turn inbound while in the procedure turn at LABER?

A— 4 DME miles from LABER.
B— 10 DME miles from the MAP.
C— 12 DME miles from LIT VORTAC.

**46.**
**4707.** What wind condition prolongs the hazards of wake turbulence on a landing runway for the longest period of time?

A— Direct headwind.
B— Direct tailwind.
C— Light quartering tailwind.

**47.**
**4737.** When may you obtain a contact approach?

A— ATC may assign a contact approach if VFR conditions exist or you report the runway in sight and are clear of clouds.
B— ATC may assign a contact approach if you are below the clouds and the visibility is at least 1 mile.
C— ATC will assign a contact approach only upon request if the reported visibility is at least 1 mile.

**48.**
**4748.** To remain on the ILS glidepath, the rate of descent must be

A— decreased if the airspeed is increased.
B— decreased if the groundspeed is increased.
C— increased if the groundspeed is increased.

**49.**
**4771.** Assume this clearance is received:

"CLEARED FOR ILS RUNWAY 07 LEFT APPROACH, SIDE-STEP TO RUNWAY 07 RIGHT."

When would the pilot be expected to commence the side-step maneuver?

A— As soon as possible after the runway environment is in sight.
B— Any time after becoming aligned with the final approach course of Runway 07 left, and after passing the final approach fix.
C— After reaching the circling minimums for Runway 07 right.

**50.**
**4789.** (Refer to figure 136 on page 53.) Which illustration would a pilot observe if the aircraft is "slightly high" (3.2°) on the glidepath?

A— 8.
B— 9.
C— 11.

**51.**
**4797.**  (Refer to figure 138 on page 49.)  What night operations, if any, are authorized between the approach end of the runway and the threshold lights?

A— No aircraft operations are permitted short of the threshold lights.
B— Only taxi operations are permitted in the area short of the threshold lights.
C— Taxi and takeoff operations are permitted, providing the takeoff operations are toward the visible green threshold lights.

**52.**
**4817.**  Which use of cockpit lighting is correct for night flight?

A— Reducing the lighting intensity to a minimum level will eliminate blind spots.
B— The use of regular white light, such as a flashlight, will impair night adaptation.
C— Coloration shown on maps is least affected by the use of direct red lighting.

**53.**
**4824.**  (Refer to figures 139 and 140 on page 265.) Which displacement from the localizer and glide slope at the 1.9 NM point is indicated?

A— 710 feet to the left of the localizer centerline and 140 feet below the glide slope.
B— 710 feet to the right of the localizer centerline and 140 feet above the glide slope.
C— 430 feet to the right of the localizer centerline and 28 feet above the glide slope.

**54.**
**4836.**  What instruments are considered supporting bank instruments during a straight, stabilized climb at a constant rate?

A— Attitude indicator and turn coordinator.
B— Heading indicator and attitude indicator.
C— Heading indicator and turn coordinator.

**55.**
**4874.**  Which instrument is considered primary for power as the airspeed reaches the desired value during change of airspeed in a level turn?

A— Airspeed indicator.
B— Attitude indicator.
C— Altimeter.

**56.**
**4891.**  What should be the indication on the magnetic compass as you roll into a standard rate turn to the right from a westerly heading in the Northern Hemisphere?

A— The compass will initially show a turn in the opposite direction, then turn to a northerly indication but lagging behind the actual heading of the aircraft.
B— The compass will remain on a westerly heading for a short time, then gradually catch up to the actual heading of the aircraft.
C— The compass will indicate the approximate correct magnetic heading if the roll into the turn is smooth.

**57.**
**4899.**  The three conditions which determine pitch attitude required to maintain level flight are

A— flightpath, wind velocity, and angle of attack.
B— airspeed, air density, and aircraft weight.
C— relative wind, pressure altitude, and vertical lift component.

**58.**
**4900.**  Errors in both pitch and bank indication on an attitude indicator are usually at a maximum as the aircraft rolls out of a

A— 180° turn.
B— 270° turn.
C— 360° turn.

**59.**
**4910.**  The local altimeter setting should be used by all pilots in a particular area, primarily to provide for

A— the cancellation of altimeter error due to nonstandard temperatures aloft.
B— better vertical separation of aircraft.
C— more accurate terrain clearance in mountainous areas.

**60.**
**4932.**  (Refer to figure 144 on page 214.)  Which illustration indicates a coordinated turn?

A— 3.
B— 1.
C— 2.

---

For additional practice tests, use FAA Test Prep software.  Call (800) 87-GLEIM to get an unlicensed diskette to review. Unlimited access to the software requires a $25.00 licensing fee.  The advantage of this software is that you cannot cheat (yourself) when taking practice tests.  You can make up as many tests as you desire and you can also have the software rearrange the question sequence and answer order.  The questions on each test are randomly selected from the FAA's actual test questions so that the coverage of topics (weather, FARs, etc.) is the same as on the actual FAA test.

## 4186895

**DEPARTMENT OF TRANSPORTATION — FEDERAL AVIATION ADMINISTRATION**

# AIRMAN WRITTEN TEST APPLICATION

TEST NO.

| DATE OF TEST | | | TITLE OF TEST |
|---|---|---|---|
| MONTH | DAY | YEAR | |

PLEASE PRINT ONE LETTER IN EACH SPACE—LEAVE A BLANK SPACE AFTER EACH NAME

NAME (LAST, FIRST, MIDDLE)

| DATE OF BIRTH | | |
|---|---|---|
| MONTH | DAY | YEAR |

MAILING ADDRESS     NO. AND STREET, APT. #, P.O. BOX, OR RURAL ROUTE

DESCRIPTION

| HEIGHT | WEIGHT | HAIR | EYES |
|---|---|---|---|

CITY, TOWN OR POST OFFICE. AND STATE     ZIP CODE

BIRTHPLACE (City and State, or foreign country)     CITIZENSHIP     SOCIAL SECURITY NO.     IF A SOCIAL SECURITY NUMBER HAS NEVER BEEN ISSUED CHECK THIS BLOCK ➤ ☐

Is this a retest? ☐ No ☐ Yes, date of last test     Have you taken or are you taking an FAA approved course for this test? ☐ No ☐ Yes (If "yes" give details below)

Graduation date:     NAME OF SCHOOL     CITY AND STATE

CERTIFICATION: I CERTIFY that all of the statements made in this application are true, complete, and correct to the best of my knowledge and belief and are made in good faith. Signature _ _ _ _ _ _ _ _ _ _ _ _ _

— — DO NOT WRITE IN THIS BLOCK — — FOR USE OF FAA OFFICE ONLY — —

Applicant's identity established by:

| CARD A | | | | | | |
|---|---|---|---|---|---|---|
| CATEGORY | TEST NUMBER | TAKE NO. | SECTIONS 1 2 3 4 5 6 7 | EXPIRATION MONTH DAY YEAR | | |

| CARD B | | |
|---|---|---|
| CERTIFICATED SCHOOL NUMBER | MECH. EXP. DATE BY SECTION 1 2 3 | ID |

FIELD OFFICE DESIGNATION

SIGNATURE of FAA Representative

**INSTRUCTIONS FOR MARKING THE ANSWER SHEET.** Completely darken only one circle for each question. DO NOT USE (X) OR (✔). Use black lead pencil furnished by examiner. To make corrections, open answer sheet so erasure marks will not show on page 2. Then erase incorrect response on page 4. On page 2 (copy) mark the incorrect response with a slash (/). Questions are arranged in VERTICAL sequence as indicated by the arrows.

1 ①②③④  23 ①②③④  45 ①②③④  67 ①②③④  89 ①②③④  111 ①②③④  133 ①②③④
2 ①②③④  24 ①②③④  46 ①②③④  68 ①②③④  90 ①②③④  112 ①②③④  134 ①②③④
3 ①②③④  25 ①②③④  47 ①②③④  69 ①②③④  91 ①②③④  113 ①②③④  135 ①②③④
4 ①②③④  26 ①②③④  48 ①②③④  70 ①②③④  92 ①②③④  114 ①②③④  136 ①②③④
5 ①②③④  27 ①②③④  49 ①②③④  71 ①②③④  93 ①②③④  115 ①②③④  137 ①②③④
6 ①②③④  28 ①②③④  50 ①②③④  72 ①②③④  94 ①②③④  116 ①②③④  138 ①②③④
7 ①②③④  29 ①②③④  51 ①②③④  73 ①②③④  95 ①②③④  117 ①②③④  139 ①②③④
8 ①②③④  30 ①②③④  52 ①②③④  74 ①②③④  96 ①②③④  118 ①②③④  140 ①②③④
9 ①②③④  31 ①②③④  53 ①②③④  75 ①②③④  97 ①②③④  119 ①②③④  141 ①②③④
10 ①②③④  32 ①②③④  54 ①②③④  76 ①②③④  98 ①②③④  120 ①②③④  142 ①②③④
11 ①②③④  33 ①②③④  55 ①②③④  77 ①②③④  99 ①②③④  121 ①②③④  143 ①②③④
12 ①②③④  34 ①②③④  56 ①②③④  78 ①②③④  100 ①②③④  122 ①②③④  144 ①②③④
13 ①②③④  35 ①②③④  57 ①②③④  79 ①②③④  101 ①②③④  123 ①②③④  145 ①②③④
14 ①②③④  36 ①②③④  58 ①②③④  80 ①②③④  102 ①②③④  124 ①②③④  146 ①②③④
15 ①②③④  37 ①②③④  59 ①②③④  81 ①②③④  103 ①②③④  125 ①②③④  147 ①②③④
16 ①②③④  38 ①②③④  60 ①②③④  82 ①②③④  104 ①②③④  126 ①②③④  148 ①②③④
17 ①②③④  39 ①②③④  61 ①②③④  83 ①②③④  105 ①②③④  127 ①②③④  149 ①②③④
18 ①②③④  40 ①②③④  62 ①②③④  84 ①②③④  106 ①②③④  128 ①②③④  150 ①②③④
19 ①②③④  41 ①②③④  63 ①②③④  85 ①②③④  107 ①②③④  129 ①②③④
20 ①②③④  42 ①②③④  64 ①②③④  86 ①②③④  108 ①②③④  130 ①②③④
21 ①②③④  43 ①②③④  65 ①②③④  87 ①②③④  109 ①②③④  131 ①②③④
22 ①②③④  44 ①②③④  66 ①②③④  88 ①②③④  110 ①②③④  132 ①②③④

# PRACTICE TEST LIST OF ANSWERS

| Q. # | Answer | Page | Q. # | Answer | Page | Q. # | Answer | Page | Q. # | Answer | Page |
|------|--------|------|------|--------|------|------|--------|------|------|--------|------|
| 1. | C | 147 | 16. | A | 113 | 31. | B | 335 | 46. | C | 234 |
| 2. | B | 159 | 17. | C | 107 | 32. | B | 66 | 47. | C | 261 |
| 3. | B | 151 | 18. | C | 133 | 33. | A | 337 | 48. | C | 269 |
| 4. | C | 58 | 19. | A | 394 | 34. | B | 341 | 49. | A | 273 |
| 5. | A | 62 | 20. | B | 394 | 35. | B | 346 | 50. | B | 53 |
| 6. | B | 155 | 21. | C | 394 | 36. | B | 70 | 51. | C | 49 |
| 7. | C | 162 | 22. | B | 393 | 37. | C | 192 | 52. | B | 205 |
| 8. | B | 32 | 23. | C | 394 | 38. | C | 200 | 53. | B | 264 |
| 9. | C | 91 | 24. | B | 395 | 39. | B | 173 | 54. | A | 221 |
| 10. | C | 94 | 25. | C | 395 | 40. | A | 181 | 55. | A | 224 |
| 11. | C | 101 | 26. | C | 395 | 41. | C | 279 | 56. | C | 23 |
| 12. | C | 104 | 27. | B | 356 | 42. | C | 283 | 57. | B | 217 |
| 13. | A | 98 | 28. | A | 188 | 43. | A | 301 | 58. | A | 37 |
| 14. | C | 116 | 29. | C | 325 | 44. | B | 313 | 59. | B | 27 |
| 15. | A | 120 | 30. | A | 333 | 45. | A | 292 | 60. | A | 214 |

# FAA LISTING OF SUBJECT MATTER KNOWLEDGE CODES

The next 11 pages reprint the FAA's subject matter codes. These are the codes that will appear on your Airman Written (or Computer) Test Report. See the illustration on page 15. Your test report will list the subject matter code of each question answered incorrectly.

When you receive your Airman Written (or Computer) Test Report, you can trace the subject matter codes listed on it to the next 11 pages to find out which topics you had difficulty with. You should discuss your written tests results with your CFII.

# DEPARTMENT OF TRANSPORTATION
# FEDERAL AVIATION ADMINISTRATION

## SUBJECT MATTER KNOWLEDGE CODES

To determine the knowledge area in which a particular question was incorrectly answered, compare the subject matter code(s) on AC Form 8080-2, Airmen Written Test Report, to the subject matter outline that follows. The total number of test items missed may differ from the number of subject matter codes shown on the AC Form 8080-2, since you may have missed more than one question in a certain subject matter code.

| | | | | |
|---|---|---|---|---|
| **FAR 1** | **Definitions and Abbreviations** | | **FAR 43** | **Maintenance, Preventive Maintenance, Rebuilding, and Alteration** |
| A01 | General Definitions | | | |
| A02 | Abbreviations and Symbols | | A15 | General |
| | | | A16 | Appendixes |
| **FAR 25** | **Airworthiness Standards: Transport Category Airplanes** | | **FAR 61** | **Certification: Pilots and Flight Instructors** |
| A03 | General | | A20 | General |
| A04 | Flight | | A21 | Aircraft Ratings and Special Certificates |
| A05 | Structure | | A22 | Student Pilots |
| A06 | Design and Construction | | A23 | Private Pilots |
| A07 | Powerplant | | A24 | Commercial Pilots |
| A08 | Equipment | | A25 | Airline Transport Pilots |
| A09 | Operating Limitations and Information | | A26 | Flight Instructors |
| | | | A27 | Appendix A: Practical Test Requirements for Airline Transport Pilot Certificates and Associated Class and Type Ratings |
| **FAR 23** | **Airworthiness Standards: Normal, Utility, and Acrobatic Category Aircraft** | | A28 | Appendix B: Practical Test Requirements for Rotorcraft Airline Transport Pilot Certificates with a Helicopter Class Rating and Associated Type Ratings |
| A10 | General | | A29 | Recreational Pilot |
| **FAR 21** | **Certification Procedures for Products and Parts** | | **FAR 63** | **Certification: Flight Crewmembers Other Than Pilots** |
| **A11** | **General** | | | |
| | | | A30 | General |
| **FAR 39** | **Airworthiness Directives** | | A31 | Flight Engineers |
| | | | A32 | Flight Navigators |
| A13 | General | | | |
| A14 | Subpart B—Airworthiness Directives | | | |

**FAR 65**     **Certification: Airmen Other Than Flight Crewmembers**

    A40     General
    A41     Aircraft Dispatchers
    A44     Parachute Riggers

**FAR 71**     **Designation of Federal Airways, Area Low Routes, Controlled Airspace, and Reporting Points**

    A60     General
    A61     Airport Radar Service Areas
    A64     Control Areas and Extensions

**FAR 91**     **General Operating Rules**

    B07     General
    B08     Flight Rules - General
    B09     Visual Flight Rules
    B10     Instrument Flight Rules
    B11     Equipment, Instrument, and Certification Requirements
    B12     Special Flight Operations
    B13     Maintenance, Preventive Maintenance, and Alterations
    B14     Large and Turbine-powered Multiengine Airplanes
    B15     Additional Equipment and Operating Requirements for Large and Transport Category Aircraft
    B16     Appendix A - Category II Operations: Manual, Instruments, Equipment, and Maintenance
    B17     Foreign Aircraft Operations and Operations of U.S.-Registered Civil Aircraft Outside of the U.S.

**FAR 97**     **Standard Instrument Approach Procedures**

    B97     General

**FAR 105**     **Parachute Jumping**

    C01     General

    C02     Operating Rules
    C03     Parachute Equipment

**FAR 108**     **Airplane Operator Security**

    C10     General

**FAR 121**     **Certification and Operations: Domestic, Flag and Supplemental Air Carriers and Commercial Operators of Large Aircraft**

    D01     General
    D02     Certification Rules for Domestic and Flag Air Carriers
    D03     Certification Rules for Supplemental Air Carriers and Commercial Operators
    D04     Rules Governing all Certificate Holders Under This Part
    D05     Approval of Routes: Domestic and Flag Air Carriers
    D06     Approval of Areas and Routes for Supplemental Air Carriers and Commercial Operators
    D07     Manual Requirements
    D08     Aircraft Requirements
    D09     Airplane Performance Operating Limitations
    D10     Special Airworthiness Requirements
    D11     Instrument and Equipment Requirements
    D12     Maintenance, Preventive Maintenance, and Alterations
    D13     Airman and Crewmember Requirements
    D14     Training Program
    D15     Crewmember Qualifications
    D16     Aircraft Dispatcher Qualifications and Duty Time Limitations: Domestic and Flag Air Carriers
    D17     Flight Time Limitations and Rest Requirements: Domestic Air Carriers
    D18     Flight Time Limitations: Flag Air Carriers
    D19     Flight Time Limitations: Supplemental Air Carriers and Commercial Operators
    D20     Flight Operations
    D21     Dispatching and Flight Release Rules
    D22     Records and Reports
    D23     Crewmember Certificate: International
    D24     Special Federal Aviation Regulation SFAR No. 14

| | | | | |
|---|---|---|---|---|
| **FAR 125** | **Certification and Operations: Airplanes Having a Seating Capacity of 20 or More Passengers or a Maximum Payload Capacity of 6,000 Pounds or More** | | **US HMR 172 Hazardous Materials Table** | |
| | | | F02 | General |
| D30 | General | | **US HMR 175 Materials Transportation Bureau Hazardous Materials Regulations (HMR)** | |
| D31 | Certification Rules and Miscellaneous Requirements | | G01 | General Information and Regulations |
| D32 | Manual Requirements | | G02 | Loading, Unloading, and Handling |
| D33 | Airplane Requirements | | G03 | Specific Regulation Applicable According to Classification of Material |
| D34 | Special Airworthiness Requirements | | | |
| D35 | Instrument and Equipment Requirements | | **NTSB 830** | **Rules Pertaining to the Notification and Reporting of Aircraft Accidents or Incidents and Overdue Aircraft, and Preservation of Aircraft Wreckage, Mail, Cargo, and Records** |
| D36 | Maintenance | | | |
| D37 | Airman and Crewmember Requirements | | | |
| D38 | Flight Crewmember Requirements | | | |
| D39 | Flight Operations | | | |
| D40 | Flight Release Rules | | | |
| D41 | Records and Reports | | G10 | General |
| | | | G11 | Initial Notification of Aircraft Accidents, Incidents, and Overdue Aircraft |
| **FAR 135** | **Air Taxi Operators and Commercial Operators** | | G12 | Preservation of Aircraft Wreckage, Mail, Cargo, and Records |
| | | | G13 | Reporting of Aircraft Accidents, Incidents, and Overdue Aircraft |
| E01 | General | | | |
| E02 | Flight Operations | | | |
| E03 | Aircraft and Equipment | | | |
| E04 | VFR/IFR Operating Limitations and Weather Requirements | | **AC 61-23** | **Pilot's Handbook of Aeronautical Knowledge** |
| E05 | Flight Crewmember Requirements | | | |
| E06 | Flight Crewmember Flight Time Limitations and Rest Requirements | | H01 | Principles of Flight |
| | | | H02 | Airplanes and Engines |
| E07 | Crewmember Testing Requirements | | H03 | Flight Instruments |
| E08 | Training | | H04 | Airplane Performance |
| E09 | Airplane Performance Operating Limitations | | H05 | Weather |
| | | | H06 | Basic Calculations Using Navigational Computers or Electronic Calculators |
| E10 | Maintenance, Preventive Maintenance, and Alterations | | H07 | Navigation |
| E11 | Appendix A: Additional Airworthiness Standards for 10 or More Passenger Airplanes | | H09 | Appendix 1: Obtaining FAA Publications |
| | | | **AC 91-23** | **Pilot's Weight and Balance Handbook** |
| E12 | Special Federal Aviation Regulations SFAR No. 36 | | H10 | Weight and Balance Control |
| E13 | Special Federal Aviation Regulations SFAR No. 38 | | H11 | Terms and Definitions |
| | | | H12 | Empty Weight Center of Gravity |
| | | | H13 | Index and Graphic Limits |
| | | | H14 | Change of Weight |
| | | | H15 | Control of Loading — General Aviation |

| | | | | |
|---|---|---|---|---|
| H16 | Control of Loading — Large Aircraft | H75 | Introduction to the Helicopter Flight Manual |
| | | H76 | Weight and Balance |
| **AC 60-14** | **Aviation Instructor's Handbook** | H77 | Helicopter Performance |
| | | H78 | Some Hazards of Helicopter Flight |
| H20 | The Learning Process | H79 | Precautionary Measures and Critical Conditions |
| H21 | Human Behavior | | |
| H22 | Effective Communication | H80 | Helicopter Flight Maneuvers |
| H23 | The Teaching Process | H81 | Confined Area, Pinnacle, and Ridgeline Operations |
| H24 | Teaching Methods | | |
| H25 | The Instructor as a Critic | H82 | Glossary |
| H26 | Evaluation | | |
| H27 | Instructional Aids | **Gyroplane Flight Training Manual — McCulloch** | |
| H30 | Flight Instructor Characteristics and Responsibilities | | |
| | | H90 | Gyroplane Systems |
| H31 | Techniques of Flight Instruction | H91 | Gyroplane Terms |
| H32 | Planning Instructional Activity | H92 | Use of Flight Controls (Gyroplane) |
| | | H93 | Fundamental Maneuvers of Flight (Gyroplane) |
| **AC 61-21** | **Flight Training Handbook** | H94 | Basic Flight Maneuvers (Gyroplane) |
| H50 | Introduction to Flight Training | | |
| H51 | Introduction to Airplanes and Engines | **AC 61-27** | **Instrument Flying Handbook** |
| H52 | Introduction to the Basics of Flight | I01 | Training Considerations |
| H53 | The Effect and Use of Controls | I02 | Instrument Flying: Coping with Illusions in Flight |
| H54 | Ground Operations | | |
| H55 | Basic Flight Maneuvers | I03 | Aerodynamic Factors Related to Instrument Flying |
| H56 | Airport Traffic Patterns and Operations | | |
| H57 | Takeoffs and Departure Climbs | I04 | Basic Flight Instruments |
| H58 | Landing Approaches and Landings | I05 | Attitude Instrument Flying — Airplanes |
| H59 | Faulty Approaches and Landings | I06 | Attitude Instrument Flying — Helicopters |
| H60 | Proficiency Flight Maneuvers | I07 | Electronic Aids to Instrument Flying |
| H61 | Cross-Country Flying | I08 | Using the Navigation Instruments |
| H62 | Emergency Flight by Reference to Instruments | I09 | Radio Communications Facilities and Equipment |
| H63 | Night Flying | I10 | The Federal Airways System and Controlled Airspace |
| H64 | Seaplane Operations | | |
| H65 | Transition to Other Airplanes | I11 | Air Traffic Control |
| H66 | Principles of Flight and Performance Characteristics | I12 | ATC Operations and Procedures |
| | | I13 | Flight Planning |
| | | I14 | Appendix: Instrument Instructor Lesson Guide — Airplanes |
| **AC 61-13** | **Basic Helicopter Handbook** | | |
| | | I15 | Segment of En Route Low Altitude Chart |
| H70 | General Aerodynamics | | |
| H71 | Aerodynamics of Flight | | |
| H72 | Loads and Load Factors | | |
| H73 | Function of the Controls | | |
| H74 | Other Helicopter Components and Their Functions | | |

**AC 00-6**   **Aviation Weather**

I20   The Earth's Atmosphere
I21   Temperature
I22   Atmospheric Pressure and Altimetry
I23   Wind
I24   Moisture, Cloud Formation, and Precipitation
I25   Stable and Unstable Air
I26   Clouds
I27   Air Masses and Fronts
I28   Turbulence
I29   Icing
I30   Thunderstorms
I31   Common IFR Producers
I32   High Altitude Weather
I33   Arctic Weather
I34   Tropical Weather
I35   Soaring Weather
I36   Glossary of Weather Terms

**AC 00-45**   **Aviation Weather Services**

I40   The Aviation Weather Service Program
I41   Surface Aviation Weather Reports
I42   Pilot and Radar Reports and Satellite Pictures
I43   Aviation Weather Forecasts
I44   Surface Analysis Chart
I45   Weather Depiction Chart
I46   Radar Summary Chart
I47   Significant Weather Prognostics
I48   Winds and Temperatures Aloft
I49   Composite Moisture Stability Chart
I50   Severe Weather Outlook Chart
I51   Constant Pressure Charts
I52   Tropopause Data Chart
I53   Tables and Conversion Graphs

**AIM**   **Airman's Information Manual**

J01   Air Navigation Radio Aids
J02   Radar Services and Procedures
J03   Airport Lighting Aids
J04   Air Navigation and Obstruction Lighting
J05   Airport Marking Aids
J06   Airspace — General

J07   Uncontrolled Airspace
J08   Controlled Airspace
J09   Special Use Airspace
J10   Other Airspace Areas
J11   Service Available to Pilots
J12   Radio Communications Phraseology and Techniques
J13   Airport Operations
J14   ATC Clearance/Separations
J15   Preflight
J16   Departure Procedures
J17   En Route Procedures
J18   Arrival Procedures
J19   Pilot/Controller Roles and Responsibilities
J20   National Security and Interception Procedures
J21   Emergency Procedures — General
J22   Emergency Services Available to Pilots
J23   Distress and Urgency Procedures
J24   Two-Way Radio Communications Failure
J25   Meteorology
J26   Altimeter Setting Procedures
J27   Wake Turbulence
J28   Bird Hazards, and Flight Over National Refuges, Parks, and Forests
J29   Potential Flight Hazards
J30   Safety, Accident, and Hazard Reports
J31   Fitness for Flight
J32   Type of Charts Available
J33   Pilot Controller Glossary
J34   Airport/Facility Directory
J35   En Route Low Altitude Chart
J36   En Route High Altitude Chart
J37   Sectional Chart
J40   Standard Instrument Departure (SID) Chart
J41   Standard Terminal Arrival (STAR) Chart
J42   Instrument Approach Procedures
J43   Helicopter Route Chart

**AC 67-2**   **Medical Handbook for Pilots**

J52   Hypoxia
J53   Hyperventilation
J55   The Ears
J56   Alcohol
J57   Drugs and Flying
J58   Carbon Monoxide

| | |
|---|---|
| J59 | Vision |
| J60 | Night Flight |
| J61 | Cockpit Lighting |
| J62 | Disorientation (Vertigo) |
| J63 | Motion Sickness |
| J64 | Fatigue |
| J65 | Noise |
| J66 | Age |
| J67 | Some Psychological Aspects of Flying |
| J68 | The Flying Passenger |

## ADDITIONAL ADVISORY CIRCULARS

| | |
|---|---|
| K01 | AC 00-24B, Thunderstorms |
| K02 | AC 00-30A, Rules of Thumb for Avoiding or Minimizing Encounters with Clear Air Turbulence |
| K03 | AC 00-34A, Aircraft Ground Handling and Servicing |
| K04 | AC 00-54A, Pilot Wind Shear Guide |
| K11 | AC 20-34D, Prevention of Retractable Landing Gear Failure |
| K12 | AC 20-32B, Carbon Monoxide (CO) Contamination in Aircraft — Detection and Prevention |
| K13 | AC 20-43C, Aircraft Fuel Control |
| K20 | AC 20-103, Aircraft Engine Crankshaft Failure |
| K40 | AC 25-4, Inertial Navigation System (INS) |
| L05 | AC 60-22, Aeronautical Decision Making |
| L10 | AC 61-67B, Stall and Spin Awareness Training |
| L15 | AC 61-107, Operations of Aircraft at Altitudes Above 25,000 Feet MSL and/or MACH numbers (Mmo) Greater Than .75 |
| L34 | AC 90-48C, Pilots' Role in Collision Avoidance |
| L42 | AC 90-87, Helicopter Dynamic Rollover |
| L50 | AC 91-6A, Water, Slush, and Snow on the Runway |
| L52 | AC 91-13C, Cold Weather Operation of Aircraft |
| L53 | AC 91-14D, Altimeter Setting Sources |
| L57 | AC 91-43, Unreliable Airspeed Indications |
| L59 | AC 91-46, Gyroscopic Instruments — |

| | |
|---|---|
| | Good Operating Practices |
| L61 | AC 91-50, Importance of Transponder Operation and Altitude Reporting |
| L62 | AC 91-51, Airplane Deice and Anti-Ice Systems |
| L70 | AC 91-67, Minimum Equipment Requirements for General Aviation Operations Under FAR Part 91 |
| L80 | AC 103-4, Hazard Associated with Sublimation of Solid Carbon Dioxide (Dry Ice) Aboard Aircraft |
| L90 | AC 105-2C, Sport Parachute Jumping |
| M01 | AC 120-12A, Private Carriage Versus Common Carriage of Persons or Property |
| M02 | AC 120-27B, Aircraft Weight and Balance Control |
| M08 | AC 120-58, Large Aircraft Ground Deicing |
| M13 | AC 121-195-1A, Operational Landing Distances for Wet Runways; Transport Category Airplanes |
| M51 | AC 20-117, Hazards Following Ground Deicing and Ground Operations in Conditions Conducive to Aircraft Icing |
| M52 | AC 00-2.5, Advisory Circular Checklist |

## American Soaring Handbook — Soaring Society of America

| | |
|---|---|
| N01 | A History of American Soaring |
| N02 | Training |
| N03 | Ground Launch |
| N04 | Airplane Tow |
| N05 | Meteorology |
| N06 | Cross-Country and Wave Soaring |
| N07 | Instruments and Oxygen |
| N08 | Radio, Rope, and Wire |
| N09 | Aerodynamics |
| N10 | Maintenance and Repair |

## Soaring Flight Manual — Jeppesen-Sanderson, Inc.

| | |
|---|---|
| N20 | Sailplane Aerodynamics |
| N21 | Performance Considerations |
| N22 | Flight Instruments |
| N23 | Weather for Soaring |
| N24 | Medical Factors |
| N25 | Flight Publications and Airspace |

| | |
|---|---|
| N26 | Aeronautical Charts and Navigation |
| N27 | Computations for Soaring |
| N28 | Personal Equipment |
| N29 | Preflight and Ground Operations |
| N30 | Aerotow Launch Procedures |
| N31 | Ground Launch Procedures |
| N32 | Basic Flight Maneuvers and Traffic |
| N33 | Soaring Techniques |
| N34 | Cross-Country Soaring |

## Taming The Gentle Giant — Taylor Publishing

| | |
|---|---|
| O01 | Design and Construction of Balloons |
| O02 | Fuel Source and Supply |
| O03 | Weight and Temperature |
| O04 | Flight Instruments |
| O05 | Balloon Flight Tips |
| O06 | Glossary |

## Flight Instructor Manual — Balloon Federation of America

| | |
|---|---|
| O10 | Flight Instruction Aids |
| O11 | Human Behavior and Pilot Proficiency |
| O12 | The Flight Check and the Designated Examiner |

## Propane Systems — Balloon Federation of America, 1991

| | |
|---|---|
| O20 | Propane Glossary |
| O21 | Tanks |
| O22 | Burners, Valves, and Hoses |
| O23 | Refueling, Contamination, and Fuel Management |
| O24 | Repair and Maintenance |

## Powerline Excerpts — Balloon Federation of America

| | |
|---|---|
| O30 | Excerpts |

## Balloon Ground School — Balloon Publishing Company

| | |
|---|---|
| 046 | Balloon Operations |

## Goodyear Airship Operations Manual

| | |
|---|---|
| P01 | Buoyancy |
| P02 | Aerodynamics |
| P03 | Free Ballooning |
| P04 | Aerostatics |
| P05 | Envelope |
| P06 | Car |
| P07 | Powerplant |
| P08 | Airship Ground Handling |
| P11 | Operating Instructions |
| P12 | History |
| P13 | Training |

## The Parachute Manual, Para Publishing

| | |
|---|---|
| P31 | Regulations |
| P32 | The Parachute Rigger Certificate |
| P33 | The Parachute Loft |
| P34 | Parachute Materials |
| P35 | Personnel Parachute Assemblies |
| P36 | Parachute Component Parts |
| P37 | Maintenance, Alteration, and Manufacturing Procedures |
| P38 | Design and Construction |
| P39 | Parachute Inspecting and Packing |
| P40 | Glossary/Index |

## The Parachute Manual, Vol. II, Para Publishing

| | |
|---|---|
| P51 | Parachute Regulations |
| P52 | The Parachute Rigger's Certificate |
| P53 | The Parachute Loft |
| P54 | Parachute Materials |
| P55 | Personnel Parachute Assemblies |
| P56 | Parachute Component Parts |
| P57 | Maintenance, Alteration, and Manufacturing |
| P58 | Parachute Design and Construction |
| P59 | Parachute Inspection and Packing |
| P60 | Appendix |
| P61 | Conversion Tables |
| P62 | Product/Manufacturer-Index |
| P63 | Name and Manufacture Index |
| P64 | Glossary-Index |

| | | | | |
|---|---|---|---|---|
| **AC 65-9A** | **Airframe and Powerplant Mechanics General Handbook** | | S31 | Cabin Atmosphere Control Systems |

**EA-ITP-G[2]**   **A and P Technician General Textbook — International Aviation Publishers (IAP), Inc., Second Edition**

S01   Mathematics
S02   Aircraft Drawings
S03   Aircraft Weight and Balance
S04   Fuels and Fuel Systems                          S32   Mathematics
S05   Fluid Lines and Fittings                        S33   Physics
S06   Aircraft Hardware, Materials, and               S34   Basic Electricity
      Processes                                       S35   Electrical Generators and Motors
S07   Physics                                         S36   Aircraft Drawings
S08   Basic Electricity                               S37   Weight and Balance
S09   Aircraft Generators and Motors                  S38   Fluid Lines and Fittings
S10   Inspection Fundamentals                         S39   Aircraft Hardware
S11   Ground Handling, Safety, and Support            S40   Corrosion and Its Control
      Equipment                                       S41   Nondestructive Inspection
                                                      S42   Ground Handling and Servicing
                                                      S43   Maintenance Forms and Records
**AC 65-12A**   **Airframe and Powerplant Mechanics**   S44   Maintenance Publications
                **Powerplant Handbook**

**EA-ITP-P[2]**   **A and P Technician Powerplant Textbook — IAP, Inc., Second Edition**

S12   Theory and Construction of Aircraft
      Engines
S13   Induction and Exhaust Systems                   S45   Reciprocating Engines
S14   Engine Fuel and Metering Systems                S46   Turbine Engines
S15   Engine Ignition and Electrical Systems          S47   Engine Removal and Replacement
S16   Engine Starting Systems                         S48   Engine Maintenance and Operation
S17   Lubrication and Cooling Systems                 S49   Induction and Exhaust Systems
S18   Propellers                                      S50   Engine Fuel and Fuel Metering
S19   Engine Fire Protection Systems                  S51   Engine Ignition and Electrical Systems
S20   Engine Maintenance and Operation                S52   Engine Lubrication and Cooling Systems
                                                      S53   Engine Fire Protection Systems
**AC 65-15A**   **Airframe and Powerplant Mechanics**   S54   Propellers
                **Airframe Handbook**

**EA-ITP-A[2]**   **A and P Technician Airframe Textbook — IAP, Inc., Second Edition**

S21   Aircraft Structures
S22   Assembly and Rigging
S23   Aircraft Structural Repairs                     S55   Aircraft Structures
S24   Ice and Rain Protection                         S56   Assembly and Rigging
S25   Hydraulic and Pneumatic Power                   S57   Aircraft Fabric Covering
      Systems                                         S58   Aircraft Painting and Finishing
S26   Landing Gear Systems                            S59   Aircraft Metal Structural Repair
S27   Fire Protection Systems                         S60   Aircraft Wood and Composite Structural
S28   Aircraft Electrical Systems                           Repair
S29   Aircraft Instrument Systems                     S61   Aircraft Welding
S30   Communications and Navigation                   S62   Ice and Rain Control Systems
      Systems                                         S63   Hydraulic and Pneumatic Power Systems

S64    Aircraft Landing Gear Systems
S65    Fire Protection Systems
S66    Aircraft Electrical Systems
S67    Aircraft Instrument Systems
S68    Aircraft Fuel Systems
S69    Aircraft Cabin Atmosphere Control Systems

**EA-TEP-2    Aircraft Gas Turbine Powerplants — IAP, Inc.**

S70    History of Turbine Engine Development
S71    Jet Propulsion Theory
S72    Turbine Engine Design and Construction
S73    Engine Familiarization
S74    Inspection and Maintenance
S75    Lubrication Systems
S76    Fuel Systems
S77    Compressor Anti-Stall Systems
S78    Anti-Icing Systems
S79    Starter Systems
S80    Ignition Systems
S81    Engine Instrument Systems
S82    Fire/Overheat Detection and Extinguishing Systems for Turbine Engines
S83    Engine Operation

**The Aircraft Gas Turbine Engine and Its Operation — United Technologies Corporation, Pratt Whitney, 1988**

T01    Gas Turbine Engine Fundamentals
T02    Gas Turbine Engine Terms
T03    Gas Turbine Engine Components
T04    Gas Turbine Engine Operation
T05    Operational Characteristics of Jet Engines
T06    Gas Turbine Engine Performance

**Aircraft Powerplants — McGraw-Hill, Sixth Edition**

T07    Aircraft Powerplant Classification and Progress
T08    Reciprocating-Engine Construction and Nomenclature
T09    Internal-Combustion Engine Theory and Performance
T10    Lubricants and Lubricating Systems
T11    Induction Systems, Superchargers, Turbochargers, and Exhaust Systems
T12    Basic Fuel Systems and Carburetors
T13    Fuel Injection Systems
T14    Reciprocating-Engine Ignition and Starting Systems
T15    Operation, Inspection, Maintenance, and Troubleshooting of Reciprocating Engines
T16    Reciprocating-Engine Overhaul Practices
T17    Gas Turbine Engine: Theory, Construction, and Nomenclature
T18    Gas Turbine Engine: Fuels and Fuel Systems
T19    Turbine-Engine Lubricants and Lubricating Systems
T20    Ignition and Starting Systems of Gas-Turbine Engines
T21    Turbofan Engines
T22    Turboprop Engines
T23    Turboshaft Engines
T24    Gas-Turbine Operation, Inspection, Troubleshooting, Maintenance, and Overhaul
T25    Propeller Theory, Nomenclature, and Operation
T26    Turbopropellers and Control Systems
T27    Propeller Installation, Inspection, and Maintenance
T28    Engine Control System
T29    Engine Indicating and Warning Systems

**EA-ATD-2    Aircraft Technical Dictionary — IAP, Inc.**

T30    Definitions

## Aircraft Basic Science — McGraw-Hill, Sixth Edition

| | |
|---|---|
| T31 | Fundamentals of Mathematics |
| T32 | Science Fundamentals |
| T33 | Basic Aerodynamics |
| T34 | Airfoils and their Applications |
| T35 | Aircraft in Flight |
| T36 | Aircraft Drawings |
| T37 | Weight and Balance |
| T38 | Aircraft Materials |
| T39 | Fabrication Techniques and Processes |
| T40 | Aircraft Hardware |
| T41 | Aircraft Fluid Lines and their Fittings |
| T42 | Federal Aviation Regulations and Publications |
| T43 | Ground Handling and Safety |
| T44 | Aircraft Inspection and Servicing |

## Aircraft Maintenance and Repair — McGraw-Hill, Fifth Edition

| | |
|---|---|
| T45 | Aircraft Systems |
| T46 | Aircraft Hydraulic and Pneumatic Systems |
| T47 | Aircraft Landing Gear Systems |
| T48 | Aircraft Fuel Systems |
| T49 | Environmental Systems |
| T50 | Aircraft Instruments and Instrument Systems |
| T51 | Auxiliary Systems |
| T52 | Assembly and Rigging |

| | |
|---|---|
| **EA-363** | **Transport Category Aircraft Systems — IAP, Inc.** |

| | |
|---|---|
| T53 | Types, Design Features and Configurations of Transport Aircraft |
| T54 | Auxiliary Power Units, Pneumatic, and Environmental Control Systems |
| T55 | Anti-Icing Systems and Rain Protection |
| T56 | Electrical Power Systems |
| T57 | Flight Control Systems |
| T58 | Fuel Systems |
| T59 | Hydraulic Systems |
| T60 | Oxygen Systems |
| T61 | Warning and Fire Protection Systems |
| T62 | Communications, Instruments, and Navigational Systems |
| T63 | Miscellaneous Aircraft Systems and Maintenance Information |

## Aircraft Electricity and Electronics — McGraw-Hill, Fourth Edition

| | |
|---|---|
| T64 | Fundamentals of Electricity |
| T65 | Applications of Ohm's Law |
| T66 | Aircraft Storage Batteries |
| T67 | Alternating Current |
| T68 | Electrical Wire and Wiring Practices |
| T69 | Electrical Control Devices |
| T70 | Electric Measuring Instruments |
| T71 | DC Generators and Related Control Circuits |
| T72 | Alternators, Inverters, and Related Controls |
| T73 | Electric Motors |
| T74 | Power Distribution Systems |
| T75 | Design and Maintenance of Aircraft Electrical Systems |
| T76 | Radio Theory |
| T77 | Communication and Navigation Systems |
| T78 | Weather Warning Systems |
| T79 | Electrical Instruments and Autopilot Systems |
| T80 | Digital Electronics |

## FAA Accident Prevention Program Bulletins

| | |
|---|---|
| V01 | FAA-P-8740-2, Density Altitude |
| V02 | FAA-P-8740-5, Weight and Balance |
| V03 | FAA-P-8740-12, Thunderstorms |
| V04 | FAA-P-8740-19, Flying Light Twins Safely |
| V05 | FAA-P-8740-23, Planning your Takeoff |
| V06 | FAA-P-8740-24, Tips on Winter Flying |
| V07 | FAA-P-8740-25, Always Leave Yourself an Out |
| V08 | FAA-P-8740-30, How to Obtain a Good Weather Briefing |
| V09 | FAA-P-8740-40, Wind Shear |
| V10 | FAA-P-8740-41, Medical Facts for Pilots |
| V11 | FAA-P-8740-44, Impossible Turns |
| V12 | FAA-P-8740-48, On Landings, Part I |
| V13 | FAA-P-8740-49, On Landings, Part II |
| V14 | FAA-P-8740-50, On Landings, Part III |

| | | | |
|---|---|---|---|
| V15 | FAA-P-8740-51, How to Avoid a Midair Collision | X17 | Missed Approaches and Rejected Landings |
| V16 | FAA-P-8740-52, The Silent Emergency | X18 | Category II and III Approaches |
| | | X19 | Nonprecision and Circling Approaches |
| | | X20 | Weight and Balance |

**EA-338**        **Flight Theory for Pilots — IAP, Inc., Third Edition**

| | | | |
|---|---|---|---|
| | | X21 | Flight Planning |
| | | X22 | Icing |
| | | X23 | Use of Anti-ice and Deice |
| W01 | Introduction | X24 | Winter Operation |
| W02 | Air Flow and Airspeed Measurement | X25 | Thunderstorm Flight |
| W03 | Aerodynamic Forces on Airfoils | X26 | Low-Level Wind Shear |
| W04 | Lift and Stall | | |
| W05 | Drag | | |

**Technical Standard Orders**

| | |
|---|---|
| W06 | Jet Aircraft Basic Performance |
| W07 | Jet Aircraft Applied Performance |
| W08 | Prop Aircraft Basic Performance |
| W09 | Prop Aircraft Applied Performance |

| | |
|---|---|
| Y60 | TSO-C23b, Parachute |
| Y61 | TSO-C23c, Personnel Parachute Assemblies |

| | |
|---|---|
| W10 | Helicopter Aerodynamics |
| W11 | Hazards of Low Speed Flight |

**Practical Test Standards**

| | |
|---|---|
| W12 | Takeoff Performance |
| W13 | Landing Performance |
| W14 | Maneuvering Performance |
| W15 | Longitudinal Stability and Control |
| W16 | Directional and Lateral Stability and Control |
| W17 | High Speed Flight |

| | |
|---|---|
| Z01 | FAA-S-8081-6, Flight Instructor Practical Test Standards for Airplane |
| Z02 | FAA-S-8081-7, Flight Instructor Practical Test Standards for Rotorcraft |
| Z03 | FAA-S-8081-8, Flight Instructor Practical Test Standards for Glider |

**Fly the Wing, — Iowa State University Press/Ames, Second Edition**

**NOTE:** AC 00-2, Advisory Circular Checklist, transmits the status of all FAA advisory circulars (AC's), as well as FAA internal publications and miscellaneous flight information such as AIM, Airport/Facility Directory, written test question books, practical test standards, and other material directly related to a certificate or rating. To obtain a free copy of the AC 00-2, send your request to:

| | |
|---|---|
| X01 | Basic Aerodynamics |
| X02 | High-Speed Aerodynamics |
| X03 | High-Altitude Machs |
| X04 | Approach Speed Control and Target Landings |
| X05 | Preparation for Flight Training |
| X06 | Basic Instrument Scan |
| X07 | Takeoffs |
| X08 | Rejected Takeoffs |
| X09 | Climb, Cruise, and Descent |
| X10 | Steep Turns |
| X11 | Stalls |
| X12 | Unusual Attitudes |
| X14 | Maneuvers At Minimum Speed |
| X15 | Landings: Approach Technique and Performance |
| X16 | ILS Approaches |

U.S. Department of Transportation
Utilization and Storage Section, M-443.2
Washington, DC  20590

# CROSS-REFERENCES TO THE FAA WRITTEN TEST QUESTION NUMBERS

Pages 467 through 475 contain the FAA Instrument Rating question numbers appearing in FAA-T-8080-20A (the FAA book of questions from which you will be taking your written test). The questions are numbered 4001 to 4943 in the FAA book. To the right of each FAA question number we have added our answer and our chapter and question number. For example, the FAA's question 4002 is cross-referenced to our book as 5-18, which means it is reproduced in Chapter 5 as question 18. Nonairplane questions (omitted from this book) are indicated as NA. The letter X denotes no answer is correct.

The first line of each of our answer explanations in Chapters 2 through 11 contains

1. The correct answer,
2. The FAA question number, and
3. A reference for the answer explanation, e.g., *FTH Chap 1*.

Thus, our question numbers are cross-referenced throughout this book to the FAA question numbers, and this list cross-references the FAA question numbers back to this book.

| FAA Q. No. | Our Answer | Our Chap/ Q. No. | FAA Q. No. | Our Answer | Our Chap/ Q. No. | FAA Q. No. | Our Answer | Our Chap/ Q. No. |
|---|---|---|---|---|---|---|---|---|
| 4001 | NA | | 4023 | A | 5-9 | 4045 | C | 5-72 |
| 4002 | C | 5-18 | 4024 | C | 5-31 | 4046 | A | 5-55 |
| 4003 | C | 5-23 | 4025 | B | 5-2 | 4047 | C | 5-78 |
| 4004 | NA | | 4026 | A | 5-15 | 4048 | A | 5-59 |
| 4005 | B | 5-44 | 4027 | A | 5-7 | 4049 | C | 5-79 |
| 4006 | C | 5-66 | 4028 | C | 5-19 | 4050 | A | 5-68 |
| 4007 | B | 5-77 | 4029 | B | 5-20 | 4051 | C | 5-69 |
| 4008 | A | 5-5 | 4030 | NA | | 4052 | C | 5-71 |
| 4009 | B | 5-4 | 4031 | B | 5-1 | 4053 | C | 5-70 |
| 4010 | B | 5-3 | 4032 | B | 5-43 | 4054 | A | 5-58 |
| 4011 | A | 5-24 | 4033 | C | 5-22 | 4055 | C | 5-67 |
| 4012 | A | 5-8 | 4034 | C | 5-17 | 4056 | B | 2-20 |
| 4013 | A | 5-11 | 4035 | C | 5-16 | 4057 | NA | |
| 4014 | B | 5-10 | 4036 | C | 5-56 | 4058 | C | 3-42 |
| 4015 | A | 5-13 | 4037 | B | 5-74 | 4059 | B | 3-38 |
| 4016 | NA | | 4038 | A | 5-75 | 4060 | A | 3-39 |
| 4017 | A | 5-12 | 4039 | C | 5-21 | 4061 | A | 3-40 |
| 4018 | NA | | 4040 | NA | | 4062 | C | 5-33 |
| 4019 | NA | | 4041 | NA | | 4063 | B | 5-64 |
| 4020 | A | 5-14 | 4042 | C | 5-73 | 4064 | A | 5-63 |
| 4021 | B | 5-6 | 4043 | NA | | 4065 | C | 5-62 |
| 4022 | NA | | 4044 | B | 5-57 | 4066 | B | 5-32 |

| FAA Q. No. | Our Answer | Our Chap/ Q. No. | FAA Q. No. | Our Answer | Our Chap/ Q. No. | FAA Q. No. | Our Answer | Our Chap/ Q. No. |
|---|---|---|---|---|---|---|---|---|
| 4067 | B | 5-34 | 4107 | B | 4-3 | 4147 | B | 4-55 |
| 4068 | C | 5-61 | 4108 | C | 4-2 | 4148 | C | 4-54 |
| 4069 | A | 3-43 | 4109 | B | 2-44 | 4149 | A | 4-53 |
| 4070 | B | 9-151 | 4110 | B | 2-37 | 4150 | C | 4-72 |
| 4071 | B | 3-69 | 4111 | A | 2-29 | 4151 | C | 4-70 |
| 4072 | C | 3-33 | 4112 | A | 4-35 | 4152 | C | 4-64 |
| 4073 | B | 3-36 | 4113 | B | 4-71 | 4153 | B | 4-67 |
| 4074 | A | 3-35 | 4114 | A | 4-29 | 4154 | C | 4-9 |
| 4075 | C | 3-34 | 4115 | C | 4-21 | 4155 | C | 4-8 |
| 4076 | C | 3-41 | 4116 | A | 4-20 | 4156 | A | 4-41 |
| 4077 | A | 3-82 | 4117 | B | 4-19 | 4157 | C | 4-52 |
| 4078 | A | 3-58 | 4118 | C | 4-18 | 4158 | C | 4-6 |
| 4079 | C | 3-29 | 4119 | C | 4-17 | 4159 | B | 4-23 |
| 4080 | C | 3-27 | 4120 | C | 4-27 | 4160 | B | 8-70 |
| 4081 | B | 5-48 | 4121 | B | 4-26 | 4161 | C | 4-66 |
| 4082 | C | 5-45 | 4122 | B | 4-25 | 4162 | C | 4-40 |
| 4083 | C | 5-49 | 4123 | C | 4-24 | 4163 | B | 4-39 |
| 4084 | NA | | 4124 | A | 4-28 | 4164 | A | 4-38 |
| 4085 | A | 5-51 | 4125 | A | 4-31 | 4165 | A | 4-37 |
| 4086 | C | 5-50 | 4126 | A | 4-62 | 4166 | C | 4-36 |
| 4087 | A | 5-52 | 4127 | A | 4-14 | 4167 | A | 4-34 |
| 4088 | C | 5-80 | 4128 | B | 4-16 | 4168 | B | 4-10 |
| 4089 | A | 2-43 | 4129 | B | 4-51 | 4169 | C | 4-33 |
| 4090 | B | 2-42 | 4130 | C | 4-50 | 4170 | A | 4-110 |
| 4091 | C | 2-46 | 4131 | B | 4-49 | 4171 | C | 4-65 |
| 4092 | A | 4-63 | 4132 | B | 4-48 | 4172 | A | 4-120 |
| 4093 | B | 2-45 | 4133 | B | 4-47 | 4173 | B | 4-147 |
| 4094 | C | 4-32 | 4134 | C | 4-46 | 4174 | A | 4-102 |
| 4095 | C | 4-119 | 4135 | C | 4-75 | 4175 | A | 4-112 |
| 4096 | A | 4-1 | 4136 | A | 4-12 | 4176 | C | 4-109 |
| 4097 | C | 4-7 | 4137 | C | 4-15 | 4177 | B | 4-108 |
| 4098 | C | 4-22 | 4138 | C | 4-76 | 4178 | B | 4-107 |
| 4099 | C | 4-69 | 4139 | C | 4-74 | 4179 | C | 4-105 |
| 4100 | C | 4-45 | 4140 | A | 4-13 | 4180 | A | 4-106 |
| 4101 | A | 4-44 | 4141 | C | 4-61 | 4181 | B | 4-80 |
| 4102 | A | 4-68 | 4142 | A | 4-60 | 4182 | B | 4-89 |
| 4103 | B | 4-42 | 4143 | B | 4-59 | 4183 | A | 4-81 |
| 4104 | A | 4-43 | 4144 | A | 4-58 | 4184 | C | 4-145 |
| 4105 | B | 4-5 | 4145 | B | 4-57 | 4185 | C | 4-114 |
| 4106 | B | 4-4 | 4146 | C | 4-56 | 4186 | A | 4-113 |

| FAA Q. No. | Our Answer | Our Chap/ Q. No. | FAA Q. No. | Our Answer | Our Chap/ Q. No. | FAA Q. No. | Our Answer | Our Chap/ Q. No. |
|---|---|---|---|---|---|---|---|---|
| 4187 | C | 4-79 | 4227 | C | 4-11 | 4267 | B | 11-9 |
| 4188 | B | 4-122 | 4228 | C | 4-104 | 4268 | C | 11-10 |
| 4189 | C | 4-121 | 4229 | B | 4-156 | 4269 | A | 11-11 |
| 4190 | B | 4-123 | 4230 | C | 4-95 | 4270 | C | 11-12 |
| 4191 | C | 4-124 | 4231 | B | 4-98 | 4271 | A | 11-13 |
| 4192 | C | 4-116 | 4232 | C | 4-97 | 4272 | B | 11-15 |
| 4193 | C | 4-115 | 4233 | B | 4-96 | 4273 | C | 11-14 |
| 4194 | A | 4-117 | 4234 | A | 4-99 | 4274 | A | 11-16 |
| 4195 | C | 4-146 | 4235 | B | 4-103 | 4275 | B | 11-17 |
| 4196 | A | 4-88 | 4236 | A | 4-101 | 4276 | B | 11-18 |
| 4197 | A | 4-136 | 4237 | A | 4-100 | 4277 | C | 11-45 |
| 4198 | A | 4-91 | 4238 | C | 4-77 | 4278 | B | 11-46 |
| 4199 | B | 4-118 | 4239 | C | 4-133 | 4279 | A | 11-44 |
| 4200 | A | 4-30 | 4240 | C | 4-134 | 4280 | A | 11-47 |
| 4201 | C | 4-111 | 4241 | C | 4-83 | 4281 | A | 11-48 |
| 4202 | C | 4-86 | 4242 | B | 4-158 | 4282 | B | 11-49 |
| 4203 | A | 4-87 | 4243 | C | 4-163 | 4283 | A | 11-50 |
| 4204 | C | 4-85 | 4244 | C | 4-164 | 4284 | A | 11-51 |
| 4205 | C | 4-84 | 4245 | A | 4-157 | 4285 | B | 11-52 |
| 4206 | C | 4-94 | 4246 | A | 4-159 | 4286 | C | 11-53 |
| 4207 | B | 4-93 | 4247 | C | 4-160 | 4287 | A | 11-54 |
| 4208 | C | 4-92 | 4248 | B | 4-135 | 4288 | B | 11-55 |
| 4209 | C | 4-149 | 4249 | C | 4-161 | 4289 | A | 11-56 |
| 4210 | A | 4-73 | 4250 | B | 4-162 | 4290 | C | 11-57 |
| 4211 | A | 4-128 | 4251 | C | 4-139 | 4291 | A | 11-58 |
| 4212 | C | 4-127 | 4252 | C | 4-138 | 4292 | B | 11-59 |
| 4213 | A | 4-126 | 4253 | C | 4-137 | 4293 | C | 11-60 |
| 4214 | C | 4-125 | 4254 | C | 4-144 | 4294 | C | 11-61 |
| 4215 | B | 4-150 | 4255 | C | 4-140 | 4295 | C | 11-62 |
| 4216 | B | 4-132 | 4256 | C | 4-141 | 4296 | C | 11-63 |
| 4217 | A | 4-131 | 4257 | A | 4-142 | 4297 | A | 11-64 |
| 4218 | A | 4-130 | 4258 | B | 4-143 | 4298 | C | 11-65 |
| 4219 | A | 4-129 | 4259 | A | 11-2 | 4299 | A | 11-66 |
| 4220 | C | 4-90 | 4260 | A | 11-1 | 4300 | C | 11-19 |
| 4221 | C | 4-155 | 4261 | A | 11-4 | 4301 | A | 11-20 |
| 4222 | B | 4-154 | 4262 | B | 11-5 | 4302 | B | 11-22 |
| 4223 | A | 4-152 | 4263 | B | 11-6 | 4303 | C | 11-21 |
| 4224 | B | 4-153 | 4264 | C | 11-7 | 4304 | A | 11-23 |
| 4225 | C | 4-151 | 4265 | A | 11-3 | 4305 | B | 11-24 |
| 4226 | B | 4-148 | 4266 | C | 11-8 | 4306 | A | 11-28 |

| FAA Q. No. | Our Answer | Our Chap/ Q. No. | FAA Q. No. | Our Answer | Our Chap/ Q. No. | FAA Q. No. | Our Answer | Our Chap/ Q. No. |
|---|---|---|---|---|---|---|---|---|
| 4307 | B | 11-29 | 4347 | A | 11-70 | 4387 | C | 6-41 |
| 4308 | C | 11-30 | 4348 | C | 11-71 | 4388 | C | 6-32 |
| 4309 | C | 11-31 | 4349 | B | 11-72 | 4389 | A | 6-33 |
| 4310 | C | 11-32 | 4350 | B | 11-73 | 4390 | B | 3-59 |
| 4311 | C | 11-33 | 4351 | B | 11-74 | 4391 | A | 6-35 |
| 4312 | A | 11-36 | 4352 | A | 11-75 | 4392 | B | 3-51 |
| 4313 | B | 11-37 | 4353 | C | 11-76 | 4393 | C | 3-54 |
| 4314 | C | 11-38 | 4354 | B | 11-77 | 4394 | B | 3-49 |
| 4315 | B | 11-34 | 4355 | A | 11-78 | 4395 | B | 3-44 |
| 4316 | C | 11-35 | 4356 | B | 11-79 | 4396 | B | 3-45 |
| 4317 | A | 11-39 | 4357 | C | 11-80 | 4397 | A | 6-1 |
| 4318 | B | 11-40 | 4358 | C | 11-81 | 4398 | C | 3-48 |
| 4319 | A | 11-41 | 4359 | B | 11-82 | 4399 | B | 6-4 |
| 4320 | C | 11-42 | 4360 | C | 11-83 | 4400 | C | 6-50 |
| 4321 | C | 11-43 | 4361 | B | 11-84 | 4401 | B | 9-11 |
| 4322 | NA | | 4362 | C | 11-85 | 4402 | C | 2-22 |
| 4323 | NA | | 4363 | C | 11-86 | 4403 | B | 3-30 |
| 4324 | NA | | 4364 | C | 11-87 | 4404 | A | 3-31 |
| 4325 | B | 10-53 | 4365 | C | 11-88 | 4405 | B | 3-26 |
| 4326 | A | 10-54 | 4366 | B | 11-89 | 4406 | B | 3-28 |
| 4327 | A | 10-55 | 4367 | C | 11-91 | 4407 | A | 5-25 |
| 4328 | NA | | 4368 | B | 11-93 | 4408 | B | 3-32 |
| 4329 | NA | | 4369 | B | 11-94 | 4409 | C | 3-65 |
| 4330 | NA | | 4370 | B | 11-90 | 4410 | A | 6-44 |
| 4331 | C | 9-138 | 4371 | B | 11-92 | 4411 | C | 6-45 |
| 4332 | C | 9-137 | 4372 | A | 5-60 | 4412 | C | 6-47 |
| 4333 | NA | | 4373 | B | 8-75 | 4413 | B | 6-5 |
| 4334 | NA | | 4374 | NA | | 4414 | B | 3-46 |
| 4335 | NA | | 4375 | B | 5-28 | 4415 | C | 3-71 |
| 4336 | C | 10-57 | 4376 | C | 6-40 | 4416 | B | 3-72 |
| 4337 | A | 10-56 | 4377 | B | 6-38 | 4417 | C | 9-148 |
| 4338 | A | 10-58 | 4378 | B | 6-34 | 4418 | C | 9-149 |
| 4339 | B | 10-59 | 4379 | C | 3-73 | 4419 | C | 9-150 |
| 4340 | NA | | 4380 | B | 3-56 | 4420 | B | 3-53 |
| 4341 | NA | | 4381 | A | 5-27 | 4421 | A | 3-60 |
| 4342 | NA | | 4382 | A | 6-42 | 4422 | A | 3-63 |
| 4343 | NA | | 4383 | B | 6-36 | 4423 | B | 3-62 |
| 4344 | A | 11-67 | 4384 | B | 6-37 | 4424 | C | 3-64 |
| 4345 | A | 11-68 | 4385 | C | 6-43 | 4425 | NA | |
| 4346 | B | 11-69 | 4386 | C | 6-39 | 4426 | C | 5-29 |

| FAA Q. No. | Our Answer | Our Chap/ Q. No. | FAA Q. No. | Our Answer | Our Chap/ Q. No. | FAA Q. No. | Our Answer | Our Chap/ Q. No. |
|---|---|---|---|---|---|---|---|---|
| 4427 | C | 5-65 | 4467 | C | 4-78 | 4507 | A | 10-43 |
| 4428 | NA | | 4468 | A | 4-82 | 4508 | C | 10-42 |
| 4429 | A | 10-1 | 4469 | C | 3-70 | 4509 | B | 10-45 |
| 4430 | B | 10-15 | 4470 | C | 9-83 | 4510 | C | 10-44 |
| 4431 | C | 10-20 | 4471 | C | 8-76 | 4511 | C | 10-46 |
| 4432 | C | 10-7 | 4472 | B | 6-2 | 4512 | C | 10-51 |
| 4433 | C | 10-22 | 4473 | A | 3-84 | 4513 | C | 10-48 |
| 4434 | B | 3-87 | 4474 | B | 3-86 | 4514 | B | 10-47 |
| 4435 | A | 10-2 | 4475 | A | 3-83 | 4515 | B | 10-49 |
| 4436 | C | 10-8 | 4476 | C | 3-85 | 4516 | B | 10-50 |
| 4437 | A | 10-9 | 4477 | A | 2-34 | 4517 | B | 10-52 |
| 4438 | NA | | 4478 | A | 2-33 | 4518 | B | 5-36 |
| 4439 | C | 5-76 | 4479 | B | 2-31 | 4519 | A | 5-35 |
| 4440 | A | 5-30 | 4480 | C | 2-30 | 4520 | C | 5-40 |
| 4441 | A | 8-73 | 4481 | C | 2-41 | 4521 | B | 5-41 |
| 4442 | C | 9-144 | 4482 | C | 2-36 | 4522 | C | 5-38 |
| 4443 | B | 3-50 | 4483 | C | 2-27 | 4523 | A | 5-39 |
| 4444 | C | 2-38 | 4484 | B | 2-26 | 4524 | B | 5-37 |
| 4445 | C | 2-40 | 4485 | A | 10-13 | 4525 | C | 5-42 |
| 4446 | B | 2-39 | 4486 | B | 3-47 | 4526 | B | 3-88 |
| 4447 | A | 10-21 | 4487 | B | 6-3 | 4527 | B | 3-89 |
| 4448 | C | 3-79 | 4488 | C | 9-139 | 4528 | B | 3-90 |
| 4449 | B | 10-16 | 4489 | A | 9-140 | 4529 | C | 3-91 |
| 4450 | A | 10-18 | 4490 | B | 9-141 | 4530 | B | 3-92 |
| 4451 | A | 10-17 | 4491 | A | 9-142 | 4531 | C | 3-93 |
| 4452 | B | 10-19 | 4492 | C | 9-143 | 4532 | B | 3-94 |
| 4453 | C | 10-25 | 4493 | C | 10-28 | 4533 | C | 3-95 |
| 4454 | B | 10-26 | 4494 | A | 10-29 | 4534 | B | 3-96 |
| 4455 | A | 10-27 | 4495 | A | 10-34 | 4535 | A | 3-97 |
| 4456 | B | 3-57 | 4496 | C | 10-30 | 4536 | B | 3-98 |
| 4457 | C | 10-23 | 4497 | C | 10-31 | 4537 | C | 3-99 |
| 4458 | A | 3-52 | 4498 | C | 10-32 | 4538 | C | 3-100 |
| 4459 | C | 3-80 | 4499 | A | 10-33 | 4539 | A | 3-101 |
| 4460 | A | 3-81 | 4500 | C | 10-35 | 4540 | B | 9-88 |
| 4461 | A | 5-26 | 4501 | B | 10-36 | 4541 | C | 10-11 |
| 4462 | B | 3-74 | 4502 | B | 10-37 | 4542 | C | 10-12 |
| 4463 | B | 3-75 | 4503 | C | 10-38 | 4543 | C | 10-24 |
| 4464 | A | 3-76 | 4504 | C | 10-40 | 4544 | B | 10-3 |
| 4465 | A | 3-78 | 4505 | B | 10-39 | 4545 | A | 10-4 |
| 4466 | A | 3-77 | 4506 | C | 10-41 | 4546 | B | 10-6 |

| FAA Q. No. | Our Answer | Our Chap/ Q. No. | FAA Q. No. | Our Answer | Our Chap/ Q. No. | FAA Q. No. | Our Answer | Our Chap/ Q. No. |
|---|---|---|---|---|---|---|---|---|
| 4547 | B | 10-5 | 4587 | A | 6-29 | 4627 | B | 9-56 |
| 4548 | C | 6-48 | 4588 | C | 6-30 | 4628 | B | 9-57 |
| 4549 | C | 6-51 | 4589 | A | 6-31 | 4629 | C | 9-58 |
| 4550 | C | 6-52 | 4590 | C | 6-28 | 4630 | A | 5-47 |
| 4551 | C | 6-53 | 4591 | C | 6-8 | 4631 | C | 9-17 |
| 4552 | B | 6-54 | 4592 | C | 6-9 | 4632 | C | 9-87 |
| 4553 | B | 6-55 | 4593 | B | 6-10 | 4633 | C | 10-14 |
| 4554 | C | 6-56 | 4594 | A | 6-11 | 4634 | C | 8-74 |
| 4555 | C | 3-55 | 4595 | B | 6-12 | 4635 | B | 9-126 |
| 4556 | C | 6-57 | 4596 | A | 6-13 | 4636 | A | 9-84 |
| 4557 | A | 6-60 | 4597 | B | 6-14 | 4637 | C | 9-86 |
| 4558 | C | 6-61 | 4598 | C | 6-15 | 4638 | B | 9-146 |
| 4559 | B | 6-62 | 4599 | A | 6-16 | 4639 | NA | |
| 4560 | C | 6-63 | 4600 | C | 6-17 | 4640 | B | 9-147 |
| 4561 | A | 6-64 | 4601 | B | 6-59 | 4641 | C | 9-91 |
| 4562 | C | 6-65 | 4602 | B | 6-26 | 4642 | B | 9-125 |
| 4563 | A | 6-75 | 4603 | A | 6-27 | 4643 | NA | |
| 4564 | B | 6-76 | 4604 | B | 6-58 | 4644 | NA | |
| 4565 | C | 6-77 | 4605 | B | 3-61 | 4645 | C | 11-25 |
| 4566 | C | 6-78 | 4606 | A | 6-66 | 4646 | A | 11-26 |
| 4567 | C | 6-79 | 4607 | C | 6-73 | 4647 | C | 11-27 |
| 4568 | A | 6-80 | 4608 | C | 6-74 | 4648 | B | 9-127 |
| 4569 | B | 6-82 | 4609 | B | 9-61 | 4649 | A | 9-128 |
| 4570 | B | 6-81 | 4610 | A | 9-68 | 4650 | B | 9-129 |
| 4571 | C | 6-83 | 4611 | B | 9-69 | 4651 | B | 9-130 |
| 4572 | C | 6-70 | 4612 | C | 9-70 | 4652 | C | 9-131 |
| 4573 | B | 6-71 | 4613 | B | 9-71 | 4653 | B | 9-100 |
| 4574 | C | 6-72 | 4614 | C | 9-64 | 4654 | B | 9-101 |
| 4575 | A | 6-67 | 4615 | C | 9-65 | 4655 | A | 9-118 |
| 4576 | C | 6-68 | 4616 | A | 9-66 | 4656 | A | 9-119 |
| 4577 | C | 6-69 | 4617 | B | 9-62 | 4657 | B | 9-132 |
| 4578 | B | 6-7 | 4618 | C | 9-60 | 4658 | C | 9-133 |
| 4579 | B | 6-22 | 4619 | B | 9-67 | 4659 | B | 9-134 |
| 4580 | B | 6-23 | 4620 | C | 9-59 | 4660 | C | 9-135 |
| 4581 | A | 6-24 | 4621 | C | 9-73 | 4661 | A | 9-136 |
| 4582 | B | 6-25 | 4622 | B | 9-74 | 4662 | A | 9-95 |
| 4583 | C | 6-18 | 4623 | A | 9-75 | 4663 | B | 6-46 |
| 4584 | A | 6-19 | 4624 | A | 9-72 | 4664 | A | 9-32 |
| 4585 | B | 6-21 | 4625 | C | 9-76 | 4665 | C | 6-6 |
| 4586 | B | 6-20 | 4626 | A | 9-77 | 4666 | B | 6-49 |

| FAA Q. No. | Our Answer | Our Chap/ Q. No. | FAA Q. No. | Our Answer | Our Chap/ Q. No. | FAA Q. No. | Our Answer | Our Chap/ Q. No. |
|---|---|---|---|---|---|---|---|---|
| 4667 | A | 9-16 | 4707 | C | 8-66 | 4747 | B | 9-26 |
| 4668 | C | 9-79 | 4708 | C | 8-67 | 4748 | C | 9-38 |
| 4669 | A | 9-20 | 4709 | B | 8-68 | 4749 | C | 9-93 |
| 4670 | A | 9-92 | 4710 | C | 8-69 | 4750 | A | 9-3 |
| 4671 | A | 9-85 | 4711 | C | 9-49 | 4751 | C | 9-145 |
| 4672 | A | 9-89 | 4712 | NA | | 4752 | C | 9-36 |
| 4673 | NA | | 4713 | NA | | 4753 | B | 9-21 |
| 4674 | C | 9-96 | 4714 | A | 9-94 | 4754 | C | 9-15 |
| 4675 | A | 9-97 | 4715 | A | 9-80 | 4755 | A | 9-45 |
| 4676 | NA | | 4716 | A | 9-13 | 4756 | B | 9-41 |
| 4677 | B | 9-98 | 4717 | B | 9-82 | 4757 | C | 9-42 |
| 4678 | A | 9-99 | 4718 | A | 9-2 | 4758 | B | 3-66 |
| 4679 | NA | | 4719 | C | 5-46 | 4759 | A | 9-12 |
| 4680 | A | 9-102 | 4720 | B | 9-39 | 4760 | B | 5-53 |
| 4681 | C | 9-103 | 4721 | B | 9-40 | 4761 | C | 3-37 |
| 4682 | A | 9-104 | 4722 | NA | | 4762 | C | 9-14 |
| 4683 | C | 9-105 | 4723 | NA | | 4763 | A | 9-19 |
| 4684 | C | 9-106 | 4724 | NA | | 4764 | B | 9-34 |
| 4685 | B | 9-107 | 4725 | C | 3-68 | 4765 | C | 10-10 |
| 4686 | A | 9-108 | 4726 | B | 3-67 | 4766 | B | 9-63 |
| 4687 | B | 9-109 | 4727 | C | 9-44 | 4767 | A | 9-78 |
| 4688 | A | 9-110 | 4728 | C | 9-50 | 4768 | B | 9-55 |
| 4689 | A | 9-111 | 4729 | C | 9-25 | 4769 | C | 5-54 |
| 4690 | A | 9-113 | 4730 | C | 9-27 | 4770 | B | 9-33 |
| 4691 | C | 9-112 | 4731 | A | 9-28 | 4771 | A | 9-54 |
| 4692 | X | 9-117 | 4732 | A | 9-29 | 4772 | B | 9-46 |
| 4693 | B | 9-115 | 4733 | B | 9-30 | 4773 | A | 9-47 |
| 4694 | A | 9-116 | 4734 | A | 9-90 | 4774 | B | 3-10 |
| 4695 | A | 9-114 | 4735 | C | 9-4 | 4775 | B | 3-11 |
| 4696 | B | 9-120 | 4736 | A | 9-5 | 4776 | C | 3-14 |
| 4697 | NA | | 4737 | C | 9-6 | 4777 | A | 3-15 |
| 4698 | A | 9-121 | 4738 | B | 3-8 | 4778 | A | 3-12 |
| 4699 | C | 9-122 | 4739 | B | 9-43 | 4779 | C | 3-13 |
| 4700 | C | 9-123 | 4740 | B | 9-53 | 4780 | A | 3-16 |
| 4701 | C | 9-124 | 4741 | C | 9-48 | 4781 | B | 3-9 |
| 4702 | A | 9-10 | 4742 | B | 9-31 | 4782 | C | 3-17 |
| 4703 | A | 9-8 | 4743 | C | 9-1 | 4783 | B | 3-18 |
| 4704 | B | 9-9 | 4744 | A | 9-18 | 4784 | C | 3-19 |
| 4705 | B | 9-7 | 4745 | C | 9-37 | 4785 | A | 3-20 |
| 4706 | B | 9-35 | 4746 | C | 9-81 | 4786 | B | 3-21 |

| FAA Q. No. | Our Answer | Our Chap/ Q. No. | FAA Q. No. | Our Answer | Our Chap/ Q. No. | FAA Q. No. | Our Answer | Our Chap/ Q. No. |
|---|---|---|---|---|---|---|---|---|
| 4787 | C | 3-22 | 4827 | C | 2-50 | 4867 | A | 8-55 |
| 4788 | A | 3-23 | 4828 | A | 2-51 | 4868 | B | 8-3 |
| 4789 | B | 3-24 | 4829 | C | 2-52 | 4869 | C | 8-39 |
| 4790 | C | 3-25 | 4830 | C | 2-13 | 4870 | C | 8-1 |
| 4791 | B | 3-1 | 4831 | B | 2-68 | 4871 | C | 8-40 |
| 4792 | B | 3-2 | 4832 | A | 8-42 | 4872 | C | 8-50 |
| 4793 | B | 3-3 | 4833 | A | 8-12 | 4873 | B | 8-57 |
| 4794 | A | 3-6 | 4834 | C | 2-1 | 4874 | A | 8-51 |
| 4795 | C | 3-5 | 4835 | A | 2-54 | 4875 | B | 8-58 |
| 4796 | A | 3-4 | 4836 | A | 8-36 | 4876 | C | 8-24 |
| 4797 | C | 3-7 | 4837 | A | 8-43 | 4877 | C | 2-2 |
| 4798 | B | 9-152 | 4838 | B | 8-44 | 4878 | B | 8-11 |
| 4799 | A | 9-153 | 4839 | A | 2-65 | 4879 | C | 2-19 |
| 4800 | C | 9-154 | 4840 | C | 8-34 | 4880 | C | 2-23 |
| 4801 | C | 9-155 | 4841 | NA | | 4881 | C | 2-47 |
| 4802 | A | 7-8 | 4842 | C | 2-53 | 4882 | B | 2-62 |
| 4803 | A | 7-17 | 4843 | A | 8-2 | 4883 | A | 2-63 |
| 4804 | A | 7-18 | 4844 | B | 8-10 | 4884 | C | 8-52 |
| 4805 | A | 7-9 | 4845 | A | 8-53 | 4885 | A | 2-49 |
| 4806 | C | 7-12 | 4846 | NA | | 4886 | C | 2-3 |
| 4807 | A | 7-10 | 4847 | A | 2-64 | 4887 | A | 2-4 |
| 4808 | B | 7-11 | 4848 | C | 8-49 | 4888 | B | 2-5 |
| 4809 | B | 7-1 | 4849 | NA | | 4889 | C | 2-6 |
| 4810 | C | 7-5 | 4850 | A | 8-45 | 4890 | A | 2-7 |
| 4811 | C | 7-6 | 4851 | C | 8-46 | 4891 | C | 2-8 |
| 4812 | B | 7-14 | 4852 | NA | | 4892 | B | 2-9 |
| 4813 | B | 7-7 | 4853 | B | 8-48 | 4893 | C | 2-10 |
| 4814 | C | 7-3 | 4854 | A | 2-14 | 4894 | B | 2-11 |
| 4815 | C | 7-4 | 4855 | B | 8-32 | 4895 | C | 8-15 |
| 4816 | B | 7-2 | 4856 | A | 2-66 | 4896 | A | 8-16 |
| 4817 | B | 7-13 | 4857 | C | 2-58 | 4897 | B | 8-17 |
| 4818 | A | 7-15 | 4858 | A | 8-47 | 4898 | C | 8-18 |
| 4819 | C | 7-16 | 4859 | C | 8-33 | 4899 | B | 8-21 |
| 4820 | B | 8-25 | 4860 | B | 2-57 | 4900 | A | 2-59 |
| 4821 | A | 2-15 | 4861 | C | 2-55 | 4901 | A | 2-56 |
| 4822 | C | 9-51 | 4862 | B | 8-31 | 4902 | B | 2-48 |
| 4823 | A | 9-52 | 4863 | C | 8-35 | 4903 | A | 8-20 |
| 4824 | B | 9-22 | 4864 | A | 2-21 | 4904 | C | 8-13 |
| 4825 | C | 9-23 | 4865 | C | 8-38 | 4905 | C | 8-14 |
| 4826 | A | 9-24 | 4866 | B | 8-37 | 4906 | A | 8-22 |

| FAA Q. No. | Our Answer | Our Chap/ Q. No. | FAA Q. No. | Our Answer | Our Chap/ Q. No. | FAA Q. No. | Our Answer | Our Chap/ Q. No. |
|------------|------------|------------------|------------|------------|------------------|------------|------------|------------------|
| 4907 | A | 8-23 | 4920 | C | 8-41 | 4933 | B | 8-8 |
| 4908 | C | 2-17 | 4921 | C | 2-67 | 4934 | B | 8-7 |
| 4909 | A | 2-12 | 4922 | B | 2-28 | 4935 | C | 8-9 |
| 4910 | B | 2-25 | 4923 | C | 2-24 | 4936 | B | 8-54 |
| 4911 | B | 2-35 | 4924 | C | 8-26 | 4937 | A | 8-60 |
| 4912 | B | 2-32 | 4925 | B | 8-27 | 4938 | B | 8-56 |
| 4913 | C | 2-16 | 4926 | B | 8-28 | 4939 | B | 8-61 |
| 4914 | B | 8-19 | 4927 | C | 8-59 | 4940 | C | 8-62 |
| 4915 | B | 8-4 | 4928 | C | 8-29 | 4941 | A | 8-63 |
| 4916 | B | 8-71 | 4929 | A | 8-30 | 4942 | B | 8-64 |
| 4917 | B | 8-72 | 4930 | B | 2-18 | 4943 | C | 8-65 |
| 4918 | A | 2-61 | 4931 | A | 8-5 | | | |
| 4919 | C | 2-60 | 4932 | A | 8-6 | | | |

# BOOKS AVAILABLE FROM GLEIM PUBLICATIONS, Inc.
## WRITTEN EXAM BOOKS

Before pilots take their FAA written tests, they want to understand the answer to every FAA written test question. Gleim's written test books are widely used because they help pilots learn and understand exactly what they need to know to do well on their FAA written test.

Gleim's books contain all of the FAA's airplane questions (nonairplane questions are excluded). We have unscrambled the questions appearing in the FAA written test books and organized them into logical topics. Answer explanations are provided next to each question. Each of our chapters opens with a brief, user-friendly outline of exactly what you need to know to pass the written test. Information not directly tested is omitted to expedite your passing the written test. This additional information can be found in our flight maneuver and reference books and practical test prep books described below.

### PRIVATE PILOT AND RECREATIONAL PILOT FAA WRITTEN EXAM ($12.95)

The FAA's written test for the private pilot certificate consists of 60 questions out of the 711 questions in our book. Also, the FAA's written test for the recreational pilot certificate consists of 50 questions from this book.

### INSTRUMENT PILOT FAA WRITTEN EXAM ($16.95)

The FAA's written test consists of 60 questions out of the 898 questions in our book. Also, those people who wish to become an instrument-rated flight instructor (CFII) or an instrument ground instructor (IGI) must take the FAA's written test of 50 questions from this book.

### COMMERCIAL PILOT FAA WRITTEN EXAM ($14.95)

The FAA's written test will consist of 100 questions out of the 565 questions in our book.

### FUNDAMENTALS OF INSTRUCTING FAA WRITTEN EXAM ($9.95)

The FAA's written test consists of 50 questions out of the 160 questions in our book. This is required of any person to become a flight instructor or ground instructor. The test only needs to be taken once. For example, if someone is already a flight instructor and wants to become a ground instructor, taking the FOI test a second time is not required.

### FLIGHT/GROUND INSTRUCTOR FAA WRITTEN EXAM ($14.95)

The FAA's written test consists of 100 questions out of the 827 questions in our book. To be used for the Certificated Flight Instructor (CFI) written test and those who aspire to the Advanced Ground Instructor (AGI) rating for airplanes. Note that this book also covers what is known as the Basic Ground Instructor (BGI) rating. However, the BGI is **not** useful because it does not give the holder full authority to sign off private pilots to take their written test. In other words, this book should be used for the AGI rating.

### AIRLINE TRANSPORT PILOT FAA WRITTEN EXAM ($23.95)

The FAA's written test consists of 80 questions each for the ATP Part 121, ATP Part 135, and the flight dispatcher certificate. This second edition contains a complete answer explanation to each of the 1,345 airplane ATP questions (200 helicopter questions are excluded). This difficult FAA written test is now made simple by Gleim. As with Gleim's other written test books, studying for the ATP will now be a learning and understanding experience rather than a memorization marathon -- at a lower cost and with higher test scores and less frustration!!

---

## FAA PRACTICAL TEST PREP AND REFERENCE BOOKS

Our new Practical Test Prep books are designed to replace the FAA Practical Test Standards reprint booklets which are universally used by pilots preparing for the practical test. These new Practical Test Prep books will help prepare pilots for FAA practical tests as much as the Gleim written exam books prepare pilots for FAA written tests. Each task, objective, concept, requirement, etc., in the FAA's practical test standards is explained, analyzed, illustrated, and interpreted so pilots will be totally conversant with all aspects of their practical tests.

| | | | |
|---|---|---|---|
| | Private Pilot FAA Practical Test Prep | 544 pages | ($16.95) |
| **NOW** | Instrument Pilot FAA Practical Test Prep | 520 pages | ($17.95) |
| **AVAILABLE!** | Commercial Pilot FAA Practical Test Prep | 432 pages | ($14.95) |
| | Flight Instructor FAA Practical Test Prep | 632 pages | ($17.95) |

### PRIVATE PILOT HANDBOOK ($12.95)

A complete private pilot ground school text in outline format with many diagrams for ease in understanding. A complete, detailed index makes it more useful and saves time. It contains a special section on biennial flight reviews.

### AVIATION WEATHER AND WEATHER SERVICES ($18.95)

This is a complete rewrite of the FAA's *Aviation Weather 00-6A* and *Aviation Weather Services 00-45D* into a single easy-to-understand book complete with all of the maps, diagrams, charts, and pictures that appear in the current FAA books. Accordingly, pilots who wish to learn and understand the subject matter in these FAA books can do it much more easily and effectively with this book.

*MAIL TO:* **GLEIM PUBLICATIONS, Inc.**
P.O. Box 12848
University Station
Gainesville, FL 32604
*OR CALL:* **(800) 87-GLEIM, (904) 375-0772, FAX (904) 375-6940**

Our customer service staff is available to take your calls from 8:00 a.m. to 7:00 p.m.,
Monday through Friday, and 9:00 a.m. to 2:00 p.m., Saturday, Eastern Time.
Please have your VISA/MasterCard ready.

> **THE BOOKS WITH
> THE RED COVERS**

## WRITTEN TEST BOOKS

| | | | |
|---|---|---|---|
| *Private/Recreational Pilot* | Seventh | (1993-1995) Edition | $12.95 |
| *Instrument Pilot* | Fifth | (1993-1995) Edition | 16.95 |
| *Commercial Pilot* | Fifth | (1993-1995) Edition | 14.95 |
| *Fundamentals of Instructing* | Fifth | (1993-1995) Edition | 9.95 |
| *Flight/Ground Instructor* | Fifth | (1993-1995) Edition | 14.95 |
| *Airline Transport Pilot* | Second | (1993-1995) Edition | 23.95 |

## HANDBOOKS AND PRACTICAL TEST PREP BOOKS

| | | |
|---|---|---|
| *Aviation Weather and Weather Services* | (First Edition) | 18.95 |
| *Private Pilot Handbook* | (Fourth Edition) | 12.95 |
| *Private Pilot FAA Practical Test Prep* | (First Edition) | 16.95 |
| *Instrument Pilot FAA Practical Test Prep* | (First Edition) | 17.95 |
| *Commercial Pilot FAA Practical Test Prep* | (First Edition) | 14.95 |
| *Flight Instructor FAA Practical Test Prep* | (First Edition) | 17.95 |

Shipping    3.00

Add applicable sales tax for shipments within the State of Florida
*Please call or write for additional charges for outside the 48 contiguous United States*
**Printed 09/93. Prices subject to change without notice. We ship latest editions.**

Sales Tax \_\_\_\_\_

**TOTAL**   $\_\_\_\_\_

---

1. *We process and ship orders within 1 day of receipt of your order. We generally ship via UPS for the Eastern U.S. and U.S. mail for the Western U.S.*

2. *Please PHOTOCOPY this order form for friends and others.*

3. *No CODs. All orders from individuals must be prepaid and are protected by our unequivocal refund policy.*

   *Library and company orders may be on account. Shipping and handling charges will be added to the invoice, and to prepaid telephone orders.*

Name _____
      (please print)

Shipping Address _____
      (street address required for UPS)

_____

City _____ State \_\_\_\_\_ Zip _____

☐ MC/VISA   ☐ Check/M.O.    Daytime Telephone (\_\_\_) _____

MC/VISA No. \_\_ \_\_ \_\_ \_\_ - \_\_ \_\_ \_\_ \_\_ - \_\_ \_\_ \_\_ \_\_ - \_\_ \_\_ \_\_ \_\_

Expiration Date *(month/year)* _____ / _____

Signature _____

060C

---

## GLEIM PUBLICATIONS, INC. GUARANTEES
### THE IMMEDIATE REFUND OF ALL RESALABLE TEXTS RETURNED IN 30 DAYS
#### SHIPPING AND HANDLING CHARGES ARE NONREFUNDABLE

P.S. We presume your local FBO or bookstore does not stock the books you are ordering from us directly. If you provide us with a name and address, we will invite them to do so.

# INSTRUCTOR CERTIFICATION FORM
## INSTRUMENT RATING WRITTEN TEST

Name: _____

    I certify that I have reviewed the above individual's preparation for the FAA Instrument Rating -- Airplane written test [covering the topics specified in FAR 61.65(b)(1) through (4)] using the *Instrument Pilot FAA Written Exam* book and/or software by Irvin N. Gleim and find him/her competent to pass the written test.

| Signed | Date | Name | CFI Number | Expiration Date |
|---|---|---|---|---|

\* \* \* \* \* \* \* \* \* \* \* \* \* \* \* \* \* \* \* \* \* \* \* \* \* \* \* \* \* \* \* \* \* \* \* \* \* \* \*

# INSTRUCTOR CERTIFICATION FORM
## GROUND INSTRUCTOR -- INSTRUMENT WRITTEN TEST

Name: _____

    I certify that I have reviewed the above individual's preparation for the FAA Ground Instructor -- Instrument written test (covering the topics specified in FAR 143.11) using the *Instrument Pilot FAA Written Exam* book and/or software by Irvin N. Gleim and find him/her competent to pass the written test.

| Signed | Date | Name | CFI Number | Expiration Date |
|---|---|---|---|---|

\* \* \* \* \* \* \* \* \* \* \* \* \* \* \* \* \* \* \* \* \* \* \* \* \* \* \* \* \* \* \* \* \* \* \* \* \* \* \*

# INSTRUCTOR CERTIFICATION FORM
## FLIGHT INSTRUCTOR -- INSTRUMENT WRITTEN TEST

Name: _____

    I certify that I have reviewed the above individual's preparation for the FAA Instrument Flight Instructor -- Airplane written test [covering the topics specified in FAR 61.65(b)(1) through (4)] using the *Instrument Pilot FAA Written Exam* book and/or software by Irvin N. Gleim and find him/her competent to pass the written test.

| Signed | Date | Name | CFI Number | Expiration Date |
|---|---|---|---|---|

# AUTHOR'S RECOMMENDATION

**The Experimental Aircraft Association, Inc.** is a very successful and effective nonprofit organization that represents and serves those of us interested in flying, in general, and in sport aviation, in particular.  I personally invite you to enjoy becoming a member:

    $35 for a 1-year membership
    $20 per year for individuals under 19 years old
    Family membership available for $45 per year

Membership includes the monthly magazine *Sport Aviation*.

*Write to:*    Experimental Aircraft Association, Inc.
              P.O. Box 3086
              Oshkosh, Wisconsin  54903

*Or call:*    (414) 426-4800
            (800) 843-3612 (in Wisconsin:  1-800-236-4800)

**The annual EAA Oshkosh Fly-in** is an unbelievable aviation spectacular with over 10,000 airplanes at one airport!  Virtually everything aviation-oriented you can imagine!  Plan to spend at least 1 day (not everything can be seen in a day) in Oshkosh (100 miles northwest of Milwaukee).

*Convention dates:*    1994 -- July 29 through August 4
                      1995 -- July 28 through August 3

# ABBREVIATIONS AND ACRONYMS IN
# INSTRUMENT PILOT FAA WRITTEN EXAM

| | | | | |
|---|---|---|---|---|
| A/FD | *Airport/Facility Directory* | | LOC | localizer |
| AC | Severe Weather Outlook Chart | | LOM | outer compass locator |
| AC | Advisory Circular | | LORAN | Long Range Navigation |
| AC | convective outlook | | MAA | maximum authorized altitude |
| AC Form | Airman Certification Form (i.e., AC Form 8080-2) | | MAP | missed approach point |
| | | | Mb | millibar |
| ADF | automatic direction finder | | MB | magnetic bearing |
| ADIZ | Air Defense Identification Zone | | MCA | minimum crossing altitude |
| AGL | above ground level | | MDA | minimum descent altitude |
| AI | attitude indicator | | MEA | minimum en route altitude |
| AIM | Airman's Information Manual | | MH | magnetic heading |
| AIRMET | Airman's Meteorological Information | | MHA | minimum holding altitude |
| ALS | approach light systems | | MIRL | medium intensity runway lights |
| ALT | altimeter | | MLS | microwave landing system |
| AME | Aviation Medical Examiner | | MM | middle marker |
| ARSA | Airport Radar Service Area | | MOA | Military Operations Area |
| ARTCC | Air Route Traffic Control Center | | MOCA | minimum obstruction clearance altitude |
| ASI | airspeed indicator | | MP | manifold pressure |
| ASR | Airport Surveillance Radar | | MRA | minimum reception altitude |
| ATC | Air Traffic Control | | MSA | minimum safe altitude |
| ATIS | Automatic Terminal Information Service | | MSL | mean sea level |
| CAS | calibrated airspeed | | NAVAID | navigational aid |
| CAT | clear air turbulence | | NDB | nondirectional radio beacon |
| CDI | course deviation indicator | | NoPT | no procedure turn |
| CFII | Certificated Flight Instructor -- Instrument | | NOTAM | Notice to Airmen |
| COP | changeover point | | NTSB | National Transportation Safety Board |
| CTAF | Common Traffic Advisory Frequency | | OAT | outside air temperature |
| DH | decision height | | OBS | omnibearing selector |
| DME | distance measuring equipment | | OM | outer marker |
| DUAT | Direct User Access Terminal | | PAPI | precision approach path indicator |
| EFAS | En Route Flight Advisory Service | | PAR | Precision Approach Radar |
| EFC | expected further clearance | | PCA | Positive Control Area |
| ELT | emergency locator transmitter | | PIC | pilot in command |
| ETA | estimated time of arrival | | PIREP | Pilot Weather Report |
| ETE | estimated time en route | | PTS | Practical Test Standards |
| FA | area forecast | | RAIL | runway alignment indicator lights |
| FAA | Federal Aviation Administration | | RB | relative bearing |
| FAF | final approach fix | | REIL | runway end identifier lights |
| FAR | Federal Aviation Regulation | | RIC | remote indicating compass |
| FBO | Fixed-Base Operator | | RMI | radio magnetic indicator |
| FD | Winds and Temperatures Aloft Forecast | | RNAV | area navigation |
| FDC NOTAM | Flight Data Center Notice to Airmen | | RPM | revolutions per minute (tachometer) |
| FL | flight level | | RVR | runway visual range |
| FSDO | Flight Standards District Office | | SA | Surface Aviation Observation Weather Report |
| FSS | Flight Service Station | | SDF | simplified directional facility |
| FT | terminal forecast | | SIAP | Standard Instrument Approach Procedure |
| GPH | gallons per hour | | SID | standard instrument departure |
| GS | glide slope or groundspeed | | SIGMET | Significant Meteorological Information |
| HAA | height above airport | | STAR | standard terminal arrival route |
| HAT | height above touchdown | | SVFR | Special VFR |
| Hg | mercury | | T&SI | turn and slip indicator |
| HI | heading indicator | | TACAN | Tactical Air Navigation |
| HIRL | high intensity runway lights | | TAS | true airspeed |
| HSI | horizontal situation indicator | | TC | turn coordinator |
| IAF | initial approach fix | | TCA | Terminal Control Area |
| IAP | instrument approach procedure | | TDZ | touchdown zone |
| IAS | indicated airspeed | | TDZE | touchdown zone elevation |
| ICAO | International Civil Aviation Organization | | TWEB | Transcribed Weather Broadcast |
| IFR | instrument flight rules | | UTC | Coordinated Universal Time |
| IGI | Instrument Ground Instructor | | VASI | visual approach slope indicator |
| ILS | instrument landing system | | VDP | visual descent point |
| IM | inner marker | | VFR | visual flight rules |
| IMC | Instrument Meteorological Conditions | | VHF | very high frequency |
| INT | intersection | | VMC | visual meteorological conditions |
| ISA | international standard atmosphere | | VOR | VHF omnidirectional range |
| KCAS | knots calibrated airspeed | | VORTAC | Collocated VOR and TACAN |
| LAA | Local Airport Advisory | | VOT | VOR Test Facility |
| LDA | localizer-type directional aid | | VSI | vertical speed indicator |
| LF | low frequency | | Z | Zulu or UTC time |
| LMM | middle compass locator | | | |

# INDEX

Please forward your suggestions, corrections, and comments concerning typographical errors, etc., to **Irvin N. Gleim • c/o Gleim Publications, Inc. • P.O. Box 12848 • University Station • Gainesville, Florida • 32604.** Please include your name and address so we can properly thank you for your interest. Also, please refer to both the page number and the FAA question number for each item.

1. _____

2. _____

3. _____

4. _____

5. _____

6. _____

7. _____

8. _____

9. _____

10. _____

11. _____

12. _____

13. _____

14. _____

15. _____

16. _____

17. _____

Name: _____

Address: _____

City/State/Zip: _____

Telephone: _____